The Gray Raiders
Volume 3

The Gray Raiders
Volume 3
Accounts of Mosby & His Raiders During the American Civil War

Mosby and His Men

J. Marshall Crawford

Partisan Life with Col. John S. Mosby

John Scott

The Gray Raiders Volume 3
Accounts of Mosby & His Raiders During the American Civil War
Mosby and His Men
by J. Marshall Crawford
Partisan Life with Col. John S. Mosby
by John Scott

FIRST EDITION

First published under the titles
Mosby and His Men
and
Partisan Life with Col. John S. Mosby

Leonaur is an imprint
of Oakpast Ltd

Copyright in this form © 2015 Oakpast Ltd

ISBN: 978-1-78282-353-7 (hardcover)
ISBN: 978-1-78282-354-4 (softcover)

http://www.leonaur.com

Publisher's Notes
The views expressed in this book are not necessarily those of the publisher.

Contents

Mosby and His Men   7
Partisan Life with Col. John S. Mosby   169

Mosby and His Men

John S. Mosby

Contents

Mosby and His Men   11

Mosby and His Men

To the Soldiers of the Battalion of Virginia Cavalry,
I Respectfully Dedicate
This Book,
As a mark of My Esteem.

It is a record of personal recollections of your achievements during the late war. Although not so elaborate a work as I could wish to offer you, yet it is a faithful and correct narrative written from memoranda made of events as they occurred, by one of your comrades, who, from the earliest organisation of our command, shared with you your hardships and defeats, until the disbanding of the command at Salem.

Although not so voluminous as it might be, yet this work contains an account of all the important movements of the command.

Some of my Northern readers may consider the work a little too "rebellious," and may charge me with presenting the acts of some of their men in colours too dark. But let them travel through the country their armies have traversed, and they will see too many proofs of the truthfulness of the picture. The once happy homes and smiling faces no longer greet the stranger. The blooming fields, the orange-groves and extensive flower-gardens, no longer cheer the tourist or protect the wearied traveller from the burning sun of the South.

The Southern flag no longer floats over its brave defenders; but the scenes and trials of the Southern people during this contest cannot be forgotten by those who saw and felt them. The history of the struggle will be written hereafter, when passion shall have cooled, and the historian shall be a philosopher, and not a fanatic. Then many things shall assume a different appearance from that which they now present; but no historian will ever say that the 43rd Battalion of Virginia Cavalry proved recreant to their duty.

To Colonel Mosby's father and mother, I return my most sincere thanks for assistance rendered me when I commenced my enterprise.

To George Palmer, Esq., of Richmond, Va., I tender my obligations for similar favours rendered in 1865; while Major Richards, Captains Glasscock and Richards, and other members of the command, will please accept my grateful remembrance for the encouragement given me in my feeble efforts to narrate the deeds of heroism done by our command.

J. M. C.

Louisville, Ky.

Chapter 1: Bombardment of Fort Sumter

The American people have just passed through a great civil war,—a war that has exceeded in gigantic proportions all the great conflicts of modern times. In its swift course of destruction it has laid many fair cities in ashes, and has left to mark its course scenes of ruin and desolation that no pencil can sketch, no pen portray.

A quarter of a million of bodies that lie mouldering in Southern soil, and the thousand of widows and orphans mourning over the loss of loved ones who will never return, attest its ferocity and the earnestness with which both sections of the country fought this contest. But it is over at last. The thunder of artillery is no longer heard, and the torch of the incendiary is no longer wantonly applied to private residences, compelling the inmates to fly from the homes of their nativity to escape the insults of a licentious soldiery. The last stray shot of a guerilla has been fired, and not a single armed foe raises his hand against Federal authority. Peace has spread her smiling wings over this once fair and glorious country, and men of all parties and all classes hail with delight the prospect of once more returning to the quiet avocations of every-day life.

It will take many long years of persevering industry and unremitting toil to build up the waste places that have been made almost a wilderness. It will be many years before the wounds made by this unhappy strife will be healed over; but wise councils and a spirit of moderation on the part of the government may yet repair the mistakes of the past, and the influence of commerce, that great peacemaker, may unite the interests of both sections in an indissoluble bond, and the Sunny South may again blossom as the rose, and her power and influence be felt in the nation as of old.

The dream of Southern independence and a separate nationality has vanished forever. The cause which the men of the South had nearest their hearts, and for which they sacrificed so many lives, so much wealth, and their whole energies both of mind and body, *has failed*, their sacrifices have all been in vain, their resources have been exhausted in the fruitless endeavour to achieve their independence, and thousands of their bravest and noblest sons have fallen in the unequal contest. At the end of four years of almost superhuman exertions, they find themselves a conquered people, with the loss of everything but their honour, seeking restoration to their former position under the Federal flag.

I was for four years in the Confederacy, having gone South almost at the very inception of the war, and having spent the last two years in guerilla warfare, in the border counties of Virginia, half of that time almost within sight of the Capital of the United States. I propose, as a part of the history of the rebellion, to give my readers a sketch of some of its main incidents, and more particularly of some of the exploits of the battalion to which I belonged, which was, from its formation to the close of the war, a terror to all the outposts and detached divisions of the Federal Army, and whose scouts and couriers gave to General Lee the most, if not all, of the reliable information he received of the enemy's movements and designs, and which enabled his lieutenant-generals to deal such sudden and heavy blows upon his adversaries. The life of a guerilla is a dangerous one, but it has its charms. Its independence and freedom from restraint, and, above all, the opportunity for bold and daring actions, which carry with them personal renown, makes this life far preferable to a position in the regular army, where men stand up like posts to be shot at, and where there is little or no opportunity for the display of personal courage.

It was in April, 1861, that the first scenes of the bloody drama were enacted. I had been holding an office in the Treasury Department at Washington for the seven years previous, and was in the civil service of the government at the time Fort Sumter was bombarded and surrendered to the Confederates under General Beauregard. The event created the most intense excitement all over the country, and no one knew what turn affairs would take. Three Confederate commissioners had been sent to Washington to negotiate for the surrender of the Southern forts, arsenals, and public property of every description, and to arrange the basis for a convention between the two governments. They had been received informally, but their mission failed with President Buchanan. They had gone home unmolested, and the policy of the new administration had not been developed.

Two of the leading Northern journals, of opposite politics, the *New York Tribune* and the *New York Herald*, were in favour of letting the South go peaceably. The Democratic party was opposed to coercion, believing that the conquest of the South was impossible, and that the country would be ruined by the war and our institutions overthrown. The Republicans, an entirely sectional party, elected on a sectional platform and for the first time in power, flushed with victory over their opponents, thought otherwise; but still they paused and hesitated before they plunged the country into a war the end of which no man could tell. Things were in this condition when the news came North that Fort Sumter had been bombarded and had fallen. It threw the whole country, North and South, into a fever of excitement, and determined the course of the new administration at once.

President Lincoln issued his proclamation on the 15th day of April, 1861, calling for *seventy-five thousand men for the term of three months*, to put down the insurrection. Massachusetts was the first State to respond to the call, and in the month of April she sent two regiments to guard Washington city; for at that time it was supposed the Confederates meditated an attack upon the Capital, and so little was known concerning the plans of the Southerners and the exact condition of affairs in that section, that the report was started and actually believed by General Scott, the government officials, and the whole North, that Ben McCulloch was marching through Virginia with five thousand Texan Rangers, supported by a large army of volunteers, on Washington, with the intention of sacking the city, destroying the public buildings, and moving northward with fire and sword.

All the roads and by-paths to the city were strongly picketed. Two companies of infantry, with artillery, were posted at the long bridge across the Potomac, to prevent any attack from that point; when the actual fact was, that with the exception of two companies in Alexandria and a picket of Confederates on the Virginia side of the bridge, including a few stragglers who had come in, there was not an armed force in the field in the whole State of Virginia,—so little did the public or the government know what was really going on in the South.

A Massachusetts regiment, passing through Baltimore on the 17th of April 1861, was attacked by a mob. Several were killed and wounded. Baltimore had always been noted for its mobocratic tendencies, and little attention was paid to the affair by the citizens, the majority of whom knew nothing of the difficulty. The regiment got through the city, however, but as the train was passing through the suburbs of the city, a member of the regiment levelled his gun, fired, and killed a highly respectable citizen (Mr. Kyle, who happened to be conversing with two or three friends) in cold blood. The news soon spread, and in a few hours the whole city of Baltimore was in a state of excitement bordering upon frenzy. The populace rose up as one man, and demanded justice in behalf of the murdered citizen. The perpetrator of the deed was not delivered up. The excitement increased. A mob collected, and the first act was to cut off all communication north of Baltimore. In one night all the railroad bridges between Baltimore and Wilmington and Harrisburg were burned and destroyed. The road between Washington Junction and Annapolis had been torn up, and the Capital of the nation was thus entirely severed from all communication with the outer world.

Had the Confederate leaders dreamed that the Federal Government intended actually to open hostilities, the State of Virginia could have thrown fifty thousand men into Maryland, taken possession of the whole State, including the District of Columbia and the Capital, and thus have ended the war, and saved all the blood and treasure that has since been wasted and squandered with such unprecedented prodigality. But they let slip the chance; they were unprepared, and a great opportunity was lost. Neither side seemed to appreciate the magnitude of the events which must necessarily have followed from what was occurring. The administration and the North thought seventy-five thousand men would quell the insurrection in three months; and the South had conceived the idea that they would, in that time, win their independence with little difficulty, and thus we gradually drifted into this great war. Neither side had counted the real cost. The South was fearfully in earnest, but they overrated their real strength and underestimated the power of their adversaries.

But to return to Baltimore. The people held a meeting at Monument Square, and resolved that no more troops should pass through the State. The city was under military rule, and twenty thousand citizens with muskets in their hands stood ready to see that their resolutions were respected. The governor of the State addressed them from the rostrum, and assured them that he would sooner see his own right arm torn from its socket than to allow any more men to go through the State, or to aid the government in opposing the South. How well he kept his word was seen when, a night or two afterwards, he slipped off to Washington and was in secret consultation with Lincoln and the Secretary of War as to the best means of delivering up his own native city to the Federal authorities. He admirably succeeded and was no doubt rewarded. A short time afterwards this same governor of a sovereign State, whose Constitution and laws he had solemnly sworn to support, we find the prime mover and instigator in the infamous plot to destroy the State Government. The legislature was *prorogued*, and the leading members arrested and imprisoned in Fort Lafayette in New York Harbour, there to languish within the confines of damp prison walls for months without trial. They were committed, and to this day no specific charges have ever been made against them.

They were finally released and allowed to return to their homes, shattered in health, and almost exiles in their own land, under the surveillance of government detectives, and subject to all the petty malice of provost-marshals, whose chief aim seemed to be to study how to exasperate the citizens of that devoted State, which for four years had been subject to all the ignominy and wrong that governmental parasites and a few native-born renegades could heap upon her. No wonder that the sons of Maryland flocked by thousands to the Southern standard to escape from such a galling despotism at home, and rushed, with avidity, to fight for that cause that commanded their sympathy and respect.

All over the North the boast was made that Baltimore should be laid in ashes. The guns of Fort McHenry were turned upon the city, her citizens were hunted down like outlaws, men were knocked down in the streets by armed ruffians wearing the Federal uniform, houses were broken open, ladies' wardrobes were ransacked, and the owners insulted, private property was confiscated to the personal use of the soldiery, and to all these wrongs and outrages the government manifested a stolid indifference that would have done honour to the Czar of Russia. Simply to be known to possess Southern opinions was cause enough to be thrown into a dungeon; and many a man, for the indiscreet expression of an opinion as to the legality of the high-minded measures then being enacted, was dragged from his bed and the bosom of his family, at the dead hour of midnight, and hurried off to provost-marshals, and, without a hearing, immediately transferred to some government prison. It created no surprise that Maryland was disaffected and still is so, for she has had nothing for which to thank the United States Government.

Chapter 2: Author Leaves Washington

Washington City was in a state of ferment and confusion. There were not more than two thousand troops there to guard the Capital of the Nation. The President and Cabinet were frightened at their supposed danger. The government clerks were called upon to enrol themselves into companies for the common protection. Arms were distributed all through the departments and stacked in every room, to be used at a moment's warning. The notorious Jim Lane of Kansas, with one hundred of his desperadoes, bivouacked in the East Room of the White House, as a bodyguard for his Excellency the President, and all day long the click of the hammer and chisel could be heard in the basements of the Treasury Building and Patent Office, preparing mines to blow up the public buildings and records in case of necessity. A gunboat at the Navy Yard had steam up all the time ready to bear away to a place of safety the precious lives of the head of the government and his official advisers.

During this time Southerners in Washington were openly leaving to join the Confederate Army. Southern communication had not yet been stopped, though a squad of soldiers from Alexandria were guarding the long bridge that crosses the Potomac at Washington. No attempt was made to stop these men. The heads of the departments caused a new test oath, unknown to the Constitution and the laws, to be administered to the clerks. Those who did not take it were summarily turned out of office. Those Southern men who took it and stayed did not remain long in office; their truculency could not save them, and the hordes of office-seekers from the New England States, who so pertinaciously beset the president and heads of departments, soon drove the remaining Southern democrats out in the cold, because they could not stretch themselves to the extreme measures of the radicals.

Not caring to be turned out of office I promptly sent in my resignation. I did not await its acceptance. Having packed up the night before, and bidding a few friends goodbye, on Wednesday, the 25th of April, 1861, I jumped into a stage coach and started to Dixie.

As we rolled over the Long Bridge I looked back upon the city I was leaving, where I had spent so many happy hours in social intercourse with friends from all sections of the country, and I cursed, in my inmost soul, the madness and folly of a sectional fanaticism that was hastening our country, with such rapid strides, into the vortex of civil war.

The spires and cupolas of Washington, with the half-finished dome of the Capitol, soon faded in the distance, and in a half-hour's time I was in the confines of the Confederacy.

The first place we arrived at was Alexandria. Here the Stars and Bars floated proudly from almost every housetop; and it was a great relief to pass from the gloom and despondency that prevailed in Washington, to the life and animation of Alexandria. All was bustle and excitement; energy and determination were stamped upon the countenance of every man I met. They all seemed to be putting their shoulder to the wheel; and the State of Virginia, having, by a solemn ordinance, dissolved her connection with the Federal Government, and joined her fortunes to the infant republic, her sons advanced with alacrity to their support, and rushed, with enthusiasm, to enrol themselves for the defence of their native State, which was so soon to become the scene of the greatest battle of .modem times. There was no flinching or holding back. The gray-haired man of sixty years, as well as the boy of sixteen summers, hastened to don the Confederate gray, and receive the congratulations of friends and brothers in arms, for the holy cause of independence which they then swore to uphold. And never did men take an oath more eagerly and with greater honesty of purpose.

For years the mad policy of the Northern politicians had been seeking to rend asunder, by their sectional onslaughts, the bonds of brotherly love that bound the North and South together. Gradually distrust and doubt, aggravated by insults and continual encroachments of the growing dominant party, settled into a firm conviction in the minds of the Southern people, that they should soon be tied hand and foot, and at the mercy of a Jacobinical party, whose genius for evil has been manifested in this country ever since the landing of the *Mayflower* at Plymouth Rock. The South felt this spirit of intolerance growing in the country day by day, and they resolved to break loose from this bondage, cost what it might, and be a free and independent nation. The heartfelt prayers of their entire home circles went with them, and they stood ready to march forth to do battle for their firesides and their freedom.

I left Alexandria the next morning, and proceeded to Charlottesville, *via* the Orange and Alexandria Railroad, where we arrived about noon, and found a large crowd waiting at the depot to hear the news from Washington, and to learn whether the Yankees would commence hostilities. I stayed that night with my brother at the University of Virginia located at that place, where he was completing his studies. I found, out of six hundred and fifty students, all but seventy-five had left for their homes preparatory to entering the Confederate service. The young men had cheerfully given up the ease and quiet and comforts of a student's life, and were prepared to bear and endure all the hardships, perils, and discomforts of camp-life. The deprivation of home comforts and luxuries, the dangers of the battlefield, and that worse than death, sickness in a camp hospital, were no drawback to their ardour, and all this *for independence* and a complete separation from our late Northern allies.

I looked around upon the desolate halls of the university, the silent quarters of the students which a few weeks ago presented so much life and animation, and where were the occupants? Gone forth in defence of the infant Republic. And where are now those noble youths, who sprang forward with such alacrity and buoyant spirits, to the mortal encounter? A large number of them have fallen on the battlefields of Virginia, fighting nobly for the cause they espoused; many have fallen victims to the cold and piercing lake winds on Johnson's Island, while languishing in imprisonment; and but a few of that gallant band, whose first exploit was the capture of Harper's Ferry, remain to tell the tale of what might have been.

From Charlottesville I went to Lynchburg, and found there that two of my brothers had already entered the service as privates, and were ready at a moment's warning to march to the seat of war. All the able-bodied young men of Lynchburg were volunteering, and crowds were coming in from all sides to volunteer their services for their country. The city was filled with recruits from the adjoining counties, and troops were arriving on almost every train of cars from the Gulf States, all eager for the fray, and all determined to fight it out to the bitter end. Such a scene would inspire the most lukewarm with the confidence of ultimate success. It might take years of labour and fighting, and oceans of blood and treasure; but what were these in comparison with independence and a government of our own? These were the thoughts and feelings that animated us all; and in that crowd of people at Lynchburg, I do not believe there was a man who would not have staked his last dollar and his last acre of land upon the success of the Southern arms.

I stayed in Lynchburg but one day, and the next morning at daylight set out on the Virginia and Tennessee Railroad, for Montgomery, Alabama, which was then capital of the Confederacy. All along the road, at Liberty, Wythville, Bristol, Knoxville, Dalton, and Atlanta, the people were very enthusiastic, and were determined to see that the Southern cause came out of the issue triumphant. There was no croaking and no drawing back; but every man was imbued with an inborn resolution to abide by the fortunes of the Confederacy.

I arrived at Montgomery in the early part of May, 1861. Nothing could exceed the enthusiasm of the people here. The streets were crowded with soldiers, some organised and marching through to Pensacola, others receiving their uniforms at the expense of the citizens, and waiting marching orders. The new government was under full headway, the departments all regularly organised and in full operation, and the machinery of government working as smoothly as in the departments at Washington. I found many familiar faces that I had seen and been in contact with in the public offices in Washington, who had followed the new government to Montgomery.

I presented my credentials in person, and was told my case would be attended to in a few days. Having resigned my office in Washington, and being perfectly familiar with all the details of the Treasury Department business, I had no doubt that I should in a few days get the same position I held under the old regime. Being acquainted with a number of the Representatives, and having letters of introduction to some of the leading members of Congress, I went to see them, and found a perfect unanimity of opinion as to the course the Southern States had taken, and the policy to be pursued. The die had been cast, the Rubicon passed, and with their eyes turned to the future and the Herculean efforts to be made, these men gave themselves body and soul to the accomplishment of their avowed purposes, and to make an era in the history of this continent which would redound to their glory. The first Congress of the Confederate States were fearfully in earnest, and to see their resolution and determination, no one would for a moment have supposed that the people whom they represented could ever be conquered or again bow the knee to a political master.

The next day the Virginia delegates to the Confederate Congress arrived. They were welcomed with open arms for upon the fidelity and endurance of that great State, the mother of States and statesmen, the success of the Southern cause depended. From her geographical position, upon the soil of Virginia would be fought the great battles of the war. That State would be the first one invaded, and to prevent the Federals from acquiring a foothold within her borders would require all the valour and undivided strength of her sons, as well as the whole power of the Confederate Government.

Though the last State to secede from the mother government, and so loath to part with all the blessings, recollections, and ties that sprang from a government of which she had been the founder and so warm an adherent, yet when she did wheel into line with her sister States in a cause that bound all her sympathies and commanded all her support, she buckled on her armour, and, like the knights of old, she went into the contest with a singleness of purpose and a high sense of honour that has extorted the admiration of the world, and commanded the respect of her adversaries, even though she has fallen from her great estate in the councils of the nation since the close of the war. But her position in the history of this country can never be mistaken by intelligent minds, and the grand old Commonwealth, though she may have for a time lost her prestige, yet another generation will soon spring up, and the State that has been styled the mother of presidents, will regain the position she has heretofore so proudly and nobly held.

With the delegates from Virginia came General Joe Johnston. He held a long consultation with President Davis and his cabinet, and urged, as a military as well as a political measure, the immediate removal of the Capital from Montgomery to Richmond. General Johnston's council prevailed. The last week in May 1861, the Capital was moved to Richmond. I returned to Virginia, and remained in Lynchburg until the first week in June. In the meanwhile suitable buildings had been secured for the departments of the government, and early in June the whole machinery was working like a clock. The president took up his residence at the Spottswood Hotel, where rooms had been fitted up for him in the most elegant and complete manner. In a short time the citizens of Richmond purchased the large and splendid residence of Mr. Crenshaw, at the corner of 11th Street and Lee, refurnished it from garret to cellar in the most elegant manner, and presented it, with a splendid carriage and horses, to his Excellency, which carriage, when the Confederate forces evacuated Richmond, General Ord appropriated to his own private use.

Chapter 3: Preparations for War in Richmond

During the organisation of the government in Richmond, preparations for a vigorous prosecution of the war were made. The greatest activity prevailed everywhere. At the old Virginia Armoury the machinists were working night and day. Old flint-locks were converted into percussion-locks. The Tredegar Works were working like bees, rifling old cannon and making new ones. Troops were coming in almost every hour of the day, from all the Southern States, and amongst the first was a company, "The Davis Rangers," all the way from Louisville, Kentucky, and composed partly of young men I knew, in my schoolboy days. Fitzhugh was captain, with A. Gale, Ed Cocke, Ivinny Colmesmil and Mat Gist as his lieutenants and sergeants. They encamped at the old Fair Grounds until other troops from Kentucky arrived, and when they were organised into a regiment with Tom Taylor as colonel, volunteers from the Border and Gulf States were arriving by every train of cars.

Schools of instruction were established all around the city. The drill-masters could be heard every hour of the day and night instructing their men. The principal school for the instruction of the cavalry was established at Ashland, the principal instructor being Captain L. L. Lomax, afterwards Major-General of cavalry, a graduate of West Point, who had served with distinction in the regular army of the United States before the war, fighting the Indians on the frontiers, but who, on the breaking out of the war and secession of his native State, Virginia, resigned and came South. Our cavalry furnished their own horses and equipments.

The latter part of June, Beauregard arrived in Richmond and was ordered to take command of the troops at Manassas, the point to which the eyes of both North and South were directed, and on the plains of which, afterwards, two of the hardest battles of the war were fought, and two of the grandest victories won. On his arrival there the keen eyes of that great soldier, after a survey of the country, soon recognised the importance of fortifying the place, as it was one of the keys to Richmond. The Yankees had already occupied Alexandria and were fortifying Arlington Heights, the home of our great chieftain, General Robert E. Lee. The first levy of troops, seventy-five thousand men, were already in and preparing for an advance right on to Richmond.

The Yankees, by some means, had conceived the idea that no resistance would be offered them on their march to Richmond; that all they had to do was to march right down and take it; and that the Rebels would fly from before them and scatter like chaff before the wind. Their implements of war had all the most modern improvements, while the Confederates were armed with old flint-lock muskets, except a few got at Harper's Ferry armoury, and some old smoothbore pieces of artillery.

Brigadier-General Magruder was on the Peninsula at Williamsburg, with a force of not more than two thousand five hundred men watching the movements of the enemy. General Butler, better know as Beast Butler, was in command at Fortress Monroe, and to have the credit and glory of being the first one to enter the Rebel Capital, he marched out of his entrenchments on the —— day of June, 1861, to ride rough-shod and disperse the mob of Magruder, which seemed to offer the only obstacle in the path to Richmond, and met at Bethel with a reconnoitring force sent out by Magruder. The Confederates had only two pieces of artillery and three howitzers, commanded by Captain Randolph, afterward General, and the distinguished Secretary of War. The enemy numbered five to one. Butler ordered the attack. The Confederates stood their ground nobly, and being accustomed to the use of fire-arms, made every shot tell.

The Yankees charged and charged, but could not stand the deadly fire poured into their ranks by our men. Randolph captured one of his "masked batteries," and at the first shot with grape and canister, the enemy broke and fled like sheep, leaving their dead and wounded on the field. The effect of Randolph's howitzers on the Yankees was like that which they have on the Indians, who will stand off and fight all day long with long-range guns, but the moment you thunder your artillery at them they drop their arms and fly for their lives. So it was at Bethel. The first discharge played such havoc with their ranks that they threw down their arms and ran away, thus adopting the principle of Hudibras,—

He who fights, and runs away,
Will live to fight another day.

These guns of Randolph's were nothing more nor less than one of those "*masked batteries*" which were such a bugbear and horror to the Yankees the first year of the war. This affair, being the first battle on the seaboard, was considered a most important one in its results. The Confederates had been longing to be led against the enemy to test their mettle. It inspired the men with confidence; it instilled new vigour into their camps.

The enemy, failing in this movement, directed their attention towards Manassas. A party of their cavalry dashed into Fairfax Court House, and captured Captain Ball and nearly the whole of his men doing picket duty. It was in this affair that the gallant Marr fell while trying to rally his men in the face of an overwhelming force. Captain Ball and his men were marched into Washington City, and being the first prisoners of war ever there, they created quite a sensation. No preparation had been made in the metropolis then for the reception and detention of prisoners. They were placed under guard on board the steamboat St. Nicholas, and the officer who made the capture was promoted to a majority.

On the 19th of July the Yankees made a reconnoissance in force, on our lines, at Bull Run. Only three hundred of our men were behind the entrenchments, commanded by Colonel Smith, afterwards Governor of Virginia. The Yankees charged our men several times, but were repulsed with heavy loss, and retreated in great confusion. On the 21st of July the first and one of the hardest fought battles of the war was fought at Manassas. The enemy, having completed all their arrangements, advanced with thirty-five thousand men, under McDowell, and commenced the attack on us at daylight. The battle raged with the greatest fury, the advantage being first on one side then on the other, until five o'clock in the afternoon, when Stonewall Jackson and Kirby Smith came up on our left and determined the fortunes of the day.

The result would have been determined sooner had it not been for the treachery of the conductor of the train, who had been bribed by the enemy to delay the train and prevent the junction with Beauregard. The conductor was bribed by the Yankees to delay the train, by paying him five hundred dollars in gold. On the approach of the train to Manassas, the cannonading could be distinctly heard for a distance of ten or fifteen miles. The eagerness of our men to engage the enemy was so great that the train was stopped ten miles from the scene of action, and the men double-quicked it from there to the field. On our right and centre we were hardest pushed, and were nearly broken down by fighting all day. Our ranks were terribly thinned, the enemy gradually pushing them back, yet every man was fighting like a hero. Indeed, so hard pushed were the Confederates, that General Beauregard sent back orders to Manassas to prepare the works for his men, as he intended to fall back to his fortifications.

While all this was going on, a shout was heard in the distance on our left. The idea of being flanked had seized the minds of the men, and everything looked indeed gloomy. The shout approached nearer, and just at the moment when Beauregard and Johnson were conferring what to do, a courier dashed up, bringing intelligence of the arrival of Kirby Smith and Jackson with two thousand five hundred reinforcements. The intelligence soon spread through the army. A new life was infused into that body of heroes; a final charge was ordered, and those weary, broken-down, and disheartened men responded to it with the alacrity of fresh soldiers. On the left Smith and Jackson's men stopped to form, and charged (half of them without bayonets on their guns) with a yell which seemed to shake the very earth.

The enemy broke and ran, followed by our men. Pressed so hard, divesting themselves of every encumbrance, they fled in the greatest disorder, and did not stop until they reached Alexandria and Washington. After a few minutes' pursuit by our cavalry, their wagon-train was overtaken; horses and mules were taken from it by the horror-stricken Yankees, to facilitate and make good their retreat, or, in fact, *flight*. The roads became blocked up with deserted and broken-down wagons, artillery, and caissons. At Fairfax Court House a Congressional party and some *ladies* had come out to witness the carnage and celebrate their victory with a splendid banquet at Manassas, and follow on with the army in their triumphal march and entry into Richmond. They, however, never realised their bright dreams. Several members of the party, including a Congressman (Mr. Ely), were captured with all their *nice things*, wines, liquors, &c., and sent to Richmond by railroad.

President Davis left Richmond Sunday morning for Manassas, and arrived there at the most critical period of the battle. A number of our best officers had fallen; our ranks so thinned that the only hope there seemed to be left for us was behind the fortifications. He rode on the field, and encouraged the men by his words and actions. That Sunday was an eventful day in the history of Richmond, and will be long remembered. None but the authorities knew that the hardest-fought battle of the war was going on then. A strange spell seemed to hang over the people. Everyone was inquiring, "What's the matter?" Something important was going on. "The president was not at church."

About noon telegrams were received for all the troops in Richmond to get ready to move at a moment's notice. About five o'clock p.m., Mrs. Davis received a dispatch from the president that "a great battle was going on." The news spread like wildfire. The people flocked to Main Street and the hotels to get some intelligence. About eight o'clock p.m., telegrams were received from the president announcing "a great but dear-bought victory." "The enemy are flying in every direction, and our cavalry in hot pursuit." On this being known, the enthusiasm of the people knew no bounds. Bells were rung, salutes fired, &c., &c.

The next day the wounded began to arrive. The hospital accommodations being very limited, the citizens took the wounded heroes to their own houses and nursed them. I went up to visit the battlefield three days after, to look after my brothers. The slaughter of the enemy was very great, for on Wednesday, three days after the battle, large numbers of the enemy were unburied, most of them Ellsworth

Zouaves. Major Haywood, of General Beauregard's staff, kindly furnished me with a horse, which enabled me to view the whole battlefield. The point where Sherman's celebrated battery was captured bore the strongest evidence of the desperation with which the combatants fought. There were seen the wheels of broken caissons, &c., perforated with musket balls, horses shot through and through,—scrub-oaks and pine-bushes with tops shot off,—men headless, &c.

CHAPTER 4: BATTLE OF SEVEN PINES

Everything remained tranquil in Richmond until the next spring, when McClellan commenced the execution of his *Anaconda* system, when by one simultaneous strike by the armies of the Potomac, the Cumberland, and that west of the Mississippi, the Confederate armies were to be crushed and dispersed. It was about this time, March, 1862, that the hero of this book attracted the attention of his superior officers. This truly celebrated man, John Singleton Mosby, was born at "Edgemont," Powhatan County, Virginia, on the 6th day of December, 1833. The place of his birth was one of those beautiful country-seats, peculiar to that region, and was owned by Colonel Mosby's grandfather, James McLaurine. His father was Alfred D. Mosby, a native of Nelson County, Virginia, and a graduate of Hampden Sidney College. Colonel Mosby's mother was a Miss Virginia I. McLaurine, who belonged to one of the best families in the State.

Mr. Alfred D. Mosby, his father, resided in Nelson County, until John was about five years of age, when he purchased "Tudor Grove," one of those lovely country residences which abound around Charlottesville, Virginia. There he resided until John was nineteen years old, when he sold out, and moved to Amherst County. John was the oldest child of his parents, and when a boy, exhibited those traits of character and energy which marked so strongly his later years. Having received a most excellent primary education, at the early age of sixteen years he entered the University of Virginia. Here he made extraordinary progress, graduating in the Greek course the first year, and being the only one who did so that session. He remained there during the years 1851, 1852, and part of 1853, when he graduated with the highest honours.

While there he enjoyed the confidence and esteem of the professors; and Dr. Gesner Harrison frequently remarked that John Mosby would make his mark in life, and that he was one of the most clever young men he had ever known among the students at the University.

He was warm-hearted and high-spirited, and consequently had many warm friends and bitter enemies; but he was never known to forsake a friend in time of need. He is generous to a fault, as his coming out of the war poorer than when he went in abundantly proves. And out of all the prisoners he captured, not one can say that Mosby robbed him. After leaving the university he studied law, and commenced the practice of his profession in Howardsville, Albermarle County, with great success. When quite young he married in Nashville, Tennessee, on the 30th of December, 1857, Miss Pauline Clark, daughter of the Hon. Beverly L. Clark, of Kentucky, and late Minister to Central America. He settled then in Goodson, Washington County, Virginia, and resumed the practice of his profession with extraordinary success, soon ranking as one of the leading members of the bar, and among that number Colonel Goodson stood foremost.

In 1860, signs of national troubles began to be visible in the horizon. The seeds of discord which the fanatics of New England had been sowing for forty years had so thoroughly poisoned the minds of the people in the Northern States that a civil war seemed inevitable. The people of Virginia had exhausted every means of saving the country from the whirlpool into which the New England politicians and fanatics were driving it, and there was no alternative left for the sons of the South but to buckle on their armour and fight it out. Mosby was among the first who responded to the call of the governor for troops to resist the invaders of her soil, by shouldering his gun and volunteering as a private in the First Regiment of Virginia Cavalry. His popularity was so great, and his friends reposed such confidence in him, that the citizens of the county presented him with a fine charger, to commence with, and well has he proved himself worthy of that confidence.

But I must return to my narrative. Our cavalry were picketing in Fairfax and Prince William Counties in March 1862. The Yankees commenced their advance. Mosby, while out scouting near the Potomac River, saw a large column of the enemy moving in a strange direction; he returned immediately, reported the fact to General Stuart, and volunteered to ascertain the object of it. Stuart gave him two men, and out they started. He penetrated the enemy's lines. He went to General Heintzelman's headquarters, and just missed him. While there he found out, from officers on Heintzelman's Staff, the whole of McClellan's plans. Distrusting them, he was provided with passes, and went down to see for himself. He found their statement correct. He returned to Stuart, and reported McClellan transporting his troops to the peninsula—and the column he saw moving was to deceive our army. In consequence of this intelligence, Johnson and Beauregard determined on an immediate evacuation of Manassas and Centreville. In a few hours the Confederate Army was moving to the Peninsula *via* Richmond. The evacuation was not an hour too soon.

By the time Longstreet had arrived at Williamsburg to re-enforce Magruder, McClellan with one hundred and thirty-five thousand men, had landed at Fortress Monroe and was moving up the peninsula. An engagement ensued at Williamsburg, a portion of McClellan's army was driven back by one division under Longstreet, who was compelled to fall back on account of the danger of being flanked by the enemy's gunboats. At West Point General Franklin's corps was repulsed by a Texas brigade. Yet McClellan telegraphed to Washington, that he was "pushing Johnston to the wall," and *"that a few hours' march would bring him to Richmond."* A great deal of apprehension that the city would be evacuated, prevailed in Richmond. General Johnson determined by one bold stroke to annihilate his adversary.

The Battle of Seven Pines was fought, and but for the wounding of General Johnston on the second day's fight, there can be no question in the minds of any military man, that McClellan's army would have been destroyed. The watercourses ran high, and the country was flooded with water. Our men fought in the swamps with water and mud up to their knees. General Johnston was wounded Sunday morning, the second day's fighting. On Saturday the battle commenced before noon. The thunder of artillery and rattling of musketry could be distinctly heard in the city. Hundreds of citizens flocked to the roof of the Capitol from which, with the aid of glasses, could be seen in the swamps of the Chickahominy, the bursting of the shells, &c.

The battles ceased Sunday about ten o'clock a.m. General Johnston was carried into Richmond to receive medical aid, his wound not being very dangerous; but he got three of his ribs broken by falling from his horse. General Lee assumed command of the army. He reorganised it—and enforced discipline, recruited his army, and fortified himself. Fears were entertained in Richmond by the citizens that McClellan would get in. Large numbers left the place; some ran off and left their houses vacant, while others sold out at a great sacrifice.

About this time the name of *Jeb* Stuart had got to be a terror to the enemy, and while McClellan was lying around Richmond, Mosby proposed to General Stuart to make a raid around McClellan's army.

Stuart requested him to put his plans in writing, which he did, and Stuart submitted them to General Lee. He approved it and authorised Mosby to take as many men as he wanted. He took two with him, and passing through Dr. Price's farm was chased by the Second United States Dragoons until dark, and the party escaped. The scouting was resumed the next day.

When near the Richmond and York River Railroad, they met the same regiment drawn up in line of battle. There was no chance of escape, and knowing their dread of Stuart he rode out with his men in full view of the enemy, and raising himself in his saddle, and looking back and beckoning with his hat, cried out at the top of his voice, which made the very welkin ring, "*Here they are Jeb!*" The enemy, concluding Stuart was in the woods nearby with his whole cavalry force, broke and ran away, with Mosby and his two men after them. The major of the regiment was killed, and his fine gray horse captured and brought to Stuart's headquarters. Mosby was complimented for this daring act, and presented with the horse.

Chapter 5: Battle of Harrison's Landing

Lee and Stuart being convinced of the practicability of Mosby's plan for a raid round the enemy's army, one was determined on. The country is familiar with that brilliant achievement, how Stuart and his men swam the rising Chickahominy, &c., &c., and returned to our lines without losing a man. Mosby was Stuart's guide on that occasion. General Lee having completed all his arrangements for an advance, started Mosby with important verbal dispatches, to General Jackson, and while resting his horse at Beaver Dam Station, on the Virginia Central Railroad, the enemy dashed in and took him prisoner. Being suspected to be a courier with important dispatches, he was searched diligently; but none were found, and he frightened the enemy away from the railroad by telling them a train of cars, loaded with infantry and artillery, would be there in a few minutes. They retreated precipitately.

Mosby was carried to General McCook's headquarters, and was asked where Jackson and Stuart were. "*He didn't know*" and "*couldn't see it.*" He was then sent to Washington guarded by seven men. His fame as one of Stuart's principal scouts had already reached the Yankee army. He was kindly treated. Lee was concentrating his whole strength around Richmond, and his army did not exceed eighty thousand men. While strengthening himself thus, Jackson was sweeping every-

A. E. RICHARDS

thing before him in the valley, and as a blind to the enemy, General Lee dispatched Whiting's division to Staunton to reinforce him; they, however, returned by rail on the next train.

General Lee's plans being now completed, by an arrangement, Jackson, after having driven the enemy out of the valley, swept, as if by magic, down the railroad to General Lee's left, and rested his army six hours at Ashland on the Fredericksburg and Potomac Railroad. One hour after his arrival there, he rode into Richmond at midnight, with no one but an orderly, conferred with the president and General Lee, and returned to commence the attack at daylight the next morning. The signal for the attack was the firing of three guns. General Lee commenced the attack, the signal was given, the firing of three guns, and promptly did Jackson respond. Then the fighting extended along the whole line of both armies. The Yankees unexpectedly found an army in their rear, as if they had dropped down from the clouds. The utmost confusion prevailed in the ranks of the enemy.

On pressed the *Stonewall*, his men mowing down the enemy. Their battle-cry "Jackson," acted as magic on the enemy. They could not realise that an army which, twenty-fours before, was five hundred miles from them, with the Big Blue Ridge Mountains between, would now be behind them, inflicting the same deadly blows on them they had dealt on their friends in the Valley. Yet it was a fearful reality to them. They retreated; they fled like chaff before the wind. McClellan, who proudly boasted he would capture[1] the city without firing a gun, was now skulking, like a whipped dog, in the morass around Harrison's Landing.

Richmond was free once more from the menace of a merciless foe. The people, who a few days before, were gloomy and almost despaired of ever realising their hope of an independent government by reason of the disasters to our arms in the West, under the great Albert Sydney Johnston, who sacrificed his life in vindicating his character as a soldier, against the malicious and dishonourable insinuations of the politicians and croakers, and the fall of McIntosh and McCullough in Arkansas, were now reanimated. Business revived, and citizens who had abandoned their property returned. Recruits began to come in rapidly.

The Sunday after the seven days' battle around Richmond, Generals Lee, Jackson, Longstreet, Polk, and others, attended divine worship in Richmond. This was Jackson's first visit to Richmond since the

---

1. See his Dispatches.

commencement of the war. The anxiety of the people to see this remarkable man was so great, that as soon as it was known he was at Dr. Hayes' church, a large crowd assembled in front of it to see him when he came out. Nothing would satisfy them short of shaking hands with him. And so strong was their attachment for him they cut all the buttons off his coat. The crowd was increasing every moment, but the crazy general would not gratify all of them. He broke through the crowd, and, taking the arm of a friend, went home with him. The next day he returned to his division.

Heretofore the Yankees would entertain no proposition leading to an exchange of prisoners, but now their great *"Little Mac"* had been beaten so badly and lost nearly half of his army, they were inclined to come to terms on that point. Every available warehouse and vacant building was filled with their wounded and prisoners; and they had become not only a burthen on the government, but a nuisance to the people. Accordingly, a cartel for the exchange of prisoners was agreed upon, and amongst the first exchanged, was John S. Mosby. The vessel he was on, when it reached Fortress Monroe, was detained several days in consequence of important military movements going on. During that detention none of the prisoners were allowed to go on deck. Mosby, looking through one of the port-holes of the vessel, discovered vessels, loaded with troops, moving; and he determined, if possible, to find out what it meant.

Conceiving the idea that McClellan was evacuating Harrison's Landing, he by some means got on deck, and saw the captain of the vessel A conversation ensued between them, and Mosby's voice having a little of that twang which is peculiar to the Yankees, he easily ingratiated himself into the confidence of the captain of the boat, who told him he had been engaged a week in carrying troops from Harrison's Landing. The next day the vessel he was on started for City Point, where he was exchanged. He mounted a horse as soon as he got ashore, and I rode that night to General Lee's headquarters, and informed him of the movements of the enemy. General Lee complimented him for his intelligence, &c., &c. The next morning the whole Confederate Army was set in motion, and on the march. Richmond was relieved of the swarms of soldiers that infested the place while the army was around it. There is nothing more injurious to an army than to be quartered near a large city.

Soon after these important events had occurred around Richmond, McClellan was relieved of his command, and General Pope, the general whose "headquarters were in the saddle, and whose back was never turned on the enemy," took command of the *finest army the sun ever shone upon*, the Army of the Potomac. My readers are perfectly familiar with his *brilliant* but brief career; how he went up like a skyrocket and came down like a stick; how the second Battle of Manassas would have been won had certain generals carried out certain orders of his, &c., &c. Jackson played the same prominent part in this battle that he did in those around Richmond. While Longstreet engaged the enemy in Thoroughfare Gap, Jackson crossed the Bull Run Mountains lower down, at Aldie. Longstreet then threw a small force through Hopwell Gap, thus flanking the enemy.

The Yankees retreated in confusion, and were followed up by Longstreet with his whole force. The thundering of the artillery in the distance told with what fury the battle was raging. Jackson was hard-pressed, but his men stood their ground. Soon Longstreet re-enforced him, and the slaughter of the enemy then it is fearful to think of now. They were routed; Pope himself left all his personal effects, including official papers, &c., and escaped in his shirtsleeves. In his flight he left his sword behind to be captured by Lieutenant Charles Minnigerode, son of Rev. Mr. Minnigerode, pastor of St. Paul's Church in Richmond.

In Richmond the greatest enthusiasm prevailed, and hopes were entertained of a speedy termination of the war. Trade revived, and new recruits came in to give the invasion of the South the finishing blow. After a short time of rest given the army, General Lee invaded Maryland. The battles of Boonsboro', Antietam, and Sharpsburg were fought. The hard fighting of this campaign, with the long and rapid marches, had nearly exhausted the troops. At Antietam the battle was a drawn one, and no victory to the enemy. If they claim it, why did not the enemy follow up their success? They incurred such a loss as to render a pursuit impracticable. General Lee recrossed the Potomac, and took a position on the Rappahannock and went into winter quarters. Fighting Joe Hooker was put in command of the Army of the Potomac. He occupied Falmouth opposite Fredericksburg, and attempted to scatter Lee's army at the Wilderness in the winter. He led his men into a slaughter-pen. They were horribly butchered, and left thousands of prisoners. Great alarm prevailed in Washington. The president and his Cabinet prepared at once to leave the city.

Urgent appeals were made to the people to send in reinforcements to defend the Capital. The draft was inadequate to furnish men fast enough for Southern bullets. The governors of the different Northern

States (particularly the Governor of Pennsylvania) called out the whole militia force of the State. This battle of the Wilderness was the severest blow the Yankees had yet received. The Border States were apprehensive the rebels would wage a war of invasion the next campaign. They were not mistaken in their apprehensions; for during the remainder of the winter General Lee was concentrating all his available men for the purpose of carrying the war into the enemy's own country.

Chapter 6: Alarm in Richmond

It was this winter, or rather during the month of March, that Mosby received his commission as captain in the Confederate States army, and authority to wage a partisan ranger war on the enemy. General Stuart first gave him fifteen men, and then increased the number to thirty, with privilege to select his own men. Generals Lee and Stuart both knew the value of Mosby as a scout, and the invaluable service he would render them in that capacity. They also authorised him to raise his company to the full quota. So when the spring campaign opened he had but thirty men.

While these preparations were going on, Burnside took command of the Union Army, then lying on the hills of Stafford opposite Fredericksburg. While there, Kilpatrick and Dahlgren make their celebrated raid on Richmond, and in which the latter lost his life. On Dahlgren's body was found a copy of the orders he was directed to execute. The substance of them was, they were to institute an indiscriminate slaughter of the innocent people of Richmond, including the president and his Cabinet, and to set fire to the public buildings. But Providence decreed otherwise. Dahlgren lost his way and was obliged to fly through the lower counties. In King and Queen County there were a few regular soldiers at their homes on furlough, who got together and determined to harass and do them all the damage they could, and knowing the road Dahlgren would take, they determined to lie in ambush for him.

Presently the Federal troops came along, Dahlgren with four or five men in advance. Hearing a rustling in the leaves, Dahlgren demands a surrender. The response he received was a volley from the Confederates. Dahlgren fell from his horse lifeless. His comrades fell back to the main column, and without a guide, in a hostile country, and their main reliance, Dahlgren, killed, the remaining officers held a consultation, and concluded to surrender, first killing their horses and destroying their weapons. Some prisoners of ours they held, however, persuaded them not to do such an insane act; that if they did, they would forfeit the respect due to prisoners of war, and would most certainly be killed. Their councils prevailed, and they surrendered the next morning to thirty men under the command of Captain ——, and were marched up to Richmond and furnished with accommodations in the Libby. The orders were published, and the citizens of Richmond were perfectly amazed at the fate they had escaped, and could scarcely believe that anyone in the nineteenth century was capable of such a diabolical scheme. Dahlgren's body—*minus* his cork leg—was brought to Richmond for identification, and buried in Potter's Field.

Kilpatrick, however, was more fortunate. He penetrated our lines on the Brooke Turnpike as far as the Hon. James Lyon's residence, and a mile and a half from Richmond, and in full view of its State House, spires, and public buildings. On reaching this point, the last line of breastworks between them and the city, and behind which there were not one hundred men, he threw himself at the head of his men, pulled off his hat, and pointing with it to the city, cried out, "*Follow me, men, and in five minutes we will have the city.*" Why they did not follow their general I have never learned. They could not realise the fact that the city at that moment lay at their mercy. They seemed spellbound, and sat on their horses like mummies. They doubtless would have followed their general, but they must have imagined there were some masked batteries between that point and the city, but no piece of artillery was nearer them than the city, and only one company of infantry behind the breastworks at the time they were drawn up in line of battle before them.

If they had got into the city, I doubt very much whether any would have got out alive. Every man in the city had a musket, and in two minutes' time artillery could have been placed in position to have raked every street. The demonstration of the enemy at this point was entirely unexpected by those in authority. They had had no intimation of this raid, for when this demonstration was made there was not a single piece of artillery behind .this inner line of works. The greatest excitement prevailed in Richmond. The town bell was rung, and the citizens were soon under arms and marching out to the entrenchments by companies and battalions, to resist and drive back the incendiaries and invaders.

This winter the star of the Army of Northern Virginia was at its zenith. The army lay on the banks of the Rappahannock River, prouder and more defiant than ever. General Hooker had assumed command of the Army of the Potomac. Before the Congressional Committee on the War, Hooker testified he was the only man in the North who could whip General Lee, and that if he had command of the Army of the Potomac, he would march rough-shod over Lee, and take Richmond without any difficulty. He would have got there, too, as a prisoner of war, but for that lamentable occurrence, the accidental shooting, by our own men, of that hero of the war, Stonewall Jackson. Everything being ready with the enemy for an advance, pontoons were thrown across the river, the Yankee Army crossed, and our batteries opened on them. The river was filled with killed and wounded; large numbers were drowned. Three times they attempted to cross before they succeeded; then ensued the bloody battle of Chancellorsville, which my reader is perfectly familiar with, and in which that great Napoleon of the war, Thomas Jonathan Jackson, fell by the hand of his own men, and in that fall the star of the Confederacy began to wane, and finally set to rise no more, at Appomattox Court House, Va., on the 6th of April, 1865.

His biographers will do more justice to him than I can; but had he not fallen that night, General Hooker's whole army would have surrendered the next morning or been killed. However, so far, it had been a most complete victory. The enemy lost over thirty thousand, killed, wounded, and prisoners. The news of Jackson's being wounded spread rapidly through the army, and so great was the confidence of the army, and the respect of the commanding general (Lee) for him, that the battle was not renewed the next morning. Hooker's generals declining to lead their men into such slaughter-pens another day, recrossed the Rappahannock the next day with his whole army. Jackson lingered only a few days, and when he passed from this earth there was one universal shriek throughout the land.

His death sounded in the ears of the Southerners like the death-knell of the Confederacy. His remains were brought to Richmond on a special train, carried to the governor's mansion, and there embalmed the next day. The most imposing and the largest procession, military and civil, ever seen in Richmond, bore the body to the Capitol, where it lay in state until the next morning. All the departments of the government were closed, and business entirely suspended, and bells tolled while the procession was moving. It was indeed a melancholy sight to see the thousands of old men, women, and even soldiers, as the coffin passed into the hearse, drop the tears of sorrow as if some dear member of their family had died.

The procession consisted of part of General Pickett's division of veterans, artillery and cavalry and citizens, together with the President and members of the Cabinet. During that afternoon some thirty thousand persons passed in single file the metallic car to get a last farewell glimpse of the features of him who only a few hours before had made the North tremble and the world gaze with wonder and delight at his deeds of valour.

Chapter 7: Remarkable Escape of Mosby

The result of the Battle of Chancellorsville again produced the greatest excitement and alarm in Washington. A new draft was ordered, from apprehension of an invasion by Lee. Hooker's army having been nearly destroyed in the Wilderness and Chancellorsville battles, there was nothing in his way to prevent Lee from going into Pennsylvania. He accordingly began to recruit and marshal his forces for an invasion of the North when the season opened. Mosby, who had been sent to the Fauquier Valley, had performed prodigies. Touching his capture of General Stoughton at Fairfax Court House, he thus wrote to a friend in Richmond:—

> You have already seen something in the newspapers of my recent raid on the Yankees, though I see they all call me Moseley instead of Mosby. I had only twenty men under my command. I penetrated about ten miles in their lines, rode right up to the general's headquarters surrounded by infantry, artillery, and cavalry, took him out of his bed, and brought him off. I walked into his room with two of my men, and shaking him in bed, said, '*General, get up.*' He rose up; and, rubbing his eyes, asked what was the meaning of all this. I replied, '*It means, sir, that Stuart's cavalry are in possession of this place, and you are a prisoner.*' We also surrounded the headquarters of Colonel Wyndham, acting brigadier-general of cavalry, but unfortunately he had gone to Washington.
> We got his assistant adjutant-general, and also his aid, an Austrian, Baron Woodsan. There was an immense amount of all kinds of stores collected there, but I was unable to destroy them. .... It was my intention and desire to reach the Court House by twelve o'clock that night, but it being very dark we lost our way, thereby losing two hours. I did not stay in the place more than one hour. On our return to Fauquier, we passed within two hundred yards of the fortifications at Centreville. We were

hailed by the sentinel. One of the prisoners, Captain Barker of New York, tried to escape by making a break for the picket, but a pistol-shot from one of the party brought him back. In the vicinity of Fairfax Court House were encamped our cavalry and our infantry brigade. We easily captured the guards around the town, as they never dreamed we were anybody but Yankees until they saw pistols pointed at their heads, with a demand to surrender.

The scout on this raid was a New Englander,—a native of the State of Maine, and a member of the Fifth New York Cavalry, who fought with distinction under the Stars and Stripes. On the proclamation of Abraham Lincoln, liberating the negroes, and the inauguration of drafting men for the army, he refused to serve their cause any longer. He was as fine a specimen of a man as I ever saw. Powerful in frame, a splendid swordsman, and good shot, he was eminent in bravery and courage. He, however, could not fight for the eternal negro. He took French leave of them, and came over and offered his services to Mosby. Mosby was a little shy of him at first, fearing some trap had been set to catch him, and the Yankees sent Ames over to be the instrument in accomplishing it. So he declined to take him at first, but gave him authority to prove the sincerity of his intentions. Ames went out and entered the enemy's camps in the night-time, gained important information, and returned the next morning with two or three horses and prisoners.

It was on one of these expeditions that he determined to capture his general. Mosby being convinced by these acts that he was all right, "took him to his bosom." Ames being perfectly familiar with all the picket-posts, the position and strength of the troops at Fairfax Court House, and the unguarded points, Mosby took him on this raid, and the capture was made without firing a shot. After this, he enjoyed Mosby's fullest confidence, and was taken by him on his most perilous expeditions. The boldness and success of this enterprise attracted the attention not only of the whole South and the army, but elicited from General Stuart the following flattering order:—

Headquarters Cavalry Division,
March 12, 1868.

General Orders.
Captain John S. Mosby has for a long time attracted the attention of his generals by his boldness, skill, and success, so signally

displayed in his numerous forays upon the invaders of his native soil.

None know his daring enterprise and dashing heroism better than those foul invaders, those strangers themselves to such noble traits.

His last brilliant exploit—the capture of Brigadier-General Stoughton, U. S. A., two captains, and thirty other prisoners, together with their arms, equipments, and fifty-eight horses—justifies this recognition in General Orders. This feat, unparalleled in the war, was performed in the midst of the enemy's troops, at Fairfax Court House, without loss or injury.

The gallant band of Captain Mosby shares his glory, as they did the danger of this enterprise, and are worthy of such a leader.

J. E. B. Stuart,
Major-General Commanding.

This bold enterprise stamped Mosby at once as another rising military character, and in due course of time to rank with Stuart, Morgan, Forrest, and the eminent cavalry leaders. As an appreciation of this piece of service, he was promoted to a majority, and designated his battalion as the 43rd Virginia Battalion of Cavalry.

On the 22nd of March, 1863, Mosby, with thirty men, attacked the enemy at Bristow Station, on the Orange and Alexandria Railroad. He captured four commissioned officers and twenty-one privates without receiving the least injury. But, owing to the difficulty of getting out, he paroled the privates, and brought off only the officers, who were sent to Richmond. In the spring of 1863, we find Lee on the banks of the Rappahannock, preparing his army for the invasion of the enemy's own country. Mosby, with his headquarters in Fauquier County, was harassing the enemy around Washington, Alexandria, and the line of the Baltimore and Ohio Railroad. He had men with him peculiarly fitted for that kind of service, men remarkable for their courage and acuteness.

There were amongst them three brothers from Fairfax County, who served with him in the regular service, and John Bush and Sam Underwood. These boys used to live in the Yankee camps, and always had plenty of greenbacks. John, one night, while scouting between Fairfax and Alexandria, had a cow-bell around his neck, and went into their camp on all-fours, and brought out five of the finest horses he could find, all belonging to officers. Morning came; and the horses were missed, and could be found nowhere. Upon inquiry, and investigating the matter, to their mortification they found they had been duped, which so provoked them that the commanding officer ordered the bells to be taken off every cow in the neighbourhood for ten miles around. Poor fellow! he lost his life by bushwhackers while on one of these expeditions near Alexandria.

In April, 1863, when scouting with ten men, and near Centreville, he heard of a wagon-train passing up to the army at Warrenton. He rode into the town in the night-time, and reported to the commanding officer as being in charge of a squad of men sent to guard the wagon-train. The officer in command put Mosby and his squad to guard the rear of the train, which they did successfully; but, when beyond their pickets, the ten rear wagons were ordered to be driven in the woods by the road, and then the horses (forty) were detached from them and carried back to Fauquier. A few days after this, with twenty-five men, he captured, below Billy Goodwin's tavern on the turnpike, forty loaded sutler-wagons. The contents were destroyed; but the horses and prisoners were brought off safely.

Early in the month of May, Mosby performed one of the most extraordinary deeds of his whole career. Passing through Prince William County, he and his men, sixty in all, were feeding their horses in the barn-lot of a farm near Dranesville, with saddles off and the gate closed. The Fifth New York Cavalry, two hundred and fifty strong, charged on them with sabres and carbines. Our men took shelter in the barn until twenty-five of them could bridle and saddle their horses; some, including Mosby, mounting their horses bareback, and opening the gate under a heavy fire, charged the enemy with pistols. Our men closed in on them, pouring a deadly fire into their ranks; indeed, every shot seemed to tell. The enemy could not stand such a fire: they broke, and fled in great confusion. We captured seventy horses and twenty-five prisoners, besides killing and wounding about the same number. Mosby and his men sustained neither loss nor injury.

In the month of May, Mosby, with thirty-five men and one piece of artillery, attacked a train of cars on the Orange and Alexandria Railroad, at Warrenton Junction. The guard to the train was driven away and the cars destroyed, and he began to retire. The enemy being re-enforced by a regiment of cavalry, pursued him. With this small body of men he fought and kept at bay, for over one hour, the whole regiment of cavalry, and then did not *take care of themselves* until his ammunition was exhausted and artillery captured, and in the retreat he lost only three men, who were captured. A few days after this, when Mosby was returning from scouting in the lower part of Fairfax County, he reached the Bull Run Mountains, and, feeling fatigued, lay down in the shade of one of the large chestnut-trees, and dropped to sleep. While in that condition two Yankees passing by recognised him. They demanded his surrender. Realising his critical situation, and knowing it would require a bold and sudden movement on his part to extricate himself, and never losing his presence of mind or expressing, in the least degree, excitement under the trying circumstances, he suddenly jumped up, and with one arm, knocked away the pistols pointed at his breast, while, with the other hand, he shot one of his would-be capturers, and the other ran away.

On another occasion during this month, while scouting with Ames, he was, during Ames's absence for a few moments, attacked by *seven* Yankees. Three Yankees were killed, and both parties having exhausted the loads in their pistols, Mosby's adversaries drew their sabres and attacked him. He was as skilful in warding off their thrusts with the pistol as an experienced swordsman, although he had never had a sabre in his hand before this war; besides, he never was partial to the use of this weapon, relying entirely on the pistol. Ames, hearing the firing, came up to Mosby's assistance and saved his life. Ames, being skilled in the use of the sabre, made two of the enemy bite the dust with his sabre, while the other two fled for their lives; and thus was Mosby's life spared to again carry terror into the armies of the invaders of his native soil.

Ames himself, in a few days, was placed in a similar situation. He was the bravest Yankee any of us had ever seen. Having determined, when he cast his fortunes with us, to never surrender or be taken alive, my readers can form some idea of the desperation with which he fought when he encountered five of the enemy. It happened in one of the gorges of the Bull Run Mountains, and the scenery and incidents would furnish a splendid theme for the dramatist for a tragedy. In a deep ravine, with a large, ugly rock projecting almost over the pass, surrounded with lofty trees &c., were five men against one. engaged in deadly combat. The one fighting for his life and a great, noble principle, and the other five fighting for a tyrant, plunder, and lucre. Ames emptied his two pistols (twelve loads,) killing two of his adversaries, and repulsing, or rather putting to flight the other three. He himself, however, was severely wounded in the right arm, which rendered him unable to do duty for nearly a year.

Chapter 8: Battle of Gettysburg

In Richmond, and throughout the South, important and beneficial results were expected from General Lee's invasion of the North. His army was as large as it ever was. The soldiers, flushed with victory, were in splendid spirits. Great and numerous were the speculations in regard to results of the invasion. He began to advance in the month of June, and met with no opposition until the Potomac was crossed. In fact the enemy were ignorant of his whereabouts until the appearance of his troops on the Maryland side of the classic Potomac. His advance guard penetrated the North as far as York, Pennsylvania. Great excitement prevailed in Philadelphia, and serious apprehension was felt that he would attack that city. In Lee's line of march the utmost respect was paid to private property. No private houses were searched for arms; no ladies insulted or robbed; no ladies' wardrobes broken open, and robbed of their clothing and jewellery.

How different were the marches of Generals Lee and Stuart, through Pennsylvania and Maryland, from that of General Sheridan's cavalry and the Army of the Potomac, when ladies were insulted and robbed of their jewellery, rings taken from their fingers by force, their entire wardrobes and bed-clothing taken and sent to families in the Northern States! Hen and turkey roosts were robbed; meat-houses broken open and meat taken, leaving not a single piece for the already ruined people; hogs shot down in the fields; sheep and cows driven off; and houses searched, for arms, they said, but in reality for nothing else than for money, jewellery, and fine clothing. Even the poor negro, for whom they expressed so much sympathy, and for whom they were fighting, had his little cabin searched and robbed of what little money he had laid aside for a "*wet day.*"

Milk-houses were broken open and robbed of their contents, and barns and stables burned. As an instance, when Ouster's cavalry were applying the torch to every barn and stable, every rick of hay, wheat, and straw in Loudon County, Virginia, a party of them, led by a major (I regret his name is not known), rode up to a house occupied by a widow lady and daughter, and asked for some refreshments. There was nothing on the place but a very fine spring. After water from that had been furnished, the major ordered his men to apply the torch to the barn and granary. The daughter, a beautiful girl of sixteen summers, came out, and pleaded with the commanding officer (this major) to spare them, declaring no soldiers had ever boarded at her mother's house. He finally consented to spare them at the sacrifice of her virtue.

The daughter returned to the house weeping, and this soldier had all the outhouses burned. If this single act is not sufficient to damn the Yankee cavalry in the eyes of the world, it is difficult to say what is so.

Where is that proud spirit of the North, with all its boasted philanthropy; those who profess a sort of Puritanical, *par-excellent* infallibility; the vicegerents of high Heaven to teach morality? Do they endorse a wholesale war upon defenceless women and children by such vandals? Alas! the human soul shudders at the conviction that these men, by such acts of oppression, were representing a faction who controlled the ship of state at Washington, and expressly obeyed the outside pressure, while those in authority secretly gloated over such outrages. They all loved the Union, *per se*, just as much as William Lloyd Garrison did. He was one of their leaders, and enunciated, as a sort of truism, that:

> THIS UNION is A LIE! THE AMERICAN UNION is AN IMPOSTURE, A COVENANT WITH DEATH, AND AN AGREEMENT WITH HELL! . . . I AM FOR ITS OVERTHROW!. . . .Up with the flag of DISUNION, that we may have a free and glorious Republic of our own; and when the hour shall come, the hour will have arrived that shall witness the overthrow of slavery.

In this connection it may not be improper to refer to the numerous arbitrary arrests of non-combatants, by *lettres de cachet*, in other portions of the country, as early as 1862, in verification of our position, that the dominant party in the North really detest the fundamental principles of self-government.

We take the following from the *Congressional Globe*. It relates to proceedings in the United States Senate:—

> Mr. Powell.—I will take this occasion to say what I was about to say a moment ago, when I was held not to be in order. It is not my purpose to enter again into a debate on this subject; but it has been intimated that the remarks I made in regard to the Secretary of State were rather harsh. I admit that they were a little harsh, sir, but I verily believe they were true. I hold in my hand a letter written to me by a very distinguished gentleman of Kentucky, in which he recites an interview that took place with the Secretary of State concerning one of the prisoners from Kentucky, as given to him by Colonel Throop, a gentleman of very high standing, and I beg to read to the Senate an

abstract from that letter:—

> While Colonel Stanton, of this city, was still a prisoner at Fort Lafayette, his brother-in-law, Colonel Throop, employed (through my agency) Mr. Charles F. Mitchell, of Flemingsburg, formerly a member of Congress from New York, and, as I knew, an intimate friend and correspondent of Seward's, to accompany him (Throop) to Washington, to promote Colonel Stanton's release. They were joined at Washington by Frederick Stanton, a brother of Colonel Stanton. The three called on Mr. Seward, Throop and Stanton being introduced by Mitchell. They opened their mission by remarking that they had called to see him in reference to the Maysville prisoners. He abruptly replied that those prisoners would not be released. Frederick asked, "What are the charges against my brother?"
>
> Mr. Seward replied, "There are no charges against him on file;" and added that the business of his office pressed him too much to entertain inquiries or give explanations. One inquired if it was his purpose to keep citizens imprisoned, against whom no charges were made. He answered, harshly, "I do not care a d—n whether they are guilty or innocent. I saved Maryland by similar arrests, and so I mean to hold Kentucky." To this it was remarked that the legislature and public sentiment of Kentucky were averse to such arrests. "I do not care a d—n for the opinion of Kentucky," he insultingly responded; adding that what he required was to hold her in the Union and make her fight for it; and then turning fiercely on Mitchell, demanded of him, "Why the hell are you not at home fighting traitors instead of seeking their release here?"
>
> This is the substance of the interview as related to me by Colonel Throop.

I will say to the Senate that Mr. Frederick Stanton told me, a few days after it occurred, this very conversation, I will not say in these exact words, but in substance; and I know Colonel Throop to be as honourable a gentleman as lives in Kentucky or any other State.

But I am digressing. We left General Lee on the north side of the Potomac River, advancing into Pennsylvania,—the last intelligence the authorities in Richmond had received of his whereabouts. Ewell was in York, Pa. His extensive line of communication being interrupted, nothing concerning his movements could be heard, except through Northern papers, and they not reliable. There was no uneasiness, however, amongst the people. They knew there was at the head of that army the greatest military chieftain of the nineteenth century. The confidence of the Southern people in him was the same as that which their forefathers reposed in the father of his country in the first revolution. The Battle of Gettysburg was fought, and the enemy whipped, as the people of the North know. If they were not, why did they begin to retreat *nine hours* before General Lee?

After long marching in the heat of summer, and the men exhausted fighting for several days, with nearly three hundred miles of communication to be kept open, out of ammunition, could a skilful general like Lee commence a pursuit of these who were supplied with abundance of ammunition, particularly when the odds were so great against him, and the enemy receiving re-enforcements every hour by their railways? General Lee had (it is estimated) about ninety thousand men in the series of engagements, while the enemy, independent of the army proper, which was estimated at two hundred and fifty or three hundred thousand, had the militia of Pennsylvania, Maryland, New Jersey, New York, and other States of the North. General Lee fell back to Hagerstown near his supplies, and waited there with his men drawn up in line of battle for three days, courting an attack from his adversary, General Meade.

Lee in the meanwhile was not idle. Fortifying himself at this place, he began to recross the Potomac, sending his trains first. If General Lee was whipped as badly as the *Baltimore American* said he was, "his army scattered to the four winds of the heavens and forty thousand of them prisoners," why did not General Meade attack him at Hagerstown, Maryland? Meade knew with whom he was dealing, and, like an able general, declined making such a dangerous and rash ,movement, notwithstanding the importunities of Stanton. The crossing was effected by Lee without opposition, and he moved thence toward his old position on the Rapidan.

The extravagant and studied falsehoods of the Northern press eventually induced the rulers to believe that Lee's army was very much crippled. The enemy threw a corps forward to annihilate Longstreet.

The forces met between Linden and Chester Gaps, in the Blue Ridge Mountains. Longstreet was prepared to meet the attack. Their attempt to dislodge him only served to teach the invaders that the Hills were too steep, Streets too long, and Stonewalls impregnable. The dashing Stewart, with his invincible cavaliers, found work for his arm of the service on the road from Leesburg to N Paris. In these engagements and skirmishes the enemy's loss in killed, wounded, and prisoners, was acknowledged to be twelve hundred.

In this memorable campaign Mosby and his partisans were by no means idle. General Lee relied upon this branch of his army for much valuable information as to the disposition and movements of the enemy's forces. His dashes into their lines will doubtless be remembered.

Lee's orders for the preservation of private property, and the protection of professed non-combatants was the subject of some censure. He had passed over the rich valleys of his native State,—on every hand were the marks of desolation inflicted by a relentless foe,—and marched with a half-naked, shoeless, and starving army, into the enemy's territory teeming with wealth; and notwithstanding the terrible examples set before him, upon his arrival in the enemy's country, no supplies were appropriated without an adequate return of the *quid pro quo*.

In reference to Mosby, who had been denounced by the Yankee scribblers with such select, choice, and classic appellations as "Land Pirate," "Horse Thief," "Murderer," "Guerilla," &c., he strictly refrained from executing the *lex talionis*. His loss during the campaign was one man severely wounded (Alfred Glasscock). To mark the contrast between our mode of conducting the war and that of our enemies, we will here give some extracts from a letter of a private soldier in the Thirty-sixth Ohio Regiment, U. S., published in the Monroe, Ohio, *Spirit of the Democracy*:

> On the evening of the 11th, five companies of the regiment started on a scout. I set fire myself to several barns, haystacks, straw-ricks, &c. It was pitiful to hear the pleadings of the wives of 'secesh' soldiers, not to destroy their property. We shot all the sheep, pigs, and calves that we could not carry off. In one or two places we came across some beehives, and then the men would pitch in and surfeit themselves on the sweet contents. The captain, at one place, sent me down to a house with three men, with orders to search the house, fire the outhouses, and bring off all the cattle that were fat enough to kill. I got the woman

to talking with one of the men, and, seizing a brand from the fireplace, set a barn full of wheat afire. I took off two horses, but left her three lean cows. There was a hive full of beautiful white honey, which the men opened, though they were already surfeited. If she had not been a widow, it would have been my duty to shoot the cows, calves and sheep, and leave them to rot upon the ground, if I could not drive them off.

At the place where we stayed over night, there were two barns full of hay and grain, two haystacks, two straw-ricks, and a large shed burning at once. A grand spectacle! But it made me feel sort of sneaking to destroy property in that way, when there was none to defend it. At two or three places where we burned property the women thought that I was an officer, and came to me and plead for an only cow or an old family horse, and when I referred them to the captain, upon whom they had already exhausted their entreaties, they begged me to use my influence to have them left. One kind-looking woman, whose barn had been set on fire, came to me while I had stopped a moment to fix my accoutrements, after the rest of the company had gone after her cattle, and offered to do anything in the world for me if I would only use my influence to have her cattle left. But I had to hurry off, thinking, as I did so, what I would do to an enemy that would treat my mother and sisters in that way. Would that the vengeance could descend upon the heads of those men who left their families to the mercy of an invader!

Alfred Glasscock, one of Mosby's most valuable men, was seriously wounded.

Chapter 9: The Writer Joins Mosby

General Lee's return to his old position, somewhat disappointed the people in the South; but when they reflected what long marches his men had made, what a long line of communication he had to keep open, how the enemy were whipped and slaughtered at Gettysburg, how he regained and reoccupied his old position, and stood as proud and defiant as ever, they became satisfied. Appeals were made to the people to come forward and volunteer. The Conscript Act was enforced with more vigour than ever. Young men, with sinecure positions in the departments, resigned and entered the army. Every able-bodied and patriotic young man manifested a desire to have his name associated in some way with the Army of Northern Virginia. Mosby's name by his heroic deeds had become a household word by this time, and all the daring young spirits were eager to join him. Of the regular service they had a holy horror. They imagined if they could only get with Gilman, Imboden, White, or Mosby, they would have an opportunity for active service, could win laurels more lasting, and, if they fell, they would have a resting-place in fame's eternal camping-ground.

But the government at Richmond strictly prohibited all persons liable to military duty from passing through the Confederate lines. Many lily-livered gentry, however, to escape service, flanked our pickets in the night-time, went to the enemy, took the oath, and remained North during the war. The cost of living by this time was exorbitant in Richmond, and the salaries of the clerks in the departments were utterly inadequate to support them. Having read with rapture of Mosby's exploits and deeds of daring, I resolved to resign my position in the Bank of the Confederate States, and cast my fortunes with him for weal or woe. My country and native State needed men in the field, and I felt it a duty to respond to her call, to the extent of my ability.

The restrictions I have just spoken of did not attach to me. By reason of the date of appointment to office, I was at liberty to attach myself to any command. Mosby had returned from Pennsylvania, and established his headquarters in Fauquier County; and, for the distinguished service he had rendered while there, had been promoted to a majority with authority to raise a battalion. Accordingly, Lieutenant Thomas Turner, of Prince George County, Maryland, and Grafton Carlisle, of Baltimore City, were sent to Richmond to get twenty recruits. They took rooms at the Spottswood Hotel, and opened their recruiting office. The first day, before noon, they had over one hundred applications. This number was more than they wanted. I was one of the lucky ones, and resigned my office that day.

Next morning, being the holy Sabbath, I sallied forth to join Mosby, accompanied by several friends on a similar mission. Our route was *via* Virginia Central Railroad, hence to Culpepper, which place we reached at noon. Culpepper was one of the most delightful towns in the State of Virginia before the war. Some of the noblest specimens of the human race hail from this ancient town. It was then occupied by our cavalry, and General Stuart had his headquarters at Brandy Station, some seven miles distant. We remained here until Turner could go to headquarters, and get passes to carry us through our lines.

About three o'clock he returned with passes. The remainder of the Sabbath was spent in travelling to "Old Church," at which point our party of amateurs initiated themselves into soldiers! life, by reclining upon mother earth, and courting *"tired nature's sweet restorer, balmy sleep,"* under the soothing rays of the silver moon. Next morning, after arranging our toilet, an aching-void convinced us that we had been fasting twenty-four hours. Our march, however, was resumed, while hunger with its thousand suggestions, forced one of the boys to descry a fair specimen of the swine, which was surrounded; the butcher and cook performed their service with dispatch, and we were served with roast pork, smoked pork, broiled pork, tenderloin, chine and spareribs, minus pepper, salt, or bread.

At the residence of Mr. Rice we were refreshed with a cup of cool, fresh buttermilk. Passing hence we reached Woodson about noon, and bivouacked near Washington, Rappahannock County, the second night. Tuesday our aquatic natures were thoroughly tested by fording, wading, and swimming the Rappahannock River some six times, which contributed to produce our quiet rest on *terra firma*, near the house of John D. Butts, Esq. Being in our novitiate, we were by this time impressed with the conviction that the life of a scout was a dreadful reality. Wednesday morning we were furnished *ex gratia* with a "square meal," so called in military parlance, and reached the place of rendezvous at Markham's, and were allowed to slumber upon the easy side of an oak board in the depot. A relative of Chief Justice Marshall furnished food for twelve of our adventurers, and others ordered breakfast with different families in the vicinity, with as much coolness as though they were *ipso facto* patriots so-called. We were advised that Mosby was making a fashionable call at Scufflebarg, on professional business. During the day we were presented to the illustrious little chieftain; and our first impulse on meeting him was, that—

> *Ours were no hirelings trained to fight,*
> *With cymbal and clarion glittering and bright;*
> *No prancing of chargers, no martial display*
> *No war-trump is heard from our silent array.*

Mosby was plainly yet neatly clad in Kentucky jeans, and sat quietly picking his dental plugs with a jack-knife. His carriage is active, easy, and graceful; his affable, genial manners are calculated to win favourable impressions. In speech, he is somewhat taciturn; but his words roll forth with a gentle fluency and decision, and reach the ear in mellow cadence. He is about five feet high, features indicate weight of character and firmness, an honest face, sharp, blue eyes, aquiline nose, light hair, and prominent forehead. In a word, Mosby possesses innate, refined, and exalted sensibilities, and is, by cultivation and education, an elegant, polished gentleman.

August, 1863, Mosby with thirty men went on a raid to Fairfax County. When he got near Billy Goodwin's tavern, on the turnpike below the Court House, he met thirty cavalry leading one hundred horses up to the army. He divided his men to attack them in rear and front,—Lieutenant Thomas Turner, in command of fifteen, to make the attack on the rear, and Mosby with fifteen, attacked in front. The enemy, seeing themselves attacked in that way, broke and took shelter in Goodwin's Tavern, and fired on us from the windows. They, however, after exhausting their ammunition, surrendered. In the engagement the gallant Mosby was wounded in the groin, and calf of the leg. Joe Calvert was wounded in the ankle, and Norman Smith killed. In this gallant young man, Mosby lost one of his most efficient men. He had rendered distinguished service under General Ewell, and was as brave a soldier as ever drew a sabre, and a splendid scout. He was a native of Fauquier County, son of Blackwell Smith (who was a lineal descendant of John Smith), and lived near Warrenton.

The enemy lost heavily in this affair. Seventy horses were brought off safe to Upperville, where the recruits were mounted, and the rest distributed among the captors. Mosby's wounds being of a serious character, and there being great difficulty in getting those little delicacies so necessary for the wounded, the surgeon of the command, Doctor Dunn, advised his removal inside our lines. The day after, he was started in an ambulance to Amherst County, the home of his parents; the command accompanying him as a bodyguard as far as Little Washington, in Rappahannock County. During the Major's absence little was done. Lieutenants Smith and Turner directed the new beginners to secure permanent boarding houses. W. B. Walston, John W. Corbin, John Dickson, Sewall Williams, and myself secured board at Mr. George Short's, and the rest around Paris and Upperville.

The enemy being so near us, we were always on the *qui vive*, and private scouting expeditions were exceedingly popular. Those not mounted would take shot-guns, and go in parties of from five to ten, to Barber's Cross Roads, and capture the enemy's pickets. Lieutenant William R. Smith, of the famous Black Horse Cavalry, but on detached service with Major Mosby on his special requisition, to whom Mosby assigned his men when he left, ordered twenty-five men to meet him at Rector's Cross Roads. Lieutenant Thomas Turner accompanied him. The party proceeded to Waterloo in the night, and attacked the picket at that place, at three o'clock a. m. The picket was composed of "Black Dutch," and easily broken without loss or injury. Twenty-five horses were brought off, with six prisoners. The enemy had five or six killed. Their new clothing, having been drawn the day before the attack, of course fell into our hands.

A few days after this affair, Lieutenant William R. Smith, in conjunction with Lieutenant Turner, took thirty men to Fayetteville, Fauquier County, a little village near Warrenton, to capture a large sutler store. The Yankee Army was on the move; and Smith, with two men, entered Warrenton in the night, with the view of finding out the object of the move. Finding it to be nothing but a feint, he rode up to the column of Yankee cavalry just passing out of the city, and held a little *tête-à-tête* for a few moments, and retired. He then returned to his men, whom he had concealed in the woods, and proceeded with them to Fayetteville to capture the sutler-store. On reaching the store Smith found the proprietor ready to follow the army next morning. The old Jew had in readiness, specially for us, four large four-horse wagons to receive his goods. The provost marshal of the army had generously given him a guard of eight infantry, but they, like all regulars, thinking they had a *soft thing* were inside the house playing cards and drinking the old sutler's champagne. The night was very dark. Smith and John Purryear rode up to the door, and knocked. One of the guard thoughtlessly opened the door, when he was politely requested to surrender and keep quiet.

In a moment the old Jew was at the door sporting his fine watch and chain, with several diamond rings on his fingers. In the meanwhile the rest of Smith's men came, and soon relieved him of his surplus jewellery and greenbacks, and secured the rest of the safeguard. Then commenced a general ransacking for clothing and other necessaries of life. I will leave my readers to conclude what thirty soldiers would do turned loose into four large rooms, filled up to the very ceiling with every conceivable thing. The men brought their sacks into requisition, and filled them. One of them, John ———, of Maryland, found a tin box containing $1,500 in greenbacks. Sixteen fine horses and three prisoners were taken off, the safeguard being set at liberty when we left. It was a rule with Mosby, his officers and men, never to disturb or detain these safeguards longer than he occupied the property on which they were stationed, which fact becoming known, duty of that nature was eagerly sought for by the Federal soldiers. I will hereafter speak of *some* of the service these safeguards rendered Mosby and his officers while their army was encamped around Warrenton.

Chapter 10: Mosby Gains Important Intelligence for General Lee

The weather being so intensely warm, nothing was done for a week, when an order was issued for a meeting at Rector's Cross Roads, a small village where the Warrenton and Snickers Gap Road crosses the turnpike from Alexandria to Winchester. Only fifteen or twenty men reported. At two o'clock, no scout reporting, we were disbanded. Owing to Major Mosby's temperate habits, his wounds, though painful, healed rapidly, and he was in his saddle again in three weeks. On resuming command of his battalion, he received a hearty welcome from his men. A meeting was ordered to take place at Rector's Cross Roads. Thirty-five men reported. Mosby took command, and at noon we moved off with the view of tapping the Orange and Alexandria Railroad at Bealton Station. It would be impossible to tell here the route we took to reach it, as on our raids Mosby always avoided the highways, and confined his marches to by-paths and through woods and fields.

We marched that day and night to within two miles of Bealton, and went into camp in the woods until day, when Mosby, W. R. Smith, and John Edmonds went out to reconnoitre. In a few minutes they returned, with the intelligence that the enemy were too strong for us to do anything. They numbered fifteen hundred infantry and five hundred cavalry. Mosby, however, was amply repaid for his trouble by the information he acquired. He saw the enemy receiving a large number of pontoons to be used in the movement General Meade made the ensuing November, when General Lee handled him so roughly on the Rappahannock. Mosby sent Horace Johnson to General Lee's headquarters with dispatches informing him of the designs of the enemy; and, finding the enemy too strong for him with his small squad of men, he changed his course for Fairfax County. On the march we passed through Grinnage to Buckland, where Mosby detailed twenty men to go with him. The rest of the men he sent back to Fauquier County. The detail consisted for the most part of new recruits.

After enjoying the hospitalities of the citizens of Buckland for half an hour, we received the order to mount our horses, and in a few moments we were moving down the turnpike in the direction of Manassas. Passing through Gainesville, we heard of the enemy's being out on a plundering expedition. Our march was over the second, and part of the first, battlefield of Manassas. On either side of the turnpike were the graves of the dead who fell in this sanguinary battle; some of the bones were exposed to the rays of the burning sun,—tops of trees shot off,—entire absence of fences,—houses riddled with bullets, and nothing left of "*the old stone house*" but the bare walls. Our survey of the field was abruptly terminated by one of the party, exclaiming, "*Yonder they are, Major*" A halt of course ensued; and Mosby, riding up on a little hill about a hundred yards ahead, saw in the distance a party of about thirty-five of the enemy returning to their camp at Centreville by the Thornton Road, leading ten or fifteen horses which they had taken from the citizens.

This Thornton Road intersects the turnpike about three miles from Centreville and just below the old stone house near "Sudley" We concealed ourselves under a small hill while the Major watched the enemy. When they had approached within five hundred yards of us he rode back, put himself at our head, and said to his men, "*Boys, I want you to go right through them.*" The charge was commenced with one of those yells peculiar to us, and which I will leave for some of our Northern friends to conjecture and describe. As soon as we were seen, the enemy, thinking we were charging with sabres (our pistols shone so bright), began to unstrap the Enfield rifles from their saddles, with the intention of getting behind the "*worm*" fence hard by; but, on the first fire from our men, they changed their minds and fled precipitately, their quartermaster taking the lead.

To reach the enemy we were compelled to charge across a deep ravine, in crossing which several of our horses fell and slightly injured the riders. This delayed for a few moments our reaching the enemy, and afforded them an opportunity to escape; not, however, before nine of them were captured, with twelve horses. Crossing this ravine, too, had the effect of scattering our men; and some of them, in their eagerness to get horses, became separated entirely from the command.

It was in this affair that one of the new recruits acquired prominence as a soldier. He was riding a very high-spirited and fine cavalry horse, without a curb to his bit. On the commencement of the firing, his horse became excited, and ran away with him. Running into a tree, he threw his rider to the ground, and passed on, leaving him afoot. The spirit of the recruit, however, was not broken. Rising to his feet, he continued his charge on foot, and overhauled a Dutch cavalryman, trying to force his horse over the rail fence. With a pistol at his head

Sam Alexander

he was politely requested to surrender and dismount. The recruit was again soon dashing over the field, and overtook Ab Wren and Walker Whaley converging from the dense pine thicket, leading horses, and in search of the command, which had disappeared. All three of the party being provided each with an extra horse, concluded to return to Fauquier.

On their way back they were overtaken by Frank Williams, who had likewise got separated from the command. While crossing Bull Run, they were overtaken by a scouting party of the enemy. The odds being too great to offer any resistance, a precipitate retreat followed, and Frank Williams's fine horse which he had just captured was mired in the stream, and the rider was compelled to seek the bushes to save himself from being captured. Mosby, after waiting on the field some time for his men to come up, resumed his march, with fifteen men, to Fairfax County, where he captured four sutler-wagons heavily laden with stores of every description. In these two little affairs, twenty-five horses and twelve prisoners were brought out, without loss or serious injury to any of his men.

On the 9th of October, Mosby ordered thirty-five of his men to meet him at Rector's Cross Roads. At noon we moved off in the direction of Fairfax. Mosby alone went ahead, and left us in charge of Lieutenant William R. Smith. The first night out we encamped in a pine forest near Frying-Pan, in Fairfax County, Mosby joining us at eleven o'clock that night. Before day next morning, the major, with John Edmonds, Ames, John W. Munson, and Dorsey Warfield, started out on a scout, and penetrated the enemy's lines as far as Falls Church. Lieutenant Smith and Lieutenant Hunter, fearing the enemy might find out our proximity to them, changed our camp, at sunrise, to a pine forest, with an undergrowth of briars, bamboo, and grape-vines so thick that a rabbit could scarcely pass through.

Here we remained until orders to move came from Mosby. In the evening of that day, Johnny Edmonds returned with orders to move that night to a certain point near Guilford. Night approached, and it was cloudy. The men could not imagine how they could get out of such a place in a dark night, on foot, to say nothing of horses. But all relied on Smith. His acquaintance with the country (and there was not a foot of ground between the Blue Ridge Mountains and Washington that he did not know) rendered him peculiarly fitted for this kind of service. At ten o'clock we commenced moving. It was so dark we could not distinguish his fileman riding a white horse. We, however, got out safe, with the exception of the loss of a few hats and some scratched faces, and reached Guilford about one o'clock in the morning. We fed our horses with new corn, and grazed them until before day (Sunday), when we rode to a point on the turnpike within five miles of Alexandria, reaching it at sunrise.

The sun never rose with greater splendour. The air was fresh and bracing, and not a cloud broke the blue sky above. Concealing the men in the dense pine forests, some three hundred yards from the turnpike, Mosby and Walker Whaley stationed themselves behind some ivy bushes on the side of the turnpike, and Lieutenant Smith with John Munson took a similar position higher up. In the distance, towards Alexandria, could be heard the tramp of horses and lumbering of wagons. Mosby, with his keen powers of perception, knew instantly what the noise meant. In a few minutes the advance of the cavalry came in full view, and passed on within twenty steps of where the major was standing. The main column consisted of three hundred and fifty men. Then came the wagons. This guard being to strong for us to cope with, Mosby let them pass on, and the wagons too. In the train there were seventy-five, and opposite Mosby there was one of those bad places in the turnpike which were very general on public highways in those days, especially those used by the government wagons.

Mosby watched this hole, and knew it would be the means of his making a capture. All the teams passed through with difficulty until the third from the last one reached it; that stalled, and the other two could not pass it. In the meanwhile the column passed on, and got a half-mile ahead before the team got out of it. Just as the last wagon disappeared behind a hill, Mosby and Whaley rode out, and politely requested the drivers to drive their teams after him. They complied readily, and turned off the turnpike into a private road leading into the pines where the men were patiently awaiting the arrival. They met with a cordial reception. The drivers, passengers, and horses were soon taken out of the wagon and sent back farther into the woods, and placed in the custody of Lieutenant Hunter.

The teams had hardly stopped when commenced one of the most exciting and amusing scenes ever witnessed by anyone. Not waiting to remove the covers off the wagons, Bob Lake and John ———, being the first to mount the wagons, out with their pocket-knives, and soon a crevice was made large enough to admit the head of a person. Insensibly the bodies were drawn in, and nothing was seen but feet projecting. Woollen shirts of every hue and style, oysters, sardines, fruits in cans, sugar, coffee, tea, &c., &c., were found. But the most acceptable of all was one hundred and seventy-five pairs of fine cavalry boots. No three wagons were ever unloaded as quick as they were; and, while this was going on, a whole brigade of cavalry passed, in full view of us, up to the army. A great quantity of necessaries were hid in the bushes, with the view of returning to bring them off. Each man being provided with a sack, and some with two, filled them. The rest that was not hid was scattered over the ground.

Lieutenant Smith, with his party, captured one stray wagon, which was about a mile behind the train, that was loaded with cigars, tobacco, candies, cheeses, sugar, syrups, &c., &c. Mosby, with two men, including myself, went over to see if anything could be brought off. On reaching the point where the wagon was, under a hill on the banks of a small stream, I was placed on picket behind a large tree on the brow of the hill, and about fifty yards from the turnpike, while the party went through the wagon. In a few minutes one Jersey wagon came along. I gave the alarm, and Mosby came up, and we rode out to bring the prize in. On reaching it the major found an old friend of his, with wife, returning empty from Alexandria, where he had been to get his groceries. He had been refused at Alexandria on account of his Southern sentiments; and Mosby invited him over to help himself, free of charge, which he did cheerfully. Out of this team we appropriated nothing but three boxes of raisins, which were kept for the ensuing winter, for a mammoth plum pudding.

Returning to the command, Mosby moved us some three miles farther into the pines, with the view of surprising a camp of black Dutch cavalry numbering about one hundred and fifty. All preparations having been completed, we only awaited the approach of night to move. The scouts, Charlie Hall and Frank Williams, had returned, after an absence of all day, and represented the camp as a *very soft thing*. But the escaping of a prisoner (Union citizen) induced Mosby to abandon the enterprise for fear he would inform the enemy of our plans. This citizen was a dangerous character, and had on former occasions given the enemy information of our being about. So soon as his escape was known, Mosby abandoned his project for the present, and moved his men back to Loudon County.

A division of the plunder was made on the farm of Mr. Kidwell, and the men disbanded, while Mosby, with two men, returned to Fairfax. Our long absence had aroused the most serious apprehensions for our safety. On former raids we had never been absent more than three days at the farthest; but on this we were out six days, and our friends in Fauquier having received no intelligence concerning us during our absence, were apprehensive all were captured. Our return was received with great rejoicing in Fauquier. On this raid not a pistol was fired, while we captured and destroyed seventy-five thousand dollars' worth of property.

Chapter 11: Attack Upon the Camp at Warrenton

On the third day after our return, Mosby ordered a meeting of all the men at Middlebury. The whole Yankee Army was on the move; and, if possible, he would capture some of their wagon trains. The guards, however, were too strong for us to do anything. We then looked out for patrols and scouting-parties. Returning from Fairfax, in Prince William County, we fell in with a detachment of cavalry, and captured twenty horses and the same number of prisoners; also forty mules they were leading to the army. On going through them, we found in their saddle-pockets, sardines, oysters, peaches in cans, &c., which they had got from the wagons abandoned by us one week before. All hands returned home without loss or injury to anyone.

One week after this, thirty of the men were taken by the major to Fairfax. Nothing was accomplished on this occasion except the capturing of six horses and prisoners at Centreville. On the day of our return, a meeting was held at Rectortown, a little village on the Manassas Gap Railroad. There was a full attendance. Mosby made a detail of thirty men with fresh horses, to meet him at sunset in Salem. At dark he moved off in the direction of Warrenton. Leaving that place to his right, he proceeded to New Baltimore, and struck here, before daybreak, a wagon-train, and captured one hundred and fifty mules, forty horses, twenty-five Yankees, and fourteen negroes, and returned the next morning without loss or injury. The appearance of such a large body of mules, horses, &c., produced the greatest excitement along the route of our return.

Our friends imagined we were the enemy, and we amused ourselves very much seeing the citizens running off their stock to the woods and mountains. The horses were divided amongst the men. The prisoners, including the negroes, were sent to Richmond, and the mules were sold to the government. Mosby, being so successful on this raid, concluded to take the whole command down to the same place next day. On reaching New Baltimore, he found he was just one hour too late. A train of over one hundred wagons had passed up without a single guard. We returned next day to Fauquier, and were disbanded until further orders.

The next meeting of the command took place at Scuffleburg, on the 1st day of October, 1863. Scuffleburg is a small village situated about midway on the road between Markham and Paris, in the hollow of the Blue Ridge Mountains, and is a place peculiarly adapted to the meeting of partisan rangers to transact business pertaining to their system of warfare. The buildings of the town consist of one blacksmith-shop with residence attached thereto, and a wheelwright's shop. The enemy had never visited the place. During the years 1863 and 1864, or rather the year after the occupation of Fauquier County by Mosby, it was considered a place of no little importance by the enemy. It was near this place the heroic and lamented Ashby was born, and over this road that Jackson made some of his celebrated flank movements.

It was also considered as the headquarters of the "guerilla Mosby," and a rendezvous of his men. The enemy imagined it a second Gibraltar, filled with all kinds of infernal machines and implements of warfare, and believed that none of them who got there ever returned. The foot of no Yankee soldier ever trod its magnificent thoroughfares, or reposed his wearied form under the stately oaks and chestnuts, from the rays of the burning sun, while the mountain breeze refreshed his burning cheek with the perfume of the wild honeysuckle, and the air was musical with the songs of birds, until General Meade occupied that country on his pursuit of General Lee, after his Pennsylvania campaign.

The meeting on the 1st of October was for the purpose of organising the second company of the Forty-Third Virginia Battalion of Cavalry, Company B. Company A had assumed the proportions of a battalion itself, and Mosby concluded to organise another company. All the men were drawn up in a line, and Mosby selected sixty therefrom, and ordered the men to go into an election of officers. William R. Smith of Fauquier County, in view of the distinguished services he had rendered the Confederacy while a lieutenant of the famous Black Horse Cavalry,—his noble spirit, generous disposition, attachment to the men, and, above all, his daring courage, and extensive knowledge of the country,—was unanimously elected captain of Company B. Frank Williams, of Fairfax, who had, since the commencement of the war, made so many of the enemy bite the dust in his own native country, and was such a terror to them, was elected first lieutenant; and Albert Wren and Bob Grey, who had rendered similar services, were elected second and third lieutenants.

Horace Johnson of Warrenton, who had served with Smith in the Black Horse Cavalry, with distinction, was appointed orderly sergeant. After the organisation, Captain Smith disbanded us, with orders to meet him the next day at Salem. Forty men reported for duty. At noon we moved in the direction of Warrenton. On the approach of night there was every indication of a storm The clouds increased in blackness, and the darkness was beyond the power of conception. Indeed, so intense was the darkness, the men could not distinguish their filemen. The rain fell in torrents, and we moved only when we had lightning. At twelve o'clock we reached the home of our captain, and sought shelter in a schoolhouse, some two hundred yards from the house, tying our horses to the trees. The captain's mother and sisters had prepared a sumptuous supper for us, after which, William Chapman and Montjoy sang delightfully for the ladies. On the break of day we moved back to the mountains and disbanded, with orders to meet at Mr. Cross's, about six miles from Warrenton, punctually, at four o'clock. We scattered over the neighbourhood, and were welcomed and hospitably entertained by the farmers.

Mr. ——, at whose house myself and friend (Foley Kemper, nephew of General Kemper) were entertained, and his accomplished daughters, and estimable lady, were particularly kind to us. We listened with delight to their performances on the piano, and their singing. And now, at this distant day, when I recall the hours I have spent so happily around the firesides of our friends in that country, in the society of their charming daughters, it seems like a dream. Our high appreciation of those kind offices shown while we were with them, has been sufficiently demonstrated by the protection we afforded them.

Four o'clock came and all hands at Mr. Cross's. Taking a private road we moved towards Warrenton, and reached an old church on the main road, some two and a half miles from Warrenton, about dark. Here we took a stand. Before us could be distinctly seen the signal lights on the cupola of the Court House. Pickets were posted, with orders to allow no one to pass either way. At eleven o'clock we moved off, observing the utmost quiet. Not even a whisper broke the stillness of the night. The night being very dark the town was flanked without discovery. Indeed, so important was it that no noise should be made, that rocky places in by-paths were covered with oil-cloths and blankets to prevent the noise of the tramp of our horses being heard by the enemy. We got three miles in the rear of the town and halted under a high hill, out of view of the enemy's pickets.

Captain Smith, William Chapman, and Montjoy went out to ascertain the exact position and strength of the enemy, who were only about one mile distant. They passed all through the enemy's camp on foot, having tied their own horses amongst those of the enemy. They found the capture of the camp a difficult matter, owing to the fact of the number of soldiers being doubled the day before; and, instead of one hundred and twenty-five men, there were two hundred and fifty. In addition to that, their position was a peculiar one. Their camp was on the brow of a hill formed like a horse-shoe. At the base of this hill, or in the bottom, were some apple-trees, to which their horses were tied, while on the slope of the hill were their tents. From the front of their camp or top of the hill, were roads diverging in every direction, and strong pickets posted thereon.

In their rear was an open, low country extending for a mile, as it likewise did on both sides, and no pickets posted. A consultation was held as to how the attack should be made. Chapman and Montjoy urged the attack in front to charge the pickets and follow them in. Smith thought otherwise. He determined to attack them with his small squad in the rear. Their long absence began to excite serious apprehensions as to their safety. Several picket-shots were heard, and it was believed, amongst the men, our raid would be a failure. Finally, about four o'clock in the morning, Smith, Chapman, and Montjoy returned. Diligent inquiries were made of the officers, by the men, as to their intentions. They received the consoling reply:

If you all will go in, there will be a horse for each of you.

The order was given to mount, and soon the camp-fires of the enemy were seen in the distance. On approaching nearer, the number of the fires increased. It was about half past four the attack was made. Not expecting a call from the rebels at that hour in the morning, they permitted us to get within ten yards of their fires (around which some of the enemy were sitting) before Captain Smith ordered the charge. The boys gave one of their unearthly yells; and, in an instant, we were in the centre of their camp, firing right and left, dealing death wherever our shots were directed. In the charge of the advance, one voice (Sam A.) could be 'heard ringing through the air like a clarion voice, "Give me your greenbacks! surrender!" Some of the men charged through the fires. The enemy rallied in a few moments, on the top of the hill, and commenced a charge down on our left flank, firing at the same time several volleys from their carbines.

Captain Smith, with his quick powers of perception, seeing the imminent danger of his small band being cut off and probably captured, gave the order to "*bring up the other squadron.*" The enemy, thinking we had a large reserve behind, commenced retreating to the top of the hill, where they contented themselves with firing over our heads. We in the meanwhile secured twenty-seven horses, six prisoners, and one negro, and retreated, under cover of night, without loss or injury to any one, although the Yankee commander of the post reported to the Secretary of War at Washington:

> He was attacked that morning by a body of guerillas. They were repulsed with heavy loss. It is supposed a large number were killed and wounded, as they could be tracked for miles by the blood of their wounded which they carried off with them.

Chapter 12: Raid to Bealton Station, etc.

In the month of November of this year, 1863, while Mosby was returning from a scout in Fairfax, in passing through the little village of Auburn, he captured two correspondents of the *New York Herald*, at Mr. McCormick's. On Mosby's appearance in front of the house, the front door was closed, and admission denied him. An order from him, however, soon opened it. The greatest excitement prevailed amongst the ladies. On tendering the correspondents the contents of two revolvers if they did not surrender, they gracefully complied with the major's request. The ladies threatened to bring down the displeasure of General Lee on Major Mosby's head if he did not release their friends. Mosby was not a man to be intimidated in that way. He invited them to their horses, which they mounted, and returned with him to Fauquier. There they were furnished with a military escort to Richmond.

A few days after this, Mosby took four picked men on a scouting expedition to Fairfax, with the intention of capturing Governor Pierpont. He penetrated the enemy's lines to the very *gates* of Alexandria. On reaching the house in which he expected to find the Governor, he learned he had left that evening for Washington City. He then proceeded to the house of Colonel Dulaney. Mosby, on entering the house, was met at the door by the colonel. Dulaney expressed delight "at meeting with Jesse scouts," and invited Mosby in, and asked him his business, when to his amazement. French Dulaney, his son, stepped in and invited his father to get on his horse and accompany them to Fauquier and Richmond.

Early in December, Mosby, with seventy men, started on a raid to Bealton Station, on the Orange and Alexandria Railroad. We arrived within three miles of the place the first night, remaining in the woods until daylight, when we moved up the railroad about five miles, and took up a position among some heavy timber, concealing ourselves from the enemy. On each side of us were encamped Gregg's cavalry, while in front, about one mile distant, on a high hill, were the general's headquarters, at which there was a morning's review of the troops. In this position we remained in the rain until noon, watching for a wagon train to return from the depot loaded with supplies for headquarters, when John Munson and Walter Whaley brought in two bluebirds, one walking and the other riding. The one riding was a guard and bearer of dispatches to General Gregg's headquarters; the other afoot was a deserter under sentence of death, and was on his way to be shot. The condemned man was set at liberty on a captured mule, and the bearer of dispatches sent to Richmond.

Mosby almost despaired of the wagon train's returning; while the men, cold, wringing wet, and the rain falling in torrents, thought of returning to Fauquier. At two o'clock those apprehensions were dispelled by the order to "*mount your horses.*" Mosby ordered Captain Smith to take Company B, and charge the enemy in front, while he took fifteen men of Company A, and attacked them in the rear. He succeeded in cutting off the rear and capturing the whole party, consisting of five wagons loaded with medical stores, and a guard of twenty-five cavalry. By a miscalculation of the distance, Mosby did not strike them until after Smith was in, and then on their flank. Notwithstanding the rain, which fell in torrents, Smith, with Company B, swept down, like a tornado, on the guard which was in the advance. The enemy made not the slightest resistance, not even firing a shot, but wheeled and made for their camp, which was about one mile distant, leaving the wagons and teams a prey to us.

Two of the guard, however, were captured, besides eight fine mules and six horses. Mosby sustained no injury whatever. The wagons were loaded with valuable medical stores, and had the capture been anywhere else than in sight of the general's headquarters, they would have been brought off and sent to General Lee. One or two men secured a few valuable articles used in surgery, and turned them over to Dr. Dunn, surgeon of the battalion. The fugitives, having reached camp, reported our audacity; and one regiment of cavalry was sent in pursuit. They pursued us until dark.

Captain Stringfellow, one of General Stuart's scouts, was our scout on this occasion, and, in company with one of our men, stopped at Mr. Skinker's, six miles from Warrenton, under the mountains, to stay all night. The rest of the men had crossed the Bull Run Mountains, and gone into camp at Salem. The enemy, thinking a number of our men would lie over at Mr. Skinker's until next morning, surrounded the house and commenced an indiscriminate firing into the windows and doors, to the great peril of Mr. Skinker's family, calling, during the firing, for Mosby's men to come out. Stringfellow, perceiving no avenue of escaping out of the house, secreted himself in one of those *secret closets* which our Southern friends always had ready for us, and escaped, although the enemy instituted a diligent search. The enemy carried back with them Stringfellow's horse and fine mare, which he had just captured of them; also Mr. Skinker and his son, whom they robbed of one thousand six hundred dollars in greenbacks. Mr. S. and son were sent to Warrenton and to Washington.

The next morning, before day, the pursuit was resumed. Taking the road direct to Salem, the enemy dashed in there at early breakfast, and captured two of our men who had been detailed to go out with the prisoners. The sergeant of the guard, Dorsey Warfield, sent our prisoners on to Oak Hill, three miles farther, while he and several of the men stopped there to see their families. It was in Salem, on this occasion, a young man, who will hereafter figure most conspicuously on every raid made by Mosby, exhibited a spirit of coolness and bravery rarely excelled by anyone during the whole war, and whose conduct pleased Mosby so much that he made him first lieutenant of Company C. When the enemy dashed into town, very few of the citizens were up; and, before he could dress himself, the place was surrounded, and all avenues of escape closed.

Fearing they would spend the day there, he determined, by one bold movement, to free himself. His horse had been taken by the enemy. He buckled on his pistols, and started out afoot, with the determination of fighting his way through them. He managed by adroitness to get some distance from town before discovery. Five cavalrymen charged him and fired. The compliment was returned by him. Being a splendid shot, he made three bite the dust. The other two retreated, and he mounted a Yankee horse and escaped; he receiving in the affray only a slight wound in the hand. This young man was Adolphus

E. Richards, of Fauquier County, Virginia, and a minister of the Presbyterian School.

Chapter 13: Bold Exploit of Montjoy

In December, 1863, Mosby took the command to Brandy Station on the Orange and Alexandria Railroad. The whole Yankee Army was moving on General Lee's lines on the Rappahannock. At the station, part of General Sedgwick's wagon-train, guarded by a brigade of infantry, was preparing to move. The large camp-fires illuminated the country for miles around. The wagon-master was riding up and down the train, hurriedly urging the teamsters to hurry up, that the rear guard had moved off. Mosby, with two men, rode up to him, and complained about the delay of the train. He also rode through the guard while they stood around the fires with their arms stacked, and conversed with them in regard to the object of the movement of the army. He thus threw the enemy off their guard, representing his cavalry as the last of their rear-guard.

Returning to his command he placed himself at their head and moved them quietly to the wagons, which were standing some fifty yards from the fires, and proceeded to detach the mules and horses, and got out one hundred and twenty mules and ten horses before the enemy was aware of what he was doing. The first intimation they had of his doings was seeing the flames issuing from forty wagons which had been set on fire by the last of his men that left the train. Before they could unstack their arms Mosby was out of their reach, with the mules and horses. They, however, fired one volley at him, without inflicting injury upon any one. The mules were sent to General Lee, and the horses divided amongst the men.

Mosby, being so successful on this raid, took both companies to Brandy Station the day after his return, with the hope of getting another train. In the meanwhile General Meade sent two regiments of Rhode Island cavalry back to *protect* the country between the Rappahannock and Hazel Rivers. After crossing Hazel River, at sunset, we halted under a hill about half a mile from the Wellford Farmhouse, now owned by a Union citizen of Richmond, to await further orders from Mosby, who had gone ahead of his men with Stringfellow. Not hearing from him by seven o'clock, Lieutenant Thomas Turner, of Company A, moved us up to the Wellford House, and occupied the out-houses which had been used by the enemy as meat-houses.

Fires were built in the old-fashioned fireplaces, out of the boxes left by the enemy, and we made ourselves as comfortable as circumstances would permit. At ten o'clock that night, Mosby and Stringfellow returned with two Yankees, belonging, they said, to an Indiana regiment. They were very soon gone through. Mosby captured them while they were out *foraging*. On examining them, papers and books were found which they had stolen from the library of a gentleman (a Mr. Thorn) in Culpepper County, whose house they had plundered and burned, turning the whole family out of doors with only the clothes on their backs, for no other reason than that he was a Southern man. The next morning we recrossed the Hazel River, and lay in the dense pine woods adjoining the farm of Mr. Majors.

Mosby having learned the position of the enemy on the other side of the Hazel River during his absence, sent Lieutenant Thomas Turner, Montjoy, Henry Ashby, and three others out reconnoitring. They recrossed the Hazel, and proceeded to the enemy's camp to see if anything could be done. Turner, concealing his men from the enemy in some bushes near their camp, began, with Montjoy, to dodge around their camp. The Yankees, seeing them, sent one man out to see who they were. He was; "gobbled up," and they sent out another who shared a similar fate. Turner and Montjoy then returned to their comrades; and, after a few moments' delay, proceeded to take a picket-post of ten men just as they were being posted some two hundred yards from the camp. The two prisoners fell into line, and accompanied them, riding in front. The weather was intensely cold, and all the party wore blue overcoats (except Turner and Montjoy) to deceive the enemy. Their movements did not attract the attention of the enemy until they were within fifty yards of the picket, when they were halted by the sergeant of the guard with,—

"Halt! who comes there?"

"*Friends*" replied Montjoy.

"What command?" again cries the picket.

"First Maine Cavalry!" responds Montjoy.

"All right,—advance!" cries the picket; and Montjoy moves up by twos to the post, each man passing on either side. After some moments' conversation, Montjoy instructed them to "*keep a sharp lookout for Mosby.*" At a certain signal nearly every picket had a pistol pointed at his head, with the invitation to follow them. Being almost paralyzed by the boldness and audacity of Montjoy's trick in the broad blaze of day (it being about noon), and so near their camps, they complied, without the least show of resistance; and all the post were soon the other side of the Hazel in a safe place. Their capture was soon discovered, and a party started in pursuit. These approached the river cautiously; and, after displaying themselves on the high hills a mile distant from us, they returned to their camps without firing a shot. Montjoy and Turner had only six men with them, and captured twelve prisoners, horses, and accoutrements, without loss or injury. Mosby, coming up in a short time, ordered us to return to Fauquier. The weather being so intensely cold, nothing was done until the 1st day of January, 1864.

Chapter 14: Affair with Colonel Cole's Cavalry

The 1st of January, 1864, was anything but a pleasant day for a soldier. The snow had been on the ground for two weeks, thawing in the daytime and freezing at night, until it was absolutely dangerous to travel on horseback. The last day of the old year, however, was very pleasant; and the snow and ice had disappeared in great measure. The sun on the morning of the new year rose with all the grandeur of which the imagination can conceive. But clouds began soon to cover the sky, and by noon snow was falling. Mosby was absent on a scouting expedition in Fairfax; and Captain Smith had ordered a meeting of the men at Rectortown, with the intention of making a new-year's call on some Yankee camp.

The enemy, however, concluded to save him the trouble; and, accordingly, eighty of Colonel Cole's battalion of Maryland cavalry, doing guard duty at Harper's Ferry, dashed into Upperville about eight o'clock a.m., on the 1st day of January, and captured two or three of our men while they were at breakfast. The party was commanded by a Captain Hunter; and, while there, they heard we were to have a meeting at Rectortown at noon. They determined to break it up. Concluding that most of the men were absent at their homes, spending the holidays, no resistance was apprehended. At noon it was snowing; and some ten or twelve had met at Rectortown, awaiting the arrival of Smith. I was at Joe Blackwell's, our headquarters, and had just left Smith with four or five men to attend meeting.

As I was crossing the railroad at Goose Creek, some two miles from the town, three of our men were seen dashing into Goose Creek at full speed. On seeing myself and companion, they exclaimed, "Don't go to Rectortown: it is full of Yankees, and we were run out of the place." I immediately returned to Joe Blackwell's, where I had left Smith, and reported the fact. He mounted his horse, and bid us follow him. During my absence, eight or ten men had assembled there. We obeyed his order, and pushed on, eager for the prey. Crossing Goose Creek, he carried us to Mrs. Rawling's, at the top of a hill, and told us to remain there until further orders to move; while he, Sam Alexander, and Frank Williams reconnoitred a little to find out the strength of the enemy, their position, &c., &c. The suspense we were in while at Mrs. Rawling's was soon relieved by the appearance of Frank Williams with orders for us to advance. In a few minutes we were in Rectortown, and were joined there by others of the command, which swelled our force to twenty-seven in all.

Not tarrying there any time, we dashed on after the enemy. The enemy, in leaving Rectortown, tried to deceive us by taking the Warrenton Road. Keeping that road for one and a half miles, they filed off to the left, and took the road by the Five Points to Middlebury. But the vigilant eye of Smith could not be deceived. While in Rectortown, Smith found out whose command they belonged to, and left orders for us to take the Five Points Road, near which place he would join us. While following them up, we were joined in Rectortown by others of our command, which swelled the whole to twenty-seven men; and, not stopping in town, we pushed after the enemy. Getting outside of the limits of the town, R. P. Montjoy, Henry Ashby, and John Edmonds, were thrown forward as an advanced guard. Just beyond the Points our advance came upon the rear of the enemy, and shots were exchanged. The enemy had taken a strong position in the road,—on one side of them a high stone wall, while on the other was an open, cleared country, extending almost as far as the eye could reach. So we could take no advantage of them. They had formed in the road, and were awaiting our attack.

Smith threw himself at the head of his men, and ordered us to charge, so that we would have the bulge on the enemy. At the first fire, Captain Hunter, their commander, had his horse shot under him; and, before waiting to see whether or no rider and horse both were killed, his men were seized with a panic, and broke and fled in every direction. An effort was made to rally them in an open field, on the right of the road: but the gallant Smith would not give them time; our style of fighting being to pitch in, and "clean" the enemy out, or be "cleaned out." In we went, when Hunter's horse fell, and himself was made prisoner. The rest retreated in great confusion, through woods and through marshes, into which some were thrown from their horses head-foremost, and stuck there some ten or fifteen minutes until extricated by some of our men who had charge of the prisoners.

Beyond this marsh, some three hundred yards, was a body of heavy-timbered land, in which a large number took shelter, hoping we would not pursue them. Generally woods do afford great protection from the attacking party; but, in this instance, they sought their own captivity. Back of these woods was a little stream called Carter's Run, very shallow and narrow, while the banks were high. In jumping their horses over this stream, some fifteen or twenty of them were precipitated into it with their horses. Sending these back to the rear, Captain Smith, with Lieutenant Turner, Bush Underwood, and ten others, continued the pursuit as far as Woodgrove, Loudon County.

Out of the eighty men brought up to "Mosby's Confederacy" by Captain Hunter, to capture Mosby and his men, and present them to Father Abraham as a new-year's gift, sixteen only got back to their camp at Harper's Ferry, to tell the tale. Eight were killed on the field; fifty-four were sent prisoners to Richmond; while the wounded were paroled, and taken by the farmers into their houses, where they received every attention. Sixty fine horses, with equipments, including thirty fine army pistols, were secured and distributed amongst the victors. The sabres and carbines we threw away, as they were weapons we had no use for.

And I will here suggest to the government agents, now collecting government arms throughout the different rebel States, that, if they will make a visit to Mosby's battlefields, they may find several wagon-loads, provided the Freedman's Bureau has not given them to the "coloured gemmen." Early in the afternoon the wind shifted around to the north; and, before sunset that day, the mercury was at zero. When we reached Joe Blackwell's with the capture, the feet of our men were frozen to their stirrups; while the prisoners, who had fallen into Carter's Run, were just one sheet of ice, and nearly frozen speechless. Smith had placed the prisoners in my custody until after the division. I moved them, including our men, to the woods on the left of Joe Blackwell's, about one hundred and fifty yards; and ordered them to build large fires, and warm themselves, while we awaited the arrival of Captain Smith, who in a few minutes rode up nearly frozen. In a short time the horses and pistols were soon divided amongst the men, and a detail made to carry out the prisoners.

This affair was of such a brilliant character, when we consider the odds against us being nearly four to one, we having nothing but pistols, while the enemy were armed with pistols, sabres, and carbines, all of the most improved kind, elicited from. Major Mosby an order of the most flattering character, complimenting Captain Smith and his small band of men in the highest manner for their bravery and success in this affair. It is a source of deep regret I cannot produce the order here to my readers; but it, with all Major Mosby's papers, reports, orders pertaining to the battalion, from General Lee, Stuart, and others, were burnt up with Joe Blackwell's house, in March, 1864. Colonel Cole met with such a brilliant new-year's reception that he made but one more expedition into "Mosby's Confederacy."

The scenery on the mountains, on the evening of the 1st of January, was of the most sublime character. In the forenoon of the day, a wet snow fell, and melted almost as fast as it fell. The air, during the forenoon and middle of the day, was fresh and pleasant; but the winds in the afternoon shifted to the north, and at sunset everything was frozen hard. Not a cloud broke the blue sky above as the sun was setting in the west behind its fiery curtains. The mountains seemed as one vast sheet of ice, and the reflection of the sun's declining rays on the scene was indeed sublime. It was a scene which would have enraptured the artist, and inspired the poet.

Chapter 15: Captain Stringfellow

Heavy and deep snows fell during this week, and the weather continued intensely cold without intermission; indeed, so severe was the cold that it was a hard matter to get the men to expose themselves at night. Notwithstanding those obstacles, Lieutenant Thomas Turner and Joe Nelson, of Company A, took twenty-five men, on the night of the 4th of January, and proceeded to a point near Warrenton, to capture a patrol of fifty Yankees. The night was one of the coldest ever experienced in that country by the oldest residents. The mercury stood below zero, and snow one foot deep was on the ground. Many of Turner's men had their hands and feet frost-bitten that night, and the hands of all were so benumbed with cold that they could scarcely use their pistols to advantage. The Yankees felt the cold almost as sensibly as Turner's men. To keep comfortable, they would ride up and down the road without dismounting. It was on their return to camp that Turner met this patrol.

As I said before, the snow was on the ground some twelve inches deep. Fortunately for Turner, the wind was blowing almost a perfect hurricane, which had the effect of drowning all noise that could be made by another body of cavalry approaching. In fact, so perfectly safe from all attack by "guerrillas" did the enemy think themselves that night, that Lieutenant Turner, with his twenty-five men, rode up within *ten feet* of them before they knew we were about, or the charge was ordered by Turner, when a yell and deadly fire was opened on them from the pistols of Turner's men. The surprise was so great and unexpected that not the slightest resistance was offered by the enemy, who begged, for God's sake, that we would not shoot them. Our firing ceased instantly. We "gathered together" forty-five horses and twenty-five prisoners, which we brought off safely. The dead and wounded were left on the field. Turner had not a man injured in this affair. However, William B. Walston lost several toes by frost; General Geary lost four fingers from one hand; and John W. Corbin, of Accomac County, Virginia, had both hands and feet frozen. With these exceptions, there were no casualties whatever on this raid.

On the 7th day of January, Major Mosby received a note from Captain Stringfellow, written in Loudon County, suggesting his cooperation with him in capturing "Cole's Battalion," doing picket duty on the Loudon Heights, opposite Harper's Ferry, stating that the enemy was picketing only one road,—the turnpike leading to Hillsboro', and that he could take Mosby and his men into their camp, and capture the whole concern without the firing of a shot.

As Stringfellow was the originator of this brilliant and unfortunate foray, I will here give my readers, by way of parenthesis, an idea of who he is and how he happened up there. Captain Stringfellow had entered the Confederate Army at the very beginning of the war, and had distinguished himself on numerous battlefields. Those actions had not passed unobserved by that great cavalier, General J. E. B. Stuart. Stringfellow's thorough knowledge of all that country stretching east of the Blue Ridge Mountains down to the Federal Capital, embracing the counties of London, Fauquier, Prince William, Fairfax, Culpepper, Orange, &c., and his bravery and dashing behaviour on the battlefield, as well as the perilous journeys he had performed for his superiors, justly recommended him to Stuart for promotion. Stuart accordingly appointed him captain of his scouts, and gave him ten men to operate with. As he was not regularly attached to the Forty-Third, little is known of his general operations. Yet I cannot restrain myself from mentioning several deeds of daring performed by him, which were unparalleled in the history of warfare.

While the Federal Army was encamped at Culpepper Court House and Brandy Station, on the Orange and Alexandria Railroad,

General Sedgwick, commanding the Sixth Army Corps, established his headquarters at the Wellford House, about two miles from Brandy Station. Stringfellow had been dispatched by General Stuart, to obtain some valuable information from the enemy. The vigilance of the enemy's pickets prevented him from accomplishing his purpose by those means which heretofore had carried him through successfully; and, as a last resort, he adopted the plan of entering the enemas camp in disguise. Providing himself with a Yankee colonel's outfit, and putting on a bold face, in the broad blaze of day he rode up to the enemy's camp. He was saluted by the pickets, and rode up to General Sedgwick's headquarters. The general, with his staff and one or two guests, was at dinner. Nothing wrong being suspected, he was invited to dismount and share their dinner with them.

Stringfellow, having lived so much in the enemy's lines, had made himself familar with all the enemy's camps, the names of the regiments, their officers, and the position of the troops. Representing himself as colonel of a regiment at the extreme end of their lines, and satisfying the officers that he was all right, Stringfellow was invited into the tent, to be one of the dinner-party. A general conversation ensued, in which he so completely gained the confidence of all around the table, that he not only found out what he was sent to discover, but more too, including the strength of the whole army, their position, and intentions. Having accomplished the object of his visit, he remounted his horse, rode through their pickets, and reported to Stuart what he had done.

On another occasion, when on a scouting expedition in the neighbourhood of Warrenton, dressed in a Yankee overcoat, five Yankees overtook him on the road. They questioned him critically in regard to the command he belonged to, and being satisfied with his representations, they passed on. When they were some fifteen steps ahead of him, he drew his two pistols and fired away at them. As he was a splendid shot, at the first fire two bit the dust; at the second fire a third one fell, and the other two fled for their lives, without exchanging a shot.

Chapter 16: Meeting at Upperville

In the spring of 1864, there was a play introduced and performed in the theatre at Alexandria, Virginia, entitled *The Guerilla; or, Mosby in Five Hundred Sutler-wagons*. The play of course excited a great deal of attention amongst us, including Mosby himself. Flaming bills were posted all over the city, and a programme was sent to Mosby. The strongest desire to witness the performance, and obtain copies of the drama, was manifested by Mosby and the men. Private expeditions to Alexandria were proposed, but obstacles beyond our control prevented the execution of them. One day, at Joe Blackwell's, Mosby, in the presence of Stringfellow and others, expressed a desire to have a copy of the play, and also a determination to go to Alexandria and see it played. Stringfellow waited until Mosby was through; then jumping up suddenly, he mounted his horse, and without telling anyone his intentions, started off alone for Alexandria.

Riding rapidly, he entered the city before day the next morning, and, stopping at a trusty friend's, spent the remainder of the day in "sightseeing" and conversing with the soldiers. Going to a bookstore, he procured several copies of the play, and awaited patiently the approach of night to see it played. The play had a great run. The house was crowded, and he found difficulty in getting a seat. At twelve o'clock that night, he was again in his saddle; and next evening, at three o'clock, was back again in Fauquier, at Mosby's headquarters, with copies of the play. The rapidity of his movements, as well as his daring conduct, completely surprised the great partisan, and ever after that expedition, Stringfellow enjoyed Mosby's fullest confidence and highest esteem.

But I am digressing too much. Mosby, on the afternoon of the 7th, reflected on Stringfellow's proposition, and thinking it practicable, ordered a meeting of the whole command at Upperville the next day at twelve o'clock. The men were reluctant to leave their comfortable log fires. The mercury ranged at zero, at breakfast that morning; and the snow was one foot deep on the ground, with a fair prospect of another fall of snow during the day. Only one hundred men reported for duty. At three o'clock in the afternoon, orders were given for us to mount and fall into line of march. We moved off from Upperville, taking the road to Union, and reached Woodgrove, in Loudon County, at eight o'clock p.m., where Mosby was joined by Stringfellow with nine men, making in all, including officers, one hundred and ten effective men.

After resting there some two hours, for the purpose of thoroughly warming ourselves, as well as to avoid being seen by the Union citizens in that part of the county, at ten o'clock we resumed our march, taking the high road direct to Harper's Ferry, alternately riding and walking, to keep our feet and hands, as well as bodies, warm. While riding, we would put the reins in our mouths, and our hands under the saddle-blankets, next to the horses' skins, to keep from being frozen. This road we followed until within three or four miles of the enemy's pickets, which were posted about one quarter of a mile from camp, at a small bridge over a mountain stream. Leaving the highway to our left, we took a by-path which led us into the mountains, and followed that in single file until we reached the Potomac River, across which could be distinctly seen the infantry camp-fires, and the sentry on his beat. Turning short to the left, we passed through a dense pine thicket, about two hundred yards, when we reached the bridge across the Shenandoah River. On the left of the road, at the top of a steep hill, and some twenty yards from the bridge, stood a two-story frame building, in which were the quarters of Colonel Cole and other officers.

Farther up the road, about twenty yards on the right, under the mountain, were quietly reposing the objects of our pursuit. To reach this camp, as we emerged from the thicket, we had to ascend a steep hill about twenty feet high, on which the snow had been trodden until it was as hard and slick as ice. The ascent of this hill was very dangerous, and was made in single file. Yet we ascended it without accident, and were in the camp. We could touch the tents with our pistols. Mosby, with one hundred and ten men, stood there in almost the very centre of the strongest fortified post of the North on that line of defences. I could scarcely realise it. Everything so far seemed to promise success to the enterprise, and render it the most brilliant affair of the war. Not a cloud could be seen. The moon seemed to shine with her silvery light brighter than ever before. The air was still and piercing cold; not even the trampling of the horses' feet could be heard. Mosby was the first to enter the camp.

He was followed by Stringfellow and his men, whom he had dispatched to the house to secure Cole and the other officers before he would take the camp, which was to be done without firing a shot. While Stringfellow was proceeding to execute his part, Mosby ordered Smith to ride back and hurry up the men, as it was of the highest importance he should make all prisoners before any alarm could be given. Montjoy was sent down the road, about one quarter of a mile, with six men, to secure the picket. He and Smith, with the rest of the men, were to enter the tents, and make prisoners of everyone in them.

But, alas! by some almost unaccountable means the plan failed in an instant, from one or the other of the following causes: in front of this house where the officers were sleeping, there was a stable which was supposed to contain the officers' horses, and around were several army wagons with mules tied to them. Some few of the men left the ranks to secure the mules; and it was supposed by many of us that they spoke rather loud, and that the officers were aroused, and a shot was fired from the house; or by Stringfellow's men leaving him after he got into the house, and crossing the road, ascending the mountain and charging into the camp in the rear, yelling and firing. At the first shot from them, Mosby, thinking they were the enemy (for he had ordered that no men should enter the camp, and particularly in that manner, from that quarter), ordered the charge. Not more than thirty of us rode up to the tents, which we completely riddled by the bullets from our pistols. The enemy soon cried out, "*The camp is yours! We surrender! Stop firing!*" The firing ceased.

Stringfellow's men charging into us, produced some confusion in our ranks, and most of the men would not come into the camp, notwithstanding Mosby's orders to "*come in and secure the horses.*" The firing alarmed the picket at the bridge before Montjoy could reach them, and they fled to the mountains. The Yankees coming out of their tents, and seeing so few to surrender to, retreated to some bushes a short distance up the mountain, in the rear of their camp, and poured a most murderous fire into our little squad. Some fifty of our men were out in the road with sixty horses when the enemy rallied, and they would not come back. The position to which the enemy retreated being so strong, and our boys having fired all the loads out of their pistols, Mosby determined to retire.

Our situation at this moment was indeed critical. The signal-gun at the ferry had been fired, and the whole garrison was under arms, and ready to march at a moment's notice. Lieutenant Thomas Turner, commanding Company A, had fallen at the first fire, mortally wounded, and was carried off the field. Captain Robinson, a Scotchman, and captain in the English Army, had been killed by our own men through mistake. Lieutenant Colston, of General Trimble's staff, had fallen while trying to rally the men. Two other brave spirits had likewise given up their lives in defence of Southern independence; and the gallant Charlie Paxon was lying at the entrance of a tent, mortally wounded.

Fearing reinforcements would arrive for the enemy before we could get out, Captain Smith, the last man to leave, was passing the tent where Paxon was lying, was recognised, and asked "for God's sake not to leave him." The appeal to the generous Smith could not be resisted. Suddenly whirling his horse around, and reaching down to place the dying youth in front of him, to bring him off, a Yankee in the tent shot him through the heart, and he fell lifeless to the earth, saying not a word. The heroic William Chapman came to his assistance in a moment; but the life of him whom the enemy dreaded equally as much as Mosby had fled. The enemy were advancing at the double quick, and Chapman was compelled to fly and rejoin the Command. Although day was near dawning, and the whole garrison alive, the retreat was conducted in the most orderly manner,—not out of a slow walk.

And, had we been pursued beyond the camp, I believe every man would have stood up like a *Stonewall* against the enemy, and revenged the death of the noble and brave spirits who had fallen that morning. The attack was at five o'clock, and in the fall of Smith and Turner, Mosby lost his ablest and most promising officers. The terror of Smith to the enemy, and the boldness of his forays, were not second to Mosby's; and Mosby's appreciation of his services as an auxiliary and an officer, and the grief he felt when told of his death, could not be better evidenced than by his crying like a child, and declining to do anything for a month. The sorrow he manifested at the loss of such a man was shared by the men and other officers.

William R. Smith was no ordinary man. Himself and his brothers before him, who had given up their lives in the cause of Southern independence, had repeatedly received compliments from Generals Lee, Ewell, and Stuart, for their bravery and daring deeds. William R. Smith was a lieutenant in the famous Black Horse Cavalry; and, when Mosby was detailed from the regular army to do this service, he requested General Stuart to let him take Smith with him. Smith was a son of Blackwell Smith, farmer, and one of the oldest, most respectable, and influential citizens in Fauquier County. He was brave and generous to a fault; his men idolized him; his conversation was of that frank and generous nature which captivated every one who met him.

Lieutenant Thomas Turner was a native of Prince George County, Maryland, and a resident of Washington City at the breaking out of the Rebellion. He was among the first from that noble old State to volunteer in the Southern cause, and was a first lieutenant in the First Regiment of Virginia Cavalry, of which Mosby was Adjutant. He was brave and courageous, and was known amongst the men as "Fighting Tom." Those qualities so essential for a partisan ranger, combined with coolness, recommended him to Mosby, who had him likewise transferred, and made him his first lieutenant. Being unable to remain on the field, Gragan and Whaley carried him to a Mr. Waters' house, about one mile from Harper's Ferry, where he lingered five days, receiving every attention our Southern friends in the neighbourhood were permitted to show him. He was buried in the cemetery at Hillsboro', a beautiful little village, some ten miles from Harper's Ferry. As soon as day broke, Mosby sent back a flag of truce, under William H. Chapman and R. P. Montjoy, to get Smith's body.

Reaching the pickets, and making known their mission, Colonel Cole declined to give them the body; but told Chapman any "citizen or member of his family could get it." A day or two after this, Captain Smith's wife, father, and mother went after it. On their arrival at Colonel Cole's headquarters, an order was received from General Mulligan, the commander of the post, to arrest them; and they remained under arrest forty-eight hours. General Mulligan declined to see them, or even hold any communication with them. Finally an interview was obtained with one of the adjutants of the post; and, before he would consent to give her her husband's body, Mrs. Smith was compelled to go down on her knees.

The enemy, in the meanwhile, had robbed Captain Smith of his money, watch, papers, &c.; and had absolutely taken every vestige of clothing from his body, except his drawers. Colston, Robinson, Paxon, and the two others were served in the same way, and all of them buried in a sink; and before Mrs. Smith could see the body of her husband, it had to be carried to the river and washed. Not only did the commandant of the post arrest Mrs. Smith's father and mother; but he threatened to place under arrest Colonel Cole and all his officers, for not sending Captain Chapman and Montjoy, under arrest, to his headquarters. General Mulligan, however, never carried his threat into execution. We brought off the field sixty fine horses, which the enemy had just drawn from the quartermaster, and six prisoners, and had it not been for the loss of the brave officers and men, it would have been the most daring and brilliant affair of the war. It was a great success, anyhow: yet Colonel Cole telegraphs to Washington:

> He was attacked that morning, before daylight, by General Mosby, Colonel White, and part of Rosser's Brigade; and, after an hours desperate fighting, the enemy were driven back, and routed with heavy loss in killed, wounded, and prisoners

The fight did not last fifteen minutes. We lost only one prisoner, Lem Brown; and he was taken the next morning bringing out two horses and one prisoner.

The loss of Smith, Turner, Paxon, Colston, and the others, was a severe blow to Mosby, and cast a gloom over the whole county, when it was known. The spirits of the men were in a measure broken; and although Smith and Turner were succeeded by able and brave officers, yet it was a long time before they enjoyed the same esteem and confidence that were given to Smith and Turner. Charlie Paxon was one of the most promising young men in the battalion, and, had he lived, would have distinguished himself.

Chapter 17: Capture of a Picket by Montjoy

Mosby had been in the habit, before this Harper's Ferry disaster, of attacking the enemy's camps in the night-time; but, ever after this, he could not be induced to entertain such a proposition, except under peculiar circumstances. This resolution was not arrived at so much from fear of the enemy's inflicting injury on him, as from the danger of his own men's firing into one another. In this case it was conceded, by all the men, that three out of the five killed were killed by our own men. So great was the despondency of the men, at the result of this affair, that nothing was done for some time. Their attachment for Smith and Turner was so great that their loss rendered the men unfit for duty. Mosby himself did not take the saddle again until February. Smith was his right-hand man; and so great was Mosby's confidence in him, that he would allow Smith to take on a raid any part or all of the command when he felt so inclined. Socially, Smith was as genial as a May day; a strict disciplinarian, who would allow none of his men to shirk duty.

In the latter part of January, 1864, R. P. Montjoy took fifteen men on an expedition to capture the United States mail, between Warrenton and the Junction on the Orange and Alexandria Railroad, the mail guarded by only twenty cavalry. It was a bold undertaking, and no man was better qualified to undertake it than Montjoy. All his men wore the regular blue army overcoats to deceive the enemy. Montjoy reached the point at which he was to make the attack, about midway between the two places, one hour too late, the mail and escort having passed by. Concealing his men in the woods, and throwing out along the road pickets to see if anything would turn up, he remained in that position a short time, when a sutler-wagon and correspondent of the *New York Tribune* came *joggling* along.

They were gobbled up in a little while. The wagon was loaded with stationery and notions. Our men, after taking what they wanted, left the wagon with the remainder of its contents in the road. The sut-

WALTER FRANKLAND

ler parted with greenbacks &c. very reluctantly; while the correspondent took it very coolly, one of the men exchanging a Confederate hat (little worn) and homespun woollen gloves for his elegant fur cap and mink-skin gloves. As he was just from New York, he was pretty flush with greenbacks, which he was advised to exchange for Confederate notes, as he was going to Richmond, and these notes were the only currency permitted by law in that city, a heavy penalty being attached to the passing of greenbacks. This arrangement he readily agreed to; and he and his companion, the sutler, were started back to Fauquier under guard of one man.

Leaving that point, it being considered not safe to remain there any longer, Montjoy proceeded in the direction of a large cavalry camp. When near it he saw a sergeant posting a picket of ten men, some three hundred yards from the camp. He at once concluded to take it. The picket was in full view of the camp. Montjoy with his men approached the post, and was ordered to halt. "What command do you belong to?" cried the picket.

"The First Maine Cavalry," responded Montjoy.

"All right," replied the unsuspecting Yankee. The party rode up to the post, dividing and passing on either side, thus surrounding them. After some few inquiries by Montjoy, at a signal, every one of the picket had a pistol at his head, with orders to get on his horse and follow, which they did without hesitation. The sergeant highly complimented Montjoy for his daring and adroitness. The affair having been observed in camp, Montjoy was obliged to retreat precipitately with four hundred Federal cavalry after him. He, however, escaped with all his capture except the sergeant and two privates. The horses captured were retained in Fauquier County; and the prisoners, ten in number, were sent to Richmond, where accommodations were provided at *Hotel de Libby*.

The boldness and audacity of Montjoy in this affair provoked the enemy beyond bounds, and the only satisfaction they could find was the promulgation of that famous order of General Pleasanton, wherein he ordered that:

"In consequence of so many pickets, patrols, &c., being captured by parties dressed in the Federal uniform, his pickets were hereby ordered to shoot or hang every Rebel soldier caught dressed thus."

This was a very sensible order,—catching before hanging. It was not the first order of the kind ever issued by the Federal generals. And General Pleasanton knew, at the time he issued it, that his men would not, and in fact were afraid to execute it; for they knew full well there was such, a law as retaliation, and that Mosby was the man to apply it without consulting the authorities at Richmond. Besides, they knew it would be rather an expensive luxury with them, as where they caught one of our men, we caught twenty of theirs; and, if they hung one of ours, twenty of theirs would pay the penalty for it. The order, however, had the effect of inducing a large number of the men to dye their overcoats black.

Chapter 18: Mosby's Men Sleep in Caves, etc.

February arrived. Mosby made a flying visit to his family, which was staying then at Charlottesville, and also to Richmond. On the night of the 5th he entered Warrenton alone, and obtained valuable information respecting the enemy's strength and plans for the next campaign, which he took to Richmond, and laid before the Secretary of War. Mosby returned to his headquarters next morning; and on the 6th of the month, with John Munson and Ben Palmer, started for our lines.

During Mosby's absence, the men were not idle, but continued to annoy the enemy. The winter had broken, and the weather was never better adapted for carrying on such enterprises. Captain William H. Chapman, of Company C, assumed command of the battalion during Mosby's absence. He took twenty into the Valley of Virginia, crossing the Shenandoah River at Berry Ferry, and captured a patrolling party of thirty cavalry, near the White Post, and returned with thirty prisoners and horses, without loss or injury.

The 18th of this month will be remembered by the people of Fauquier, or rather of "Mosby's Confederacy," for all time. A trifling white man, by the name of John Cornwall, had been dodging, for twelve months, the enrolling officers, to keep out of the service, and had been employed by Captain Walter Frankland, our quartermaster, to make one trip to Charlottesville, with an ambulance, to bring back a load of ammunition. On his return, he presented a bill of expenses, a portion of which Frankland disallowed. Cornwall appealed to Mosby, who sustained Frankland. Leaving headquarters, he swore vengeance against Mosby, Frankland, and the whole command.

On the 17th he went to the enemy at Warrenton, and had no difficulty in entering their lines; for it was established as a fact, after he left, that he had been going backwards and forwards for some time, carrying information to the enemy, and stealing all the fine horses in the neighbourhood, and selling them to the enemy. Going to headquarters, he stated his grievances, and offered to capture Mosby and his whole command if they would give him five hundred men. The enemy, considering his plans practicable, complied with his request; and the night of the 18th was selected for the purpose. The residents of Fauquier, and the enemy themselves who participated in that affair, will remember it as the coldest night of that severe winter.

The column started from Warrenton on the 17th, at nine o'clock p.m., and reached Salem at one o'clock a.m. At this place they commenced, and searched every house up to the Blue Ridge Mountains, along and under them to Middleburg, embracing an area of about fifteen square miles. At Rectortown they divided, one half—two hundred and fifty—going by Middleburg and Upperville, where both reunited at sunrise; the other column taking in its march, Piedmont, Oak Hill, Markham, and Paris, at the foot of Ashby's Gap, thence to Upperville. One squad of fifty even penetrated the mountains, and visited Slice Barbour's. on the top of one of the spurs of the Blue Ridge, where Cornwall behaved most disgracefully. Learning that Mosby was absent, the enemy thought they had a sure thing of it, and that, on the return of the great partisan, he would find himself minus his command; and their scheme came very near proving successful. But the Fates were against them, and a beneficent Providence had decreed otherwise.

Two things conspired in our favour,—the darkness of the night and the cold. Although their visit was unexpected, and a perfect surprise, as we had not thrown out pickets, they did not capture more than twenty-five of our men. You see we boarded and slept at the farmers' houses; and the enemy thought all they had to do was to ride up, surround the houses, go in, and take us out of bed. But the weather being so bitter cold, and they nearly frozen, the enemy could not act with much celerity. At the house of Mr. Jamison Ashby, uncle of the lamented Turner Ashby, where Captain Frankland lodged, one hundred and fifty surrounded the house, and Cornwall himself superintended the search. He said he was bound to have Frankland. The room was entered; but the bed was empty, yet warm. The cage had been opened, and the bird had flown, but not out of the house. The building was searched thoroughly three times; but Frankland could not be found.

The little negroes were questioned, and threatened with instant death if they did not tell where Frankland, Henry Ashby, and Hamner were. All they could get out of the servants and little darkeys was, they did not know anything about them. The party never executed their threats, but went off disappointed, saying they would come back; but they did not do so that morning. While one set were searching the house, there was another in the stables and fields, getting the horses and mules of Mr. Ashby and his boarders. Not content with all the horses on the place, they stole every turkey, chicken, duck, and goose on the plantation. I will here state, for the information of my readers, that Captain Frankland could see and hear all that was going on in the house.

When the enemy approached Ben Triplett's, where Lieutenant Albert Wren and Jim Wren boarded, the men jumped out of the second-story window in their night-clothes, and fled across the fields, pursued by the enemy, and sought refuge in a straw-rick, under the mountain, on the opposite side of "Crooked Run." The enemy ceased their pursuit at the Run. In this rick the two remained for three hours, and at daylight were found nearly frozen; but, by proper remedies, they were soon restored, and enabled to participate with the heroic Chapman in his efforts to recapture our boys that day. Others made equally narrow escapes, and suffered from the cold as severely.

At Mr. Gibson's, Sergeant Corbin, when the enemy declared that if he, Walston, and the three Gibsons did not come out and give themselves up, the house would be burnt, came out and surrendered, to save the others. While all this was going on, the brave William H. Chapman was collecting together what men he could. He succeeded in getting thirty, and attacked the enemy about one mile from Paris, on Mrs. Betsy Edmond's farm. The enemy retreated to a field in front of her house, and drew up in line of battle behind a stone fence. Not wishing to sacrifice his men by attacking them in that position, Chapman retired a short distance to watch their movements. In a short time the enemy received reinforcements from Paris, when they all retreated to that place, and remained until three o'clock p.m., when they started back to Warrenton.

About noon Mosby returned from Richmond; and, hearing of the calamity Cornwall had brought upon him, determined, if possible, to rescue his men, and capture Cornwall. Collecting every man he possibly could, he tried to divide the enemy so as to attack him in detail; which, if he had succeeded in doing, he would have not only got his own men back, but a large number of the enemy. The enemy, however, kept well closed up on their return; and there was no possible chance of cutting any of them off. Then, as a last resort for the recapture of his men, he determined to attack the enemy near Warrenton. Taking a private road, he expected to reach the point at which he intended to make the attack some time before the enemy, and to stretch a large piece of telegraph wire across the road, and, when they approached it, to charge them in the rear, and run them against it in the dark. But they, apprehending some trick would be played upon them by us in the dark, marched in a trot, and reached Warrenton at sunset, with all their prisoners, turkeys, chickens, &c. They took back with them two hundred of the finest horses in the State of Virginia. The citizens of Warrenton told us that this raiding party, on their return, had turkey and roast chicken for dinner one whole week afterwards.

After this night raid to "Mosby's Confederacy," the boys built huts in the mountains, but would take their meals as heretofore, and after supper, or at dark, would repair with their horses to the huts, and repose as comfortably as in feather-beds. Some slept in caves in the mountains; some continued to remain as before, but had burrowed holes in the ground under the houses, which were entered through a trap-door. When the "British" (Sam Alexander's name of the enemy) came, they could seek refuge in the holes; the houses being hid in the woods. Others had niches, with small holes for the eyes made in the walls of the houses; these niches being entered by private doors. Some few would secrete themselves up the chimneys. Mosby, with one or two of his staff, and often by himself, would generally, at dark, mount their horses, and go down to some good friend's house near the enemy's camps, and stay all night, thinking that the safest place.

Chapter 19: Attack Upon Colonel Cole

The success of this last raid produced the greatest rejoicing throughout the North. The enemy were sure they had crippled Mosby beyond his ability to recuperate. The officers commanding the expedition were lauded to the skies. The California battalion, stationed at Vienna, concluded to finish him entirely, and terminate his career as a partisan. Accordingly, a raid was made by two hundred and fifty men, who, after scouring the upper portion of Fauquier, without seeing him, his men, or anything else, returned in the hope that he had left the country, as he could no longer hold it. Mosby, hearing them coming, collected eighty of his men, and started for Dranesville, a little village in Prince William County. Knowing the enemy would pass through the place on their return to camp, Mosby placed twenty-five of his men in ambush, on each side of the road, just outside of the town, and divided the rest, so that one half should attack in front, while the other half charged them in the rear, thus subjecting them to a fire all around.

In the course of an hour, the enemy approached in a very careless manner. The men in ambush opened on them with Colt's army-pistols, producing confusion in their ranks. Before order was restored, they were attacked in the rear and front; Mosby leading the latter. Desperate was the fighting, and terrible the slaughter; a large portion of the fighting being hand to hand. Numbers fought their way through our thin ranks, and escaped. Fifty of the enemy were killed and wounded and left on the field; seventy prisoners and ninety horses were brought off the field. The most remarkable feature about the 'affair was, that Mosby lost only one man killed (Chapplier of Fauquier,) and three wounded.

In the month of March, Colonel Cole made his farewell raid into our "Confederacy." Mosby was at Piedmont, receiving the congratulations of some of his men on his promotion to the rank of Lieutenant-Colonel. Cole dashed in on the party, and dispersed them, capturing two or three. Mosby, rallying his men, and by the coming in of others having his forces increased to seventy-five effective men, followed up Cole, whose force numbered two hundred and fifty, and attacked him at the schoolhouse, three miles from Upperville, on the road to Bloomfield, and routed them, driving them ten miles, killing and wounding twenty. One killed they left in the road, and he was buried in the lot adjoining the schoolhouse; Mosby sustaining no loss. Twenty horses were secured in this little affair.

The rest of this month no raids took place; but numerous *private* scouting-parties operated on the enemy, obtaining valuable information, and doing good service. The brave and lamented Watt Bowie, of Maryland, Bush and Sam Underwood, John W. Puryear, of Richmond, John Russell, of Clark County, Virginia, and others commanded these parties. Bowie operated in Maryland, the Underwoods in Fairfax, Russell, Puryear, and others operated in the valley. They would return, some mornings, loaded with plunder, prisoners, and horses, captured from the enemy.

Early in April, Colonel Mosby received information, from a reliable source, that the enemy at Warrenton contemplated another raid into his Confederacy. There was general rejoicing throughout the command at their expected visit. Mosby, acting on this information, ordered every man to repair to Somerset Mills, on the road from Piedmont to Ashby's Gap. Two hundred men reported for duty. At dark we moved from Somerset to the woods adjoining Mrs. Shacklett's farm, one mile from Piedmont, and lay there three consecutive nights, awaiting the approach of the enemy; but the enemy did not come; and most fortunate was it for them that they did not, for very few would have got back to camp to tell the tale. Each of our men was armed with a double-barrelled shot-gun (each barrel with twenty-four buckshot in it), besides three brace of Colt's pistols, which were good for twelve more shots. What execution these would have done, I leave for my readers to determine.

General Grant, having assumed command of the Army of the Potomac about this time, commenced his advance "on to Richmond," expecting to walk rough-shod over General Lee, and celebrate his Fourth of July in that city. Warrenton was evacuated, much to the relief of its citizens. At this place they left articles which betrayed the traps they had set for us, which consisted of wires stretched across the streets, to sweep us off our horses if we dashed into the place during their occupation of it; but we had warm friends there, who kept us always posted in regard to the intentions of the enemy and what they were doing. Nothing could transpire in Warrenton during the day, which we would not know at headquarters before twelve o'clock the same night.

A few days after the evacuation of Warrenton, Chapman and Montjoy carried fifty of us down to the place to capture a scouting-party of the enemy, numbering seventy-five or a hundred. We arrived in town too late, the enemy having gone about one hour before. Our entrance into Warrenton was very gratifying to the men. Smiles and waving of white handkerchiefs, from fair young ladies, greeted us from every house; and there was a general rejoicing. Cakes, wine, &c. (just think of it, kind reader), were handed around by pretty ladies to a set of guerillas, who had nothing to drink in their Confederacy but new wheat whiskey and apple brandy just from the still. As we entered the town, desolation met the eye from every quarter. Warrenton, which, in time of peace, abounded in beautiful groves, flowers, and green fields, was now like a deserted ship at sea.

The beautiful groves had been cut down to afford fuel to the soldiers; fences gone; private grounds and buildings converted into stables; and, in the place of the luxuriant fields, ugly mud huts could be seen as far as the eye could reach. Everything inviting and pleasant to the sight had disappeared, except the pretty girls and the houses they lived in. Remaining in town not more than an hour, we returned to headquarters to prepare for a raid into the valley the next day. Agreeably to orders, we met at Paris the next day. Colonel Mosby made a detail of twenty-five men, and started for the valley. Crossing the Blue Ridge at Ashby's Gap, and swimming the Shenandoah River at Berry's Ferry, near Winchester, he captured a small wagon-train and ten horses and six prisoners, and sent them out to Fauquier, by Cuper and three others.

Pushing on with the rest of his men (twenty), he reached Martinsburg a little after midnight. After a little reconnoitring he dismounted part of his men (the rest holding their horses), and entered the enemy's camp about one mile from town. The officers being absent on a frolic in the town, the guards were careless. Our men entered the stables, and brought out twenty fine horses. The guards were aroused; and our men, upon leaving the stables, were fired upon, but no one on our side was injured. Some of the men entered the officers' tents, and secured their entire wardrobes. Mosby and Wirt Ashby entered the town, and inspected the enemy's fortifications, rejoining the men without discovery. The Yankee officers, on their return to quarters, did not miss anything until ten o'clock the next morning, when, to their astonishment, they discovered that twenty of their finest horses were gone. By the time the discovery was made, Mosby was across the Shenandoah River, in Paris, distributing the prizes amongst his men.

There were horses in this lot which Louis Napoleon would have been proud to own; yet Mosby would not appropriate a single one to his own use. During his whole career as a partisan, of the many thousand horses—and very fine ones too—which he captured, he appropriated but one captured horse to his own use. This he did when General Lee invaded Pennsylvania, in 1863. General Stuart was passing through Upperville upon a very indifferent horse. Mosby, feeling a little mortified at the condition of the general's horse, dismounted from a very fine mare, and presented it to the general. Mosby then mounted Stuart's horse, and, crossing the mountains into the valley, captured a vidette that night, and returned to Fauquier before day the next morning.

Chapter 20: Visit of a German Baron

Lieutenant Samuel Chapman, brother of Captain William H. Chapman, who had distinguished himself on several battlefields by his bravery, was this month transferred to the battalion from the regular army, at the special request of Colonel Mosby, who appointed him his adjutant, with the rank of First Lieutenant. Lieutenant Chapman, a few days after his arrival in Fauquier, took fifty men, crossed the mountains at Slice Barbour's, and the Shenandoah River at Howardsville, and attacked, in the night-time, a picket-post of one hundred of the enemy at Guard Hill, and captured thirty prisoners, including one captain, and fifty horses, besides killing and wounding several, and returned without loss.

Mosby's fame as a successful partisan ranger, was at its zenith, and had reached the Old World. Officers in the European armies came over, and joined him as privates. One German baron came out from Washington to see Mosby, and learn his *tactics* and the great secret of his success. On his way up to our headquarters, from Washington City, he met with some of our scouts in Fairfax County. He told them his business: but they took him to be an impostor and spy; and, acting upon that supposition, they *"went through him."* As I have used this phrase very often, I deem it proper my readers should know what it means, and the *modus operandi*. Meeting an enemy after his surrender, you demand his greenbacks. If he is slow in shelling out, you simply insert your hand into his pocket and take them, or present a pistol to his head.

The latter was the most popular method; and, finally, it got to be a common course on both sides, that the captured, after his arms were taken away, always handed the captor his pocket-book without being asked. If he had a watch, he was relieved of that, lest it might be taken from him on his way to Richmond. If his hat was better than yours, you exchanged with him, and the same way with boots and everything else. My readers will please to understand we were not the only ones who indulged in this luxury. Our enemies indulged in it in every instance, and particularly the officers, even those as high in rank as colonel.

But to return to our baron. He remonstrated with his captors all in vain. After relieving him of his valuables, they let him pass on; and he reached Mosby's headquarters. He reported his treatment, and asked redress. After an examination of his papers and his business, he was politely informed that that "was part of our tactics." The baron returned to Washington a poorer but wiser man.

During this month, details were made to go to Loudon County, to collect forage for the ensuing campaign, which promised to be a very active one. Grant had fought the Battle of Spotsylvania Court House, and was repulsed. General Lee, fearing his supplies would be cut off, reoccupied his old lines at Fredericksburg, and gave his adversary a severe drubbing there. Citizens of that ancient town were turned out of their homes to accommodate the enemy's wounded, which numbered thirty thousand.

Just after the Battle of Fredericksburg, Mosby took fifty men, well-mounted, to King George's County, below Fredericksburg, and captured a wagon-train, and brought out forty mules and horses and ten prisoners, without loss. He was absent five days. Having been so successful on the last raid, Mosby ordered fifty more of us to meet him at Joe Blackwell's, the day after his return, with five days' feed for our horses. Rations for ourselves we never carried, depending on buying or having them given to us by the citizens. We moved from headquarters at noon, and bivouacked the first night out near Catlett's Station, on the Orange and Alexandria Railroad.

At daylight the next morning we crossed the railroad, and took the old telegraph road to within a mile of Stafford Court House. Leaving the highway about half a mile, we entered one of those deep ravines which abound in that rugged country, and remained until the next afternoon, when we resumed our march, passing through Stafford Court House, thence across the Acquia Creek Railroad, to a secluded point about three miles from Belle Plains. Here we were rejoined by Mosby, Charlie Hall, and John Edmonds, who had been on a scouting-party to find out the wagon-trains from the Plains to Fredericksburg. While out, they captured a wagon-master, who had strayed away from his train, from whom they obtained all the information necessary for Mosby to carry out his plans. While they were interrogating him, a brigade of infantry was seen approaching them. Mosby sent his prisoner into the woods, out of their view, while he and Edmonds remained in the road.

As the brigade passed, Mosby and Edmonds exchanged salutes, and conversed with the officers "on the situation." After the column had passed, Mosby and his party returned to the command, reaching it early in the afternoon. At midnight we started out to find the wagon-camp. On the march we had a fine view, by moonlight, of the enemy's fleet at the mouth of Acquia Creek. It had the appearance of a large city lighted by gas. A diligent search was instituted for the camp, but it was not found until near daylight. It was not guarded; but, daylight being so near, Mosby deferred the attack until next night, with the view of making a sure thing of it. Had the nights that season of the year been one or two hours longer, Mosby would have made a capture which would have eclipsed all his former deeds.

From Belle Plains to Fredericksburg the distance is nine miles, and the enemy had a train of wagons hauling supplies from this place to the latter for the army. Indeed, so numerous were the enemy, that, to facilitate this immense amount of transportation, two roads were required, one for the wagons to go up, and the other to return. The remoteness of this country from our headquarters, Fauquier, induced the enemy to believe we would not molest them; consequently, they dispensed with the usual guards. Besides, Grant had lost so heavily at Spotsylvania and Fredericksburg, that every soldier was needed in the field. When it was known the camp was found, the men were anxious to "go into it" anyhow. The temptation was great, but had to be resisted; for had we attacked it, and captured five hundred or a thousand mules and horses, we could have at that hour been cut off and captured. Mosby took us back to the dense pine woods, to await the return of night. At ten o'clock Mosby left us in charge of Alfred Glasscock, who was to make the attack, and went scouting to Fairfax County.

The enemy, in small squads, started out the next morning, to see if any rebels we're in that country. Seeing the tracks we made the night before, they returned to camp, and reported. Then a force of one regiment of cavalry and one regiment of infantry were started out to capture us. While most of us were indulging ourselves in a nap, under the shade of the trees, some with their horses unsaddled, our men were suddenly confronted with a large column of infantry. They, not knowing our force, halted, which afforded our pickets time to get back to camp, and apprise us of our danger. In a few moments we were mounted, and ready to move; but our guide, Charlie Hall, was gone. We, however, commenced the retreat, going in the direction of the railroad. Meeting a citizen hiding from the enemy, we were advised by him not to "go that way;" that "the whole country was filled with the enemy." There being no one amongst us who knew the country, he guided us to the railroad, where we met another detachment of infantry marching down the railroad with labourers to repair it. Being thus cut off, Glasscock adopted the daring plan of dashing on (we after him), and crying out, "Mosby is after us! get out of the way!" The enemy broke, and ran for the woods; we passed, and got out safe.

That morning, early, Charlie Hall (our guide) and John Edmonds had started out scouting; and, as they had not returned before we left, the greatest anxiety was felt for their safety. They came out safe, with three prisoners and horses, but with some difficulty. On their return to camp, they met this same force, and were compelled to change their course. Whatever way they went, the enemy's pickets were seen. Finding themselves surrounded, to save their prisoners and horses, they concluded to represent themselves as a federal scouting-party looking for Mosby. Riding up to the pickets, and representing themselves as such, they were permitted to pass out of their lines, and got back safe to Fauquier with their booty.

Chapter 21: Disappointments

In a few days after our return, Mosby (not seeing anything in Fairfax for us) took one hundred and fifty men to the valley, crossing the mountains at Ashby's Gap, and swimming the Shenandoah River at Berry's Ferry, pushed on under cover of night to Martinsburg, to capture one hundred cavalry and two hundred artillery horses. We reached the suburbs of the town about three o'clock a.m., without being seen by anyone, and halted under a hill near the railroad, while Mosby and John Russell should reconnoitre, and find out the best way to get in. To their surprise, three hundred infantry were found guarding the horses, and videttes were found posted a hundred yards apart all around the camp. Mosby at once abandoned all idea of attacking the camp, and ordered us to retire. On going out we had not proceeded more than one hundred yards before the command, "Halt! who comes dar?" rang in our ears. John Russell, our guide, being in the advance, rode up to him. He was a German, and asked Russell, "Vot you want?" his carbine pointing at Russell's breast. Russell pushed his carbine aside, and, pointing a pistol in his face ordered him to throw the carbine down.

"Vot you want me throw it way for? Me pay for it."

After the exchange of a few more words, Russell, with his prisoner, joined the command, and all started back for Fauquier At sunrise Mosby ordered A. E. Richards, who had been promoted to the captaincy of Company B, for meritorious conduct, to detail twenty men, and return to the Baltimore and Ohio Railroad, and take that express-train which passed while we were lying near Martinsburg the night before. Richards made the detail, including Lieutenant Harry Hatcher, alias "Deadly," of Company A, and returned the next night. They reached the railroad without being discovered by the pickets. There were two tracks, the old one and a new one; and they, thinking the train would pass over the new, removed a rail on it, and retired to a small piece of woods some twenty yards from the road, and then patiently awaited its arrival, each one having visions of greenbacks, gold watches, &c., &c., looming up before them. In a few moments the train came dashing by, but on the old track. One fellow, thinking it would stop for him, mounted his horse and made for it; but it soon disappeared behind a mountain, and Richards returned without accomplishing anything

The season for a vigorous campaign approaching, Mosby, to be prepared for it, sent Companies B and C to Loudon County, to get forage for the battalion. Chapman, with Company C, collected it near Lovettsville, and pressed wagons from the farmers to send it to Fauquier. Richards, with Company B, operated in the neighbourhood of Waterford, sending out with each load one or two men as a guard. Chapman gathered his without interruption. Richards, after collecting the tithe around Waterford, took his remaining men, six in number, and moved over towards Berlin to find corn for another occasion. While going down the grade beyond General Wright's (who was a wealthy and influential farmer at the commencement of the war, but was broken up by the enemy), we were attacked by Reyes's cavalry, sixty in number.

We retreated to the woods; and, striking a private road, we followed that, which led us to the mountains, pursued all the way. Bob Walker, with Captain Richards, while gallantly trying to keep back the foe, had his horse shot under him. Being near a wheat-field, he retreated to that, climbed an apple-tree, and escaped, although the enemy instituted a diligent search for him. Reaching the mountains, we ascended them; and, resting our horses until the cool of the evening, we then resumed our march back to old Fauquier.

This affair being the first time Reyes's men ever pursued any of us, they were very much emboldened, and afterwards would cross the Potomac River at the Point of Rocks, in squads of fifteen and twenty, and scout up as far as Hamilton, Woodgrove, and Waterford, robbing the citizens who sympathised with the South, and getting whiskey at Downey's Stillhouse, the owner of which was President of the *bogus* Virginia Senate, then holding its sessions in Alexandria. This place was a great rendezvous for them, at which they captured quite a number of our men; and from this place they would come up to Waterford, a distance of only five miles, to see their parents and sweethearts. It was on one of these trips, that Lieutenant Frank Williams, of Company B, gave a drubbing to a party of them, which effectually terminated all future expeditions of the kind.

Lieutenant Williams, with six men, visited Waterford with the view of capturing one of these parties. Passing through the town, he concealed his men behind an old house near the bridge, at the lower part. In a short time fifteen of Keyes's men dashed into the village, and commenced having "a nice time" with their friends; telling them how they had chased "those horse-thieves," meaning Mosby's men, and expressing a strong desire to met them again. Williams, with one man, rode up to where they were, and fired into them. They soon mounted their horses, and gave Williams chase. When they had reached their comrades, they halted; and the rest of his men charged the enemy. Keyes retreated in confusion, and was pursued three miles. Six of his men were captured, one killed in the town, and three wounded. Williams secured ten fine horses in this little affair. When he returned to Waterford, to convey the prisoners, and look after the wounded, the most affecting scenes took place between the prisoners and their friends at parting. Williams sustained neither loss nor injury.

Chapter 22: A "Trap"

The enemy, while we occupied that country, very ungenerously accused us and our Southern friends living inside their lines with being bushwhackers. Now I will venture to say here to the world, and to state it without fear of contradiction, that there were not two persons, soldiers or citizens, in that whole country, extending from the Blue Ridge to Washington, who were regular bushwhackers. The only instance of the kind that ever came to my knowledge was that of a darkey (whom the Yankees had driven away from his home) near Salem, while General Meade's army was lying around Warrenton, and scouting-parties were roving over the whole country. This darkey would take his double-barrelled shot-gun, secrete himself in the corner of the fence, amongst some bushes, and pick up the stragglers. What he did with his prisoners was never known; but I learned, from a reliable source, that he sent them to Culpepper. This darkey would frequently have eight and ten horses at a time. This explanation, I trust, is satisfactory, so far as regards Southern bushwhackers.

Now, a word concerning the Union citizens in and around Waterford. That place, in my judgment, afforded more of that class of people, during the war, than any other town or county in Eastern Virginia. Whenever we were in that particular portion of Loudon, our pickets were invariably fired upon by them. Information reached Mosby that the enemy had laid a trap in Loudon to capture him; and he, being a person ever ready to acquire knowledge, ordered a meeting of the command at Upperville, on the 1st of June, that they might go up with him. One hundred men reported for duty. Captain Richards, with Company B, he sent ahead to the neighbourhood of Point of Rocks, to toll the enemy over the river, while he took Companies A and C with him. Our movements were made under cover of night, the main roads being shunned, to avoid being seen, and to keep the people ignorant of our actual strength.

In the daytime we stayed in the woods, and were not allowed to expose ourselves to anyone. Reaching the turnpike leading to Berlin, Mosby distributed his men in squads along this thoroughfare, in striking-distance of each other, and patiently awaited the approach of the enemy. Captain Richards being unable to draw the enemy across the river, from their stronghold at Point of Rocks, Mosby and ten men went to Harper's Ferry, to draw them out from that place. The men had not smelt gunpowder for nearly one month now, and were "spiling for a fight." Company B was ordered to Hillsboro', in hopes the enemy could be tolled from the Ferry. In such a contingency, they were to hold them in check until the rest of the men could be brought up. Company B remained here three days, and no signs of an attack. We returned to Fauquier, and to this day have never learned what that trap was which the enemy had set for us. During our stay we were most hospitably entertained by some of their citizens. Mr. Janney's and Mr. Hoe's accomplished wives and daughters were unremitting in their attentions to us; and music, dancing, card playing, &c., was the order for three whole days.

On the 22nd of June, the battalion met at Rectortown, where we had roll-call for the first time since our organisation. Two hundred and sixty men answered to their names; and, for the first time, we had one piece of artillery (twelve-pound howitzer). Detail of artillerists was made to man the gun, and Lieutenant Sam Chapman placed in command of it. At noon the men fell into ranks, and moved off in the direction of Fairfax. On reaching Anandale, we found the enemy prepared to receive us, and also re-enforced. Declining to attack them, Mosby ordered us back to Fauquier by companies, Captain Richards, with Company B, taking the road, *via* Centreville and Manassas. When near Centreville he met with a large squad of the enemy, grazing their horses and surveying land (for what purpose the writer never learned). Charging them before they could form, he took thirty-five of them prisoners, killed, wounded, and dispersed the rest, secured fifty horses, and got back to Fauquier County without loss.

On the 28th day of June, a meeting was held at Upperville. Two hundred and fifty men responded to their names. At noon we moved up the turnpike through Paris; thence across the mountains at Ashby Gap. One mile from the gap, at Mount Carmel, we took the mountain road, which carried us to Shepperd's Mills, crossing the Shenandoah River there. Resting our horses an hour or so, we resumed our march, passing through Cabletown, on to within one mile of Charlestown, on the turnpike, where we halted and drew up in line of battle on either side of the road, with one piece of artillery posted on an eminence commanding the turnpike up and down for one mile. A party was sent into town to draw the enemy out, if any were there; if not, to Halltown, near Harper's Ferry.

After waiting half an hour to be attacked, and the party sent out to draw the enemy on having returned with intelligence of no enemy nearer than Harper's Ferry, Mosby determined to strike the Baltimore and Ohio Railroad. Passing through Charlestown, where we were greeted with waving of handkerchiefs and smiles from pretty ladies, we filed off to the left, outside of the town, and made for Duffield Station, leaving Company A (twenty-five men) with Lieutenant Joseph Nelson, to prevent, if possible, our being cut off by troops from the Ferry. Reaching the railroad without opposition, Mosby sent Captain Richards into Duffield. with flag of truce, demanding an unconditional surrender, on pain of being shelled in two minutes; Mosby in the meanwhile having posted his howitzer in good position, with Company C to support it.

So great was the surprise that the lieutenant of the post had to arrange the terms, the commandant being taken very suddenly sick. Richards returned with the terms, and we occupied the place. The camp was burnt, and all government goods in the depot confiscated, including Union men's shoes, and ladies' and gentlemen's dress and fancy goods. Groceries were found in great quantities, with which each man filled his sack. The whole guard was surrendered, but only seventy infantry prisoners were brought away. Mosby, apprehending a large force might be sent from Harper's Ferry to intercept him, ordered the retreat to where Nelson was.

Mosby's expectations were realised. Before we were out of sight of Duffield, a courier came to direct us "to hurry back, as Nelson was engaging an overwhelming force." We hurried back as fast as our horses would carry us, with the loads on them, but arrived too late for the *fun*. Nelson had already, with his twenty-five men, fought and routed one hundred of Siegel's cavalry, killing two captains, and taking twenty of them prisoners, with their horses. Nelson drove the enemy as far as Halltown. Apprehending a stronger force would be sent after us, the whole command started for Fauquier. On the way out, when above Charlestown a short distance, Siegel came down from his stronghold with a force, and displayed them one mile and a half from us, and marched back. No further attempt was made to pursue, although this dispatch was sent to Washington:

> A competent force has been sent in pursuit, and a fair prospect they will be overhauled.

We recrossed the Shenandoah River at Shepperd's Mills that night, and camped, on the Fauquier side. Next morning at daylight our march was resumed, and we reached Paris at late breakfast. Here a division of the property was made amongst the men, who were then disbanded, and the prisoners sent to Richmond.

Chapter 23: Skirmishing Across the Potomac

The weather being so very hot, nothing was done until the 3rd day of July, when the whole command met at Upperville. The men turned out on their finest horses, each provided with a large sack strapped to his saddles, for the purpose of bringing home the plunder. The men had a presentiment that Mosby was going into Maryland, and a very correct one it was; for Generals Early and Breckenridge had commenced that celebrated movement on Washington City, and the advance was crossing the Potomac River at Williamsport. At noon the men were formed by companies, and moved off with one piece of artillery, taking the road to Bloomfield. On reaching Green Garden Mills, one mile from Upperville, the battalion was halted, horses fed, and ammunition distributed (two rounds to a man). The sun being so intolerably hot (mercury at ninety-six in the shade), we remained here in the shade until four o'clock in the afternoon, when we formed again and moved off.

All villages, Union men's houses, and public roads were avoided on the march until night. Strict orders were issued by Colonel Mosby, prohibiting the men from straggling, and telling the people to whose command they belonged. The first night out we bivouacked near Purcellville, Loudon County. At daylight, on the 4th, we resumed our march; passing through that portion of Loudon in which resided a great many people who, to curry favour with the enemy, and get pay for so doing, were continually giving information concerning our movements. It was of the highest importance, to insure success to Colonel Mosby's plans, that the citizens should be kept ignorant of the name of our command and commander; so, when any citizen inquired who we were, the men would say, "the advance guard of Longstreet's corps," knowing that it would be immediately communicated across the river, and operate to our advantage. To give plausibility to the statement, they had received intelligence that Early and Breckenridge were already in Maryland, and marching on Frederick City.

At eleven o'clock we reached the Potomac opposite Berlin, and in full view of the place; then filing right down the river through a large orchard, a few miles' march brought us to the farm of Mr. B. There we rested our horses for fully one hour, to await the return of a small scouting-party. Colonel Mosby had sent to the Point of Rocks, to look at the "situation." While waiting, and enjoying the delightful shade of the woods, a large number of the men were hospitably entertained by Mr. B.'s lady and amiable daughter, although they were strong Union people. At noon the scouting-party returned, and the order was given to "mount your horses." We then moved farther down the river, to a private ford, one mile from town, the battalion halting some two hundred yards from the river, in the woods.

Sharpshooters and "long-range" guns were ordered "to the front," and skirmishing across the river commenced, Colonel Mosby superintending and participating himself in the luxury. The enemy, apprehending an attack on this stronghold, had increased the garrison at this place, and thrown up a very formidable earthwork on a knoll of ground at the lower end of the village, with a canal and river between us, in which fifty resolute men could have kept at bay, and even repulsed, at least one thousand cavalry, after the bridge across the canal was torn up. This fort commanded the river up and down for miles. The enemy's cavalry (about one hundred), commanded by Captain Keyes, were stationed half a mile in the rear of the town, while their infantry, some five hundred in number, were distributed on the side of the mountains for a mile up the river, and kept up a very brisk firing, without inflicting any injury to our men.

While this sharpshooting was going on, Lieutenant Sam Chapman moved his piece of artillery up a high hill directly opposite the town, and screened from the sight of the enemy, by the thick undergrowth, part of Company C supporting it. Some of the enemy were having a 4th of July dinner on a canal-boat. The dinner was over, and refreshments were being served. The sun was a little past meridian; and they seemed to be enjoying themselves so much, that it looked like a pity to break up their "sociable" in such an unceremonious manner. But the view of the enemy by the gallant and impetuous Chapman aroused that inordinate desire in him to engage them whenever and wherever he could. Placing his gun in position, he determined to fire a salute. The salute was fired, and the shell exploded under the dinner-table on the boat.

A panic ensued in the town, which soon extended to the garrison. The cavalry tore up the bridge across the canal, and retreated to Frederick City, while the infantry dropped their guns, and sought refuge in the mountains, some concealing themselves in the crevices of the rocks, with the impression on their minds that the whole of Longstreet's corps was after them. Companies A, B, and D charged across the river, while the sharpshooters waded across with water up to their armpits. The scene was new to me, and the most exciting I ever experienced in my life. A few of the enemy's sharpshooters continued to fire on us while crossing, without injury to anyone. The Potomac was very broad at the place we crossed, but the Maryland shore was soon reached, when our course was directed down the tow-path to the town, each man spurring on his horse, and trying to be the first in the place.

On reaching the bridge across the canal, it was found that the enemy had removed the flooring. A few minutes' time was all that was required to replace it with boards from an old warehouse on the river-banks, which the enemy occupied as quarters. In their hasty retreat from it, they forgot their colours, which we secured. A temporary floor to the bridge being laid by this time, over the boys dashed, led by Wirt Ashby, a relation of the heroic and lamented Turner Ashby. The telegraph wires were cut to prevent communication with the enemy at Harper's Ferry. On the men dashed to the enemy's camps, which, after a critical examination "for arms," were burnt.

Captain Richards, with eight men, pursued the cavalry five miles beyond the town towards Frederick, but could not overtake them, when he ordered us back to the command. Passing through the burning camps, the boys, after collecting what relics they wanted, pushed on back to town. Such an exciting and laughable scene few have ever witnessed or enjoyed. They had secured a huge pound-cake, which had been prepared by some ladies, who were to give the officers of the garrison an entertainment that evening.

The history of this cake is as follows: The officers of the garrison had signified to some of their lady friends their desire and intention of celebrating the Fourth of July in a becoming manner; so their lady friends went to work and prepared a monster cake for the occasion. This cake was moulded in the form of a spread eagle, the mould being made in Boston, and measured twenty-five feet from the tip of its bill to the tip of its tail. It was a complete eagle in all its parts. It had glass eyes, talons, &c., &c., and in the baking of it, which occupied three days and nights, it was burnt (intentionally I presume), so that it looked like a real eagle. But the most remarkable thing about it was, that inside of it there was some machinery that every time one of the boys thrust his sabre into the eagle to cut off a piece, the bird would scream. What their idea was in inserting this instrument into this spread-eagle cake, I have never been able to learn or conceive. I inquired diligently of the residents of the place, but they would give us no satisfaction. Colonel Mosby would have brought it across the river, and sent it to Richmond; but the enemy had destroyed all the boats, so the boys concluded to take it to pieces; which, being done, it was with great difficulty got across the river in the evening by means of a raft. A six-horse team belonging to Mr. S. was pressed into service, the cake put into it, and started for Fauquier County. A guard of five men accompanied the wagon.

While in camp on Goose Creek, the second night they were out, the guard got drunk on "blockade," and all of them lay down and went to sleep. The driver being a strong Union man, and having conceived the idea he would be made a hero, if he could save what was left of the great American bird, availed himself of the opportunity, and drove his load in the night to a Mr. ——'s farm, in Loudon County, situated on Goose Creek. Securing four of Mr. ——'s most reliable coloured servants, he secreted his precious load in one of those safe places which abound on that stream, and which are known only by those patriotic and loyal coloured men, and started back with his team. Sunrise next morning, found him in the bosom of his family, on the banks of the classic Potomac.

This Union driver kept the part he had played a profound secret, until General ——, occupied the valley, when he divulged his secret to him. On General ——'s retreat from Washington, a portion of his wagon train and eight hundred prisoners crossed the Blue Ridge mountains at Ashby's Gap. This portion of his army was pursued by

General Durfea, with two thousand five hundred cavalry. After occupying the gap three days, Durfea fell back to Snickersville, where General Wright was encamped with a division of the Union Army. On their march to Wright, they passed by Mr. ——'s house, and found these coloured Union citizens, who conducted them to the spot where the treasure was hid, and carried it off with them.

But the fates seemed opposed to having the remnants of the bird ever reaching the shores of Maryland again. Notwithstanding its long captivity, it retained signs of life still; and as it approached the soil on which the stars and stripes had never ceased to wave, those symptoms of vitality increased. An escort was sent with it; while crossing the Shenandoah River at Rock Ford, the wagon upset, and the load was precipitated into the river. By an eye-witness of the scene, I was told that it was beyond description. Suffice it to say, the greatest confusion prevailed. Everyone wanted his own plan adopted to save the bird, and before any one that the men suggested could be adopted, to their utmost dismay and horror the bird gave one shriek, and then sunk to rise no more. I never learned whether or no it was recovered; the presumption is that it was not.

But I find myself digressing from my narrative. The boys enjoyed the spread-eagle cake and "blockade" hugely, and many a toast was drunk, "hoping the Yankees would soon give us another thing as good as this." The contents of five stores were appropriated to themselves by the men. Some, "to make it pay," doffed their hats, and substituted a dozen Shaker bonnets, &c., &c. One fellow (Sam), the very personification of a partisan ranger, seeing the excellent "blockade" poured into the streets, thought it a wanton destruction. He conceived the idea of carrying some of it to Fauquier in his sack, which was already filled to overflowing with ladies' and gentlemen's dress and fancy goods, tea, sugar, coffee, &c. Taking this sack and putting the mouth of it to the spigot in a barrel of very fine "old rye," he began to fill it.

After drawing several gallons, a friend informed him of his mistake. But it was too late; the whole contents of the sack were saturated with "spirits." Abandoning that one, he picked up another, which was soon filled. Only a few prisoners were captured here, and they escaped, while the men "went through" the stores. After all the men had provided themselves with what their necessities required, orders came to recross the river. In crossing the river the men presented a novel appearance, being completely enveloped in goods, with nothing visible of them but their heads and horses.

After the crossing had been accomplished safely, we moved back from the river one and a half miles, and bivouacked on the Hon. James Mason's farm, and on the road leading to Leesburg. That night three wagons were pressed into service, and our plunder sent back to Fauquier. While the men were loading these wagons, the owner of one of the stores we had gone through, came up to Colonel Mosby, who on certain representations made to him, gave him permission to take from the men all goods that had his mark. Two of the wagons had already started out, which he reported to Colonel Mosby; whereupon, Mosby gave him an order permitting him to proceed to Fauquier County unmolested, and search, and take his goods wherever he found them. A large quantity of his goods were taken out of the lot in camp, and the men turned around and bought them at the owner's own prices, just in the same manner as a person would go into a store to make a purchase.

In Fauquier, what goods the merchant found were carried to Middleburg, and sold to the citizens. In the opinion of all rational men, this statement will effectually refute the charge the enemy made against us of being a pack of robbers. The next day the enemy scouted down to the point, to see what was done. They approached the town very cautiously, and finding no "Johnnies" in the place, they became careless. The officer in command detailed a squad to go up the river to the abutments of a burnt bridge, and reconnoitre.

The eagle eye of Mosby, having from the "lookout" seen them approach the town, he took a few, picked men, and reached the river before they did. With him he had a young man named Martin, from King and Queen County, Virginia, who promised to vie with Colonel Mosby in deeds of daring, &c. On the battlefield he was the bravest of the brave, and in the charge his impetuosity knew no bounds. Being a splendid shot, he was always in the front with Colonel Mosby; and when the charge was sounded, his soul seemed fired; and away he would go, frequently ahead of his commander, right into the enemy, firing right and left, every shot telling; and when his ammunition was exhausted, he has been frequently seen using the butt-end of his pistols over the heads of the enemy, and always with telling effect.

The keen eye of this young man, as he approached the river, observed in the distance on the opposite side, several of the enemy behind one of the abutments of the burnt bridge. He snatched a Sharp's rifle from one of his companions, and seeking a good position opposite the abutment, he spied a Yankee taking sight at one of his party, while only a few inches of his head could be seen. Colonel Mosby was standing by, when Martin asked if he saw "that fellow on the other side behind the abutment." Before Mosby could reply, the crack of the rifle was heard, and the head suddenly disappeared. The enemy retreated in great haste, Martin mounted his horse, dashed across the river, went to the abutment, and lo! there lay one of the enemy dead, with his gun cocked ready to fire at his Johnny; but another Johnny was too quick for him. The fellow was shot as if the muzzle of the gun had been placed to his head. Martin brought his gun and accoutrements to the Virginia side of the river, and did good service with it afterwards. For this piece of service, Colonel Mosby complimented Martin before the whole command. After this affair the enemy retreated from the river, towards Frederick, Maryland.

Chapter 24: Mosby's Life Saved by Tom Richards

The battalion was formed at three o'clock p.m. on the 5th, and moved in the direction of Leesburg, with the view of crossing the Potomac again at Muddy Branch. The battalion, numbering about one hundred and fifty men (the rest having flanked out and gone home), went into camp that night within five miles of Leesburg. At nine o'clock, after all had fed their horses and lain down to sleep, scouts came in and reported that "Leesburg was full of Yankees, who were looking after us." Horses were resaddled in one moment, and mounted. Our present position being considered unsafe, Colonel Mosby moved up across the mountains by a private road to a point one mile above Waterford, and remained there the rest of the night. During the night scouts were sent out to ascertain the strength of the enemy, and who they were.

They returned by sunrise next day, and we broke up camp at seven o'clock, going directly to Leesburg. Arriving there at nine o'clock a.m., we found the enemy two hundred and fifty strong, under the command of Major Forbes, of Boston. He had left the place about one hour before, threatening to annihilate Mosby if he came across him, saying that they came out expressly to meet him, and had been looking two days without finding him. While in Leesburg, Colonel Mosby ascertained that they were picked men from three regiments of cavalry stationed at Falls Church, Anandale, and Fairfax Court House, and under the command of Major Forbes, "fighting major," as Colonel Lowell used to call him.

Colonel Mosby determined to follow him up, and, if he could

George Baylor

overtake him, to offer him battle, expressing, at the same time, a desire to meet him at or near Mrs. Skinner's, below Aldie, on the Alexandria Turnpike. Meeting with no detention in Leesburg, we moved rapidly to Ball's Mill, on Goose Creek, a great rendezvous for the enemy when scouting up to our Confederacy. Here we expected to meet them. Mosby, disposing his men to the best advantage, waited a few minutes for them. No enemy making their appearance, we struck for the turnpike below Mrs. Skinner's. Companies A and B were sent off, under the gallant Richards, by one road, while Mosby took Companies C and D with him. The turnpike was struck one mile below Mrs. Skinner's, by both squads at the same time. Colonel Mosby, with John Waller and Munson, had preceded his men, and found the enemy feeding their horses at the very place he wanted to meet them, in a large field one mile square.

Mosby was seen by the enemy's pickets, who gave the alarm. They soon bridled their horses, and formed in line of battle across the turnpike, before Mosby's men arrived. Mosby, with six men, charged their advanced guard, which fell back to their main column. He then fell back himself, and formed his men in the turnpike. The artillery was then brought up, and one shell fired into their ranks, which broke them. Simultaneous with the firing of the gun, the charge was ordered, and before the enemy could re-form, we were into them. Major Forbes, the bravest Federal officer we ever met, tried to rally his men in the field on the right of the road, three times failing in his efforts. His last effort was a beautiful retreat behind a fence which stretched across the field. Drawing his sabre, he cried, "Rally around your major for the last time, and repulse them." But so impetuous was our charge, that it was beyond a possibility for them to rally. Some, how ever, did so, and fought gallantly. Our men closed in on them, and a hand-to-hand fight ensued.

It was here that Mosby would have been cut in two by Forbes's sabre, but for the brave Tom Richards, who warded off the blow with his pistol, and received a severe flesh wound on the shoulder, from Forbes's sabre. Forbes, seeing no chances of escape, surrendered like a brave soldier. Then ensued a fight of the most exciting character. The enemy were armed with Spencer's seven-shooters, pistols, and sabres, while we had nothing but pistols; and this compelled us to close in on them. The enemy retreated precipitately by the Braddock Road, pursued by us for six miles, they pouring into us Mr. Spencer's *unpalatable pills* the whole distance, but without injury to anyone. The enemy fought like soldiers, and ought to have engaged in a better cause ;. but when first broken, we would close in on them, and afford them no opportunity to rally.

This was a proud day for Mosby. He had vanquished, in fact annihilated, with one hundred and fifty men, two hundred and fifty men picked out of three regiments for their bravery and fighting qualities, who had been out three days looking for Mosby. Colonel Mosby had one man (Smallwood) killed and three wounded. The enemy lost fifteen killed, including two commissioned officers; on the field, twenty-five wounded and sixty prisoners, including Major Forbes and two commissioned officers. Seventy-five horses were also captured and distributed amongst the men. The wounded were kindly cared for by Mrs. Skinner until next day, when Colonel Lowell came up with ambulances and removed them to camp. Night coming on, we moved up the turnpike, and went into camp. Next morning at sunrise we passed through Middleburg; thence to Piedmont, on the Manassas Gap Railroad, where there was a division of the property, and a detail made to carry the prisoners to Richmond.

Mosby was not unmindful of Tom Richards's endangering his own life to save that of his colonel. The Secretary of War at Richmond had written to Mosby for an officer to go on the Northern Neck to break up the blockade-running carried on in that quarter. Mosby replied he had "none to spare; but the bearer of this is a young man who is every way worthy of any trust or confidence you may be pleased to repose in him." Richards, in due time, presented this to the Secretary of War, who appointed him captain. Men were given him, and he was sent to the Neck, rendering there good service.

In this engagement with Forbes, there were acts of heroism performed, which, but for fear of making invidious distinctions, I would present to my readers. There was one, however, of which I cannot refrain from speaking. It was the conduct of young Martin, who, having his horse shot under him early in the action, pursued the enemy afoot, and at dark returned to camp, mounted on a fine horse, with one prisoner.

Chapter 25: A Brilliant Feat

On the 12th of July, Captain William H. Chapman, with one hundred men, crossed the Potomac River at Muddy Branch. Having burned the cavalry camp there, he occupied Adamstown. On account of the behaviour of the men at Point of Rocks, Captain Chapman issued stringent orders against the men's plundering the stores in this place. Finding no enemy here, he recrossed the Potomac, and returned to Fauquier with a few government horses.

Between the 1st and 18th of July this year, important events had occurred on the soil of Maryland. Generals Early and Breckenridge had crossed the Potomac, dispersed the Union troops and militia under General Wallace at Frederick City, and were marching triumphantly on Washington. His orders were to only threaten the place; but Early could have captured the city as easily as threaten it; and had General Lee been advised of the strength of the garrison, I am sure he would not have hesitated one moment as to the orders he would have given Early. Almost every available soldier had been sent to Grant; and I am correctly informed, two thousand five hundred regular troops could not have been brought into action. The greatest consternation prevailed in the Capitol of the nation. President Lincoln had fled to Philadelphia; Stanton and the other members of the Cabinet were on a monitor in the Potomac, ready to escape down the river; and our Southern friends confidently expected the Rebels to come in and take the place.

Early, however, confined himself to carrying out General Lee's orders. He made a demonstration on their works a mile and a half from the city, threw a few shells into Seventh Street, and retired. Had he pushed on after the engagement at Frederick City, transcended General Lee's orders by going into the city, and destroyed the public buildings and captured some prominent and lending officials, he might have terminated the war. But no: he had executed his superior's order to the letter, and retired without opposition, bringing with him large numbers of horses, mules, cattle, &c., and several thousand prisoners. He recrossed the Potomac below Berlin, and the Blue Ridge Mountains at Snicker's Gap, with his army, sending his prisoners, wagon-trains, and cattle up to Ashby's Gap, to cross Friday night.

On the 18th, we had a meeting at Upperville, and moved off at noon. Early had been pursued, and the enemy's army, under Wright, was already at Snickersville. The afternoon of the 18th, the enemy's cavalry, three thousand strong, under Durfay, dashed into Upperville. It was garrisoned by five hundred men; the rest pressed on up the turnpike to Paris and Ashby's Gap that night, which points they occupied. Camping that night in the woods, next morning we entered Middleburg. Then, Colonel Mosby sent Captain A. E. Richards with Company B, to Fairfax County, to engage a party of the enemy scouting up every day to Thoroughfare Gap; Companies A and D, Captain Montjoy, he took to operate on the grade between Leesburg and Snickersville; while Company C, under William Chapman, went to Ashby's Gap, to operate there.

The enemy had tried to force a passage across the Shenandoah at Castleman's Ferry, but were repulsed with terrible loss. Durfay had likewise attempted a passage of the same river at Berry's Ferry, three times, under a galling fire from Imboden's men behind some light breastworks on the valley side, and fared even worse than Wright did lower down at Castleman's Ferry. Durfay lost five hundred men killed and wounded, and the river was almost dammed up with dead men and horses. Chapman, who was in the gap, was not idle while this was going on. He was continually firing into and harassing the enemy, picking off one man here, and another there, until Durfay, imagining Early had sent a large force around to attack him in the rear, sounded the retreat. Chapman suddenly concentrating his men (only sixty) dashed between their advance and their picket of sixty men, posted in the Gap at the old Poplar tree, swept them off down the mountain, through Paris, to a safe place beyond Semper's, with General Durfay and two thousand cavalry after them. Durfay, however, pursued him no farther than Paris, when they moved down the turnpike, and rejoined the army at Snickersville.

Chapman, in this affair, captured forty horses and thirty prisoners; the rest jumped behind the stone fence, and hid until the main column came up. Chapman lost one man, his orderly sergeant, who was thrown from his horse, and injured so severely that he died a few days afterwards. Richards, with Company B, did nothing of consequence. The scouting to Thoroughfare Gap had been discontinued. John Atkins, Sam Alexander, Walter Whaley, and two others, while scouting near Union Mills, met with a squad (ten) of the enemy, captured five, including one lieutenant, with their horses, &c. Returning to command, Richards ordered us to return to Fauquier. Mosby, with Companies A and D, captured one hundred and two infantry, and sent them to Richmond.

On the 28th of this month, Company E was organised, Sam Chapman as Captain, Font Beatty (Mosby's confidential friend), First Lieutenant, Ben Palmer, of Richmond, Third Lieutenant, and the impetuous Martin, Second Lieutenant, all elected for their daring and fighting qualities. After the organisation of Company E, the battalion started for Maryland again. Crossing the Potomac at Nolen's Ferry without opposition, Mosby pushed on to Adamstown, occupied it, and captured twenty prisoners and thirty horses, again refusing to let the men plunder the stores. Recrossing the river with his prisoners, he left Company E, on the Maryland side, to scout and report to him. On their return to the rest of the command at night, Chapman was attacked by the Eighth Illinois Cavalry, and his men retreated in confusion. Lieutenant Beatty, with six men, formed a rear guard, and by charging the enemy and falling back a little, and recharging, succeeded in getting his men across the river, all safe but one, who, being a little tight, fell off his horse and was captured.

Mosby, having got all his men across the Potomac again, moved off the next day to the Valley, crossing the Mountains at Snicker's Gap, and sent William Chapman back to Fauquier with prisoners, and ordered him to bring every man back, with the alternative of going into the regular service. Chapman brought back with him, the next day, thirty men, and met Mosby four miles above Charlestown. Waiting there several hours, and no enemy making their appearance, Mosby ordered his men back to Fauquier. Walter Frankland, our quartermaster, took twenty men with him to thrash wheat in the valley, for the battalion. The enemy, during their occupation of Snicker's Gap, tried to see how much damage and suffering they could bring upon the people in the vicinity of the Gap. Their horses and cattle were turned loose in the cornfields, gardens were destroyed, poultry, pigs, and cows killed, and not a thing left to the helpless people.

On the 6th of August, Mosby took thirty-five men from Company A to Fairfax, and accomplished one of the most brilliant feats of the war. While scouting with two or three men (the rest being hid in the woods) he ran into one hundred and five Yankees, between Fairfax Court House and Fairfax Station, on the Orange and Alexandria Railroad. The enemy, suspecting it was Mosby, mounted their horses and formed in an open field. Mosby sent for his men and charged them. The enemy reserved their fire until he was within forty yards of them. They then opened on him with carbines. This fire was harmless, being too high. After the first volley, seeing none of their foe fall, they broke and retreated in great confusion, with Mosby after them. Ten were killed, including one captain, and twenty prisoners were taken, besides twenty-seven horses, which were brought away; and, strange to say, Mosby and his men sustained no loss. A few hours, however, before the engagement, one man was bushwhacked, receiving a slight wound.

Chapter 26: Plans Defeated

In compliance with orders, two hundred and fifty men reported at Rectortown, on the 12th of August, for duty. Two mountain howitzers, presented to Colonel Mosby by General Stuart, were taken along for an emergency. They moved off at noon, passing through Snicker's Gap, and fording the Shenandoah River at Castleman's Ferry just at dark. From there our course was directed to the vicinity of Berryville. Concealing the men in the woods, four miles from the town, and one mile from the turnpike leading to Charlestown, Mosby, John Russell, and two others went out to pike to see what was going on. In a few minutes, an ambulance drawn by four mules, with a guard of two men, approached them.

Mosby, concluding he might possibly learn something from them regarding the wagon-trains, rode up to them, and before letting them know who he was, inquired how long since his train had passed, and would camp near Berryville. The enemy, regarding him as a Union officer, promptly replied that it had just passed up. Demanding their surrender, and sending them back to the command, he and Russell pushed on to ascertain the whereabouts of the train. One mile from Berryville they found the train in camp, with a guard of one regiment of infantry and five hundred cavalry. The infantry, however, were in Berryville, and the cavalry two and a half miles beyond.

Returning to his men on the morning of the 13th, at daylight, Mosby moved to make the attack. Reaching their encampment at sunrise, just as they were breaking it, he took Company A with him to disperse one hundred infantry at the head of the train; A. E. Richards, with Company B, was to attack the train on the left; Company D supported the artillery, and Company C was to secure the plunder. The signal for attack was the first shot, which fell into a group of teams and men standing about midway of the train. Companies A and B, to reach the point from which they were to attack, were compelled to pass in full view of the train for half a mile, and the artillery a quarter of a mile to two hundred yards of the train for a position. The enemy made no preparations to resist an attack, thinking we were their own men trying to play a trick on them. The artillery fired one shot, which fell short by one hundred yards. Still they all stood gazing at our movement, and moved not a step.

Another shot was fired which fell and exploded in their midst. Then came the charge on our side, and the stampede amongst the wagons, some with drivers, others without, they taking refuge behind a stone fence fifty yards from the road. The infantry retreated and sought refuge in a church in the suburbs of Berryville, and from its windows opened a galling fire on Company A, which compelled them to fall back to the train. But few of the wagons escaped. Five hundred mules, one hundred horses, two hundred and twenty-five head of cattle, and two hundred prisoners were brought away.

The train belonged to the Sixth Army Corps, and in it was the baggage of all its officers. There were also two iron chests filled with greenbacks, to pay off a whole corps, and the one hundred days' men, whose time was about expiring. That we did not learn until we had left; and even had we known it before, I doubt very much whether it would have done us any good, for as soon as the attack was made, an officer in charge of the chests threw them out of the wagon on the ground, and there being no powder along to blow them open, they would have been the means of some of our men being captured. Had the boxes remained in the wagon, we would have hitched every mule and horse in the train to it, but that we would have got them out. The wagons were loaded with commissary stores and forage; one hundred of them were burnt. Before the match was applied to the wagons containing the officers' baggage, our men *froze* on the valises, and brought them away; and after our return to Fauquier, the officers of the Sixth Army Corps would have enjoyed seeing our boys *swelling* in their new uniforms, which had been provided for them with so much expense in New York.

In this engagement Mosby lost two killed, (Sergeant Welby Rector, of Company A, and Private —— Heddy, of Company B,) and one wounded, Ed Rector, who was wounded slightly, but painfully, in the ankle. The mules were turned over to the Confederate Government, and one hundred and twenty-five head of the cattle were presented to General Lee, for the Army of Northern Virginia.

On the 18th of August, a meeting of the command was held at Rector's Cross Roads, four miles from Middleburg, to go on a raid to the Valley again. At three o'clock the command moved off. Crossing the mountains at Snicker's Gap, we moved on to the Shenandoah River, and halted, while Mosby sent a scout across to see if the road was clear. Returning in the course of an hour, they brought intelligence of two regiments of cavalry encamped a mile and a half from the river, with dismounted men, or infantry pickets out. Mosby, seeing in a moment he could not accomplish anything (that is, if he made a capture, he could not bring it out, Berry's and Castleman's Ferries being strongly guarded), changed his whole plan of operations. Company A he sent to Fairfax County; Company B, down the Shenandoah River, by a mountain road, to Rock Ford, where we crossed into the valley, under cover of night. Lieutenant Alfred Glasscock, of Company D, took six men, returned to Fauquier, crossed the Blue Ridge at Ashby's Gap, and the Shenandoah at a private ford, penetrated the enemy's lines as far as Strasburg, where he surprised and captured twenty Yankees and twenty horses, and brought them out safe, without loss or injury.

Company A returned without accomplishing anything; and likewise Company B, although it scoured the country as far as Charlestown, without seeing any of the enemy.

The weather being intensely warm, a few days were afforded our jaded horses to recuperate. A meeting was called at Rectortown, and the roll called. Three hundred men, with two pieces of artillery, reported for duty. At noon the men were moved off, Mosby at the head of the column. Mosby had for some time been contemplating a foray on one of the enemy's camps in Fairfax. He now determined, if possible, to carry his plan into execution.

Anandale, six miles from Alexandria, was the camp; crossing the Bull Run Mountains at sunset, he pushed on rapidly, under cover of night, to the camp. The enemy, though, through some of their emissaries who were scattered all over the county of Fairfax, had obtained information of Mosby's designs, and to his surprise, at daylight the next morning Mosby found the enemy had sent all their horses to a camp lower down, and the garrison were placed in the stockades, and were waiting our approach.

Finding his plans frustrated, in a measure, by treachery, Mosby determined to make a demonstration notwithstanding; and Captain Montjoy was sent, with a flag of truce, to demand a surrender, with a threat of shelling in case of refusal. Five minutes were allowed the commander of the post to decide. Feeling secure against any attack successful in his strongly fortified position, he sent to Mosby the laconic reply, "to shell and be damned." Mosby opened on him with his artillery, commanded by Sam Chapman. The artillery made no impression on the stockades, and hearing of reinforcements on the way from Falls Church, Mosby abandoned the attack, and returned to Fauquier with his command. The officer in command of Anandale, for his heroism on this occasion, was promoted to a colonelship for "*gallant services.*"

Chapter 27: Unsuccessful Attacks

The wonderful success which attended Major Mosby on all his forays on the enemy, had elicited from Generals Lee and Stuart frequent recommendations to the War Department for his promotion. No officer in the Army of Northern Virginia (and there was many a gallant one) had accomplished as much with a brigade of cavalry as Mosby had with his small band of men. With this small squad he kept the enemy in the Valley, and made them *hug* their fortifications around Washington, at Point of Rocks, Berlin, and Harper's Ferry, Maryland, besides extending the arm of protection to the farmers in the counties of Fauquier, Loudon, Prince William, and the upper portion of Fairfax. Order and respect for private property prevailed all over these counties; and whenever there was the least trespass on private property, whether it was upon Union or upon Southern farmers, by his own men or by other persons, the trespassers were arrested and sent to Richmond, to be tried by court-martial. In consideration of all these services, the President promoted Mosby to the office of lieutenant-colonel, and a merited promotion it was.

A few days after Mosby's return from Fairfax, Captain Sam Chapman of Company E, and Montjoy of Company D, took portions of their companies (sixty men) into the valley on a raid. When near Berryville, they met a party of the enemy applying the torch to every barn, stable, and out-house in their march, shooting and killing stock in the fields. Innocent women and children and old men were turned out of doors, and their houses and all burnt to the ground. The sight presented to Chapman and his men aroused all the worst passions of the soldier; and there was one general shout of "no quarter!" Chapman and Montjoy, with their sixty men, swept down on the enemy like a whirlwind. Forty were killed on the spot. Thirty-five horses and two prisoners were brought off. The prisoners were sent to Culpepper by a German baron.

On the 28th of August, Colonel Mosby ordered fifty men to meet him in Middleburg. At noon we moved off down the turnpike, passing through Aldie, and bivouacked that night near Mr. Cross's, in Fairfax County. At daylight, the next morning, scouts were started out in all directions, to find *game*. Mosby, hearing a large body of the enemy's cavalry were moving up the turnpike towards Middleburg, took Bob Walker and myself out with him. We went back to within two miles of Aldie, before we learned anything definite as to the strength of the column which had just passed up. There we learned six hundred cavalry and several wagons had gone up one hour before. Deeming it unnecessary to follow them further, we retraced our march to the men who still remained in the woods near Mr. Cross's.

When half way back, on the turnpike, we were met by Bush Underwood and John Sinclair, running for their lives, with one hundred and eighty New York cavalry after them. The whole party were then chased up the turnpike about two miles, when Mosby dodged into the woods, and let the enemy pass. When they disappeared, Mosby returned to the turnpike, and learned "they were going up to reenforce the Eighth Illinois at Middleburg." Refreshing ourselves with a glass of hard cider at Mr. ———'s, Mosby returned to his men. After an hour's rest, he moved us lower down in the county, to the farm of Mrs. Moore. Here we remained in the woods until the afternoon of the next day. We were then divided into three squads; Harry Hatcher, lieutenant of Company A, *alias* Deadly Hatcher, took twelve men; Lieutenant Albert Wren, of Company B, took fourteen men; and the rest were under Mosby.

The intention of Mosby was to take every picket-post around Alexandria that night. The enemy, however, heard we were in the neighbourhood, and trebled the strength of their pickets; and instead of six or eight men on duty, there were twenty-five at each post, besides several scouts started out to scatter or capture us. Mosby sent ——— Mason, John Dickson, Fred and John Hepkins, to take the post at Falls Church. The attack was before day, but not successful. Mason fell wounded, but escaped to the bushes, under cover of night, and reached Colonel Elgey's, in Loudon County, the next day, having marched forty miles with a ball in his leg. The rest of the party escaped uninjured. Lieutenant Albert Wren and his party were chased out by a scouting-party before they had got even a sight of their work.

Harry Hatcher and Bush Underwood, with their party, had been charged with the duty of taking the post at Lewinsville. Hatcher, with Bush Underwood as guide, had managed to get in sight of his work without being seen by any of their scouts; but unfortunately for us, we were seen by a sergeant, who reported the fact in camp, and a large scouting-party was sent after us. Night coming on, we sought refuge in the thick pines, and remained there until nine o'clock, when the enemy returned to their camp. We then emerged from our hiding-place, and started back for Fauquier, taking in our route Mrs. Swinks', a great rendezvous for Federal officers, expecting to pick up a few of the French gentlemen; unfortunately, none were there that evening.

Lieutenant Hatcher, Bush Underwood, Bally Rowser, and myself were invited into the house by Miss Mattie, Mrs. Swinks' accomplished and amiable daughter, and handsomely entertained. Cold ham, crackers, cheese, preserves, &c., &c., were served in great profusion to the half-starved rebels; and we were half starved, for we had not had a "*square meal*" for three days. As we were leaving the house, Miss Swink called us back, saying she had forgotten something. Stepping upstairs, she returned in a moment with a black bottle covered all over with gold, with the stamp of "old Bourbon" on it in large letters. A Federal captain had presented it to her that afternoon, and she told him at the time she never indulged, but would take it and treat her friends with Mosby the first time they came there. It was opened, and after drinking our hostess' health, we drank that of the captain too, hoping he would again open his heart soon, and let there be a larger flow of that great panacea.

Miss Swinks' parents were Unionists, but she a most uncompromising Southerner; yet she enjoyed the confidence of the Federal officers in and around Washington and Alexandria, and could pass and repass to Alexandria, Washington, and Georgetown at will; and the members of the "old Forty-Third" will always remember her with feelings of gratitude for the offices of kindness she showed them while we occupied Fauquier. Leaving Mrs. Swinks' at ten o'clock, our faces were once more directed to headquarters. On the road we learned that dismounted men were sent out every night to bushwhack us. Fearing we should run into them, we bivouacked that night at Peacock's, and at daylight the next morning resumed our return to Fauquier.

Chapter 28: Mosby Wounded

In Middleburg the enemy behaved most disgracefully, searching and robbing private houses, and insulting ladies. They nearly pulled the finger off one young lady, Miss Nolen, in their efforts to take a ring. She fought like a rebel for it, and kept it, too. The cowardly wretches, however, bruised her arms until they were blue.

One remarkable fact about the enemy's cavalry around Washington and Alexandria was, that of all the scouts they ever made to Mosby's Confederacy, invariably every one was made when Mosby was absent on a raid with his men. How it happened so it is impossible for me to say, and I should like to have some of the Federal officers commanding those troops explain it. I know of no explanation, unless it was to afford their men an opportunity to plunder, and see how much misery they could heap on a people who sympathized with a government which was struggling with the whole world for their dearest rights.

On the 2nd day of September, the whole command met at Rectortown. Colonel Mosby took Companies A and B and crossed the Blue Ridge at Snicker's Gap; then taking the road down the Shenandoah River, a march of seven miles brought him to Rock Ford. Hiding his men in the mountains, Mosby, with Captain A. E. Richards and ten men, went on a scout across the river in search of Captain Blaze. Blaze had crossed the river at that ford that morning, had gone up to the stillhouse a few miles from the river, and it was supposed had returned to the valley by another road; but, instead of returning to the Valley from the stillhouse, they took the road up to Snickersville. Reaching there, they learned Mosby had passed through the gap on a raid. Getting on our track and following it up, they found us with horses unsaddled and half the men asleep.

Charging us from the rear, they created the greatest consternation amongst the men. Lieutenant Joe Nelson, of Company A, and Horace Johnson, of Company B, rallied fifteen or twenty of the men and charged the enemy, and were driving them back when Nelson unfortunately fell from his horse, dangerously wounded in the thigh. The men no longer tried to keep the enemy at bay, but commenced a disorderly retreat. They were pursued by the drunken foe, and suffered heavily, three being killed and several wounded; but few were taken prisoners. Although these Yankees were drunk, I must say they had more of the instincts of men, and feelings of humanity about them on that day, than any we ever met before. Our wounded they carried to houses in the neighbourhood, and requested every attention to be shown to them until removed.

Captain Sam Chapman, with the other squadron, crossed the Blue Ridge at Ashby Gap, and the Shenandoah River at Shepherd's Mill; then directing his course towards Berryville, half a mile below the town, he met the Sixth New York Cavalry, and routed them, killing twenty and capturing thirty horses and thirty prisoners, including two officers. It was a dear capture, though, and made at the expense of some of the brightest ornaments to the battalion,—Lieutenant Frank Fox, of Company C, and Jarmain, of Company E. Fox was one of the bravest of the brave, and by his genial nature and social qualities, had won the confidence and heart not only of Mosby, but of the whole command. His loss was serious, and much deplored. His horse carried him into the midst of the enemy, where he was wounded seriously in the arm, and taken prisoner. He was kept in a private house for three days, and then sent to Harper's Ferry in an oxcart.

At the ferry his arm was amputated, not from necessity, but to render him unfit for future service, should he survive the operation. He lingered only three days, when a merciful God snatched him from the hands of his torturers. Jarmain, although a new member, had, by his manly bearing and unflinching courage, gained the confidence and esteem of all, and was looked upon as a rising star of the Forty-third. Clay Adams, who fell mortally wounded in this engagement, was as brave a soldier as ever drew a sabre. Exempt from military duty by disability (being deaf), he entered the service as a private soldier, and fought with a *vim* that would have been creditable to the heroes of old. He was shot through the sides, by which the whole lower portion of the body was paralyzed. The enemy carried him to a neighbour's house, and were kindly treating him. John Russell, Sidney Ferguson, and one or two others crossed the river in the night, went to the house, and brought him away, although the house was strongly guarded. He was brought the next day to his father's, in Paris, where he lingered for six months. His death was lamented by all who knew him.

Mosby, with his squad, returned, with twelve mules and five prisoners, which he had captured near Charlestown. Nothing of any consequence was done for nearly two weeks. Colonel Mosby, with two men, Walter Whaley and —— Love, started on a scouting expedition to Fairfax, and when in the neighbourhood of Centreville, they were attacked by a party of seven of Colonel Lowell's men. Two of the enemy were killed, two wounded, and the other three took to flight. In the engagement Mosby received a painful wound in the groin of the leg. After the enemy's retreat, he was brought by Whaley and Love to the White Plains, where his wound was dressed, and the next day he started for his father's, in Amherst County. Captain William H. Chapman, of Company C, being senior officer, assumed command. During Mosby's absence, scouting in small squads was all the rage.

Lieutenant Alfred Glasscock took ten men, crossed over in the valley, entered Sheridan's camps, and rode through them as Provost Guard, with orders to take all men found absent from their camps, to Sheridan's headquarters. Glasscock met fifteen men and officers, mounted them on the finest horses in the camp, and, instead of carrying them to Sheridan's headquarters, he started for Mosby's headquarters in Fauquier. On the way, when near Berry's Ferry, three surgeons were met. The usual halt and questions passed. Glasscock, satisfying the surgeons he was "all right," advanced to where they were, and after a few inquiries where they had been, and if they had seen or heard of any rebels, ordered them to fall in and follow him. The surgeons complimented Glasscock very highly for his skill in the management of this affair, and complied with his order with very good grace. Glasscock reached Fauquier with eighteen horses and prisoners, without firing a shot, or having a man injured.

Chapter 29: Mosby Attacks the Enemy at Salem

Lieutenant John Russell, of Clark County, —— Magner, of Mississippi, Dr. Lowers, of the Valley, and Ab Suttle crossed the Shenandoah River every night, attacked picket-posts, and harassed the enemy at every point in the Valley, giving them no rest night or day. Every trip they made was a successful one, in securing prisoners and horses. Lieutenant John Russell established daily communication with General Sheridan's headquarters at Winchester. Daily Baltimore papers (the *Gazette* and *American*) were received in Paris at nine o'clock the night after they were issued.

Mosby being still absent, on account of his wound, large numbers of the men availed themselves of the opportunity (business being very dull) of getting a short furlough, to go home, and take with them what had been captured during the summer campaign in Maryland and the various camps. I availed myself of the opportunity, and paid a flying visit of two days to Richmond. I met there my Captain, A. E., and Tom Richards, and also John Atkins, of County Cork, Ireland, who had crossed the Atlantic "to join Mosby." Mr. Atkins was a younger brother of Captain Atkins (now Lord ——) of General Elzey's staff.

The day after my arrival in Richmond, Fort Harrison was taken by the enemy, and the greatest alarm prevailed in the city. The town bell was rung, militia called out, and guards placed at every corner, to take up furloughed soldiers and officers (with which the city was filled) to go to the entrenchments, and check the advance of the enemy. After being picked up on the street, they were marched by a guard to what was called the Soldier's Home, there organised into companies, and then marched out to the army. Atkins and myself were amongst the fortunate ones they desired to go out; but having completed our arrangements to leave the city the next morning for Fauquier, our captain had no idea of spending the remainder of the campaign in those agreeable places, "the entrenchments;" and having learned the art of flanking pretty well with Mosby, I determined to apply it in this instance. I got to my room safe, and coming out of it to see my captain at the Spottswoods, was picked up the second time. I flanked out the second time, and reached my room.

While looking out of the window, I observed most of the guards were dressed in citizen's dress; and having an old musket and cartridge-box in my brothers office, I conceived the idea of playing guard; so shouldering my musket, and adjusting the cartridge-box, I went forth in quest of men to go out and defend their Capitol. Every man was made to show his papers. The first person I ran against was my old comrade-in-arms, Charlie Hall, who had likewise got into the same trouble as myself. I took him into custody, and he took me by turns; by that means we managed to get through our little business, and have everything ready to leave by the morning train, with my Captain, A. E. Richards. My reasons for acting in this manner I considered the very best. I thought I could do my country more good in Fauquier, with the great partisan; besides, I had no idea of spending the fall in the entrenchments.

Atkins pursued a different plan, and much bolder. At the armoury, when handed his musket, he refused to take it, stating his reasons to the officer commanding the company, and to General Barton. They "couldn't see it," but marched him back to the Soldier's Home. He, however, was released the next day, through the intercession of Captain Ed Hudson, of General Elzey's Staff, and formerly of the Prussian army. That night orders were issued to allow no one to leave the city. Guards were stationed at daylight at every corner in the city, to pick up men who could not show proper papers. Having procured passports to leave the city the day before, and before the enemy made this 'movement on our lines, I had no difficulty in reaching the depot, although my pass was examined very critically by at least twelve soldiers. At the depot, agreeably to arrangements, I met Captain A. E. Richards. We left Richmond at nine o'clock, and reached Gordonsville at the usual time. There we found Mosby, returning to his command. He and Richards went by rail to Culpepper, where their horses were, and I by Madison Court House, Washington, Rappahannock County, and Barber's Cross Roads, reaching Fauquier in three days.

Colonel Mosby had not entirely recovered from his wound, yet he resumed his seat in the saddle immediately. On reaching Fauquier, he found the enemy coming up the Manassas Gap Railroad through Thoroughfare Gap, in strong force of infantry and cavalry. They occupied the Plains and Salem. A meeting of the whole command was ordered at Piedmont. Mosby attacked them at Salem, with two hundred and fifty men, and drove them back to the Plains, and burned the depot there, with a large quantity of stores, &c. In the engagement Mosby made a narrow escape with his life. His horse, stumbling, fell on him, and sprained his ankle. Before he could get up, a Federal soldier galloped over him, and fired as he passed; but a wise Providence changed the direction of the ball, and it missed him.

The enemy receiving reinforcements at the Plains, Mosby fell back to Piedmont, without losing a man. At Piedmont he rested his men one day. In the meanwhile the enemy occupied Rectortown, and fortified themselves. Two thousand constituted the garrison. On the west side of Rectortown is a range of high hills, overlooking the town. The enemy having no cavalry, Mosby determined to shell them out of the place, if possible. Concealing one half of his men in the woods, with the other half he took a position on one of these hills on Mrs. Rawling's farm, and opened on them with two pieces of artillery (one gun and a howitzer). Skirmishers were thrown out. The enemy retreated, but soon rallied and sought refuge under their entrenchments, from which retreat they could not be drawn. Several, however, were killed and wounded. After an hour's shelling, our ammunition gave out, and Mosby ordered us to fall back and renew the attack next day.

Promptly at eight o'clock, all met at Joe Blackwell's, two miles from Rectortown. With the assistance of glasses, the enemy could be seen, working like beavers, strengthening their works. The attack was to be renewed at nine o'clock. Mosby and his men became impatient for the fray, which was delayed by the artillery's not coming up. It finally reached us at three o'clock, and Mosby attacked them in their fortifications. They started off a train of cars down the railroad, with one thousand Infantry on it. Mosby attacked it; but by the late arrival of the artillery the train was lost. The enemy, however, were driven from it, and it flew down the railroad to Salem. The enemy retreated across the fields towards Salem, pursued by Mosby and his men. They took a position on a mountain to the right of Salem, with a high stone fence at its base, and could not be dislodged, on account of the natural strength of their position. Mosby formed his men in line of battle, and opened on them with his artillery, but without effect.

While the enemy were in this position, Albert Wren, Bully Rowser, John Iden, Dr. Sowers, Sidney Ferguson, and Reub Triplett distinguished themselves by their bravery in charging up the mountain to the enemy, and discharging their pistols at them.

Mosby, finding he could not dislodge the enemy, retired at sunset and disbanded his men. The enemy that night were re-enforced by two thousand five hundred cavalry from Washington and Muddy Branch. The next day we met at Freds, on the top of one of the spurs of the Blue Ridge. One hundred of us started down the mountain, under Captain William H. Chapman, to engage a force of about one hundred and fifty of the enemy, at Mrs. Shacklett's, half a mile from Piedmont. Having got in the rear of Mrs. Shacklett's house, Lieutenant John Russell, who had gone ahead to see if the country was clear, suddenly came dashing down the mountain on the opposite side of Crooked Run, warning us of our danger, and telling us to fall back. No sooner had we seen him than the brow of the mountain was black with the enemy, the foremost about ten rods behind Russell. The enemy complimented us with three rounds, when we retired. Anticipating our attack on the party at Mrs. Shacklett's, they had sent a force of three or four hundred around and concealed them under this mountain to attack us in the rear, should we bite at the bait they had set for us; but the keen eye and sagacity of Russell frustrated all their nice-laid plans.

While this was going on near Piedmont, the enemy, concluding all our men had left the country, except those with Chapman, sent a party of sixteen from Rectortown, *via* Upperville and Paris, with dispatches to General Sheridan in the valley. Their arrival in Upperville, in such a small squad, was a surprise to all. Captain Montjoy being in the neighbourhood and hearing of them, sent John Thomas, John Horn, Ab Fox, James Keith, and two others, who followed them through Ashby's Gap and attacked them at the tollgate, between the gap and the river. Nine were captured without making any resistance; the other seven dismounted and fled to the mountains, and, getting lost, came down in the evening to Paris and gave themselves up. Sixteen horses and the dispatches were secured. The dispatches, being in cipher, were sent to Richmond, and the character of them never known.

The morning after this, thirty-five men of Company B met Captain A. E. Richards at Paris, and started on a raid to the valley, crossing at Ashby's Gap. and the Shenandoah River at Island Ford. When near Strasburg Richards attacked fifty cavalrymen and one ambulance belonging to General Sheridan's headquarters. The enemy were routed; six were killed, including Sheridan's chief quartermaster; twenty-eight horses and twelve prisoners were taken. The ambulance, also, was captured with contents, including valuable papers, giving reports of the number of cavalry and artillery horses &c., &c.; these were sent to Richmond.

Chapter 30: Capture of Mosby's Artillery

Harry Heaton of Company D, one of the valley scouts, came in and informed Mosby of a fine opening in the valley on the Baltimore and Ohio Railroad. Mosby ordered a meeting for the next day, the 13th of October, at Bloomfield, in Loudon County, a small village five miles from Snicker's Gap. Seventy men reported for duty. At noon the mountains were crossed at Snicker's Gap, and the Shenandoah River at Castleman's Ferry. Pushing on through Cabletown, night overtook the party at Dr. William's, in Jefferson County. Here Colonel Mosby, the officers, and a few men, were very hospitably entertained by the doctor and his accomplished daughters. At nine o'clock the march was resumed. The scout having learned the hour the train was due at Duffield Station, the railroad was struck half an hour before it was due, obstructions were placed on the track at the depot, and all awaited anxiously the arrival of the train.

In due time the express came lumbering to the station and stopped. A guard was placed over the engine and the men entered the cars. Two paymasters were found with one hundred and seventy thousand dollars of government funds. The greenbacks were confiscated, and started out to Fauquier by Lieutenants Briscoe, Grogan, of Company D, and two men. Some of the men commenced "going through" the passengers. One Southerner was put through the mill by being relieved of a fine watch, which Mosby found out, and made the fellow return it, through him, to the owner in Baltimore. A number of the men exchanged overcoats, hats, gloves, &c. with the passengers. One hog-drover, who was returning to his home in the West, from Washington, where he had drawn his money for a lot of hogs sold to the Government, was relieved of the burden of five thousand dollars. John Horn, who commenced going through a big Prussian officer, was seized by the throat and choked until his tongue hung out, but was extricated from his perilous situation by Puryear's dispatching his assailant. The cars were destroyed, and Mosby started back with twenty prisoners and fifteen horses, without loss. The following is General Lee's dispatch to the Secretary of War in Richmond:—

Army of Northern Virginia,
October 16, 1864.

On the 14th instant Colonel Mosby struck the Baltimore and

Ohio Railroad at Duffield Station, destroyed a United States mail-train, consisting of locomotive and ten cars, and secured twenty prisoners and fifteen horses. Among the prisoners are two paymasters, with one hundred and sixty-eight thousand dollars Government funds.

R. E. Lee, General, &c.

The money was divided equally amongst the men, officers and men sharing alike. Mosby, however, refused to take a cent.

During Colonel Mosby's absence on this raid, the enemy captured his artillery, through the treachery of one of his men, who, for a purse of gold, told them where it was. When the enemy occupied the Manassas Gap Railroad, Captain Franklin, commanding the artillery, imprudently hid it in the Cobblar Mountain, instead of the Blue Ridge. Lunsford, the traitor, told them where it was. The enemy surrounded the mountain in the night, with a large force of cavalry, and sent two hundred dismounted men up into the mountain to its place of concealment. These captured it, and the men guarding it.

The loss of our artillery was a serious one, but did not terminate our forays on the enemy. The enemy, however, made a great fuss and hurrah over its capture, and also that of one wagon-train. Mosby had two wagons at this time; and I know, from my own personal knowledge, they did not get these, for no Federal soldier was ever in the Blue Ridge Mountains where they were hid; and in April, 1865, when I left Fauquier County, the same wagons were there then; so General Augur was mistaken about a wagon-train being captured belonging to us. If his men captured any wagons that night, they *captured* them from the citizens.

The enemy having fortified themselves at Rectortown, the Plains, and Salem, with a large force at Piedmont, scoured Fauquier County, with the view of driving us out of the country. All the men except those living in and right under the mountains changed their boarding-houses to the southern side of the railroad. Lieutenants K., S., and Y., with a few picked men, amused themselves by tearing up the railroad. Lieutenant K. threw a train, of cars off the track between Thoroughfare Gap and Gainesville in the night, killing and wounding several, and smashing up the locomotive and cars. Lieutenants S. and Y. placed torpedoes in the road between Piedmont and Markham. One exploded, and blew a cavalryman and horse to pieces. That stopped their scouting up to Front Royal.

To prevent a repetition of these annoyances, General Augur ordered the arrest of five of the most prominent citizens in the county. The victims of Augur's wrath were Messrs. Jamison, Albert and Samuel Ashby (three brothers, and uncles to the lamented and renowned Turner Ashby), Benjamin Triplett, and another citizen, all old men. These old men were dragged from their beds and the bosoms of their families in the dead hour of night, carried to Rectortown, and made to ride in the front car, to keep us from throwing the trains off the track. Providence, however, relieved Mr. Jamison Ashby from the hands of his persecutors.

While sleeping with his neighbours and old friends on the floor of the car one night, he was shot in the head by a guard without any provocation whatever. He was carried to a hospital in Alexandria, and his friends were not only prevented from seeing him and showing him some attention, in alleviating his sufferings, and supplying his wants, but the authorities absolutely refused his daughter the privilege of simply seeing him, at a time, too, when he was in the very throes of death; and the almost heartbroken girl was compelled to return to her home in Fauquier, without ever again in this world gazing upon the face of an affectionate and doting father. This is a sad. tale, my readers, and may appear to some as being exaggerated, but it is true. If anyone questions the statement, let him visit Fauquier, and inquire of parties who witnessed the deed.

Chapter 31: Treachery

A few days after Colonel Mosby's return from the valley, he led about two hundred men to Fairfax, to attack a train of two hundred wagons at Burk's Station, on the Orange and Alexandria Railroad. Each wagon was guarded by three negro soldiers. Fifty of these wagons would go out at a time, and were engaged in hauling wood to the depot. We arrived there, however, one hour too late; the wagons and niggers had gone into camp, and six hundred infantry in wagons,' were almost too much of a good thing for two hundred cavalry, armed with nothing but pistols; and Mosby concluded to let them rest for another time.

From Burk's Station we went down to Billy Goodwin's tavern, on the turnpike, some ten miles from Alexandria. Meeting with little or no encouragement there, Mosby moved us lower down, in sight of Anandale. Two men were sent to take the picket, and draw the garrison out. One prisoner was taken, the other retreated to camp.

The garrison, however, declined to come out. Night approaching, Companies A, B, C, and E, were sent back to Fauquier. Company D, Captain Montjoy, was sent to Falls Church, to capture two hundred cavalry and two stores. Bush Underwood was the guide, and but for the treachery of a citizen, named Reed, Montjoy would have made a clean sweep of the place. The pickets had been flanked, and our men in their camp and at the stables, leading out the horses, when this Union citizen (a spy), gave the alarm by blowing a horn, as we were going into the camp. The men, not suspecting anything, paid no attention to it, but thought somebody was going out a 'possum hunting, though no barking of dogs was heard.

The enemy had taken a position behind some breastworks, and when our men commenced leading out the horses, a volley was fired into them. Lieutenant Glasscock rode out a few paces in the direction the firing came from, and told them to stop firing into their own men. The reply he received was another volley. Thinking prudence the better part of valour, he retired. Passing Reed's house, the boys found out what the blowing of the horn meant, and shot Reed. Had it not been for Reed, the enemy would have been spared the trouble and expense of trying that notorious character Charlie Been, a deserter from Mosby. We regretted exceedingly that we were compelled to leave him and Yankee Davis undisturbed in their slumber in the store at Falls Church that night, with their sable companions. Three negroes, however, were killed, five prisoners taken, and ten horses brought off. Montjoy sustained neither loss nor injury.

On the 22nd of October, 1864, a meeting of the command was held at Bloomfield. Very near four hundred men were present, the largest number ever out. We crossed the mountains at Snicker's Gap, and the Shenandoah River at Castleman's Ferry about dusk. That night we camped near Summit Point, and next morning resumed our march at sunrise.

Colonel Mosby took ten men (Sam Alexander, John Russell, John Dickson, Fred Hipkins and others), and went on a scouting expedition, the command following. When on the turnpike between Winchester and Martinsburg, near Mrs. Allen's, six miles from Winchester, he fell in with General Durfay and twenty-five cavalry (Durfay riding in an ambulance), being the advance guard, consisting of three thousand infantry. Fourteen pieces of artillery, and five hundred cavalry, to a train of one thousand wagons. Mosby captured the general, one staff officer, and four privates; the rest retreated to the main column. Russell and Sam Alexander followed them up, but were obliged to retreat or rather get out as fast as they went in.

Mosby then came back to the command, threw himself at the head of the First Squadron, Companies A and B, and commenced charging the train. Their cavalry ran off; but their infantry (*Zouaves*) formed in line of battle, and opened on us with two pieces of artillery. We fell back under cover of a piece of woods and a hill. The enemy parked the wagons, and posted some of their infantry behind and in them, but did not advance. Mosby was in fine spirits, and riding along the column in front of Company B, cried out,—

"Well, ———, which would you rather have,—the general or the wagons?"

"Both," replied ———.

Just then a shell exploded near the colonel, which terminated the colloquy, and we moved off towards Fauquier.

The battalion dividing below Berryville, the Second Squadron, with Chapman, recrossed the Shenandoah River at Berry Ferry, and passing through Ashby's Gap, proceeded to Markham, Fauquier County, to watch the movements of the enemy on the Manassas Gap Railroad. The First Squadron, under command of Captain Frankland, of Company F, crossed the Shenandoah River, at Castleman's Ferry; thence through Snicker's Gap to a point (Mum's) between Rectortown and Middleburg, in the hope of intercepting some small scouting-parties of the enemy. After we had lain in the woods watching for them all day, and had neither seen nor heard anything of them, orders came from Captain Richards to disband and go home.

On the 29th of October, Colonel Mosby ordered a meeting, at Middleburg, of a portion of the command. Lieutenant Wren, with fifteen men, reported, and found the colonel had gone. From there we pushed on to Carter's Mill. Reaching there, we learned Mosby had just left, without stopping. Getting track of him, we pushed on and overtook his party in the woods one mile and a half from the Mill. Lieutenant Harry Hatcher, of Company A, riding up to us, told us to rest our horses; that two hundred Yankees had just started out from Rectortown, scouting, and that he and Colonel Mosby had been watching them.

Orders soon came to *mount our horses*. The party with Mosby coming up, our number was swelled to one hundred and ten men. Learning the enemy were at Hatcher's Mill, on the Alexandria turnpike, we pressed on in that direction, in high glee, and found them dismounted and feeding their horses. Deeming it hazardous to attack them then, we waited in the woods until they resumed their march, and followed them on until we reached Henry Dulaney's house, about one mile from Upperville. In the meanwhile Mosby left us in charge of Captain Frankland, while he went on the opposite side of the turnpike, at Green Garden Mills, to see Captain A. E. Richards, who had just returned from scouting in the Valley.

Frankland having given up the office of Quartermaster of the battalion, to take command of Company F, a short time before, thought it an excellent opportunity to make his "*Jack*." The Yankees, knowing we were after them and in that neighbourhood, drew up in line of battle in three columns behind a ditch four feet wide, with a six-rail fence over that. The centre numbered about one hundred men, with columns of fifty men on either flank, and were patiently awaiting an attack from us. Frankland, brave and impetuous, could not resist the temptation, although he had received orders just to watch them, and nothing more. He determined to attack the enemy at all hazards. Riding back to his men, he divided them into two squadrons; the first, with forty-five men, being parts of Companies A and B, commanded by the gallant Wren; the Second Squadron, numbering sixty-five men, was commanded by Lieutenant Grogan, of Company D. The First was to charge the enemy, and the Second to support us.

Having formed in fours, and all things being ready, orders came to charge. On we dashed, Wren at the head, over the hill with a yell with which the very mountains in the distance rung. Charging up to within twenty yards of the foe, and seeing their strong position, we looked back for our supports. None being in view, the men began to waver. The enemy, appreciating our position, fired one volley, and then charged through a gate, pouring into the little squad a deadly fire from their Spencer rifles. No assistance coming up, a precipitate retreat was commenced. Our loss in killed, wounded, and prisoners, was heavier than in any previous engagement during the war. Four men were killed, and ten captured. Among the killed was John Atkins, of County Cork, Ireland, and brother of Captain Atkins, late of General Elzey's staff, but now Lord ———.

No higher compliment could be paid to a brave soldier than that paid by Mosby to the noble patriot, as he lay stretched on his bier in Henry Dulaney's house. Someone came in the room while the colonel was there, and commenced explaining the part played in the affair by certain officers. The colonel replied, pointing to the dead body of

Atkins,—

"There lies a man I would not have given for a whole regiment of Yankees."

John Atkins left home, friends, wealth, and position, and came three thousand miles to fight for a cause which every true Irishman holds most dear. He was brave as he was generous. He knew not what danger was. Fearless as a lion, he was gentle in his manners as a lamb. How touching are those last words he spoke while pouring out his heart's blood at the foot of the shrine of liberty: "Oh, my mother! my poor mother! "He was a man of fine education and most agreeable manners, and enjoyed the esteem and confidence of the whole command. A neat coffin was furnished by his friends, and he was buried in the cemetery at Paris. Mosby, who stood in Captain Richards' front, and witnessed the charge of Companies A and B, complimented Lieutenant Wren very highly for his gallantry on the occasion, in his having displayed all the qualities of a good soldier.

Captain A. E. Richards, the evening of this disaster, had just returned from scouting in the valley, with only eight men. He was eminently successful, having captured twenty horses and prisoners without loss.

Chapter 32: General Powell's Raid

About this time there appeared in the valley another conspicuous character, Captain Brasher, *alias* Blazer, whom the authorities at Washington had selected from their whole army for his bravery and daring, and sent to the Valley, with one hundred men selected by him from their cavalry, and distinguished for their fighting qualities, to "clean out Mosby." Captain Brasher made Cabletown his headquarters. His first act was a proposition to Mosby to take fifty of his men, and whip one hundred of Mosby's best and tried men. Mosby took no notice of his challenge, but bided his time.

In the meanwhile, Brasher, with his men, with a degree of boldness and daring unprecedented in the cavalry of the Army of the Potomac, made frequent forays into *our Confederacy*, and scoured the Blue Ridge Mountains from Harper's Ferry to Ashby's Gap; which was something no other Federal officer had ever done, unless he had a brigade or a division of cavalry with him. In those expeditions he did nothing very damaging to us, except here and there picking up a Mosbyite and a horse or two. One circumstance which distinguished Brasher and his men above all other Union soldiers that raided into that country, was the respect he and they paid to citizens and private property. The consequence was, his visits were not looked upon with that feeling of dread that was inspired by the raids of other parties.

But we must leave Captain Brasher for a little while, and see what was doing at Rectortown, on the Sunday following. The enemy had left the Manassas Gap Railroad, taking with them all the iron rails and even clamps. Colonel Mosby started on Sunday with two hundred men for Prince William County to Gainesville. Crossing the Bull Run Mountains by a private road, we camped that night on the other side of them. At daylight we moved down to the woods on Mr. Pickett's farm near Gainsville, and remained there all day. Scouts were sent out to draw the enemy's cavalry away from the railroad. Not being able to get them out, Colonel Mosby ordered Lieutenant Hatcher, with Company A, to a point near Centreville; and the rest of the men, under Lieutenant Grogan, to St. John's Church, near Sudley. There we remained until next day at noon, when orders came to disband and go home, returning by way of Hopewell Gap and the Plains. Hatcher returned without doing anything.

During our absence on this raid, General Powell, with two thousand five hundred cavalry, and four pieces of artillery, made a raid into the Confederacy by way of Front Royal, Linden, Markham, Piedmont, Rectortown, Upperville, and Paris, stealing, in their route, all the stock, cattle, and poultry they could find, and returned to their camp by Ashby's Gap and the Shenandoah River, at Berry's Ferry. The day after Mosby's return from Prince William, he took twenty men to the valley, and captured seventeen Federals, with their horses, near Winchester. These prisoners belonged to Custer's cavalry, and participated in the shooting and hanging of our men in Front Royal, in the month of September.

Returning to Fauquier with his prisoners, Mosby called a meeting of the men at Rectortown. The prisoners were drawn up in a line, and all drew to see which should be hung in retaliation for those hung and shot in Front Royal, amongst whom were some of the most respectable citizens of Fauquier. One was Anderson, a justice of the peace, visiting at Markham. A short time before that bloody affair, the same brigade hung, at Sandy Hook, Mr. Willis, a Baptist preacher, and a member of the Forty-Third. This was done in retaliation, they said, for one of their men whom Chancellor killed.

The history of that case is this: A short time before one of their numerous raids into and through that country, they sent a man ahead

Thomas W. S. Richards

to find out who had fine stock, and where they hid it. This fellow represented himself to the farmers as a Confederate soldier, escaped from prison. Some of our men who were travelling through that portion of the country, hearing of him, concluded he was nothing more nor less than a spy. He was sought out, and found at Mr. Chancellor's. Being questioned as to his business, &c., his true character was found out. He was then taken out and shot. A few days after this, a large column of the enemy made a raid through there, and, hearing of this, burned Mr. Chancellor's house, in retaliation for the deed.

Not satisfied with that, on their return, Willis was overtaken, and hung for the same thing. For these outrages and violations of all the laws of war, this scene was being enacted at Rectortown. One lieutenant and six privates drew black balls, one of the lucky ones being a newsboy, who had no connection with the army except in vending newspapers to the soldiers, and in no way connected with those that did the hanging. Mosby threw his name out, and another drawing, to make up the seven, was held. The number being now complete, the unfortunate and doomed men were placed under guard, and started back to the valley, to pay the penalty for their atrocious deeds. In the valley Montjoy was met, returning with some prisoners. The lieutenant being a Mason (as. Montjoy was one), he was exchanged for a private, and the lieutenant went a prisoner to Richmond, instead of to the gallows. The night being very dark three escaped, but four were hung in sight of the enemy's camp. They were amazed, the next morning, to see their companions in arms dangling in the air.

The next day Mosby wrote to General Sheridan, explaining the reasons which compelled him to adopt this summary and disagreeable method of checking their treatment of his men, and hoped he would never be obliged to do it again; but that if he or General Custer persisted in treating his men in that manner, he was ready to fight them under the black flag. Mosby then stated to him the number of his (Sheridan's) men he had taken prisoners of war, who were kindly treated, and how many he (Sheridan) had captured of his; and if he, with those facts staring him in the face, continued that system of fighting, he would be greatly the loser, and the responsibility of his (Mosby's) course would rest on his (Sheridan's) shoulders.

General Sheridan would not reply to Mosby, or recognise him as an officer in the Confederate Army, but wrote to General Early, then commanding in the valley, that he had received a communication from Mosby, and that what had been done to (Mosby's) men, was done entirely without his knowledge and authority, and that hereafter Colonel Mosby's men would be treated as prisoners of war.

This hanging had the desired effect. It convinced the enemy how terribly in earnest we were, and that we were entitled to the same privileges that regular soldiers were entitled to. Before this, General Sheridan's and Kilpatrick's cavalry would offer our men every species of indignity. Instead of having a guard placed over them while awaiting transportation to prison, they were invariably thrown into loathsome jails and dungeons in Warrenton. Winchester, and Martinsburg. At Point Lookout, Johnson's Island, Fort McHenry, Fort Delaware, Camp Chase, and other prisons, we were special objects of insult, torture, and bad treatment. One brave soldier, Robert Harrover, of Washington City, whom they captured in Fairfax, on a scouting-party with Frank Williams, and who the enemy imagined was behind every pine-tree and little bush in Fairfax, with his unerring rifle, was carried to Washington and tried for his life by the Military Commission:

> For leaving Washington City after he had been enrolled, and attaching himself to a band of guerillas.

Bob stood his trial, and the night after his condemnation to the Albany Penitentiary for fourteen years, took French leave. Confined in the third story of the Old Capitol Prison, in the dead hour of night he tore up his bedclothes, and made a rope by which he let himself down to the pavement, and escaped, although the sentry fired at him. The night being very dark, he quickly disappeared, and sought the house of a friend in the city, who provided him with a suit of citizen's clothes. Sallying out the next morning, he passed through Georgetown and Rockville as a member of the Sanitary Commission, bargaining for poultry and supplies for the hospitals. Beyond Rockville he overtook a party of five Marylanders, going South. All being provided with pocket-pistols, they took a picket post, and mounting themselves, pushed on rapidly to the Potomac, and crossed over into Virginia, near Leesburg, and reached the Confederacy, after eleven months' imprisonment.

Chapter 33: Escapes from Prison

During this year, 1864, no less than thirty of our men escaped from prison and the guards over them. Charlie Hall, who was a prisoner of Colonel Cole's, and was awaiting transportation to prison at Harper's Ferry, obtaining a Federal overcoat, asked of the guard permission to go to Colonel Cole's headquarters. Instead of going to Colonel Cole's headquarters, he walked out of camp uninterrupted, and reported at Mosby's the next day.

Magner, of Mississippi, was captured in Paris in the night, by taking the enemy for our own cavalry. He was carried to Harper's Ferry a prisoner. Having on a very fine uniform of the Confederate gray, he exchanged it with a Jessie scout for a Federal uniform. While waiting for transportation to Camp Chase, a large body of troops passed through Harper's Ferry, to re-enforce Sheridan in the Valley. At a moment when he was not watched closely, he fell into the column as a common soldier, limping, as if wearied with his march. His *comrades* asked him where his gun was. "In the wagon," replied Magner, and passed on, without attracting any further notice. Watching his chances to escape, he straggled, and sought refuge in the mountains, where he remained all night. Next day he was discovered by a scouting-party, who gave him chase. Jumping down an embankment of fifty feet, which dislocated his shoulder, he plunged into the Shenandoah, swam across with one arm, and was free once more. The next day he reached Fauquier.

On the 11th of November, an inspection of the battalion was held at Rectortown. Five hundred men reported to their names at roll-call. This inspection was held at the request of Mosby. A large number of men had connected themselves with the battalion, whose names were on the rolls of the regular army, and who, thinking to shirk military duty, came up and joined the Forty-Third. They were a set of men who very seldom went on a raid; and when they did go, and there was any fighting or horses captured, would lag behind, and when it was all over, would lead the horses out, take the greenbacks from the prisoners, and when near their homes would flank out with a horse, and never come up to a division of the property. In that way they lived. This kind of men Mosby did not want, and would not have; and he adopted this method of getting them together with the determination of sending them to Richmond, to be put in the trenches.

Captain Meade, of General Early's staff, was the inspecting officer. The names of these men had been previously obtained from the captains of the companies. When their names were called, and they appeared before the colonel and inspector, they were relieved of the equipments furnished by Mosby, and placed under guard. Eighty names were struck from our rolls that day, and started for Richmond under a guard of twenty-three men. Out of the eighty, only twenty-three were turned over to Major Boyle, provost marshal at Gordonsville. Some of them escaped by jumping out of a window in the third storey of a house; others would leave their horses, &c. After inspection, the men were disbanded, to go to their homes and await further orders.

On the 16th of November, a meeting of Company D was held at Paris. Thirty men reported for duty, and started on a raid into the Valley, commanded by Captain Montjoy. They passed through Ashby's Gap at noon, and the Shenandoah River at the Island Ford one mile below Berry's Ferry. Montjoy then shaped his course in the direction of Winchester, avoiding on his march the public roads and highways. His movements in the Valley being entirely under cover of night, he succeeded in reaching the vicinity of Winchester without being observed by any one, either friend or foe. Concealing himself and men in a piece of woodland until day, and resting and feeding their horses at sunrise, he sallied out in quest of *game*.

It was not long before Montjoy, who was ahead some distance *prospecting*, came back and reported the enemy advancing in a force he intended to attack. He drew up his men for the charge under a hill about one hundred yards from the road leading from Winchester to Newtown. The enemy moved up slowly and carelessly, and little dreamed they were marching into the lion's jaws, or that a mere handful of *Johnnies* (one third their number) were lying a few rods from them, eager for the fray. When they were directly opposite his men, Montjoy ordered the charge. The enemy were struck on the flank and rear. So great was the surprise, and impetuous the charge, that little or no resistance was shown by them. They all, to a man, put spurs to their horses, to escape the best way they could. Twelve, however, bit the dust in the space of about one mile, and seventeen were captured, including the same number of horses.

On Montjoy's return to Fauquier, while passing through Berryville, he met Captain Brasher, *alias* Blazer, with about seventy-five men. The meeting was a surprise to both parties, and had Captain Montjoy, instead of inquiring who they were, charged through them, as Mosby would have done, Brasher would have been routed, and his men scattered over the whole valley. But during the colloquy, time was afforded Brasher to form his men by one of his lieutenants (Cole), and thus get the bulge on Montjoy, which resulted in a precipitate retreat. Captain Montjoy and his men were pursued to the Shenandoah River, losing two men killed and five wounded, besides abandoning all his capture.

Chapter 34: Magnanimity of Brave Men

On the 17th of November, the First Squadron, Companies A and B, met at Bloomfield, while the Second Squadron, Companies C, E, and F, met at Paris, and went into the Valley, capturing four horses and three prisoners near Winchester, and returned on the 18th. The First Squadron, commanded by Captain A. E. Richards, crossed the mountains at Snicker's Gap, and the Shenandoah River at Castleman's Ferry. From there Richards pushed on down the valley to Cabletown, in search of Captain Brasher. Reaching Cabletown, Richards learned that Brasher had just gone in search of him, in the direction of Rock Ford. Getting on his track, Richards followed him up, and, when about midway between the ford and Cabletown, met him in an open field.

Company B halted under a hill, while Company A was sent ahead, to pull down a fence. Brasher, thinking A retreating, charged them; but before reaching Company A, Richards, with Company B, charged them on their flank. A desperate fight ensued, a portion of which was hand-to-hand. The enemy broke and retreated in confusion, and were pursued for several miles. The field was strewn with their dead and wounded. Brasher, who fought as no Federal soldier ever fought before, after a hand-to-hand fight with Sidney Ferguson, who knocked him off his horse with a pistol, surrendered. Thirty-one of the enemy were killed and wounded; nineteen were taken prisoners, together with thirty-nine fine horses.

Brasher, when he made the attack, had six prisoners with him,— three of General Lomax's men, and three of ours, whom they had captured the day before in the valley. Puryear, one of them, as soon as he was liberated, picked up a club in one hand, and with a pistol which he had borrowed, in the other, went in, knocking down on one side and shooting on the other. Richards had one man killed and six wounded. He had only seventy-five men with him, while Brasher had his whole command (one hundred men) with him. Brasher complimented Richards highly for his bravery and skill in the management of his men, saying he never saw men fight better, and that he had been whipped fairly, a compliment that affected Harry Hatcher so sensibly, that he could not refrain from embracing the old soldier, although he was a foe.

When the North heard of this complete overthrow of the man who had been taken from the regular army, and sent to the valley with one hundred picked men, to *"clean out Mosby"* by one third fewer men than he had, and armed with nothing but pistols, their newspapers teemed with explanations, and insisted that the case was not so bad as was at first supposed. It might not have been so; but one thing is certain, Captain Brasher was so crippled in this engagement, that his men who escaped never made another raid into our Confederacy, or exchanged shots on the battlefield. When he was exchanged, the authorities gave a Confederate colonel for this captain.

On the 20th of November, a meeting of the members of Company F was held at Paris. Lieutenant Frank Trurun, commanding, took twenty-five men, crossed the mountains and entered the valley, and captured, near Summit Point, eight prisoners, and the same number of mules and horses. Sending them out with a guard of five men, he pushed on with the remaining twenty to the neighbourhood of Winchester, and captured on the 22nd fifteen prisoners and fifteen horses, and returned to Fauquier, on the 23rd, without loss.

On the 21st, Companies C and D met at Paris, Montjoy commanding. Mosby took them into the valley, and on the 22nd, when near Winchester, captured nineteen prisoners and seventeen mules, which were brought out and sold to the government.

On the 23rd of November, Companies C and E met at Paris. Only sixty-five men reported for duty. At four o'clock p.m., led by Lieutenant John Russell, they passed through Ashby's Gap, and crossed the Shenandoah River at Berry's Ferry. Russell then moved in the direction of White Post. Here he hid his men in the woods, until Mosby and Captain William Chapman should come up. They arrived at midnight, after a short rest. Lookouts were posted on all the roads, to watch for wagon-trains. Seeing nothing, they were called in, and Mosby moved his men nearer Winchester. While emerging from a piece of wood, they saw a train of wagons in the distance. Pushing up his men, Mosby charged the train, and followed it into General Powell's cavalry camp of two thousand men. The enemy fled in all directions, leaving Mosby to start out with one hundred and fifty prisoners and two hundred horses and mules. The enemy, however, rallied and pursued Mosby. Mosby's horse became unmanageable, broke his bit, and ran away. The men followed him, and were pushed so close as to necessitate an abandonment of all the prisoners and captured property.

In the retreat, Captain Chapman had his horse killed under him. John Kirwin, one of his men, dismounted from his Rosinante, and gave him to his captain, while he himself jumped up behind another man, and came out safe. Young Bolling had his horse shot, and fell with him, playing dead. The enemy came up, took one thousand two hundred dollars out of his pocket, and passed on. After they had all disappeared, Bolling got up, shook himself, and started afoot to Fauquier. Angelo, alias Mocking-bird, was captured, and taken to Martinsburg and put in jail. During the first night of his incarceration, he opened the jail door, walked out, and escaped, reaching Fauquier the next day. These were all the casualties on this raid. The pursuit terminated at Millwood, five miles from the Shenandoah River.

Chapter 35: Raid of Custer and Others

On the 26th of this month, the First and Second Squadrons met at Bloomfield. Two hundred men reported for duty. Mosby, placing himself at the head of the column, moved off to Snickersville. Passing through the Gap and crossing the Shenandoah River, he pushed on to Charlestown, to attack a cavalry camp at that place. On reaching Charlestown, it was found that Captain Baylor, of the regular army, had attacked them the night before, and they had been re-enforced with three hundred infantry posted in a church near by. Deeming it inexpedient to make an attack, Mosby. abandoned the expedition, disbanded his men, and all returned. The Second Squadron met the same day at Paris, crossed over into the valley, and captured only three horses and three Feds, and returned.

Montjoy, with Company D, went to Loudon County after Keyes, who had been raiding there with impunity. Entering Leesburg, Montjoy met and attacked him. Keyes made a precipitate retreat towards his rendezvous, the Point of Rocks, with Montjoy after him. Three miles from town, Montjoy, being far ahead of his men, was bushwhacked, and received a mortal wound in the head, just over the eye. He was carried to Leesburg by his men, and left in charge of kind and warm friends. Here he lingered only a few hours.

In the fall of Captain R. P. Montjoy, Mosby lost one of the most brilliant officers in his command, gallant and brave to a fault. A poor boy from Mississippi, he raised himself to the command of Company D by his own industry. Through his sobriety, skill, courage, and amiable manners, he enjoyed the esteem of his men and the confidence of his commander. Twenty-four horses and fifteen prisoners were brought away, the fall of Montjoy being the only casualty. Jim Chilton and Bob Crawford distinguished themselves in this engagement by their dashing conduct.

While we were absent this month on a raid, the enemy came up from Falls Church and burnt Joe Blackwell's house, Mosby's headquarters. Their treatment of Mr. Blackwell's family was of a most unsoldierly character. The family were turned out of doors, and not even permitted to take with them a change of clothing. Nothing was left on the plantation but the spring-house. They even applied the torch to the chicken-coops. In the destruction of this house, Colonel Mosby lost all his reports, correspondence, and other valuable papers pertaining to the command. After the destruction of Mr. Blackwell's house, Colonel Mosby established his headquarters at Holland's Factory, two miles and a half from Rectortown. This factory derived its name from the owner, Mr. Holland, a Union man. Attached to the factory was the private residence of Mr. Holland, who owned the factory.

While Holland was absent in Washington, the tolls from the carding of the wool were very heavy; and after a large quantity had accumulated on Mrs. Holland's hands, she would communicate the fact to Mr. Holland. He would then bring a large force of the enemy up to the factory, by whom the wool was carried out in the road and set on fire. The enemy leaving immediately, a stream of water was turned on it and the fire extinguished. Holland would return to Washington, file his claim, and get pay for his wool; and it is a notorious fact in Fauquier, he has told reliable citizens there, that he received pay from the government for every pound burnt, and in some burnings treble the amount that he had on hand. Here Mosby held his headquarters until the surrender, and although the enemy made repeated visits to this factory, they never disturbed anything.

On the 28th of November, a dense fog hung over Fauquier all day: so thick was it that objects could not be distinguished a distance of ten yards. The enemy, availing themselves of it, crossed the Shenandoah River at Berry's Ferry with three divisions (about eight thousand cavalry), and made that celebrated raid through Fauquier and Loudon Counties, in which they burnt every barn, stable, wheat, hay, and straw-rick, and mill, and everything that man or beast could subsist upon, and all the stock, cattle, &c., they could see were driven off. The divisions consisted of Custer's, Torbert's, and Merritt's. Commencing at Peter Hartman's, Mrs. Edmonds', and William Hopper's, they burnt every mill,—including the celebrated Reed Mill, whose flour took the premium at the World's Fair in London,—barn, stable, hay and straw-rick and wheat-stack, and even shocks of corn in the field; every cow, horse, sheep, and hog they could see was driven off, not a single thing being left for the people to subsist upon except a little the people had hid in the mountains, for an emergency.

When hogs had been killed by the farmers and hung up to cool off, these men would take an axe, chop the hams off, and drop the remainder in the mud. One mile from Upperville, where they camped the first night, a widow lady, Mrs. Fletcher, was having a load of hogs brought home from a neighbour's to salt. When the wagon crossed the turnpike going to Mrs. Fletcher's, the enemy took her oxen to their camp and burnt up the wagon with the pork. This was all the meat that poor widow had to feed her children with the ensuing summer.

The next day they established their headquarters at Snickersville, and remained there for three days, and during that time applied the torch to everything except the houses: these they robbed. In some portions of Loudon, Quakers and Union citizens were spared; but along under the mountains, from Semper's Mill to Leesburg, none escaped the fury of the enemy. The poor people, with only one cow for their subsistence, were deprived of it. If old Satan himself had thrown open the gates of hell, and turned loose all the devils in there, they could not have inflicted greater misery and woe than Custer's, Torbert's, and Merrill's cavalry inflicted on these people in this raid.

To see that they did their work of destruction thoroughly, General Custer himself, the second day after he crossed at Berry's Ferry, with a large force scoured the Blue Ridge Mountains from Snickersville to Ashby's Gap. On entering Paris, and halting with his bodyguard in front of Mr. Adams's, keeper of the hotel, he ordered his men "to get to work and complete the destruction of everything that might be of service to Mosby," and to show his men no quarter. Two of his bodyguard went to Mr. Hartman, to get their *rations*. While one was in the milk-house, doing his dirty work, Sid Ferguson rode up and seized him by the collar and carried him off. General Custer, fearing he might meet with the same fate, made a hasty retreat to Mrs. Hicks's, two miles down the turnpike, where he rejoined a portion of his men, who had swept everything before them.

How agreeable must have been General Custer's reflections, as he viewed from the top of the Blue Ridge, immense clouds of smoke and flame, arising from smouldering ruins, as far as the eye could reach,— the ruins of the houses of a once happy and prosperous people, now reduced to absolute beggary by his hand and edict. Recollections of that character may be drowned in the excitement of active life and the storm of the battlefield, but on the deathbed they will rise up as they appeared to him on the 29th day of November, 1864.

About fifty of the burners were captured and shot. One was taken to Mount Eddy, and with his eyes looking down on the smoking ruins wrought by his own hands, was hung. At Mrs. Burns's, near Upperville, they caught John Thomas, of Company A, and beat him, as they thought, to death. He, however, "played possum," and, after they left, got up, minus his pistols and pocketbook. Fully realising his situation, John took a position on the roadside, and waited for something to turn up. While he was reflecting on the vicissitudes of a partisan ranger's life, a straggler came along. Thomas seized the reins of the horse with one hand, and with the other hand dismounted his adversary before he had time to draw his pistols. Securing them, and mounting the fellow's horse, he escaped to the mountains just as the rear-guard was coming in sight.

Chapter 36: Mosby Severely Wounded

On the 2nd of December, Mosby started to Richmond, to make arrangements for forage for his men's horses for the next campaign, and lay the matter of this burning before the President.

On the 3rd of December, a meeting of the whole battalion was held at Upperville. The First squadron went into the valley, crossing at Snicker's Gap and Castleman's Ferry. Proceeding then to Charlestown, and finding no enemy, Captain A. E. Richards pushed on to the Baltimore and Ohio Railroad at Duffield Station, placing obstructions on the track, to capture a train of cars. After waiting patiently all night for one to approach, and none making its appearance, the men were disbanded, and all returned to Fauquier. The Second squadron, commanded by Captain William H. Chapman, crossed over into the valley at Berry's Ferry, and when near the White Post, were attacked by an overwhelming force of the enemy, which necessitated their retreat. That was effected without loss or injury.

On the 7th of December another inspection of the command was held at Rectortown. Captain Clary, of General Early's staff, was the inspecting officer; but no further details were made to the regular army. After inspection, Captain Richards, of Company B, and commandant of the First squadron, detailed forty men, with fast horses, to meet him the next day (Thursday), at two o'clock, at Snickersville.

In compliance with Richards's order, the men met him. He then started on a raid to the valley, crossing the mountains at Snicker's Gap, and Shenandoah River at Castleman's Ferry. Penetrating the enemy's lines to within five miles of Martinsburg, and capturing only two federals, he changed his course, and struck for the Baltimore and Ohio Railroad, near Duffield Station. When about halfway a violent snowstorm set in and compelled him to return to Fauquier. As it snowed all that night, Richards's men suffered severely. He reached headquarters, however, without loss or serious injury, although the mercury stood below zero during his entire absence.

On the 10th of December, Captain Sam Chapman, commanding Company E, took thirty of his men into the valley, crossing at Ashby's Gap, and the river at Island Forde, in a terrible snowstorm. He bivouacked that night on the banks of the Shenandoah, and at four o'clock the next morning mounted his men and attacked a picket post at the tollgate, near Millwood, before day, with great success, capturing five Federals and eleven horses, without loss.

On the night of the 21st of December, Colonel Mosby, with only one man (Love), was surprised and wounded. He fell into the hands of the *Philistines* at Mr. Lake's, near Rector's Cross Roads. Colonel Mosby, with young Love, was returning from a scouting expedition in one of the lower counties, and, feeling very much fatigued, they stopped in at Mr. Lake's, at nine o'clock at night, to refresh themselves with a cup of genuine coffee. Believing no enemy to be nearer than Middleburg, he went into the house. However, to guard against any accident or surprise, he put Love on picket, to watch the road leading to the cross roads. He had been in the house but a few minutes, when a party of one hundred of the Eighth Illinois Cavalry came up the Salem road and captured Love before he could give any alarm by firing his pistol.

Mosby, hearing an unusual noise, like the rattling of sabres, in the road, jumped up from the table and went to the door to see what was the matter. On his opening the front door, a large squad was waiting for him, who instantly demanded his surrender. Closing that door, he retreated to the back door, but found no avenue of escape through it, as a large squad were there. He then concluded, as a last resort, to try one of the front windows, thinking that by jumping through it into the darkness amongst them, he might, in the confusion, escape unobserved. Divesting himself of his elegant military coat and jacket, with no insignia of rank on, or of his being a Confederate soldier, except a pair of gray pantaloons, he approached the window, when he was fired upon from the road, and fell, dangerously wounded.

The Miss Lakes, fearing Mosby's rank would betray him, took his jacket (which had two stars on the collar), and hid it under a lounge. The enemy, as soon as Mosby fell, rushed into the house to see what officer it was they had shot, through the window. They were met at the door by Miss Lake, who told them *"That man you shot is dying!"* Several of them went into the room where he was stretched out on the floor, in the throes of death. He could yet speak a little. On being asked what his name was, and where shot, he told them he was "*Lieutenant Johnson, of the Third Virginia Cavalry.*" His speech failing him at that moment, and the enemy imagining he was really dying, relieved him of his boots, military cloak, pocketbook, and papers, and left him. Love, who was a prisoner in the road, had all this time kept silent as to who the officer was in the house. In the meanwhile, some of the party who were in the house, rejoined the column in the road, and related what had transpired. Love, overhearing the conversation, and feeling the greatest anxiety for the safety of his colonel, and seeing they did not know who it was, "took the cue," and determined not to tell them, and thus afford Mr. Lake an opportunity (if Mosby was not too dangerously wounded,) to carry him to a safe place.

Love was carried to Middleburg. On the road he was interrogated as to who that officer was in the house. He replied that he was a stranger to him, but he understood his name to be Lieutenant Johnson, of the Regular Service. The enemy, satisfied it was not their great terror (Mosby), troubled themselves no further about him until they reached their camp, when on examining the papers in the pockets of the clothes they had taken from Lieutenant Johnson, to their utter amazement, they found it was no other person than the veritable John S. Mosby, and not Lieutenant Johnson! The greatest excitement prevailed in and through the camp. The command "to horse," was instantly given by the officer in command, and the whole force started back to Mr. Lake's, to secure Lieutenant Johnson, and bring him to camp, dead or alive.

The return was a most exciting march. Men vied with their officers to reach Mr. Lake's first. Mr. Lake, however, who was a great admirer and warm personal friend of Colonel Mosby, had not been unmindful of the colonel's critical situation, and what a serious loss his capture would be to the people of Fauquier, and the Confederacy. Without considering the treatment he would receive at their hands, Mr. Lake, as soon as the enemy left the house, yoked up his steers, and placed him in an *ox-cart*, in an almost dying condition, and drove him through the fields, (to prevent the enemy's getting on his track) to Mr. Quilly Glasscock's, father of Lieutenant Glasscock, a mile and a half distant on Goose Creek, and off the public road. Ere Mosby had reached Mr. Glasscock's, the enemy were back to Mr. Lake's for their prize; but the bird had flown. The house was searched diligently, but no one found. They raved. The ladies of the house were taken out and interrogated as to where that wounded man was, and told that if they did not tell, their house should be burned down. The only reply they received was, "Burn on, we do not know where he is."

The enemy, satisfying themselves he was not on Mr. Lake's premises, and not knowing at what moment they might be attacked at that hour of the night, fell into line and moved back to their camp, with the intention of renewing the search the next morning.

At Mr. Glasscock's, Dr. Dunn, surgeon of the battalion, and Dr. Eliason, late of General Stuart's Staff, were soon at his side. His wound was pronounced dangerous and painful, being through the side, just below the ribs, producing internal bleeding, so that he was not in a condition to be moved. Yet he was kept in an ambulance, with fleet horses harnessed up, ready to be moved in an emergency.

The enemy returned next day, and after a fruitless search returned that evening to Fairfax. Doctors Dunn and Eliason pronouncing Mosby's wounds too dangerous to admit of his being moved, the men were employed in picketing all the roads, to give notice of the approach of the enemy. For fear the enemy might find out Mosby's whereabouts, he was moved in the night from one neighbour's house to another, by which means they were not only ignorant of where he was, but even his own men did not know. His men, however, knew he was in the neighbourhood, and that was all.

The Monday night after he was shot, he was carried to Salem. Tuesday morning five thousand Federal cavalry arrived in Salem, on their return to the Valley from a raid through Rappahannock and Madison Counties, to Gordonsville. They had heard of Mosby's being wounded, and were looking. out for him, knowing his friends would endeavour to get him inside of our lines, or to his father's in Amherst County. In Salem all inquired where he was, and large rewards were offered for the information. "*No one knows*" was all they could get out of the citizens of Salem; yet Mosby was amongst them at that moment. The enemy, dividing their force there into two columns, instituted a rigid search for the "guerilla." One column moved in the direction of Middleburg, destroying and burning everything in their route, except private residences. The other column moved through Rectortown and Piedmont, and camped on Joe Gibson's farm, two miles from Paris, that night. Generals Custer and Torbert establishing their headquarters in the mill, the roads and lanes were barricaded, to keep us from disturbing them.

Lieutenants Beattie and John Russell, with some few men, annoyed the enemy all night. Sky-rockets were thrown into their camp, and the cattle and stock they had stolen from the citizens along their route were frightened and stampeded. Their camp being between two mountains, and our men being on the sides, they amused themselves by throwing hand-grenades in amongst them, rolling large rocks down on them, and firing into them. Their situation, and the sleep they had that night, can be better imagined by my readers than I relate to them. The enemy visited Jim Lew Adams, and charged him with having boarded and given aid, comfort, and sympathy to our men. According to Judge Lynch (under whose code they decided such cases), accusation and conviction being synonymous terms, they destroyed every article upon which his family might subsist, including bedding, clothing, corn, and poultry, carrying off such articles as suited their fancy.

They likewise made a call upon Mr. William Hopper, near the Gap. Mrs. Hopper had anticipated the object of their mission, and secreted the contents of the smoke-house under the wood-pile. Just as her undertaking was completed, the squad came into the yard and ordered refreshments, which were not furnished according to a regular bill of fare, when they broke into the smoke-house and feloniously captured two rolls of sausage. At Mrs. Margaret Edmonds's, they discovered some good bacon in the garret, which was hastily confiscated. The sanctity of her private chamber was broken, and the men acted without restraint. From thence they crossed the mountains at Ashby's Gap, in the direction of Winchester. In the gap. there lived at the house of Peter Marshall, a faithful old black woman, who, for the love she bore her *true* friends, had received and given shelter to our pickets on divers occasions. By some means not known to the writer, the Yankees had learned of this old woman's fidelity, and forthwith she was robbed of all her food and little "traps."

Captain Richards and Bob Walker, with fifteen Virginia boys, followed close in the wake of these plunderers as they crossed the river, and even to the vicinity of Millwood, from whence our men retraced their steps, encountering a dense fog, under cover of which the remaining division of the Yankee forces came upon our men unawares. Our men were very "impressionable" at this juncture of affairs, and effected their escape with some rapidity and considerable *éclat*, by taking to the mountains.

It was on the day of these occurrences that several promotions were made in the command, for gallant services, and meritorious conduct, Mosby receiving a colonel's commission, Captain William H. Chapman, that of lieutenant-colonel, and Captain A. E. Richards, that of major.

December 29th, was the day on which another search was inaugurated for Mosby. Some three hundred men of the Eighth Illinois Cavalry came from Fairfax, and worked with great industry in their hunt. Mosby was hard by, and on two occasions was completely in their power, if they had known it. Some of the prisoners captured were at a loss to account for Mosby's ubiquitous character, charged our men with making underground railroads, and acting *à la Mosby* above ground, while the original Mosby escaped through some subterranean passage.

The last forty-eight hours of the old year brought us violent snowstorms, gloomy and freezing-cold rains, hail and sleet, and consequently not much activity was displayed.

The Second Squadron, consisting of Companies C, E, F, and G, met at Salem on the 3rd day of January, 1864, and made preparations to take up winter quarters on the Northern Neck, comprising the Counties of King George, Westmoreland, Northumberland, Lancaster, and Richmond, lying between the Rappahannock and Potomac Rivers, a section of country not having been occupied or visited by the forces of either side, and one of the richest portions of the Old Dominion. Forage and commissary stores existed in abundance, and food was a *desideratum*, as the Yankees had swept the country around the Neck, with a sort of patent broom, which deprived men and non-combatants alike, of the necessaries of life.

Our preparations, however, were completed, when it was whispered that the Graces desired to honour us with an entertainment, and friendly reception. A *déjeuner* was prepared under the auspices of the beautiful Virginia girls, Misses Cochrane, Murray, Welch, and their lovely associates, which did honour to the donors and the occasion. We were served with dressed turkey, roast pork, beef *à la mode*, cake, hot coffee, etc. Notwithstanding these savoury viands met a cordial welcome with the physical man, the nobler impulses of our soul were gently touched with admiration and emotions akin to love for the accomplishments and unostentatious hospitality of our fair friends. It was, moreover, a feast of reason, beauty, grace, and refinement, and an interchange of wishes, hopes, and prayers for the success of our sacred cause.

During the *tête-à-tête*, and amidst the fugue of voices which rung in every tone, semi-tone and key, falling in sweet cadence, and enriched ever and *anon* by bursts of sparkling wit and pathos, one of our boys brought the house to breathless silence. In a stentorian voice the question was asked: "Why are Virginians engaged in war?" Immediately Miss ——— arose, and extemporaneously alluded to the cause of the war with a modest diction which nerved every fibre of our souls with the sentiment, that:

Thrice is he armed who hath his quarrel just.

She said in substance:

> Soldiers! Liberty is your watchword. Causes which are not ephemeral have led you to seek the establishment of an independent government, organised with such powers as may be derived from the consent of the governed. You have never denied to others the rich boon you seek. Aggression, and open declarations, and overt acts of hostility to our wronged and injured people, have impelled you to defend your altars and homes. Our enemies know the honesty and justice of the struggle, but systematically falsify history.
>
> Recur, if you please, to the published crusade contained in the infamous Helper Book, the teaching of the Stowes, Beechers, Dickinsons, Phillipses, Greeleys, and abolition conclaves, the Nat Turner Insurrections, John Brown raid, Kansas Border wars, Lincoln's *dictum* that the *government cannot endure permanently, half slave and half free,*—the organisation of Manufacturers' Leagues in the North, forcing us to pay tribute by exorbitant tariffs, accompanied by their "Wide Awake" mobs and Personal Liberty-Free-Negro-Bills, the declaration of an Irrepressible Conflict, the dogma of Federal consolidation and infringement of reserved, vested rights.
>
> These are some of the causes which inspire and move you. The instinct which drives the worm to turn under the tread, is engrafted in your natures; hence you resist coercion and subjugation by the natural laws of self-defence. Nay, you fight to perpetuate and hand down to posterity, the patriotic principles enunciated by our Washington, Jefferson, Monroe, Madison, Marshall and Henry.

Company D travelled from Hooper's shop, on the turnpike near Middleburg, to the vicinity of Fairfax, touching at Centreville, thence to Gainesville. Night, darkness and foul weather were wholly disregarded. The command, being in charge of Major Richards, were occasionally divided into squads, one of which, led by Captain Glasscock, attacked a train on the Orange and Alexandria Railroad, near Alexandria, without material success, more than to remind our enemies that we had not "froze out"

Major Richards resolved to strike a blow which should be felt by the sentimental, infallible gentry, and accordingly ordered eighty men to concentrate at Bloomfield. From hence they hastened across the mountains, via Snicker's Gap, fording the river at Castleman's Ferry, passing through Cabletown and Charlestown, and called a halt at Duffield Station, on the Baltimore and Ohio Railroad. Simultaneous with their arrival, a richly laden freight train hove in sight. Upon an exchange of cards, the train was confiscated. A vote of thanks was extended to the provident Yankee quartermaster, for our supplies of coffee, sugar, clothing, crackers, fish, &c. Indeed, the success inspired the men with delight to such a degree that the visit was prolonged for several hours, trusting that the express train would run into their tender embrace. An alarm was sounded, but before the command had fully retired, the Express train came thundering forward, like a shooting star, and was suddenly brought to a complete smash-up by the debris of the freight train. This was a casualty of war, and the curses heaped upon Mosby were neither select nor elegant. The Union-savers soon repaired the damage and arrested sundry non-combatants, to surfeit their revenge.

Chapter 37: Rumours of Peace Negotiations

The dawn of the morning of February 1, 1865, was heralded by still another exploit of Major Richards with twenty-five men. They made another crossing at Castleman's, and captured five patrolmen, from whom, by the exercise of strength, awkwardness, and a mixture of deception, they succeeded in obtaining the countersign, and thus armed were enabled to effect the loan of five noble chargers from the Yankee garrison at Charlestown. The conditions of the loan not being fully understood, several leaden messengers sung around their ears as they made their exit. The riders of the captured horses were induced to remain in the saddle until we could furnish them quarters. Upon the return of Major Richards, he was advised that Jim Wilcher and Bob Eastham, (*alias* Bob Ridley), with ten men, had attacked a train between Harper's Ferry and Winchester, without success. The engineer, however, fell from the train in his frenzied efforts to save his charge, and was instantly killed.

About this time rumours were in circulation of peace negotiations, and a conference to that end was said to be on the *tapis* at Fortress Monroe, between Vice President Stephens, Hon. Mr. Hunter, and Campbell, and Messrs. Lincoln and Seward. The news was brought by Bush Underwood, who had been scouting in Fairfax with four men. The intelligence cast a gloom not only over the officers and men, but over the whole of Mosby's "Confederacy;" and, although the farmers and soldiers were living on half allowance, gold at one hundred, and the citizens refusing to take Confederate money, we did not relax our efforts in the least degree. The officers and men unanimously resolved that if the Confederacy went down, the present generation and those that came after them should not say we did not discharge our duty. The men began to accumulate forage for their horses for the approaching campaign. They commenced collecting the tithe in Fauquier, but that was discontinued, by order of Colonel Mosby, in consequence of the heavy tax which the people had already paid, in boarding his men.

On the 6th of February, Major Richards started with five men on a scouting expedition to Fairfax; but was obliged, before he got half way, to return, in consequence of a violent snowstorm which set in. The snow fell to the depth of two feet, and in many places where it drifted, it was one hundred feet. Roads were blockaded with it, and the stock in the mountains died for the want of grazing. While this condition of the roads lasted, the men amused themselves with the exciting sport of fox-chasing. Day and night could be heard the barking of dogs and the music of the horn reverberating in the mountains. A grand chase was proposed by some of the old hunters, and it came off on the 8th of February. The snow was about eighteen inches deep. Hunters came from the adjoining counties with their dogs. The foxes had become very annoying to the farmers in this portion of Fauquier, and as all kinds of business and work were suspended, it was thought an excellent time to terminate the career of some of them.

The old hunters, Wm. Hopper, Reuben Triplett, Bob and Phil Eastham, Hand, and John Carr had the management of it. One hundred citizens and soldiers participated in the chase. There were one hundred hounds, and the reverberations of their barking through the mountains, combined with the sight of a hundred men engaged in the chase, was a thing long to be remembered by the people of Fauquier. In dashing over the ravines men would sometimes be precipitated into the banks of snow, but soon recovered themselves. The chase commenced at ten o'clock a.m., and terminated at sunset. Five foxes were caught, and a large number chased to their caves.

On the 18th of February, one hundred and twenty-five of the Fourteenth Pennsylvania Cavalry, commanded by Major Gibson and Lieutenant Baker, of General Merritt's staff, crossed the Shenandoah River at Shepherd's Mill, nine miles from Paris, at eleven o'clock p.m., and made a night raid into our Confederacy, confident that we had abandoned our huts and holes in the mountains during this severe weather, and were sleeping in the farmers' houses again. The weather was, and had been for some time, intensely cold. Snow was deep on the ground, and they were sure of making "*a good thing of it.*" After crossing at Shepherd's Mill, they took the road under the mountains and struck the turnpike at Mount Carmel Church.

Here they were joined by another party of two hundred, who had crossed at Berry's Ferry. Passing through the Gap, they reached Paris at the foot of the mountain. Here they separated. The party of two hundred, which crossed at Berry's Ferry, were to proceed down the turnpike to Upperville, and capture Major Richards at his father's, two miles beyond, at Green Garden Mills; thence to Rectortown and Piedmont, where they were to meet the other party, after searching every house in their route. The other party, Major Gibson's, was to take the mountain road to Markham, and from there proceed to Piedmont.

The first party, after searching every house on the turnpike, entered Upperville. There they found a government agent, with five barrels of apple brandy, which he had brought up to Fauquier to trade with the farmers for hospital supplies. This was confiscated. The heads of the barrels were knocked out, and all hands got drunk. By the time they reached Major Richards, they were too drunk to effect anything. They, however, surrounded the house. A party knocked at the front door, and were admitted by the major's father. Taking him at first for the major, they subjected him to a little rough treatment, until, by showing them his locks, frosted by many winters, he induced them to release him. The major, who heard them before they entered the house, secreted himself in a place in the wall, which he had specially prepared for this exigency. The house and premises were searched diligently; but the object of their visit was not to be found. However, they appropriated to themselves every stitch of clothing he had in the world, including a magnificent dress uniform and overcoat, which he had received but a few days before from Baltimore. Being too drunk to proceed any further, this party returned to the valley before day.

Major Gibson performed his part like a soldier, searching every house diligently on his route, except Mr. Hopper's and Mr. Hartman's at the foot of the gap. How they overlooked them I am unable to comprehend. Had they given Mr. Hopper a call, five would have been caught sleeping in a feather bed, including the writer. Soldiers, however, you know, are inclined to be superstitious. They remembered the last 18th of February, and that their friends were languishing in Northern prisons from the treachery of one of their own countrymen. Some of the old members had become careless, and returned to their feather-beds. Those that returned, and new ones, were all captured.

While at Mrs. Betsy Edmonds', Clem Edmonds, George Triplett, and Sam Alexander, heard them from their *ranch* in the mountains, about half a mile in rear of the house. Saddling their horses, and convincing themselves who they were, they started out and gave the alarm. Proceeding ahead to Lieutenant Wren's, who was staying at Mr. Brown's, about one mile distant, they were joined by him and a few others, and followed the enemy up to Piedmont. Reaching this place at daylight, Gibson expected to find the other column. Not hearing anything from them at sunrise, he started back to the Valley, taking the turnpike to Upperville, and thence up to Paris, Lieutenant Wren following him, but not doing anything except keeping them closed up. Every chicken and turkey-roost in their route had been robbed by them, and each man had his turkey or old hen strapped behind his saddle, together with the clothing, &c., which they had taken from the citizens.

At Mr. Chapplier's, two miles from Piedmont, on the turnpike to Upperville, J. Wright James, our quartermaster, was captured. By this time their presence in our midst became generally known amongst our men; who displaying themselves on the hills and mountains, the enemy became alarmed, and pushed on rapidly from Mr. Chapplier's to Upperville. Not finding any of our men there except Grafton Carlisle, they pushed on rapidly up the turnpike, and reached Paris about nine o'clock a.m.

Major Richards, in the meanwhile, heard of this party, and having no clothes of his own, he put on a suit of his father's brown jeans, mounted his horse, and started after them. At Upperville he met with Lieutenant Wren, with a few men. Pushing on up the turnpike, at

Paris he was joined by others, who swelled his party to *thirty-eight men*. In Paris some skirmishing took place between the enemy's rear-guard and Richards. The enemy retreated rapidly though the Gap, and formed on the other side of the mountain, at Mount Carmel Church, two miles from Paris. The pursuit of Richards was conducted without any order whatever. His thirty-eight men were strung out for one quarter of a mile. But on dashed the gallant Richards. At the foot of Mt. Carmel he ordered the charge.

The enemy, seeing with what resolution the charge was made, and imagining five thousand guerillas were after them, broke and retreated by the road they came. It was a narrow defile through the mountains, just large enough for one wagon to pass. Through this defile or road they had to retreat seven miles, where they were to cross the Shenandoah River by a dangerous ford, before they could entertain any idea of being safe. When they broke and got into this road, Richards' men closed in on them, and the slaughter was terrible. Along this road, clean down to the river, were strewn the dead, wounded, and prisoners. It was indeed a sickening sight. The snow this entire distance was crimson with the blood of the dead and wounded. Every man of ours they had captured (twenty-five) was retaken, besides one hundred mules and horses they had taken from the citizens (which were returned to them by Richards). Ten or fifteen were killed, eighty odd were captured and wounded, and brought to Paris. Major Gibson was wounded, captured, brought to Paris, and paroled with nine other badly wounded men.

Amongst the prisoners was Lieutenant Baker, of General Merrit's staff. When he was asked how he happened to be absent from his general, he stated that he had been on one or two of the night "excursions" in the valley, had found them quite exciting and pleasant, and as his friend, Major Gibson, was going on this one, he concluded he would accompany him, and render his assistance in "arresting" us. But he counted the chickens before they were hatched. Their raid as far as Upperville was a decided success. And here their hopes failed them. They knew not at what moment they would be attacked by a set of *wolves*. Surrounded by these circumstances, very few men would fight with an enemy they did not understand. The men that were able to walk were sent to Richmond. Lieutenant Baker was furnished with a horse, by one of the men, to ride to Culpepper, where they took the cars for Richmond.

Major Richards, in this affair, had one man (John Iden) killed, already a wounded soldier, and one (Dr. Sowers, of Clark's County,) wounded. The enemy captured John Iden at his brother Tom's, and took a watch, a family piece, from John. As they were carrying him off prisoner, his aged mother, hearing of the captors' having taken the watch, went to Lieutenant Baker, stated her case, and he promptly had it returned to her. The enemy, rather chagrined at the conduct of Baker, after they got him away from the house, on the public highway, robbed him of everything. The writer was detailed by Major Richards to take charge of the prisoners and guard. In due course of time we reached Culpepper Court House, on the Orange and Alexandria Railroad. From there they were sent by rail to Gordonsville, and were that night turned over to Major Boyle, Provost Marshal of the Army of Northern Virginia.

The next morning, while in Major Boyle's office, awaiting the arrival of the cars, he handed me a lock of hair, which he said Baker had taken from one of the prisoners, who had taken it from the young man that was killed, and asked that it might be returned to his mother. Such an act of feeling was so uncommon in the Yankee Army, I have deemed it worthy of notice here. Feeling a curiosity to know who the person was, I inquired of Major Boyle, who told me he was an Englishman, and the lieutenant I brought out.

I expressed to Major Boyle a desire to visit Richmond, and he placed the prisoners in my charge. The train coming up in a few minutes, after a short stoppage we were soon on our way to the capital. Reaching Richmond at seven o'clock p.m., we marched down Main Street to the Libby Prison, and turned over our prisoners to Major Turner.

Chapter 38: Sheridan's March

At that time, in Richmond, it was melancholy to contemplate the condition of affairs. Hemmed in on three sides by the enemy, their supplies cut off, and only one avenue over which they could escape or draw supplies; and that portion, the Virginia Central Road already exhausted, there seemed to be nothing in prospect but starvation. Bacon was twelve and fifteen dollars a pound; flour twelve hundred dollars a barrel; sugar fifteen dollars a pound; oysters five dollars a dozen; eggs one dollar apiece; corn seventy-five dollars a bushel; and board at the Spottswood, fifty dollars a day. Considering these prices rather extravagant for a private soldier, who was getting only fifteen dollars a month, I remained in Richmond only two days. Taking the cars to

Gordonsville, I there met Colonel Mosby, on his way to rejoin his command.

Mounting my horse, and swimming the Rapidan, night found me at Jack's shop. At daybreak the next morning I was wending my way through Madison Court House, thence through Washington, Rappahannock County, and reached Fauquier the day after the Colonel. The day on which Colonel Mosby rejoined it, the command was ordered to proceed immediately to Loudon County, to collect forage for the ensuing campaign. The citizens were very kind to us, especially the Quakers. Mr. Elijah Holmes, the head of their church in that county, entertained eight or ten of us every night for a month, without charge. Mrs. Hoge and her accomplished daughters (another strong Union family) likewise contributed all in their power to make our stay amongst them as pleasant as possible. In Waterford, the stronghold of Unionism, every attention imaginable was shown us. In Leesburg, the people, especially the ladies, rejoiced to see their Southern friends once more. Private entertainments were given to us, and all was mirth for several days. Our men, notwithstanding these attentions, were collecting their tithes, and sending it back to our little Confederacy, all anticipating a prosperous and active campaign.

Early in this month Sheridan commenced his march up the valley, to join Grant, then lying around Petersburg and Richmond. The people are familiar with the misery and woe he brought upon the people along the line of his march. Mosby had anticipated this movement, and ordered his men to meet him in Markem. The elements, however, prevailed against him. The spring rains had set in, and the water-courses were so swollen as to prevent their passage. Had it been otherwise, many of Sheridan's cavalry would have "gone up "on their march from Charlottesville to Tyre River, on the Lynchburg Railroad. Mosby, learning the condition of the watercourses, ordered us back to Loudon.

On the 12th of March, Mosby ordered fifty men to meet him at Leesburg. Twenty-five of them were sent to Fairfax, under Captain Glasscock; the other twenty-five, under Lieutenant Ed Thompson, were sent to Munson's Hill, near Washington City. Thompson captured a patrol of ten men and horses. Captain Glasscock. hearing of a scouting party of thirty of the Sixteenth New York Cavalry near the Court House, prepared to engage them, and, if possible, capture the whole party. Learning the road they were on, he divided his men, one half being under Lieutenant Briscoe, the others under himself. Concealing themselves in the woods until the enemy should pass, as soon as the rear-guard went by Briscoe, he charged them, while Glasscock charged them in front. The enemy fought gallantly, and in their efforts to cut their way through all were killed except three, who escaped, and a few who surrendered. Glasscock brought off eighteen horses, without sustaining any loss.

On the 18th of this month (March), Lieutenant Ed Thompson was ordered by Mosby to take a squad of men and visit Occaquan. Selecting fifteen tried men, he visited that historic ground, and captured fifteen cavalrymen, with their horses, without loss on his side.

On the 20th of March, our gallant men were advised that an expedition of five hundred Yankee cavalry and one thousand infantry had been dispatched from Harper's Ferry, for the purpose of driving us from our native heath. They marched out to Hillsboro, with songs of mirth and self-admiration ringing through hill and dale. The ground over which they marched had been rendered classic by marches, counter-marches, skirmishes, and repeated engagements. Many noble spirits had already been buried in this soil, and the little mounds here and there were but so many memorials or guide-posts, reminding the living soldier of the sacredness of his struggle for liberty.

The 21st of March, as the dawn illumined the eastern horizon, we were summoned by our gallant leader to assemble at Hamilton. The clarion notes of the bugle rallied one hundred and twenty-eight as noble hearts as ever beat in the bosom of man. Hamilton was the point at which the Yankees expected to make their grand *coup de main*. The Southern boys were posted, and ordered to lie in hugger-mugger near Quaker Church, whilst Captain Glasscock, with a scout of four or five picked men, should ascertain the designs of the invaders. The Yankees reached Hamilton about noon, and moved down the road toward our position without delay. Colonel Mosby arrived on the field, and after a brief consultation prepared to meet the invaders, and to,

> Strike for the green graves of our sires,
> God, and our native Land.

Fifty Yankees were sent out to meet us as decoys; and their charge upon our rear and left flank struck us like a young hurricane, and then rebounded. Their blow was not irresistible, neither were our men immovable, but their retreat was as sudden and precipitous as their charge. Mosby, Glasscock, and Bob Eastham, promptly rallied the men, and determined to return the compliment. The retreat was closely followed up until within half a mile of Hamilton, where the Yankees were posted in full force, and in all the splendour and pomp of martial array. There was no halting or hesitation, and our men went in to the feast set before them. As we neared them, an exchange of volleys took place, and before our sabres could reach their front rank it gave way, and so confused those in the rear, that they at once sought safety in the houses and sheds of Hamilton.

This was rather to our wish, as we were fully equal to the task of taking any single house. Colonel Mosby, however, called the men forth and formed them in an open field near the town. This movement was mistaken for a retreat; but Mosby, after the men were marshalled into line, waved his hat and shouted for the Yankees to advance. They came from their hiding-places, but seemed unwilling to meet us. We cannot apologize for their hesitancy in accepting the challenge but upon the conjecture that our handful of men must have been mistaken for the advance guard of a large force. A spirited exchange of shots was kept up until late in the evening, when the Yankees drew off and passed through Hamilton, and admitted in their exit that they had lost fifty-two killed, wounded, and missing.

Their men who were taken prisoners acknowledged a defeat, with a loss of two captains killed. Among our boys, James Keith and Binford were killed at the head of the column. Captain Manning, John Chew, and Ben Fletcher, wounded. Among those complimented by Colonel Mosby for distinguished prowess, were Corbin and John Hipkins, the colonel himself having one horse killed under him during the engagement. We lost, also, two of our men captured, who, no doubt, have met the sad fate of many others, under the convenient pretext of being guerillas.

That night we bivouacked near Hamilton, and at dawn of day next morning discovered that the condition of the roads and fair weather had induced the invaders to make an advance on Snickersville, Bloomfield, and Middleburg. Mosby determined to follow, and in doing so resorted to a series of strategems and devices to draw the enemy into another engagement. Their infantry, however, formed and marched in hollow squares, with the cavalry in the enclosure. This novel mode of protecting gay cavaliers did honour to the infantry, but the cavalry must have left their "*grit*" at the ferry. We continued the pursuit below Middleburg, where the enemy were re-enforced by three hundred cavalry from Fairfax, which made their force too formidable for us to cope with, and having one man wounded during the day (John Foster, of

White Plains), Colonel Mosby ordered his men to be in readiness for subsequent emergencies, and to retire from the vicinity of Middleburg.

On the 24th, we were ordered to return to Loudon, and continue to collect the tithe, which was done under very great difficulties. A great many, in fact most of the farmers who had teams, had run them across the Potomac into Maryland, to prevent us from taking their corn and bacon. In addition to collecting the tithe, squads of men had been detailed to destroy all the distilleries in the county. The proprietors of these institutions had been ordered by Mosby to stop distilling the grain of the country; but no attention was paid to his orders. These houses had been broken up, and the stills cut to pieces in Fauquier, and Mosby was determined to terminate their traffic in Loudon. In addition to the injury the operations of these institutions would have on his men, they were consuming the very life-blood of the people.

The principal one in Loudon County was Downey's, the proprietor of which was President of the Virginia Senate, under the Pierpont dynasty. He had fled to Maryland, and only returned when his property was occupied by the enemy His absence, however, did not interfere in the least degree with the distilling of grain. It was carried on as successfully by his wife as if he had been present. It was a rendezvous for the enemy, and had become an intolerable nuisance. A detachment of men were sent there by Mosby; and the stills were cut to pieces, and the liquor poured into the creek. Mrs. Downey determined to have her revenge. She had secreted in her house a squad of the enemy; and when Captain James, our quartermaster, Major Hibbs, and John Bolling went to Downey's a few days after the destruction of the concern, to collect the tithe of bacon, they were, while dismounted, and in the house, seized by the enemy and carried prisoners across the Potomac River to Berlin, Maryland. Throughout Loudon County there was a general rejoicing when this nuisance was abated, and deep regret expressed at the capture of their benefactors.

Chapter 39: News of the Fall of Richmond

On the 31st of March, Mosby surprised his men in Leesburg. While they were enjoying the society of the charming ladies of this place, he dashed in and ordered all of them to Carter's Mill, to do picket duty.

On the 2nd of April, a meeting was held at the Quaker Church but nothing was done worthy of record.

On the afternoon of the 4th of April, heavy firing was heard on the other side of the river in Maryland. At dark, reports said, "It is in honour of the fall of Richmond." No credit was attached to it by our men. That night there was a great deal of speculation about it. The reports of those guns sounded like the death-knell to all our hopes and aspirations. We retired that night to awake in the morning and find it a fearful reality. The Baltimore papers received that evening revealed the fact to us. The intelligence produced great rejoicing among the loyal men of Loudon. Mosby and his men, however, did not despair, or give up the cause.

A meeting was forthwith called (the 5th of April), at North Fork, at which there was a full attendance of the men. Mosby was much concerned about the news. In conversation with Sergeant Corbin and myself, he said, "*There is nothing else for me to do but to fight on*" The men declared they would stand by him. A new Company was organised, and George Baylor, of Charlestown, Virginia, was elected Captain, Ed. Thompson First Lieutenant, Jim Wilcher Second Lieutenant, and Henry Carter Third Lieutenant; all elected for meritorious conduct.

Captain Baylor was a lieutenant in the regular army, and had distinguished himself on many a battlefield, although a mere youth. By his daring and heroic conduct he had won the confidence and esteem of Lee, Stuart, and Hampton. As a successful scout he had no superior in the army, and on all important and hazardous expeditions, Stuart and Hampton called on him to execute them; and he did it successfully. His fame was not confined to our own army, but extended to that of the enemy. The foe in the valley dreaded him as much as they did our own chieftain, Mosby. Mosby had been for a long time anxious to have Baylor attached to his command. There was no way he could be had without promoting him to a Captaincy. He was already a First Lieutenant in the regular army, and if he resigned was liable to conscription. So this company was organised especially for him; and how worthy did he prove himself to lead brave men into battle! His first foray on the enemy will attest that. After the election of officers and appointment of non-commissioned officers, Mosby told Baylor to go out and see what he could do.

Baylor ordered his men (fifty), "to fall in," and moved off, with the best wishes of Mosby and the other men. The command was then ordered to return to Fauquier, and await further orders. Baylor passed through Snicker's Gap, thence down the Shenandoah River to Rock Ford, when he swam the river, under cover of night, pushed on down the valley, and stormed Bolivar Heights at Harper's Ferry before day, capturing seventy-seven horses and forty-seven prisoners, belonging to Keyes' Loudon Cavalry, without a man of his receiving an injury. Captain Baylor, in this affair, annihilated Keyes, leaving him not a man or a horse; and had Keyes been there, he would have gone up too.

Chapter 40: Mosby Invited to Surrender

It may prove interesting to the searcher after truth, to speak somewhat more in detail of our operations subsequent to the fall of Richmond. Gloom and despondency seemed to hang over the spirits of the people like a pall, notwithstanding the stout heart of our brave leader indulged the last ray of hope that we might yet be free,—that some stone would be cut from the mountain that could roll and carve the road to liberty. Mosby was not a guerilla; the tongue of calumny had made him such. He fought for liberty and independence, and conducted his campaigns not after the fashion of *Don Antonio Espozy Mina*, but as a brave, humane and Christian soldier.

On the 8th of April, the command made a rendezvous at Upperville. Mosby ordered Companies D and H to operate near Fairfax, and with Companies A and B repaired to the Valley, crossing the Blue Ridge at Ashby's Gap, and Shenandoah River at Ab. Ferguson's. After swimming the river, a halt was ordered near Ferguson's. Mosby took John Munson, Hifflebower, and Ed. Hurst, and dashed forth on a scouting expedition during the night and following day. In fact, the men went to work as though our star of destiny was unobscured by the clouds of adversity. John Russell, with seven men, captured and scattered the picket at Berryville, consisting of eight men with horses. Three of the men were killed, and three captured, two escaping, and of the horses seven were taken. The next day, the 9th, Lieutenant Ab. Wrenn, took the detachment up the river, and bivouacked at Bethel Church, returning the following day to Ferguson's.

Mosby having returned, brought tidings of the capture of General Ewell, Custis, Lee, and others at Amelia Court House; but there remained yet a short time in which we could strike; and forthwith each detachment and squad lost no time. Twenty men, under Lieutenant Frank Turner, and twenty under Lieutenant Wrenn, were assigned to the Turnpike, between Berryville and Charlestown. Ed. Hurst went to Bunker Hill with ten men, while Mosby took Company A to Winchester, for the purpose of capturing a supply train from the enemy; but ascertaining that if he captured it (of which he seemed to entertain no doubt), it would be necessary to burn or destroy it, and thus lose the provender, &c., he declined to take it. Hurst and Turner returned without tangible results. Lieutenant Wrenn, however, under the auspices of an inferior guide, was carried into the meshes of the enemy's camp. Speed was then the essential attribute of a good soldier, and was called into requisition; for we fled with inconceivable rapidity. We did not debate the order of our flight, but *went* at once, and plunged across the old Shenandoah at Robinson's. Once safe across, we turned to behold the Yankees on the opposite side indulging in frantic demonstrations at our escape.

In this connection we must not neglect to mention the exploits of the brave Baylor, in Fairfax County, and his portion of our command, who were busy (not as Beast Butler was at New Orleans), but whilst searching for *armed* enemies, were surprised and attacked in the rear by a large force of the Eighth Illinois Cavalry, under Captain Gibson. At the first fire Baylor's charger, which was a wild, unbroken animal, became wholly unmanageable, and went plunging into the woods and across ravines as though ten thousand demons from the lowest realms of perdition were in pursuit. In the skirmish Baylor lost two men killed and five or six captured, including Lieutenant Harney, whose loss was irretrievable.

The Second Squadron had been operating industriously on Northern Neck, under Captain Thomas Richards and Colonel Chapman; and whilst there, Richards embarked with several men in a frail scow, and attempted the capture of two schooners in the bay. They were fired upon by a Yankee gunboat, and so closely pursued that the men were forced, as a *dernier resort*, to jump into the water and swim for dear life, until they reached the shore. It is needless to remark that our man-of-war fell into the hands of the enemy.

After gaining *terra firma*, the remainder of the detachment were collected together under Colonel Chapman, and during his efforts to procure arms for those who had been unfortunate in the Naval Expedition, word came that a detachment of infantry, artillery, and unbleached Yankee cavalry, had been dispatched from Washington, with orders to show no quarter, but drive us into the bay. Colonel Chapman resolved to fight it out, and as the shades of night approached made a charge upon them. In the *mêlée* Captain Samuel Chapman was severely wounded. The roads being in excellent travelling condition, the Yankees returned to Washington early next morning, and reported many daring adventures. Colonel Chapman's men then returned to Fauquier, not to engage in the approaching campaign, but to surrender, and lay down their arms.

Alfred Glascock

On the 13th, a national salute was heard at Winchester, in honour of the Yankee successes and the downfall of our cause. As the sound of each discharge echoed and reverberated through the hills, it fell like the knell of departed glory upon the hearts of our people. On the 14th, General Hancock dispatched a courier to Mosby, inviting his surrender with comrades-in-arms, representing that General Lee, under whose command he was acting, had surrendered his whole army, and that surrender included Mosby and his command, giving a pledge, moreover, that his men should be paroled, and allowed to retain their side arms and horses, that were the private property of the men, but that Mosby himself would not be included in these terms. Mosby did not reply. A second courier came, offering and pledging to Mosby equal and fair terms with the balance of the army. Colonel Mosby was not a stranger to the studied and wanton vituperation of a mercenary press, and the malice and hatred cherished against him by the devotees of a senseless and degrading calumny. He concluded to delay an answer until he could communicate with his government

Alas! man's whole life is a tragedy, and here is the afterpiece. The last act in our drama had been played; the curtain was falling; we had no government. Coercion was indeed a success, and whatever else might be our status, we were now conquered. The government of our choice, which had flourished like a young giant, had been suffocated and crushed.

General Hancock's solicitude for the fate of our command was further developed by a proposition that an officer of equal rank with Mosby would be sent with orders to parole him, and Millwood designated as the point to consummate the business. Colonel Mosby lacked confidence, and postponed the matter. Colonel Chapman, Captain Thomas Richards, Adjutant William Mosby (brother to the colonel), Lieutenant John Russell, and Surgeon Montero, visited, by special leave the headquarters of General Hancock, at Winchester. Each of these gentlemen will in after life recur to their kind reception and hospitable entertainment at the hands of General Hancock and his staff, with the most profound feelings of gratitude. Much anxiety and curiosity was manifested to see and converse with them, and they spent the whole Sabbath very pleasantly at the general's headquarters.

General Hancock revoked the order outlawing Colonel Mosby. A suspension of hostilities for ten days was agreed upon, and Colonel Mosby was allowed to confer with the authorities, fully, and learn the real desire of all good and brave men as to his future treatment. The lawless *banditti*, and cowardly, stay-at-home, white-cravat enemy, he knew would not entertain propositions for him to return to peaceful pursuits unmolested. He desired to know fully and fairly if the government at Washington would receive his surrender in good faith as a finality, first to learn explicitly their terms, and then prepare to comply, and perform his part without reservation. There was an ominous Board of Military Justice, located in Washington, whose inquisitions were a novelty in modern civilization, and here was the rock on which many a poor unarmed Confederate, it was feared, would split. Their crimes were the more revolting because of their hypocritical pretence about *justice* and the public weal in their trials and semi-barbarous murders, their ex parte, manufactured, second-hand, newspaper evidence, their higher-law convictions, and their sanctimonious abuses of their victims, made it much more desirable with brave and honest men, to die with arms in their hands on the field of battle, than to be murdered by such a tribunal.

All the officers with whom Colonel Mosby conferred during the interim, were gentlemen, and who honoured the uniform they wore, with great unanimity promised protection, but could not promise definitely, at that time, what would be the conduct toward him by this Board of Military Justice, so-called.

During the pendency of negotiations, the father of General Torbert visited headquarters at Winchester, and to gratify the earnest wish of the old gentleman, Colonel Mosby granted him an interview at Millwood. He expected to see a rough, uncouth *demi*-savage in the person and manners of Colonel Mosby, and was rather abashed when he was introduced to a Lilliputian, physically,—one whose easy and unobtrusive bearing impressed his visitor of his rare qualities, his accomplishments, and gentlemanly deportment. Still the old gentleman seemed not to be able to overcome his prejudice and fears, and urged Mosby, with much earnestness and feeling, not to harm his son. Mosby having failed to obtain reliable assurances from the Military Commission at Washington, at length ordered his whole command to meet him at Salem.

Chapter 41: Mosby Takes the Oath

The men drawn up in line for the last time in the streets of Salem, calmly considered the fact that they must sever forever the cords which had so long bound their destinies in one common cause. It needed not the hand of the painter or poet to picture our emotions; they shone forth from every countenance, and spoke from every eye.

The crisis had come; this ordeal could not be ignored; the trials of the war were severe, but this cup contained the concentrated bitterness of all our trials.

Adjutant William Mosby read to the command the following *farewell address*:

Headquarters 43 Va. Bat. Vol. Cavalry,
Fauquier Co. VA., April 21, 1865.

Soldiers:

I have summoned you together for the last time. The vision we have cherished for a free and independent country has vanished, and that country is now the spoil of a conqueror. I disband your organisation in preference to surrendering to our enemies. I am no longer your commander. After an association of more than two eventful years, I part from you with a just pride in the fame of your achievements, and a grateful recollection of your generous kindness to myself: and now, at this moment of bidding you a final *adieu*, accept the assurance of my unchanging confidence and regard. Farewell.

J. S. Mosby.

The common sense and eloquent simplicity of this address, with the information it conveyed, was received by the men as the fond mother receives the announcement that her offspring has departed; its words were watched as we would watch and gaze upon the form of some dear one whose life was giving out its last ebbing pulsations; and then as each man grasped the honest hand of his brave leader, and pronounced the fatal word *farewell*, all eyes were moistened with tears of affection and sorrow. No one knew what was to be the fate of him who had just addressed us.

During the two succeeding days, Colonel Chapman and the greater portion of the officers and men visited Winchester, and were naturalised upon their native soil, and then returned to their respective homes.

Major Richards and Adjutant Mosby visited Amherst County on a mission of reconciliation and reconstruction. They there learned that General Joe Johnson had surrendered his command, and that the tide of war was rapidly flowing into peaceful channels.—Divested of all misgiving as to the final issue, they returned to Fauquier, and accepted the parole.

In the meantime, Colonel Mosby put himself in full communication with the government at Washington, and undertook to comply with President Johnson's proclamation, if the government would give him a *quietus*, and full receipt for all dues and demands, political, civil, military, and financial. The momentous question was decided in the affirmative, and the government, after mature deliberation, accepted in a spirit of amity his proposition; and accordingly he returned to his allegiance by subscribing the prescribed oath. There were many men professing humanity and Christianity, and even styling themselves patriots *par excellence*, who thirsted for the blood of this noble man. Among such creatures, whose virus poisoned the atmosphere, were many persons who had never been injured or harmed by Mosby or his men; but they prayed for an opportunity to bathe their hands in his blood, and to take his life would have been esteemed a most refined luxury. Notwithstanding this fact was well known to the Virginia hero, after taking the oath, he laid aside his arms and visited Charlottesville, and other points, sometimes *incog*, and occasionally he made himself known to his former foes.

During a visit to the University, a Yankee accosted him, and asked him if he knew Mosby, the guerilla, and requesting him to describe the individual. He then dwelt with ecstasy upon the fact that a reward of ten thousand dollars had been offered for his capture, and wished to undertake the contract, and gain the reward. Mosby informed the *blood* speculator that he had seen the individual in question, but could not gratify him by giving him a reliable description. Mosby then mounted his horse, and went to Elijah Murray's house, about a mile distant. There he remained a few minutes, and departed for his father's in Amherst. He had scarcely got out of sight, when two hundred reward-hunters, calling themselves soldiers, dashed up to Murray's house and demanded Mosby as their prisoner. Their language on the occasion was not very select, nor by any means chaste, and the originality of their anathemas gave graphic evidences that they felt no personal risk in their undertaking. Every nook and corner was overhauled, and the outhouses, stables, negro quarters, sheds, &c., underwent a thorough search.

These modern humanitarians, who, no doubt, had entertained numerous weak minded dupes at church-meetings, with most heart rending accounts of the slave lash, and the brutalities of the "Slave Oligarchy," land pirates, horse thieves, &c., like Tam O'Shanter's wife, nursed their wrath to keep it warm, and were slightly enraged at the disappointment. A daughter of Mr. Murray, who was an invalid, had just entered the carriage at the side door, and was about departing for an evening drive, when several *patriots* rode up and shouted, "there's our game." The young lady, and the carriage, of course, had to be subjected to their *gentle* questions and searching gaze, and after an officer had removed her veil, the command retired with great *éclat*, in their usual good order.

When our hero reached his father's, he learned that General Gregg and Colonel Duncan, of the United States Army, had honoured the family with a visit. They spoke of having a fighting acquaintance with Colonel Mosby, complimented him in very flattering terms, and expressed a warm desire to form his acquaintance. General Gregg, like a true patriot, soldier, and gentleman, offered old Mr. Mosby any protection he desired. On reaching home, Colonel Mosby expressed his gratitude at this manifestation of fraternal kindness, but he was forced by necessity, to forego the pleasure of returning the visit. At night he remained with a relative, William, Hamilton Mosby, and daring the day, spent most of his time at his father's.

During one of his first visits in this neighbourhood after the surrender, the garrison at Lynchburg were advised, doubtless by some "*intelligent contraband*" that the brave cavalier was stopping with his father. Immediately an expedition of twenty-five men, led by a lieutenant, departed under the sable protection of night to win unfading laurels by his capture, albeit the moving cause was the ten thousand dollars, and visions of greenbacks danced through their heads. They reached a point within one mile of the house of Colonel Mosby's father, when a courier from General Gregg's headquarters overtook the party, with orders for their immediate return. They turned back, not however, without indulging in some trite phrases about "copperhead," traitor, rebel sympathizer, &c., &c. The demon of avarice continued to rage in the hearts of wicked men, and prowling bands were covertly scouring the country to such an extent, that General Gregg deemed it necessary to place a guard at the bridge across James River, with orders to allow no egress or ingress, unless the party held a pass, or his business was known.

Many incidents such as these go to make up the epilogue to the grand tragedy which had just been played. The acts of bad men sometimes served as a foil to set off the noble deeds of other men. Whilst Colonel Mosby now enjoys the seclusion of his home in Warrenton, Fauquier County, his grateful recollections of the kind services rendered him by the true soldiers of the Yankee Army, will be cherished by him. as the happiest emotions of his life.

The capture of Bolivar Heights, the action at Hamilton, and a few unimportant skirmishes, were the closing acts of the eventful scenes through which this hardy band had passed. Our boys, at the beginning of their campaign, did not have the glittering gems of wealth to lure them, nor the certainty of success to invite them onward; but actuated solely and honestly by inborn love for liberty, they bade adieu to the comforts and luxuries of home, and embarked their fortunes, honour, and lives in the sacred struggle for human freedom.

The capture of Richmond, the surrender of Generals Lee and Johnson, and the capture of our chief executive, thoroughly completed the work of subjugation. It then became our imperative duty, as faithful, humane, and honest soldiers, to contemplate the solemn task of coming under the yoke of the old government, in a restored and unbroken Union of the States. Our men, not only as a body, but individually, at once turned their attention to the proper duties of good, law-abiding citizens. In proportion as each man had previously displayed activity and engaged in daring exploits for the *"lost cause"* he seemed to run to the opposite extreme, in adapting himself to the new order of things.

Mosby and his men never evinced the slightest vindictive feeling on the subject of reconstruction. They seemed willing, in good faith, to accept the arbitrament of the sword as deciding the issue against them. We speak for ourselves, as well as the command, that however much against our wish the tide of battle has turned, in common honesty and fairness we must adopt the axiom as true, *"once in the Union, always in the Union"* Its truth has been sealed by the blood of nearly half a million brave hearts. The problem of disintegration and the establishment of two governments with separate laws and distinct powers, has been definitely solved. Some of us contended that we were right, by virtue of an inherent right of revolution; others believed in the abstract right of secession; while another class denied the power or right of the general government to coerce a sovereign State, and upon this theory took the Declaration of Independence as their *magna charta*; but whatever might be the ruling motives, all united to resist oppression from the dominant faction in the North.

The primary issue of the war upon the part of our enemies was, *"the Union" an unbroken Unio*n; and relying upon these professions, we were willing upon our surrender to recognise the hand of fate, frankly and honestly to acknowledge our mistake, that we had *not* been out of the Union during the four years of war, but that the Government of the United States is one, and must be as it was, minus the institution

William R. Smith

of slavery. It is a well settled fact, both in theory as well as practice, that the primary object of all just governments under the aegis of civilization, is to impart the greatest amount of domestic tranquillity and happiness to the greatest number of people: we vainly indulged in the flattering belief that it was to be,

> *A union of hearts, a union of hands,*
> *A union that no one can sever;*
> *A union of lakes, a union of lands,*
> *The American Union forever.*

The axiom "*that all just and free governments are founded in the consent of the governed,*" was finally ignored, when the last gun was fired, and with feelings of hope and confidence, we trusted in the magnanimity of a conquering foe. Speeches, proclamations, military orders, inaugural addresses, newspaper editorials, and private discussions with our prisoners during the struggle, had led us and the world to believe that the war was waged by the so-called Republican partisans, in good faith and honesty, to restore the Union and the dear old flag. In this we have been disappointed, as well as in our dreams of independence.

Partisan Life with Col. John S. Mosby

Contents

Preface — 175
Partisan Life with Colonel Mosby — 179
Appendix — 510

Dedication

TO

MRS. GENERAL HOWARD, MRS. J. HANSON THOMAS, MRS. JOHN H. B. LATROBE, MRS. JAMES HODGES, MRS. SAMUEL K. GEORGE, MRS. A. DUBOIS EGERTON, MRS. ROBERT H. CARR, MRS. RICHARD NORRIS, Jr., MRS. THOS. MURDOCH, MRS. BULLOCK, MRS. DR. C. JOHNSTON, MRS. CHARLES HOFFMAN, MRS. CHARLES J. BAKER, MRS. LURMAN, MRS. RYAN, MRS. ANDREW REID, MRS. PEYTON HARRISON, MRS. C. HUGHES ARMISTEAD, MRS. J. S. GITTINGS, MRS. CHARLES HOWARD, MRS. WM. GEO. READ, MRS, ISABELLA BROWN, MRS. THOS. T. HUTCHINS, MRS. GEO. PATTERSON, MRS. WM. HENRY NORRIS, MRS. E. LAW ROGERS, MRS. DR. JAS. A. STUART, MRS. GEO. W. WEBB, MRS. E. M. GREENWAY, MRS. BENJ. E. CATOR, MRS. J. HARMAN BROWN, MRS. JOHN MERRYMAN, MRS. T. PARKIN SCOTT, MRS. GEO. M. GILL, MRS. R. H. MITCHELL, MRS. THOS. C. JENKINS, MRS. NEALE, MRS. MATHIAS, MRS. WM. R. HODGES, MRS. CHARLES TIERNAN, MRS. SAMUEL W. SMITH, MRS. BAYARD SMITH, MRS. JAMES WILSON, MRS. WINN, MISS EMILY HARPER, MISS DORA HOFFMAN, MISS. FRICK, MISS MARY GRACE, MISS LAURA ROBINSON, MISS FLORENCE PATTERSON, MISS LOUISA HOFFMAN, MISS NANNIE HOWARD,

And other Noble Ladies of Baltimore.

As a testimonial not unworthy of the noble sympathy which, during the late war, under the most trying circumstances, you displayed for the cause of justice and truth, I dedicate to you the history of one of the most brilliant and devoted heroes which those stormy times produced—Mosby—a young man who, rising by the native force of genius and courage from the obscure position of a private soldier, with a command of his own creation, at no time numbering more than a few hundred kindred spirits, planted himself in a district abandoned to the occupation of the enemy, and, besides capturing a multitude of prisoners and destroying many millions of public property, kept in a defensive attitude, according to their own admission, thirty-five thousand of their troops, which would otherwise have been employed on the active theatre of war. But this was not all. More than once, with his band of followers, he compelled the invading armies to relinquish actual and projected lines of communication, to fall back from advanced positions, and if we may credit the assertion of the Federal Secretary of War, occasioned the loss by the enemy of an important battle.

Such deeds deserve the pen of History; and when recorded on her scrolls—though in a manner far below the merit of the subject or the dignity of this occasion—are worthy to be laid at your feet, ladies of Baltimore.

This mode of defensive warfare, as original as it proved effective, deserves to be understood both in its principles and details, the mode of execution in war, as in every other practical science, being of the first importance to success. With this object kept constantly in view, I have observed a great particularity in the relation of what may appear to some minor details, as they constitute a part of the system of defensive warfare which it is the purpose of this book to develop and explain.

By the advocates of rectitude and justice in every age and country, by all the lovers of good and haters of evil, let this matchless chief be remembered, for he has invented, and in arms developed, a mode by which, in a more auspicious era, mankind may be enabled to defend their homes and their altars against those wasting and bloody conquerors who murder the independence of nations.

My advantages in composing this work have been unusual; my diligence has been great, but it remains for you to declare the measure of success.

   Respectfully,

              John Scott,
            of Fauquier, late C. S. A.

Historic truth ought to be no less sacred than religion.
      Napoleon III., *Life of Caesar.*

There is game in every bush if we will beat for it.
      Sir Isaac Newton. Dedication

Preface

As soon as the surrender of the army of General Lee rendered it probable that the sanguinary contest which for four years had raged between the hostile sections was about to be brought to a close, and it was understood that I was to undertake the laborious task of writing the history of the Partisan Battalion, its origin, its growth, its exploits, I set about collecting the facts which were to compose my checkered narrative. Of these, very imperfect records had been kept, and they had to be obtained by interrogating the memories of the actors in the scenes which I proposed to commemorate.

I had conceived and drafted the Partisan Ranger Law, shown it to Secretary Randolph, and, with his approbation, had carried it before the Joint Military Committee of the two houses of Congress, whose chairman was Mr. Miles, of South Carolina. I found the table of the committee covered with all kinds of projects relating to the irregular service. Mine was preferred by the committee, reported to the two houses, and, without debate, became a law: Colonel Mosby has often told me that upon that basis rested the superstructure which he afterward reared, and that it was but just that I should write the history of the command which vindicated the correctness of the principles of the Partisan Ranger Law. The principle of that law is but the application of the prize principle of nautical warfare to land war, yet it was one, I believe, which had not been made before.

Amid the many failures which occurred in the Confederate service in the application of this law, Mosby alone brought to the work all the high qualities necessary to command success and write his name so high upon the column of Fame.

I was born in the district of country which constituted his field of exploits, and have, in consequence of a familiar and wide-spread acquaintance with its inhabitants, enjoyed peculiar advantages in collecting from them incidents and anecdotes with which to enrich and enliven my pages. Regarding my task in the light of a trust, I set about its execution with a diligence which has not deserted me at any time. My mode was to visit all the officers and men of the command to whom I had access, and from their lips to obtain full accounts of all they did, or knew to be done. These accounts, under appropriate headings, I reduced to writing, until my notes had increased to many volumes. From many of the officers and men of the battalion whom I could not visit, I received voluminous notes, which, together with the facts and explanations furnished by the Partisan chief himself, have enabled me to compose a full and authentic history.

To enable me the more perfectly to attain this end, I resided in Colonel Mosby's family for some time, and from that central point rode with him to inspect the most interesting localities. The following letter, addressed to me by him, will display to the reader the lively interest which he took in the prosecution of my work, and how ready, at all times, he was to render me assistance. The intimate association which thence ensued enabled me, by a strong and steady light, to peruse that great man's character and discover the springs of those actions with which he astonished friend and confounded foe.

Leesburg, January 10th, 1866.

Dear Major,—The bearer of this letter is James G. Wiltshire, who was a lieutenant in my command. He visits you at my request, that you may avail yourself of the fund of anecdote and adventure which he possesses—for his dash and spirit of enterprise led him to participate in all the prominent events connected with the command in which he could, with truth and propriety, say, '*Quorum magna pars fui.*'

I have no doubt but that he will add much to your stock of information. I am very anxious for you to accompany him to Clarke and Jefferson, for I consider it all-important to the success of your work that there should be great accuracy in the description of localities which you expect to make historical. You must, by all means, see John Russell, who lives near Berryville, for he saw more service than any man in the command, as he always acted as guide in the valley. I have just received a letter from him saying he was anxious to see you. Russell and Wiltshire could make every thing plain to you; besides, you could see a great many persons whom you could put on inquiry to assist you. You must, by all means, go to Charlestown, and visit my charming friends at the Bower; also those at the vineyard, near Berryville, where you will meet with John Esten Cooke. George Saddler, of Charlestown, can supply you with a good stock of anecdote. He was in my confidence, is a man of great shrewdness, and exerted himself to get information for me. Your book can not be complete without seeing him. You must make a visit to Duffield Station, to see how we gathered them there; to Berryville, to see how we mauled them there; to Cabletown, where Richards destroyed Blazer; to Millwood.

By making one such visit, you will put everybody to thinking and remembering what they know of us. You may depend upon it, you will find this unexplored country an El Dorado.

I am now in Leesburg, *under arrest*, I was ordered yesterday, by the commanding officer here, to report by what authority I was in Leesburg. I reported 'that I had been in the habit of coming here for two years, and didn't know anybody that had a better right.' He put me under arrest, and I am now paroled to the limits of the town, to await orders from Winchester. If I am released, as soon as I get to housekeeping come down and make my house your home.

Yours, truly,   John S. Mosby.

Major John Scott.

With the mass of information thus accumulated, I retired, toward the close of the summer of 1866, to compose my varied narrative, having been delayed in its execution by frequent indispositions and one violent attack of illness.

Before I conclude this preface, it is only just to say that the names of many members of the battalion, of signal merit, do not appear in this book, for the sufficient reason that they were not associated in a particular manner with events, the relation of which would add variety to my page; or, to borrow Mosby's language, "You could not call the roll in every fight."

Truth is the religion of the historian, and I feel conscious that I have not been governed by partiality or prejudice, and that if I have not adorned, at least I have not dishonoured the shrine of the Historic Muse by the most odious of all vices—falsehood.

The Author.

Philadelphia, May 14th, 1867.

Partisan Life with Colonel Mosby

CHAPTER 1: HOW MOSBY BECAME A PARTISAN.

Upper Fauquier, January 2nd, 1863.
My dear Percy,—You have doubtless received ere this my letter giving an account of the decisive Battle of Fredericksburg, accompanied by a rude drawing of the battlefield, which, I trust, has enabled you to appreciate that fight. Since that time I have accompanied the gallant and enterprising General Stuart from the camp of the Confederate army, near Fredericksburg, on an expedition to Dumfries, and, strangely enough, find myself now with a small detachment of cavalry which he has left behind him, under the command of Captain Mosby, as he is generally called, though his military rank is, I believe, entirely honorary.

My acquaintance with Captain Mosby was begun in the earlier stages of the war, and since that time I have been often associated with him, particularly on some of the daring scouts which he has made, and which have excited the admiration and won the applause of General Lee himself. Mosby, I am sure, is a remarkable man. He has often explained to me in conversation a mode of Partisan warfare which he is persuaded, if fully developed, would enable the Confederate government to cripple the invading armies of the enemy, retard their progress, and ultimately enable the opposing forces to overwhelm them with, disaster. He thinks the most vulnerable point of every invading army is in its rear—an opinion which he formed from his own observations on the communications of the Northern army.

In order to afford a practical illustration of the value of this opinion, and doubtless to gratify, at the same time, his thirst for action, and satisfy an honourable desire for fame, he has proposed to General Stuart, from time to time, to allow him to take a small detail of men, and with them to operate in the rear of the enemy and upon his communications, but until now his proposition had met with no favour.

However, as Stuart was returning from his ineffectual raid upon Dumfries, he called, in company with several of us, to make a visit to Miss Laura Ratcliffe, who resides near Frying-pan Church, in Fairfax County. As our party rose to bid this lady farewell, I was surprised and pleased to hear the general address her in the following language:

> You are all such good Southern people through this section, I think you deserve some protection, so I shall leave Captain Mosby, with a few men, to take care of you. I want you to do all you can for him. He is a great favourite of mine and a brave soldier, and, if my judgment does not err, we shall soon hear something surprising from him.

We were soon again upon the march, with the column headed toward Middleburg, in the county of Loudon, on the Little River Turnpike, very near to the Fauquier line. I was riding alone, between the advance guard and the head of the column, when I was joined by Mosby, who, in high spirits, informed me that at last fortune had begun to smile on him, for Stuart had promised to leave him with a detail of *nine* men to operate on the outposts and communications of the enemy. He invited me to join him, promising, as an inducement, an adventurous life. I consented, and am now in Upper Fauquier, with Captain Mosby and his nine men.

My letters henceforth will contain but little of the movements of large bodies of troops, and nothing of political events, but I hope to compensate you with accounts of skirmishes, surprises, and personal adventures.

Chapter 2: Mosby's Raid on General Percy Wyndham's Outposts.

Upper Fauquier, January 18th, 1863.

Dear Percy,—Since the evacuation of Manassas by General Johnston in the spring of 1862, the enemy have kept at Fairfax Courthouse a military force composed of infantry, cavalry, and artillery, as an outpost of Washington City. The cavalry consists of a brigade, which is composed of the Fifth New York, the First Vermont, the Eighteenth Pennsylvania, and the First Virginia regiments, commanded by Colonel Percy Wyndham, formerly, it is said, an officer in the English Army. This brigade maintains a chain of picket-posts, within a half mile of each other, from Centreville to Dranesville, and from that place to the

Potomac River, a distance of twenty miles. On this line of outposts Mosby began his operations.

On the 10th of January we started from the neighbourhood of Middleburg for Fairfax County, and proceeded to the house of a farmer who lives very near to Herndon Station, on the Loudoun and Hampshire Railroad. As we approached the dwelling, Mosby observed a man pass rapidly out of the back door into the pines which cover the rear of the house with their dense growth. We found no little difficulty in convincing the farmer of our Confederate character, for in Fairfax a gray uniform often conceals a Yankee. As soon, however, as his doubts were removed, he became more cordial, and, by a peculiar whistle, called from the pines the man to whom I have gust referred. He seemed about thirty years of age; his person was short and thickset, and he had a shock of white hair, which stood erect in unrestrained independence. His whole appearance was that of a wild man, but his eyes, ever in motion, indicated watchfulness and an intelligent mind. His name is John Underwood, whose value as a guide Mosby's penetrating eye soon discovered, for he is distinguished, above all other men whom I have known, by a wonderful faculty which enables him to thread with unerring certainty, in the darkest night, the intricate forests and tangled brushwood of the country in which he lives. Without much difficulty Mosby prevailed upon Underwood to join him, and, being thus furnished with a guide, prepared at once to strike the enemy near Herndon Station, where they had a cavalry picket.

His small command being dismounted, they were conducted at night to the rear of the Federals, whose forms were distinctly visible by the ruddy light of their campfire. A pistol-shot from Mosby was the signal for attack, and we rushed upon the picket, which was composed of seven men, of whom we wounded one, and captured six unhurt. With his prisoners and captured horses Mosby retreated deeper into the pines, where he paroled the men and divided the horses. A fine horse, with its equipments, was, together with a pair of cavalry pistols, allotted to his first recruit, John Underwood, who was overjoyed at this unexpected stroke of fortune.

Two nights afterward, with Underwood still for our guide, our leader, with the same party, started in search of other game, which he found a few miles from Herndon Station, where Cub Run flows across the Little River Turnpike. Our former mode of attack was adopted, the picket being surprised and captured from the rear, the two vedettes alone effecting their escape. Five prisoners and as many horses, with cavalry equipments, rewarded this enterprise.

Not content with this success, Mosby determined to signalize the night by still another. At Frying-pan Church there was a cavalry picket of ten men, who had already been apprised, as we afterward learned, of our presence in the neighbourhood. We found two of their number posted as vedettes, while the others were asleep in a small house hard by, with a sentinel stationed at the door. When he had arrived within a few hundred yards of this place, Mosby ordered his prisoners to dismount and stretch themselves on the ground. Their horses were then led away and concealed in the woods. This done, he left one man to guard the prisoners, while with the rest of his party he approached the picket-post from the direction of the Federal camp. The sentinel, taking us for a patrol, allowed us to come within a few steps of the house before he gave the order to halt. Mosby then ordered the house to be surrounded and pistols to be fired through the thin weather-boarding upon the inmates. Gunshots were returned, and one of the assailants, in a loud tone, ordered up the infantry—a stale and childish device, as our leader appeared to think, for he called to the Yankees that his party was not larger than their own, but, at the same time, demanded an unconditional surrender. It was at once made, and we returned in triumph to Loudoun County, taking with us our twofold captures, amounting to thirteen prisoners and a corresponding number of cavalry horses, with their equipments.

The next morning our party, re-enforced by the prisoners, took breakfast at the hotel in Middleburg, and soon after the latter were paroled and dismissed to their Mends, highly pleased with the indulgent manner in which they had been treated. The horses and arms were then divided among the captors.

I regret to add, as a concluding paragraph to my letter, that we have to return to the army, for Mosby yesterday informed me that, not feeling authorised to keep the detail longer on this detached service, he had ordered the men to return to their command, while in person he would report to General Stuart the result of his recent operations. I was not aware until then of the temporary nature of our stay in this district, and feel sadly disappointed at this abrupt termination of our Partisan service.

CHAPTER 3: COLONEL WYNDHAM DRIVEN OUT OF MIDDLEBURG

Upper Fauquier, February 8th, 1863.

Dear Percy,—You will be surprised to receive a letter from me dated again from Upper Fauquier, for, contrary to expectation, Mosby is here again on detached service in rear of the enemy.

As soon as we reached the cavalry headquarters, near Fredericksburg, Mosby proceeded at once to Stuart's tent, where he recounted his performances since they had parted at Middleburg. The general was so well pleased at the recital that. General L. Armistead coming in, he requested the enterprising scout to repeat the account, and then ordered him to retire to the office of his adjutant general, and make a full report in writing.

Mosby then said to Stuart that, with a detail of fifteen cavalry, he would undertake, in two months' time, to compel the enemy in Fairfax to abandon their advance line of outposts, and give up ten miles of country.

"Very well," said the general, "let it be so; "we will destroy them in detail."

The future now loomed up before Mosby, and he felt, he said, like Columbus when, having been often repulsed, he obtained, from the favour of Queen Isabella, three small ships with which to explore the mysterious deep, and develop the idea over which he had so long brooded.

On the 18th of January, with a detail of fifteen men from the First Virginia Cavalry, then camped at King William Courthouse, Mosby started again for Upper Fauquier, and, crossing the Rappahannock at Fox's Mill, we soon arrived at Warrenton. As our little band marched through the town, we were stopped by the citizens, who expressed surprise when they heard that we had come to make war, for, they said, we resembled rather the retinue of an embassador, or a company of missionaries, than a band of warriors. After leaving Warrenton the command was dispersed, with orders to rendezvous on the 28th instant at Mount Zion Church, on the Little River Turnpike, a mile and a half east of Aldie. This interval of eight days was not, however, wasted by Mosby; for, while his men and horses were being recruited at the houses of citizens, he himself was occupied in collecting information about the position of the enemy, and in gaining a more accurate knowledge of the country in which his operations are to be carried on.

In pursuance of orders, the command met Mosby, and marched down the Little River Turnpike, but turned in the direction of Fryingpan Church, where we captured a patrol of two men, and then proceeded toward Old Chantilly Church, where we regained the turnpike. At the church was stationed a picket of nine men from the Eighteenth

Pennsylvania Cavalry, which our leader determined to attack.

Covering his movements by the pines, he formed his men, and moved cautiously forward, for, contrary to his former plan of attack, he decided to assail the picket in front. Taking with him one man, Mosby dashed forward and captured the two vedettes without resistance. The command then charged the reserve, using at the same time their revolvers. The fight was a short one, and bloodless but for the wounding of one man, who was shot by Mosby when attempting to make his escape. With eleven prisoners, and their arms, horses, and equipments, we returned in high spirits to Middleburg, where, as before, the prisoners were paroled and the spoil divided.

Roused by our assaults upon his outposts. Colonel Wyndham, with a body of two hundred cavalry, pursued us the following day, and arrived at night at Middleburg, denouncing, on his march, vengeance against the guerrillas and their adventurous chief, as well as against the citizens among whom they found aid and protection. As Wyndham drew near to the town he passed the house of Mr, Lorman Chancellor, at which Mosby and his devoted friend Beattie were asleep. Being roused by a negro with this information, they were soon in the saddle, and having by the morning collected seven of his men, Mosby entered Middleburg as Colonel Wyndham was leaving it.

He boldly charged the enemy's rear, killing one and capturing three of their number, and then retired to the farther end of the village. He there stopped and allowed the Yankees to shoot at him as he sat upon his horse, a piece of temerity which greatly astonished the citizens, but which was not without its good effect upon the men. The rest of his command having been brought up—for Colonel Wyndham had entered Middleburg with only one hundred of his men—he ventured to open an attack. Before the vigour of this onset Mosby was compelled to retreat, losing Beattie and two others, who were taken prisoners.

As soon as the enemy halted in the pursuit, our leader, with one man, returned to a hill-top but a few hundred yards distant from the head of the Federal column. Colonel Wyndham, believing them to be members of his own command who had pressed too far in the front, dispatched a courier to order them back; but Mosby received the order very quietly, and sent the messenger back with the reply that *he couldn't come yet.*

Soon after the return of this expedition to the Federal camp there appeared in the Northern papers a very animated account of the victory which Colonel Wyndham had achieved at Middleburg over Stuart's cavalry.

In consequence of Colonel Wyndham's threats to burn the town of Middleburg, and ravage the country between it and Fairfax Courthouse if our attacks upon his outposts were repeated, a petition from certain prominent citizens was presented to Mosby, requesting him to withdraw from their midst. But it drew from him only the following spirited and conclusive reply:

Fauquier County, February 4th, 1863.

Gentlemen,—I have just received your petition requesting me to discontinue my warfare on the Yankees, because they have threatened to burn your town and destroy your property in retaliation for my acts. Not being prepared for any such degrading compromise with the Yankees I unhesitatingly refuse to comply. My attacks on scouts, patrols, and pickets, which have provoked this threat, are sanctioned both by the custom of war and the practice of the enemy, and you are at liberty to inform them that no such clamour shall deter me from employing whatever legitimate weapon I can most efficiently use for their annoyance.

The day after this affair with Wyndham our command was convened at Middleburg for the purpose of striking again the Federal outposts. A deep snow had fallen, followed by a chilling rain; but, undeterred by the inclemency of the weather, Mosby proceeded in the direction of Fairfax, but stopped for supper at the house of his friend, Mat Lee. Here we left the turnpike and went toward Frying-pan, halting at the house of Ben Hatton. Ben had that day returned from a visit to the Yankees, to whom, according to the warning which Mosby received, he had been giving information about his movements; so Ben was given the choice between a visit to Castle Thunder, or guiding us to the Federal picket-post, which was not far distant. Without the least hesitation he consented to act as guide, a service for which his recent visit had well qualified him.

The picket stood on the Lawyer's Road, near Tyler Davis's house, and consisted of twelve men from the Eighteenth Pennsylvania Cavalry. A patrol of two men passed between this picket-post and another half a mile distant once in every hour. Our men, being concealed near the road along which the patrol passed, succeeded in capturing them both, and then sent them under guard to the point where our horses had been left. Guided by the light of the Yankee camp fires, Mosby ordered the men to creep close to the picket, and then charge. The result was that the Yankees were all captured without resistance. Two mounted vedettes, however, attempted to escape, but Hurst and Keys, mounted each on a captured horse, followed close upon them, killing one and taking the other prisoner. The capture had scarcely been effected and the prisoners carried off when a squadron of Federal cavalry reached the spot. It had been stationed a short distance off by Colonel Wyndham's order, in anticipation of our assault upon the pickets, but failed, as I have said, to come up in time. Thus was Colonel Wyndham a second time foiled in his efforts to catch his harassing enemy.

In his report of his operations, which he sent to General Stuart, up to February 4th, accompanied by the correspondence between the citizens of Middleburg and himself, Mosby remarked of this last affair: "He set a very nice trap a few days ago to catch me in, but, contrary to Colonel Wyndham's expectations, I brought it off with me."

In this report Mosby proposed to Stuart to make a dash with the brigade then lying in Culpepper upon Dranesville. He said:

> In Fairfax County there are five or six regiments of cavalry; there are about three hundred at Dranesville, who are isolated from the rest of the command, so that nothing would be easier than to capture the whole force. I have harassed them so much that they do not keep their pickets over half a mile from camp. They have no artillery.

But, for some unexplained reason, this plan, which appeared to be so feasible, was not acted upon.

Chapter 4: Mosby Saved by an Angel

Upper Fauquier, February 24th, 1863.

Dear Percy,—The issue which was raised between certain of the citizens in and around Middleburg and our leader has been determined by General Stuart, and Mosby is more firmly established than before in Loudoun and Fauquier, unless, indeed. Colonel Wyndham can, by craft or force, expel him; for, after highly commending his late operations. General Stuart, in a letter to Mosby, concluded by saying:

> I heartily wish you great and increasing success in the glorious career on which you have entered.

The 7th of February had been designated for our assemblage at Ball's Mill, on Goose Creek, not far from the Loudoun and Fairfax line. But only five of the men appeared at the rendezvous, six of them having been captured by raiders the night before at a dancing party which they had attended in violation of orders. It was the purpose of Mosby to have renewed the attack on the picket-line in Fairfax, but, hearing of a foraging-party in the neighbourhood, he resolved to follow them. The plunderers, for they were robbers rather than soldiers, had not only taken with them the horses of citizens, which in this war are regarded as contraband, but had stripped such dwelling-houses as lay in their course of all valuables which they could carry off, including silver spoons, jewellery, and the clothing of ladies. They even carried their thieving so far as to deprive Dr. Drake, whom they met on their march, of his medical saddle-bags. When the foragers had reached a point within a few miles of Dranesville, we overtook a party of seven, who had halted to examine their "captures." Throwing ourselves between them and their main body, the spoilers, with their spoil, were without difficulty captured. The former Mosby sent to Richmond to be detained as robbers, but the latter he returned to its owners.

The next day, with eight men, Mosby started again for Fairfax with the intention of striking a picket-post near Frying-pan Church, which proved to be a trap that had been set for him, but from which he was saved by the activity and courage of Miss Laura Ratcliffe. She was informed by a soldier who came to the house to ask for milk that Lieutenant Palmer, of the First Virginia, with a party, had placed himself in the pines, near Frying-pan Church, leaving a few of his men in sight of the road as pickets. He added, "We will surely get Mosby this time. On his next raid he will certainly come by Frying-pan, and it will not be possible for him to escape. I tell you this, though I know you would give Mosby any information in your possession; but, as you have no horses, and the mud is too deep for women folks to walk, you can't tell him; so the next you hear of your 'pet' he will be either dead or our prisoner." After the man left, the ladies wondered what they could do in that emergency.

At last Miss Laura concluded to go across the fields and leave word with the Southern families to watch for Mosby and put him on his guard. While she was at Mr. George Coleman's in execution of this purpose, she beheld from the window a small body of men, and, in company with a lady friend, proceeded to intercept them. But, as she approached, she saw among them so many blue-coats that she feared she had fallen in with a band of Yankees, but was soon relieved from her suspense by John Underwood, who rode up to inquire the news, and was soon followed by Mosby, whom she informed of the ambuscade prepared for him. Not having men enough to justify an attack on Lieutenant Palmer, we turned aside to Herndon Station, where we fell in with a blockade runner, who had just returned from Washington. It was night, and, in an old barn, by the light of a candle, the peddler displayed his goods, and we purchased from him with Federal currency such articles as we desired.

While here, a citizen, who was in the confidence of the Federal authorities both military and civil, apprised Mosby of the position of a picket-post near Dranesville. From the description, John Underwood recognised the spot, which, under the guidance of our skilful pilot, we reached without difficulty. The vedette, as usual, made his escape, but the reserve of fifteen men, together with their horses, arms, and equipments, we captured, and carried in safety to Middleburg. On our arrival we were informed that Alexander Davis, a Union man who lives near Aldie, but who has been compelled by the violence of Southern feeling to take refuge in the Northern army, had been to the neighbourhood with six wagons, guarded ostensibly by eighteen cavalry, but in each of which were concealed twelve infantry from the Bucktail Regiment of Pennsylvania, but, not finding Mosby, had returned to camp with his six wagon-loads of live Yankees. Thus Lieutenant Palmer's second device miscarried.

Chapter 5: Attack at Thompson's Corner

Upper Fauquier, February 28th, 1863.

Dear Percy,— Notwithstanding the capture of almost half of his detail, which I mentioned in my last letter, Mosby's band has, by the process of accretion, almost doubled in number since we left camp, for the fame of his exploits has gone abroad, and adventurous spirits are gathering around him. This attraction has extended even to the camp of the enemy; for the other day, while Mosby was in Middleburg, Sergeant Ames, from the Fifth New York Cavalry, sought admission into our little band. His application created quite a stir among our men, who expressed a violent objection to receiving a Yankee deserter, as they called Ames, into their fellowship. In this objection they were fortified by the sage opinions of the citizens, who gravely shook their heads and talked of treachery.

Deserters are a class necessarily suspected, and the risk of betrayal is one of those dangers which appeals most strongly to the imagination. But Mosby is the last man in the world to be affected by the suspicious fancies of soldier or citizen. Relying rather upon his own penetration, and won by the frank and soldierly bearing of the proposed recruit, he conversed with him about the condition of things in Fairfax, comparing what he heard with the information of which he was already possessed, and about the verity of which he was convinced. The result of the interview was the adoption of Ames into our command; and as he attracted by his antecedents the suspicion, and since, by his courage and fidelity, the admiration and confidence of the men, I will give you a description of his appearance.

He is large and muscular, with determination stamped in every line of his face. His black eye is quick, clear, intelligent, while his bearing is manly, and his manners and conversation are pleasing. Sergeant Ames had been a seafaring man ere he became a soldier, and carries about him all the characteristics of that profession. The cause of his desertion, he said, was the Emancipation Proclamation of President Lincoln, for which he never meant to fight. As soon as the object of the war was changed from the reconstruction of the Union to the abolition of slavery, he regarded his military engagement as annulled.

In addition to his proper command, there is another element, composed of loose and unemployed material, which Mosby is now able to combine and hurl against the invaders of his country. His custom is to advertise, about a week in advance, a meeting to be held at one of his rendezvous, and to it repair those who love adventure or plunder. But the most abundant and useful source from which these temporary recruits are derived is from the members of the regular cavalry at home, on detail or furlough. Hence it is that members of the Black Horse Company, originally recruited from, this county, have so often taken part in our expeditions, and are weaving their history into Mosby's career. Convalescents from the hospitals also will sometimes join him for a single raid; but when the Yankees come in pursuit, as in the case of Colonel Wyndham, they find them languidly stretched on their pallets. These several classes of recruits are called by Mosby his "Conglomerates."

But there is another element of greater durability and value which is gradually forming itself around him, and will constitute, I think, the nucleus of a large and independent command. It is composed of discharged soldiers, youths under the conscript age, and young gentlemen from Maryland, who prefer service under the standard of Mosby to that in the regular army.

Success is the charmed word by which this strange man attracts and embodies the scattered material around him.

But this growing fame has produced an inconvenience of a serious nature. Deserters from the regular army have begun to rally to this new and brilliant standard, under which they may partake of the comforts and pleasures of social life, and at the same time discharge the duties and receive the emoluments of the Partisan soldier. I feared at one time that this evil, more potent than the enemy, would destroy our infant command; but I find Mosby has an uncompromising sense of military honour and duty, which has preserved him in this trial. Instead of allowing his command to become a refuge for deserters, he is, on the contrary, a most efficient ally of the conscript officer. In this way Mosby has obtained the respect and confidence, as well as the admiration of his military superiors and the officials at Richmond.

On the 26th of February, the day after the date of my last letter, we started from Rector's Cross-roads to attack a picket on the by-road at Thompson's Corner, not far from Germantown. During the preceding night a heavy snow had fallen, which by morning had changed into a slow but steady rain. The roads were so deep as to be almost impassable, and any man but Mosby would have been content to remain by the fire. With twenty-seven men he proceeded down the turnpike, and about nightfall struck off in the direction of the proposed place of attack.

Among our band was Sergeant Ames, mounted, but unarmed, for the men, still distrustful of his fidelity, had insisted that this precaution should be taken, and Ames had willingly agreed. As the command was passing near her residence, Mosby stopped to consult his intelligent friend. Miss Ratcliffe, and then resumed his place at the head of the column, which was guided by the unerring Underwood, When within a short distance of Thompson's Corner, our leader was informed by a citizen residing in the vicinity, with a view of dissuading him from making the attack, that the outpost was furnished with a hundred men.

"Well, well," replied Mosby, "if you are right they will suppose that a hundred at least have come to attack them."

The night was very cold, and so dark and rainy that no living wight but John Underwood could have found the route. When he had neared the post, Mosby halted his men that he might ascertain the true strength of the picket, and whether it could be approached in rear; but, foiled in this, he resolved to dismiss stratagem and approach boldly in front, hoping to be mistaken for the patrol coming from Chantilly, Frank Williams and Joe Nelson were ordered to the front, and the column moved on. Strange were our sensations as we pressed forward in the darkness, which was so intense that a man by your side could not be recognised. Soon a voice from the front ordered us to halt, and when Nelson and Williams replied that they were friends, they were allowed by the vedette to approach nearer.

But when he saw them he fired his carbine and retreated rapidly, closely pursued. Our commander at once ordered a charge, and we dashed forward through the mud and snow, ever keeping Nelson and Williams in sight. The reserve were sleeping in an old house on the roadside a short distance off, and toward them the vedette directly retreated. When we arrived at the house the Yankees were, under arms to receive us, and poured a volley into our ranks. The men wavered for an instant, till reassured by the voice of their chief. "Close on them, men," he shouted. The command dashed forward, and the Yankees, fifty in number, fled and scattered in the pines.

The time had come at last for Sergeant Ames to settle all doubts and suspicions with regard to his loyalty to his new commander. All unarmed as he was, he rushed on a mounted soldier, seized him by the collar, and threatened him with immediate death if he did not surrender. He surrendered and delivered up his revolver, his carbine, his sabre, with which Ames plunged into the woods in pursuit of the flying enemy. From that time "Big Yankee" has been a great toast with Mosby's men, and no man doubts now either his loyalty or his courage.

The enemy lost in this midnight encounter a lieutenant and three men killed, five prisoners, besides several wounded. We also trotted off thirty-nine fine horses, which stood saddled and bridled in the pines, and were soon on the return march to Fauquier.

The outpost at Thompson's Corner was but a short distance from the camp of the First New York Cavalry, from which a heavy detail was sent out to intercept us. As soon as our command had reached Rector's Cross-roads, George Slater, of Baltimore, one of the bravest and most trusty men, was sent down the turnpike as far as Middleburg to ascertain if there was a pursuit by the enemy.

In the meantime the Federal detachment had proceeded to a point near Aldie, where they fell in with a citizen, of whom they inquired if he had seen "a horse-thief named Mosby." The citizen laughed at the polished wit, and pointed up the road. Off they dashed, expecting to overtake the "horse-thief" very soon. Thus they continued till they reached Middleburg, beyond which point their horses, from sheer exhaustion, could not proceed. The result of the pursuit was that half of the Yankees returned to their camp leading their lame and jaded

"Close on them men."

animals.

When Slater returned to notify Mosby of the approach of the enemy, he found the rendezvous deserted; for, in his absence, the prisoners had been sent off, the spoil had been divided, and the men had scattered through the country.

Chapter 6: Daring Exploits

Near Upperville, March 3rd, 1863.

Dear Percy,— I shall begin my letter today with narrating a daring personal exploit performed by Sergeant Ames and Walter E. Frankland, of Fauquier, a new recruit. The latter, in company with George Whitescarver, from the same county, attended on foot our recent meeting at Rector's Cross-roads. Whitescarver managed in some way at once to mount himself, but Frankland was not so fortunate. Ames was induced, with Mosby's approbation, to propose to Frankland to enter with him the camp of the Fifth New York, for the purpose of each bringing off an officer's horse. Frankland readily assented, and the two adventurers set forth on foot for the camp, which was then near Germantown, on the turnpike, one mile from Fairfax Court-house.

Having selected the hour of midnight for the execution of their plan, they succeeded in secreting themselves in the bushes within a short distance of the line of sentries. About nine o'clock the lights were extinguished, and soon all was quiet in the camp. But, as midnight approached, and Ames and his companion were preparing to go forth from their hiding place, the bugles in two regimental camps were sounded, and very soon they saw detachments of cavalry from each move off in the direction of Fauquier. When the lights were again extinguished, and the camp was again sunk in repose, the two men crept from their place of concealment, and stealthily crossed the sentry-line. As Ames was familiar with the arrangement of the camp, he proceeded at once to the stalls where the officer's horses were to be found, followed by his companion. They found the guard on duty as usual, but he was engaged in conversation with a soldier, and did not appear to observe them. The Rangers marched boldly into the stable, and, selecting two of the best horses, proceeded at leisure to bridle and saddle them. As soon as this was done, the horses were led forth and mounted, and slowly ridden from the camp. Their riders, once more on the road, soon struck into a gallop, and hastened to inform Mosby of the Federal raiders who had started in search of him.

The cavalry force in Fairfax, commanded by Colonel Wyndham,

is at this time distributed as follows: The Eighteenth Pennsylvania is encamped at ———, the First Virginia and Fifth New York are near German town, as we have seen, while the First Vermont is at Dranesville. This force performs the outpost duty, as well as the scouting and raiding for the artillery and infantry stationed at Fairfax Court-house, under command of Brigadier General Stoughton. Mosby's unremitting and successful attacks render his destruction an object of primary importance to both of these commanders.

In consequence, an expedition of four hundred men, under command of Major Gilmore, was sent on the 2nd of March to Middleburg, and at an early hour entered the town, hoping to surprise some of our men, and perhaps Mosby himself. Failing in this, Major Gilmore captured several old gentlemen, whom he caused to mark time on the streets, and then started on his return march.

Mosby had ordered a meeting of his men on the same day at Rector's Cross-roads, his purpose being again to assail the picket-line; but, as soon as he was informed of Major Gilmore's presence in Middleburg, he withdrew his command a short distance from the turnpike, with the view of falling in behind the raiders and harassing their rear. The sudden return of the Yankees disconcerted this plan, and Mosby approached Middleburg only to ascertain the number of the enemy and the route they had taken. He at once announced his purpose to pursue. The ladies of Middleburg came out and besought him earnestly not to do so, for, they said, "There are Yankees enough to eat you up." But, nothing daunted, our fearless commander started off in pursuit, taking with him seventeen men.

At Aldie we came in sight of a party of the enemy, which we supposed to be Gilmore's rearguard. Some of them were riding from house to house, others had dismounted and were lounging about the streets, while the larger portion were grouped around the door of a mill, engaged in feeding their horses. A charge was immediately ordered, and the Yankees scattered, offering but slight resistance. Some of them sprang to their unbitted horses, some fled to the adjacent mountain, while others concealed themselves in the stone mill and the adjoining buildings.

Mosby was then in undisputed possession of the west end of the village; but, seeing a Federal officer on the other side of Little River, which passes through the town, he inferred that the enemy had rallied, and were preparing for a fight. He ordered Turner to take one man, and proceed in that direction to watch the movement. Turner discovered that Mosby's conjecture was unfounded, and at once attacked the officer, who proved to be Captain Worthington, of the First Vermont Cavalry. The combat was a short hand-to-hand fight, but the Federal officer did not surrender until he had had his horse shot, and had inflicted on his captor a serious wound.

A HAND-TO-HAND FIGHT.

Mosby was still under the belief that he had engaged the rear-guard of Major Gilmore's command, and that the entire column would soon return to attack him. He therefore ordered his men to return to Middleburg, and take with them the prisoners and horses, leaving himself and one other, the only Confederate soldiers in Aldie. Thinking all danger over, three of the Yankees, who had escaped to the mountain, returned to the village and were captured, and sent off under charge of Mosby's companion. Then, for the first time, Mosby learned that the enemy whom he had fought were not Major Gilmore's command, but a party of fifty-nine men from the First Vermont Cavalry, under command of Captain Huttoon, who, at his own request, had been allowed to go on an independent expedition in search of the guerrillas.

In less than two hours from the time we had left Middleburg we had travelled eight miles, and, in an encounter with a greatly superior force, had captured nineteen prisoners, among whom were two captains and twenty-three horses.

In the fight at Aldie Mosby's horse became so unmanageable that he was compelled to leap from the saddle, and allow the animal, which had been recently captured, to rejoin its old friends. At this juncture

Furlong Carter dismounted and offered him his horse, which enabled Mosby to rejoin the command and again enter the combat.

Chapter 7: General Stoughton's Capture by Mosby.

Upper Fauquier, March 15th, 1863.

Dear Percy,—I am now about to relate the most brilliant personal exploit of the war. A few days ago, Mosby put in execution a plan which he had gradually matured for the capture at Fairfax Courthouse of the Federal officers, whose headquarters were at that place.

With twenty-nine men he started down the turnpike from Rector's Cross-roads, and halted at Aldie, where he disbanded his men to meet again the following day, hoping that an escort, which had been sent off in charge of prisoners, would rejoin him by that time. Disappointed in this, the next day he continued his march for eight miles, when he stopped to have the horses fed and await the approach of night.

A steady rain had been falling since early in the evening, but, notwithstanding, we set forward as soon as it became dark. When we had reached a point within three miles of Chantilly, we turned to the right, and struck across the country in the direction of Fairfax Courthouse. So intense was the darkness that, as we were passing through a dense body of pines, the command was separated into two divisions, Mosby, with the head of the column, going forward, while the rest of it stopped under the impression that a halt had been ordered. When our isolated position was discovered (for I was with the party left in the pines), we were in a great quandary as to what course we ought to pursue. Without a guide, in a dark night, in an intricate forest, in a strange country, the situation in which we were placed was one of no little embarrassment. Some of the men advocated a return to Fauquier, while others thought it best to remain stationary until Mosby should send back for the missing detachment; but the most of us preferred to press forward and endeavour to overtake our leader. After some deliberation this counsel prevailed, and, having proceeded a short distance, the wanderers discovered a faint light glimmering through the pines. Advancing toward it, we found, to our great joy, that it proceeded from a woodman's hut, where we found Mosby with the rest of the command.

We were now near the enemy's outside picket-line between Centreville and Chantilly, and, by the use of great caution, we succeeded in passing through without being discovered, and again resumed our march. Feeling our way very carefully, we next struck a point on the turnpike midway between Fairfax Court-house and Centreville, and cut the telegraph wires by which the Federal force at the court-house could communicate with the cavalry at the latter place. Moving down the turnpike until he came within a mile and a half of the court-house, Mosby flanked off to the right to avoid some infantry camps, and proceeded in a south-easterly direction until he struck the road which leads from Fairfax Station to the court-house, on which he moved toward the village.

By this movement he hoped to disarm the suspicions of sentinels and pickets as to the true character of his party. As we drew near the town, the camp-fires of the infantry burned brightly in every direction. These encampments we avoided as we pressed rapidly on, yet necessarily, passing sometimes quite near the sentries. But we were. not challenged, as no soldier suspected that a handful of Confederate cavalry could have penetrated without being detected so far within the Federal lines, or would have the hardihood to attempt it.

At two o'clock in the morning we entered Fairfax Court-house, and found the streets deserted and scarcely a light any where visible; every one seemed buried in sleep, officers, soldiers, citizens. Swiftly and silently we marched along the street which leads from Fairfax Station to the point where it intersects the Little River Turnpike in front of the village hotel now used as a hospital. Here Mosby left Ames and Frankland, and with the rest of the command proceeded to the house of a citizen farther on in the village. The two Rangers were soon discovered and challenged by the sentinel who was pacing his beat in front of the hospital. Ames promptly responded that they were members of the 5th New York Cavalry, waiting for the return of Major White, of that regiment—an answer which appeared to satisfy the man, for he resumed his beat. Ames then called him as if to whisper something in his ear, and, when he approached, took him prisoner.

Very soon Mosby returned to the spot where he had left Frankland and Ames, and proceeded to make his dispositions for the night's work. A party under the guidance of Ames was sent to capture Colonel Wyndham, another party was detailed to collect the horses in the stables, while with a third Mosby proceeded to pay his respects to Brigadier General Stoughton.

When Ames arrived at his point of destination he discovered that Colonel Wyndham, the object of his search, had that morning gone to Washington. Meantime one of the men stepped into an adjoining room, and aroused from his sleep an officer with the information that

Mosby desired his presence. Appreciating his situation, he very warmly protested against being carried off, as he was only a sutler, and at the same time, in confirmation of his words, pointed to a quantity of confiscated merchandise which was lying about on the shelves and chairs. The Ranger was deceived by these representations, and was about to turn off from the supposed sutler, when Ames came up and recognised him as Captain Barker, of the 5th New York Cavalry, to whose company he had belonged. As soon as the captain recognised Ames, he acknowledged his stratagem and prepared to accompany his captors.

While this scene was being enacted, the horse detail were plying their work with busy hands in the officers' stables, where they secured many a prize. Almost a hundred horses were at short notice collected in the streets awaiting Mosby's return.

Mosby, meantime, had gone to the house of Dr. Gunnel, which stands apart toward the west of the village, at no great distance from the Little River Turnpike, toward which it fronts. With six men he approached the door, at which he knocked for admission. Soon a voice from a window above demanded their business at so unusual an hour.

"Dispatches for General Stoughton," replied Mosby. The door was soon unlocked, and the general's nocturnal visitors proceeded to his apartment on the upper floor.

It appears that Brigadier General Stoughton had the night before given a dancing-party at his headquarters. The revellers had tarried long, and the gallant officer was now in the soft embrace of the first sleep. With a rude shake Mosby roused him from his slumber, and it may be from his dreams. The general demanded the cause of so unseasonable a visit. Mosby curtly replied,

"Stuart's cavalry is in possession of the town."

"Impossible," exclaimed Stoughton; nor could the incredulity of the Sybarite be removed until he was informed by his captor that his name was Mosby. As obedient as to the summons of death, the Federal officer arose, and without another word proceeded to put on his clothes; but, while thus engaged, informed the intruders that if they had only come the night before he would have been prepared for their reception, but that, inasmuch as they were expected at Chantilly that night, arrangements had been made there to receive them.

While these events transpired in the chamber of General Stoughton, George Whitescarver and Welt Hatcher had explored some tents in the rear of the house, and had captured seven of the 1st Vermont Cav-

Capture of General Stoughton

alry on duty as a bodyguard to the general.

As soon as his *toilette* was finished, Stoughton, who was a philosopher as well as a general, in a cheerful voice called to his servant to bring out his horse, but some handy Ranger, for Mosby's men are all handy, had more than performed this service, for *two* beautiful animals from the general's stud, all caparisoned, were standing in front of the house. But I regret to add that the general's cheerful spirits did not last long, for instead of being allowed to mount one of his own fleet-footed steeds, he was requested politely to ride a horse of lower mettle which had been provided for his service.

Just as we were about to depart an incident occurred which I think worth relating. Frank Williams approached General Stoughton and handed him his watch, which the Ranger said in the hurry of the departure had been overlooked. Thus you see that, so far from being a band of plunderers, Mosby's men scrupulously respect private property.

With his prisoners Mosby returned to the rendezvous in front of the hotel, and as soon as the several detachments had come in, bringing with them their captures, we prepared to return in the same direction from which we had entered the town. We had been an hour and a half in the village, garrisoned as it was by a considerable body of infantry, and yet our presence had not been discovered except by the sentinels, all of whom we had captured.

After we had started on our return, encumbered with thirty-two prisoners, two of whom were captains, and fifty-eight horses, which were all that we could bring off with us, a window of a house which we passed was thrown open, and a voice imperatively demanded what command that cavalry belonged to. A laugh from the men was the only reply. The column, however, was halted, and Nelson and Welt Hatcher were ordered to dismount and search the house for the person from whom. the voice had proceeded.

This duty they proceeded to perform, but found, instead of the officer whom they expected to meet, only a lady, who proved to be the wife of Colonel Johnson, of the 18th Pennsylvania, then acting quartermaster of the post. The colonel's uniform they found lying on a chair; his gold watch was hanging on the wall, and his hat was on the table, but the colonel himself was nowhere to be found. It was a clear case of desertion, and, instead of capturing the officer, Nelson only brought off his hat, to supply the place of his own, which he had lost a few nights before. After their fruitless search the two men rejoined the column, which proceeded on its march without farther delay, for it was now half past three o'clock, and our commander was desirous of repassing the outposts before day should dawn.

As we were flanking around the fortifications at Centreville, and passing so near as to be hailed by the sentinel on the redoubt, and distinctly to see the bristling cannon through the embrasures. Captain Barker set spurs to his horse and attempted to make his escape; but a pistol-shot from his guard, which grazed his head, induced him to return. The sentinel challenged again, but no answer was returned, and the column moved on.

We were soon outside of the Federal pickets, and, crossing the Warrenton and Centreville Turnpike, we struck Cub Run about one mile above the Suspension Bridge. This stream was now much swollen by the recent snows, but we soon swam our horses across it. Mosby plunged in first, followed by General Stoughton, who, as he emerged from his cold bath, remarked, "Captain, this is the first bad treatment I have received at your hands."

From Cub Run we proceeded to the Sudley Mills, and again struck the turnpike at Groveton. Here Mosby left us, and, with George Slater, galloped ahead of the command, to ascertain if any danger threatened his line of march. They rode to the crest of a high hill, which commanded a view of the road far back toward Centreville, and it was with an anxious heart that Mosby's eye swept the horizon in that direction. But he could see no indications of pursuit, and for the first time since his departure from Fairfax Court-house did he feel confident that his daring exploit had been crowned with success, nor until then had the captured general abandoned all hope of being rescued.

Apprehending no danger in his front, Mosby ordered the command to proceed directly to Warrenton, while with Slater he lingered in the rear, and did not overtake us until we had reached the town.

The citizens, who had been notified of our approach by Walter Frankland, had prepared for our hungry band a plentiful breakfast, and received us with hearty cheers.

The next day, at the headquarters of Brigadier General Fitz Lee, at Brandy Station, Mosby turned over his captives, and then divided the spoil among his brave companions.

General Stuart was as this time still encamped near Fredericksburg, but he arrived the next day at Brandy Station, having been summoned to attend a court-martial at that place. He had met at Gordonsville Stoughton and his fellow-captives, and when he saw Mosby he expressed in the strongest terms his appreciation of the brilliant exploit which he had just performed.

Mosby's services had already attracted the attention of Governor Letcher, who, in acknowledgment of them, had sent him, through General Stuart, a captain's commission in the Provisional Army of Virginia, an organisation which had long ceased to exist. On this occasion Stuart delivered it to Mosby, and added that he thought it possible that the Confederate government might be induced to recognise its validity. But Mosby, not a little indignant, refused to accept so nominal a dignity, for the governor's commission was in truth about as valuable as would have been His Excellency's warrant for a tract of land in the moon.

In a few days after this, the following order was published to the cavalry corps of the Army of Northern Virginia:

> Headquarters, Cavalry Divisions, Army of Northern Virginia, March 12th, 1863.
> General Orders, No. —.

Captain John S. Mosby has for a long time attracted the attention of his generals by his boldness, skill, and success, so signally displayed in his numerous forays upon the invaders of his native state. None know his daring enterprise and dashing heroism better than those foul invaders, though strangers themselves to such noble traits.

His late brilliant exploit—the capture of Brigadier General Stoughton, U. S. A., two captains, thirty other prisoners, together with their arms, equipments, and fifty-eight horses—justifies this recognition in General Orders.

This feat, unparalleled in the war, was performed in the midst of the enemy's troops, at Fairfax Court-house, without loss or injury.

The gallant band of Captain Mosby share the glory, as they did the danger of this enterprise, and are worthy of such a leader.

> J. E. B. Stuart, Major General commanding.

Great was the surprise at Fairfax Court-house the next morning when it was discovered that during the preceding night Mosby had been there and had carried off the commanding officer, besides a large number of prisoners and horses. Some censured one officer, some another, but it was agreed on all hands that so daring a feat could not have been performed without the aid of accomplices in the town. Upon the strength of this suspicion, wholly devoid of foundation in fact, eight prominent citizens of known Southern sympathies were thrown into the county jail, from which they have been sent to spend many a weary month in the Old Capitol Prison.

The vengeance of the military authorities at Fairfax Court-house was at the same time wreaked upon the head of an innocent and interesting young lady of the village, Miss Antonia Ford, who has been torn from the bosom of her family, and sent likewise to the Federal Bastille, an act of harshness and tyranny which deserves the reprobation of all good men in whatever country they reside.

A few days after I called to see Miss Laura Ratcliffe, and was told by her that the day after our expedition the Yankees came out in swarms, but looked very sullen, and would have nothing to say. "We knew," she said, "there was some cause for the unusual excitement. At last one of them came up, seeming greatly amused, and told us that they were ordered by their officers not to tell what had happened in 'Devil's Corner,' as they call this neighbourhood, as it would delight us too much. But he thought the smartest thing that had been done in either army since the war ought not to be kept secret He then told us that Stoughton and his staff had been captured in bed the night before by Mosby. The news," she said, "was too good to keep, so we went round among our neighbours to tell it, and that day was one of rejoicing among us all."

Thus you see, my friend, that Mosby has begun to expand his wings, and you may expect from him soon a higher flight.

Chapter 8: Capture of the Pickets at Herndon's Station.

Upper Fauquier, March 21st, 1863.

Dear Percy,—So harassing has been our warfare on the Federal outposts in Fairfax, that a brigade of Michigan cavalry has been added to the force on that theatre of the war, to enable the commander at the Court-house to strengthen his pickets to such an extent as to render it impossible for Mosby, with his small command, to attack them with any chance of success.

In order to strengthen his command to meet in some degree this heavy re-enforcement of the enemy, Mosby proposed, while at Brandy Station, to take the dismounted men of General Fitz Lee's cavalry brigade, promising to mount and equip them in return for a short term of service—a proposition which he thought reasonable enough, as he was interposed between the brigade and the enemy in Fairfax. But it was declined, and the dismounted men were sent in charge of a brigade officer to obtain horses and equipments from the enemy.[1]

About this time, the original detail with which Mosby crossed the Rappahannock, and with which he had performed such brilliant services, was recalled to the brigade in Culpepper County on the ground of some informality in the manner in which it had been made. But Mosby appealed to his good friend General Stuart, and obtained from him an order by which the period of service was extended, and, once more on his old field of operations, one which had by common consent been abandoned to him, he began again to unwind the threads of destiny. A proclamation was at once made of an intended raid, and his little band, and all others disposed to unite in the enterprise, were notified to meet at Rector's Cross-roads on the 16th of March.

In response to his call, forty men assembled, of whom the usual proportion were "conglomerates." The command was drawn up, and General Stuart's order in reference to the capture of Stoughton was read, and was received with a round of cheers. We then proceeded down the Little River Turnpike till we reached a point below Middleburg, where we struck across the country to our left till Ave reached the neighbourhood of Ball's Mill. Here the men were divided into two parties, one of which was sent with Dick Moran to find quarters at the house of a citizen, while Mosby, with the other party, passed the night with Nat Skinner, his faithful friend and supporter.

At an early hour the next day the command was brought together, and marched in the direction of Dranesville. Except the direction of the march, no one, save the guide Underwood, knew aught of our leader's purposes. As we tramped through the mud and snow, we occupied ourselves with many a conjecture on this head, but such was the confidence with which he had inspired all hearts that not a man doubted but that ahead somewhere there was a good thing in store for us. Underwood, of course, determined the route. At one time we were on a highway, at another traversing the blasted and unenclosed fields of Fairfax, and anon we were treading unfrequented by-paths, which pursued their devious course through some dense and tangled forest of pine.

Toward noon we struck the Loudoun and Hampshire Railroad, about three miles northwest of Herndon's Station, and, crossing it, we entered a pine forest which stretched along the railroad toward

---

1. The result was, that the dismounted men were soon all captured; for it was not so easy as it appeared to be to gobble up Yankee cavalry, and get their horses and equipments.

Alexandria. After about an hour's ride we discovered that Underwood had conducted the command to the rear of the picket at Herndon's Station, and that we were approaching it on the road leading from Dranesville.

Mosby now prepared to attack. His first step was to send forward two men to capture the vedette, whose attention was engaged with a newspaper. He had seen the party as they drew near, but had taken it for the relief which was expected at that hour. His capture was in consequence effected without difficulty, and the command pressed forward at a rapid pace. As soon as we emerged from the woods and were in full view of the object of attack, the force at the station, fifty in number, were distinctly seen lounging about the place, wholly unconscious of the impending danger. A charge was now ordered with drawn sabres, and the men dashed forward on the surprised Yankees. Some were at once taken prisoner, but the most found shelter in the houses about the Station. The sabre was then exchanged for the pistol, and soon an effective fire was opened on the enemy through the thin weather-boarding with which the houses were encased, A speedy surrender was the consequence.

A considerable number of the Yankees, however, had sought refuge in a saw-mill close at hand. Into this building Mosby entered, accompanied by John De Butts, and demanded and received the surrender of the whole party without a shot being fired. After the prisoners were mounted, and the command was ready to begin the homeward march, Mosby had his attention called to several horses which were fastened near a dwelling which the assailants had passed in the impetuosity of their charge. A search was ordered. When the house was entered, the men discovered in a lower room a table set out with a plentiful meal, but none to partake of it. The two lower rooms being found empty, the searchers ascended to the upper floor. But no one was there, unless men were concealed in a garret over one of the lower rooms, which communicated by a small door with the upper floor on which the searching-party stood. One of the men (it was Ames, I believe) approached this door, and looked into the dark garret, but could see no one.

He then called to the Yankees, whom he supposed to be there, to come forth and surrender. There was no answer. The demand was repeated, and still no answer. The bold partisan then fired his pistol into the obscure apartment, and heard a whispered conference between parties within. A peremptory demand was then made, to which no response was returned. Another shot, and Captain Schofield soon made his appearance. But his companion, Major Wells, made a more direct and precipitous descent into the room below by treading on the lathing of the ceiling, which gave way, and landed him among the partisans.

As soon as the officers had delivered up their arms, the men attacked the dinner on the table, and soon dispatched it. Mosby, with these two prisoners, then rejoined the command, who were awaiting his return before taking up the line of march.

But Major Wells, under pretence that he could not mount his horse, sought to delay our departure until the expected relief should come up, seeking by this artifice to repair his misfortune. But his guard was a rude fellow, and, penetrating his design, with cocked pistol, bade him mount at once. The major leaped nimbly into the saddle, and the partisan column moved toward Fauquier.

The prisoners, with a sufficient guard under John Underwood, who was ordered to use all expedition, were started in advance; the rest of the command, in charge of Dick Moran, following Underwood's trail, with the exception of twelve men, who, with Mosby, lingered behind to protect the rear from being assailed by the expected relief. In this order we proceeded until we crossed the Horse-pen, where the rear-guard overtook Moran. Just as we passed this stream the Federal relief galloped up and opened fire on us from the opposite bank. There is a lane, formed by two high fences, which leads from the margin of the stream to a hill-top distant about one hundred yards in the direction of Underwood's retreat. On the crest of this elevation, Mosby, strengthened by Moran's party, halted, and challenged the Yankees to cross the water-course.

The stream was deep, and his plan was to wait until the most of his pursuers had crossed it, and then to cha.rge them. He doubted not, as he told me afterward, that in this event he would have captured or destroyed almost the entire party. The enemy, however, dismounted a force, and attempted with their carbines to drive us away. Mosby stood his ground until Underwood, with the prisoners, was safe from pursuit, and the day following rejoined the command at Chappelier's, on the Upperville Turnpike, near Piedmont. Having become satisfied that Wyndham's threats were only an empty boast, he again paroled the privates among his prisoners, twenty-one in number, and started them off for Harper's Ferry. They were in high spirits, and thought it not a bad thing to be captured by the guerrilla Mosby, and get a furlough until they could be exchanged. The officers, however, were placed on a different footing, for, after being put on their parole of honour, they were ordered in charge of Jake the Hungarian, to report to General Fitz Lee in Culpepper.

Now Jake, who had been a soldier with Kossuth, had the least possible confidence in a parole of honour. Accordingly, when the party stopped for the night on the route, he resorted to the following cunning stratagem to prevent the Federal officers, while he was asleep, from slipping off to their countrymen. As soon as they had retired for the night, Jake appeared, and in the politest manner offered to black their boots; for, while he had so little confidence in a parole, he was yet perfectly convinced that no gentleman would go off without his boots. According to the principles of this Hungarian code, all that Jake had to do was to hold fast to the boots through the night, and this he very carefully did.

Up to this time, Mosby, while he declined participating in the spoil taken from the enemy, had yet been in the habit, when he needed it, of reserving a captured horse for his own use. As he is ever in the saddle, such a reservation is in a manner necessary to his full efficiency; but even this *peculium* he has determined to resign, rather than afford the slightest colour to the accusation preferred against him by the enemy, and repeated sometimes in the South, that he is a mere mercenary, and makes war subservient to avarice. So careful is this remarkable man to vindicate the high motives which govern his conduct from the taint of suspicion, that he will not take even so much as a halter-strap or a saddle-girth from the rich spoil which he daily captures from the enemy.

Chapter 9: The Raid on Chantilly.

Upper Fauquier, April 8th, 1863.

Dear Percy,—Before Mosby disbanded us at Chappelier's, he designated Rector's Cross-roads and the 24th of March as the time and place for our next meeting. This ample notice was given for the benefit of the "Conglomerates," of whom Mosby on that occasion pleasantly remarked, "They resemble the Democratic party at least in one particular, for they are held together by the cohesive power of public plunder."

As soon as we were disbanded Mosby procured a fresh horse, and, accompanied by John Underwood, proceeded on a scout to Fairfax. At the end of the sixth day he was at the rendezvous, where he found fifty-five men assembled to follow his standard. Among them was Captain Kennon, who had served with distinction in Wheat's celebrated Tiger Battalion, and Captain Hoskins, an English officer, who brought back a medal from the Crimea.

As soon as this American war broke out, Hoskins resigned his commission and sought service in the Southern army. At his own request, he was ordered to report to Mosby, which he did on the 24th, when, for the first time, I met him. He seems formed for a soldier. His temper is brave, elastic, and generous, and his frame, though small, is muscular and firmly knit. His favourite weapon is the English sabre, which he wears always on service, and uses with great skill.

By his scout to Fairfax Mosby ascertained that the enemy, three thousand strong, composed of infantry, artillery, and a brigade of cavalry, were posted at Ox Hill, which is about three miles from Frying-pan and Chantilly, at which points they had established outposts, composed each of one hundred men of the 5th New York Cavalry. The troops stationed at these two places our leader determined in succession to surprise. In pursuit of this object, he marched down the Little River Turnpike, and, at a point about six miles from Chantilly, struck out to the right, and then followed the direction of the road. As we emerged late in the evening from a body of wood about a mile from Chantilly, we encountered two vedettes, who galloped off in the direction of the outpost. Besides these, we saw five or six others, about six hundred yards in front of us, observing our movements.

Finding that his plan for a surprise had miscarried, it being late in the evening and our horses very much jaded, Mosby concluded to return. But, as soon as the command came in view of the vedettes, a party of our men, seven or eight in number, broke from the ranks, and dashed across the field in pursuit of them. Suddenly they came upon a picket of ten men on the turnpike, which had been thrown out by the force at Chantilly. They were engaged in cooking their rations, but soon mounted their horses and hurried after the vedettes. Keys and Seibert, who were better mounted than the rest of their comrades, pressed close upon the flying enemy, and were only a few paces in their rear when they reached a small stream. Here Keys demanded a surrender; but one of the Federals responded by turning in his saddle to shoot his pursuer.

With a quick eye and steady aim Keys anticipated the action, and his ball penetrated the forehead of his antagonist. Subdued by the fate of their companion, seven of the fugitives halted and surrendered to their two pursuers. The party then returned with their prisoners and horses to report their success to Mosby, whom they found on the summit of a hill which commanded a view of Chantilly, for he had left the command at the Double Tollgate, and had come to look after the party with Keys and Seibert,

From that point he could clearly discern a large detachment of cavalry move out from Chantilly, and proceed slowly in the direction of the Double Toll-gate, and soon saw them joined by a body of equal strength, numbering in all about two hundred men. Mosby at once hurried back to the command, and fell back up the turnpike, feigning a retreat, until he reached a point where the Yankees had blockaded the road with fallen trees. Here he formed to receive them, for, as he afterward said, from his knowledge of Yankee character, he knew they would imagine themselves fallen into an ambuscade. When the enemy had come within a hundred yards of us, Mosby ordered a charge, to which the men responded with a vim that swept every thing before them. The Yankees broke when we got within seventy-five yards of them, and it was more, of a chase than a fight for four or five miles.

We killed five, wounded a considerable number, and brought off one lieutenant and thirty-five men prisoners. Mosby did not have with him more than fifty men, some having gone on with the prisoners, and others having gone on ahead when we started back, not anticipating any pursuit.

All the men behaved with distinguished gallantry in this combat, but Ames seemed fired with a peculiar zeal, and his eyes grew brighter as he pressed forward in the front to engage his old regiment. As we mingled in among the flying enemy, he shot right and left, as if possessed by the demon of battle. In the hurly-burly one of the 5th New York recognised him—

"How are you, Sergeant Ames?"

"Well," was the reply, and with a shot from his pistol he brought his old acquaintance to the ground.

Josh Fletcher, of Fauquier, one of the "Conglomerates" in the pursuit, came upon a thick-set Dutchman, and dealt him no gentle stroke with his sabre, which induced the fugitive in his guttural tones to propose to surrender. But Josh had never studied Dutch, and, as he swept, by, he dealt him another blow across the head which brought the unfortunate man to the ground.

William Hibbs, known in the, command as Major Hibbs, had acted in this fight with so much gallantry that Mosby acknowledged it in the presence of the command. The major, who is the most excitable of men, overpowered by this unusual honour, laughed and wept in turn, exclaiming, "Well, captain, I knew the work had to be done, and that was the way to do it."

In reply to his dispatch announcing this success, Mosby received the following communication from General Stuart:

> Headquarters, Cavalry Division, Army of Northern Virginia, March 27th, 1863.
>
> Captain,—Your telegram, announcing your brilliant achievement near Chantilly, was duly received and forwarded to General Lee. He exclaimed upon reading it;
>
> "Hurrah for Mosby! I wish I had a hundred like him!"
>
> Heartily wishing you continued success, I remain your obedient servant,
>
> J. E. B. Stuart, Major General commanding.
>
> Captain J. S. Mosby, commanding, etc., etc.

I will now give you an account of a surprise which the Yankees gave Mosby a few days ago, that you may see how he extricates himself from such difficulties.

At his next meeting, which was on the 31st of March, 1863, Mosby mustered a command of sixty-nine men, the usual proportion of which was composed of volunteers from the regular cavalry, at home on detail and furlough. Taking the direction of Dranesville, he left the Little River Turnpike at Mat Lee's house. Herndon's Station, where he paused on his route, he found to be no longer a Federal outpost, nor did he find the cavalry camp which he proposed to attack still at Dranesville; for the fight at Chantilly had induced the enterprising General Stahl to draw in his line of outposts behind Difficult Run, a stream which well deserves its name, for it is narrow and deep, and rolls over a broken and rocky bed. Its steep banks are, moreover, heavily skirted with timber, which had been felled in order to strengthen this barrier of Nature against the assaults of the all-seeing and ever-present Mosby.

Mosby had now redeemed his promise, given to General Stuart as the inducement for that officer to *lend* him fifteen men, that in two months' time he would compel the Federal commander in Fairfax to contract his lines. The means of fulfilment was the detail of fifteen men, but re-enforced by such auxiliaries as his genius, enterprise, and brilliant success had attracted to his standard.

In Dranesville two sutlers were found who had not yet removed their stores, but the men were prohibited from interfering with them. Disappointed in his expectations, Mosby marched his command several miles up the Leesburg Turnpike, and camped for the night at Miskel's house, which is on the northern side of the road, and is situated on the summit of a hill, at the northern base of which, at the distance of half a mile, rolls the Potomac.

From this point could be plainly discerned the highlands on the opposite side of the river, and a cantonment of Northern troops. On the south side of the house, and between it and the turnpike road, are first an in closure of cultivated land, and then a considerable body of wood. The barnyard, in which the command was encamped, is surrounded by a high fence, and connects with the narrow enclosure which surrounds the house; and it opens, through a plantation gate, into the field of cultivated land, through which the road runs leading to the turnpike. There is a fence between this field and the body of wood already spoken of, in which is a high and strong gate where it is crossed by the road, and along the side of this road another fence runs back to the barnyard gate.

From the position of these enclosures it will be seen that Mosby was effectually cut off, in case of a sudden attack, from a retreat in the direction of Dranesville, while Broad Run empties into the Potomac at a short distance from Miskel's house, and is an effectual barrier to all egress in the direction of Loudoun and Fauquier. This was the spot which Mosby had been compelled to select for the night's encampment, for it was the only place where forage could be procured in the country around. The men slept in the barn and in the dwelling, which was an ordinary farm-house, while their horses were fastened to the fence.

On account of the temporary and precarious nature of his control over the conglomerate body which he commanded, Mosby did not, in such inclement weather, send out pickets, but kept on duty, as a camp guard, only one sentry at the barn.

As the command marched from Dranesville, Dick Moran, who came from that neighbourhood, stopped to pass the night with an old acquaintance, Mr. Green, who lives on the margin of the road, about midway between Dranesville and Miskel's.

The presence of the Northern army in Fairfax County had unsettled and perverted the loyalty of a portion of the people. Among these was a woman who lived at Herndon's Station. Intent upon mischief to the Southern cause, as Mosby passed that place in the afternoon, she counted the number of his men, and when her brother returned home at night posted him off to the camp of the 1st Vermont Cavalry on Difficult Run, with this information, coupled with the fact that they had been marched in the direction of Dranesville. As soon as this intelligence was communicated to the officer in command, he resolved not to allow so favourable an opportunity to escape for the destruction of his troublesome enemy.

Captain Flint, for his bravery and skill, was chosen for this important service; and a call was made for volunteers from the regiment, which, in so gallant a command, he found no difficulty in obtaining. Two hundred men were selected from those who came forward, and were divided into two squadrons, the first being armed with the revolving pistol, the second with the carbine and sabre.

About daylight Captain Flint, after passing through Dranesville, stopped at Green's house, where he learned that Mosby was then camped at Miskel's.

As the confident officer moved off, he exclaimed, "All right, boys; we will give Mosby an April fool!" and was answered by cheers from the men. As soon as the surprise-party had passed, Moran, who had been concealed in the house, speedily mounted his horse, and rode through the intervening farms to apprise his friends of their impending danger.

About sunrise, one of the command informed Mosby that the enemy on the Maryland side of the river were making signals. He arose and went out to make observations, when he heard Dick Moran shout, as he rode toward the house, "Mount! mount! The Yankees are coming!" In a moment the camp was all alive with excitement, and the men hurried to resume their arms and saddle their horses. Mosby passed out of the house by the front door which looks toward the barn, and as he did so, beheld Captain Flint's first squadron marching through the gate into the field which separates the barnyard from the wood. He at once called to his men to rally, and told them they had to fight! Mosby's horse was unsaddled, and, as he gained the barnyard, the first squadron was pressing forward, and extending itself in a semicircle so as to prevent, as they hoped, any of the guerrillas from effecting their escape.

As the Federals came within pistol-shot of the fence which encloses the barnyard on the side toward the wood, they opened a rapid fire upon Mosby's men, who were there engaged in saddling and bridling their horses. The fire was warmly returned by the partisans, and when Captain Flint called out to his men to "shoot the d—d cowards," he fell from his horse pierced by eight balls.

But the decisive blow was not struck at this point. As the right wing of the Federal squadron was pressing down on the barnyard gate, which is near the house, making the air resound with their cries and shouts, Mosby still on foot, but with twenty men mounted and ready for service, with rare intrepidity and presence of mind threw open the gate and advanced pistol in hand, at the same time ordering a charge. The twenty dashed forward, and engaged the enemy in a hand-to-hand combat. Harry Hatcher, of Fauquier, a private in the 7th Virginia Cavalry, seeing his commander on foot, with a noble generosity which ever distinguishes his character, sprung from his horse in the *mêlée*, and offered it to him.

In a moment Mosby was in the saddle, and, with a wild pleasure in his heart, plunged into the thickest of the fight, while Hatcher, mounting a Yankee horse, whose rider had been shot, soon followed him. The impetuous charge of Mosby, who was each moment re-enforced, broke through the semicircle, and the assailants at once gave way. The right wing of the first squadron was routed, and driven back on the second squadron. These, instead of advancing to restore the fight, wheeled their horses and united in the headlong retreat, while the left wing passed around the barn toward the river, and were ultimately all captured.

When the flying enemy had reached the wood, they were brought to a halt by an obstacle of an unusual nature, and of their own contrivance. Captain Flint had ordered a detail from the second squadron, after it had passed through the gate on its route to Miskel's house, to obstruct it with rails so as to enable him the more effectually to destroy the doomed party. The obstacle was certainly of a formidable nature, for on each side of the gate the fence was both high and strong. Here the slaughter of the Federals was the greatest; our men riding among them as they herded to this corner, shooting right and left. Before so great a pressure the gate at last gave way, and the disordered and frightened men scattered through the woods, and along the road leading to the turnpike.

Dick Moran overtook in the woods a Federal trooper, and demanded his surrender. But the man was made of better stuff, and, being an accomplished swordsman, he closed with Moran, who would certainly have gone down in the conflict had not Harry Hatcher come to his relief, and by a blow from his pistol terminated the combat.

A portion of Captain Flint's party succeeded in reaching the Dranesville Turnpike, but the partisans hung fiercely upon their rear. The Rev. Sam Chapman, on this occasion, illustrated his faith by his works. With flashing sabre he was among the foremost of the pursuers, and, having already killed two Yankees, he dashed in between two others, demanding their surrender. But he met with the fate of Dick Moran; for the soldiers, instead of laying down their arms, vigorously attacked him, one of them giving him a severe sabre-cut on the head. The reverend gentleman was now in an embarrassing situation, when Hunter (afterward lieutenant) came up, and both of the Yankees surrendered. The pursuit was continued to Dranesville by the command, and two miles beyond by George Whitescarver, Seibert, Welt Hatcher, Wild, Harry Hatcher, and the Rev. Sam Chapman. During its progress Captain William Chapman was overtaken and captured; but one of his command, who witnessed the occurrence, soon brought assistance and set him at liberty.

The two sutlers were called upon to partake of the fortune of their countrymen, and their merchandise, including a quantity of confectionery, was divided among the victors. As soon as the prisoners and booty were collected, Mosby hurried off toward Fauquier.

The loss sustained by the Yankees on this April-fool's day was ten killed, fifteen wounded so badly as to be left on the field, eighty-three prisoners, and ninety-five horses, besides the animals that were killed. Mosby's loss was one killed, a gallant young fellow from Kentucky, Davis by name, who belonged to the artillery service, and three men wounded, Ned Hurst, of Fauquier (who has a run of luck in that line). Keys, of the 1st Virginia Cavalry, and R. A. Hart, of Fauquier, a private in the original Black Horse Company, and one of the most gallant men in the cavalry service.

At Rectortown the captures were divided, and from thence the prisoners were sent to Culpepper, where they were turned over to Brigadier General Fitz Lee.

Frank Williams, of Fairfax, when Mosby was attacked by Captain Flint, was in the neighbourhood hunting up a breakfast, and, in consequence, was not in the fight. Indeed, he had been cut off from his command, and inferred, from the formidable array that had gone to attack Mosby, that his entire party was captured or destroyed. Under this belief, he set off for Middleburg, but not until he had captured and taken along with him two Yankee soldiers whom he had fallen in with down the road. Frank had just reached his destination, and was relating to the listening and afflicted citizens the bad fortune which had at last overtaken the gallant Mosby at Miskel's, when up rode old Dick Moran in charge of the prisoners and horses. There was a loud laugh at Frank's expense as the citizens came forth to greet Mosby at the head of his victorious partisans, and to congratulate him that his star was still bright and riding in the ascendant.

Chapter 10: Desperate Fight of the Hatcher Brothers

Upper Fauquier, April 20th, 1863.

Dear Percy,—I will give you an account of one of those accidental encounters which are occurring every day between small parties of our men and the Yankees, from which you may learn the sanguinary nature of the warfare which is now raging all around us. Not only is army pitted against army, and squadron against squadron, but man against man wherever they are brought in proximity to each other, for this war is now being waged with all the fierceness of individual hatred.

A few days after the surprise at Miskel's house, that notable April-fool's-day, a brigade of Michigan Cavalry proceeded from Fairfax toward Fauquier for the purpose of retaliation. Halting about a mile and a half above Middleburg, on the Little River Turnpike, the news of their advance spread rapidly through the country.

Captain Dan Hatcher and his brother Harry, of the 7th Virginia Cavalry, were at home on furlough at Hatcher's Mill, on the Little River Turnpike, a few miles higher up the road than the point at which the brigade had halted. As soon as they heard of the enemy's presence in the neighbourhood they mounted their horses, and stationed themselves on the turnpike. Here they met Ames, who had come thither for the purpose of gathering intelligence, and, if opportunity offered, of inflicting damage on the advancing column.

Thus re-enforced, the Hatchers moved toward the Yankees, but had not gone more than a mile when they were met by a party of five, under command of a sergeant, the main column following at a short distance. Captain Hatcher, with his two men, immediately fell back toward the mill, his purpose being to draw the sergeant's party farther from their command. The Federals, nothing loath, pursued until they had gained a point on the road where a high stone bridge spans Cromwell's Run, which, after turning Hatcher's Mill, crosses the turnpike at this point. Here they halted. The Confederates immediately charged them from a distance of one hundred and fifty yards, both parties being armed with the revolver, and both retaining their fire until within a few paces of the point of collision.

Ames had discharged but one shot when he was disabled by a bullet which passed through his right shoulder. The brothers were now left alone to contend with their five opponents. Soon Harry Hatcher's horse was shot and tumbled over the bridge, but not until its rider had sprung to the ground. But whether on foot or on horseback mattered little to Harry, and the fight was continued with unabated fury, though in its progress both of the Confederates had been wounded. Nor had the Yankees escaped unhurt in this desperate encounter. One of them lay dead in the road, another was desperately injured, and the other three had each received his wound. In this condition of things the Federals wheeled, and retreated toward their column, leaving behind, in addition to their two comrades, two of their horses. During the fight forty shots were exchanged, and at its close the pistols of the two Hatchers were empty.

This skirmish with the advance put the Yankee commander on his guard, and the brigade advanced cautiously, with dismounted flankers, until it reached Goose Creek Bridge, from which place, satisfied with their retaliation, the Yankees returned to their encampment.

Soon after the Miskel fight, Mosby sent John Underwood, Prank Williams, Walter Frankland, and two others to Fairfax on a scout, which deserves notice, as it is the first expedition which he has not accompanied in person. They proceeded to the vicinity of the camp of the 1st Michigan Cavalry, where, from an ambush, they soon captured Lieutenant Wallace of that regiment, and two men. Starting off with their prisoners, they called at the house of a citizen, where a Yankee surgeon was found engaged in courting the citizen's daughter, a young lady of known Union proclivities. She had something of the lioness about her, and planted herself in the doorway, refusing to allow the intruders to pass. But the Rangers pushed rudely by her, and, on the very scene of love and courtship, captured the love-sick doctor.

Lieutenant Wallace was known to many of the citizens of Fauquier and Loudoun from his gentlemanly deportment when on raids to the upper country, and when it was known that he had been captured, many regrets were expressed that, instead of him, it had not been one of those brutal creatures who sometimes wore and always disgraced the uniform of a Federal officer.

When, on the 6th of April, we assembled again by appointment at Rector's Cross-roads, we were disbanded, with instructions to meet a week later in Upperville. But Mosby reserved eight men, with whom he went to Fairfax to discover, if it could be found, an assailable point of the enemy. He now experienced the effect of his own activity, for the Federals were so well protected by the barrier of Difficult Run that he could not assail them. Only particular fords were kept open, and these were guarded by large and vigilant bodies of cavalry. Mosby has thus been compelled to widen his area, or rather to explore new fields of enterprise. You must bear in mind that he possesses as yet no recognised organisation, yet sixty men, on the 11th of April, met him at Upperville, a village which lies at the base of the Blue Ridge, in Fauquier County, and is within a stone's throw of the Loudoun line. With this command he proceeded toward Harper's Ferry, but was unable to entice from that stronghold a party of cavalry to pursue us, and was consequently compelled to return empty-handed.

A few days after this fruitless expedition, Tom Turner, W. L. Hunter, and Walter Frankland were surprised and captured at the house of Mr. Utterback, near Warrenton. Turner attempted to fight through his captors and effect his escape, but was badly, and, as it turned out to be, mortally wounded. He was carried to Kinloch, his father's residence, near the Plains, where he died soon after. This was a serious loss to Mosby, for Tom was one of his coolest and bravest men. He had been with us but a short time, yet long enough to justify the following letter of recommendation which he brought with him from Stuart to Mosby, in which the general said:

> I can cheerfully recommend Turner as of the right sort of stuff for such daring enterprises. He has served with distinction in the infantry, had his horse killed under him in Maryland, and has on several occasions shown great courage, coolness, and gallantry. Give him a chance.

The other two prisoners were carried to the headquarters of General Davis, where they were examined by him, apart from each other, as to Mosby's whereabouts. They would not respond to such interrogatories. Hunter was sent to the guard-house, but Frankland was compelled to walk the circle for several hours.

It is no more than justice to the Federal Army to add that many of the officers who witnessed the punishment expressed their indignation at this cruel, unusual, and unjustifiable treatment of prisoners of war.

On the 17th instant, one hundred men, the largest command which he has yet had, assembled at Upperville to accompany Mosby to his new theatre of operations. He had been long casting his eyes across the Shenandoah and over the huge mountain-rampart at whose base it flows, and watching the movements of the Federal troops in the valley, but never until now had he been able to collect men enough to justify him in undertaking so hazardous an enterprise. General Milroy was at Winchester, drawing his supplies by railway from Harper's Ferry, and this line of communication Mosby determined to assail, thus exchanging his attacks on the enemy's front in Fairfax for a far more harassing and dangerous warfare upon their rear in the valley. But when we reached the banks of the Shenandoah, that "beautiful but disloyal stream," as it has been called, we found the river-god unpropitious, and, being unable to cross the angry waters, we were compelled, for the nonce, to relinquish the expedition.

But I must not let you suppose, in justice to the Confederate Government, that a commission in the Provisional Army of Virginia has been the only offer of promotion which has been made to Mosby as an acknowledgment and a reward for his brilliant services, for President Davis, as soon as he heard of the capture of Stoughton in the midst of his camp, at once sent him, through the official channel, a commission of Captain of Partisan Rangers. But this commission brought with it a difficulty of an embarrassing nature, which for a time induced Mosby to decline the proffered honour, for along with it came the following letter of instructions from General Lee:

> Headquarters, Army of Northern Virginia,
> March 23rd, 1863.
>
> Captain J. S. Mosby, through Major General Stuart.
>
> Captain,—You will perceive, from the copy of the order herewith enclosed, that the President has appointed you Captain of Partisan Rangers.
>
> The general commanding directs me to say that it is desired that you proceed at once to organise your company, with the understanding that it is to be placed on a footing with all troops of the line, and to be mustered unconditionally in the Confederate service for and during the war. Though you are to be its captain, the men will have the privilege of electing the lieutenants so soon as its number reach the legal standard. You will report your progress from time to time, and when the requisite number of men are enrolled, an officer will be designated to muster the company into the service. I am, very respectfully, your obedient servant,
>
> W. W. Taylor, A. A. G.

At the same time he received a letter, dated March 25th, 1863, from Stuart, stating that, according to General Lee's "accompanying instructions, you will be continued in your present sphere of conduct and enterprise." At the same time he urged Mosby to call his new command "Mosby's Regulars," and not by any means to insist upon recruiting a body of Partisan Rangers, on account of the bad repute into which that branch of the service had fallen with the government.

Almost any man would have at once yielded to this command from General Lee and recommendation from Stuart, but Mosby had other views.

According to the law which governs the regular service, the captures made from the public enemy become at once the property of the government, and must be turned over to its authorized agents. This Mosby knew, and that there was no power in the military authorities to prevent this legal consequence. With the power to distribute the spoil among his men taken from him, which was the meaning of the letter of instructions, he felt conscious that his opening career in the partisan service must necessarily be brought to naught, for he had said before that his command resembled the Democratic party at least in one respect, that it was held together by the cohesive power of public plunder. But this was not the only ground upon which he rested his opposition to General Lee's construction of the President's commission. Though he doubted not Stuart's disposition to continue him on the frontiers of the two armies, or General Lee's, though his letter contained no ground for this opinion, he still knew that, once mustered in the regular service, his hope for developing the new mode of warfare, which I have before explained to you, would be lost, or at least put to jeopardy. Moved by these considerations, he wrote to Stuart in these terms:

> I have received from the War Office a notice of my appointment as Captain of Partisan Rangers. The letter of Captain Taylor says that they are to be organised with the understanding that they are to be on the same footing with other cavalry. The men who have joined me have done so under the impression that they are to be entitled to the privileges allowed in the Partisan Ranger Act. If they are to be denied them I can not accept the appointment. Please let me know.

This letter of Mosby's. was forwarded to General Lee, who returned it with the following endorsement:

> No authority has been given to Major Mosby to raise partisan troops, nor has it been so intended. He was commissioned as

such to give him rank, pay, and command until he could organise companies that could be mustered regularly into the service. He was so informed when his commission was sent him, to prevent mistake. His commission was limited to himself, and did not extend to his troops.

I have failed to mention until now (because the two commissions were depending on the decision of the same point of law) that, as soon as General Lee received information of the Chantilly fight, he caused a major's commission to be sent Mosby in recognition of his high merits. The question at issue was the construction which was to be put upon the President's commission. Not satisfied with the correctness of General Lee's opinion, Mosby appealed to the Secretary of War, who determined that Major Mosby's commission entitled him to recruit a command for the partisan service, a decision which was acquiesced in by all parties.

Chapter 11: General Stahl's Grand Campaign

Upper Fauquier, May 2nd, 1863.

Dear Percy,—I have today something quite out of the common course to relate—a grand expedition to Upper Fauquier, under General Stahl. But first let me dispose of some matters.

The command of the Army of the Potomac having been transferred to General Hooker after the Battle of Fredericksburg, he sent a cavalry force to occupy Warrenton preliminary to taking possession of the Orange and Alexandria Railroad. As soon as this was done, and the railroad began to be used for transporting troops and supplies. General Stuart requested Mosby to interrupt, if possible, this line of communication. In a letter dated April 26th, he said,

> There is *now* a splendid opportunity to strike the enemy in the rear of Warrenton Junction; the trains are running regularly to that point. Capture a train, and interrupt the operation of the railroad, though it may be, by the time you get this, the opportunity may be gone. Stoneman's main body of cavalry is located near Warrenton Junction, Bealton, and Warrenton Springs. Keep far enough from a brigade camp to give you time to get off your plunder and prisoners. Information of the movements of large bodies is of the greatest importance to us just now. The marching or transportation of divisions will often indicate the plan of a campaign. Be sure to give dates, and numbers, and

names, as far as possible.

This letter displays, I think, in a very striking manner, the importance into which Mosby has raised himself as an intelligent and successful co-operator with the army of Northern Virginia. In compliance with Stuart's request toward the last of April, Mosby assembled at Upperville about one hundred men, intending to strike the railroad at some point between Warrenton Junction and Fairfax Station. He was, however, turned aside from this purpose by an event which I will now relate.

General Stahl had been put in command of all the Yankee cavalry in Fairfax, and determined to signalize that event by the destruction of Mosby and his troublesome guerrillas, who, he was informed, had erected a formidable earth-work at Upperville. To accomplish this object, he had determined upon an expedition to Upper Fauquier, which should strike terror into the country, administer a quietus to Mosby, and, what was of greater importance still, be worthy of General Stahl's reputation, his dignity, and high command. With two of his best brigades of cavalry, numbering twenty-five hundred men and four pieces of artillery, he left camp. When the expedition reached Cub Run, the advance-guard captured three of Mosby's men—Jack Barnes, Taliafero, and Ab Wren, who were travelling on foot to Fairfax for the purpose of mounting themselves on Yankee horses.

It was proposed to General Stahl by one of his officers to send these prisoners under a guard to Fairfax Courthouse; but he replied that it was impossible for him, while on so important and hazardous an expedition, to weaken his force for any purpose whatever. "No," said the general, with an air of profound cogitation, "the prisoners must be made to accompany the expedition on foot." The column, which had been halted until this important affair could be disposed of, again moved forward with all the pomp and circumstance of glorious war, while all the precautions worthy of a prudent commander were observed on the line of march. At Aldie the band of prisoners was increased by the capture of seven citizens and three of Mosby's men, Thompson, Green, and Hutchison,

After passing through Middleburg, General Stahl determined to camp for the night, and sent forward his engineers to select suitable ground for the purpose, for he reflected that the best military men are agreed that the location of a camp in an enemy's country is always a matter of the first importance. The Romans, he knew, always put their troops in fortified camps on such occasion, and while he could not revive that ancient custom, he yet determined to adopt the best substitute in his power. The engineers having reported a body of wood, a mile beyond Middleburg, as the most eligible point within reach, General Stahl ordered up the artillery, and opened upon the wood a concentrated fire, very much to the destruction of the saplings and the grievous injury of the trees. Satisfied that not even guerrillas could live under so destructive a fire, this prudent commander proceeded to limber up his guns and take possession of the camping-ground.

Each piece of artillery was then placed in such a position as to be most serviceable in case of a night attack. The horses were then unbitted, but only long enough to enable them to eat their corn, and the men, after a hasty supper, were ordered (that they might be ready in case of a surprise) to sleep by their horses. The night was cold and rainy, yet not a fire would General Stahl allow to be kindled; for he very prudently remarked that he did not intend to light signal-fires to direct guerrillas in a nocturnal attack upon his camp. But there was still another precaution taken before the commanding officer would consent to lie down for the night. Strong scouting-parties, under enterprising officers, were sent out to scour the country in every direction, who, if they performed no other service, recommended themselves to the favour of their general by bringing with them fifty citizens whom they had kidnapped in their beds, and double the number of horses taken from their stalls.

General Stahl had formed the profound hypothesis that Mosby's depredations were committed, not with soldiers, but with citizens, who were either too old or too young for the action of the conscript law, and had therefore been left at their homes. In consequence, none escaped him; the halt, the lame, the blind, were all carried off in obedience to his rigid and undiscriminating orders. One old man had been on crutches from boyhood; he was dragged from his home and his flannels on the evidence of a Federal soldier, who swore he saw him leading the charge at the Miskel fight. This motley crew was afterward sent on broken-down horses from Fairfax Court-house to Washington City, and were paraded :through the streets as Mosby's gang, whom General Stahl had captured, their chief being said to have narrowly escaped with his life.

The day following the Yankee general set forward to destroy the formidable earth-work at Upperville, of which he had heard; but Fortune was not propitious on this occasion. Before the invading force had advanced half way to Upperville, Tom Richards, with five or six men, met the advance-guard, and opened fire upon it. Supposing this to be but a prelude to a general engagement, the Federal commander halted his column and placed it in line of battle, posting his artillery on neighbouring elevations. He held this position unmolested for an hour, but at the end of that time, that he might disappoint the calculations of the guerrillas and avoid all their snares, General Stahl moved abruptly to the left, in the direction of Salem, proposing to return to Fairfax through Thoroughfare Gap.

But it is time to return to Mosby. Disregarding the presence of the enemy at Middleburg, of which he had been duly informed, and desirous of complying with General Stuart's request, he marched through Salem on his route to Thoroughfare Gap, through which he intended to pass on his way to the railroad. When he came within a few miles of the Gap, he was overtaken by Alfred Glasscock and Norman Smith, whom he had left on the road, and informed that five hundred of Stahl's cavalry were on his track. He at once expressed his intention to turn upon his pursuers, for he said to the command, "They are the same men whom we whipped at Chantilly and at Miskel's, and we can do it again." So saying, Mosby reversed his column and proceeded in the direction of the Plains; but, after going a few miles, he was informed of the true state of affairs, which was that General Stahl had altered his plans, and was trying to make good his retreat to Fairfax through Hopewell Gap; for he had been informed by someone who had seen Mosby on his march thither that Stuart's cavalry were at Thoroughfare Gap waiting to intercept him.

Mosby now abandoned for the time his intention of striking the railroad, and determined to harass the retreat of General Stahl through the difficult pass of Hopewell Gap. With this intent he left the road on which he was matching, and struck across the country to the road leading from the Plains to the mountain pass. As fortune would have it, when he reached the road he fell in with the advance-guard of the Yankees, which immediately fell back, and informed General Stahl, who was then at the Plains, that Stuart's cavalry had likewise occupied Hopewell Gap, and were then pressing forward to attack him. Upon the receipt of this alarming intelligence the Federal general again prepared for action, and drew up his forces in line of battle on a hill near the Plains, henceforth to be known as Stahl's Hill.

From an eminence in the neighbourhood of Kinlock Mosby could plainly observe this movement. The general, on a milk-white steed, surrounded by a brilliant staff, could easily be distinguished as he sent off and received couriers bearing important dispatches. Mosby's classical imagination was carried back to the Retreat of the Ten Thousand as that devoted band, surrounded on all sides by barbarians, was preparing to cut its way back to the Hellespont.

General Stahl considered himself in a situation of extreme peril, surrounded by enemies who were doubtless waiting for the hour of midnight to begin a murderous attack. He had been met by Confederate cavalry on his march to Upperville, and had turned aside to avoid them; they had been seen to hover on his flanks at Salem, his scouts had reported them on the road to Thoroughfare Gap, and his advance-guard had been just driven back by them on their route to Hopewell Gap. This was a desperate situation of affairs, from which he could only be extricated by the utmost coolness, secrecy, and expedition. What was to be done? An inspiration of genius suggested a night march. Yes, a night march, thought he, will do the business, and thus would he give the slip to Stuart, to Mosby, and all evil-disposed persons, and get back sound in wind and limb to his camp in Fairfax.

As soon as it was dusk the column was again formed, and headed, this time toward Middleburg, the only avenue of escape left open to the beleaguered general. The route selected was a private road which leads through the premises of Mr. James William Foster. Mr. Foster was astonished at the procession, and inquired of an officer,

"Why, sir, where in the world are you going?"

The Yankee cunningly replied,

"Ah, sir! this is too unhealthy a country for us."

General Stahl assuredly deserves to be classed with the most prudent commanders who have ever carried on aggressive war, or graced the page of history. On his march, as wakeful and vigilant, he counted the watches of the night; he caused not only all the bridges in his rear to be torn up, but also fences to be built, and trees to be felled across his track, by which means he proposed to prevent the fierce guerrillas from charging his rear, and spreading confusion and alarm through his ranks.

Arrived in the neighbourhood of Middleburg, General Stahl went into camp, but this time in an open field, for he was determined to avoid the ambuscades which he felt confident had been prepared for his destruction.

It so happened that by this nocturnal stratagem Mosby came near being captured. He had left, as he supposed, late in the evening the

Federal cavalry about to go into camp at the Plains, and, upon that supposition, had dispersed his command for the night, and gone himself to the house of a friend near Middleburg. Great was his astonishment when he waked the next morning to find himself in the midst of General Stahl's camp.

When asked why he did not attack and disperse the raiders on their midnight march, he replied, "I knew nothing of it, and I had no right to suppose that an idiot had been placed in command of two brigades of cavalry and four pieces of artillery."

Chapter 12: Desperate Fight at Warrenton Junction

Upper Fauquier, June 2nd, 1863.

Dear Percy,— On account of the lameness of my horse, I did not accompany Major Mosby on the expedition which resulted in a severe fight at Warrenton Junction, but I will give you the particulars as I have received them from Captain Hoskins, Alfred Glasscock, and others who were present

With about one hundred men, on the 2nd of May Mosby started with the intention of striking in the rear of General Hooker at Falmouth, who had commenced the movement which soon after resulted in the battle of Chancellorsville. At Warrenton our men were received with cordial demonstrations by the citizens, who brought food to them on the streets, and, when ranks were broken, entertained them in their houses. The command bivouacked about two miles from the town, where the horses were plentifully fed on grain which had been left by the Yankees.

By sunrise the next morning it was moved off in the direction of Warrenton Junction, to which point the enemy's cavalry were reported to have retired, for Mosby expected to be able to capture the force at that place, and then proceed to carry out his original plan. But the event did not justify his expectation, and he was compelled to abandon his designs on General Hooker's communications. When Mosby came in sight of the camp, he discovered that the force, although cavalry, was yet quartered in a dwelling-house and two outbuildings, situated in an angle made by the two railroads. The soldiers were lounging about, and everything denoted a feeling of security on the part of both officers and men.

Their horses were without saddles or bridles; some were tied about their quarters, but a considerable number were turned out to graze in an adjoining field. Mosby's men, coming from the direction of Warrenton, were at first mistaken by the Yankees for a detachment of the 5th New York, which had been sent out on a scout; but they were soon undeceived, for the major, at the distance of three hundred yards, ordered the charge to be made, but it was checked by a miry branch over which the men had to pass. This delay gave the Federals time to recover in some measure from their surprise, and prepare to defend themselves in the houses. As our men approached, they poured a hot fire into them with carbines and pistols, wounding several men and horses.

Those who had taken refuge in the outhouses, however, soon surrendered and Mosby, with thirty men, proceeded to attack the main building, in which were crowded about a hundred Yankees, commanded by Major Steele. Here the resistance was stubborn. The Confederates would ride up to the windows and shoot those within as fast as they appeared, and in this way greatly diminished the advantage derived from the possession of the house. When the fight had thus lasted for about half an hour, Mosby, in order to spare the lives of his men and bring the contest to a close, directed Alfred Glasscock to set fire to a lot of hay and burn the building. But before this order could be executed, Sam Chapman, Mountjoy, Harry Sweeting, and John De Butts dismounted and forced themselves into the house.

Chapman advanced to the foot of the staircase and demanded a surrender from those above. Twenty men came down and delivered up their arms. At the same time the inmates of the room on the right hand surrendered to his companions, but those in the room on the left still held out. John De Butts then fired through the closed door, and killed a man who was leaning against it; whereupon Sweeting and the others burst into the room, where the smoke from the gunpowder was so dense as to conceal the respective strength of the two parties. Here a number of Federals were killed and wounded, and the resistance was continued until the officer upstairs, finding that the storming-party had broken into the house below, and seeing the preparations on the outside to burn it, hung out a white flag as the emblem of capitulation.

Mosby was now undisputed master of Warrenton Junction, having captured, after a sanguinary struggle, the 1st Virginia Regiment of Cavalry (three hundred officers and men), with all their horses, arms, accoutrements, camp equipage, and a fine ambulance. But this success had not been purchased without serious loss to the victors. Templeman, a gallant soldier, and one of Jackson s best scouts, lay dead near the house, while about twenty of the men, among whom was Captain

Ducheane, were wounded or captured. General Stahl, in his report, admits a loss of six officers, including a major, and fourteen privates killed and wounded.

Flushed with success, the partisans were in the act of saddling up their horses preparatory to leaving, when the alarm was given that reenforcements of the enemy were coming. Just then, about three hundred yards off, Mosby saw a column of cavalry approaching from the woods in the direction of Cedar Run Bridge. The command was entirely disorganised and dispersed over the fields, catching loose horses and fugitive Yankees. Our leader used every endeavour to rally and form the men, but it was impossible, and there was no alternative left but retreat.

The pursuing party, as soon as they arrived at the scene of conflict, divided, the 1st Vermont being sent round on the left to intercept Mosby's retreat, while the 8th New York charged in the rear. When the men saw the Federals swarming in upon them on all sides, the retreat became a precipitate flight. Prisoners, horses, and other booty were hastily abandoned, and those who but recently had fought with such determination were now compelled to trust to the fleetness of their steeds.

Mosby, with a small party, had turned aside into a body of pines, where he soon came in contact with the Vermonters, who pressed him hard with their pistols and sabres. At this point Willie Jones fell from his horse badly wounded, and his brother Jasper, roused by the spectacle, turned fiercely upon the pursuers. But what can one man, even if he have the courage of Jasper Jones, accomplish against overpowering numbers? Sabred and shot, the revengeful soldier reeled and fell to the ground. Mosby, with the rest of his party, sheltered by the friendly pines, eluded his pursuers, while the body of the command scattered through the country, but succeeded, nevertheless, in bringing off eight prisoners, thirty horses, and a large number of pistols and sabres.

The affair at Warrenton Junction, though a victory as well as a disaster, had the effect of damping the ardour of the "Conglomerates" to such a degree that only thirty-seven men met Mosby on the 9th of May at Upperville. They had been instructed by that event that war, even with him, was not an uninterrupted flow of victory, and that, if they made a habit of going with him, they would have blows to receive, as well as blows to give.

General Stahl was at Fairfax Court-house, with portions of his command disposed in large detachments for the protection of the rail-

The Partisans' first retreat

road from Fairfax Station to the Rappahannock River. These were too strong for Mosby to attack with success, in consequence of which he determined to adopt a line of action which would compel the Federal general to split his forces into smaller bodies. The means which he selected to accomplish this result exemplify the fertility of his invention. He proceeded to break the unguarded railroad track and burn all unguarded bridges, and in this way reveal to General Stahl other vulnerable points. He struck the railroad between Catlett's and Bristoe's Station, and, after destroying the track, proceeded to burn the bridge over Cedar Run. As soon as the fire was in full blast, the men were marched by a circuitous route to Kettle Run Bridge, where the same destructive measures were resorted to, but were defeated in an unusual manner. During the time occupied in making the circuit, a train of cars with a heavy infantry guard had passed, but were compelled by the conflagration at Cedar Run to return, and was so fortunate as to reach Kettle Run before the fire at that point had progressed to a dangerous extent. The cars disembarked their infantry, the partisans were compelled to retire, and the bridge was saved.

As the command returned homeward, Harry Sweeting and Dan Thomas captured two infantry soldiers with muskets—a bad investment, the Partisans considered, of time and trouble, and at Greenwich the prisoners were paroled, and the command disbanded. This raid was called a water-haul by the Conglomerates, yet it compelled the enemy to suspend the use of the railway for *two days*, which paid Mosby.

In his report made about this time to General Stuart, Mosby says:

> If you would let me have a mountain howitzer, I think I could use it with great effect, especially on the railroad trains. I have several experienced artillerists with me. The effect of such annoyance is to force the enemy to make heavy details to guard their communications. I have not attacked any of their railroad trains, because I have no ammunition for my carbines, and they are pretty strongly guarded with infantry.

About a week later, Mosby, with twenty-five men, penetrated within the enemy's line to within one mile of Dumfries, his object being to interrupt their transportation on the telegraph road, which connects Alexandria with Fredericksburg.

We were feeding our horses at the house of a citizen, when the alarm of "Yankees" was given. Quickly bridling up, we did not await their attack, but, led by Mosby, went to meet them. After a short hand-to-hand encounter, we succeeded in putting our assailants to flight, leaving on the field two dead, and five too badly wounded to be brought off, besides taking four prisoners, eight horses, arms, etc. The lieutenant who commanded the party was badly wounded in his right arm, and was so conspicuous for his gallantry, that after the fight Mosby said to him,

"Lieutenant, you are too brave a man to fight in so bad a cause."

As the enemy had taken the alarm, our leader did not deem it prudent to remain longer inside their lines, and returned, having sustained no loss. An account of this expedition was without delay sent to Stuart by Fount Beattie, who was instructed to communicate to the general all the information which Mosby had acquired with reference to the number and distribution of the enemy's troops.

Chapter 13: Another Defeat

Upper Fauquier, June 10th.

Dear Percy,—On the 28th of May, in company with Willie Foster, I stopped for the night with Major Mosby at the residence of Mr. Hathaway, Fauquier County, a few miles from Rectortown. We were aroused from sleep by Fount Beattie, who informed us that he had left the Yankees at Rectortown, *en route* for Mr. Hathaway's, in pursuit of Mosby. We dressed and saddled our horses with all expedition, but when we were ready nothing was to be heard of the Yankees. We waited a while, and still heard nothing of them, but concluded, as a precautionary measure, to betake ourselves to a piece of woodland near the house and finish the night. Here we slept, without the slightest disturbance, until the sun was several hours high the next morning. As we were returning to the house, Mr. Hathaway's little son met us, and said,

"Major, they have taken off pa and all your horses."

"Who?" inquired Mosby.

"The Yankees," responded the boy. "Didn't you know they had been here?"

"How long have they been gone?"

"Not fifteen minutes."

So we dispatched our breakfast, sent out for some of the men to meet us at Middleburg, and started after them, but they had gotten too far ahead. So we came back, and Major Mosby disbanded the little party, with orders to make it known that there would be a meeting of the command the next day at Patterson's.

The morning was bright and warm, and at an early hour forty eight men had assembled. After the men selected for artillery service had been drilled for an hour by Lieutenant Sam Chapman, an ex-officer of the Dixie Battery, but then detailed on conscript duty in Fauquier, the command started for Catlett's Station, to intercept a train of cars. At Greenwich we stopped to get supper, and then marched several miles farther, and camped for the night near the residence of Mr. Marstella.

In the morning we proceeded to the railroad not far from Catlett's Station, and near the residence of Squire Stone, where we cut the telegraph wires, slipped a rail from its place, and put the howitzer in position.

When it was announced that the train was coming, Major Mosby ordered Willie Foster, who appears to enjoy a large share of his confidence, to hold the men in readiness. The train came dashing along at headlong speed, and at the appointed place ran off the track. The guard, consisting of two hundred infantry, opened fire upon us, but were quickly dispersed by a round of grape from the howitzer, accompanied by a charge from Foster's men. Thus we were left in undisputed possession of a train of twelve loaded cars. We had but little time to plunder, as there were cavalry camps on either side within a mile of us. Some of the boys, however, took out morning papers, several bags with the United States mail, boxes of oranges and candy, leather for boots, and nearly everyone got a fresh shad. We then sent a shot through the locomotive, fired the cars, and started on our homeward march.

After passing Stone's house we struck the Burwell Road, which leads from Catlett's Station to Haymarket, and had not marched more than a few miles when we observed the advance-guard of the 5th New York on a hill immediately in our front. Discovering by the dust that the main body were out of sight in a depression beyond, Chapman sent a shell, which fell in their midst, killed an officer's horse, and created great confusion. Eager for the charge, Willie Foster dashed forward, and had just started the Yankees in flight when he was recalled by Mosby, in consequence of erroneous information which he had received.

The command was again started through the fields, Foster being left behind in command of a rear-guard.

Soon after we had passed Squire Stone's, the 7th Michigan Cavalry, under command of Colonel Mann, came up and searched the house for Mosby, but did not immediately commence the pursuit, for the

Plundering and destroying the railroad train at Catlett's Station

reason that he was informed by a coloured woman that the party who had destroyed the train were only a portion of a much stronger force which had been held in reserve. Soon, however, being largely re-enforced, Colonel Mann followed our retreating column. The rearguard under Foster checked the pursuers several times by firing on them from an ambuscade, but was finally driven back. A few shots from the howitzer, however, arrested for a time the pursuit, and thus we continued to skirmish until within half a mile of Warren Fitzhugh's house. There discovering the overwhelming numbers by which he was followed, and that it would be impossible to get off the howitzer, Mosby resolved to make the Yankees pay for it as dearly as possible. With this intent Chapman was sent in advance to select an eligible position on which to post the gun, while Mosby, with six men, lingered in the rear to retard the progress of the enemy. Soon a hand-to-hand conflict began with the advance-guard, consisting of about fifteen men, whom we succeeded in driving back, but we lost in the encounter the gallant Captain Hoskins, who fell from his horse mortally wounded.

Chapman took up a position on a hill at the head of a narrow lane which turns abruptly to the right from the Burwell Road, and is about a hundred yards distant from the Fitzhugh House. The Federals came up in gallant style, and, in column of fours, crowded into the lane. At a distance of eighty yards we opened on them with grape, followed by a vigorous charge of cavalry, and drove them before us half a mile in confusion. Twice again did they rally, and as often were sent reeling back. At last our ammunition was exhausted, and we were forced to abandon the gun, but not without a fierce hand-to-hand struggle, in which many of the enemy were made to bite the dust.

In the *mêlée* Mosby received a slight sabre-cut on the arm. Lieutenant Chapman and privates Mountjoy and Beattie stood by the gun until surrounded by the enemy. Chapman and Mountjoy were captured—the former having been shot through the thigh when fighting with the rammer of the gun. George Turberville, one of "Mosby's young roosters," acted on this occasion with great gallantry as driver, and drove the caisson from the midst of the Yankees out into the woods, where it was not found for several days. The gun which we lost on this occasion only returned to the hands of its original owners, for it had been captured from the Yankees at Ball's Bluff, near Leesburg, in the battle of the 23rd of October, 1861. The enemy lost in this fight, by their own admission, five killed and fifteen wounded; and Stuart sent Mosby word that he would send him another gun of the same size if he would sell it as well. The brave Hoskins was carried from the field to the residence of Mr. Charles Green, where he soon after died. His remains are buried in the Greenwich churchyard, and the spot will be respected by all who honour the character of a gallant soldier and thorough gentleman.

Chapter 14: Fight at the Frying-Pan Church

Upper Fauquier, June 20111, 1863.

Dear Percy,—On the 3rd of June fifty men assembled at the invitation of our leader, and marched to the vicinity of Frying-pan Church, with the view of assailing parties from the 5th and 6th Michigan Cavalry, camped at Fox's Mill, which is situated half a mile from the by-road, and six miles from the church. The night was cool, and, according to Mosby's invariable custom, the men were allowed to build fires in the pines in which they were camped. A party, consisting of Bush Underwood, Sowers, Frank Williams, Minor Thompson, and John Saunders, was sent, under the charge of John Underwood, to attack a patrol from the Michigan camp which passed on the Ox Road during the night Mosby's object in this was to induce the commander at Fox's Mill to send out one or more parties for the purpose of looking after the nocturnal assailants.

Underwood placed his men in ambush, and fired upon the patrol as they passed, killing one horse and wounding three of the soldiers. The stratagem succeeded. A little after daylight, Underwood, who had been watching the road leading from the enemy's camp to Frying-pan Church reported fifty Yankees marching toward the latter place. Mosby immediately ordered us to mount and march down the road in their rear; but before we came in sight of them, Underwood galloped up and reported that the first party had been re-enforced by about sixty men, and had halted at the church.

"The more the better," replied Mosby; "I am in their rear. Forward, trot, charge!"

Their rear-guard, which had likewise halted in the road, was driven before us in so thick a cloud of dust that their comrades at the church could not fire upon us for fear of injuring their own friends. But not so with us. Amid yells and exploding revolvers we rushed upon them, and, after a short and desultory resistance, put them to flight. It is Mosby's opinion that we would have captured the entire force, but for the presence of a squadron of Michigan cavalry who were posted across the road a few hundred yards lower down. As soon as this discovery was made he drew off his men from the pursuit and returned to Fauquier, bringing with him seven prisoners and ten horses. In the fight the enemy had three killed and several wounded, but we sustained no loss, except the capture of Dr. Alexander, a volunteer surgeon, who was with us on that occasion.

On the morning of the 10th of June one hundred men assembled at Rector's Cross-roads, thirty of whom belonged to Captain Brawner's company of independent cavalry. On this occasion Mosby's first company, A, was organised by the election of James William Foster, Jr., of Fauquier, Captain; Thomas Turner, of Maryland, First Lieutenant; William L. Hunter, Second Lieutenant; George Whitescarver, of Fauquier, Junior Second Lieutenant.

CAPTAIN FOSTER.

Captain Foster entered the regular service in May, 1862, as a private in Captain Turner Ashby's cavalry company, where he served without any casualty, except having his horse killed under him at Kernstown. During the latter part of his service with this company he was made a sergeant, and was frequently put in command of small detachments. He had been sent to Fauquier with a squad of twelve men who had been furloughed for the purpose of recruiting their horses, but when he disbanded them at Salem they agreed to join him and go with Mosby on his next raid. This was the Chantilly fight, an account of which I have given you in a previous letter. In this encounter, Sergeant Foster, with Ames, Willie Brent, and Tom Turner, composed the first set of fours who charged the enemy, and bore himself with such distinguished gallantry as to induce Mosby to confer upon him the honour of being his first captain. Thomas Turner, of Maryland, won his commission in this same engagement. Lieutenants Hunter and Whitescarver have already been brought to your notice as prominent actors in the Miskel fight.

As soon as the company organisation was completed, Mosby set forth for the purpose of making a night attack on two cavalry camps of the enemy on the Maryland side of the Potomac. About ten o'clock at night we reached the river at a point opposite to Muddy Branch, where we procured a guide to pilot us across. Finding the water at this point too deep, our guide undertook to conduct us to another ford lower down, but unfortunately lost his way, and did not find it until daybreak. Thus was Mosby's plan for a night attack frustrated.

When the command reached the ford, Nelson, Glasscock, and Trunnel were sent across to capture a cavalry patrol on the tow-path of the Chesapeake and Ohio Canal, if possible, without firing a shot. Having crossed the river and secured their horses, the three men concealed themselves in the bushes, and, on the approach of the patrol, sprang out, seized their horses by the bridle reins, and presented their cocked revolvers. The patrol, which was composed of only two men, quietly surrendered, and were taken back to Mosby, who had crossed the river, impatient at the approach of day.

With Nelson, Glasscock, and Trunnel, re-enforced by three others as an advance-guard, the command moved up the tow-path, and soon overhauled a canal-boat, from which were taken five mules. We proceeded then at a trot, and the advance-guard met and captured another patrol, consisting of four men, but not without firing. This alarmed a picket who was stationed at a bridge over the canal not far distant. He immediately turned the bridge and fled to the camp, which was a half mile distant. This occasioned some delay, and gave the Yankees time to prepare to receive us. As we approached, we saw the officer in command ride along his ranks waving "the old flag" and exhorting his command to stand firm. But it was to no purpose. His men, ninety in number, before we got within pistol range fled in confusion toward Poolesville.

Mosby ordered his command to halt and destroy the camp, but Captain Foster, with Lieutenant Turner, Alfred Glasscock, Major Hibbs, Ned Hirst, Carlisle, and a few others, not understanding the order, pressed on in pursuit about a mile, when they reached a bridge, on the farther side of which, near Seneca Mills, the enemy were drawn up to dispute the passage. Here the fight was continued until Mosby came up. He at once called out, "Men, we will charge them;" and, with Frank Stringfellow at his side, dashed across the bridge, followed by the command. The enemy again gave way, and this time to rally no more. A running fight was kept up for a mile beyond the bridge, in which Captain Brawner and Lieutenant Whitescarver were killed.

The enemy's loss was seven killed, a considerable number wounded, seventeen prisoners, thirty horses, and "the old flag." Our loss was the two officers mentioned and Alfred Glasscock, who was badly wounded. The remains of Lieutenant Whitescarver were carried by his relation, Joe Nelson, to the house of a citizen, and by him interred near the spot where he fell. Those of Captain Brawner were recovered the next day by his company. Alfred Glasscock, at his own request, was taken across the river and left at the house of an acquaintance. While here he was visited by the Federal officer who had been in command at the fight at Frying-pan Church. He said to Glasscock,

"You belong to Mosby?"

Glasscock "I do."

Federal Officer. "I fought him once at Frying-pan Church."

Glasscock "I was there, but I did not see much fighting."

Federal Officer, "Mosby did not fight fairly. He surprised me, and the night before had bushwhacked some of my men."

Glasscock "The bushwhacking was to draw you from camp; the surprise to whip you, and, the odds considered, I think the fight was a fair one."

This affair created a great excitement in Washington. A cavalry force was dispatched at once to Leesburg to ascertain what it meant, and De Forest's cavalry, camped at Kettle Run, marched to Upper Fauquier to intercept our return. General Stahl, too, again unfurled his battle-flag, and moved his cohorts from Fairfax, One of these bodies of cavalry, in passing through Middleburg, captured Captain Foster and the splendid gray horse which Mosby had given him as a mark of his appreciation.

CHAPTER 15: MOSBY'S ADVENTURES IN SEARCH OF INFORMATION.

Upper Fauquier, June 25th, 1863.

Dear Percy,—When we returned from our expedition to Maryland, our horses were so much broken down that we found it necessary to recruit them a while.

When General Lee was pressing Hooker toward the Potomac, Mosby called to see Stuart, who was at Middleburg, with his command thrown forward toward Aldie. After a short conference with the general, he returned to the party who had accompanied him, and started again for the neighbourhood of Seneca. We had not proceeded more than two miles, when firing was heard in the direction of Aldie. The cause of it, as we soon learned, was a collision between Kilpatrick and Rosser, who had met unexpectedly at that place. Mosby, with sixty men, moved around by Oatlands, the residence of Mr. George Carter, so as to gain a position in rear of Kilpatrick on the Little River Turnpike.

A corps of infantry had reached Gum Spring, another had gone to Leesburg, and Mosby thus found himself interposed between the cavalry and infantry of Hooker's army. With this information a courier was sent to General Stuart, who, for the first time, learned where Hooker was.

It was dark before we reached the turnpike, and on our march thither we had captured a number of prisoners.

Leaving the command concealed in the woods, Mosby, accompanied by Charlie Hall, Joe Nelson, and Norman Smith, proceeded to the road, where they espied three horses fastened near a dwelling-house, with an orderly standing by them. He rode up to the man, and was informed by him that the horses belonged to Major Stirling and Captain ————. In a whisper, he then said to the orderly, who was an Irishman,

"My name is Mosby; keep quiet."

The man understood him to say that he (the Irishman) was Mosby, and very indignantly replied,

"No, sir, I am as good a Union man as ever walked the earth."

"Those are the very sort I am after," replied Major Mosby.

Just then the officers made their exit from the house. When sufficiently near, Hall stretched out his hand to take the major's arms. Supposing him to be an acquaintance, Major Sterling offered his hand, and was thunderstruck when he was informed that he was a prisoner. And well he might be, for he was the bearer of important dispatches from Hooker to Pleasonton, his chief of cavalry.

Mosby proceeded to a house near by, where, after procuring a light, he discovered what a treasure he had captured. The dispatches informed Pleasonton of all Hooker's plans, and all the information which he wanted to obtain.

This information, so important, was entrusted to the courage, the prudence, and the fidelity of Norman Smith. At twelve o'clock at night Norman set forth, and just as the first faint dawn appeared the dispatches were placed in General Stuart's hands.

After the prisoners had proceeded a short distance, they were informed by Hall that Mosby was their captor. At this they were highly amused, and, when asked the cause, replied, "We have laughed so much at our men for being gobbled up by Mosby, that we can not help laughing at being caught ourselves."

We slept that night in the woods within half a mile of the camp of the 5th Corps, and early the next morning moved lower down the turnpike near Pleasant Valley, where farther important information was obtained about the disposition of Hooker s army. Here we captured two well-stored sutler-wagons drawn by six horses, which we gutted in the woods. One sutler was indeed a prize, for he had six hundred dollars in greenbacks on his person, and was leading a very fine mare, which belonged to the lieutenant colonel of the 73rd Ohio. The mare was at once dedicated to the partisan service.

With thirty prisoners and horses. Major Mosby returned to report in person to Stuart, and crossed Bull Run Mountain by an unfrequented bridle-path, as Hancock's corps was at Thoroughfare Gap, and Pleasonton still at Aldie.

Two days after these occurrences, Mosby, with sixty men, started for Fairfax across Bull Run Mountain. It was night, and one of the men dropped his hat, and, stopping to get it, halted that portion of the column in his rear. The command moved forward, and thus became separated. The men who had thus been cut off despairing of finding Mosby amid such wild scenes, disbanded and returned to their respective quarters, while he at a farther point on the mountain camped for the night.

Early the next morning we passed through Dr. Ewell's farm, and were near Ewell's Chapel, when we discovered fifty cavalry in our front. Mosby was in the rear, and the column, thirty-five strong, halted for him to come up. Instead of attempting to retreat, our leader, with that heroic impulse by which he is ever animated, ordered a charge, determined to burst through the impediment thus suddenly presented to his progress. The cavalry broke and fled. With Hall and Mountjoy at his side, he discovered, on approaching the church, that the cavalry had been put there as a bait, and that he was, in fact, involved in an infantry ambuscade. The infantry poured a volley into the advancing partisans, wounding Hall, Mountjoy, and Ballard. Extricating himself by the exercise of great coolness and courage from this perilous situation, Mosby halted at a point about a mile distant, from which he sent off the wounded. General Meade had been informed the night before by a negro, who had seen Mosby go into camp, that he would pass Ewell's Chapel early the next morning. The general rejoiced greatly at the opportunity thus thrown in his way of ridding the Federal army of so harassing an adversary, and proceeded to prepare for him the deadly snare.

But Mosby, undismayed, started again at midnight for the Little River Turnpike, which he proposed to make the scene of operations. Stuart's quarter-master was deficient in animals for transportation, and this want our leader was desired to supply. His first capture consisted of four wagons, each drawn by six mules. These animals, together with several prisoners and horses, were dispatched to the Confederate camp, while Mosby pursued and overtook a train of twenty wagons. As soon as the horses and mules were unhitched they were started for the same destination along with their negro drivers. The cavalry escort was in advance of the train. Taking the alarm, they soon returned to avenge the affront and recapture the prize. Our men, only fifteen in number, took to the woods in order to save the plunder, but lost a good many of the animals in their flight, as well as three of our number, who were taken prisoners. This capture was effected within a mile of General Birney's camp, who, in retaliation, came down and caused the house of a citizen near by to be pillaged and burnt.

About this time Mosby received a note from Stuart, requesting him to ascertain for General Lee if Hooker was crossing the Potomac. In compliance with this request he took with him two men, and, crossing the Bull Run Mountain, entered the turnpike below Mat Lee's. While he was conversing with a citizen in relation to the movements of the Federal army, two soldiers rode up, who were captured and sent to the woods in charge; of one of his companions. Soon after four lieutenants, approached him, and without suspicion, for both he and his companion had oil-cloths over their shoulders to protect them from a drizzling rain. After some conversation Mosby introduced himself to the startled officers. Having procured a good deal of valuable information, he sent a dispatch to General Stuart along with the six prisoners in charge of his two men.

Mosby was now alone, and proceeded toward Frying-pan, but stopped to visit his trusty friend. Miss Laura Ratcliffe, who lived not twenty yards from the highway. From her I received the following account of his visit:

When Hooker's army was watching General Lee, trying to find out his intentions, Reynolds's corps was camped at Guilford Station, and the wagon-trains, with cavalry escorts, were constantly passing our house to and from the railroad. One day a soldier on a white horse, with an oil-cloth around him, rode up to the house, and we could scarcely believe our own eyes when we found it was Major Mosby. He dismounted, and came in to see if we had late papers or any news, and left his horse standing at the front door. One of my sisters was so afraid the Yankees would come while he was here that she led his horse behind the barn, and kept him there till the major was ready to start; but he did not appear the least uneasy, nor did he make a hurried visit. That evening two Yankees came to our house and told us that it was rumored that Mosby had ridden several miles with them between here and Guilford; that when he got ready to turn off he had said 'good-evening,' and then dashed through the woods, and was out of sight in an instant I told the men the story was improbable, but suppose it was really true.

Having procured from Miss Laura the information of which he was in search, Mosby proceeded to the house of John J. Coleman and called for him. Just then two cavalry-men approached and stopped under a tree in Mr. Coleman's field to pick cherries. Mosby rode up, and, presenting his pistol, demanded a surrender, and two members of the 5th New York Cavalry submitted as prisoners. In consequence of this capture on his premises the Yankees threatened to burn Mr. Coleman's house, and would have done so, but for the generous interposition of General Reynolds.

Mosby then returned to the turnpike, along which a large wagon-train was passing, guarded by a cavalry escort. But nothing daunted, he determined to pass through the wagons and the escort, carrying his prisoners with him. Accordingly, after tying the halters of their horses together, he started off. Sometimes he was so close to the cavalry as almost to touch them, and nothing prevented the prisoners from giving the alarm but the certainty that immediate death to at least one of them would be the consequence. In this way Mosby proceeded until, reaching a convenient point, he turned off and directed his course to Fauquier. He reported without delay the important intelligence he had gained to Stuart, who was charmed with the boldness as well as the success of the exploits by which it had been obtained.

At this interview General Stuart communicated to Mosby his intention of crossing the Potomac .between Hooker and Washington, and, at the same time, the wish that he should command his advance. He agreed to the proposition, and, collecting about twenty of his men, proceeded to cross the Bull Run Mountain for the purpose of meeting Stuart where Cub Run crosses the Little River Turnpike, the place of rendezvous. But the plan was frustrated by a movement of General Hancock, who, interposing his command, compelled Stuart to make a circuit by Brentsville.

In consequence of this derangement of their plans, Mosby the next day disbanded his men at the Sudley Springs, but reserved eight, with whom he went on a scout to Pleasant Valley, where in a little while he captured a surgeon and a trooper. He then crossed the Braddock Road, which he found occupied by soldiers, artillery, and droves of cattle for the army. But the smallness of his party forbade an attack.

The captured surgeon, who expressed his surprise at the appearance and bearing of Mosby and his followers, as well as at the good treatment which he had received at their hands, was soon after released on condition that he would procure the liberation of Dr. Alexander—a condition which was readily agreed to by the medical gentleman, and speedily complied with by the authorities at Washington.

Chapter 16: Adventures Between the Lines of the Opposing Armies

Upper Fauquier, July 30th, 1863.

Dear Percy,—I take my pen today to give you a rapid survey of our operations from the time that the Confederate Army crossed the Potomac until the time that the Rappahannock again became the dividing line of the hostile armies. It forms a novel and interesting chapter in Mosby's military life, and shows how fertile he is in expedients when pressed by difficulties.

After failing to connect with Stuart, Mosby returned to Middleburg, where he collected about thirty men, and crossed into the Valley for the purpose of joining General Lee in Pennsylvania. He struck for Mercersburg, where he understood a portion of the Southern army could be found, but, on reaching that place, discovered that it had moved. Finding himself in a hostile country with a mere squad of soldiers, and ignorant of the position of Lee's army, Mosby determined to return to Virginia, but brought with him about three hundred beef cattle, which he turned over to the Confederate States commissary at Winchester. At that point he heard of the defeat of our army at Gettysburg.

Prom Winchester Mosby visited Richmond on official business, and on his return appointed a meeting for his command at Rector's Cross-roads. But the advance-guard of General Meade having reached that point, he was compelled to change the rendezvous to Rectortown, where he collected about thirty men. In order to reach the rear of the invading army, he made a detour by way of the Plains, and camped that night in sight of the 11th Corps, which was about Mountsville, in Loudoun County. On his way to this point he met Bush Underwood who, with two men, had captured at Benton's Ford of Goose Creek a lieutenant colonel, a major, and an orderly.

Early the next morning Mosby captured three heavily-laden sutler-wagons and forty-five prisoners, and while thus engaged fell in with General Carl Schurz, who was riding out, and chased him with hot speed into his camp.

The next day the horses were divided among the men, and the prisoners were put in charge of Tom Lake, with a detail of five men, to be conducted to Culpepper Courthouse—a task of no little difficulty when we remember that the country through which Lake had to pass was occupied by hostile troops.

These results got the citizens (who are chiefly Quakers) into trouble, for the next morning the Yankees, infuriated, sent out and arrested many of those living in the vicinity. A very ludicrous occurrence happened in this connection, for several of Mosby's men who had ingratiated themselves with the Friends were captured along with them. But the boys all got Quaker hats and Quaker coats, and it was laughable in the extreme to hear them, with sanctimonious looks, *theeing* and *thouing* the Yankees. But it all passed off well, for the Quakers were soon turned loose, having found no difficulty in establishing their innocence.

Two days later Mosby started from "Camp Spindle," which he had established in the Bull Run Mountain since the occupation of Fauquier and Loudoun by the Northern army, and returned to its rear. Near Circleville he came in sight of nine wagons prepared to forage among the Quakers, and such was the feeling of security that no guard had been deemed necessary for their protection. The wagons were captured and set on fire, and with fifty-six horses and mules and twenty prisoners Mosby returned to the Bull Run Mountain. This affair got the Quakers again into trouble, and another order was issued for their arrest.

Mosby next began to operate farther to the front of Meade's army, between Salem and the Plains. As he was marching from his mountain fastness to the latter place, he captured two cavalry-men loaded with the spoils of a poultry-yard. By them he was informed that a large number of mules had been turned to pasture near the Plains, guarded by forty artillerists. Upon these he made a swoop, and, in full view of the enemy's camp, carried off mules and guard to his mountain rendezvous, laughing at the infantry who were sent in pursuit of him.

The untiring partisan returned in the evening, and, concealing his command in the woods, took with him Fount Beattie and Norman Smith to a hill-top, and presently saw two officers ride out from camp. When they had advanced far enough for him to get in their rear he charged them, and for three miles the exciting chase continued. With bloody spurs, the bare-headed officers made for a wood at the extremity of a lane into which they had entered. But as they approached it they came upon two ladies, who, appreciating the situation, drew up their horses to witness the sport. As Mosby and his two companions passed them, they cheered with waving handkerchiefs, and pointed out the direction which the fugitives had taken. The race was then soon brought to a close, and the two Federals were taken to the Bull Run Mountain, from the crest of which could be plainly seen the Northern army camped in the Plains below.

With five or six men Mosby then rode to Fishback's, almost within the purlieus of the Yankee camp. Here he found a dozen cavalry-men, mounted on officers' horses, and foraging for an officers' mess. These were added to his list of prisoners, and sent to join the captured officers.

I will now give you a personal adventure of Mosby's; which happened about this time, which illustrates strikingly, I think, one of the remarkable traits of his character. With Fount Beattie he was one day asleep in a piece of woods a little above Hathaway's, when a party of Yankees came and searched the house for him. While they were thus occupied, one of the soldiers rode to the woods to look for horses that might there be concealed, and approached the sleepers. As he was levelling his pistol to shoot Mosby awoke, and, springing to his feet, wounded his assailant's horse in the head. He turned to fly, and, as he did so, the partisan chief lodged another bullet in his saddle. Before the searchers could be summoned to the spot, the Rangers were "*over the hills and far away*."

Meade's army now took position in the vicinity of Warrenton.

While the movement was being made Mosby followed the various corps, and hung upon their rear. After the last corps had passed, a major, with thirty men, was sent back to look after him, but fell in with Norman Smith and another man near Mrs. Lewis's house, who were riding some distance in advance of their command, and chased them to the mountain. In the meantime Mosby rode up to inquire the news from Mrs. Lewis. She came out and implored him to save himself by instant flight, for the major, she said, had breakfasted under her roof, and had declared that if he captured Mosby he would hang him to the first tree. But our leader laughed at her fears. At this moment the Yankees were seen coming across the mountain toward the house, and, as fortune determined, Mosby's command of eighteen men appeared on the scene at the same time. They were led instantly to the charge. Up the mountain-side they dashed, leaping over two stone fences which lay across their track. The Yankees broke and fled round and round the mountain, followed by the guerrillas, the fun equalling that of any fox-chase.

The boastful major who had so wrought upon the fears of Mrs. Lewis was caught squatting under a bush. Thirteen men and a lieutenant were also captured. But the lieutenant was the last caught, and not until he had several times made the circuit of the mountain, and, like Reynard when the mouthing dogs are at his heels, had struck out in the direction of a pine forest. Mosby, however, was upon his tracks, and, after the chase had continued thus for more than a mile, his horse, entirely spent, refused to proceed farther. The lieutenant was still fifty yards in advance, and had reached the top of a high hill, when his pursuer resorted to an expedient which succeeded well. He fired at the Yankee, shouting "halt!" The officer reined up, and rode back with his pistol down, Mosby thought, to fight. But it was to surrender.

The prisoner was mounted on a magnificent gray horse, and in the most piteous accent said,

"You won't take my horse, will you?"

"The devil I won't," replied his captor, "what do you suppose I was chasing you for?"

This gallant officer was a lieutenant of the 17th Pennsylvania Cavalry.

During the period of General Meade's advance through Loudoun and Fauquier, Mosby was entirely cut off from all communication with Lee's army, and was compelled by the enemy, who swarmed in every neighbourhood, to abandon his usual haunts. He did not, however, as you have seen, retire before them, but established his camp on the crest of the Bull Run Mountain, from which he descended like a mountain wolf and made daily forays upon the enemy. The amount of his captures during this period was one hundred and eighty-six prisoners, one hundred and twenty-three horses, twelve wagons, fifty sets of fine harness, arms, etc.

Encompassed as he was with enemies, a general belief prevailed that he and his band had been destroyed; but Stuart, who knew him better, said, "No, he'll turn up yet, right side up." And so it was.

CHAPTER 17: "THE ICE-CREAM RAID."

Upper Fauquier, September 1st, 1863.

Dear Percy,—As soon as the army of General Meade had taken a position around Warrenton Mosby broke up his camp on the Bull Run Mountain, again dispersed his men among the citizens, and resumed his warfare upon the enemy's communications. Meade's base of supply was now Alexandria, and Centreville, in the line of his communications, was occupied by a strong detachment of troops. With this object in view, Mosby, with twenty-six men, proceeded to the vicinity of Germantown, a group of hovels which stands, or rather stood, for it has since been destroyed by the Yankees, at the junction of the Little River and Warrenton Turnpikes. In a short distance of this place, on the road to Fairfax Court-house, he captured a sutler-wagon, accompanied by three men, which he sent to Germantown in charge of two of the Rangers to await his return.

At the court-house several other sutler-wagons were found, and also several Yankee stores. One wagon was loaded with cavalry boots, others with a variety of merchandise suited to the use of the army, and one contained ice cream, which in the command has given its name to the raid.

A suitable guard was detailed for these captures, while Mosby, with the rest of the command, proceeded to a wagon-camp one mile below the town. Near the camp the men were halted under cover of a hill, and Bush Underwood and Welt Hatcher were sent forward to reconnoitre. They found the wagons without a guard, and the drivers all asleep except two—one a Dutchman, whom Hatcher treated in a very uncivil manner. They were drinking, and as he passed him Welt pulled the bottle out of the Dutchman's hand, an unwarrantable liberty for which he received a sound cursing. The wagons, twenty-nine in number, were soon captured, and, as they were laden with valuable stores, Mosby determined, contrary to his custom, to attempt to bring off the rich booty—a hazardous enterprise, with a large force of the enemy at Centreville, from which point parties could easily be sent out to intercept him, and with Union men strung along the road to play the part of informers.

Having collected his prizes into one train, as he proceeded on his return, Joe Calvert, a brave and reliable man, was sent to the front to notify Mosby of the approach of any force in that direction. Mosby for a similar purpose remained in the rear. After advancing in this way up the Little River Turnpike for eight miles, an ambulance-train, guarded by twenty-five cavalry, was reported in his front. "All right," he remarked to Bob Gray, who communicated the information, "we will just take them too." At Mat Lee's, just as day was breaking, Mosby rode to the front for the purpose of attacking the ambulance escort, when he saw the flash of a pistol. With eight men, the amount of his available force, he dashed forward, and found that Joe Calvert had been attacked and driven back by a party stationed on the road, and that Bush Underwood, who had been the first to go to his support, had received a severe sabre-cut.

The Yankees were then charged, routed, and hotly pursued to within a hundred yards of Mount Zion Church, when, lo! a regiment of cavalry appeared in line of battle across the road, and at once moved forward. It had marched, under command of Colonel Lowell, from Centreville during the night, in consequence of information that Mosby was below, and had thrown out, as a picket, the force of twenty-nine men which he had encountered on the road.

It was now time for Mosby to retreat, but he first attempted to deceive the enemy as to his strength, while he dispatched a courier to inform the men with, the wagons of the overwhelming attack in his front. The wagons were hastily abandoned, but fifteen of the prisoners, with many horses, were carried to Landmark, in the Bull Run Mountain. To that point Colonel Lowell pursued and rescued all the prisoners.

The enemy lost on this occasion two men killed and four wounded; Mosby's loss was one man wounded and one taken prisoner.

The day after the loss of the sutler-wagons Major Mosby collected about twelve of his scattered forces and started again for Fairfax Court-house, near which he found a wagon-train camped for the night and guarded by cavalry. As he rode across the field he came upon seven of the escort, who had left their command to have a comfortable sleep in a hay-stack. They were captured and ordered to saddle up, never doubting but that they were arrested by their own provost-guard for straggling. Early the next morning, after making additional captures from the neighbouring cavalry-camp, the command was moved to a position on the turnpike about one mile below the town, where it was left, and Mosby took Harry Sweeting, Jack Barnes, and another, and went on a scout. Between Anandale and Alexandria they encountered three wagon-masters lying in the shade, with their pistol-belts unbuckled. From them the partisan leader learned that a large wagon-train was loading in the woods at no great distance, and that the cavalry escort had gone off on a scout. He then told them his name was Mosby, and ordered them to give up their arms, which they did promptly.

Presently the train emerged from the woods on the turnpike, and, as each wagon drove out, it was ordered by Mosby to be taken to a designated spot. The teams from about forty, together with their drivers, were started up the road. Jack Barnes being put in front When he returned to his command, Mosby found that the men had overhauled seven sutler-wagons. It was a rich spoil, and all hands, prisoners included, were allowed to plunder. It was a jolly sight to witness the delight with which the Yankees appropriated the good things of which their countrymen had been despoiled.

News of Mosby's presence on the turnpike below reached Centreville, and a party was dispatched to anticipate his return, but this time without success.

A few days afterward, with a party of twenty men, he captured two hundred wagons, but was only able to bring off the horses and a part of the spoil.

Mosby among the wagon-trains

In an expedition to Paget's about this time, near Alexandria, thirty prisoners and thirty wagons were captured, with about seventy horses and mules, but many of them were lost, in consequence of the party being compelled on their return to travel unfrequented paths.

During this month's operations four hundred prisoners were sent to Stuart. Innumerable expeditions from Meade's army and from the force around Washington were sent to capture our chief, but with no success.

Among the captures which were made that I have not mentioned was a train of nineteen wagons and twenty-five prisoners, which was secured near Anandale, and seven sutler-wagons on the Little River Turnpike, where it is crossed by Accotinck Creek. So much of the contents as they desired was appropriated by the men, and the wagons and the rest of the merchandise were then destroyed. Being in want of information which he could not otherwise obtain, Mosby, with a companion, entered a sutler's camp at Bailey's Cross-roads. As the weather was warm, he wore only his shirt and a pair of blue pantaloons, and, thus habited, approached one of the wagons, the owner of which was standing behind his table ready to serve all customers. The partisan chief called for a glass of beer and a piece of cake, and, at the same time, entered into conversation with the unsuspecting merchant, and extracted from him the information of which he was in search. He then bade the sutler a courteous farewell, and proceeded to avail himself of the knowledge he had acquired.

I shall now pass over several similar captures to those I have related, and only give you the details of one other, which is known in the command as the Boot Raid. It consisted of a number of sutler-wagons, and was made between Fairfax Courthouse and Alexandria, at a point where Mosby had left his command, under Lieutenant William Smith, concealed in the woods, while he, with two men, had gone on a scout. The prize, as soon as secured, was removed from the road into the pines, and then followed its examination. Boxes were broken open, and their contents scattered on the ground. Boots, hats, and other clothing were first appropriated, and the men, dressed in their new clothes, strutted about, objects of mutual admiration; cans were despoiled of their delicious fruits, while champagne bottles poured forth the precious liquor. As the bottle circulated the scene became more noisy and grotesque, and was becoming riotous, when Lieutenant Smith, with an air of authority, arrested it by ordering the men to prepare to return to Fauquier.

Three Rangers were left behind to inform Mosby of what had been done, who, on his return, ate heartily of the canned oysters, fruits, etc., which had been left, for him, and then set out to overtake the command. Night had set in before he joined them, and, as they had to pass a point where a party of his men had been bushwhacked on a previous occasion, he expressed some concern lest the attack might be repeated. This suggestion produced a general state of excitement, and as they entered a wood, the object of their apprehension, all were on the alert for the first sound of the bushwhackers. Soon a great rustling was heard among the leaves, and each man wheeled his horse to avoid being shot from the ambush. Down the road they galloped for a quarter of a mile, scattering in their flight the boots, clothes, boxes of cigars, hats, and other articles of which they had just despoiled the sutlers. At last they rallied, and, after a careful reconnoissance, discovered that their dreaded adversary was a prolific old sow with her fifteen pigs. When the plunder was divided near Mat Skinner's, each man got three pair of boots, besides his share of the other articles.

I will, before concluding this letter, give you an account of the fight at Gooding's tavern, in which our leader was badly wounded, and in consequence of which he is still absent from his command.

On the 23rd of August, Mosby, with thirty-five men, reached a position near Anandale, and, after posting them in a wood, took with him Norman Smith and Jack Barnes to go on a scout. Late at night the party stopped to sleep in a haystack at Ravensworth, a private residence, and when they awoke in the morning found, themselves in full view of and close proximity to an encampment of Yankees. Without being suspected, they quickly saddled up and returned to Anandale, having discovered several unguarded bridges. From the wood Mosby saw a drove of a hundred horses pass up the road under guard of forty cavalry. He at once decided to attack this party, and to postpone burning the bridges until night.

Mounting his command, he followed in their rear until he came within half a mile of Gooding's tavern, where the Yankees halted to water their horses. Mosby also halted, and detached Lieutenant Tom Turner, with half the command, to make a circuit so as to attack the escort in front, while he fell upon their rear. While this movement was being executed, twenty non-commissioned officers on furlough, under charge of a captain, came up. This was an event for which Mosby had made no calculation, but there was no help for it. So at them he dashed, driving them back toward the escort, which was still at the tavern. With Norman Smith at his side, Mosby led the charge upon the combined parties, and routed and scattered them in all directions. A few took shelter under cover of the houses, but were soon silenced. At the very moment of victory, Mosby was shot through the side and thigh, and was borne to the woods by Dr. Dunn, the surgeon. The men, not understanding it, followed their leader, which gave the Yankees time to escape. But for this accident they would all have been captured. As soon as Mosby was aware of it, he ordered the men to go back, which they did just as Lieutenant Turner came gallantly charging up, having attacked and routed another party above. Six of the Yankees lay dead on the field.

Over a hundred horses fell into the possession of the partisans (though a good many were lost in bringing them off at night); also twelve prisoners, arms, etc. Mosby's loss was two killed and three wounded. Lieutenant Shriver, of Maryland, a gallant soldier, was one of the victims of this fight; the other was Norman Smith, of whom Mosby said, "He has left the memory of a name which will not be forgotten till honour, virtue, courage, all shall cease to claim the homage of the heart." Lieutenant William Smith, of the Black Horse, on duty with us, acted on this occasion, as he always does, with conspicuous gallantry.

Lieutenant Turner succeeded to the command, and, after dispatching the prisoners and horses to Fauquier, proceeded to burn the bridges before alluded to.

Chapter 18: The Partisan Chaplain at His Devotions

Upper Fauquier, September 22nd, 1863.

Dear Percy,—On the return from a scout to Fairfax I broke off at New Baltimore, and crossed the Pig-nut range of hills, determined to execute a purpose which I had long entertained, of paying a visit to the Rev. Dr. Gog, the chaplain of our command. In my rambles and adventures in many parts of the world I have acquired, as you know, no small degree of skill as a woodsman and land pilot. This, added to some knowledge of Upper Fauquier, enabled me, without difficulty, to find his abode. As the doctor is a character the like of whom is not met every day, I will give you some account of the exterior of his dwelling. In front of it was a grove of forest trees, from which was cut off, by a dilapidated post-fence, a spacious and level yard, covered with luxuriant greensward, which in some places was eaten close to the ground. It was an ordinary farmhouse, constructed of wood, with the first floor on the ground. The owner had abandoned it when the Northern army first penetrated the country, and had left it in the custody of a family of negroes, who still occupied one of the outhouses. In a corner of the enclosure was a copious spring, of clear cold water, at which a woman was engaged in washing clothes, some of which had been hung to dry on the fence, while others had been spread over several snow-ball bushes which grew hard by, a row of which appeared at one time to have formed a half circle in front of the house.

A large and powerful iron-gray horse, marked with the United States brand, which I at once recognised as the property of the parson, was fastened by a halter-chain to a heavy block, and was quietly cropping the verdant sod. But these rural features did not complete the picture. To the trees in the grove full fifteen horses, with military equipments, were fastened, and I reasonably inferred that their riders had sought this holy place for religious consolation. The only important peculiarity in the interior arrangement of the building was, as I afterward learned, a large hall or dining-room on the east side of the house, which the present occupant called "the chapel." Judge, then, of my surprise, when, as I approached this parsonage, or "glebe," as the doctor himself sometimes calls it, I heard sounds of revelry issuing from the interior of the chapel.

I determined to reconnoitre the position, for it occurred to me as far from improbable that a raiding-party had invaded these sacred premises, and were desecrating them with ribaldry and song. With a stealthy step, as catlike as that with which a North American savage approaches his victim, I drew near an open window from which the noise proceeded. It was mantled by vines and running roses, which clung to a trellis, and were then trained up the sides of the window. Standing here, my concealment was complete, while, by putting aside the branches of a honeysuckle, I obtained a view of the interior of the apartment.

All apprehension was at once set at rest by the appearance of the chaplain himself, not occupied with sacred meditation, prayer, or penitential hymns, but instead I beheld a scene which has shaken my confidence in the severity at least of his religious code. The floor of the room could not, I am sure, have been swept since the owner had left the house, or *refugeed*, in the phraseology of the day. In addition to an astonishing accumulation of trash, it was scattered over with odd boots and shoes, sword-belts, broken bridles and discarded gear of that kind. But one article of furniture deserves a more particular notice. It occupied one of the corners of the room, and was a very large brass-plated saddle, with stirrups and bridle-mounting to suit, the property of the worthy churchman. It was the pride of his heart, and had been presented to him, he told me, by his parishioners, as, in ecclesiastical phrase, he called the men of the battalion. Broken chairs and broken benches added to the decorations of the chapel. I did not find, as I have said, Dr. Gog engaged in the exercises of religion, but instead he was sitting at the head of a table in a huge armchair, engaged in the unclerical employment of playing cards with his visitors.

A red flannel shirt, open at the breast, with the sleeves tucked up to the elbows, blended in horrid sympathy with a suit of coarse red hair as it fell upon his shoulders. In his lap lay a cat of unusual size, purring and sleeping, and *anon* looking gravely in his master's face as he would pass his hand along the animal's back and striped tail with evident pleasure. This was the parson's principal pet, his "chief of staff", he would pleasantly say, and had been trained to fly at any object upon which it was set. It had been named Ajax on account of its bellicose disposition, and the master's love for his fierce quadruped was of no ordinary strength. How it delighted him to take one of Ajax's paws, expand it on the palm of his hand, and admire the length and sharpness of its claws!

MOSBY'S CHAPLAIN AT HIS DEVOTIONS

At the doctor's feet and under his chair lay several terriers—Brindle, Trip, Mustard, Ring, and Sweetheart, which at intervals shared with Ajax their master's caresses. A large tumbler of spirit was set on his right hand, from which the doctor would often sip with evident relish. Some four or five of the company were engaged with the game, while the others stood around the players, but not uninterested spectators, for from time to time they would make special or by bets, as they are called, as the game progressed.

At the other end of the table was seated Mr. Blackwell Magog, the friend, the relative, and often the boon companion of his host Like his great "contemporary," as he often called the parson, he is of large proportions, is much encumbered with flesh, and is by several inches the taller of the two. There are a great many points of dissimilarity between the two men, yet there exists still what might be called a family likeness, for, as the parson has often remarked with great emphasis, "blood will show."

This observation, as remarkable for its truth as its originality, is strikingly illustrated in the persons of the portly cousins. Some of the men, struck, doubtless, by the covert and unexplained resemblance, call them "The Twins," though so monstrous a brotherhood is evidently excluded by the possibilities of nature. Still the astronomers call them "Gemini," the Castor and Pollux of guerrillas, and no star-gazer could, on the score of magnitude at least, contest the right of two such figures to form a constellation in the zodiac. With so grand an apotheosis, even such powerful spirits as Gog and Magog ought, in all reason, to be content. Outside, or rather inside of these physical points are many coincidences of disposition, which add strength to the parson's emphatic but unoriginal apothegm. Both of these gentlemen enjoy keenly the pleasures of the table; both like a relish of brandy, or new-dip, if better can't be had; both are devoted to the chastened society of cultivated females; both love cards, at which one of them is an adept; and both are fond of war, at least the quartermaster's department of it, and would follow a wagon-train or hang round a corral of horses with the pertinacity of a famished jackal or a Cossack wolf; and, finally, both are avowed devotees of the grape.

This trait is so conspicuous in the character of each of the worthy relatives, that Mr. John B. Jeffries wittily called them "Grog and More Grog." This alteration in their patronymics took the rounds of the battalion, very much to the scandal of the parson. One of the "young roosters" thought it so good a thing that on one occasion he addressed the chaplain as Dr. Grog, and was very properly knocked down for his impertinence. A blow from the parson's fist soon became proverbial in Mosby's confederacy, and was called a papal bull, and no one was ever so contumacious as to have it thundered against him a second time. After that the joke fell into disrepute, or was never alluded to except behind the doctor's back.

Dr. Gog, as you already know, is the inducted chaplain of the Rangers, and Mr. Blackwell Magog is the chief of staff—both high officials.

Turning once more to the other person of this duality, we will find much to admire in Mr. Blackwell Magog, and I am sure you will be entertained by a more particular account of him. The most conspicuous trait, then, in the chief's mental organism is a high poetical temperament—a mind of an imaginative cast. This is a rare endowment, and makes the chief a very extraordinary person. I do not assert that he has ever composed a great poem like the Iliad, or Childe Harold, or any other masterpiece that elevates human genius almost to the rank of the archangels, or even that he has ever amused his leisure with the lighter productions of the muse, such as sonnets, odes, madrigals, or lyrics. No, the chief has devoted himself to the active pursuits of life, and has had no time for such literary flirtations. But still, I repeat, he is a poet. "Let me illustrate," as the puzzled lawyer says when he is entangled in the meshes of his own argument, "let me illustrate."

If the chief were to undertake to relate any occurrence that he had seen or heard, no one could possibly recognise the story. His creative genius being brought immediately into play, he would brood over the subject, and a transformation would at once take place. The egg would hatch, and a bird of Paradise would come forth with its brilliant plumage; the dull and commonplace, becoming electrified, would be sentimental or heroic, tragic or comic, according to the nature of the subject, the condition of the atmosphere, or the mood of the mighty magician, or "the great Dundidler," as the guerrillas sometimes call him. As a Walter Scott, by a magical process known only to men of genius, would transform a rustic lay or a wild legend caught from the lips of some untutored peasant into an immortal poem or a prose-drama destined to be embalmed in the memory forever, or a Homer would turn an obscure and half-remembered tradition into an Iliad, with its divine and human actors blended in a wondrous harmony, so Mr. Blackwell Magog can metamorphose the most ordinary transaction into an astonishing romance, investing it with the brilliant hues of a fervid imagination. This is what I mean by being a poet, for the best critics are agreed that it is the creative power that forms the poet.

A practical inconvenience, however, has resulted from this exuberance of fancy not generally felt by the children of song. His friends and admirers—and Mr. Blackwell Magog has a great many friends and admirers—not knowing where the poem ends and where the history begins, are puzzled in the attempt to separate the golden ores of fancy from the dross of fact. But little by little this inconvenience has abated, for his intimate associates have come to regard the chief as a rich placer, indeed a nugget in which there is little else than the pure metal. A singular result has ensued from the outpourings of this abundant spring of fiction, the enrichment of the English tongue by a new and very expressive word—*blackwellism*, which the parson uses to designate these flights of fancy. It is an ill wind that blows nobody good, and a redundant imagination has added a very beautiful word to the dictionary—another key to the wondrous organ of human speech. To sum the whole, Mr. Blackwell Magog is an example of a man in whom the faculty of memory is overwhelmed and confounded by the energy of a creative imagination.

The chief and the parson, or rather the parson and the chief, for among Mosby's men the Church is always piously preferred, were on this occasion sitting, as I have said, at opposite ends of the table. Contrasted with some of the figures around them, they looked like hippopotami on the banks of the Senegambia, come forth from the liquid element to bask in the warmth and radiance of an African sun.

Parson. "By the groves of Venus and the wine-presses of Bacchus, never was a man so persecuted by Fortune as I have been today. I have lost not a dollar under three hundred in greenbacks, as good as Chase ever issued from his paper-mill. Ministers of grace! and all this bad luck has been brought upon me by that profane, awkward, heavy-built, whisky-drinking, calico-stealing guerrilla, Mr. Blackwell Magog. I have never had any luck when that fellow has been about, especially at cards. I believe he would ruin the fortune of a saint, much less of a humble minister like me."

A voice from one of the bystanders responded with emphasis,

"Well, doctor, I am not surprised at that. You will have to keep a sharp look-out in this crowd. These are stirring times, I tell you, reverend sir!"

Parson. "You are quite right. A man, or woman too, for that matter, must keep wide awake here. But that fellow has ever been a bird of ill omen to me."

John De Butts. "Egad, you might with more propriety call him a bird of prey, for he has plucked many a pigeon in his time."

"No, no," responded a very youthful soldier, "Mr. Blackwell Magog is a vulture."

"Why?" inquired several voices.

"Because," responded the youth, "he preys on Dr. Gog."

Parson (with dignity). "I am offended, and I shall take no farther notice of yon."

Johnny Alexander. "I humbly ask your pardon. I do, on my honour, parson."

Parson. "I can not understand why Mosby, who appears to have some sense about other matters, should take these young chaps into his command. They are like two-year olds, fit neither for the saddle nor the collar, yet are able to consume the provender and fill the room of a valuable beast. By Pluto! he will have to build a nursery for them. How I would like to have charge of the establishment with a keen cowhide!"

Mr. Blackwell Magog. "Indeed, I think it would suit you much better than the Church."

George Smith. "That's not my opinion. He would corrupt the morals of the youth committed to his care, but here he can at least do no harm. Mr. Blackwell Magog will next propose him as the principal of a female academy. Wouldn't that position suit his style?—regulating the dress and behaviour of young ladies, and putting on the last touch for society!"

"Yes," exclaimed several voices, "the parson would make a splendid *duenna.*"

Johnny Munson. "Are you not afraid, parson, lest your dissipated habits come to the colonel's ear? He would without doubt dismiss you from your post."

Parson. "What, I should be pleased to know, has he to do with the discipline of the Church? He knows enough of business to mind his own affairs. As long as my code of religious morals does not forbid murder and horse-stealing, I do not know what the like of you have to object to it. You may learn from the page of history, John Munson, and I suppose you have been flogged through enough of it to learn that this thing has been often tried by worldly men, but the Church has always come off victorious. Kings and emperors have been made to bow to the mitre. Besides, this Mosby of yours is a good deal of a humbug."

Several voices, "How? tell us how!"

Parson, "Because, sirrahs, I never knew a man of real genius who wasn't fond of French brandy. But your master never touches a drop of the ardent. Look at Alexander the Great how he went it! Didn't he die in an orgy? Then there's Mark Antony, one of the best soldiers of Rome, and Plutarch thinks one of the greatest men of antiquity, he was drawn through Italy on a car crowned and attended as the god Bacchus. Go to our own army, too; have I not seen, while the troops lay at Manassas, a revel among high officers that would shame a Bacchanal?"

Johnny Munson. "Noble models you propose for the imitation of our commander—a drunken Greek, a degenerate Roman, and Confederate officers who ought to have been cashiered. You are doubtless prepared to recommend him to borrow the dusky hues of the African, that he may resemble a Hannibal or Othello."

Doctor Gog turned with contempt from the last speaker, and in a mincing, mocking tone, continued,

"It is all coffee, coffee, coffee! He never enters a Southern woman's house but it is, 'Colonel Mosby, will you have a cup of coffee?' I have seen him on horseback, in the streets of Leesburg, as he was returning from a successful expedition, surrounded by ladies. One miss, with flowing curls, held the coffee-pot, while another, it might be a summer younger, held the sugar-jar from which your master would from time to time be supplied. From that hour I lost all confidence in your guerrilla chief If it had been a flask of cognac, or even a glass of your brave Loudoun whisky, I could have understood the thing."

Johnny Munson. "I have no doubt, parson, if your places were changed, you would set him adrift for being a coffee-drinker, and it is just possible that Mosby may some day exhibit toward you a similar illiberality."

Parson, "I'd like to know, sirrah, who would suffer most by that? How do you think the command would do without me?"

Johnny Alexander. "Do without you, doctor? Listen, and I will tell you what they would do without you."

Parson, "Well, Mr. Jackanapes, what?"

Johnny Alexander. "Why, chaplain, they would go to h—ll their own way instead of yours."

This sally produced much applause, which for a moment disconcerted Dr. Grog, but he soon rallied.

"You saucy, ill-mannered, ill-contrived, ill-thriven, withered, wizen-faced, half-fed monkey, what knowest thou about sacred things? I tell thee, sirrah, thou art not fit to be the lackey of a monastery, or to carry water from a pump, or to bear a lighted taper, or ring a silver bell, or dust the altar, or unloose the latchet of mine own shoe, or, in fine, to do aught that appertains to holy things, much less unsought to pass thy censure on the high concerns and mysteries of the Church. I tell thee roundly I mean, at my convenience, to take thee in hand, and administer a well-merited castigation. I do, thou untaught, thou unwashed, unchristened varlet, thou unlicked cub! You ought to be at school, sir; and thy mammy, if perchance thou hast one, ought to smack thee and send thee to bed. If I were she, or she but knew the duties of maternity, boy, the stars wouldn't find thee abroad, unless those early sentinels which morning sets in the sky to tell upon the lazy plough-boy. With all the Christian charity that doth possess my soul, I can not abide these half-fledged, scratching, crowing, spurless roosters. Bad luck to you, you impudent starling! Lord, how I have prayed for them, the graceless *banditti!*"

Here the good parson bowed his head on the table, as if overwhelmed by ingratitude. The company appeared to be touched by this unexpected demonstration, and looked reproachfully at Johnny Alexander for his unkind, or at least thoughtless words—those envenomed shafts which are scattered so wide and driven so deep. But the youth was nothing daunted, and even smiled good-humouredly at the philippic of the offended churchman. He did not blink an eye, but was ready to let fly another arrow at his adversary as soon as he should detect a crevice or vulnerable point in his armour. The minute and watchful martin was he, perched on some withered twig, his bright, piercing eye turned oft askant, but ready to pounce upon the hawk or crow, his hereditary enemy, as soon as he should unfurl his wings and expand them on the ambient and buoyant air.

"Dr. Gog," inquired a young gentleman, who, from the texture of his clothes and his fair hands, seemed to have just joined the command, "Dr. Grog, to what society of Christians did you belong before the war?"

Parson, "I was a Black Rock Baptist, and had been a Southern Methodist."

The youth again inquired: "Were you in the ministry, reverend sir?"

Parson, "My master, you are over inquisitive for a newcomer, but I have no objection to satisfying your curiosity, as it may perchance be of service to you. It will teach you, at least, to begin where I ended. I commenced my religious life as an Episcopalian, but soon grew offended at their starch and gentility. I next tried the Presbyterians, and abode with them until they got to looking into my life, as they called it. I then got with the Methodists and Baptists. I tried the Campbellites, too, for a time, and lodged a few weeks with the Free Communion Baptists, passing from one to the other like a bad shilling. I have now the honour to inform you, my master, that I am a preacher in the great Universalist Church, where I expect to remain for the rest of my natural life."

All. "Good, good! That's the very church for Dr. Gog."

Parson. "Yes; and, let me inform you, it is the very Church for every one of you; for what chance have any of you for heaven unless through the general amnesty which that Church has proclaimed to all sinners? Your master knew this when he besought me to take charge of your souls."

The game had been suspended during this conversation, and Mr. Blackwell Magog, in company with several others, had left the room for some sinister purpose, as I was afterward led to suspect. Upon their return a renewal of the game was proposed, and acceded to by all but the parson, who demurred because, as he said, the jade Fortune was against him that day; but he finally agreed to play if Munson would pay the fifty dollars he owed him. The proposition was promptly agreed to, and the debtor handed over a fifty dollar Confederate note.

Parson, "I lent you, sir, fifty dollars in Yankee money, and I'll let you know that I understand how to collect the dues of the Church."

Munson, "Why, parson, I only meant it for a proposition. I will pay you, if you prefer, in greenbacks."

Parson, "Your proposition was at least cool—yes, sir, devilish cool; but I leave others to determine its morality. Under the cloak of the figures on that bill, you proposed to transfer just forty-nine dollars and fifty cents from my pocket to yours."

Munson. "Forgive me, doctor, but I thought you so good a patriot as to seize with avidity any opportunity to display to the world how much more you value the Confederates than the Yankees. Besides, you know, everybody says that, as soon as the war is over, Confederate money will be as good as gold."

Parson, "Then keep it yourself, John Munson, for your patriotism stands fully as much in need of illustration as mine."

One of the Rangers here remarked, if the politicians would restore the credit of the finances they must take their ugly faces off the notes, for they are enough to destroy any fiscal system.

"Yes," responded Mr. Blackwell Magog, "and put old Abe's, I suppose, in their place."

Parson. "No, no, my beauty; when Congress sets about to reclaim the currency by the employment of such means, they'll certainly photograph your full moon."

Mr. Blackwell Magog. "And your red head."

Munson. "Excellent! what a combination, to have the strong points of two such paragons! Gog's curls and Magog's blushes! Wouldn't that be to add a perfume to the violet! Ha! ha! ha!"

All. "Ha! ha! ha!"

John De Butts. "Capital idea that. The notes would soon be at a premium, at least with the young ladies, for you know they dote on the parson."

James Keith. "I don't know how it is with the guerrillas, but in the regular service we are opposed to blending the perfections of two such different styles of beauty; indeed, I might with more propriety say, orders of architecture. A Greek artist is said to have tried this, and the result was a picture so shockingly ugly as to drive him mad."

Johnny Alexander. "That's the most sensible thing I've heard today."

Parson (with a severe manner). "Gentlemen, your remarks are growing personal. I trust you will not forget that you are within the precincts of a chapel. Though I would not be boastful of the gifts of nature, nor value myself too highly on the vain article of beauty, but would, with all humility, acknowledge the perishable nature of such external advantages, yet do I entertain the opinion that Cousin Magog and myself are by all odds the handsomest men in the room. Such, at least, would be the verdict of any jury of maidens in Fauquier. In Lilliput, or among the Bushman race, such a shrimp and manikin as Johnny Alexander might be received, but not here—no, not in Virginia. What think you, Mr. Blackwell Magog?"

Mr. Blackwell Magog. "I would think, cousin, the better of your proposition if you had left yourself out; but, for the life of me, I can not reconcile a red head with my ideas of beauty."

Parson. "The devil you can't! Pray, then, what do you think of your own bull-pup features? Do you think the Apollo looked like that? You blunderer, you don't understand that I put you along with myself only out of respect for your family. Auburn locks, let me assure you, in all ages, have been thought, among people of taste, far handsomer than the dirty sheepskin you wear on your head."

"Hurrah!" shouted one of the company, "the twins, are pulling at each other;" and Johnny Alexander jumped up into a chair, and flapped his wings, and crowed at Dr. Gog. The mirth and confusion having subsided, and Munson having discharged his debt in the desired currency, the game recommenced with renewed ardour. Loo it still was. Silence reigned at the board, broken only by the muttered curses of unfortunate players. To the parson Fortune was again unpropitious, and he staked his last note.

"They have gutted my pocket-book," said he, as he returned it to his breast pocket. "They have gutted my pocket-book, and I shall be compelled to draw again on Secretary Chase."

A Ranger. "You have bad luck, doctor. Why don't you try the widow?"

Parson. "I have tried her already three hands in five, and the bitch has almost ruined me. But I begin to suspect that Fortune does not preside at this board, and that the cards do not have their own way." The doctor's last stake was up, and he had become somewhat nervous as he exclaimed with energy, "I believe there has been foul play at this board all day; yes, a conspiracy to pluck me. I have not lost less than five hundred dollars in greenbacks and gold."

The players all protested their innocence, and Mr. Blackwell Magog expressed his indignation at the injurious suspicion thus cast on a company of gentlemen.

Parson. "Since you are so sensitive you can give me the cards, for a shuffle will soon disclose whether there has been any rascality here."

After some demurring on the part of his great relative, the cards were handed to the parson, who remarked as he took them,

"You have such a sleight of hand at cards that I believe you have had something to do with a *faro* bank."

But events now hurried to a catastrophe. The chief's arrangement of the cards now had been disconcerted, and soon the foul play was apparent. The parson threw on the board the evidence of fraud, and seized a scourge of knotted and twisted ropes which lay near, which he kept to preserve peace among his favourites. He sprang to his feet, overturning the table, the cards, the money, and the glasses, shouting at the same time, "Thieves and moneychangers in the temple of the Lord." He seconded his words with blows, and uproar and confusion reigned.

The gamblers rushed to the door, for the desire to escape that dreadful lash was uppermost in every breast. In the meantime, Ajax was not idle, using his claws and teeth with terrible effect, and adding to the din by his fierce battle-cry, while the terriers annoyed and delayed the retreat.

As soon as his guests had departed, the parson made haste to purse the money which lay scattered on the floor, and then threw himself in a chair, and began to whistle the "Mocking-bird."

Soon I knocked at the door of the mansion, and was most graciously received. Supposing that I had been a witness of what had just occurred, my host remarked with a laugh,

"I reckon, Mr. Arthur, you never saw anything like that in the old country. It will be several weeks before these fellows come again to cheat me at cards. Ha! ha! ha!"

After spending an hour with the parson, during which time he furnished me with a substantial lunch, I rose to depart, waiting only until Juniper could bring my horse from the stable, where he had been carried to get a bait of corn.

Parson, "Well, Mr. Arthur, glad to see you always. Come and spend a week with me."

I assured him I would often visit him, but insisted as a condition that he should spend several days with me at my ranch on the Blue Ridge.

Parson. "To be sure I will. I hear you have quite a little town up there, but I hope the Yankees won't find it. When I come, it will not be, remember, to get the blockade you were telling me of, though I have no objection to that, but to talk about the Old Country, for I begin to think it was not such a clever thing after all to have torn us from the old mother. I think General Washington would have done better had he left the cubs with the dam a while longer. I am coming up to have a gossip about the old Revolution—that is, after I have looked through several volumes which I received the other day from a blockade runner in Fairfax."

The reverend gentleman, I must explain, is something of a bookworm, reading suiting his sluggish disposition. He has been known to lie about the house for weeks, silently absorbing volume after volume. In this way his acquirements are considerable, though very much diversified.

I bade *adieu* to my hospitable friend, and, as I did so, he took me cordially by the hand, and, walking toward my horse, said,

"I have taken a liking to you, Mr. Arthur, and I don't care if you know it. "When I meet an English gentleman, I feel that I have found a man it will do to tie to."

We parted with many expressions of mutual esteem, and I turned my horse's head homeward.

All hail, Doctor Grog!

CHAPTER 19: CAPTURE OF COLONEL DULANEY

Upper Fauquier, October 25th, 1863.

Dear Percy,—After a few weeks' absence, in consequence of the wound received in the fight at Gooding's tavern, Major Mosby returned to the command, and at once recommenced his harassing assaults upon Meade's communications. He expressed himself as highly pleased with Lieutenant Turner's activity during his absence, and said, in his official report to Stuart, that he had proved himself in every way fully equal to the trust.

This interval I shall pass over, for I have devoted it to society rather than arms, as I was anxious to acquire a definite knowledge of the country, and an acquaintance with the people among whom Mosby's idea of partisan warfare is to be developed.

One incident, of rather an amusing nature, I will relate to you, which occurred on an expedition under Lieutenant William R. Smith to Warrenton Junction, in which he captured several wagons, a large amount of sutlers' goods, eighteen horses, and ten mules. The goods were found stored in a house in front of which three wagons were standing. John Munson, with a fire-brand in his hand, approached one of them, and found two sutlers asleep on a buffalo robe, with a pack of cards and a candlestick at their heads. He waked them up, and said he wanted that robe. In reply, one of them bade him go to h—ll; but Munson, anxious to find out where their horses were, said, "The guerrillas are coming; you had better hitch up."

The Yankee responded, "Damn the guerrillas; I have been bothering myself to death, ever since the army began to move, to keep out of their way, and now I don't care much if they do catch me."

Munson then informed the sutler of his connection with Mosby, and he at once handed over the buffalo robe, and various other articles useful to a man in Munson's line of business.

But to return to Mosby. His first act was to organise Company B at Scuffleburg, a hamlet at the base of the Blue Ridge, not far from Markham. The recruits had been gathered in the country north of the Rappahannock River, and most of them had seen service with the partisans. In accordance with the system which he had determined on in the very outset of his career, Mosby had selected the officers for this company, and required the men by their votes to ratify his choice, and stamp it with the authority of law. He saw at a glance that the law of Congress, which ordained the election instead of the appointment of officers, would, if executed, prove even more destructive in his command than it had done in the regular service. He did not hesitate, therefore, to put it aside with that vigour and promptitude which belong only to men qualified for command.

William R. Smith, of Fauquier, a lieutenant of the famous Black Horse Company, had been selected by Mosby as the captain of the new company. He is a man in the prime of life, is remarkable for his personal strength, is cool, bold, and possesses in a remarkable degree the qualities necessary to command. (See note following).

******

Note:—It may interest some readers if a brief account of the Black Horse Company of Cavalry, in which Captain Smith was a lieutenant, is appended to this page. It was organised the spring before the repose of the country was broken by the irruption of John Brown, and in what is popularly known as the John Brown War it was remarked for its activity and zeal. These gay cavaliers, even at that period, had adopted the disunion flag, and they greatly shocked, by their free utterance of disunion sentiments, the conservative opinion of Jefferson County. As soon as the war broke out the officers and men of the Black Horse— for they had nothing of the Carpet Knight about them—took the field, and faithfully did they perform their part. If the flag of Southern independence did not wave in triumph at the close as it did at the beginning of the war, it was not the fault of the

Black Horse Company; for it was at the birth of the Army of Northern Virginia at Manassas, accompanied it in its bloody progress through the war, and was present in the hour of its dissolution at Appomattox Court-house. William H. Payne, its captain, rose to be brigadier general of cavalry, and was distinguished, wherever he fought, for uncommon gallantry. Robert Randolph, the first lieutenant, became lieutenant colonel of the 4th Regiment of Virginia Cavalry, and fell in battle, near Richmond, toward the close of the war. If the virtues of men live after them, those of Randolph will gather around his tomb and adorn it as a garland of fragrant flowers. A. D. Payne, who at the formation of this famous company was a private in its ranks, became during the progress of the war, its captain, and well sustained its dear-bought reputation for constancy and valour.—Original Editor.

★★★★★★

CAPTAIN SMITH

Frank Williams and Ab Wren, from Fairfax, and Robert Gray, from Loudoun, completed the list of commissioned officers. Each of them had served with Mosby, and had won his promotion by the exhibition of superior merit. On the 21st of August we started, Mosby in command, to attack Meade's line of communication on the Orange and Alexandria Railroad. At a point between Warrenton Junction and Bealton we discovered an immense pontoon train moving in the direction of the Rappahannock River. Mosby thought this indicated the intention of the Federal general to cross the river, and immediately retired to the pines, and communicated the fact to General Lee in a dispatch, which he sent by Horace Johnson, of the Black Horse, who, in order to deliver it, had to pass through the hostile army.

The railroad Mosby found too closely guarded for him to effect any thing at that point. In consequence, he proceeded in the direction of Fairfax Court-house in search of farther information, and when he reached Buckland, a point on the turnpike between Warrenton and Bull Run, he sent back the command in charge of Captain Smith, reserving for himself a party of ten. When we reached the battlefield of Manassas we met thirty Yankee cavalry, each with a led horse, for they were out on a horse-stealing expedition. We charged and routed them, taking thirteen prisoners, who were immediately sent under guard to Fauquier. At night our party slept in a pine thicket, and we were aroused in the morning by the reveille from a Yankee camp only a few hundred yards distant, of the existence of which we had been perfectly unconscious. We were soon mounted, and, passing around the camp, struck out in the direction of Burke's Station, with the design of capturing the trains engaged there in hauling wood.

But we found the work had been suspended, and the mules turned out to graze in a field near an infantry camp. The guard was captured and the animals driven off in sight of the regiment, who, in their doubt and amazement at the boldness of the exploit, made no effort to recapture them. After making a circuit of several miles through the pines, in order to baffle pursuit, the mules were trotted off under an escort to Fauquier.

Mosby then, with four men, proceeded on his scout toward Alexandria, and rode to the heights in the vicinity, where he spent several hours watching with his glasses the movements both on the Virginia side and around Washington. Night putting a stop to his observations, our scouting-party slept in the woods, and the next day returned to Fauquier.

On the 27th of September, Mosby, with eight men, left Fauquier, his object being to capture Colonel Dulaney, aid to Governor Pierpont. We travelled toward Alexandria by unfrequented roads, but following the direction of the Little River Turnpike. Flanking around Fairfax Court-house, we slept in the pines between that place and Alexandria. The next day was spent in collecting information and picking up stragglers, a half dozen of whom were sent off under guard late in the afternoon. This reduced our party to five.

About sunset we started again for Alexandria, and soon after nightfall struck the Telegraph Road two miles from the town, Mosby inquiring as he proceeded for Colonel Dulaney's residence. He was informed that the colonel had passed but a few hours before on his way to Chestnut Hill. He had been to Fairfax Court-house during the early part of the day, where he heard that Mosby had passed through the lines, and had hastened to communicate it to the authorities at Alexandria.

The road on which we were travelling was a thoroughfare leading to Alexandria, and we galloped rapidly along, the citizens whom we passed little suspecting that darkness alone concealed from their view the renowned Partisan chief. It was not long before our guide pointed out Chestnut Hill, where the object of our search was supposed to be. We approached the door, and knocked for admittance. An upper window was thrown open, and Mosby pleasantly inquired, "Is Colonel Dulaney in?" Being told that he was, Mosby replied that he was just from Alexandria with dispatches from the governor, which he must deliver in person. Colonel Dulaney, not at all surprised at this nocturnal visit, soon appeared to receive the dispatches. As he opened the door, Mosby asked, in a polite tone, "Is this Colonel Dulaney?"

"Yes, sir," was the reply. "Walk in, gentlemen, and be seated."

As he advanced, our leader added, "My name is Mosby."

This startling announcement confused the staff-officer for a minute, but the situation was soon explained, and, after giving a simple promise not to attempt to escape, he was allowed the liberty of the house for the purpose of preparing for his trip to Richmond. After some delay on this account, we mounted, and, accompanied by the prisoner, were soon again on the road leading to Alexandria. This we followed until we struck the railroad where it crosses Cameron's Run. Here we collected combustible materials and burned the bridge, under the guns of two of the most formidable forts erected for the defence of the town. We then returned to Fauquier, from which point the prisoner was sent to Richmond.

As soon as Mosby discovered that Meade was making a retrograde movement to Fairfax Court-house, he started from Middleburg with fifty men for the purpose of attacking the trains of the retreating army. Below Mount Zion he fell in with the battalion of cavalry commanded by the gallant and distinguished Colonel Elisha V. White. After a brief consultation between the two officers, Mosby determined to leave this field of operations to White, and strike the enemy farther down their line of march.

With this intention he made a detour, and about sunset secreted his command near Frying-pan Church. Leaving Captain Smith in command, Mosby, with a small party, proceeded to Chantilly, where they concealed themselves until a wagon-train which they heard approaching had rolled by. Discovering that the train had no escort, Mosby, with his seven men, in the most natural way, fell in behind the wagons, and, as train-guard, passed through the Yankee camps, which, with their blazing fires, were strung along on either side of the turnpike. Martial figures, collected in groups around the fires, with their rugged and often savage countenances, presented a picturesque appearance. They were infantry, and their stacked muskets reflected the light from their polished bores. The night was dark and cloudy, and when the train, with its strange escort, passed the line of camp-fires, all was again wrapped in darkness.

At a signal from our leader, we rushed upon the wagons, and easily effected their capture. In the meantime, several officers and mounted men, as they passed to and fro, were made prisoners and disarmed; among them Captain Barton, the adjutant of an infantry regiment.

This was a rich harvest-field; but, our presence being discovered, we were compelled to retreat, carrying off with us thirty-six mules, seven horses, and thirteen Yankees.

The prisoners were sent to Fauquier in charge of Walter Frankland and five men, and Mosby returned to the command, which he had left with Captain Smith. Taking with him another detail of seven men, he returned to the Federal camp, but entered it at a different point. He was, however, soon discovered, and sentinels were posted around to prevent his escape. But this proved no obstacle to Mosby, for he captured the sentinels, and carried them off to Frying-pan.

The next day Lieutenant Turner, with Company "A," was ordered back to Fauquier, while, with twenty-five men of Company "B," commanded by Captain Smith, Mosby proceeded a mile below Fairfax Court-house in quest of information. It was obtained from a citizen, who furthermore informed him that his presence on their flank having been discovered by the Federal commanders, several parties had been dispatched in pursuit of him. One of these had been sent on the very road on which Mosby had been travelling, but, fortunately, had passed up before he struck it. Proceeding to the junction of the Ox Road and Little River Turnpike, the command was halted by a mounted picket. Making use of the information which he had obtained from the citizen, Mosby replied,

"We are friends, and the same party that just left you."

"Is that you, Sergeant Hough?" said the sentinel.

"Yes," replied Mosby.

The picket of thirteen men was then easily captured, and conducted for the distance of half a mile into the pines. Here we halted, and gathered around our leader to listen to. a cross-examination of the prisoners. It was conducted in the most approved legal style; for, if the Federals hesitated to expose the situation of their friends, Mosby, adroitly changing the point of attack, would wring from them the desired information before they perceived the object at which he was aiming. The picket proved to be a portion of General Meade's body-guard, which had been stationed at the junction of the two roads to forward reports from the different parties who were searching for Mosby. The officer in command having made his escape while we were marching through the pines, Mosby considered the present position unsafe. The prisoners were in consequence sent off, and the scene of operations removed to the vicinity of Anandale.

Concealing fourteen men a quarter of a mile from the road, with six others Mosby took a position on the turnpike in order to capture travellers to and from the army. Very soon six men, with their horses and equipments, were in the hands of the partisans. A captain, with eleven men, next approached. They were attacked and routed, six of the men, with their officer, being taken prisoners. But this party proved to be the vanguard of six hundred cavalry who soon came in sight, and, expecting to be attacked, formed in line of battle. Taking advantage of this interval, Mosby ordered Captain Smith to withdraw the command and prisoners as rapidly as possible by means of a route not discernible by the enemy. With his three men he held his position on the road, the enemy still supposing that he represented an attacking force, until Smith had had time to make good his retreat. Mosby then dashed off in an opposite direction to the one taken by the command, and, when closely pressed by a pursuing party, made his escape, together with his three comrades, by leaping over a deep gully, over which the Yankees were unwilling to follow him.

Captain Smith reached Fauquier in safety, but Mosby, for a day and night, still hovered about the Federal camps, and experienced extreme difficulty in escaping the patrols and pickets which were thrown out in every direction for the purpose of effecting his capture.

About this time Mosby instructed Ab Wren to select a party, and proceed to the vicinity of Fairfax Courthouse, and capture a picket that was stationed about one mile from that place in the direction of Middleburg. On account of the frequent captures which had already been made, the cavalry picket was withdrawn at night and replaced by infantry, but at reveille would again be sent to that point. The result was, that the capture had to be effected by daylight and in sight of the numerous camps, some of which were almost in gunshot of the outpost. During the night Wren and his party passed to the rear of the infantry camps, and took up his position in a hollow, where, as long as night lasted, he was secure from discovery. Here the party lay benumbed with cold till daylight, when Charles Grogan, who had been sent out to reconnoitre, crawled back from the crest of the hill, and reported twelve cavalry-men proceeding toward the picket-post to relieve the infantry according to custom. The Rangers quietly mounted their horses and dropped in behind the Federals, whom they overtook as they were in the act of dismounting. The Yankees very quietly surrendered, and were trotted off to Fauquier in full view of their astonished countrymen.

CHAPTER 20: "THE BILLY SMITH RAID"

Upper Fauquier, December 28th, 1863.

Dear Percy,—As soon as Meade's advance made the Rappahannock River again the picket-line of the two armies, Mosby directed his efforts against the rear of General Sedgwick's Corps, which was encamped about Warrenton, and was drawing its supplies by wagon-trains from Gainesville. With seventy-five men secreted in a wood at Chestnut Fork, a crossing of the Warrenton and Gainesville Turnpike, he awaited the approach of one of these supply-trains.

The guard, composed of cavalry and infantry, were inarching, he discovered, only in front and rear, instead of being distributed among the wagons. Mosby then ranged his command along the turnpike, and ordered Captain William H. Chapman, after the guard in front had passed, to take ten men and attack the train near the centre, while he held the rest in reserve to support him if necessary. But Chapman stopped the wagons without resistance, for the guard both in front and rear were entirely unconscious of what was being done.

An additional detail was then sent forward, and one hundred and thirty mules, thirty-three horses, one quartermaster, and twenty other prisoners were secured. Having now as large a booty and as many prisoners as he could conveniently manage, Mosby retired in the direction of the Blue Ridge, and the next day sent his captures across the headwaters of the Rappahannock: thus, without the loss of a man, supplying the Confederate Army with teams for forty wagons.

In consequence of the attack at Chestnut Fork, the wagon-trains were ordered to follow the line of the Orange and Alexandria Railroad and the Warrenton stem—a change which removed them several miles farther from Mosby, besides placing them under more efficient military protection. In consequence of this arrangement, a large number of wagons were often parked near Warrenton, and upon one of these camps Mosby decided to make a descent. It appeared to be impenetrable, for it was heavily guarded by infantry, with a line of sentinels posted around it. But Mosby, ever fertile in resources, resorted to the following ingenious expedient to defeat these precautions.

A portion of the command was dismounted, and John De Butts, of Loudoun, and Harn, from Louisiana, were sent forward, disguised as negro drivers, to capture the sentries on that portion of the line through which he proposed to enter the camp. The stratagem succeeded, and the dismounted men were thus introduced among the wagons and teams. Two hundred mules were driven out, and the men mounted in order to conduct them to a place of safety. They had heard that mules would with great eagerness follow a white horse at night; so several men thus mounted were placed in advance, and the drove was started. Everything worked well until the animals reached their usual drinking-place, about a mile distant. Beyond this point they would not go, and when urged, broke from their drivers and galloped back.

Unwilling to relinquish so valuable a prize, Mosby, with a party, again entered the wagon-camp, but the mules were now intractable, and rushed wildly about. As the Rangers were preparing to lead them out by the halter, the guard was aroused and the intruders expelled, taking with them only thirteen mules and two prisoners.

And now let me call your attention to a new feature of Mosby's system of warfare, in the development of which you appear to be interested. He has begun to send out parties under command of his officers, and in this way will be enabled greatly to increase his aggressive power. On two occasions Captain William H. Chapman, in conjunction with Captain Smith, has captured pickets on the edge of Warrenton, not more than a few hundred yards distant from where the garrison was quartered. These successes led to the conception of a bold design for the capture of the garrison itself. It was this: Chapman, at night, was to introduce himself into the town, there to remain concealed the next day in the house of one of the elect, in order to ascertain the enemy's strength and position. If the plan was found feasible, he was to communicate the ensuing night by preconcerted signals with Captain Smith, who from the outside was to make the attack. Chapman's attempt to enter the town was, however, defeated, for as he was creeping over a fence in the rear of a dwelling-house, he was discovered and fired upon by a sentinel not many paces from him. With his revolver he returned the shot, inflicting a wound, and then made haste to rejoin Smith, who was awaiting the resu.lt of the adventure at the foot of the hill.

The day following the events just related. Captain Smith, with forty-five men of his company, gained the rear of one of Gregg's cavalry camps, which were established along the road between Warrenton and the Warrenton Springs. The camp selected for attack lay in a deep gorge of Lee's Ridge, about one mile from the town, and was occupied by four companies of the 12th Pennsylvania Cavalry. The surprise was complete, and amid the confusion and uproar produced by it the Rangers carried off thirty-nine horses and twenty-five prisoners, besides leaving twelve of the enemy too severely wounded to be moved. The Yankees rallied as their assailants were about to leave, and opened upon them a rapid fire, which, however, inflicted no injury.

As he was about to withdraw from the camp, Captain Smith halted a soldier just as he was passing a blazing fire. The man replied, "I am one of your own men," but at the same time seized a carbine and levelled it at Smith, who, being on the alert, shot him with his revolver. The wounded man fell across the blazing fire, rolled in agony for a few moments, and then expired. The partisans reached Salem by daybreak, and divided the booty. This nocturnal expedition is known in the command as "The Billy Smith Raid."

Our next expedition was for the purpose of capturing one of the supply-trains which our leader had been informed by Captain Stringfellow, one of General Stuart's scouts, were passing from time to time from Bealton Station to Warrenton. Stringfellow at the same time offered to be our guide. We left Rectortown with about sixty men, and at night halted for a few hours at Mr. James K. Skinker's, where a refreshing repast was furnished to the command, and a party of us most agreeably entertained with music by the ladies. While thus engaged, the order to mount was given, and about daylight we reached the point at which the attack was to be made.

The usual precaution of placing the men out of sight in the woods was adopted, and we remained there for several hours, waiting for the train, to pass. But fortunately a courier, carrying the mail to the garrison at Warrenton, soon fell into our hands, and we amused ourselves during the tedious interval by examining its contents. When the approach of the train, guarded by-about fifty cavalry, was reported, Mosby divided his command. One detachment he entrusted to Captain Smith, the other he reserved for himself, his plan being for the two parties to fall simultaneously upon the front and rear of the escort. The plan was successfully executed, and we brought off about forty prisoners, as many mules, and a large quantity of medical stores. The work accomplished, we prepared to retreat, for the proximity of the garrison at Warrenton, and an encampment of infantry at Bealton, made it very certain that we would be pursued. About sunset we arrived at Mr. Stinker's, where Mosby detailed private A. E. Richards, of Company B, to accompany Captain Stringfellow on a scout the next day to the Rappahannock River. The column moved on to Salem, where, the following morning, the property was divided, and the prisoners were sent to Richmond.

A few days previous to this raid, Baron von Massow, a Prussian lieutenant, had joined our command, bringing with him letters of introduction to Major Mosby from General Stuart, and also from his fellow-countryman. Major Heros von Borck, with whom he had served in the Prussian Army, and who was now a member of the general's staff. He is about twenty-five years of age, and very striking in his appearance. His forehead is ample, his eye black and piercing, and he wears a very heavy moustache. Dressed in his rich army overcoat

BARON VON MASSOW

of dark cloth, with a slouched hat, from which floated two large black plumes, he presented a truly martial appearance, as, mounted on a fine charger, he dashed among the foremost upon the cavalry escort. He is an accomplished swordsman, and with his flashing blade pressed forward in the pursuit of the flying Federals for about a mile. When he returned from the chase, he quietly remarked, "This beats the fox-hunt of England."

But it is time to return to the two scouts whom we left to pass the night at Mr. Skinker's. The day had been cold and rainy, and, after being furnished with supper, they joined the family circle around the fire, where they found Ludwell Napp, a member also of Mosby's command. As they were discussing the events of the day and the probabilities of a pursuit, a servant-girl hastily entered the room and announced the arrival of a number of soldiers, who had inquired if Mosby or any of his men were in the house. Supposing them to belong to the command which had so recently left there, and to be in search of their comrades, she had admitted the fact, and only became aware of her mistake when she saw them making preparations to surround the house.

The lights were at once extinguished, and the Confederates were hurried to the garret, where they hid under the loose flooring, and were covered over with rubbish by the faithful servant, who was most anxious to atone for her mistake. But Richards was less fortunate than his companions, for, in attempting to ascend the staircase, he fell, and, finding himself thus left behind, he determined to attempt to escape from the house, trusting for success to the darkness and his revolver. With a pistol in each hand he leaped into the yard, and, after encountering and putting to flight two Yankees, succeeded in getting off.

The Federals threw open the hall door and fired several shots within. Then, having procured a light, the search was begun, the officer in command ordering his men to give no quarter to any soldier found concealed in the house.

But, just as they were about to enter the attic, the servant-girl stepped forward and offered the Yankees to lead them to the garden, whither she said the Rangers had escaped. With well-feigned surprise she searched among the bushes and shrubbery, and at last accounted for her failure by suggesting that they must have escaped when the attention of the searchers had been drawn off by Richards. The Yankees, who always on such occasions place implicit confidence in information furnished by the contrabands, were imposed on by the story, and contented themselves by arresting Mr. Skinker and his little son, whom they have since committed to prison. They then took the road to the Plains, searching citizens' houses all along the route, and from thence to Salem. Here they again fell in with Richards, who in the meantime had been mounted by a friend, and started in pursuit of him. But he led them through the open fields around the town, occasionally returning their shots, and finally eluded them, having received no other injury than a slight flesh-wound in the arm. During this pursuit a party of the enemy had charged through Salem, and captured Sergeant Warfield and two other Rangers.

From Salem the Yankees returned with their prisoners to Warrenton.

On the 28th of November Mosby started on a raid to Fairfax, but was met at Middleburg by Captain Smith, who had just returned from a scout, and reported that the Yankees who had been camped at the Warrenton Springs had crossed the river, and that Meade's whole army was in motion. The partisan chief at once abandoned the raid to Fairfax, and directed his attention to the army in Culpepper. Having sent out couriers to notify the men to assemble at Rectortown, he ordered Lieutenant Turner to take command, and join him the next day at the' Springs.

Arrived at that point, the command, numbering one hundred and twenty men, was transferred to Captain Smith, with instructions to march to Coon's Mill, and there to await farther orders. Mosby then, with Mountjoy, Walter Whaley, and Guy Broadwaters, crossed the river, and proceeded to the house of a friend, where, about sundown, he saw a large train of wagons loading at Brandy Station, which confirmed the opinion which he had formed that Meade had made that place a depot of army supplies, and upon which he had acted when he planned his expedition.

Mounted upon his fine gray horse, Mosby, with his companions, rode unsuspected for a mile through the Federal camp, talking with the men, and getting from them much valuable information. But, as the party were about to leave, a sentinel challenged them, and although at first he seemed satisfied with the reply "We are a patrol," afterward fired, but too late to inflict any injury. Having rejoined the command at Coon's Mill, Mosby, with Captains Smith, Chapman, and a few others, again crossed the river to reconnoitre the enemy's position.

The result of this second visit was a determination to attack Meade's wagon-camp that night, for the whole army-train was collected at Brandy Station, with only infantry stationed around as a guard. Having dispatched a courier to Lieutenant Turner, now in command at Coon's Mill, to move forward as rapidly as possible, Mosby laid down within a hundred yards of the Federal camp, and slept soundly until aroused by Chapman with the information that the command had come up. He at once made the following dispositions for attack: Mountjoy, with twenty-five men, was ordered to fire the wagons, Smith and Chapman, each in command of a party, were directed to drive off the mules, while Lieutenant Turner was told to hold the rest of the men in reserve in case of an attack by cavalry. The plan worked well, and one hundred and seventy-five mules, in addition to a lot of cattle, were brought across the river.

The crackling flames and the braying of the frightened mules roused the sleeping guard, whose arms were stacked, but not loaded, and before they could prepare for resistance the partisans had made good their retreat. A body of Yankee cavalry pursued as far as Welford's Ford on Hazel River, but to no purpose.

As Captain Chapman was about to leave the camp, he saw four fine mules hitched to one of the burning wagons, which he determined to bring off. While he was thus engaged, the negro driver rolled out of the wagon, exclaiming, "Who, in de name of God, set dese wagons on fire!" Chapman ordered him at once to unhitch his team, which he promptly did, thinking the Ranger some good-natured person who had volunteered to help him in his difficulty, nor did he discover his mistake until he was trotting away merrily for "Mosby's Confederacy."

Having returned to Fauquier, our indefatigable leader collected a fresh band, and proceeded again on an expedition, known in the command as the Second Culpepper Raid. This time he only succeeded in bringing off eleven prisoners, but learned from two of them, who belonged to the brigade whose wagons had been captured at Brandy Station, that Meade had sent his supply-train to the fork between the Rapidan and Rappahannock Rivers, and had detailed a brigade of cavalry from the front to protect it. The men furthermore stated that their brigade, in consequence of Mosby's recent capture, was on short rations, as the country around was too impoverished to afford any supply for man or beast.

On the 7th of December, Company C, which had been recruited for the partisan service, assembled at Rectortown for the purpose of electing their officers, or rather, as we have seen, of confirming Mosby's appointments, which were as follows: William H. Chapman, captain; A. E. Richards, first lieutenant; Frank Fox, from Fairfax, second lieutenant; Yager, from Page, junior second lieutenant.

Captain William H. Chapman was twenty-one years of age the very day that the Ordinance of Secession was passed at Richmond. He was at that time a student at the University of Virginia, and belonged to a company of students which was ordered to Harper's Ferry for active duty, but was soon disbanded by Governor Letcher for the sufficient reason that those who belonged to it might return to their homes, and there recruit, drill, and officer troops for the Southern army. Chapman was elected lieutenant in the Dixie Battery, which went from Page, his native county, and was afterward promoted to the captaincy, a position which he filled with great credit until the consolidation of batteries in January, 1863, by which act so many meritorious officers lost their commands. Still holding his artillery commission, he was assigned to duty as enrolling officer for Fauquier County, but his official duties were often interrupted by the incursions of the enemy. This, however, afforded him an opportunity for mingling in more congenial scenes, and he often volunteered to go with Mosby on his raids. By his intelligence and courage he has so won our leader's confidence as to be frequently sent by him in command of expeditions, an account of several of which I have already given you.

Lieutenant A. E. Richards, from Loudoun County, first served in the valley under General Turner Ashby, and was afterward on the staff of his successor, General William E. Jones; but, having a taste for the partisan life, be resigned his commission, and enlisted as a private in Company B. In that capacity be served for six weeks, during which time I have on several occasions introduced him to your notice. The captain elect, who still held his artillery commission, proceeded at once to Richmond to obtain a transfer to the Partisan Ranger service, and as Lieutenant Richards had not yet recovered from the wound which he received in escaping from Mr. Skinker's, the command of Company C at once devolved upon Lieutenant Fox.

About this time Mosby experienced a slight reverse, which shows some ingenuity on the part of the Federals in guarding against his nocturnal assaults. Attempting to charge a picket of forty men between Luinsville and the Chain Bridge, they were found to have stretched a telegraph-wire across the road high enough to pass a horse, but not its rider. By this device some half dozen of the assailants were unhorsed, and, amid the confusion and delay thus created, the picket effected their escape.

Chapter 21: An Exciting Chase After Mosby

Upper Fauquier, January 8th, 1864.

Dear Percy,—Mosby has recently had an exciting adventure and a narrow escape from the Yankees, while, with Lieutenant Turner and Dr. Alexander, he was at the house of Major Richard H. Carter, who was at home on furlough.

Soon after dawn, a neighbour sent Major Carter intelligence that a detachment of Federal cavalry was marching from Rectortown toward his house. Very soon the soldiers were mounted, and started to make a reconnoissance. At a short distance from the house, they drew up their horses in a lane, with high stone fences on either side, and beheld, within a few hundred yards of the outer gate, the head of the column coming down the road.

The morning was foggy, and just at that moment the sun arose, and, partially dispelling the fog, fully revealed the Yankees to the colonel and his party, while it was doubtful whether they in turn had been seen.

The question immediately arose as to the best mode of retreat. If they retired by the way of Major Carter's house, it would certainly draw the enemy in that direction, and expose a family of ladies and children to insult, and his house to plunder, and probably destruction.

After a hasty consultation, it was determined, in order to avoid, if possible, that risk, to dash across a field to the right, which, however, would bring the fugitives nearer, and expose them more to the view of the enemy. They hoped, however, to shield themselves from view by means of a hill and skirt of woods until they had gained a sufficient distance to preclude danger of successful pursuit.

But in this they were disappointed. They had scarcely entered the field when they discovered that they had not only been seen, but were pursued by a large detachment, who had broken through the fences, and were within one hundred and fifty yards of them. It was now clear that the only chance for escape was in the fleetness of their horses. The race then began in earnest. As soon as the Yankees reached the summit of a hill they opened fire with their carbines, and in this way continued the race for about two miles, when the colonel and his party, leaping a stone fence, entered a wood, and, dashing down a ravine, they were for a short time hid from their pursuers, and were thus enabled to increase the distance between them. "When they emerged from the woods, they discovered that the Yankees had halted at the fence, from behind which they continued to fire until the Confederates were out of range.

When the pursuit began the main body of the enemy occupied a small piece of woods immediately in front of Major Carter's residence. The family, aroused by the firing, rushed into the yard, and witnessed, with painful anxiety, the race in which death or capture seemed inevitable to the objects of their deep solicitude. One incident connected with this escape is deserving of especial notice, as it illustrates in a striking manner the cool courage and almost unparalleled presence of mind of Lieutenant Tom Turner, of Maryland. Dr. Alexander did not leave the house with the rest of the party, and was not aware of the near approach of the enemy until he saw Colonel Mosby and his companions dashing across the field. He started to join them, and at one time was not more than fifty yards from the Yankees; in fact, they were a little ahead of him; but, fortunately, he was under the hill, and was not at once discovered.

He had nearly accomplished his purpose, when, in attempting to pass through the gate leading into the second field, the doctor's horse ran against the post and threw him on the ground, leaving his foot fastened in the stirrup, while his pursuers, about twenty in number, were not more than sixty yards behind. Colonel Mosby and Major

Carter had passed through the gate, but Lieutenant Turner, discovering the accident which had befallen his friend, determined not to leave him in such a condition. Without hesitation, he wheeled his horse, and when Colonel Mosby and Major Carter looked around, they saw him standing erect in his stirrups, and, waving his cap about his head, they heard him urge his pursuers to come on. The Yankees, evidently suspecting a ruse, immediately halted, and, wonderful to say, for the moment ceased firing. Taking advantage of the pause, Turner jumped from his horse and assisted the doctor to remount. Before the pursuers had recovered from their surprise they had rejoined their companions.

It is due to the doctor to state that, while running the severe gauntlet, he did not forget to return the enemy's salute. Finding that his carbine was likely to be in his way in the race, he determined to drop it, but first turned in his saddle and discharged its contents in the face of his pursuers.

A few days after. Miss Roberta P——, from the neighbourhood of Warrenton, displayed, in an enterprise which she voluntarily undertook, courage not inferior to that of Lieutenant Turner. I record it not only as an instance of female heroism, but because it vividly displays the romantic devotion of the ladies of the Upper Piedmont to the Southern cause.

A cold December morning this young lady walked to Warrenton, in and around which was stationed a considerable detachment of Federal troops. Upon her arrival she was informed by Miss L—— that she had seen a negro, evidently a newcomer, pass toward the office of the provost-marshal, accompanied by several officers. They concluded at once that he must be the bearer of intelligence, and Miss Roberta determined to get possession of it.

In execution of this purpose, she went to the house occupied by the provost-marshal, and, by means of a bribe, induced the sentinel on duty to allow her to enter the basement, under the pretext of wishing to transact business with the woman who occupied it; but instead, as soon as she entered the building, turned into a dark and uninhabited room immediately under the provost's office, and there heard the negro volunteer to conduct a party of cavalry to a house in which Mosby and many of his men could be captured, and where, in addition, a large quantity of corn could be seized. About the grain, the officers said, they cared nothing, but that Mosby would be indeed a prize. With this thought they waxed warm, and, speaking in loud and confident terms, informed the fair listener that an expedition, with the negro for a guide, would start that night, if certain expected re-enforcements arrived; if not, certainly the next night.

Her resolution was at once taken to communicate this conspiracy to the partisan chief or some of his men, and, having control of no agency, she was compelled to bear the tidings herself It was late in the afternoon when, unaccompanied, she mounted her horse. The weather, as night approached, had become intensely cold, the wind had risen, and the face of the sky was covered with masses of black cloud which cast their gloom over the landscape. She stopped at the house of a neighbour and friend, whose little son, Walter, agreed to accompany her on her perilous enterprise; for, in order to reach the Salem Road, she would be compelled to pass through the Watery Mountain, on the summit of which was stationed a body of Federal troops. In making this hazardous attempt darkness overtook her, and, ignorant of the route, she was soon compelled to grope her way through the forest. Thus bewildered, the benighted lady came suddenly upon a large fire, at which she paused to enjoy its genial warmth, not remembering that the light might reveal her to those whom she wished most to avoid. Soon she again set forth to attempt to thread the labyrinth in which she was involved; but the farther the wanderer proceeded the deeper in its intricate mazes did she plunge.

> *A thousand fantasies began to throng into her memory*
> *Of calling shapes and beck'ning shadows dire,*
> *And airy tongues, that syllable men's names*
> *On sands, and shores, and desert wildernesses.*

Weakness would have sunk by the wayside, but the braced nerves and daring spirit of this heroic girl carried her forward amid all dangers and through all obstacles. Her faith was in her high purpose, and she trusted to unseen guardians to direct her steps. Suddenly the moon shone forth, and revealed to Walter a party of Federal soldiers, and as suddenly again passed under a cloud. Sheltered by the friendly darkness, she pursued her way, until she was ordered to halt by a horseman immediately in her front. With rare presence of mind, she determined to work upon the dread of surprisal with which Mosby had inspired the Federal pickets, and in a voice hoarse from exposure she ordered him to surrender. In reply, she heard the sound of retreating hoofs. Her spirits rose with this adventure, and believing this to be the last picket she would encounter, she pressed rapidly forward.

On reaching a higher point on the mountain, she beheld with dismay the lights from the town of Warrenton, and discovered that, instead of progressing on her journey, she was returning to the point from which she had started. But the lights from the town, while they discovered to the lady her mistake, yet furnished her with the means of rectifying it, and from this new point of departure she struck out again in the direction of Salem. But her adventures were not yet over, for she had not proceeded very far when she saw before her a horse, and standing beside it his rider. He approached, and, laying his hand on her bridle, said,

"Stop, lady; you can go no farther. To what place are you bound?"

In a tone of innocence and candour, which so well became her youth and beauty, she replied that she had started to visit a sick friend in Salem, but night coming on she had lost her road. The soldier then told her it was his painful duty to conduct her to the reserve, where she would be detained till morning.

"I will not go," she replied. "You may shoot me, but I will not go. I am not willing for you to perform your duty."

"Nor will I perform it," generously replied the soldier. "No one could be so cruel as to detain you or turn you back on such a night as this."

He then pointed to the light from a neighbouring farmhouse, and bade her go there, while at the same time he led her horse by a circuitous route, to prevent her running into the reserve. The soldier then turned and said,

"Goodbye. I have yet three hours on picket to think of a freezing lady."

That sentinel was not made of common earth!

The wanderer soon reached the friendly shelter, and communicated to the lady of the house the object of her midnight adventure, who the next morning accompanied her to a rendezvous of Mosby's men in the mountain.

The day after this nocturnal adventure a Federal soldier came to the residence of the farmer, and gave an animated account of the alarm which they had had the night before on the mountain in consequence of a threatened attack from the guerrillas. "They had sent," he said, "one of their number in advance to capture the vedette, but he was sharp enough to escape the trap."

Chapter 22: The Chaplain's Visit to Baltimore.

Upper Fauquier, January 12th, 1864.

Dear Percy,—I am again alone at my abode on the Blue Ridge, my visitors having all left me this morning. About a week since, and soon after his return from a secret mission to Baltimore, I received, through his servant Juniper, a letter from the chaplain of our battalion, the Reverend Adolphus Adam Gog, informing me that on the ensuing Thursday he would pay me his long-promised visit for the purpose of canvassing the political events of 1776 in their connection with the present condition of affairs in the United States.

Attended by his faithful henchman, the doctor arrived at my abode in due time for dinner, and met the two guests whom I had invited to assist me in his entertainment—Colonel Nicholas Spicer, a gentleman who lives on the eastern declivity of the Blue Ridge, and a friend and neighbour of his, known among his friends as "The Philosopher," an appellation which has been bestowed on him as well from the calmness of his deportment as from the cast of his conversation. "The Philosopher" is a peculiar person, and, as he will be often mentioned in my letters, deserves a few words of description. Self control appears to be the primary law of his existence, and no Spartan ever obeyed its behests with sterner punctuality.

His character is ennobled by many high traits, and though the exterior is cold and sometimes forbidding, yet is he generous, indulgent to the faults of others, and characterized by great love of truth and scrupulous politeness. He is much given to reflection and to books; is solitary in his habits, and prone to silence; but, if roused and interested, talks with freedom, and like a man of positive opinions. "The Philosopher" has been in the Southern army, but was discharged from the service in consequence of a disabling wound. He is an old acquaintance of the chaplain, and was much gratified at again meeting with him.

While seated at dinner, the doctor was called upon to give some account of his visit to Baltimore, where Southern sympathy burns with so bright a flame, though in the trans-Potomac country. This is particularly true of the ladies of that city, who very early signalized their devotion to the Southern cause by voluntary sacrifices which involved pecuniary as well as personal inconvenience. In response to a remark from me embodying the statement, the chaplain said,

"Yes, sir, I heard and saw enough of that during my sojourn in that city, and I dare say that scarcely a Southern prisoner who has passed that way but will add his testimony to mine. It will not require a great weight of testimony to convince you, gentlemen, that while I remained in that Federal garrison I led a very retired life. But it was impossible to conceal the fact from the knowledge of the elect that the chaplain of Mosby's Battalion was in the city, who made haste to show me attention in the most gratifying forms. Both gentlemen and ladies of the first consideration visited me at the house of the friend where I lay concealed, and never before were my powers of entertainment so severely tasked. But I trust," added the parson, with a satisfied air as he turned toward Colonel Spicer, "I trust the honour of the battalion did not suffer in my hands."

Colonel Spicer, who is apt to look to the main chance, here interposed: "I admire the people of Baltimore; but, doctor, tell us, did their sympathy for our cause expend itself in kind words and compliments?"

Doctor Gog. "By no means. Colonel Spicer; on the contrary, they gave me the most substantial evidences of their regard. My wardrobe was soon overstocked, and I have a box full of mementoes from the *belles* of Baltimore."

Colonel Spicer. "Was that all?"

Doctor Gog. "You unconscionable guerrilla, no! Money, sir— money that can be carried in a man's belt, was showered on me. So plentiful was my supply of Federal currency when I returned to Virginia that you would have sworn I had been upon the greenback raid."

Colonel Spicer. "Do you think, doctor, if I were to go to Baltimore, the ladies would call to see me?"

The chaplain hesitated in his reply, as if unwilling to divide honours; but "The Philosopher" smilingly said,

"Beyond all doubt. Colonel Spicer."

Colonel Spicer. "It is true I am not a member of Colonel Mosby's command, and am not sure that I ever killed a Yankee, though I shot at night at an intruder into my garden whom I always supposed to be one; but then I am remarkably well acquainted with the colonel, and have seen him often as he returned from his raids with his spoil and captives. Moreover, I was once myself colonel of a militia regiment in Virginia, and I suppose all well-informed people in Baltimore are apprised of that fact. My family, too, have always had the military cast. They were distinguished both in the last war with England, and in the revolution which won our independence, an event which The Philosopher, by-the-way, once told me crowned America with misfortunes, and was but the mother of anarchy and civil war."

The parson was not willing that Colonel Spicer should divert the conversation from his recent visit, and lead it, at that time, to so grave a subject as the political effects of the Revolution of 1776, so he resumed the thread of his conversation, and remarked:

"Among the devoted partisans of the South whom I met in Baltimore was Mrs. T——s, a native of Virginia, whom some of us can remember when she first appeared at the Fauquier Springs, at that time the resort of beauty and fashion."

Philosopher. "Yes, Miss A—ie Gr—n, we all remember her, with her brilliant dark eyes and chestnut hair. She was the ornament of the circle in which she moved. I see her now, through the *vista* of years, as she stood alone on a summer's morn, arrayed in simple white, by the fountain which occupied the centre of those cultivated grounds. She looked like a *naiad*, ready to plunge again in the crystal wave from which she had emerged; or it might be the Genius of the place, come to bless the spot on which she stood. As I gaze at that youthful form, adorned by Love and the Graces, I am carried back to the beautiful garden where love and the worship of God were the sole occupation of mankind."

Colonel Spicer. "Bravo, Philosopher, bravo! I remember now to have heard that you once entertained an amiable sentiment toward that lady."

The face of The Philosopher flushed deeply as he turned away, and Dr. Gog, who did not consider the subject of his visit to Baltimore yet exhausted, continued:

"Not only did a full share of the troubles and dangers which surrounded her class fall to this elect lady, but she gave freely the highest testimony of devotion in a mother's power to afford. Two of her sons, Hanson and Raleigh, were officers in the Southern army, and her third son, Douglas, a youth of only fifteen years, was captured in an attempt to join the army of General Lee. But the object of greatest curiosity and interest which I found in Baltimore was a gentleman whom I shall introduce to this company as 'The Philosopher of Springfield.' I never saw anyone who resembled him before, and I studied him as I would a specimen from the Zoological Gardens. There is nothing like him in the modern world, and comparisons will have to be sought far back in classical history.

"He looks for all the world like one of the old Greek philosophers. In person he resembles Socrates, but his shrewd and sarcastic observations on the drama of life and its actors declare him to be of the race of Diogenes. Now he will utter a sage apothegm that sounds like Doctor Franklin, but a biting jest soon brings the old cynic before you again. Like him of Sinope, he would reform society, and put folly and vice to the blush by satirical reproofs; but he meets, I suspect, with no better success than his antecedent and prototype. Hobbes has said that war is the natural state of man—a sentiment which is at least true here, for he lives in a state of amiable hostility with his whole acquaintance. The consequence is, if any one has a keen observation to make, he is sure to point it at this cynical philosopher, who, to do him justice, pays back the debt with a promptitude that would establish the credit of any merchant on change.

"During my sojourn in the city in so peculiar a manner associated with the memory of Washington, I met this gentleman at an entertainment given by a mutual acquaintance, and witnessed an encounter which he provoked with the sprightly and attractive Mistress M——. In a moment she was under arms, and retaliated on her adversary with a nimble and caustic wit. As she baffled him with her dazzling fence, and at the same time pierced him with a handful of shining darts, the company seemed all to agree that he had at last met his match, or, at any rate, had found an adversary worthy of his steel. The Philosopher gazed at his adversary with a surprise and wonder that might have possessed some redoubtable hero when he met Bellona in the field.

"But here the parallel between the ancient and the modern philosopher ceases, for The Philosopher of Springfield does not live in a tub, but at a most charming country place, where he entertains himself with books and the rearing of Devon cattle of the purest breeds. Thither his friends—or, if you choose, his enemies—often repair to partake of his hospitality and taste the nectared sweets of philosophy."

Colonel Spicer. "Parson, I like thy picture well, and would be gratified to meet this Philosopher of Springfield, though methinks I would not be over-pleased to provoke his satirical wit. But, prithee, have you nothing to tell of the *belles* of the trans-Potomac? You once had an eye for beauty "

Doctor Gog. "And have it still—yea, a most lively appreciation of all female perfections. Well, this philosopher has a fair daughter, the sweetest damsel that ever my foolish eyes looked upon."

Philosopher. "I am interested. Paint me the nymph in her sky robes laced with sunbeams, and in all the bright colours of her beautiful youth."

Doctor Gog. "The language of prose has no application to her. Poetry alone should attend her footsteps, garland her brow, and embalm her memory."

Colonel Spicer. "Why, parson, she must be a tasty lass."

Doctor Gog, "But let the truth be spoken, the lady has her drawbacks—yes, most serious drawbacks and disqualifications. Her name is fickleness. You might as easily fix the transient meteor as her thoughts. I had a mind to make an investment in the matrimonial stocks, and abandon forever Mosby and his guerrillas, and listen for the rest of my natural life to the teachings of philosophy under the lindens which whisper to the winds and render Springfield umbrageous, but I could not fix the inconstant sprite, this modern Titania. I lost the lady, but then I did not lose my revenge, and revenge is a morsel delicious even to the gods. Like the Parthian, who is most dangerous when discomfited and flying, I shot back an arrow at her, or rather shot a paper bullet at my fair foe."

Colonel Spicer. "These guerrillas have most singular ideas about property. Here is their chaplain, with the air of a bankrupt, tells us he lost the maiden, though from his own account it appears he had never won her. Just so the partisans sometimes return with downcast visages, and tell you they have 'lost a million of dollars,' because they have made an unsuccessful attack on a train loaded with greenbacks. A most singular mode, upon my soul, they have of estimating their effects! If one of them took a fancy to my farm, he would say with a sigh that but for an accident he would have been a landed proprietor."

Philosopher. "A paper bullet! Then of course you addressed her in the language of poetry. Repeat the verses. The marble-hearted fair ought, for the safety of mankind, to be banished to the cloister, there to wear

"The livery of a nun,
Chanting faint hymns to the cold, fruitless moon."

After some persuasion, the chaplain repeated, in a most affecting manner, these lines, which, after the custom of the poets, he inscribed to the lady under a fanciful name:

> To Silvia.
> Silvia's love is like a fountain
> Bubbling from a green-clad mountain;
> Never still, but ever flowing,
> Be it calm or be it blowing.
> Now madly in a cascade rushing,
> Now in the sunshine gently blushing;
> Then to the ear its murmuring tone
> Is on the gentlest zephyr borne.
> Each mossy bed and rough stone favouring.
> In tone, and speed, and motion wavering,
> It is a thing to chance e'er bending.
> To storm or calm its influence lending.
> To know new things 'tis ever learning,
> To once-seen objects ne'er returning;
> Now 'tis here, and then 'tis gone,
> In beauty yet still flowing on.
> On the water's shifting tide.
> As gently on their course they glide.
> Words or marks make with thy finger,
> Then write love on Silvia's mind;
> A moment gone, no traces linger
> Of either that was left behind.

Colonel Spicer, "A pretty parallel, and well worded! But if that was all you could effect, you ought to be unchurched. Tell me not of love-verses when the honour of the battalion is at stake! You ought to have brought the lady back with you. Her hand was the trophy we all had a right to expect."

Doctor Gog, "Well, colonel,! did make a raid on her, but not a step would she budge; and when I held up before her the charming vicissitudes of our partisan life, she quietly replied that she had no taste for guerrillas, and that when she became a soldier she meant to enlist in the regular service. What could be done with a perverse woman like that ?"

Colonel Spicer. "That's no excuse whatever in this command, where there is a regular professor of love and courtship. "Why, the professor assures me that, according to his method, a young woman stands no chance at all, and that the winning of her is as certain as a mathematical calculation—yes, as certain as that twice one makes two. If this thing gets out you will lose all your religious influence. No, sir, a raid wasn't the thing. You should have laid siege to the fortress, and established your parallels, as the professor would express it. You have been defeated, notwithstanding all the advantages of a scientific education, in a general engagement by a young lady, who, I dare say, is not out of her teens, and have seriously compromised the reputation of the battalion for gallantry.

"At the first opportunity that offers itself I shall strongly advise Colonel Mosby to take away your commission, or send you to follow your vocation of soul-saving in the regular army, though I scarcely think you would do for the chaplain of Stonewall Jackson. I am deeply mortified, parson, at your inglorious defeat at 'the Battle of Baltimore,' as some future chronicler will call the engagement; and, old a man as I am, if I had not some seventeen or twenty blooming angels, I would brush tip and take a paragraph at the young beauty myself If I could step back some twenty summers on the path of life, it would afford me a great pleasure to solve that scientific problem. By my faith, the lady would soon discover that King Agamemnon had taken the field! The next best thing to be done is to send Charley Grogan, or some other brave from 'Company Darling,' to try the effect of the mathematics upon her."

Doctor Gog, "But the man to whom I laid the closest in Baltimore was old Dan Tucker—they call him 'King Tucker.' Old Dan is one of the merchant princes of Baltimore, nay, of America, for that matter, and his name would be honoured by the Bank of England for a million. But I scorn in these high times to speak of such ignoble things as ledgers and bills of exchange, and tell you that he is as nice a piece of company as ever you tied to, Colonel Spicer."

"Tucker, Tucker," said Colonel Spicer, with a very profound air; "Tucker; that name sounds not unfamiliar in my ears. Does he belong to the family of the old judge, or that pleasant fellow, Ran?"

Doctor Gog. "The same breed of dogs—the old Bermuda stock."

Colonel Spicer, "It is certainly a very good breed of dogs. There is Dave, the best doctor they ever had in Richmond, and 'Bev,' who is known to all the crowned heads and pretty women in Europe."

Doctor Gog, "Well, old Dan is worth them all put together, even if they are made of pure gold. The truth is, Colonel Spicer, old Dan is a trump. Many a time have I gone on the sly to his elegant home with that prince of gentlemen and good fellows, Hughes Armistead, and, I tell you, we made his Champagne and Madeira talk!"

Colonel Spicer. "I think it far more probable, parson, that old Dan's Champagne and Madeira made you talk. Ha, ha, ha !" and with this bit of pleasantry the colonel rose from his chair, and walked to the fire to light his pipe, which he "set great store to," as he said, because it was the gift of Colonel Mosby.

The Philosopher appearing somewhat annoyed at the personal attack made upon him by Colonel Spicer, as soon as dinner was over, arose and proposed to adjourn to the adjoining room, where we could discuss at leisure the subject which had procured me the homer of the chaplain's visit.

The Philosopher here engaged in the examination of the causes which produced the American Revolution, and some other matters not of interest in this connection.

Chapter 23: Death of Tom Turner.

Upper Fauquier, January 21st, 1864.

Dear Percy,—Mosby had determined to celebrate the advent of the New Year by a raid into Fairfax, and had ordered the men to assemble on the morning of the 1st of January for this purpose. But, before he arrived at the rendezvous, Sam Underwood rode rapidly into the village and reported that he had been pursued by a party of Federals who were not far off. Captain Smith, who was on the ground, ordered Underwood to take his brother Bush and another man, and follow the enemy, and report their movements to him at a designated point. He then galloped off to where he knew his company was assembling preparatory to the proposed raid. Finding twenty-five of his men in place, he moved them to the point agreed upon with Underwood, and was met there with the information that the Yankees were a detachment of Major Cole's Maryland Battalion, who had been sent, under command of Captain Hunter, into "Mosby's Confederacy" to capture the guerrilla band, and that they had gone to Five Points, a place where five roads meet, and distant a few miles from where Smith's command then was.

Captain Smith frankly told his men that they were outnumbered three to one, but that he meant to fight, and added that any man who shrank from the combat upon such terms was at liberty to withdraw. The captain was answered by hearty cheers, and at once moved off in the direction of the enemy. Just as the Federals had entered an open field for the purpose of forming in line of battle to receive the attack, the Partisans dashed in upon them. They broke and fled, the bulk of them in the direction of Middleburg, hotly pursued for several miles. When Smith's company, exhausted and burdened with prisoners, were about to relinquish the pursuit, Mosby, with six fresh men, took it up, and followed the routed enemy through Middleburg and into the country beyond, in the direction of Harper's Ferry, from which place the expedition had started. Thus the raiders returned, having lost ten of their number killed and wounded, forty-one taken prisoners, and fifty horses, with their equipments. Smith's loss was Corporal Dulick slightly wounded.

With Captain Smith in this fight was James Keith, of Fauquier, adjutant of the 4th Virginia Cavalry, and a member of the original Black Horse Company. He bore himself with conspicuous gallantry, and well sustained the reputation of his command.

About a week after the fight at Five Points, Captain Stringfellow reported to Mosby the situation of a Federal camp, which, he thought, might be easily surprised, at the eastern base of the Blue Ridge, on the road from Hillsboro to Harper's Ferry, and within a mile of the latter place. Captain Stringfellow is well known in the army as a successful and reliable scout, is employed alike by Lee and Stuart, and upon information derived through him often depends the march of large bodies of troops. Without hesitation, therefore, Mosby prepared for an attack upon Major Cole's camp, whom he was eager to capture, on account of his rough treatment of the people living along the border. With Companies "A," "B," and "C," he began his march on the afternoon of the 9th of January, and halted for a few hours soon after nightfall at Woodgrove, the residence of Mr. Heaton, where cheerful fires blazed in every room, and a plentiful supper had been prepared for both officers and men.

Several hours glided pleasantly away, until, as had been agreed upon, a courier arrived from Stringfellow (who, with a party of ten men, had remained to watch the camp) with the information that every thing was favourable for the execution of the plan. At nine o'clock we were ordered to resume the march. The night was clear, but intensely cold, and the snow lay six inches deep on the ground, muffling the sound of the horse's feet as the column moved on. Within a mile and a half of the camp we were joined by Stringfellow's party, and, leaving the grade at right angles, we struck across a narrow skirt of country to the base of the Short Hill Mountain. Here the command was halted and the horses fed, while our leader, accompanied by Stringfellow, went forward to reconnoitre the camp. In about two hours they returned, and our column marched along the base of the mountain until it reached the Potomac River. Then we proceeded along the river bank toward Harper's Ferry, ascending on our route a wooded cliff, which could only be done by leading our horses, and grasping in our ascent the thick bushes with which it was covered.

Along the crest of this cliff ran the grade, which we gained at a point midway between Harper's Ferry, where several thousand troops were quartered, and the camp which we wished to surprise. At this place Mosby made his dispositions for attack. Captain Smith, with a party, was directed to secure the horses which were standing around the hospital building; Stringfellow, with his party of scouts, to capture Major Cole and the officers at his headquarters, while Mosby, with the bulk of the command, was to attack the camp.

In order to make the surprise complete, our leader had dismounted a portion of the men, and had succeeded in capturing the first row of tents, when Stringfellow's party, contrary to orders, came galloping into the camp. The Partisans, supposing them to be Yankees, fired, killing or wounding six of them before the mistake was discovered. The firing and the confusion which began to prevail roused the Federals, who, being rallied by Captain Vernon, of Maryland, poured a rapid fire upon their assailants. Seeing that his plans had miscarried, and that his men were falling beneath the fire of friends as well as of enemies, and hearing, too, the signal-gun on Loudoun Heights, Mosby ordered a retreat in the direction of Hillsboro.

But this order was not heard by those on the outskirts of the camp. In a little while Captain Smith, uniting with Captain Chapman, dashed in among the tents with fifty men, but was soon driven out. The two officers, unattended, then returned to the camp to look after their wounded, and had not gone far when they recognised Charlie Paxson, of Loudoun, extended on the ground, so badly wounded that he was unable to rise. He besought them in moving terms to carry him off, which Smith was preparing to do, when he was fired upon from one of the tents and instantly killed. Chapman, supposing his companion was only wounded, hastened to obtain assistance to bear him away, when he was met by Lieutenant Gray, who communicated to him Mosby's order to retreat.

They had not proceeded more than a few hundred yards toward

Hillsboro when they overtook the Baron von Massow, who, touched with a generous compassion, had just lifted a wounded soldier on his horse to convey him to a place of safety.

At this time, two miles farther on, Mosby was standing by the bedside of Lieutenant Tom Turner, who had been mortally wounded early in the fight, and had been borne to the house of Levi Waters, which stands on the margin of the road. It was an affecting spectacle to see the men gathered around the wounded officer, to look for the last time on him whom they had followed in so many fights; but hope still kept her vigils by his couch, and in cheerful accents he assured his sorrowing comrades that in another week he would be with them again. It was, however, but the delusive voice of a charmer. Never again will he mount the neighing steed; never again, with throbbing pulse and kindling eye, will he listen to the trumpet's loud call, nor carry aloft amid a hundred foes the crimson banner of his chieftain.

TOM TURNER DYING

The race is run, the battle has been fought, the fitful dream is over. Brave spirit, rest! The youthful warrior now sleeps in Arnold Cemetery, near Hillsboro, and his name will be held in honour as long as the annals of the battalion endure.

The command reached Woodgrove by sunrise the next morning, from which place a flag of truce was sent to Major Cole by Captain Chapman to propose an exchange of prisoners, and request the permission to remove our dead and wounded. But Major Cole refused to receive any communication from Mosby, which shows the embittered feelings of the enemy toward him.

We brought off ten prisoners and forty-five horses—a poor compensation for the grievous loss which the battalion had sustained; for, in addition to those already mentioned, William E. Colston, William H. Turner, of Maryland, and Robertson had been mortally wounded, while Boyd Smith and several others had received less serious injuries.

Thus sadly ended one of Mosby's most daring enterprises, which promised to be a perfect success, but was defeated by one of those strange occurrences which are beyond the power of the most prudent to anticipate.

The defeat at Harper's Ferry was enough to damp the ardour of any spirit but Mosby's. But so great is its elastic vigour that soon he was as busily engaged in new enterprises as though he had sustained no reverse. *"Ever superior to Fortune, he endures her frowns with serenity, enjoys her smiles with moderation, and shows himself alike in victory forbearing and in defeat undaunted."* His countenance and deportment correspond with his character—firm, collected, intelligent.

Chapman, a deserter from the California Battalion, who had been received into the partisan command, reported the Federal camp at Vienna to be in a condition to be easily surprised. He was anxious for Mosby to accompany him in person to ascertain the correctness of the information, but to this Captain Chapman objected, thinking that the temptation to betray our leader might prove too strong for the guide's fidelity. Instead, he proposed to go himself and inspect the camp, taking with him Flannegan, a daring soldier, to shoot the deserter guide in case he proved treacherous. This was agreed to, and the adventurous party set forth. It was very cold, and a crust of ice had formed over the snow, which crackled under their feet as they proceeded. At one o'clock at night they entered the camp, which they found had been protected by barricades to guard against nocturnal assaults.

While making his observations, Chapman had seen a number of stables, and, finding that the proposed surprise would be impracticable, he determined to carry back a lot of horses. Upon his return, Mosby, who, with twelve men, was awaiting the result of his visit to the camp in a wood about four hundred yards distant, determined to repeat the operation. A second detail was made, of which Baron von Massow was one. They were equally successful; but the baron, as he brought off a fine horse, exclaimed, "Ah! Chapman, this is not fighting; this is stealing." The guide, who had now proved his fidelity, was allowed, in charge of a party, to try his luck, and succeeded in getting a third supply of horses. The next morning, when the animals were missed, and a diligent but fruitless search had been made for them, it was. agreed among the Yankees that Mosby must have called for them.

I will now give you an account of a raid into the Valley, undertaken by Captain Chapman during the temporary absence of Mosby in Richmond on official business. Up to this time it had been the impression that the stone fences in that district, and the absence of bodies of wood to be used as a cover, rendered it unsuited to partisan warfare, and Chapman was ordered not to attempt any thing in that direction unless confident of success. But on the 2nd of February, with thirteen men, he crossed the dreaded Shenandoah and proceeded to Berryville, where he learned that a party of the enemy, about equal in strength to his own, had just left and gone to Charlestown. He at once struck across the country with the design of cutting them off, but instead, when he entered the turnpike, found himself immediately in their rear. A pursuit ensued, during which nine of the enemy were killed, wounded, and captured. From the prisoners Chapman learned that the garrison at Charlestown had gone on a raid to Winchester, to intercept General Rosser on his return from an expedition, and had left their camp and a large amount of military stores with a slender guard.

Chapman at once returned to Fauquier and assembled the battalion to attempt the capture of this camp, but when he arrived within six miles of Charlestown he discovered the raiders on their return, and was compelled to abandon the enterprise. He, however, captured a good many prisoners, which was accomplished by calling stragglers to the woods, who, thinking themselves invited by their comrades to participate in the spoil taken on the raid from citizens, would unhesitatingly obey the summons, and so fell into the trap which Chapman had set for them.

Mosby returned from Richmond on the 18th of February, and was informed upon his arrival at Piedmont late in the afternoon that a party of raiders was out, guided by Cornelle, who had deserted from the Partisan battalion to Gregg's cavalry at Warrenton, and that they had captured several of the Rangers at their boarding-houses. He hastily collected a small band, with which he lay in ambush, hoping to intercept the raiders, but he was too late, for they had already returned to their camp at Warrenton.

While in Richmond he had procured the transfer of the Rev. Samuel J. Chapman to the Partisan Battalion as adjutant, with the rank of first lieutenant. He is a brother of Captain Chapman, with whom he served as lieutenant in the Dixie Battery, and was then assigned, along with him, to conscript duty in Fauquier. While thus employed he often joined Mosby in his raids. At the request of General Deering he had been ordered to Caskie's Artillery Battalion, in which he served with distinction until the time of which I am writing.

Chapter 24: The Two Brides

Upper Fauquier, February 6th, 1864.

Dear Percy,—I have recently attended wedding festivities at B——d, in Loudoun County, an account of which I will give you today.

Two sons of the house had brought home their brides, friends had assembled from all directions to greet them, and all things were prepared for the reign of pleasure. During the evening a laughable scene occurred between one of these brides and the chaplain of our command, the Rev. Adolphus Adam Gog, and, as you have requested me to relate the adventures of the worthy clergyman, I will give you a somewhat full account of the incident to which I refer. You say that the chaplain is certainly a character of marked originality. I feel sure you will be more decidedly of that opinion than ever after you have heard the story I am about to tell you. I am pleased to hear that Sir Anthony, your wife, and the rest of the family have received pleasure from hearing my letters read, and that the names of the chaplain of Mosby's Battalion and of his chief of staff are as familiar in the household as the names of Mosby, Chapman, and Richards.

With a party of eighteen or twenty, of whom your correspondent was one, Mosby set out from "Heartland," and reached B——d, our "objective point," as the chief called it, a full half hour before the guests began generally to assemble. After throwing off our wrappings and overcoats, we advanced into one of the rooms thrown open for the reception of guests, and were soon met by young Mrs. Carter, upon whom, in consequence of the indisposition of the mistress of the house, had been devolved the graceful duty of presiding for that evening, though she was herself a bride of a few weeks' duration. Here, then, is one of the brides. The other was a beauty from the Lower Rappahannock, but with her I contracted only a slight and formal acquaintance. But I shall have occasion to introduce you more particularly to the hostess-bride, to whom, in turn, several of us were presented by Mosby. She received us all with graceful courtesy, but no one in so distinguished a manner as the chaplain of our command. The doctor was highly pleased, for the lady extended to him her hand, on which sparkled a costly gem. She was prettily habited in a light-coloured silk, so fitted as to display to advantage an elegant and graceful figure. Her eyes, large and black, were filled with light and sentiment, and her hair was so glossy and redundant as to make you marvel at the skill which could dispose of the superfluous tresses. The doctor has a great fancy for "pretty women," as he curtly expresses it, nor did he on this occasion withhold the homage of his admiration. But this was not all, for the parson, whose heart has not been wholly purged of worldly thoughts, determined to extort admiration in return. It was with satisfaction that he cast his eyes at a mirror, on whose polished surface he saw reflected his own person arrayed in Confederate gray of Shafer's latest and best cut, and with the cross on his breast, the customary badge of Southern chaplains, to denote his holy office.

I would not have you, my friend, to imagine that the parson expected to inspire that beautiful lady with the belief that he possessed a large amount of physical beauty—no, that was not the doctor's mark. But there was a class of charms to which the dignified churchman aspired, by means of which he hoped to carry off the prize of Mrs. Carter's admiration—fine manners, a genteel and self-possessed bearing, and a copious flow of learned, eloquent, and impressive conversation, seasoned, perhaps, with occasional sallies of wit. Here was a field in which he meant that night to shine a constellation of unrivalled splendour. While he held in just contempt mere symmetry of form and feature, he yet considered that so intellectual a part would be highly appropriate to his great fame, and the eminent position he held in Mosby's Confederacy. So Doctor Gog deliberately selected his line of battle, threw out his skirmishers, put his artillery in position, and prepared to open on the enemy.

It falls to the lot of the historian of these events to relate that, among the many perfections with which a generous Creator had endowed Mrs. Carter, there yet dwelt in her one small fault, if, indeed, so harsh and unhandsome an appellative could be applied to any of her qualities. But the swart fairy had intruded at the auspicious hour of her birth, and had cast into the golden urn of her virtues this fault. She was truly pious, and Christian piety, even *infidels* allow, imparts to a lady's character the highest finish. It is the celestial gloss which shines on the plumage of the angels. Do not suppose for a moment, therefore, that I mean to enumerate Christian piety as a fault—no; but it was in the excess of this principle that the fault consisted. Perfection is found in harmony and proportion; but here was a discord—a disproportion—a fault. Mrs. Carter, at least so thought her unconverted friends, set too high a value on the ministers of the Gospel, or "the parsons," as that self-denying brotherhood are called in Mosby's Confederacy.

Throughout the range of her acquaintance, even before her marriage, Mrs. Carter was known as the steadfast friend of Colonel Mosby and the Partisan Battalion. Yet was there one thing about it which she did not like—the battalion had no chaplain. It was a great scandal, she thought, and felt that it boded no good. Some of Mosby's men, she reflected, were being killed every day, and, what made the matter worse, many of them were mere boys, who, by rights, ought to be at home with their sisters, instead of being here, belted with pistols, and swearing strange oaths. The thing did not suit her at all, and she was resolved not to let the matter drop. So much importance did she attach to it, that on the very next occasion which offered itself she remonstrated with Mosby on the subject, and received from him the assurance that, as soon as a suitable person could be found, he would provide his command with a religious instructor. It was easy enough, he said, to pick up an army chaplain, but one suited to his command ought to possess all the higher qualities of a missionary—piety, learning, zeal, courage, added to a force of character that would enable him to impress the consciences of so peculiar a body as the Partisan Battalion. And Mrs. Carter could not but acknowledge the justness of this observation.

Her gratification, then, was very great, when to the pleasure of that evening was added an introduction to the Reverend Adolphus Adam Gog, C. M. B., as he always signs himself. Happy Mrs. Carter! Contrary and perverse things had conspired to render that evening blessed. How the bright smile hung upon her lips and laughed in her eyes. It was with a peculiar grace, in which joy mingled, that this lady, so debonair, placed her small hand in the huge fist of Doctor Gog, and invited him, by a courteous gesture, to a seat not far off. I followed them, and, seating myself near the lady, am enabled to report a portion of the conversation that ensued.

Mrs, Carter. "How honoured, Dr. Gog, we ought to feel that you have brought yourself to cast your lot with us on this neutral ground of the two armies. But of this, reverend sir, be assured, however things may go, you will be repaid for the sacrifice by the consciousness of doing good—the only guerdon, after all, to a well-poised mind. You could scarcely have chosen, for the exercise of your pious energies, a more extensive field of labour than the one before you."

Dr. Gog. "True, Mistress Carter; as the sacred volume declareth, *The harvest is plenteous, but the labourers are few.*"

Mrs. Garter. "What circumstance, doctor, first directed your attention to Mosby's Confederacy?"

Dr. Gog, "Mistress Carter, the incident is quite out of the common course, and carrieth a complexion of romance. As I strolled through the public square in Richmond, and was standing at the base of the monument erected by the gratitude of Virginia and the genius of Crawford to the men who broke our union with England and contracted it with the North, a party of well-favoured youths passed by, dressed in the manner of soldiers. Inquiry elicited the fact that they were of the band known as 'Mosby's men,' a reprobate and lost crew. Furthermore, Mistress Carter, I learned that they were entirely destitute of the means of Christian grace, no ecclesiastic having been found bold enough to attack, as it were, the Prince of Evil in that, his impregnable strong-hold. My informant, a quiet and ancient citizen, presented to me a cup brimful of horrors. I was deeply impressed by the recital, and at once resolved to go forth, with oaken staff and sandal shoon, among those anthropophagi, like another apostle of the Gentiles, and dispute with Satan so goodly a heritage. My propositions were promptly acceded to by their chief, and I entered without delay on my ministry."

Mrs. Carter. "That evening's stroll looks almost providential, but it only shows by what trifles the human destiny is shaped."

Dr. Gog. "Mistress Carter, it was altogether providential, and is well matched by a romantic incident related in church history. The story is told by Ranke, but more fully and pathetically by Mosheim and Milner. Robert Southey, too, in his account of what he calls the origin of the Established Church, gives it in his usual diluted style."

Mrs. Carter. "Do tell me the incident to which you allude, for it is so seldom that we meet nowadays with a clergyman so erudite and instructive."

This sly and well-timed compliment produced a fine effect on the parson. His sympathies underwent a marked expansion, and his companion rose many degrees in his good opinion. "Handsome," said he to himself; "and so devilish clever. Clearly a woman of great discernment." The chaplain then mustered all his energies, and having in a very deliberate and impressive manner cleared his throat, proceeded to comply with the lady's request.

"About the period of the arrival of the Saxons in England—that is, in the sixth century of the Christian era, Mistress Carter—Pope Gregory was strolling through the Roman Forum, when he beheld a group of blue-eyed, fair-haired captives exposed for sale. He was informed that they had been brought from Britain, once an insular possession of the Romans, where Gospel truth had, according to tradition, been once planted, but did not then shine, but where the inhabitants were abandoned to the sanguinary superstition of the Druids, or else were doing abhorred rites to Thor and Odin. *'Alas! alas!' exclaimed the good pope,'* that the Prince of Darkness should possess countenances so luminous, and that so fair a front should cover minds destitute of eternal grace.'

"As the result of that fortuitous, or, as I call it, providential happening, the mission was resolved on of Augustine 'the monk' (as he is called in ecclesiastical history, to distinguish him from the illustrious father of the same name), or 'Augustine and his forty monks,' as Gibbon irreverently styles the sacred embassage."

The lady bowed her head in a very instructed manner as the reverend doctor paused and looked grandly into her splendid eyes. He thought they looked brighter than ever, for the power of appreciating the intellectual superiority of another is a faculty rarely bestowed on young ladies.

Mrs, Carter. "Have you, doctor, a chapel in which to collect your congregation for instruction?"

Dr. Gog. "Yes, madam, I have an edifice for that purpose, where I sometimes thunderise the guerrillas; but, on account of their irregular mode of life, I am compelled to administer instruction wherever I find them—in the highways, in the forest, in the camp, or at the bivouac. But the most potent influence which I bring to bear on them is the force of mine own example; for. Mistress Carter, an inquisition into the heart of man will teach us that the true way to govern that wayward child is through his affections, and by holding up before him a model for imitation."

A prolonged whistle of astonishment was, as he said this, heard at the parson's elbow. He started, looked quickly around, but beheld only a receding figure. His face, however, flushed a deeper carnation as he turned to listen again to his companion.

"Has your ministry, Doctor Gog, been attended as yet with much success?"

Dr. Gog. "Rarely, Mistress Carter, has so large a measure of success been vouchsafed to the proclamation of the Word. Last Sabbath day one month ago, a mighty concourse gathered to hear me. It was a second day of Pentecost; all counted who that day professed a quickening—furloughed soldiers, Yankee prisoners, contrabands, and citizens, besides my own proper charge, amounted to a trifle less than five hundred souls, that is—if Yankees have souls, a question on which divines are much divided."

Mrs. Carter. "Five hundred souls, doctor?"

Dr. Gog. "Yes, Mistress Carter, five hundred souls."

At this period of the conversation the whistle again sounded in the chaplain's ears, and his eyes kindled with ire as he beheld the figure of a soldier disappearing in the crowd. Mrs. Carter was herself offended at the rudeness of this interruption, and inquired the name of the intruder.

Dr. Gog. "That youngster, madam, is an idiot boy, who has eluded the vigilance of his parents, and attached himself, to the command, where the good nature of Mosby allows him to remain. He entertains himself, and sometimes others, with uncouth gestures, whistlings, and strange exclamations."

Mrs. Carter. "Where do his parents reside? You have not told me his name."

Dr. Gog. "In Richmond, madam; and his name is John Munson."

Mrs. Carter was here called off, and Adolphus Adam Gog, C. M. B., was left alone,

"I have rarely seen a pretty woman take more stock in a parson," said he, with a chuckle, while a prolonged visit to "Oatlands," and visions of devilled turkey and roast pig, of which he was so uncommonly fond, rose before the divine. He thought, too, of Mr. Carter's cellar and his baronial mansion; how he would saunter along the avenue of grand old oaks, the contemporaries, it might be, of Columbus, having at his elbow a library of old English authors—books that *"a man might tie to."* "I have rarely seen a pretty woman take more stock in a parson," repeated the doctor, as he drew on his gloves, and began to saunter through the rooms.

When Mrs. Carter again met the partisan chief, she thanked him for bringing his chaplain to their marriage feast.

"I am charmed with him, he is so intelligent and dignified, and his intelligence and dignity are accompanied by such unaffected piety. He is so learned, too, that he almost reminds one of St. Paul."

Here the gray eyes sparkled as, with a polite bow, their owner assented to the lady's remark, but a minute observer would have detected a smile lurking in the corners of the mouth. But Mrs. Carter was far too happy that evening to be prying into the mystery of smiles, and seeking to interpret the enigmas of the countenance. At that moment she was informed by a servant that Dick Buckner and his guerrilla band were ready to strike up the music, if such was her pleasure.

"Not for the world," exclaimed the hostess, "until I know the wishes of the Rev. Dr. Gog on the subject. Do you think, colonel, he would object?"

Thus appealed to, Colonel Mosby referred the question to the parson himself, who was not far off. Bowing with great politeness to the lady, the reverend gentleman, in his own style, thus answered her question:

"Music, and dancing, Mistress Carter, I esteem appropriate to this occasion and this company. Believe me, they are the reverse of disagreeable to my feelings. I approve, indeed, of all kinds of innocent pleasure, particularly where it creates

"'The pert and nimble spirit of mirth.'

"I so love and admire innocence in all its forms, that I should be loath to confound it, by a prohibition, with wrong and error. Dancing, which embraces music, I consider, of every species of enjoyment, the most to be preferred on every fitting occasion, for 'the reason that it combines exercise with grace, innocence, and pleasure—three which, if they be personified, could not be considered out of place, if, to their own untaught harmonies, they were to tread a measure on the ivory floors of Paradise. Mistress Carter, we best praise the All-giver when, within the pale of innocence, we are happy. When I see one who, at suitable times, condemns the dance and the song, I suspect the presence of a weak head, a sour heart, or a hypocritical conscience."

Such liberal sentiments greatly pleased the lady, who, yet fearing lest the good parson had been somewhat governed by politeness in what he had said, determined to save his sensibilities the slightest shock by conducting him to an apartment aloof from the dancers, where he would find company of a graver cast, among whom she knew were several elderly ladies who would be delighted with the opportunity of becoming acquainted with the chaplain of Mosby's Battalion.

But the chaplain of Mosby's Battalion had formed, it soon appeared, other plans for the evening's entertainment; so he stoutly opposed the arrangement, and when urged by Mosby to accept the invitation, abruptly crossed the room and joined Miss Josephine Stevenson, one of the fairest ladies present, where I must leave the reverend gentleman until a later period of the night. I have neglected to mention that before they parted company Mrs. Carter had engaged Doctor Gog to preach at Upperville the ensuing Sunday, and had, in order to secure a large attendance, made the arrangement generally known to her guests. Thus things stood when she was both surprised and pained to see the chaplain lead the fair Josephine to the dance.

His manners had undergone an entire change, and were now as sportive as before they had been grave. She looked at him with an expression of surprise and reproof; but her glances of displeasure produced no more effect on Doctor Gog than the darts of the Lilliputian archers did on the person of Lemuel Gulliver. The truth is, the parson had taken about half a pint of "blockade," and did not care the snap of a finger for the reproachful looks of all the black eyes in Christendom. It was perfectly clear, too, that he had forgotten all about his appointments, and was now engaged in quoting from Byron and Moore, instead of the fathers, to the sprightly Josephine.

Mrs. Carter, much displeased, withdrew from that part of the room, and saw no more of him until late in the evening, when she observed a general movement toward the spot where he was dancing. I, too, was attracted thither, and, to my surprise, discovered that the dance had been broken up with the exception of the chaplain, who was violently engaged in performing a solo. With arms akimbo and head thrown back, he was executing with great vigour and minuteness all the steps learned from an old-fashioned dancing-master—the double-shuffle, the pigeon-wing, the back step, etc. Never did mortal ears hear so great a clatter made by a single pair of feet.

I looked up and saw standing before me Mrs. Carter, as if petrified with surprise and mortification. Her husband was at her side, and I heard him say to her,

"You have a gay parson, my love. He preaches for us, does he not, the next Lord's day?"

"Yes," responded she, in a faint and troubled voice, and, as she said so, moved off to a remote part of the room. As she turned away her dejected visage reminded me of the woeful faces that throng the halls of Eblis.

THE PARSON'S STAG DANCE.

A pause in the music at this time occurred, and the unhappy lady looked as if relieved from a great torture; but no, no, it was only to be increased, for in noisy tones she heard the parson exclaim, as he advanced toward the musicians,

"Holloah, Mister Nigger, give us the 'Ringtailed Roarer!'"

Dick Buckner. "Don't know it, parson."

Doctor Gog. "The thunder you don't! Give us, then, 'Billy in the Low Grounds,' or 'Sugar in the Gourd,' or 'The Arkansas Traveller,' or some hell-bender of your own!'

This sally produced immense laughter, in which it is needless to say Mrs. Carter did not unite. Instead, she buried her face in her handkerchief and wept with very vexation. She then arose, and, with a resolute air, approached Colonel Mosby, who, as soon as he was informed of the nature of her perplexity, annulled all the chaplain's engagements, set Mrs. Carter at liberty, and restored smiles to her countenance. As she turned from him I heard her say, "Never again will I invite one of these army men to preach—no, not if he be an archbishop."

CHAPTER 25: DEFEAT AND DISPERSION OF CAPTAIN REID'S CAVALRY BATTALION.

Upper Fauquier, February 26th, 1864.

Dear Percy,—I have omitted to tell you that, about the date of the "Chestnut Fork Raid," Major Mosby established his head-quarters at the residence of Mr. Blackwell Magog, his chief of staff, who lives within a short distance of Piedmont. Two days after the Cornelle Raid, a party, composed of the major, Jake Lavender, Johnny Edmunds, and Johnny Munson, were seated at breakfast, when Jimmy Edmunds ran in, and said that the turnpike, which was about a mile distant, was "full of Yankees." At first they were incredulous, but Major Mosby said they had better saddle up and see for themselves. When they reached the road they discovered that it was crowded, as the little boy had said, with Federal cavalry, who proved to be Cole's Battalion on a march from their camp at Harper's Ferry to Front Royal.

The party proceeded to Mrs. Chappelier's orchard, where the major determined to open the fight—Johnny Edmunds and Johnny Munson each being armed with a long-range gun—and trust to the sound of the firing to attract his" men to the spot. This unexpected attack upon his column arrested the march of Major Cole, who doubtless thought the guerrillas prepared to harass his march, which lay through the Blue Ridge Mountains. In consequence, he reversed the head of his column, and returned toward Upperville. As it approached Gap Run, Mosby, with his three men, took position on a hill immediately above the ford, where the major said he would try his hand, and, taking Edmunds's carbine, he and Munson fired into the Yankees. The effect of this was to wound a man, kill a horse, and quicken the speed of the retreating column. This irregular fighting was kept up until the Federals reached Upperville, the partisans having from time to time been re-enforced along the route.

At this place Major Cole halted to have his horses fed, a pause which proved very advantageous to Mosby, for during the interval fifty of his men gathered around him. The mode of attack was now changed from sharp-shooting on the hills to assaults on the enemy's rear, which induced Major Cole to keep out a strong rear-guard of sharp-shooters. About two miles farther on we charged the rearguard, drove them in, and threw the column into some confusion, but soon scattered before a counter-charge. As soon as they resumed the march we again charged, and this time with success, for, getting into close quarters, we drove them as far as Blakeley School-house. In this charge Mountjoy encountered Captain Morgan, and, after a personal contest, in view of both commands, killed him. Mosby witnessed the duel, and in warm terms congratulated the victor when it was over, assuring him that he had that day won a commission.

At the schoolhouse the fighting was very animated, charging and counter-charging until the enemy took refuge behind the stone fences which form the cross-roads at that place. From these, as a breastwork, they continued the fight, until Mosby, resolving not to be held at such disadvantage, flanked their position as if to throw himself in their front. While executing this movement he was brought in full range of the enemy, who, having identified him among the assailants, opened upon him a concentrated fire. His appearance was conspicuous, dressed in a dark overcoat, the cape of which, lined with scarlet, was thrown over his shoulder, and a light felt hat, with a black plume. He was mounted on a gray horse, remarkable for its beauty and activity, and Major Cole offered a reward to any one who would kill the Partisan chief.

The Federal officer, seeing the dangerous position in which he was about to be placed, resumed his retreat, but with his flanks and rear still exposed to galling attacks, which were kept up for several miles farther. Mosby's loss was Lieutenant Fox and Starke wounded, while Major Cole lost one officer and five privates killed, and eight men, with their horses and equipments, taken prisoners.

During their advance through Fauquier the Federals captured two of the Rangers, John and Bartlett Bolling, at the residence of their father, and killed M'Cobb, of Baltimore, who, when surprised at his boarding-house, mounted his horse, and, in attempting to leap a fence, was thrown, and there killed.

Before disbanding the command, after the fight at Blakeley School-house, Major Mosby ordered it to rendezvous at Piedmont the next day, for the purpose of escorting the remains of M'Cobb to the grave. About nine o'clock on Sunday morning the men began to assemble—small squads arriving from time to time, while Mosby was at the house of John B. Jeffries writing a report to General Stuart of the proceedings of the last few days. He had not finished it when information was brought him that the Fairfax Yankees were in Fauquier on a raid, and were then in the vicinity of Middleburg. Without waiting to pay the last sad tribute of respect to the memory of our comrade, the command, numbering one hundred and fifty, was marched, under Captain Chapman, in the direction of the enemy, while Mosby, with a small party, hastened forward to reconnoitre his position. He learned that the Yankees were a detachment of cavalry from Vienna, commanded by Captain Reid, and that they had gone from Rector's Cross-roads across the country to Mountsville.

Without delay, he started Sam Underwood and another man to follow their line of march, and report to him at a designated point below Mountsville, on the road leading from Snickersville to Aldie, where he would meet him with the command. Mosby's object in this was to have it in his power to intercept Captain Reid in case he should attempt from Mountsville to return to his camp at Vienna. But Underwood reported that, instead, he had proceeded in the direction of Leesburg. With the object still in view of keeping between Captain Reid and his camp, Mosby marched his command to Carter's Mill, on Goose Creek. Here he left it, with instructions to Chapman to have the horses fed at the corn-crib of a Union man in the neighbourhood, whose principles Underwood had reported, and from thence to proceed to the farm of Mr. Harrison, lower down on Goose Creek, and farther in the direction of the Leesburg and Dranesville Turnpike, along which he thought Captain Reid would return toward his camp, and there to await farther orders. Mosby then took a party to act as couriers, and proceeded toward Leesburg for the purpose of watching the movements of the enemy and directing those of his own command. He now felt sure of success; for, while his men were moving on the shorter interior line, the Yankees, as Sam Underwood expressed it, were marching on "the rainbow."

Finding himself correct in his conjecture as to the route which Captain Reid would follow from Leesburg, Mosby, by a courier, ordered Chapman to move the command still nearer the turnpike, where at night he joined it, after he had discovered that the enemy had camped at Mr. Kephart's, who lives a short distance from the turnpike, and had been joined by one hundred and fifty cavalry, under command of Major Frazier. The next mornings with a cheerful countenance, Mosby assured his men that it was all right, and they would certainly catch the Yankees before they got to their camp. He then marched still farther down the turnpike in the direction of Vienna, and posted the command in a body of pines on the right of the road, and a little beyond Anker's shop.

But there was a point in his rear on the turnpike where a road branched to the right, by which it was possible the raiders might return to their camp. Here he stationed Walter Whaley, to report to him which road they took; for, in the event of their leaving the turnpike, it was still in his power to strike across the country, and again throw himself in their front.

Soon Whaley came dashing up with the information that the Federals had separated—Major Frazier having taken the country road, but that Captain Reid, with the California Battalion, was still travelling the turnpike.

Mosby at once made his disposition for attack. Mountjoy, with twenty dismounted sharp-shooters, was placed in the centre of the position. The command was then divided into two parts; one, under Frank Williams, was posted forty yards to the right; the other, under Captain Chapman, forty yards to the left; while "Red Fox" and another man were stationed a short distance farther down the road, to attract the attention of the advancing column. The orders issued were as follows: Mountjoy and his sharp-shooters were to fire their carbines, and simultaneously Williams and Chapman were to rush upon the exposed flank of the enemy at the sound of Mosby's silver whistle, which he would blow when the column was in the act of passing. Strict silence was then enjoined, and we lay awaiting the approach of the enemy with breathless anxiety. During this interval of suspense we distinctly heard the deep peals of the great siege guns around Washington as they thundered forth gratitude and praise to the memory of the man who, above all others, founded the American Union, for the maintenance of which this destructive war is now being waged.

As soon as the raiders arrived at Anker's shop, which is on the slope of the hill toward Leesburg on which we were posted, their advance-guard, numbering about twenty men, discovered "Red Fox," and at once dashed forward in pursuit of him; but the column halted at the shop. Mosby, finding himself thus exposed to the danger of discovery by the vanguard if he waited for it to come up, gave the signal, which was followed by the crack of Mountjoy's rifles, and in another moment by an onset from Williams and Chapman. Mosby, with Adjutant Chapman, charged at the head of Williams's detachment down the hill upon the front of Reid's column, while Captain Chapman, from his position, passing by a circuit through the pines, fell upon its rear. Thus assailed, resistance on the part of the enemy was of short duration. They broke and fled in every direction, but the bulk of them up the turnpike toward Leesburg closely pursued, and, in attempting to crowd through a gate on the roadside opening into a barnyard, near which stood Mosby, with a party of his men, many of them were killed.

Baron Massow, who was with Chapman's party, distinguished himself in the fight. Having emptied his pistol, he recurred to his sword, and dashed into the midst of the flying enemy. Captain Reid, whom he passed in his rapid career, by a shot from his revolver inflicted upon him a dangerous wound, which brought him to the ground. Chapman, seeing his friend fall from his horse, spurred forward to engage the man by whom he had been shot, and, when within three feet of Reid, fired, killing him instantly. The baron was carried to the house of a citizen near by, and tenderly nursed by a lady until he could be moved to Oatlands, the elegant residence of Mr. George Carter, where he still is.

Mosby's loss on this occasion was Pendleton and Chappelier killed, John Munson, Thomas Burke, Harry Sweeting, and the Baron Massow wounded. The Federals had fifteen killed, fifteen wounded, seventy taken prisoners, and lost one hundred horses, with their equipments.

This raiding-party was guided by Charlie Binns, a deserter from Company "A" to the Federal camp in Fairfax, where he is in great favour with his new friends, or rather employers, by whom he is often sent on expeditions to "Mosby's Confederacy." Great exertions were made to capture him in the pursuit, but, mounted on a swift horse, he escaped in the direction of the Potomac.

At Piedmont, on the 23rd, the captured property was divided, and the prisoners sent to Richmond. As they moved off, Mosby remarked,

"Well, I have stopped a few more of you from sucking eggs."

CHAPTER 26: MILITARY BOUNDARIES OF MOSBY'S CONFEDERACY

Upper Fauquier, April 2nd, 1864.

Dear Percy,—At this time "Mosby's Confederacy" is compassed about by enemies. On the south it is hemmed in by the garrison at Warrenton; on the east by the numerous camps stretching across Fairfax; on the north by General Sullivan's command at Harper's Ferry; and on the west by the forces always swarming in the Valley. It would seem as though he must be crushed by these opposing bodies, as it were between huge icebergs; yet does this remarkable hero maintain an undaunted front. Not only does he hold his ground, but, as we have already seen, has driven off two invading forces, and destroyed another, and is still, with his indomitable Rangers, ever hovering about the hostile camps with which he is begirt. General Crawford, who commands a detachment of cavalry stationed at Bristoe for the protection of that section of the Orange and Alexandria Railroad, had been sending daily a patrol to Greenwich, varying in strength from fifty to a hundred men.

Lieutenant Richards, with a party, had, without success, attempted its capture, and Mosby now determined to try it. With forty men, he stationed himself in ambush on the road from Bristoe Station to

Greenwich. Leaving the men in charge of Lieutenant Hunter, he proceeded, in company with Lieutenant Chapman, to a hill from which he could see the patrol approaching. Having rejoined Hunter, he waited until it passed the ambuscade, and their charged its rear. The Yankees scattered through the pines, and in this way escaped with only nine prisoners and horses.

The day after the little affair at Greenwich which I have just related, Lieutenant Richards obtained permission from Mosby to take a party of forty-five men and go on an expedition to the valley. He had been informed by John Chew, a member of Chew's Battery, of the exposed position of a Federal picket-post near his father's house on the road leading from Cabletown to Charlestown. The picket consisted of two companies of the 1st New York Veterans, commanded by Lieutenant Bryandt, and was stationed in a skirt of wood bordering the road. About sunset Richards crossed the Shenandoah, and at midnight arrived at Cabletown, two miles beyond which place he halted his command, and, accompanied by Chew as a guide, made a visit to the Federal camp.

Finding everything quiet, he returned for his men, and by a circuitous march approached the picket-post about daylight from the direction of Charlestown. This enabled him to impose his command upon the sentinel as the relief, and thus, without exciting alarm, entered the camp, which was found in profound repose. But one man was astir, and he, poor fellow, was killed by the signal-shot from Richards as he was kindling a fire from the embers of the preceding night. The surprise was complete, and the Rangers met with no resistance until the return of a scouting-party of twenty men, who came gallantly charging up while the intruders were in the camp, but were soon driven off.

With twenty-five horses and as many prisoners, among whom was Lieutenant Bryandt, Richards left the camp at a gallop, for he feared pursuit from Charlestown.

On the return march, one of the most gallant fights of the war was made by six of Richards's men, Robert Walker, Fount Beattie, Dr. Sowers, Rucker, John Hearn, and Ben Syd Edmonds. They had lingered at Cabletown, and were there overtaken by Major Sullivan, who had come in pursuit of Richards from Charlestown with a party of thirty cavalry. There was no commissioned officer among them, but, at the invitation of one of their number, the heroic little band faced about and charged back oil their assailants^ killing a lieutenant and wounding a captain. This checked the enemy's advance, when the

Rangers again renewed the charge, and this time routed their pursuers, killing Major Sullivan and two others. With six prisoners and as many horses, they then pressed forward, and rejoined the column before it recrossed the Shenandoah. But I must not omit, in this narration, the part borne by Willie Martin, one of the bravest of Mosby's men. He was captured before his comrades were overtaken, and thus took no part in the fight; but, as soon as the rout began, he wrested the carbine from his guard, and, seizing it by the muzzle, stood in the road, and with the butt end of it fought the fugitives as they fled by him.

Lieutenant Bryandt wore, when he was captured, a sword which had been presented to him by his company. It was encased in a silver scabbard, on which was inscribed:

"Presented to 1st Lieut. Bryandt as a mark of esteem, by Co. L, 1st New York Veterans."

He pleaded hard to retain the costly present, but was told that Mosby's men never returned captured arms. It now hangs at the gallant Mosby's side, but with a new inscription:

"Captured March 9th, 1864, and presented to Lieut. Col. John Singleton Mosby, by Lieut. A. E. Richards."

About the middle of March Mosby captured a picket of fourteen men at Germantown, which had been thrown out by the garrison at Fairfax Court-house. A few hours later, a hundred cavalry were on his track, inquiring at every house if Mosby had passed. They were informed that he had returned to Fauquier, in consequence of which they retraced their steps, determined to be more vigilant in future.

About this time Captain William H. Chapman was married to Miss Jeffries, of Fauquier, and was indulged with a furlough of thirty days. Lieutenant Richards, being left in command of Company C, again looked to the Valley as a theatre for activity. Taking with him ten men, he set forth for the purpose of attacking the pickets near Charlestown, but found upon his arrival that they had been withdrawn to Halltown. Proceeding to that vicinity on the 20th, he was informed that both cavalry and infantry had, during the afternoon, been ordered to retire within the fortifications at Harper's Ferry, but that a sutler, whose goods had been stored in a temporary building, had been allowed to remain outside for the purpose of packing his wares, upon condition that he would move in during the night.

Richards determined to make the sutler a visit before he moved, and about one o'clock at night called at his establishment. He was promptly answered by two men at the door, from one of whom he demanded, in a tone of authority,

"Why, sir, didn't you move into the Ferry this evening, as you were ordered?"

"It was late before we finished packing," replied the merchant, in a humble voice, "so I concluded to wait till morning."

"That will never do," said Richards. "The Rebels were in Charlestown several hours ago, and will have your goods before morning."

"Never!" replied the sutler, with a tragic air. "Never! With the aid of camphene, I will, in case of emergency, lay my whole establishment in ashes."

Richards, as if highly pleased with this sentiment, volunteered to assist in the removal of the goods, while the sutler withdrew to make ready his wagons, thinking himself the luckiest man in the world to have fallen in with so good-natured a fellow. But great was his dismay when he returned to the house, for he found that the soldiers had left behind the heavy merchandise, and were only moving such light articles as could be carried away on horseback. The truth at once flashed upon the merchant, and, folding his arms across his breast, he exclaimed, in an imploring voice,

"Gentlemen, I know now who you are. Take whatever you desire from my store, but, for God's sake, spare my life"—doubtless as sincere a prayer as was ever offered up.

Richards then mounted his horse, and stood picket on the road leading to Harper's Ferry, while his merry men, with many a word of condolence for the sutler, loaded their horses from the contents of his booth.

This brings my record to the end of March, for three months previous to which the weather was so stormy and inclement, and the roads so deep, that our leader was compelled to operate only with small parties, who could be accommodated at the houses of citizens. Of their operations I have only received the. meagre account which I have given you; but Mosby, in his report to Stuart, which I have seen, states that during this period he has captured an average of one hundred and fifty prisoners and horses a month. My own attention has been somewhat engaged in establishing a temporary abode on the Blue Ridge Mountains, about midway between Markham and Paris. I have selected this location, first, because it is convenient to the Shenandoah Valley, henceforth to be with us a scene of great activity, and, secondly, because it is so sequestered as not to be exposed to the incursions of raiding-parties.

Chapter 27: Freedom of the Ballot

Upper Fauquier, May 8th, 1864.

Dear Percy,—On the 1st of April the battalion was ordered to rendezvous at Paris, for the purpose of organising Company "D." Many murmurs had been heard at the arbitrary manner in which Mosby had conducted the previous elections, and a formidable opposition had been silently formed. But he met the issue in a prompt and characteristic manner. As soon as the men who were to form the new company were drawn up in line, the names of a list of candidates were read aloud by the officer appointed by Mosby to superintend the election. During the pause which ensued Mosby stepped in front of the electors, and very quietly informed them that any one not willing to ratify by his votes the nominations which had been made was at liberty to leave the ranks, and would, without delay, be sent to the regular service. This alternative no man was ready to adopt, for the regular service is regarded by the Rangers as Mosby's Botany Bay. So the nominations were all confirmed. This was a crisis, and through it the command passed safely. All felt it, and Mosby is now more firmly seated than ever in the dictatorship he has assumed over his men. This combination was the first, and will probably be the last ever formed against his authority.

E. P. Mountjoy was elected captain; Alfred Glasscock, first lieutenant; Charles E. Grogan, second lieutenant; William Trunnel, junior second lieutenant.

Captain Mountjoy.

Captain Mountjoy is by birth a Mississippian, and at the beginning of the war entered the Provisional Army of the South as a private in one of the infantry regiments contributed by his native state. At an early period of its formation he obtained a transfer to the Partisan Battalion, and by the gallantry of his bearing soon attracted the general attention. At Ewell's Chapel, as I have mentioned, he was wounded while pressing forward in the lead, and since that time has been a prominent actor in other collisions.

Lieutenant Glasscock, of Fauquier, at the breaking out of the war was a private in Captain Turner Ashby's cavalry company, in which he rose to the rank of lieutenant, an office from which he was afterward ejected when the Confederate Congress reorganised the army by exchanging the old principle of authority for the new principle of popularity. This loss of rank proved in the end to be a benefit, for it enabled Glasscock to enter the Partisan service, for which he has proved himself to be so well fitted.

Lieutenants Grogan and Trunnel are both from Maryland. The former served for a time on General Trimble's staff, and with him was captured at Gettysburg, and confined on Johnson's Island. From that dreary prison he made his escape, under circumstances of extraordinary peril, and immediately afterward joined the battalion. Lieutenant Trunnel was, it is needless to say, a good soldier, and was among the first of the bold spirits who were attracted to the partisan banner when unfurled by Mosby. He stood high with his commander, and his promotion had been postponed in consequence of a captivity from which he had but recently been liberated.

This company was formed almost entirely of young gentlemen from Maryland, who have cast their lot with the South in this great trial of arms. Its members, as conspicuous for gallantry in the parlour as they undoubtedly are in the field, have won for it from the ladies the endearing name of "Company Darling."

At the same time another of "Mosby's elections," as such occasions are jocularly called in the battalion, was held, to supply the vacancy produced by the death of Lieutenant Turner. Lieutenant Hunter having been promoted to the vacant rank. Lieutenant Joe Nelson to the position which Hunter had filled, Harry Hatcher, from the 7th Virginia Cavalry, was "elected" to succeed Nelson.

Company "D" was but just organised when it was called upon to choose again a junior second lieutenant, for Trunnell, before his promotion could be communicated to him, was killed while scouting in the Valley, With Boyle, of the 12th Virginia Cavalry, he had attempted to capture a party of Yankees who were concealed in a house near Martinsburg; but, as the soldiers approached, they were fired upon and killed by those within the house.

David Briscoe, of Baltimore, was elected to succeed Trunnell.

On the 8th of April Mosby started from Middleburg, with twenty-five men of Company "A," under command of Lieutenant Hunter, to attack a picket-post, guarded by a company of cavalry, at Hunter's Mill, on the road from Silent Hill to Fairfax Court-house. On a previous scout he had visited this camp, had seen the corporal of the guard station the vedettes, and had heard him take leave of them with the injunction, "Now don't let old Mosby get you." His plans were therefore matured; so, marching to a point distant a quarter of a mile from the mill, he dismounted his men, and, leaving two of them in charge of the horses, with the rest charged the camp with a yell. Twelve prisoners and twenty horses were secured, but many of the fugitives escaped, sheltered by the darkness, and carried the news of the disaster to the brigade at Vienna, two and a half miles distant, to which their regiment was attached.

As soon as the capture was made, Mosby ordered Lieutenant Hunter to take the command back to Fauquier by the route which passes Gum Spring and Mat Lee's, while he, with Bush Underwood, went, at the request of General Stuart, in search of information, which he expected to obtain from a citizen living near the Orange and Alexandria Railroad, who had just been to Washington,

Lieutenant Hunter, instead of pursuing the route by Gum Spring, for some reason struck across to Chantilly, and from thence proceeded up the Little River Turnpike. Colonel Lowell, in the meantime, who was in command at Vienna, had, with a detail of cavalry from the California Battalion (which the Rangers think the most formidable of their opponents), started in pursuit of the assailants. At the Double Toll-gate he came in sight of the stragglers from Hunter's command and the pursuit was pressed with new vigour. Some of the stragglers who had lingered on the road to get breakfast harassed the march of the Californians by firing upon them, then plunging into the pines which skirted the road. At Aldie, in consequence of the freshness of Lowell's horses, the Partisans were overtaken. Hunter at once sent forward the prisoners in charge of five men, while he and Lieutenant Nelson, with the remaining ten of the command, faced about and charged their pursuers. The combat for a short time was severe, but the overwhelming numbers of the enemy obtained the victory. Hunter was taken prisoner, and Nelson severely wounded; but he managed, in spite of it, with nine men, to make his escape, the pursuit being abandoned at this point.

After the death of Captain Smith, President Davis, at the recommendation of Colonel Mosby, appointed Lieutenant A. E. Richards to fill the vacant office, which promotion was announced to the battalion in the following order:

> Headquarters, 43rd Va. P. E. Battalion,
> April 26th, 1864.
> Special Order, No.—.
>
> First Lieutenant Adolphus E. Richards, Company 'C,' having been promoted by His Excellency, the President, to the captaincy of Company 'B' for gallantry and skill displayed in action, will be respected and obeyed accordingly.
>
> J. S. Mosby, Lieutenant Colonel Commanding.

The next day, Captain Richards, with thirty-five men, and Henry Heaton for a guide, started on a foraging expedition to Loudoun. At Hillsboro, where they arrived about ten o'clock at night, he was informed that Captain Keys, with forty-five men, had passed through the village about sunset, and had gone in the direction of Wheatland. This company of cavalry was recruited in Loudoun County for the Federal service, and is called the "Loudoun Rangers"—a name which they richly deserve, for they have plundered half of the poultry-yards, milk-houses, and stables in the county.

Richards determined to abandon the object for which he had come, and turn his attention to Captain Keys. In the morning, he was informed by a citizen that Keys was in Waterford, quartered in an old church, where he had passed the night. Falling upon a picket of six men, which had been thrown forward by the commander at that place, Richards drove them back upon the reserve, hoping to draw them out into the open field; but his effort was not successful; for Captain Keys, as soon as apprised of the danger, put it to the vote whether they should fight or run, adding, at the same time, "Boys, they greatly outnumber us"—an application of the Democratic principle to the army which had not occurred even to the sages at Richmond.

As Richards came thundering into the village, the gallant company, with a unanimous voice, shouted that the interests of the public service demanded an immediate retreat, and Captain Keys left Waterford at a charge, taking a circuitous route to the Point of Rocks. Mounted on the picked horses of Loudoun and the adjoining counties, the "Loudoun Rangers" fled like the Arabs of the desert, pursued by the partisans for five miles. Richards's horse at this point fell from exhaustion, and thus ended the chase. Keys having lost in his rapid career twelve prisoners, three of whom were wounded, and fifteen horses, while his pursuers had sustained no injury at all.

Fisher's Hill is an abrupt eminence that lies across the track of the Valley Turnpike, two miles beyond Strasburg. At its base flows the north branch of the Shenandoah, the banks of which are so steep as to render it impassable except by means of the bridge here thrown across it. The road is, dug out of the hill, and gradually winds around its western face until it reaches the summit, where it resumes its original direction. This hill was the culminating point of a raid that Captain William Chapman started upon on the 5th of May from Piedmont. With twenty men, he marched to a point between Strasburg and Middletown, for the purpose of attacking a supply-train, which passed from Winchester to General Hunter's camp at Newmarket. Posting two of his command so as to watch the road in the direction of Winchester, he and Willie Gibson stationed themselves so as to be on the look-out toward Strasburg.

Late in the day, four cavalrymen, under command of a lieutenant, approached from the direction of Strasburg. Chapman at first attempted to deceive them as to his true character, but, failing in this, he and his companion fell back before them until they reached their comrades on the road, about a quarter of a mile distant. The two parties, then being equal in strength, rushed upon each other, and a fight ensued, which resulted in the capture of the five Yankees. Chapman at once sent the prisoners under guard across the river, and the command then bivouacked for the night. Early the next morning he resumed his march on the turnpike, and very soon a supply-train approached from the direction of Winchester, guarded by three hundred infantry and eighty cavalry. With his men disguised by the oil-cloths which they wore as a protection from the rain, he followed in its rear until the wagons were ascending Fisher's Hill, with the guard strung all along the road winding up its side. In this situation of affairs, the bridge blocked up with wagons, and the guard unable to come to the rescue.

Chapman charged the rear-guard. Twelve were killed and wounded, nineteen made prisoners, and twenty-three horses secured. With these captures, Chapman, with all expedition, retraced his steps, and was saved from pursuit by a lady, who assured the Federals there was no chance of overtaking him. The next day the prisoners were turned over to the provost-marshal at Luray, and the Rangers disbanded, to return to Fauquier by routes of their own selection.

Chapter 28: Capture of the Picket at Grant's Hill

Upper Fauquier, May 15th, 1864.

Dear Percy,—There is a low range, called the Pine Hills, which extends from the North Branch of the Shenandoah, in Warren County, through Clarke and Frederick, and terminates in the counties of Berkeley and Jefferson. Guard Hill is an elevated point of this range, and rises abruptly where Crooked Run crosses the turnpike leading from Winchester through Cedarville to Front Royal. Its name is said to be derived from its having been the site of a fort constructed by the early European settlers in the vicinity, to defend themselves from the Indians. On this eminence a detachment of Federal cavalry was encamped, which Mosby proposed to attack, and, with this object in view, left Paris on the 7th of May, with a hundred men. Upon arriving at the Shenandoah, it was found to be so swollen by recent rains as to render fording impossible, in consequence of which the command under Richards was ordered back to Mount Carmel Church, where it bivouacked for the night, while Mosby, with six men, crossed the river in a boat, and proceeded to the neighbourhood of Winchester on a scout.

The next morning Richards brought the command over the river in boats, their horses being driven after them. This operation was tedious, and before it was over a courier arrived from Mosby, with instructions to Richards to move to the vicinity of Cedarville, two or three miles from Guard Hill. At eight o'clock at night Mosby joined the command at the designated place, and was informed by M'Kay, a resident of that neighbourhood and one of his men, that the Federals had that day been re-enforced, and that their number was not less than two hundred men.

"Excellent!" replied he; "then each of us will get two horses apiece."

The command was then conducted around Cedarville to the residence of Dr. Melton, who lives near the base of the Pine Hills. Here Mosby left it, and, with Harry Shaw and four others, approached Cedarville, and on the turnpike captured a party of Federal cavalry, upon whom he imposed himself for a patrol from Guard Hill. At the village he made other captures, and then rejoined the command, after an absence of several hours. Unable to gain any satisfactory information from his prisoners, Mosby marched the command by a country road which runs along the crest of the Pine Hills to Guard Hill, so as to enable him to approach the cavalry camp from the rear. When within half a mile of it the men were halted, and Mosby, accompanied by Sam Chapman, proceeded on foot to reconnoitre the enemy's position. But a severe cough which at this time harassed him soon compelled him to return, and Lieut. Nelson was sent in his stead. Chapman, who knew the ground thoroughly, reported the encampment to be situated on the road that passes along the back-bone of Guard Hill, which is thickly covered with wood.

Upon the receipt of this information, Mosby ordered him to proceed to the camp, with fifteen dismounted sharp-shooters, while Richards, with Company "B," was directed to support him. The rest of the command followed under Mosby, first at a trot, then at a gallop, and finally, when a volley from Chapman was heard, in a headlong charge upon the enemy, dispersing them in every direction, wounding three, and taking seventeen prisoners. To enable you to understand what follows, I must state that the Yankees were divided into two parties, one being camped, as already described, on the crest of the hill, while the other lay around Stenson's house, which is situated at its base, and commands an extensive view of the river flat which here separates the North Branch of the Shenandoah from the highlands. Mosby was ignorant of this division, and was about moving off, when Captain Auer, of the 15th New York Cavalry, rode up from the camp near Stenson's house to inquire into the cause of the disturbance, which he supposed to be a repetition of some rioting which had occurred the previous night. His question was addressed to Sam Chapman, who responded by demanding his arms, and then turning him over to the custody of Harry Shaw, to be escorted to Fauquier.

At daybreak the homeward march was begun, which had not proceeded more than four miles, when, for the purpose of expediting the passage of the river, the command and captures were divided into two equal parts, one of which was entrusted to Mountjoy, to cross at Howellsville, the other to Captain Richards, to cross at Berry's Ferry, while Mosby, with a small party, lingered in the rear to watch the movements of the enemy.

The capture of Captain Auer was the means of explaining a mysterious circumstance which had occurred in the fight at Blakeley schoolhouse. One of the Rangers had killed a horse which was ridden by an officer whose uniform was plainly seen; but, on going to the spot, a private was found standing by the dead animal. On the, march from Guard Hill, Captain Auer stated to Harry Shaw that he was the officer whose horse had been shot on that occasion, and that he had been saved from capture by the generosity of one of his men, who had given him his horse, and remained behind to be taken prisoner in his stead.

As the command was charging into the Yankee camp, Phil Lee, of Fairfax, bethought him of a stratagem which he straightway put into execution. He raised a mighty shout of "Imboden, Imboden is upon you," by which war-cry Phil hoped to spread consternation into the ranks of the enemy. The next day, at the division of the horses, seventy in number, Mosby remarked to the Ranger, in allusion to this circumstance, that, like Peter, he had denied his master, and that, in justice, he ought to be sent to finish the campaign with General Imboden.

About this time the Federal Army was passing on toward Staunton under General Hunter, who had an arrangement for communicating with his rear by couriers, which he maintained until he reached that place. Mosby sent out small parties to harass his march, one of which, consisting of thirteen men under Captain Richards, entered Newtown, and so quietly captured and sent off a party of Yankees that the citizens knew nothing of the occurrence. Richards then marched toward Winchester, having heard that one of Hunter's couriers, whom he wished to capture, would pass along that section of the turnpike about nightfall, with an escort of twenty-four men. On his march he soon heard the sound of approaching hoofs, and at the distance of thirty paces an officer in command of a detachment of cavalry ordered him to halt, and demanded,

"Who are you?"

"First New York Cavalry," was the reply.

"All right," responded the Yankee; "we are some of the 21st boys, but at first I thought you were Johnnies."

In the meantime the two parties drew near to each other, Richards continuing the conversation, and in the course of it was informed that a supply-train, with a large escort, was only a few hundred yards behind.

During this time the partisans had ranged themselves along the column of the enemy, and were engaged in disarming them as quietly as possible, when a man refused to surrender and was instantly shot. Secrecy, of course, could no longer be observed, and pistols were freely used. But the Federals soon retreated to their wagon-train, leaving ten on the ground killed and wounded. The escort pressed forward in pursuit of the attacking party, but Richards and his men were quickly lost to view in an adjoining wood.

When Mosby returned from Guard Hill he found at his headquarters a; communication from General Stuart, stating that Grant, who was now in command of the Army of the Potomac, was in motion. The indefatigable partisan, although he had been on duty for two days and two nights, issued orders for the meeting of the battalion at Rectortown, after a rest of two days, and then, mounting a fresh horse, proceeded to Warrenton, which had been recently evacuated by the Yankees, in search of additional information. Upon his arrival he found several of his men, and among them Captain Mountjoy, attending a dancing party. Mosby at once started him with a small party upon a scout to Germana Ford, with orders to report to him the next morning at Brandy Station, while he indulged in a few hours' rest before repairing to the rendezvous. Having received Mountjoy's report the next day, he met the battalion at Rectortown.

Parties under Richards and Chapman were first detailed to operate during his absence at different points in the valley, and then, with a command of sixty men, Mosby set forth to cross the Rappahannock at the United States Ford, and assail the rear of Grant's army, at that time fighting in the Wilderness, having the year before started to perform the same service for Hooker, when he was stopped by the reverse at Warrenton Junction.

When the command passed near Bealton, Glasscock, with a detail of ten men, was left to tear up the rails, and to burn several railroad bridges and store-houses, for the road and some buildings were still used by Grant as his principal line of supply and depots. When Mosby reached the river, he found the ford guarded, Grant being at Chancellorsville; but, supposing that the Federal general must maintain a line of communication through Fredericksburg to the Potomac, he determined to push on, and assail him in that quarter. Passing through Falmouth that night, he marched into King George County, and camped near the house of a citizen, who fed both men and horses abundantly. The next morning, taking with him Willie Martin and Bowie, he made a reconnaissance in the vicinity of Belle Plain, and on the route fell in with a body of Federal cavalry, by whom they were closely pursued.

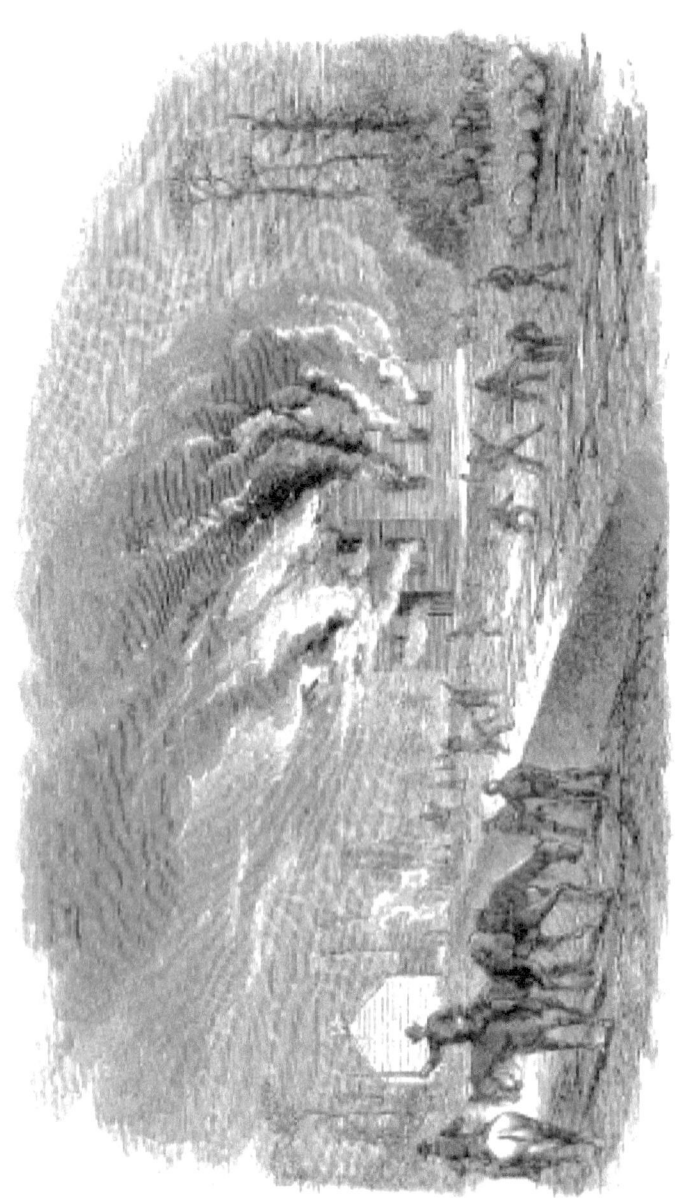
Destroying the railroad in Grant's rear

The fruit of this exploration was an attack at night on a train of fifty wagons, which was passing between Fredericksburg and Belle Plain.

The command was divided into two parts, one of which was sent, under Lieutenant Grogan, to capture and turn off the road the rear half of the train, while the other, under command of Ben Palmer, of Richmond, was sent to take charge of the wagons in front—a service which was handsomely performed. Mosby, with Fount Beattie, was in the road, waiting for Grogan to perform the allotted duty, when a surgeon and wagon-master rode up to look after the missing wagons. Being informed that they were prisoners in the hands of the guerrillas, they manifested both surprise and alarm, and the doctor at once handed out his pocket-pistol, but was told that he might keep his pistol, but must give up his horse. Encumbered with prisoners and horses, the command then returned to Fauquier.

When Mosby, in a few days, returned to this line of communication, he found that a brigade of cavalry had been sent from the front to guard it, in addition to the line of infantry posted along the road. No more captures were now possible with his small command, but his object had been attained, for General Grant had been compelled to detach from his aggressive force a considerable body of troops to protect his rear.

I will now give an account of the operations of the parties entrusted to Capt. Richards and Lieut. Sam Chapman, to operate in the valley during Mosby's absence.

At Paris the two commands, numbering twenty-five men each, met, and the officers agreed to cross the river together, and to separate on the farther side, if it should be found expedient. As the combined party was about to take up the line of march, Captain Chapman, who, with a few men, had been scouting in the valley, made his appearance, and was invited to join the expedition.. As soon as it crossed the river, the command was left in a wood near Berry's Ferry, and Richards, taking with him John Russell, proceeded to Millwood, to find out the strength of a party of Federal cavalry reported to be there. But he found they had left, and, without delay, endeavoured to rejoin Chapman; but Chapman could nowhere be found; so Richards and Russell went in search of him to the Valley Turnpike on which it had been proposed to operate.

Here they saw unguarded trains passing, for General Hunter relied upon the cavalry at Berryville and Charlestown for the protection of his transportation from Martinsburg to Winchester. But, as they had no force at their command, the two Rangers were compelled to recross the Shenandoah.

Lieut. Chapman, in the meantime, becoming impatient at the absence of Richards and Russell, had marched the command to Millwood, where he ascertained that the Yankees came every day in scouting-parties from Winchester to that place. Instead, therefore, of repairing to the Valley Turnpike, as Richards supposed he had done, he determined to lie in wait for one of these, and accordingly went into camp in a skirt of woods two miles distant, and in sight of the Winchester Turnpike. The next day, about twelve o'clock, a party of twelve Yankee cavalry were seen crossing the fields in the direction of Berryville, and Captain Chapman, with a party of about equal strength, started in pursuit of them. They had stopped to plunder a dairy, and were soon overtaken and charged in the rear, with a loss of two killed, five taken prisoners, and eight horses.

Upon his return, Captain Chapman represented to his brother that the party which he had attacked belonged to the 1st New York, which was out on a scout, and would, in all probability, be in pursuit of him in a few minutes, and urged an immediate retreat. The words were scarcely spoken when the regiment appeared. But the advice did not suit the reverend gentleman, who, whether in the regular service or with Mosby, had never been known to deny himself the luxury of a fight. Instead, therefore, of retreating, he charged the advanced guard, drove it back on the regiment, and then, with the prisoners and a portion of the command, fell back toward Millwood, while his brother, with the rest of the men, retired in another direction.

Lieutenant Chapman, finding himself followed by only seven of the enemy, thought that another chance for a fight was offered; so he sent off the prisoners, and then, with six men, faced about, and ordered a charge upon the pursuers. But the order was only partially obeyed; for, after firing a few shots, his men rejoined the retreating party. But not so Lieutenant Chapman; for, unattended, he charged through the seven Federals, who proved to be the advance-guard of the regiment, and, drawing up his horse on the side of the road, awaited their shots as they dashed past him to rejoin their command. In this unequal contest three of the Federals were wounded, while Chapman had his horse killed, but himself escaped unhurt. Thus dismounted, he took refuge in a patch of briers until the regiment had passed, and then returned on foot to Fauquier. Thus ended this series of adventures without the slightest injury to one of Mosby's men.

The incident which follows represents the anxiety of the Federal commanders to capture Mosby, and the dangers by which, in consequence, he is ever beset. Late on the 18th of May, 1864, a detachment of several hundred cavalry set forth from Vienna for an expedition into Upper Fauquier, to effect the capture of the "guerrilla chief," under the guidance of a man who had recently deserted from the battalion, and who sought to recommend himself to his associates and employers by this signal service. He had often known his former leader to stop at the house of Mrs. Rawlings, near Rectortown, and had taken up the idea that it was his boarding-house. To this point, accordingly, the Yankees were conducted.

The night was far spent when the party reached the neighbourhood, and, avoiding Rectortown, where a picket was sometimes stationed, they proceeded to a wood about two miles distant, and there were halted. About half of their number were dismounted, and, under cover of night, were conducted across the fields. The dwelling was surrounded, the doors burst open, and the search begun before the sleeping inmates had notice of the enemy's presence. Mosby was not there, and the angry and disappointed soldiers were compelled to content themselves with the plunder of the house and the capture of several unfortunate Rangers.

The raiders were then conducted by their guide, who sought to win the approbation of his masters by zeal, if not the success of the enterprise, to the house of a citizen in the vicinity of Mrs. Rawlings's, where but a few days previous the deserter had been entertained by the family. Here several additional prisoners were captured; among them Richardson, of Baltimore, and the raiding-party hastened to return to their camp by the way of Upperville; but their retreat was annoyed and delayed by small parties which had collected, and which hung on their, flanks and rear.

CHAPTER 29: RAIDING IN THE REAR OF GENERAL HUNTER'S ARMY

Upper Fauquier, June 17th, 1864.

Dear Percy,—With one hundred and fifty men, Mosby crossed the Blue Ridge Mountains at Manassas Gap, for the purpose of operating upon Hunter's communications. At Mr. Ashby's, in Front Royal, where he stopped for supper, Chapman introduced to him, as a reliable guide for the expedition, Charlie Richardson, with whom he had served in the "Warren Rifles." Chapman and Richardson were dispatched the next day to the town of Strasburg to collect information, and, on their return, reported that detached parties were passing from time to time between Winchester and Hunter's camp, and also that a wagon-train was expected up that day. Mosby, with a small party, stationed himself on a wooded bluff of North River, from which point the track of the turnpike could be seen for the distance of a mile above and below the town of Strasburg.

A wagon-train, escorted by several hundred infantry and thirty cavalry, was soon observed descending Fisher's Hill, but, on account of the strength of its escort, it was allowed to pass unmolested to Newtown, where it was parked for the night. Early the next morning the wagons moved off without the guard, who remained behind to watch Mosby's movements, whose presence in the wood had been discovered.

Seeing their exposed situation, Mosby ordered Lieutenant Chapman, with twenty-five men, to move around the guard and capture the wagons. Then he, with a few men, advanced toward the guard, and, when charged by them, retreated past the position occupied by the command in charge of Captain Richards, who was ordered, through a courier, to interpose his men between the enemy's infantry and cavalry, and thus isolate and destroy the latter. But, this order was misunderstood, and, instead, Richards charged the Yankee cavalry and drove them back upon the infantry, who fired a volley at the pursuers, which killed Emory, and wounded Hines, of Company "B." Just as the cavalry were put to flight by Richards, Chapman, with his party, gained a position on the turnpike, where he could easily have captured the wagons, but, seeing the escort coming toward him, he charged them with great impetuosity, and drove them back again upon their infantry support, killing several and wounding three. But the wagons, meanwhile, had been suffered to escape, which Mosby thought ought not to have been done; but between a capture and a fight, how could the reverend gentleman hesitate?

A few days previous to the affair I have just related a train loaded with commissary stores had been captured in this vicinity by Major Harry Gilmor, and it had so irritated General Hunter that he had ordered all houses in the neighbourhood where an attack was made to be burned. Prompt to obey a command so much to their tastes, the Yankees, while Mosby was engaging them in front, had burned Stickley's house in the rear, the incendiary being a Union man from Martinsburg, who, for the sake of his principles, had been made a wagon-master in the United States Army.

GENERAL HUNTER'S HOUSE-BURNERS AT WORK

He was afterward captured by Chapman, and, having been identified as the man who urged the burning of Stickley's house, and as having himself applied the torch to the barn, and also as having threatened the ladies of Newtown to turn the Federal soldiers loose upon them in case of farther assaults upon the trains, this son of rapine and murder was ordered to be led to the ruins of White's house, which had been burned by Hunter's own direction, and there to be shot to death. This placard was left fastened on his back:

Shot for house-burning.

Mosby then dispatched a letter to the Federal commander in the Valley, which contained an account of this transaction, and a declaration that he would continue to have all house-burners executed who might fall into his hands.

I send you a copy of Hunter's order, in virtue of which these acts of incendiarism were committed, and as an explanation, and, in the opinion of atrocious men, a defence of it, an extract from a recent Northern newspaper. They are as follows:

> You are hereby notified that for every train fired upon, or soldier of the Union wounded or assassinated by bushwhackers in any neighbourhood within the reach of my cavalry, the houses and other property of every secession sympathizer residing

within a circuit of five miles from the place of outrage shall be destroyed by fire, and that for all public property jayhawked or destroyed by these marauders, an assessment of five times the value of such property will be made upon the secession sympathizers residing within a circuit of ten miles around the point at which the offense was committed.

The payment of this assessment will be enforced by troops of the department, who will seize and hold in close military custody the persons assessed until such payment shall have been made. This provision will also be applied to make good from the secessionists in every neighbourhood five times the amount of any loss suffered by loyal citizens of the United States from the action of bushwhackers whom you encourage."

By-the-way, Stanton attributes Siegel's recent defeat in the valley to the fact that he had to keep half his force in the rear to protect it from Mosby's attacks.

With the battalion, Mosby left Paris on the morning of the 1st of June, for the purpose of capturing a corral of horses near Martinsburg. He had obtained from a negro, whom he had made prisoner, the information which induced him to undertake the capture, but upon his arrival at the expected scene of action he found that it was impracticable. He then retired to the Opequon Creek, or rather river, at a point near "The Bower," the elegant and hospitable residence of Mr. Dandridge, where he left Richards, with twenty-five men with orders to capture the express train on the Baltimore and Ohio Railroad the following night, and returned with the rest of the command to Fauquier.

Richards at once moved to a wood between Smithfield and the railroad, where he spent the rest of the day, and when night closed in proceeded to execute the orders of his chief at a point between Kearneysville and Duffield Station. The railroad was closely guarded, in consequence of the capture of an express train which had recently been made by Major Harry Gilmor, of distinguished reputation, and camp-fires were visible to the raiders on both sides of the road; but, being inexperienced in this branch of the Partisan service, Captain Richards only tore up the track upon which he was told the train would pass in moving westward, and then divided his command into boarding-parties. Soon the express from Baltimore came rushing and hissing along the route, but, to the inexpressible mortification of Captain Richards, passed safely by on the unobstructed track. The Rangers laughed heartily at his discomfiture, and uttered many a jest at his expense, for it was then clear enough that Captain Dolly's informer had put him on the wrong track.

On the 8th of June thirty-five picked men met Colonel Mosby at Rectortown, for the purpose of accompanying him to Alexandria, with the hope of capturing his Excellency, Governor Pierpont, in the capital of his imperial domain. "When they arrived at the Plains, they found a company of twelve Yankees who had just been brought in as prisoners. Capt. Julian Lee and Stenny Mason had discovered them as they were passing between Hopewell Gap and the Bull Run Mountain, and, having procured the assistance of Bush Underwood and five of his comrades, had without difficulty effected their capture. The prisoners were sent to Piedmont, and Mosby, with his band, proceeded toward Alexandria.

About the middle of the next day they halted in a body of pine until within an hour of sundown, and during this interval the dispositions for the night were made. Two men had previously been sent off to procure a covered wagon, and have it in readiness at a designated point on the Telegraph Road, near Alexandria. Mosby, with his followers, was then to drive to the picket post, and, claiming admittance for a market-wagon, was to secure the picket, thus thrown off their guard. The way to the town being opened, the command, divided into three detachments, was to march in. The first, under Mosby, was to look after the governor; the second, with Captain Richards at its head, was to pay its respects to General Slough, who commanded the department; while the third, directed by the Reverend Sam Chapman, was to provide, from the government stables, horses for the use of the prisoners, and perhaps some for general distribution.

But the best conceived plans sometimes miscarry, and such was the fate of the one which I have just detailed. The guide lost his way in coming to the rendezvous, and, in consequence, it was too late to attempt the capture that night, for, if successfully accomplished, several hours of darkness would still be necessary to enable Mosby to elude the pursuit which would certainly be made. But this mishap only made him determine to postpone the hazardous adventure till the following night, and during the next day the command remained concealed in the wood, and were fed by friendly citizens. The hours were tedious, and the men began to dispose of the captured property in anticipation. Bush Underwood and another had a high dispute as to who should have the governor's watch, some selected his horse, some his boots, and some his coat; but George Turberville was moderate enough to say that he would be satisfied with His Excellency's greenbacks.

But, in the meanwhile, the plot had been discovered, and Mosby, being informed by a citizen of the preparations which had been made to receive him, prudently determined to return to his own confederacy. But for an unpropitious fortune, Governor Pierpont and General Slough would have had a merry gallop that starry night with Mosby and his men.

Three days later, the battalion, numbering two hundred and fifty men, with a twelve-pound howitzer in charge of Lieutenant Chapman, left Rectortown, under command of Colonel Mosby, for the purpose of attempting the capture of a wagon-train employed in hauling wood at Springfield Station, on the Orange and Alexandria Railroad; but, upon inspecting the position, he found the infantry guard too strong to make the effort advisable, and the command was ordered back to Union Mills. From that point two scouting-parties, one under Walter Whaley, the other under Ned Thompson, were sent out to collect information from Fairfax Court-house, Anandale, and Centreville. Mosby did not await their return, but early the next morning marched the command toward Centreville, and on his route he was met by Whaley with the information that forty Yankees were at that place. Taking with him the squadron composed of Companies "A" and "B," he advanced upon the town, but found that the Federals had, a few minutes before, taken their departure. Company "A," under Lieutenant Nelson, was at once ordered to strike across the country and intercept their march, while Mosby, with Company B, under Captain Richards, followed their trail.

The Yankees were overtaken near Machen's barn, where they had dismounted, and were found, some of them up the cherry-trees, some asleep, and others engaged in feeding their horses. Mosby, who, with six men, was in advance of Company "B," charged and routed them, inflicting a loss of four wounded, thirty-two made prisoners, and thirty-six horses. Captain Richards's command, although close upon his heels, finding nothing to do but secure the captures. A courier was then dispatched to inform Lieutenant Nelson that the work had been accomplished, and to order him to halt at the Double Toll-gate until rejoined by the command. From that point Mosby proceeded to Hooper's shop, where the captured property was divided and the battalion disbanded.

Chapter 30: The First Calico Raid

Upper Fauquier, July 1st, 1863.

Dear Percy,—On the 19th of June, Colonel Mosby left Upperville in command of the battalion, and took with him a piece of artillery, intending the next day to capture the passenger train on the Baltimore and Ohio railroad. Soon leaving the rest of the command to follow, under Captain Chapman, he took with him Company "A," and pressed forward several miles in advance, and by night reached the vicinity of Charlestown, whither Lieutenant Russell had been sent for the purpose of ascertaining the strength and position of the enemy in that vicinity. He reported General Mulligan at Smithfield, seven miles distant to the left, with several thousand troops, consisting of infantry, artillery, and cavalry; and Averill, only five miles farther, at Bunker Hill, with his entire cavalry command. On the right, at Harper's Ferry, eight miles distant from Charlestown, but only six from Duffield Station, the proposed point of attach on the railroad, he reported General Max Weber, with over a thousand men, belonging likewise to the three branches of the service.

At ten o'clock on the morning of the 20th, Captain Chapman, who had camped the previous night at Cabletown, united with Mosby on the Berryville Turnpike, about one mile from Charlestown. After waiting for the return of a lady from Duffield Station, from whom he gained accurate and reliable information of the enemy's force at that point, Mosby stationed Lieutenant Nelson, with Company "A," numbering twenty-two men, on the Harper's Ferry Turnpike, with instructions to fight any force arriving from that direction which did not twice exceed his own. Then, having learned from a time-table which he had procured that the train was due at Duffield Station at one o'clock p.m., at half past eleven he set out with the command for that point, distant five miles. In order to conceal the battalion from the signal posts at Harper's Ferry, Mosby, instead of passing through Charlestown, made a detour into the country, but it came, nevertheless, in full view of the Maryland Heights before it had advanced a mile.

About this time we passed the home of Willie Gibson, our guide, a boy only fifteen years of age. He had joined Mosby without the consent of his parents, and a messenger was sent by his mother to meet him, and demand his return. But the major, as he is called in the battalion, refused to comply with the summons, saying, "Tell her the success of the expedition depends upon my presence." When within a mile of the station four infantry-men were taken prisoners, who informed

Mosby that the train from Baltimore had just passed, but that the one going eastward was expected in about fifteen minutes. In addition, he learned from them that the station was garrisoned by sixty-five men, posted in a-stockade, commanded by a lieutenant. Surrounded on all sides by overwhelming numbers, it was clearly our leader's policy to capture the place without firing a gun, in order to accomplish which, the command was secreted in a wood, and two parties dispatched, one under Lieutenant Wren, to secure a party of Yankees guarding a flag on the railroad, and cut the telegraph wires to prevent communication with the neighbouring camps, and another to the eastward for a similar purpose.

These objects accomplished. Captain Richards was ordered to go forward, under a flag of truce, and demand the unconditional surrender of the post and the troops by which it was garrisoned; Mosby adding, as he was about to leave, "Inform the officer in command by whom and with what force he is attacked." As he galloped off, accompanied by Walter Whaley, Mosby posted the command in line of battle on an eminence a quarter of a mile from the stockade, and ordered the howitzer to be trained on it.

As Captain Richards approached the post he was halted by a sentinel, and the officer of the day summoned. A young man, wearing a lieutenant's uniform, soon appeared, and, with an air of authority, demanded the object of the visit. The summons to surrender was then delivered, and the young man changed countenance as he turned off, saying, "I will call the senior officer." He soon appeared, and inquired the conditions of surrender, but was informed that none were offered, but that he was at liberty to see the attacking force, if he desired to do so. Mounted on Whaley's horse, the lieutenant was conducted to Mosby, who advanced to meet him, and repeated the demand for a surrender, at the same time pointing to the howitzer and the command stationed near it.

No alternative was now left the Federal officer, and he promptly complied with the terms demanded. Mosby then ordered the gun to be advanced so as to command the expected train as it came from the west, and Captain Mountjoy's company, on account of his great authority over his men, was sent to support it, while Companies "B" and "C" were directed to take charge of the captured property. A large stock of dry-goods was found in the possession of a Pennsylvanian, who was preparing to open a shop, and the men, first loading themselves with as much calico and other dry-goods as they could carry off, then packed the artillery-carriage and limber-box with sacks of coffee.

Mosby waited an hour for the arrival of the train, which had been stopped at Martinsburg, for the flames of the burning camp at Duffield Station had revealed the presence of the partisan chief. At length, having despaired of its arrival, he ordered Mountjoy, with the howitzer and prisoners, to proceed directly to Charlestown, while Richards and Chapman, with their companies, followed at intervals of a quarter of a mile, so as to deceive the enemy, by the cloud of dust thus raised, in regard to the strength of his command, which, as it moved along, laden with merchandise, resembled rather a caravan of merchants than a column of soldiers. Mosby was in advance, and was met by a courier from Nelson with the information that he had encountered a party of sixty of the enemy (nearly three times his number), who had been sent out to reconnoitre from Harper's Ferry, and had killed, wounded, and captured twenty-five men, and secured twenty horses.

This cheering news was sent back to the command, with instructions for it to join Nelson as soon as possible, preparatory to a fight, for the courier had furthermore reported that the enemy, in heavy force, were advancing upon him from Harper's Ferry. Mosby found Company "A" drawn up in line of battle, and was welcomed by them with enthusiastic cheers. The howitzer was then stationed in the centre of the position, with "A" and "D" on its right and left, ready for action, while Richards and Chapman, with their companies, were concealed half a mile back on the Duffield Road, with orders to attack simultaneously the enemy's flanks as soon as the firing on the road was heard. Mosby's calculation was that the enemy, seeing only Companies "A" and "D," would charge down upon them in heavy force. With spherical case at short range, he intended to check the attack, and then, with another volley from the howitzer, throw them into confusion, while a combined charge upon their front and flanks by the four companies would, he was confident, complete the work.

But the Federals, deceived, no doubt, by the column of dust on our line as to our numbers, declined an engagement, and greatly disappointed our leader, for he said that, with his men in such spirits, he could whip any cavalry in the world, provided only they had fine horses. But as soon as the column was in motion the Yankees again advanced. A line of battle was a second time formed, and Mosby halted a quarter of an hour, awaiting an attack; but, despairing of bringing on a fight, he ordered Captain Chapman to recross the river with the command and prisoners. They bivouacked for the night on the eastern bank of the Shenandoah, without food for men or horses, making for themselves beds with their captured merchandise.

On the homeward march, Mosby, with six men, had lingered, as was his custom, in the rear of the column. Placing five of his party in ambush, he and Carlisle decoyed seven Yankees into giving them chase. They fled past their comrades' position, and then wheeled upon their pursuers, who, being assailed at the same time in their rear by the party in the woods, had one of their number killed, one wounded, and the remaining five captured.

During the pursuit Mosby's horse became unmanageable, and he was about to be shot, when Carlisle fired, killing his antagonist.

One of the captured Yankees, who had been foremost in the pursuit, urged his release upon the ground that he was a member of the Sanitary Commission, and a non-combatant; but Mosby only threatened to have him shot for impudence if he mentioned the subject again.

Upon his return from this raid, sometimes called in the command the First Calico Raid, a lady, after complimenting Colonel Mosby on his success, remarked, "I hear you have a large supply of calico, an article which I greatly need, and I suppose you will sell it very cheap?" To this interrogatory the partisan chief abruptly replied,

"Madam, you have mistaken my profession: I am a soldier."

Chapter 31: The Fight at Mount Zion Church.

Upper Fauquier, July 10th, 1864.

Dear Percy,—I will now give you an account of the "Point of Rocks," or the "Second Calico Raid," and its supplement, the fight at Mount Zion Church. In the afternoon of July 2nd, near Rectortown, Mosby, accompanied by Fount Beattie, met Hugh Swartz, who is employed in Early's quartermaster's department, and from him learned for the first time that Early was on the march to Maryland, and would that night camp near Winchester. Without delay, he dispatched runners to collect his men, two hundred of whom met him at Upperville the next day. The object which he had in contemplation was to strike the enemy's communications between Washington and Harper's Ferry, for he considered that in this way he could most effectually co-operate with the advancing army.

On the 3rd of July Mosby started with this force, taking along a twelve-pound, brass Napoleon in charge of Lieutenant Chapman, and about noon the following day reached a crossing of the Potomac, one mile above the Point of Rocks. Accompanied by the guide, our leader entered the water, and had proceeded about halfway the stream, when he was fired upon by sharpshooters, who were concealed in the bushes on the other side, and was compelled to retrace his steps. He then ordered the Napoleon to be put in position on an eminence which commanded the Maryland shore, and detailed from the respective companies a party of *carbineers*, under command of Lieutenant Wren, to wade the river. Protected by the fire from the artillery, they had reached an island midway the stream, when the first squadron, under command of Captain Richards, was ordered forward to support them.

As the Rangers approached the Maryland shore, the Federal sharpshooters fled to the mountains, and Captain Richards's command proceeded down the tow-path in the direction of the Point of Rocks. Soon they overtook a steam-packet freighted with government clerks going on an excursion to Harper's Ferry, there to celebrate the national anniversary. As soon as the pleasure-seekers discovered the command, notwithstanding they had left Washington armed with revolvers for the express purpose of shooting the guerrillas, they leaped from the boat, and with clean heels made for the mountain. Our men fired at them as they scrambled up its rough and shaggy sides, frightening the valiant clerks nearly to death, and killing one poor fellow, less lucky than his companions.

POINT OF ROCKS, HARPER'S FERRY

The partisans then hurried on to the Point of Rocks, which is situated on the opposite side of the canal, and was garrisoned by three hundred and fifty troops, consisting of two companies of infantry, commanded by Captains Bainford and Hardesty, and two of cavalry, which were no other than the redoubtable Loudoun Rangers. At the village the canal is crossed by a bridge, which is within easy musket-range of a circular rifle-pit which crowns an adjacent hill; but its flooring had been torn up before the Rangers reached it. Richards promptly ordered it to be replaced with plank torn from the building occupied by the provost-marshal; while this was being done, Harry Hatcher crossed on the sleepers, tore from the flag-staff "the stars and stripes," and, wrapping the national emblem around him, returned in triumph to his comrades.

While the work on the bridge was going forward, the enemy kept up a brisk fire from the rifle-pit, but as soon as it was accomplished, and a detachment advanced to dislodge them from the hill-top with as much prudence as valour, they scattered in the forest in their rear, not waiting to have their defences stormed. The retreat of the Loudoun Rangers was so precipitate that they neglected to carry off their flag, and was not discontinued until they reached Frederick City, thus placing a distance of twelve miles between themselves and their remorseless pursuers. Captain Richards, with a small party, started in pursuit of them, but he might as well have undertaken to follow a crow, and returned, having captured only a lieutenant and three privates, who belonged to the infantry.

As soon as the command entered the village, the fighting being over, they began the work of plundering, first the camp, and then the store-houses. Most of the men went into the dry-goods business, and soon four regular shops and one sutler's establishment were emptied of their contents. Some invested in calico, some in one article, and some in another; while still another element in the command, represented by our susceptible surgeon, supplied themselves abundantly with confectionaries of various kinds to carry to their favourites whom they had left behind.

While the men were occupied in making investments in calico at the Point of Rocks (and it must be remembered that calico, with Mosby's men, is a generic for all dry-goods). Lieutenant Chapman, in command of the artillery on the Virginia store, fired upon a train of cars, but without inflicting any damage upon it.

As soon as the camps were destroyed and the Rangers had loaded themselves with every thing they could bring off, Mosby ordered the command to recross the river by the Coney Island Ford, and proceed to a wood not far distant, where it halted until late in the evening, which gave the men time to overlook their plunder. But on their way to the wood an incident occurred which I will relate, as illustrative of the popularity of Mosby's men with the fair sex. A party of mountain nymphs, attracted to the spot, doubtless, by the noise of the fight, were ranged along the road which leads from the river. One of them, addressing Charlie Hall, asked him to give her a pair of shoes.

"Certainly," responded the gallant Ranger, "but you must give me a kiss in return."

On these terms the bargain was concluded, and the shoes handed over to the girl, who, with a smile and a blush, turned her cheek to the soldier.

Late in the evening the men resumed the march, bedecked in a very grotesque and original manner with their captured goods. As they passed along the road, some arrayed in crinoline, some wearing bonnets, and all disguised with some incongruous and fantastic article of apparel, they looked like a company of masqueraders. Mrs. Dawson, who was in her garden, as she beheld the strange procession drawing near, was seized with alarm, and, rushing to the house, exclaimed to her daughters,

"Run, my children, run to the garret! they are coming, they are coming! They ain't Yankees, and they ain't Rebs: they must be Indians. Oh, they'll scalp us! they'll scalp us!" But her fear was turned into pleasure when she learned that they were only Mosby's men returning from the calico raid. That night the Rangers camped in a wood not far from her house, and the next morning impressed wagons in the neighbourhood to transport their captured property to Fauquier.

Colonel Mosby, as soon as the command had halted for the night, made a visit to Mrs. Dawson, who brought to his attention the following order, which had been issued by the officer in command at Harper's Ferry, and the notice which had been served upon her in virtue of it.

Office Provost-Marshal, Point of Rocks, Md.,
June 23rd, 1864.

To all Southern Sympathizers and Rebels:

Your attention is called to the vandalism and destruction of private property by a party of Mosby's guerrillas. On the 17th inst. Some of this lawless and undisciplined band came to the premises of Mr. Sydney Williams, and, without cause or provocation, burned his house, barn, and other buildings. It is hereby ordered that the rebels of Loudoun County at once take steps to reimburse Mr. Sydney Williams, by raising sixteen thousand dollars by contribution among themselves, and pay the same to the provost-marshal at Point of Rocks, Maryland. Any failure on the part of the above-named to pay their part of the required fund will be taxed double the amount required. You have until the 6th of July next to pay the above amount. By command of

  Brig. Gen. Max Weber, commanding at Harper's Ferry, Va. Official.—R. E. Bainford, Capt. and Prov.-Marshal, Point of Rocks, Md.
Printed: Schley, Reefer & Co., Frederick, Md.

       Office Provost-Marshal, Point of Rocks, Md.,
               June 27th, 1864.
Mrs. Dawson:—Madam,—Your attention is called to the within bill, in accordance to order issued by General Max Weber. The amount of tax levied on you is four hundred dollars, which tax you will promptly pay, as designated on the within bill.

       R. E. Bainford, Capt. and Prov.-Mar.
       Per A. R. Roderick, Clerk.

It is difficult for a man bred in the ideas of civilized life to find words to express his indignation at this act of military license. From what code, unless that of General Hunter, did General Max Weber learn that it was just to punish one man for the unlawful acts of another? Even the forms of an inquiry were not observed, and the whole case rested upon the assertions of the man who was to get the money thus obtained.

Mosby emphatically denied that the burning had been committed by his men, and added, in the presence of a Union citizen who would certainly tell it to General Weber, that if any money were exacted on such a pretence, he would indemnify the sufferers twofold out of the Union men of Loudoun. This declaration from a man who never threatened in vain set the matter at rest.

Before the captured goods were sent off from the woods near Mrs. Dawson's, an incident occurred which well illustrates the authority which Mosby exercises over his men, and the principle of equity by which he is guided in such cases. Mr. Lewis Meens, a gentleman of Southern principles, was one of the merchants at the Point of Rocks whose property was carried off by the Rangers. He appealed to Colonel Mosby to have it restored, who at once ordered all the merchandise which had been taken at that place to be brought forward, that Mr. Meens might identify and recover that which belonged to him. The men murmured at this surrender of their spoil, but there was no appeal from that iron will.

In virtue of his confidential relations with the commander, the chief, in advance of all others, had been informed of the projected expedition, and had, in pursuance of a promise, notified his friend and admirer. Bill Lake, to hold himself in readiness to accompany him, for of all things Bill most desired to go with him upon one of his plundering excursions. The most extravagant visions danced before him, and, rubbing his hands, he said, in a confidential manner,

"Why, Chief, it will be better than a lottery-ticket."

True to the objects which had induced them to accompany the expedition, the two friends, as soon as the flooring of the bridge was relaid and the rifle-pits carried, rushed into the store-houses along with the crowd, but their exertions were rewarded with different measures of success. The chief was almost concealed as he sat upon his horse by the merchandise which he had managed to pack before, behind, and on every side of him, while Bill, in the crowd of eager and experienced plunderers, managed only to secure a tin coffee-pot. The two were together when Mosby's order for restitution was delivered. The chief swore roundly that he would not submit to such arbitrary treatment, and be despoiled of the property which he had acquired by the exposure of his person to Yankee bullets. Bill, too, was equally intractable, and one would have thought, from his brave words, that he would have died sooner than surrender his valuable trophy. The messenger was urgent, but the chief cut the matter short by striking across the country for home, attended by the faithful Bill.

The morning after the fight at Point of Rocks, two hundred Federal cavalry, under command of Major Thompson, of the California Battalion, arrived at the village, and were followed late in the day by two companies of infantry, one of which was placed in the rifle-pit, and the other posted on the hills above the town. These facts being communicated to Colonel Mosby, he broke up his encampment near Mrs. Dawson's, and returned to a point near the river and opposite to Point of Rocks. From this point he dispatched a party of sharpshooters to the river-bank, who, as soon as they were seen, were fired upon by the infantry from the opposite hills, and a desultory fire was kept up between them for two hours, during which a ball fired by one of the sharpshooters fell short of its mark and killed Miss Ellen Fisher, a young lady residing at Point of Rocks. Mosby, meanwhile, had posted the Napoleon on an eminence below the town and opposite to Major Thompson's cavalry, which was drawn up about half a mile from the river; but, owing to the premature bursting of the shells, no damage was inflicted, so the duel across the Potomac was abandoned, and the Partisan Battalion marched several miles down the river, for the purpose of crossing at Poland's Ferry, and thus gaining the rear of the Federal force.

But, in order to conceal this movement, Mosby left a party under Lieutenant Ab. Wren in the vicinity of the village, to keep up the impression that his command was still there. In the neighbourhood of Greenville the Rangers went into camp, and while Mosby was taking his supper at the house of Mr. Henry Ball, John Thomas and Harry Hatcher returned from a scout with the information that two hundred Yankee cavalry were then at Leesburg.

In consequence of this announcement, farther designs against the force at the Point of Rocks were abandoned, and Colonel Mosby moved his command across the mountain for the purpose of attacking Major Forbes, who was in command of the cavalry whose movements had been reported by the scouts. At Waterford he halted and threw out a picket on the Leesburg Road, with whom he passed the night, and at daylight dispatched Carlisle and Puryear to Leesburg, who soon returned, and reported Major Forbes still at that place. Mosby at once started in pursuit, but, as he passed Fort Johnson, a mile from the town. Major Forbes was discovered in the act of leaving it. At Leesburg the partisan chief was received with enthusiasm, but he did not linger, for there was work ahead, and, with all the energy of his nature, he proceeded to perform it.

Having discovered that the Federals had gone toward Aldie, Mosby, instead of following their track, took the road leading to Ball's Mills, from which point he would be able to throw himself in their front on their return to the camp at Falls Church, thus pursuing the same military policy which had resulted in the success at Anker's Shop. Leaving the command in charge of Captain Chapman, the next morning he took with him Willie Mosby, Wat Bowie, Bush Underwood, and a few others, and went on a scout for the purpose of ascertaining the whereabouts of Major Forbes, who, in the meantime, had come from Aldie to Mount Zion Church, two miles below, on the Little Kiver Turnpike. Soon the scouting-party encountered a detachment of the enemy, before whom they retreated to the command at the Mills, where Mosby, supposing that he would soon be attacked by Major Forbes's entire force, posted himself in an advantageous position to receive the anticipated charge.

But his expectations were not realised, and, finding that no attack was intended. Colonel Mosby marched to a point on the Little River Turnpike, two miles below Mount Zion, in the hope that Major Forbes would pass his position on his return to Falls Church. But, after waiting in vain for the space of two hours for the fulfilment of this expectation, he determined to seek his antagonist, and fight him in the open field. When he came in sight of Mount Zion Church, he found the enemy drawn up on the left of the road, in an open field, which had a gradual slope to the turnpike, with one squadron posted in advance of the other. Mosby's dispositions for attack were then made as follows. A body of sharp-shooters, under command of Harry Hatcher, was sent forward to occupy a skirt of woods on his left, while he stationed the Napoleon in the road, supported by Company "D," commanded by Lieutenant Glasscock, and disposed the rest of the command in a position from which they could charge the enemy.

The fight was opened by an ineffectual shot from the Napoleon, followed by an impetuous charge, led by Mosby. Major Forbes's advance squadron for a time stood firm, but, finding itself overpowered, and attacked in front and flank, wheeled and fell back upon the squadron in the rear. This movement soon became a retreat, in which the rest of the command united. About six hundred yards in their rear, the Federals were checked by a high fence, and here a party of twenty-five men turned upon their pursuers, and fought with determined but useless valour, in a hand-to-hand combat, for in a little while half of this gallant band were either killed, wounded, or dragged to the ground by their wounded horses. As soon as the fence gave way the retreat became a rout; but at a point farther on in the direction of Sudley Mills, another party of the enemy, numbering about fifteen, rallied and drove back a few of the pursuers; but they were soon reenforced, and this second party, like their comrades, were forced to seek safety in flight.

Mosby, with Johnny Edmunds, continued the pursuit to Sudley Mills, a distance of ten miles from Mount Zion Church, where the fight began, from which point they returned, driving before them about fifteen loose horses.

Mosby's loss in the engagement was Henry Smallwood mortally wounded. Bob Walker, Tom Richards, and Tom Lake severely wounded, and Willie Martin badly bruised by blows with a carbine. The enemy lost twenty killed and mortally wounded, twenty-five badly wounded, sixty taken prisoners, and ninety horses, with their equipments.

As soon as it was reported that Major Forbes, well known as a successful raider, was in command of the opposing force, several of the Rangers expressed their determination to be his captor. But fortune favoured Tom Richards, who, after a fierce hand-to-hand conflict, in which he received a dangerous wound, succeeded in making the Federal officer his prisoner. The next day the booty was divided at Piedmont, and the prisoners sent to Richmond. Thus terminated one of Mosby's most brilliant expeditions, for in the period of five days he had crossed the Potomac, captured the Point of Rocks and dispersed its garrison, and then had turned upon an unexpected adversary in superior force, and had routed, pursued, and captured him. (See Appendix for Mosby's Reply to Early.)

> Note.—I inspected the scene of this combat with Mr. Alexander Davis, of Loudoun County, who was at the time an officer in the Federal army. The version of the fight which he received a few days after, at Falls Church, was, that Major Forbes ordered his advanced squadron to fall back to the position occupied by the other, and Mosby, quick to seize the advantage thus afforded, charged while this movement was being executed.

CHAPTER 32: RAIDING IN MARYLAND

Upper Fauquier, August 2nd, 1864.

Dear Percy,—In my account of the raid on Point of Rocks I omitted to mention a scouting-party which Colonel Mosby sent, in charge of Wat Bowie, to Maryland the day after the capture, and while his command was camped in the wood near Mrs. Dawson's.

Having crossed the river at Noland's Ferry, Bowie halted on a canal bridge to take a survey of the country, and soon saw two men advancing up the river bank. Charlie Vest and Charlie Dear were sent to bring in the strangers, who proved to be citizens residing in Virginia, and from them information was obtained of the advance of Colonel Thompson's command to Point of Rocks. With Munroe Heiskell and Lowndes, Bowie then proceeded to the house of a citizen in search of farther intelligence, and while there cut the telegraph wires.

Upon his return to his party a courier was sent to report to Colonel Mosby all that had been learned, and Bowie then proceeded to attack a party of Yankees, who, he was informed, was guarding a number of canal-boats at Monocacy, a place situated at the junction of the river of the same name with the Potomac. They were driven off after a short resistance, in which two were killed and four taken prisoners. The partisans, before leaving, made a descent upon a store, from which, in addition to other things, they procured greenbacks enough to give each man a dividend of five dollars. Bowie and his party then recrossed the river, and rejoined their commander the next day at Waterford.

A few days after the Mount Zion fight, Bowie was again furnished with a party to return to Maryland, and on his march to the river was told by a citizen that a party of twenty-seven Yankees, dressed in Confederate uniform, had passed up the Leesburg and Dranesville Turnpike on a plundering expedition. With his nine men he started in pursuit, but soon met them coming back down the road, and charged them at full speed, but they all escaped under cover of night to the woods, with a loss of only three horses, while three of Bowie's party were wounded, and Frank Carter seriously injured by a fall from his horse.

While General Early was in the vicinity of Washington, Mosby, in command of the battalion and a piece of artillery, crossed the Potomac at a ford near Leesburg. At Poolesville he halted long enough for the command to be hospitably entertained by the citizens, and then marched several miles beyond the town to camp for the night. The next morning he proceeded to the camp of the 8th Illinois, which was on Muddy Branch, but found it deserted, with evident signs of having been hastily abandoned, although it was very defensible, being situated on the crest of a high hill, and protected by fortifications. The camp equipage and a large quantity of supplies, which the Lincoln boys would not defend, were destroyed, and Mosby then set out to return to Fauquier.

As Early's rear-guard was crossing the Shenandoah on the return of the expedition from Maryland, Mosby sent Captain Richards, with a party, to the vicinity of Snickersville to get information. They were urged by the village people to leave the neighbourhood, and were informed that a Federal column had just disappeared in the gap of the mountain. During this parley, Richards's attention was directed to two men dressed in citizen's clothes, who were riding leisurely along the grade toward him. Willie Martin and Gibson were sent to discover who they were, and, disappearing from view behind a hill, a single shot was heard. They returned, bringing with them one prisoner and a led horse.

"Yankees, captain," said Willie. "This fellow is a lieutenant, the other was an orderly sergeant."

The prisoner, when asked why he was absent from his command, replied that he had been sent back, with a squad, to burn some broken-down caissons.

"Where is your squad?" inquired Captain Richards.

"They are behind, sir, with the first lieutenant."

"How many, and how far behind are they?"

"Ten, besides the lieutenant," answered the officer; "and I guess they can't be more than a quarter of a mile back."

"Good luck, boys," exclaimed Captain Richards. "Here is your chance; a horse a piece if we manage right. Here, Robinson," continued he, "take the prisoner to headquarters; and now, men, forward by twos, and quietly."

Holding their arms and horses in readiness, the Rangers moved silently along the road until, from the top of a hill, they saw the squad approaching, apparently unsuspicious of danger. But soon the lieutenant, who was in advance, reined up, and remained for a moment as if puzzled to know by whom he was to be met. But discretion quickly got the better of valour, and, suddenly wheeling his horse, away he flew, followed by his men. But for this very action Richards was prepared, and the Federal officer had hardly turned his horse when the partisans dashed upon him. In five minutes the business was accomplished—eight of the squad killed, two captured, the lieutenant missing, and eight horses, with their equipments, secured. The Rangers afterward learned that the lieutenant's horse, blinded by the cloud of dust, fell with him, but that, not being seriously hurt, he extricated himself, and escaped on foot.

Richards then ordered the prisoners, horses, and arms to be collected, and feeling sure that Colonel Mosby could extract from the prisoner already sent to head-quarters all the information he desired, he conducted his command by a circuitous but safe road back to Upperville. Just before nightfall he ordered a halt, and divided the horses by lot, Harry Shaw having the good fortune to draw the lieutenant's bay, which he forthwith named General Lee, and sent to his boarding-house to be taken care of

While the enemy in pursuit of General Early had their outposts at Bloomfield, Colonel Mosby divided his command into several parts, each of which was entrusted to a separate officer. Richards, with Company "B," was sent to Fairfax, while the other detachments, under Mosby, Lieut. Glasscock, and Captain Chapman, operated upon Hunter's army, then lying at the base of the Blue Ridge. The artillery was sent, for safety, to the mountains. For the sake of convenience, these detachments were afterward broken up into small squads, and I will only give you a few specimens of their mode of harassing the enemy.

A detachment of the enemy's cavalry was camped near the Aldie and Snickersville Turnpike, when Lieutenant Glasscock, with seven men, from a position on a wooded eminence which overlooked the camp, saw a party of ten Yankees issue from it. The weather was warm, and Glasscock ordered his men to take off their gray coats and strap them behind their saddles, relying upon the blue pantaloons which they wore to. make them pass for Federal soldiers. Then, placing himself at the head of the column, he emerged from the wood, carelessly whistling Yankee Doodle, and marched for some distance in the rear of the Federals before he was observed. Presently they halted, and a sergeant rode back toward Glasscock, but did not suspect his true character until too late to retreat. With great presence of mind, his captor, without halting him, in an under ton^ ordered him to the rear, and his companions, seeing him pass on apparently unmolested, concluded that all was right, and resumed their march at a slow walk.

The Rangers, as soon as their backs were turned, drew their revolvers, and, trotting briskly up on their flanks, ordered them to surrender. Without resistance they complied, only remarking, "Pretty cool, that; but we mistook you for our own men." They were all well armed and finely mounted. After they had gone a few miles, one of the prisoners, who was riding a fine blooded mare, tried to make his escape, but was pursued by Fount Beattie, and captured, after an exciting race of about a mile, during which he was twice wounded. The wounded man was carried to a neighbouring farmhouse, and the surgeon of his regiment summoned to attend him. Those who represent our command as composed of robbers and bandits would be surprised to learn that he was assisted to dismount by Lieutenant Glasscock.

While Lieutenant Glasscock was piping Yankee Doodle on the Snickersville and Aldie Turnpike, Chapman attacked an outpost which had been left in the rear of General Duffie's cavalry division, which had gone toward Berry's Ferry. He found, upon reconnoitring, that the picket of sixty men was stationed at "the big poplar" which marks the corner where the counties of Fauquier, Loudoun, and Clarke unite, and stands in the gap of the mountain, near the turnpike, and that they were dismounted, and had their horses tied together. Acting upon this information. Chapman divided his command.

One of the divisions he entrusted to Lieutenant Fox, for the purpose of making a simultaneous attack on the picket from opposite points, which would have rendered its capture or destruction certain. But the party under Fox, in executing their part of the plan, came upon some marauders who were plundering Mrs. Crear's house, and fired upon them. Chapman, supposing from these shots that Fox had opened the fight, charged the picket, two of whom were killed, five wounded, and thirty taken prisoners. In addition, thirty-eight horses were secured, and Chapman decoyed the enemy to pursue him and a few others, in order to afford time for the rest of the command, in charge of the prisoners, to reach, by a mountain road, the house of Slice Barbour, where the captures were disposed of.

When Hunter fell back toward Leesburg, after the disaster at the Parker House, Harry Hatcher, with a detachment of thirty men, was sent by Mosby to watch the turnpike, and, before nightfall, captured one hundred of the retreating and demoralized army. About the same time, Mosby, with a party, camped near Woodgrove to pass the night. As he dismounted he ordered Major Hibbs to take a detail and procure corn with which to feed the horses the next morning. The major demurred, pleading fatigue and the lateness of the hour; but Mosby insisted; so the chief of the Corn Detail, who made it a rule to obey nobody else, started off. At daylight Mosby awoke, and discovered, outstretched among sacks of corn, the major, who had long since erased from his lexicon the word "impossible." After gazing at the sleeper for a moment, he turned away and said, "What a misfortune to the country that my chief of the Corn Detail is not quartermaster general!"

With a portion of his company. Lieutenant Glasscock about this time crossed the Shenandoah at Rocky Ford, and camped near Charlestown. The next morning he concealed his men in a wood near Locust Grove, and soon three sutlers' wagons appeared, escorted by twelve cavalry-men. Without firing a shot, the wagons and escort were captured and carried to Loudoun.

Soon after the events just related, Mosby, with eight men, went to the valley on a scout. Leaving the command in Campbell's Wood, he, with John Russell, went toward the turnpike to make observations. The first train which they saw pass was too heavily guarded to be successfully interfered with; but soon eight wagons approached, escorted by three infantry and eight cavalry. Mosby's command was then brought forward, but the advance of two hundred Yankee cavalry on the march to Winchester compelled them to desist from making the attack until the train had reached Stuart's farm. At this point Mosby remained to watch the road, while Russell and the seven others made the capture, and, in addition, secured a sutler's wagon, which they rifled, supplying themselves with hats, boots, over-coats, and other articles of convenience, to say nothing of some excellent liquor. The captures were conveyed to Campbell's Wood, from which point they were sent in charge of Russell and five others to Fauquier. Mosby, with two men, remained in the Valley, where Richards, with the command, was ordered to join him.

Upon Richards's arrival he was dispatched with ninety men toward Winchester, while Sam Chapman, with a party of twenty, was sent to capture a picket-post near Bunker Hill, and Mosby, with the remaining twenty, proceeded to the neighbourhood of Martinsburg.

About three miles from the village they halted in a wood, and were furnished by a citizen with oats for their horses and food for themselves, including the luxury of Lincoln coffee. During this interval Wirt Ashby was sent to Martinsburg to look around—a duty requiring some delicacy in its performance, as there were several thousand Federal troops in and around the place. After the lapse of several hours the scout returned, and reported that it was practicable to enter the town with the command, and that in it would be found a stable filled with officers' horses, a jewellery store, and an establishment for furnishing military outfits.

Mosby, as soon as he heard the situation of affairs, divided his command, leaving half of it in charge of the horses, and, taking with him ten men, followed Ashby to the village. Ever thing was astir, and Federal soldiers met the Rangers face to face, but, on account of the friendly darkness, did not recognise them. The guide at once proceeded to the stable, which he entered through a window, and then opened the door for his comrades. They had no time to look about for saddles and bridles, but each, selecting the best horse he could find, mounted bareback, leading the animals by halters. Just as Mosby's men were leaving the stable, a man in the loft awoke and inquired who was troubling his horses.

This unexpected interrogatory alarmed several of the party, who, excited by the novelty and peril of the situation, dashed through the streets, and the horses becoming unmanageable, the headlong rush was continued for several miles beyond the town. A little later, Mosby, who thought the night's work but just begun, returned to Martinsburg, but, finding every thing in a state of excitement, and the enemy on the alert, he was compelled to abandon his intention of visiting the store-houses, and with difficulty escaped detection by passing out of the town by a back street. Foiled in this attempt, Mosby then conducted his men to a camp on a neighbouring hill. The inmates were asleep, and the officers absent on a frolic in the village. Without creating alarm, several horses were secured, and many articles of value were taken from the tents, among them officers' trunks, which were carried off to the party in charge of the horses in the wood, and there made to deliver up their contents.

A few days after this affair Captain Richards captured a Federal soldier, who, in narrating the circumstances, said that it was the work of a party of the 1st New York Cavalry. He was incredulous when told that it was an achievement of Mosby's, for he was slow to believe that even he would have made so bold an attempt.

CHAPTER 33: SOCIAL LIFE OF THE GUERRILLAS.

Upper Fauquier, August 10th, 1864.

Dear Percy,—Would you have, my friend, another feature of the little world which Mosby, with plastic art, has created around him? Listen, and I will tell you; or, rather, read what is here set down, for, as the day is rainy, I will give a veritable record of an amusing scene which recently transpired in the Partisan Battalion.

As Mosby, with an advance party, was resting by a patriarchal spring under a thick shade, when we were on the Point of Rocks Raid, and was engaged in some light talk with Mr. Blackwell Magog, Bill Lake, who is called by the ladies "Sweet William," several others of the command, and myself. Dr. Dunn, our surgeon, passed near. We had along a plenty of coffee, procured at Duffield Station a few days before, and Carlisle and Henry Heaton had just started to have some of it prepared at a house a short distance off. The colonel called to the medicine-man to join the circle, which, after loosening the girths of his saddle, the doctor proceeded to do.

Now it was a fact notorious in the command that our excellent surgeon had had the misfortune to fall over head and ears in love with a beautiful and attractive lady in our Alpine Confederacy, Miss K———, of the P———, or *Dulcebenietta*, as, in his peculiar nomenclature, Mr. Blackwell Magog calls her. A lively interest was manifested in this affair of the heart throughout the battalion, and the bets ran high on the result of the doctor's love-suit. Horses, spurs, cavalry-saddles, and, profanely, many jugs of blockade, were staked on the issue. The bets, I repeat, ran high, and one Ranger offered as much as a hundred in greenbacks that the surgeon, if properly supported, would capture the fair *Dulcebenietta*, and lead her in triumph to the altar. It was Fount Beattie, who had come from the doctor's country, who was willing thus boldly to back him. Others, however, more sagacious or more desponding, expressed the opinion that there would be a spirited, perhaps an obstinate defence, and that the garrison might hold out as long as old Troy.

In this state of things, what was to be done? Why, the most natural course was to refer the matter to Mr. Blackwell Magog, whose opinion in such affairs carries with it a just weight. After several days' deliberation the oracle spoke, and in a very grave and erudite manner declared that, unless the surgeon of Mosby's Battalion had help, and a good deal of it, a sally from the fortress might relieve the garrison and scatter the besiegers. The priest of the Delphic art added with great emphasis, "What the siege requires is engineering talent—yes, sir, engineering talent—sappers and miners, and then a storming-party."

It must be known that "the chief" ever speaks in military phrase. Indeed, it is one of the glories of his life, that he has at least that distinctive badge of a soldier; for, like other military men, he entertains a just contempt for civilians. So thickly strewn is his phraseology with such words, so constantly do his sentences bristle with the terms of the military art, that you would swear he was educated at West Point. So far does he carry this form of expression, that he talks of flanking young ladies, and taking their defences in reverse.

As soon as the opinion of "the chief" was noised abroad, Dr. Dunn was considered a ruined man. The Rangers began to avoid him as a man of ill omen, and not a guerrilla of them would venture even so much as a halter-strap on his chances of success. Bets were drawn and forfeits paid up; and even Fount, the ever-faithful, showed a loss of confidence, and evident signs of backing out, and leaving Dr. Dunn to his fate. *Dulcebenietta* was clearly the favourite now, and, disheartened by the unpopularity of his cause, the surgeon was almost ready to embrace the last consolation of the wretched, and close his miserable life by the rash hand of self destruction.

When the great augur and high-priest was informed of the effect which his words had produced, he was induced by his kind heart, but as much by a secret desire to have a hand in such affairs, to interrogate the stars a second time, or, in stricter conformity with the customs of the old Romans, to auspicate the event by consulting the flight of birds, and by other oracular signs, by which the will of the gods can be ascertained, but which are known only to the initiated. For several nights he was engaged with these prognostications.

Oft, amid vigils and fastings, the astrologer might be seen on the mountain top or in the fields, observing the course of the heavenly bodies. At such times the men would gaze at him with secret awe if they met him in his solitary rambles, and would regard him, when he returned again to the haunts of men, as a messenger, or rather plenipotentiary of some higher power. He mounted the tripod, and declared the decree of Fate to be, "If Dr. Dunn would win the virgin, he must follow the path of the honey-bee, which seeks its treasure from afar." The interpretation of the response, in simple prose, was understood to be, that Dr. Dunn must not rely upon himself altogether, but must be governed by the advice of his friends. Thus the case stood.

Now this son of the healing art was the most teachable of men, and of this trait in his character Mr. Blackwell Magog was well apprised when he interpreted to him the Delphic response which has just been related. He knew full well that he would be called on in the critical juncture at which affairs stood, and he rubbed his hands and rejoiced greatly at the opportunity thus publicly and notoriously offered to supersede the coarse and vulgar method of love-making by the elegant and refined teachings of science. Mr. Blackwell Magog was an amateur, and, like all amateurs, adored his art. When the surgeon had joined the party before described, Mosby addressed him:

"Come, doctor, come and tell us how you prosper in love-making—how you and Miss K―――― are getting on."

Dr. Dunn. "I regret to say, colonel, that I can not gratify your curiosity, for, in truth, I know not the signs of prosperous love."

Colonel Mosby here inquired of the chief if he could not instruct the doctor in the symptoms of love, and the mode in which to conduct a courtship to a happy conclusion.

"Certainly, certainly," responded Mr. Blackwell Magog, with the air of a professor.

So the man of science arose, and, with a look and gesture that imparted weight to his words and dignity to his subject, thus addressed the doctor, who, duly impressed with the dignity of the occasion, assumed an air of attention, and humbly and reverently looked up into the instructor's face.

It ought to be mentioned, in justice to the orator, that he first poised and settled his person, wiped the perspiration from his red face with his handkerchief, and then, with a very solemn look, fixed his great ox-eyes on his scholar. The colonel rested his chin on his right hand, and gazed with interest at the speaker; the rest of the company were lying around in curious silence, while I drew forth my tablets, a mark of consideration which the speaker acknowledged by a graceful wave of the hand. His style was animated, copious, fluent, and free from meretricious ornament; his matter was well arranged, his manner impressive, his utterance clear and agreeable.

THE LECTURE ON LOVE

Mr. Blackwell Magog. "It is not unknown to you, oh surgeon of Mosby's Battalion, that I am the Professor of Love in this command; that, as such, I rank all the officers save the colonel, and, in the parlour and *boudoir*, the colonel himself. Yes, wherever the ladies are, there is my realm, there am I paramount, there bear undisputed sway; or, in the language of the poet,

My flag the sceptre all who meet obey.

"I perceive, Dr. Dunn, that you are a novice—a mere rustic, indeed, in love; but, simple youth, I pity rather than blame your ignorance, as you come from-a region much infested by barbarians. I will therefore, by way of preliminary, observe, that in the educated and refined circles of society love is just coming to be regarded as one of the sciences, or, with a greater precision of language, one of the fine arts. In this higher sphere of life it is classed with music, poetry, painting, sculpture, and, like them, has its established laws. The ancients—to whom, in matters of taste, the world still bows—ever so regarded it, and allotted a muse or presiding divinity to this, the most excellent of all the arts. Indeed, as if in recognition of this superiority, they assigned it a more exalted sphere when they called the divine Venus, the model of elegance and beauty, from the stars, to preside over the affairs of the heart. Among the moderns, it is true, who have materialized every thing—I speak not, to be sure, of the age of chivalry, when all Christendom built altars to woman—among the moderns, love has lost something of its exalted, or, rather, its ethereal or celestial dignity.

"But, oh surgeon, though love is no longer adored in temples, and honoured with sacrifices and games, it still occupies a respectable position and wields a potent sceptre. To sum the whole, the ancients honoured love as a powerful deity, while with the degenerate moderns it is only a terrestrial potentate, into whose dominions Mammon—who still is, and ever will continue, a god—makes destructive incursions. Here I put in a caveat. I speak not, oh neophyte, of love as a passion. As such, banish it to the *wigwam* of the savage, or to company with the swinish multitude. Once for all, I tell you, with love as a passion I will have nothing to do. I mate not with so gross a companion! Would you have lessons in such beastly materialism? Go, hapless youth, to the Yankees, with their miscegenations, their passional attractions, and free-love societies.

"But I speak alone of that refined, softened, delicate, sentimental affection of the heart which the best people entertain, and which ladies and gentlemen are not ashamed to acknowledge—an inspired emotion rather, a glowing and impassioned friendship. It is. Dr. Dunn, with love as an exalted, filtrated sentiment, an operation of the mind even more than an emotion of the soul, that I treat—or Love in his ambrosial weeds, as he fascinates and ensnares the gods. Have I, oh disciple of the excellent Galen, have I, with sufficient caution, guarded myself against misconception and error? For it is not unknown to me, the strong proclivity of your brotherhood to materialism—that, in defiance of the divine oracles, you would convert the temple of man's soul into a perishable structure of clay, not for the indwelling of holy thoughts forever, but as the companion and food of worms. Disciple of the chirurgic art, dost comprehend the sage doctrine I would unfold to thy untutored mind?"

Here Dr. Dunn humbly and reverently bowed, as under the ferula of a master, and after a short pause the professor again spoke: "Love, Dr. Dunn, hath ever been the companion of the Graces; nor can they be severed except by violent and unnatural means. When, therefore, you prepare to enter the presence of the fair *inamorata*, the object of thy soul's adoration, be ever circumspect, and assume thy most graceful carriage. The candidate for the honours of matrimony should take his hat in the right hand, and, after adjusting his oiled and perfumed locks, should hold it about six inches from his breast, opposite the region of the heart, to indicate that it needs a shield against the powerful glances to which it is about to be exposed. This done, he should throw himself in the attitude the most affecting to the fair sex—I mean the Grecian curve or bend, as it is vulgarly called—and with the heels drawn close together, and the points of the toes well turned out, he should, with a light, springy tread, and the most fascinating smile, approach the fair one. Thus, Dr. Dunn."

Here the professor, in conformity with these directions, and with the most enchanting expression of countenance, stepped off a few paces.

Rangers, "That's it. Professor, that's it." Having regained his position, he again began: "The preliminaries of introduction and acquaintance over, which I will assume to occupy three hours or three hours and twenty minutes, though in extreme cases I have known the period prolonged as much as four hours, you will take your seat by the damsel, so placing yourself as to have the free use of the right hand and arm."

Here the professor paused to observe that in the case of a left-handed lover the instructions must be modified to suit the case.

"Having placed yourself beside the patient— you will surely understand that here the patient is a blushing young girl, trembling with the soft tumult of love, her heart wildly beating to its intoxicating music—having placed yourself, I repeat, by Dulcinea's side, you will carelessly take her hand in yours. But, Dr. Dunn, be particular that this introductory act be performed in a manner of unstudied elegance and unpremeditated carelessness. Assume, if you can, an air of abstraction, as though you took no thought of the act, for the enemy must not, by any means, be apprised of your intentions. These evolutions represent your line of skirmishers, Dr. Dunn, thrown out to bring on the engagement, which they invariably do if the generalship be able.

"When you take the soft, tremulous hand in yours, mark the downcast eye, the heaving breast, the quick beat of the heart, the kindling blush—those innocent shames that mount in the cheek—for they are all harbingers, and portend success in love. Having taken the maiden's hand, for it is only with such as have the aroma of first love about them, as the young violet its perfume, that the higher and abstruser branches of the art are called into requisition, you will begin to examine and compliment her rings.

"Dr. Dunn," exclaimed the professor, throwing up his eyes and clasping his hands in the most affecting manner, "Dr. Dunn, by the order and economy of the universe, all things, whether created by the Great Father or by man, have their uses. The sun is lord of the day, and the moon, in her reflected splendour, is regent of the night. To shine upon and bless this opaque globe, and render it fit for the habitation of man, are their ordained objects. The wind, when it comes from its desert home, has its uses, as have the eyes, the ears, and the hands of man. As the winds, and the heavenly bodies, and the eyes, the ears, and the hands of man have their uses, so the rings on the fingers of young ladies have their uses, their functions, their purposes, their occasions. These, excellent physician, are to serve as a preface, a preliminary, a preamble to love—an easy, natural, recognised introduction to courtship. It was obviously on account of this inbred connection between the ring and love that the ring was selected by Hymen as the emblem and pledge of the most sacred and interesting of all terrestrial relations.

"Having examined her rings with a gentle emphasis, oh surgeon— it must be a very gentle emphasis, accompanied with a scarce audible sigh—you will observe that one ring alone is wanting to the perfect adornment of that fair hand. This every woman will understand to convey a delicate allusion to the wedding-ring, at once the object of all the hopes and fears of every young woman. You will then gently press the hand, gradually tightening the grasp as the occasion would require."

Here the Professor again paused, and fell into a fit of abstraction, looking like Galileo among the stars.

Mosby. "Well, chief, what next?"

Mr. Blackwell Magog (with great deliberation of manner). "Having encompassed the nymph's hand in yours, and bestowed on her a melting glance, thus, you will gently slide the other hand, being your left, around the fair one's waist, and, resting it on the side farthest from you, begin again the system of gentle pressure. Every system. Doctor Dunn, has its nature and principle, and the principle of my system is that of gradual approaches. It is rarely that I venture to storm a breastwork— indeed, never, unless the rampart is low and the garrison weak."

Rangers. "That gets her!"

Here ensued another pause.

Mosby (impatiently). "Tell us what comes next. We are all deeply interested in your proceeding. Do go on. A man might almost imagine himself an actor in so interesting a piece."

Holding up the first digit of the right hand as if in admonition, the professor continued:

"Here two distinct lines of action lie open before an enterprising lover, either of which may conduct to a successful issue, but I generally take the lips next."

Mosby. "Well, chief, what next?"

*Mr, Blackwell Mago*g. "What next? Great God! does any man under eighty ask me what next? Ha! ha! ha!"

DULCEBENIETTA

All. "Ha! ha! ha!"

Munson. "The fort surrenders without firing a gun."

About a month later, when we were again on the march, we assembled under a great oak—a favourite halting-place with Mosby's men when they passed on the route near which it stood. The shade was dense, the breezes cool and nimble, and Colonel Mosby called up the surgeon to report upon the efficiency of the professor's rules for courtship; in short, to tell what success he had met with at the hands of *Dulcebenietta.*

Dr. Dunn. "Success! Why, I was devilish near getting the side of my head slapped off for impertinence. The lady was highly insulted, and hasn't spoken to me since. I believe Mr. Blackwell Magog to be an impostor."

At this Mosby cast a serious and reproachful glance at the professor, as much as to say, "See what mischief you have wrought—what snares you have set for our surgeon's feet !"

Mr. Blackwell Magog (much excited). "Sir, Dr. Dunn is a bungler, and deserves to have his ears boxed. The mode is excellent. I have tried it a hundred times, and never had it to fail."

Mosby (laughing). "Ah! chief, I see how it is. The medicine is good, but the administration has been bad."

The professor was deeply chagrined at the surgeon's discomfiture. It might have the effect of bringing contempt upon science, and that he could not endure. In consequence, he took great pains to vindicate his method, and throw the whole responsibility of failure on Dr. Dunn's own blundering management.

Dr. Dunn (in an ill humour). "D—n it, Professor, if you are not pleased with my handling, you had better try it yourself, for I have done forever with Love, considered as one of the fine arts."

The proposition was considered a fair one, and it was settled that this high-priest of love should attempt in person to subdue the intractable fair—an attempt the more easily made, as he was only known by reputation to *Dulcebenietta.* But the professor, ever a devoted spouse, stipulated, as was right, that "Bob" should first give her consent.

On our return to Fauquier, I was sent as embassador to solicit the concurrence of Mrs. Blackwell Magog, after explaining and unfolding all the circumstances of the case. Arrayed in my best clothes, I accordingly proceeded to "Heartland," where I had been often before, but never on so absurd a business as this. But it was not until I was seated in Mr. Blackwell Magog's parlour, and had sent up my name to his wife, that the full sense of the awkwardness of my position broke upon me. The proposition of which I was the bearer was not only ridiculous and unusual, but might be regarded as positively disrespectful. Often did I wish that I had left the business with Dr. Dunn and his instructor, and heartily repented of the part which I had agreed to play. But how vain are regrets! They serve only to plague and unnerve a man.

While my mind was thus engaged, the lady entered, leading by the hand her bright-eyed daughter, little Madge. Her smile was so bright and good-humoured that I thought Mr. Blackwell Magog, of all men, might afford to erect his altar at home, and abandon his scientific pursuits. With as much delicacy and skill as I could command, I explained to the lady the object of my mission, and I dare say that never, in the whole range of diplomacy, was an affair so awkwardly managed. But Mrs. Blackwell Magog, as soon as she comprehended the scope of the business, instead of betraying anger, only laughed gayly, and without hesitation consented to the arrangement. She knew, she said, her husband's devotion to science, and nothing could induce her to be an impediment to its progress. I was charmed, and thought Mrs. Blackwell Magog not only one of the most attractive ladies in Mosby's Confederacy, but one of the most sensible. As I rose to depart, however, the lady carelessly remarked that she had a single condition to annex to her consent. I respectfully bowed, and inquired the nature of that sole condition. She replied,

"I stipulate that, in my husband's absence, I too shall be allowed to amuse myself with love considered as one of the fine arts." I bowed again and departed, but much believing that the condition would greatly impair the value of the concession. So it proved; for when I reported the result of my embassage to the professor, he exclaimed, in a loud voice,

"No, sir, no, sir, I'll be d——d if I consent to any such arrangement. The science of love was only designed for young ladies. Do you suppose I'll consent to have a score of these palming puppies sighing and making love to Mistress Blackwell Magog? Zounds, no! But I can't, for the life of me, think how Bob got such notions in her head. Egad! I must be getting home. By the Lord Harry, it's my opinion, if this war doesn't stop, every thing will be ruined— yes, sir, turned upside down, and there will be nothing left worth fighting for."

Munson. "But, chief, where is your respect for science? You don't stick to your own principles, man."

Mr. Blackwell Magog. "D——n your principles; they weren't made for married women."

So saying, the professor posted off to look after his domestic interests.

Chapter 34: Raiding on Phil Sheridan's Communications.

Upper Fauquier, August 18th, 1864.

Dear Percy,—About the 1st of August, Company "E," of the Partisan Battalion, was organised. Adjutant Sam Chapman was, after the fashion in "Mosby's Confederacy," elected captain; Fountain Beattie first lieutenant; Willie Martin second lieutenant; and Ben Palmer junior second lieutenant—all gallant soldiers, and worthy of the confidence reposed in them by their commander.

About the 8th of August Mosby crossed into the valley, and learned from a citizen that Sheridan was in Early's front, with his lines extending from Berryville to Summit Point. The first night he spent with his men concealed in a deep ravine in a dense wood, and the next morning went on a scout, with a small party, along Sheridan's rear, from which he returned bringing a lieutenant and six prisoners. Having ascertained the exact situation of general headquarters, which were in a house in rear of the army, and several hundred yards distant from any formidable force, Mosby determined to capture him. At a distance of

Captain Chapman

three hundred yards from the house he left the command, and went forward to reconnoitre. He discovered camp-fires blazing all around the headquarters, and selected John Hearn, on account of his coolness and intrepidity, to ascertain the strength of the force.

Hearn proceeded cautiously, until, leaping a fence, he found himself in the midst of six sleeping soldiers, near whom stood an infantry sentinel, who demanded his name. Hearn replied, still advancing, that he was in search of a New York regiment to which he belonged, and, springing upon the Yankee, wrenched from him his musket. In piteous tones he cried "Murder, murder," and the Ranger was compelled to retreat, but brought off the gun as a trophy. In consequence of this misadventure, which roused the camp, Mosby was forced to abandon his enterprise. During the night he returned to Fauquier, leaving the command in the valley with Richards, who the next day captured a captain and thirteen men; but the enemy discovering his presence in their midst, he was in turn compelled to retire.

About the middle of August Colonel Mosby again sent Captain Richards to the valley with twenty-eight men. He selected a position on the turnpike leading from Charlestown to Berryville, along which Sheridan communicated with his depot of supplies at Harper's Ferry.

In a short time, two men, coming from toward Berryville, were captured, but one of them proved to be a citizen, and was released, while the other, a reporter for the *New York Tribune*, although a noncombatant, was kept in custody. Richards again started to go to the turnpike, but was arrested by hearing the most heart-rending cries proceeding from the direction of his command. In haste he returned, and found the cause of the disturbance to be as follows: Puryear, having thoroughly searched the reporter, or "gone through him," in the technical language of the battalion, had thus addressed him: "Now, sir, which do you prefer, to be hung or shot?"

The idea that he was in the hands of the guerrillas, and about to be executed for being a Yankee, had then flashed upon the reporter's mind, and caused him to utter cries of distress. But Richards told him that, although the crime of his nativity was certainly a great one, he should not be murdered for it if he would keep quiet, which assurance so excited the captive's gratitude that he informed his deliverer that twelve of his countrymen would soon be along, and that if he would "lie snug" he could get them all.

Soon, in confirmation of the reporter's words. Captain J. S. Walker, a bearer of dispatches, and Lieutenant Ware, Commissary of the

5th United States Cavalry, made their appearance, with an escort of ten men. Richards, to remove any suspicion, advanced to meet them, whistling a song. When very near each other, Captain Walker, discovering his mistake, ordered his men to fire, but Captain Richards ordered his men to charge. A Yankee sergeant and private were killed, and the rest of the party fled toward Berryville. In the pursuit which followed Captain Walker and one private were killed, and Lieutenant Ware and three men captured.

In Captain Walker's pocket was found a miniature likeness of his bride, with her name and the date of her marriage inscribed upon it—sad words when the bridegroom lay stark and cold before us. Buck Watkins, touched with sympathy, obtained possession of the picture, and gave it to a lady, who sent it to Mrs. Walker by the hands of a Federal officer.

Captain Walker's horse—young, handsome, and well-limbed—was presented to Captain Richards; and proved to be the fastest horse in the battalion. After the fight was over, this animal was running away as fast as possible, when Willie Martin tried to overtake him. Finding it impossible, he ordered an infantry-man ahead of him to stop the horse, who promptly obeyed, and held the reins until Martin came up, who, to the man's surprise, ordered him to mount and go along with him.

When the captured property was divided, it was discovered that some lucky fellow had found in Lieutenant Ware's pocket-book five hundred dollars in greenbacks, and about an equal amount in drafts.

As Captain Richards, on his homeward march, halted on the side of the Blue Ridge, he saw a column of Federal cavalry march to the scene of the recent encounter, but it was too late, for Mosby's men were "*over the hills and far away.*"

On the 15th of August, Colonel Mosby ordered Lieutenant Glasscock, with fifteen men, to go to the Valley, with the view of assailing Sheridan's communications. The result of this expedition was the capture of twenty-eight men and horses, and I will now describe the mode in which the work was performed. After leaving Kernstown with his men, who had oil-cloths over their shoulders in front and in rear of his column, Glasscock discovered a company of Federals approaching him, but was prevented by a bend in the road from ascertaining its strength. "If they're too many for us, we'll pass them; if not, we'll demand a surrender," said he; and added, "Now, boys, I'll show you how to capture Yankees." Just then two men from the column came forward, with drawn pistols and threatening looks, to see whom they were meeting. But Glasscock laughed at the idea of his men being suspected of being rebels, and passed on to the main body. As he came up, the commanding officer exclaimed, "Holloa, boys, I took you for Johnnies."

"No, indeed," replied Glasscock, "Uncle Sam never had truer soldiers." By this time he had reached the rear of the enemy's column, and his men were ranged along its flanks. With a simultaneous movement, the Rangers presented their pistols, and demanded and received a surrender from the entire party. These captures were all made without firing a shot, or the enemy being aware of Glasscock's presence on the turnpike. The soldiers were missed from their command, but whether they had been killed, captured, or had deserted, who could tell?

While Sheridan was still drawing his supplies from Harper's Ferry over the turnpike which passes through Berryville, Mosby determined, with his battalion re-enforced by two howitzers, to strike that line of communication, and compel the Federal officer to make a retrograde movement, it might be at a critical time. After crossing the Shenandoah, a scout informed him that a wagon-train was then moving through Berryville in the direction of Harper's Ferry. Halting the command a few miles from that place, Mosby, with two men, proceeded to the turnpike, which he struck a mile from Berryville toward Rippon. Here he dismounted, and leaving the horses in the custody of one man, with the other went to inspect more closely the train which was then on that section of the road. But he discovered, in addition to the down train already spoken of, an up train heavily loaded with supplies. Without delay the battalion was brought up, with the intention of attacking both trains. When it arrived, however, day had dawned, and the down train had entirely passed out of hearing. But the richest prize was still where Mosby had left it, though in the act of moving off.

The first act was to dispatch John Russell, with a party of eight men, to capture what he supposed was a picket, but which proved to be a broken-down wagon, around which were gathered a wagon-master and his assistants, who were taken prisoners, and, with their mules, conducted to Mosby. From them he learned that the train consisted of one hundred and fifty wagons, and that it was guarded by two hundred and fifty cavalry, and a brigade of infantry, under the command of Brigadier General John R. Rentz, of Maryland. The infantry was disposed, they said, principally in front and rear, but was also strung along the train in the proportion of a company to about every ten wagons.

The artillery, supported by Company D, under command of Lieutenant Glasscock, was now posted on an eminence in full view of the turnpike, and not more than a quarter of a mile from it. Captain Richards, with the first squadron, and a piece of artillery in charge of Lieutenant Fray, was sent toward Berryville, while Chapman, with the second squadron, was drawn up in line of battle to the right of the gun.

The signal for the attack was to be three shots from the howitzer. The first scattered a body of cavalry; the second exploded among the wagons, producing great confusion; and at the third the two squadrons dashed forward, soon joined by Company "D." Up to this time, so complete was the delusion as to our character, that while Richards's men were drawn up in readiness to execute their part of the plan, several Federal officers rode to an eminence in front of him to witness, as they thought, the artillery practice.

When Richards charged, a company of infantry just at that point sprang to their feet, fired a volley, which severely wounded Sergeant Ned Rector, and then scattered. Dashing furiously on toward Berryville, he created the greatest alarm and confusion among the wagons, their drivers and attendants, and rode over and through several companies of infantry. Arrived at Berryville, instead of entering the town, he cut across the angle formed by the road leading from Harper's Ferry to Berryville, and the one which leads from Berryville to Winchester, both of which were occupied by the moving train, striking the latter a few hundred yards from Berryville, and cutting off about twenty wagons, with their guard. But, not satisfied with this handsome result, Captain Richards continued the charge nearly a mile toward Winchester, spreading consternation as he went.

But at this point he was driven back by a volley from the enemy's advance-guard, who were posted behind a stone fence, and commanded by General Rentz in person. As he was falling back across the angle, a volley proceeding from a brick church a little out of Berryville, toward Charlestown, arrested his attention. He discovered that a party of infantry, which he had cut off by his dash to the Winchester road, had taken refuge in this building, and had fired upon a party of Rangers who were passing in charge of a large number of prisoners, horses, and mules, and killing Welby Rector, wounding another man, and scattering the whole party.

Lieutenant Fray, with his howitzer not far distant from the spot, was now ordered to open fire on the church, which compelled the enemy soon to evacuate it, and fall back in the direction of their advance-guard. While this was being done, Lieutenant Willie Martin, with that audacious courage which on all occasions he is ready to display, rode boldly into the midst of the retreating party, and disarming a mounted officer, conducted him to Captain Richards, while his men, in dumb amazement, witnessed the exploit, but showed no disposition to interfere.

Chapman struck a point on the turnpike opposite the position which his squadron occupied, where there were about one hundred and fifty infantry. These, surprised by the suddenness of the onset, took refuge in gullies and behind fences. But a portion of them retreated to an orchard in the vicinity, and, being there re-enforced, made a stand. Chapman at once charged the combined party, and routed them without difficulty, but in the charge lost Lewis Adie, of Leesburg, a young soldier of the highest promise. As soon as this resistance was overcome, it was reported to the captain that a drove of several hundred beeves was following the wagons, which he at once took possession of and sent off.

Mosby had remained with the piece of artillery which opened the fight, to superintend operations in both directions, and to send off the prisoners and spoil to Castleman's Ferry as fast as they were reported to him. As soon as the work had been accomplished, he issued an order for the destruction of the wagons, and a scene of the liveliest interest was soon presented, for it was the richest prize that the Partisans had ever captured. Among the articles tumbled out on the road was a box, which contained, as we afterward learned to our distress, a million of dollars, designed for the payment of Sheridan's troops, but it was overlooked by the men in the scramble for officers' trunks. The next day its owners sent and took possession of it. As soon as the wagons were in flames the command moved off toward the ferry; but Mosby, with a rear-guard, remained at Berryville until the enemy cautiously approached the town.

Among the captured articles were a number of violins, and it was a droll sight to witness the rude attempts of the Rangers, as they moved off, playing, as they said, Dixie "for General Sheridan to dance to."

By this brilliant success Mosby secured three hundred prisoners, seven hundred mules and horses, which were sold to General Lee's quartermaster, and two hundred and thirty cattle, half of which was presented to General Lee for the use of his army, while the rest were put to pasture in Fauquier, and served out to the command.[1] But the chief advantage derived from the blow which had been struck was, that Sheridan's army was compelled to fall back from Strasburg to Winchester, and to subsist on short rations for a week.

CHAPTER 35: AGAIN IN SHERIDAN'S REAR

Upper Fauquier, August 24th, 1864.

Dear Percy,—Lieutenant Sam Chapman having been promoted to the command of Company "E," it became necessary to organise an artillery company. The officers—appointed by Mosby, of course, under the mask of an election—were, Peter Frankland, Captain; ——— Fray, First Lieutenant; John Page, Second Lieutenant; Frank Rahm, Junior Second Lieutenant.

I will now resume the account of Mosby's assaults upon General Sheridan's line of communication. On the 19th of August, with two hundred and fifty men, he crossed the Shenandoah at Castleman's Ferry, where he was informed by Jim Wiltshire, who had been sent in advance on a scout to Berryville, that there was a brigade of Federal cavalry camped at that town, with a picket thrown out within a mile of Castleman's Ferry, In consequence of this information, Mosby divided his command into three parts. "C," "D," and "E," were assigned to Captain William Chapman, with orders to operate on the section of the turnpike between Berryville and Rippon. Company "B" he assigned to Captain Richards, to whom was allotted that portion of the road between Rippon and Charlestown, while he reserved Company "A" for his own command, and that part of the road between Charlestown and Harper's Ferry. This partition of the command was resorted to because it was too large to be kept together in safety in the midst of the hostile army, and particular sections were assigned to particular officers for the twofold purpose of prolonging the line of attack and of preventing collisions during the night.

Having received his instructions. Captain Chapman marched his command to the house of a citizen in the neighbourhood, from which Mountjoy, with a party, was sent to acquire farther information about the position of the enemy, while he went on a similar expedition. Mountjoy soon returned, having recruited for the night's service six estrays from the 6th Virginia Cavalry. But Chapman's scout was more

---

1. The amount of captures given above is accurate, although, it exceeds the amount reported by Mosby to General Lee, for the reason that the dispatch was forwarded by John Munson the same night from Rectortown, while many horses, mules, and cattle were brought in afterward which had strayed on the way.

adventurous. He attempted to capture the picket before referred to, but the man, who belonged to the 7th Michigan Cavalry, refused to surrender, and was in consequence killed—an event which you will presently see was fraught with the most calamitous consequences to several families in the neighbourhood.

Having rejoined his command, it was moved to a position near the turnpike which leads from Berryville to the ferry, with the purpose of assailing a cavalry patrol which often passed to the river. From this point Captain Chapman, taking with him Hefflebower and another, proceeded to the house of Hefflebower's father, not far from the cavalry camp near Berryville, in order to obtain additional information. There he fell in with three Yankees, upon whom he imposed himself for a provost guard, and captured them without resistance. On his route with the prisoners back to the command, as he passed near the house of Colonel Josiah Ware, a party of Yankees who were there saw him, and immediately started in pursuit. This accident saved that beautiful mansion, for it had been already fired by these men, who being thus diverted, the family were enabled to extinguish the flames.

Not long after this adventure, Captain Chapman saw smoke and flames bursting from the house of Mr. Province M'Cormick, distant about two miles. He hastened to the spot, and was informed that it had been fired by a detachment of Federal soldiers, acting under an order which condemned to the flames five of the best houses in that neighbourhood belonging to Southern sympathizers, as a retaliation for the death of the picket who had been shot the previous night. The Rangers were soon brought up, and the command started on the track of the burners. When they reached the residence of Mr. Sowers, which had likewise been embraced by the cruel order, the roof had fallen in, and the ladies and children of the family were gathered in a corner of the yard, exposed to the falling rain. The forlorn ladies, as soon as they saw Mosby's men, dried their tears, and with exclamations of vengeance urged them to follow quickly the inhuman Yankees who had just destroyed their home.

"Smite and spare not," they cried, "for, though we have lost our home, we are still for the South—yes, as true as ever." The effect of this appeal, added to the piteous spectacle before them, maddened the soldiers. As they galloped off they shouted, "No quarter, no quarter today."

The elegant and hospitable residence of Colonel Morgan stood at the distance of half a mile, and was already fired when Chapman's men approached. The incendiaries, numbering ninety, were still on the ground, and, when they saw the hand of vengeance uplifted to strike them, hastily formed their ranks to receive the attack. They were charged with fierce impetuosity, and immediately broke, every man seeking safety in flight. The partisans pursued them for a mile, and then returned to put to death all the prisoners who had been taken, and all the wounded who had fallen by the way. Twenty-nine Federal soldiers thus perished, victims of the bloody code of retaliation.

Leaving the dead to bury the dead, the Rangers, with their captured horses, arms, and equipments, recrossed the Shenandoah at Berry's Ferry. As they ascended the mountain, it was discovered that a solitary prisoner had escaped the fate of his comrades. Mountjoy, who remembered those houseless ladies and his oath of vengeance, demanded that this man, too, should pay the forfeit. He was accordingly conducted deeper in the forest, and ordered to prepare for death. It was a solemn spectacle to see this brave young soldier kneel in the solitude of the mountain, and pour forth a fervent prayer to the Great Father to pardon his sins and forgive his own officer, whom he regarded, he said, as the true author of his death. The young man then rose slowly to his feet, and, tearing open his shirt, with unquailing eye received the fatal shot. An accusing spirit flew up to heaven with an appeal to the good God against the atrocious deeds perpetrated in this war. In his report to General Lee of this affair, Mosby says, "They returned with thirty horses, and no prisoners."

We will now accompany Captain Richards on his nocturnal expedition. At Myerstown, in the character of a Federal officer, he roused a citizen from his bed, and from him learned that Sheridan's army was then camped at the turnpike between Rippon and Charlestown. He then resolved to enter the Federal encampment, and carry off, if possible, the general, thus severing from its huge trunk one of the strongest limbs of the Northern army. It was a bold conception, but, under the favour of night, what might not strong nerves, directed by a cool head, accomplish? At all events, Captain Dolly meant to try it, and play a game with Fortune. When within a mile of the turnpike he halted Company "B," and, with eleven picked men, advanced cautiously toward the sleeping army. Passing through a wood, he was halted by a sentinel, to whom he advanced on foot, and represented himself to be in command of a detachment of the 21st New York Cavalry, with whom he had been on a scout toward the Shenandoah.

"Does that satisfy you?" he added, in a tone of injured innocence at having his flag called in question.

"Yes," replied the Yankee, "you are all right." The adventurous party entered the camp of the 19th New York, but could not ride through it, so thickly were the wearied soldiers strewn over the ground. Richards then determined to return and penetrate the camp at another point.

As they passed the sentinel, Lieutenant Willie Martin, in a stern voice, ordered him to hold his gun properly, and added, "That's no way for a man to stand on duty." Very much to the amusement of the Confederates, he at once assumed the position of a soldier. Continuing his search for the officers' quarters. Captain Richards stopped at Roper's house, near the turnpike, and, observing the yard full of sleeping soldiers, roused one of them, and inquired if he could tell him where to find headquarters. But the man knew nothing; so he proceeded to the turnpike, hoping to meet with better fortune. There, representing his party to be the provost-guard, he arrested a straggler from the 7th Michigan Cavalry, and compelled him to go with him. The prisoner stated that he had passed along the turnpike through the entire army without being halted, and Richards determined to try the same experiment.

He again entered the camp of the 19th Corps, resolved this time to try his luck with an officer, who might with more reason be supposed to be able to direct him to headquarters. But, as the partisans were about to enter an opening in a wood, where Richards supposed, from seeing tents and horses, that he would find an officer, the prisoner, who had discovered that he was in the hands of the enemy, put spurs to his horse, and rode into an infantry regiment asleep on the roadside, and exclaimed," Wake up! wake up! the rebels are among you." In an instant the Rangers wheeled their horses and galloped from the camp to rejoin their company, which, with all haste, was conducted to a place of safety. Thus, by an accident— the fruitful cause of so many miscarriages in military life—this bold enterprise was thwarted, and Richards thought it prudent to relinquish for the time farther operations. At the residence of Mr. Henry Castleman, where Mosby's men are always received with a cordial welcome, he stopped with a few of his men, and fortunately in time to capture four Yankees who had just begun to pillage the house.

When Richards's company had reached a place of safety, it was discovered that Harry Shaw's horse was without saddle or rider; but he afterward made his appearance, and gave the following account of his adventures. He had been thrown in attempting to leave the camp, and while on the ground was run over by a horse and left senseless. When consciousness returned he found himself in the midst of an army, which had been suddenly aroused from sleep by the cry "The rebels are upon you." Drums were beating, bugles were sounding, officers were calling loudly to their men to fall into line, while the confusion was increased by excited men rushing about, and by one hundred and fifty cavalry galloping to the turnpike. It was a novel situation for one of Mosby's men, but Harry Shaw was just the one to cope with it. He mingled freely with the Yankees, and talked loudly, until, seeing an opportunity to escape, he rushed by a sentinel, who took him, it might be, for a ghastly apparition, and made his way the house of Mr. Roger Chew. He was met at the door by the fair Miss Jennie, known in the battalion as the Rose of the Valley. To her he made known his sad plight, and was conducted to a surgeon by chance in the house, who rendered him the needful assistance.

Now we will follow Mosby. Having ordered Lieutenant Hatcher to report to him the next morning at Mr. Chew's, at the appointed hour Mosby was on the spot, and, declining an invitation from the ladies to take breakfast, said, "I have a piece of work on hand, but after it is done I shall pass this way, and will call and take a cup of coffee." With six men he rode across the country to Roper's, where Richards had stopped the previous night, and found there three horses tied to the gate. As there was some difficulty in gaining admittance through the front door, two of the Rangers ran around the house. Wiltshire advanced upon and captured a party who were buying butter and eggs from Mrs. Roper. O'Bannon saw, through a window in the basement story, five cavalry-men seated at breakfast with the family. With a gallantry that belongs to the Stonewall Brigade, with which he had served at the first Manassas, he bounded, with a cocked pistol, through the casement, looking like a gladiator in a den of lions.

The boldness of the exploit carried with it the means of safety, for the Yankees, supposing themselves surrounded, quietly slipped off their arms and surrendered themselves prisoners of war. Meanwhile Mosby, accompanied by Carlisle and Dan Thomas, had, in sight of a brigade of cavalry, charged and dispersed twelve infantry in the barn-yard. He then, according to agreement, returned to Mr. Chew's, where he subdivided the company among Hatcher, Wiltshire, and himself These parties then dispersed, and after operating actively on the outposts of the enemy, returned to Fauquier. As Captain Richards was returning, an event occurred which threw a gloom over the battalion. Lieutenant

Willie Martin was shot by an accidental discharge of a pistol in the hands of one of his comrades. He was buried in Upperville, regretted alike by citizens and soldiers. Mosby attended the funeral, and was deeply moved when he saw the earth close over the gallant officer.

Chapter 36: Captain Blazer's Defeat of Lieutenant Nelson

Upper Fauquier, September 5th, 1864.

Dear Percy,—I will now resume the account of our operations in the valley. Sheridan's army was lying between Charlestown and Berryville. General Torbert, who commanded the Federal cavalry on that theatre of the war, had been sent up the Valley in the direction of Front Royal, supported by a corps of infantry. On the 25th of August the battalion rendezvoused at Rectortown, when Mosby made the following dispositions: Mountjoy, with Company D, he ordered to cross at Berry's Ferry, for the purpose of harassing Torbert's rear; Captain Sam Chapman, with the 2nd squadron, was sent to operate between Berryville and Millwood, while Mosby, with the 1st squadron, under command of Captain Richards, proceeded to cross the Blue Ridge at Wormley's Gap. We will now follow these detachments in the order in which they have been mentioned.

When Captain Mountjoy reached Berry's Ferry, he was prevented from crossing the river by the presence of the enemy's cavalry. Captain Sam Chapman, however, succeeded in crossing at Sheppard's Mill, near which he camped for the night. From thence he sent Lieutenant Russell to Berryville, who returned about eleven o'clock, bringing the information that a large body of Federal cavalry had marched through the town in the direction of Front Royal, accompanied by wagons and ambulances. Early the next morning, with Henry Kerfoot for a guide, Chapman marched to his allotted scene of action, and halted his squadron within a mile of Berryville. From that point Kerfoot was sent on a scout toward Milwood, while Chapman, with a party, entered General Kershaw's lines, which were established near Berryville. He was there informed more accurately of the movements of the enemy—that their cavalry, as we have already seen, had passed up the day before, but that General R. H. Anderson, with Kershaw's division, had intercepted the 8th Infantry corps as it attempted to follow, and that a fight had ensued, in which the latter were repulsed and pushed back several miles.

Chapman at once determined to follow the enemy's cavalry, and with that intent rejoined his squadron. At White's burned shop, not more than a quarter of a mile from his rendezvous in the woods, he met General Torbert's advance-guard, the 6th New York Cavalry; that officer, when he reached White Post, hearing the sound of cannon, and seeing that his infantry support had not followed him, had determined to rejoin General Sheridan. As soon as he had satisfied himself that no other troops were in supporting distance of this force, Chapman at once resolved to charge them. They were marching in a column of four, with a considerable body of skirmishers on the flank next to their assailants, and had no time to change their formation before they were attacked by the squadron in line of battle, Chapman leading Company "C," and Beattie Company "E."

The Yankees did not withstand this impetuous assault, but slowly retreated. Their officers could be distinctly heard to say, "Fall back to the woods; we will give them h—ll there." But Chapman and Beattie pressed them so closely that, by the time they gained the desired point, the column had been thrown into confusion, and the retreat was suddenly checked by the interposition of a high fence, through which a gate furnished the only means of escape. The pursuit was kept up for a mile, and resulted in the capture of thirty prisoners and forty horses.

The loss of the squadron was severe. Jarman and Iden were killed, and Clay Adams and the brave Lieutenant Fox were mortally wounded. The fight was scarcely over when the main body of Torbert's command came in sight; but, upon receiving a few shells from Anderson's batteries, they flanked off toward Charlestown, where they encountered Mosby, of whose movements I will now give you an account.

With the 1st squadron, after passing through Snickersville, he proceeded to cross the Blue Ridge at Wormley's Gap, with the intention of camping in the Valley, but was compelled, by the darkness and a storm of rain, to stop all night on the mountain. The next morning he crossed the Gap, and halted the command near Myers's Ford, where it was left in charge of Lieutenant Nelson, and with a detachment of fifteen men crossed the river. This done, the detachment was divided, Richards being sent with six men to inspect the turnpike at Rippon, while Mosby, with nine men for a similar purpose, went to the section of the road between Charlestown and Harper's Ferry, on which, to use his own language, he found "plenty of game." In consequence of this discovery, he sent Harry Heaton and Kennon with orders to Nelson to bring up the squadron.

Richards had not advanced more than a mile when he came to a grove where Captain Blazer, with ninety men, had camped the night before, and, following his trail, discovered that he had crossed the river three miles farther up. He at once returned to the squadron, from which he detached Company "B," and with it went in pursuit of Blazer. Finding, however, that Blazer had taken the mountain road to Snickersville, he relinquished the pursuit, and sending Company "B" to rejoin Lieutenant Nelson, with a detail of ten men started again for Rippon.

At Snickersville Blazer was informed that Mosby had passed the evening before, going in the direction of Wormley's Gap. At once he started in pursuit of him, and when he had arrived within a mile of Myers's Ford, was informed by a citizen that Nelson, with one company, was there encamped, for the citizen was not aware of the return of Company "B" to the command. Captain Blazer was in high spirits at the prospect of surprising a single company with ninety men. He considered that he was playing at certainties, and the result proved the opinion to be true. It was midday, and Nelson's men were lying around, some sleeping, some amusing themselves with games, while many, with a feeling of blind security, had, contrary to orders, taken the saddles from their horses, when Blazer charged among them.

Assisted by Sergeant Johnson, who was in command of Company "B," Nelson attempted to rally and form the squadron, but in vain, for Blazer, who had opened the fight with his seven-shooting rifles, was pressing close upon them. Nelson, in this extremity, preserved his well-earned reputation as a soldier. He placed himself at the head of twenty-five men, and charged into the midst of the assailants, driving them back. But Blazer soon rallied his men, and led them again to the charge. At this critical juncture Nelson was severely wounded in the thigh, and was compelled to retire to the rear—a movement which the men construed into an abandonment of the fight. They, in consequence, gave way, and in a headlong flight rushed through Wormley's Gap, and descended into Eastern Virginia near the residence of Mr. Jonah Osborne. In this fight Nelson's loss was Mallory and M'Quinn killed, Wolfe badly wounded, and Corporal George Skinner, Dick Moran, Willie Flinn, and several others captured.

Captain Blazer, in the hour of his triumph, proved himself to be a gentleman, as well as a soldier, by the humanity and courtesy which he extended to his prisoners.

In the meantime, Captain Richards had taken a position in a wood near Rippon, where the turnpike presented a similar condition of things to that which Mosby found lower down—wagon-trains and ambulances moving without guards or with insufficient escorts. He was about to attack one of these trains, when the ladies residing in a house near by implored him to desist, for the Yankees, when Captain Walker was killed at the same point, had sworn that if another attack were made by Mosby's men in that vicinity the citizens should all be burned out. These entreaties induced Captain Richards to transfer the scene of capture to another point. He joined the wagon-master, who was in front, and, drawing upon his imagination, entertained him with an account of the battle then in progress between Early and Sheridan until they reached a road which turned off toward the river. The Yankee was then informed that he was a prisoner, and ordered to move to the left, and he could not be persuaded that it was not a joke until a cocked pistol was presented to his head.

With twelve mules and five prisoners the Rangers galloped off to Myers's Ford to inform Mosby of the unprotected condition of Sheridan's communications. But, instead of finding the squadron bitted for an expedition, Captain Richards, when he reached the ford, was apprised by a lady and a shot from the opposite bank of the fate that had overtaken Nelson. He therefore moved up the Shenandoah, and crossed at Mosby's Ford on his route to Fauquier.

After sending off Heaton and Kennon, Mosby left his party concealed in a wood, and, with Joe Owens, rode to the turnpike. Soon there came from the direction of Harper's Ferry two ambulances, containing fifteen infantry-men on their way to Sheridan's army, accompanied by two cavalry-men. Without resistance they were all captured, and sent across the river under an escort, which left Mosby with only five men. While waiting with this reduced party for the appearance of the squadron, a train of ambulances, containing furloughed soldiers returning to duty, passed on toward Charlestown. Not deeming it expedient to assail the train on that part of the road, he followed it beyond the town, where, without difficulty, he turned it off the road, and proceeded to unhitch the teams.

In this occupation Mosby was assisted by an unusual ally—a newsboy whom he had captured before the ambulances came in sight. The lad begged to be set at liberty, and was told by Mosby that he would turn him loose if he would assist in the capture he was about to make. To this proposition he readily assented, and, when the work of unhitching the teams was begun, was the most efficient man present, for with threatening gestures he compelled the prisoners to do the work. At this juncture General Torbert arrived on the scene, and the partisans were compelled to leave their prey, taking off with them only eighteen horses and prisoners. The fate of the newsboy is not known, though a clever fellow like that, ready to turn his hand to any business, doubtless made his peace with the Yankees, and is now at his old trade again.

Arrived at Myers's Ford, Mosby was informed of the disaster which had overtaken Nelson, and followed the track of the fugitives through Wormley's Gap, and from Mrs. Jonah Osborne learned that they had, in the most disorderly manner, after the pursuit by Blazer's men, passed on toward Fauquier.

Soon after the events which I have just recorded transpired. Brigadier General Chapman, of the Federal army, with a brigade of cavalry, crossed the Shenandoah at Castleman's Ferry, and, moving across the mountain, camped at Snickersville, from which point he dispatched a body of three hundred men to Upperville. On the eastern bank of the river he had left fifty men, with orders to join him at the expiration of two hours. But, instead of complying with this order, they proceeded up the river bank for several miles, and then by a wolf-path reached the crest of the mountain, along which they marched until they reached Snicker's Gap, where they halted to await General Chapman.

Captain William Chapman, as soon as he learned the presence of the enemy at Upperville, collected about sixty of his men, with whom he pursued the Yankees, who by that time were on their return to Snickersville; but, failing to overtake them, he, at the trap, ascended the ridge, and on its top struck a cavalry trail, which led him to the spot at which the fifty had halted, as already stated. As soon as he had reconnoitred the position and discovered the strength of the enemy, he charged them with a yell. They were surprised and fled, some toward the river, pursued by Captain Peter Frankland, but most of them dashed headlong down the mountain toward the Federal camp at Snickersville, hotly pursued by the Rangers. General Chapman from this summer excursion carried back to the valley five of his men killed and many more wounded, besides leaving behind thirteen prisoners and forty horses. The partisans lost Johnson, of Leesburg, mortally wounded, and Hooe and Fletcher taken prisoners.

CHAPTER 37: THE RAID TO ADAMSTOWN

Upper Fauquier,—.

Dear Percy,—I will begin my letter today by an account of Lieutenant Nelson's raid to Adamstown, though a little out of the order in which it occurred. The situation of affairs was as follows: Early was in Maryland. The Federal troops had been withdrawn from the Valley, and there was no assailable point to be reached except on the Baltimore and Ohio Railroad before it crosses the Potomac.

The battalion assembled at Upperville for an expedition into Maryland. After marching down the Little River Turnpike, the men were well-pleased with the order to turn to the left and proceed toward the Potomac. About dark Wat Bowie was sent with twelve men in advance of the battalion to inspect certain fords of the river, to ascertain the strength and position of the pickets, and at an early hour the next day to report to Mosby at a designated point. After an hour's brisk riding Bowie reached the river, and at the house of a lady obtained all the information he desired. She was one of the elect of the purest strain, and though compassed about by enemies who would have destroyed her, yet she received Bowie and his party with a hospitable welcome, and, after supplying grain for their horses, invited them to partake of a plentiful supper. A woman's patriotic devotion, when once it is roused, is always the strongest principle of her nature; and here this daughter of Virginia, dwelling on the remote banks of the Potomac, although within sight of Federal pickets, allowed the Confederate scouts to sleep in her shrubbery, and at daylight sent them off, after having refreshed them with a first-rate Loudoun breakfast.

Soon after the sun had lifted his bright face above the mountains of Maryland, Bowie reported to Mosby, who, in consequence of the intelligence he had obtained, determined to send only one squadron across the river. Lieutenant Nelson was put in command, and ordered to proceed to Adamstown, a station on the Baltimore and Ohio Railroad a few miles distant. Near the village the Rangers broke into a gallop and dashed suddenly in upon the affrighted citizens. A storehouse was soon crowded with soldiers, and a scene of confusion followed not easily described. The first impulse of the proprietor was to flee; but soon he returned, for the instinct of self-preservation yielded to the instinct of preservation of property; but the "rights of things," as Mr. Justice Blackstone would say, were as little regarded in that house as the rights of persons.

The more experienced of the intruders turned their attention in the outset to the money drawer, while others climbed up on the shelves and began to toss to partners below merchandise of various kinds—rolls of cloth, dress-patterns, hats, bonnets, boots, shoes, and bottles of whisky, while yells and shrieks added to the wild uproar. In the midst of this scene, the proprietor, a pitiable spectacle, was rushing to and fro, now shoved this way, now that; now dodging a package of goods, now tumbling over somebody's pile, and loudly protesting that he was a first-rate Southern man, and declaring that if his visitors would only stop a minute, he would prove it to their satisfaction. But, unfortunately for him, a box of brass thimbles struck his head before this reasonable compromise could be considered, and he fell groaning on the floor. As soon as he could scramble on his feet again he escaped to the back part of the shop, and stood silently weeping. But just as some of the men who were loaded with plunder had begun to strap it on their horses. Lieutenant Nelson came up, and at once changed the aspect of affairs.

"Put these things back—right back," said he, "every one of them. This merchant is a Southern man, and the colonel said his goods must not be disturbed ;" and, seconding his words with acts, he dashed from the arms of a soldier who stood neat him the calicoes and silks with which they were filled. The lieutenant then pushed into the shop, and, pulling and hauling right and left, soon had all the plunder scattered again over the floor.

"Now get out of here, every one of you; not an article shall be taken from this store unless it is paid for."

The law was a hard one, but the concluding part of it was construed by some of the men so as to pluck from it the sting, for I saw one of them who had reached the door turn back and squeeze three hats on his head, leaving his old one "for pay." He also strapped a parcel of dry goods to his saddle, which, with a very innocent manner, he said he had paid for according to orders. But this was not the only case in which the lieutenant's order received, this liberal construction. Johnny Munson, for example, left a five dollar Confederate bill on the counter (old issue at that) in payment for merchandise worth several hundred dollars in greenbacks. But Joe saw nothing of this, or he would certainly have made them disgorge. As soon as his unexpected auxiliary arrived on the scene of action, the weeping proprietor cheered up, and was at once all smiles and gratitude.

Nothing was too good for his new ally. He took him behind the counter and forced upon his acceptance a pair of cavalry "boots, a fine hat, and cloth for a suit of clothes, to say nothing of boxes of collars and cigars. Nor was this all. He uncorked a bottle of the best Bourbon whisky, and the two. Lieutenant Joe and the merchant, sat down to drink it. Coming on the heels of so signal a service, the liquor made them the best friends in the world. The merchant threw his arms around his deliverer's neck, and insisted upon introducing him to his wife and sister. This was accordingly done, and Joe, rubicund with the whisky, made the ladies his best Virginia bow.

So daring in love and so dauntless in war,
*Have ye e'er heard of gallant like young Lochinva*r.

With a sigh of regret, whether for the liquor or the lady is not certainly known. Lieutenant Joe left the house to look after his fierce guerrillas, to tear down the telegraph wires, and then to depart from hospitable Adamstown. The little merchant was a sight to gladden the heart of a philanthropist as, with a wave of his hand, he bade Mosby's men *adieu*, he piously hoped, forever.

Nelson determined to cross the Potomac at a ford a little below the mouth of the Monocacy, but, when he came near it, was informed by a citizen that the Yankees were there lying in wait for his party.

"How many are they?" inquired the lieutenant.

"Only fifty," was the reply; "some of them are at the ford, but the rest are on the hill near by to surprise you."

"All right," said Nelson, undismayed. "Maybe we will surprise them."

As soon as the position of the ambuscade was reconnoitred, Harry Hatcher was sent, with a party of twelve men, to attack in the rear, while Nelson, it was agreed, should march down the road, as if ignorant of its existence. The attack of the two parties was to be simultaneous; but, owing to an accident. Hatcher was delayed. The Yankees, thinking, that Nelson had fallen into their trap, fired two volleys at him as he ascended the hill, by which Johnny Alexander alone was wounded. They had overshot their mark. Hatcher soon broke upon their rear, and rarely has such a scattering been seen. Some ran down the hill and hid in the bushes, while others mounted their horses and struck wildly across the country. The result of the attack was four of the enemy killed, and eight, with their horses, captured.

A charge on the party at the ford was then ordered, but, having witnessed the collision on the hill, they had already taken to flight. After a fatiguing pursuit, about six of them were taken prisoners.

Nelson then rejoined Mosby on the Virginia side of the river, and reported the result of the expedition.

"Where are your goods?" said the colonel to some of the men, who had not availed themselves of the paying clause of the lieutenant's order. The explanation was then given, to which Mosby replied,

"I gave no such order. That shopkeeper is the worst Yankee in Maryland. You ought to have taken everything from him." These words doubtless eased the conscience of Munson, but they gave but little comfort to the bulk of the command.

During the absence of Nelson's squadron two other companies had crossed the river, but were attacked by a large cavalry force, and only by dint of great exertion, both in fighting and retreating, had returned in safety to Virginia.

Chapter 38: Mosby "Goes Through" the Yankees

Upper Fauquier, September 22nd, 1864.

Dear Percy,— During the last summer Mosby received frequent dispatches from General Lee, urging him to prevent any raid from being made from Alexandria on Gordonsville, as his was the only Confederate force in a position to be interposed for the protection of that place. Accordingly, when Sheridan fell back under cover of the guns at Harper's Ferry, he turned his attention to Fairfax County. About the 1st of September, Mosby sent Harry Hatcher, with a detachment, to alarm the outposts about Chain Bridge, while, with another detachment, he drove in their pickets on other parts of the line, and captured eleven men and horses. On his return, in company with Willie Mosby and John Waller, he was pursued by a squad of eight Federals to a point beyond Fairfax Court-house.

On reaching the top of a hill he halted, which induced his pursuers to halt likewise. He then requested Dr. Baker, who happened to be passing, to tell them to come and get their horses, and at the same time to inform them who he was. But the Yankees replied, they did not mean to fall into any such d—d trap, and, after firing a few shots from their carbines, posted back to their command.

With Company "A," Lieutenant Joe Nelson in command of it, Mosby proceeded to a point between Union Mills and Centreville, and camped for the night. On the march, Walter Whaley, with five men, was sent to capture a picket near Alexandria, a duty which he handsomely performed, and, with three prisoners and four horses, returned to the command the next morning. Soon after his arrival, Lieutenant Nelson, with twenty men, and Ab Minor for a guide, was sent to capture two pickets stationed on the old Braddock Road, near Alexandria. The first of these got notice of the contemplated attack, and had retired; but the second, composed of twelve men, posted near Triplett's house, had taken refuge in a school-house, having concealed their horses in the pines. The schoolhouse was charged; its inmates fled, and, it being twilight, all effected their escape except three, who, with their horses, were captured.

Nelson, having accomplished his mission, prepared to return to his command. But here an unexpected difficulty intervened. Ab Minor, the guide, proved to be the only man present who knew nothing of the road, and the consequence was that we were all lost in the pines. Now we would follow one road and now another, and the farther we marched the more our confusion increased. At length, in the midst of the bother, our guide drew up his horse, and said if he could only find the "Bone Mill" it would be all right. Again we started, every body being on the look-out for the "Bone Mill"—a fixed star that was to guide us through all the perplexities of our route. But devil a bit could the "Bone Mill" be found, and the consequence was that we had to lie all night in the pines. Ever after Minor went by the name of "Bone Mill" till he shot Bill Trammell about it. From that time the joke lost all its relish, and our excellent guide was restored to his baptismal appellation.

When we arrived the next morning at Arundel's Mosby had departed, in consequence of an event which had occurred during our absence, which I will now relate.

As soon as Nelson had set forth, Mosby dispatched two scouts, one toward Centreville, the other toward Arundel's. Very soon information was received from George Slater and Whaley, who composed the latter party, that the Yankees had been at Arundel's searching for Mosby, and were still in the neighbourhood. In consequence, the command, consisting of thirty-six men, was moved thither, and Whaley and Slater were sent forward to follow the enemy to Fairfax Station. As the two scouts were riding at a lively pace through a body of pines, they were bushwhacked by thirteen Federals, Slater was shot in the thigh and his horse in the neck, but, notwithstanding, managed to escape with his companion and report the adventure. With five sharpshooters, Mosby, followed by the command, galloped to the spot, but the birds had flown, taking the direction of the Station. They were rapidly pursued, and half an hour's gallop brought the Rangers within view of the Catholic church, which is situated not far from the station, on the road leading to Fairfax Court-house.

There they beheld a body of one hundred and ten Federal cavalry, composed of two detachments, one from the 16th, the other from the 13th New York, commanded respectively by Captains Fleming

Mosby "Going through 'em."

and Minimum. They had started in pursuit of Walter Whaley in consequence of the capture of the picket near Anandale, and, failing to overtake him, had determined to make a raid into Fauquier or Loudoun. When Mosby first came in sight the Yankees were feeding their horses preparatory to the expedition, but were quickly formed across the road, with their left flank resting on the church. The railroad, when it leaves Fairfax Station, crosses the country road above referred to, and passes, as it approaches the church, through a deep cut of some length. Mosby, approaching the railway from the direction of Arundel's and Sangster's Cross-roads, was compelled, by this deep cut, to make a circuit toward the Station in order to attack the Federals, which afforded them the opportunity of estimating the number of their assailants.

After gaining the public road, Mosby closed up his ranks, and, rolling up his sleeves, said, "Men, I want you to go right through them." He was answered by loud cheers, and the command sprang forward in the charge. The corresponding order of Captain Fleming to his men was to fire a volley from their carbines, and then, with drawn sabres, to charge. They held their fire until the partisans were within fifty yards of them, and then, after firing one volley, broke and fled toward the Courthouse. They were fiercely pursued by Mosby and his men, who fired into them at every jump. Before the pursuit reached Fairfax Court-house many of the fugitives had been wounded and many killed. Among the latter was the commanding officer, who, after wounding Frank Turner, was shot by Ned Hurst, and had received, before he fell to the ground, a bullet also from Johnny Waller. When the fugitives reached the courthouse, one of them broke off to the right through the grounds of Mr. Thomas, hoping in this way to shorten his course to the camp at Anandale; but Ames, like the angel of death, was close upon him, and with a pistol shot him at the distance of thirty yards.

Captain Minimum throughout the retreat proved himself worthy of his rank. From time to time he attempted, but to no purpose, to rally his men, and bring them back to the fight. No; the fear of Mosby wrought within them, whom they feared more than any other living wight. They would not have rallied to the trumpet of an archangel.

While Captain Minimum was engaged in one of these fruitless attempts, he was attacked by Whaley and Will Anderson with empty pistols, but he drove them off. Then he continued his retreat, but from time to time halted and fired back at his pursuers, who, having procured loaded revolvers, returned to assail him. But they succeeded only in making the gallant officer desist from any farther attempt to rally his flying soldiers. After the pursuit had passed the court-house, Walter Whaley, who had been separated from his antagonist, again attacked Captain Minimum, but had his horse killed for his pains.

The loss of the Federals, besides their wounded, was six killed, and thirty-three men and horses captured.

After the fight was over, a splendid bay horse was seen without a rider in one of the open fields. A great effort was made by the Rangers to capture the gallant steed, but to no purpose. They drove him through the village, but the horse, who appeared to have no taste for guerrilla life, and a great affection for the "Constitution and the laws," broke through all barriers. Unable to effect his capture, the men next resolved to destroy this fleet-footed animal. The chase then became most animated, and many revolvers were emptied. As a bullet would strike him, he would bound wildly in the air, and again lead off toward the Federal camp. The last that they saw of the gallant bay was as he disappeared behind the hills of Fairfax, bleeding from many a wound, but his head and tail still up.

About two hours after Mosby had departed a body of cavalry arrived from Anandale. As soon as the officer in command had ascertained the facts of the recent fight, he expressed his indignation, saying, "Thirty soldiers have whipped a hundred cowards."

Soon afterward Mosby returned to capture a quartermaster's establishment at Falls Church, about three hundred yards from which a cavalry brigade was stationed. With two men he entered a tent and brought off a butcher, who was sleeping near a beef he had killed to issue the next morning, and with him a fine pony. He protested against moving, supposing that some of his comrades were playing a joke on him; but his captors soon found means to convince him of his error. Having discovered the condition of affairs in the camp, and that there were about seventy-five horses in an exposed condition, he sent a lieutenant, with a party of men, to bring them off. But, in consequence of delay in the execution of this order, the camp was alarmed, and the plan defeated. The command was then sent back to Fauquier, but Mosby, with Tommy Love and Guy Broadwaters, lingered at the house of a citizen.

On their return they met in the turnpike, near Centreville, a regiment of Federal cavalry, with an advance-guard of seven men. By a feigned retreat he induced the latter to follow him for the distance of a quarter of a mile, and then turned suddenly upon them. Being dressed in full uniform, Mosby was recognised by the Federals, and made a mark for their shots. One ball shattered the handle of his pistol; another entered the groin, wounding him so badly that he could with difficulty keep the saddle. But Broadwaters and Love continued the charge, and drove their pursuers back upon their column, after killing two of their number. They then returned to their commander, and, procuring a light wagon in the neighbourhood, carried him to the Plains, where he was cordially and kindly nursed by the family of Major Foster. As soon as it was noised through the neighbourhood that Mosby lay wounded at the Plains, the ladies and gentlemen of the country around flocked to see him, and vied with each other in expressions of admiration and sympathy for the wounded hero. In a few days he was removed to the residence of his father, near Lynchburg. A day or two before he was wounded. Colonel Mosby had sent to General Lee a report covering his operations during the spring and summer. It was forwarded to the adjutant and inspector general for the information of the department, with the following endorsement:

> Attention is invited to the activity, and skill of Colonel Mosby, and the intelligence and courage of the officers and men of his command, as displayed in this report. With the loss of little more than twenty men, he has killed, wounded, and captured, during the period embraced in his report, about twelve hundred of the enemy, and taken more than sixteen hundred horses and mules, two hundred and thirty beef cattle, and eighty-five wagons and ambulances, without counting many smaller operations. The services rendered by Colonel Mosby and his command, in watching and reporting the enemy's movements, have also been of great value.
>
> (Signed), R E. Lee, General.

Chapter 39: Wat Bowie's Adventures

Upper Fauquier, September 30th, 1864.

Dear Percy,—The Partisan Battalion is growing apace. The feeble germ slowly put forth its tender shoots, but, now that the sunlight has fallen upon it, it is spreading fast into the vigorous oak. The sixth company, "F," was recently organised at Piedmont, with Walter Frankland, of Fauquier, Captain; Walter Bowie, of Maryland, First Lieutenant; Ames, of New York, Second Lieutenant; and Frank Turner, Junior Second Lieutenant.

In the latter part of February, 1863, in company with George Whitescarver and Joe Nelson, Captain Frankland was on his way to

Captain W. E. Frankland

join Colonel White's Cavalry, then on detached service in Loudoun County, but, when they reached Upper Fauquier, they determined, instead, to connect themselves with Mosby, whose reputation then was just taking wing. After seeing some service with the partisan leader, he was made quartermaster of the battalion, with the rank of captain, but was returned to field-service as captain of the new company.

With Ames you are already acquainted.

Lieutenant Turner joined Mosby in the fall of 1863, and had been designated by him as one of the officers of Company "D," when he was captured and detained in prison until July, 1864.

The first lieutenant I purposely passed by, that I might give you afterward a more extended notice of him.

When the war broke out between the hostile sections of the republic, Lieutenant Bowie was a lawyer in good practice in Upper Marlboro, Maryland. Obedient to the impulses of his nature, as well as to the convictions of his understanding, he did not hesitate as to the part he would act in that painful conjuncture, and without delay joined the Confederate Army, but did not join Mosby till the spring of 1864. His love of adventure and a certain cool daring soon made his name familiar in the battalion, and attracted the notice of his commander. His chosen field of enterprise was Maryland, and he eagerly sought opportunities to cross the Potomac, with every ford of which he was acquainted from Harper's Ferry to Washington. He is now dead, and every incident connected with his daring career is invested with a melancholy interest. Some of these I will relate, for they illustrate not only the character of Bowie, but the qualities which are cultivated and admired in the Partisan Battalion.

During his expeditions to Maryland he had many strange adventures and wonderful escapes, for his name was well known to the Federals, and they made strenuous exertions to capture him..

On one occasion, he was passing the night at the house of a friend, when it was surrounded by a troop of cavalry eager to catch him. As soon as their business was known, Bowie commenced to disguise himself by blacking his face. He next slipped on the gown of an old and faithful cook-woman, and, tying up his head in her handkerchief, seated himself by her side in the chimney-corner as if stupefied with fright. As the day began to dawn, the old woman, fearing detection, said to her companion,

"Come, child, we must go to the spring and get some water to cook the white folks' breakfast." She then picked up a pail, and, giving a bucket to the pretended girl, the two moved toward the spring. As they passed out of the door one of the Yankees remarked,

"That's a d—d tall nigger."

When the cook returned unattended, Mr. Yankee inquired for her companion.

She readily replied, "How I knows? You skeered the gal so I suppose she done run away." After a close search, the Yankees found Bowie's hat, coat, and pistols, but concluded that, as usual, the eel had slipped out of his skin.

On another occasion he was at a country tavern in Maryland, where two Federal soldiers dismounted, and asked for something to drink. The landlord had nothing better than apple jack or new dip at the bar. Bowie, however, stepped up, and offered his own flask, from which the party took a social glass. After some conversation, he bade the officers a courteous farewell, but as he did so inquired,

"Have you got Wat Bowie yet?"

"No," replied they, "but we will have him before long. We know. where he is to be this week, and all is fixed for his capture."

"All right," said he. "Be sure you hold him this time, for he is a slippery chap, you know."

"Ah! trust Stanton for that. He will make sure of him when he is taken again. Goodbye." And, so saying, the officers rode off.

In this last remark reference was made to his escape from the Old Capitol Prison, the circumstances of which I will relate in this connection, as they exemplify, in a very striking manner, that self command in sudden danger which Nature has bestowed and partisan life developed in him. The night was dark as Erebus, and a drizzling rain was falling, as he got out on the roof of a wooden shed, fourteen feet from the ground. There he rested until the sentinel, who paced the street below, had passed, when he let himself down to the ground, but in the act sprained his ankle. He at once called to the sentinel,

"My good fellow, help me up."

The sentinel turned, and, approaching him, asked how he came there.

"Why," said Bowie, "it was so dark that I came on the wrong side of the street, and have trodden on something which, caused me to fall and sprain my ankle. How am I to get home? It is late, and no one is going my way."

"Get up," said the sentinel; "I will help you to the end of my beat, and then maybe you can get on. But you must not come this way again, or you will get worse hurt."

"Thank you, thank you, my friend," said Bowie; "I assure you I find that this is not a safe place, and will not be likely to pass this d—d street again."

The sentinel, true to his word, gave him the promised assistance, and as he was not as much hurt as he represented himself to be, he limped off, and, after a walk of four miles, hired a horse, and was twenty miles from the Federal Bastille before sunlight irradiated its lofty towers.

When Bowie was asked why, when he fell, he did not run from the sentinel instead of calling to him, he laughed and said,

"That would have made him fire upon me, and might have caused my rearrest."

But his adventures did not end here, for a few days later, and while his trail was still warm, he came upon a party of soldiers who were on the look-out for him. They were seated in a bunch of pines around a fire made of fence-rails. Bowie, without hesitation, walked up to them and said,

"Holloa, men, you make free with my rails. I think you might have taken the wood, and not destroyed my fence. But Uncle Sam, I suppose, must have his own way; but," he added, "don't do more harm than necessary."

One of the soldiers inquired,

"Who the d—l are you?"

"Who else," replied Bowie, "but the owner of this land and of those rails?"

After some farther words, one of the men inquired if he knew any thing of Wat Bowie, proceeding to describe his person with considerable accuracy.

"Yes, I know him well. He was in the neighbourhood, it is said, a few days ago, but has gone to the upper part of the country, where he was born." Seeing that he was closely eyed, he added,

"I am glad I met you on my own ground, else you might have given me trouble, for I am said to be much like him." And, turning off, said,

"Success to you. If you want a drink, come to my house about dusk, when I shall be in."

"Thank you, sir," said the soldier, giving a military salute; "you are of the right sort."

As soon as the organisation of Company "F" was completed. Lieutenant Bowie, with twenty-five men, started on an expedition to Maryland, the purpose of which was to capture and bring off the chief executive of that state. Governor Bradford. His route carried him through Falmouth and King George Court-house. At the latter place he halted and organised his little command by appointing Jack Randolph and Jim Wiltshire second and third in authority. He then directed his march to the Potomac. Having dispersed his command through the neighbourhood, he pressed the boat of Long, a blockade-runner, whom he compelled to accompany him, and then, with Randolph, Wiltshire, and the young widow of a Georgia soldier, on her way to visit her friends in New York, proceeded to cross the river.

The water was very rough (for the Potomac at this point is four miles wide), but the lady was as calm as the widow of a Southern soldier ought to be when the frail bark was trembling on the heaving waves. The party landed at "The Walnut," a large tree which gives its name to the crossing, and remained three days in the neighbourhood, during which time Bowie acquired the information he desired. In the afternoon of the third day, on their return to The Walnut, they encountered two of Bowie's friends, who had come out from Port Tobacco to see him, having been secretly informed that he was in the neighbourhood. After a brief interview, a shake of the hand, and a glass of Bourbon, they departed.

Concluding that it was impracticable to conduct in safety so large a command as he had brought with him through Maryland, Bowie determined to send it back to Fauquier, reserving only O'Bannon,

Charlie Vest, Ratcliffe, George Smith, Haney, Jack Randolph, and Jim Wiltshire.

As soon as this arrangement had been determined upon, Wiltshire was sent to cross the river with Long, to have the order executed. When the boat was midway the stream. Long became alarmed at the number of boats that were passing, and expressed a determination to return to the Maryland shore. But Wiltshire was not in the habit of doing business in that way; so he cocked his pistol, and presented it at the head of the astonished blockade-runner, bidding him continue his course. Having executed his mission on the Virginia shore, Wiltshire, with the men before enumerated, recrossed the river, and dismissed Mr. Long, to ply again the profitable and patriotic business to which he had devoted his industry and talents.

Bowie, with seven of Mosby's Rangers, was now afoot in Charles County, Maryland, embarked upon the hazardous enterprise of leading into captivity the highest official in the state. But the distance to be travelled made it necessary for the lieutenant to mount his followers, for if His Excellency should be captured a forced march to Dixie would, beyond doubt, be necessary. But where were the horses to be obtained? It would never do to take them from the citizens of Charles County, who were so zealous for the cause of Southern independence. There were Yankee cavalry at Port Tobacco, however, and "Old Abe" was a quartermaster from whose stables Mosby's men had, for many months, been in the habit of supplying themselves. To Port Tobacco they accordingly repaired. It was night when they arrived. The men were halted outside of the town, while their leader went in to reconnoitre. He soon returned, and conducted them to B——'s tavern, where they were provided with crackers and cheese. Liquors and cigars followed, and then came Ratcliffe's oyster story.

A cavalry camp was within half a mile of the town, but a provost-guard of fifteen or twenty men was quartered in the court-house building. Here, then, were horses, and Wat Bowie determined out of that stud to mount his foot-sore and weary followers. The sentinel who guarded the horses was first captured by Bowie and Wiltshire, and turned over to one of the command. Bowie then proceeded to the court-house. Charlie Vest was stationed to guard the door, Randolph, Haney, Ratcliffe, and O'Bannon were directed to hold themselves in readiness, while Bowie and Wiltshire entered. The room was very dark, and the former, having lighted a match, was passing about among the sleeping Yankees, when a stalwart Dutchman sprang up, and, running his pistol against Bowie, threatened to shoot. The two Rangers at once shouted, "If any man shoots we will murder the whole party." At these, words Randolph and his comrades rushed upon the scene. There was not even the show of resistance made; the warlike Dutchman fell back upon the floor, protesting that he did not mean to shoot.

The prisoners were then paroled to remain in the courthouse till sunrise—an engagement to which they were faithful, for Bowie told them by that time he would be able to recross the river. The horses were then distributed among the Rangers, Bowie selecting for his own saddle a handsome gray, not because it was the best, but because it would be most conspicuous in the fight, and would, on account of its colour, Le a good guide-horse at night, Thus equipped, they started for Upper Marlboro, a small town about thirty-six miles distant. The following night, weary and hungry, they entered the town, and found it difficult to procure food, for even the Southern sympathizers were afraid to give it to them. The ladies of Upper Marlboro, in the article of pluck, are not equal to the heroines of Baltimore, who would have defied the whole Northern army before they would have seen one of Mosby's knights lack for a mouthful of food.

But the ladies of Baltimore are of a higher type, and it is not just to compare mere mortals with them. They belong to the order of angels—yes, ministering angels to the sick and imprisoned soldiers of the South. There was, however, a hospitable old negro, who carried the strangers to his humble cabin, and there gave them a ham of bacon and a crust of bread. He was the single righteous man that saved the city from utter condemnation. After the lapse of an hour the Partisans again set forth, and, after less than a day's ride, arrived at the house of one of the elect, where they were received with a most cordial welcome, and waited upon at table by the daughters of the house, the servants having been purposely all sent out of the way. Mosby's men felt like gods, with dimpled Hebes to give them nectar in the likeness of Lincoln coffee—no bad substitute either to hungry and toil-worn soldiers. As they took their departure from this hospitable roof, Wiltshire, in the most enthusiastic manner, exclaimed,

'Twas bright, 'twas heavenly, but 'tis past!

A few hours later. Lieutenant Bowie, with three men, started to visit a neighbouring county, and left Wiltshire, with the rest of the party, concealed in a forest. Here Brune Bowie joined them. He had been a member of the 1st Virginia Cavalry, but now enlisted under

Mosby. The wanderers slept soundly by their camp-fires in the woods until, at dawn, Ratcliffe was aroused from his slumbers by a hunter's dog. Springing to his feet, the Ranger found himself face to face with a forester, who carried a fowling-piece on his shoulder. Ratcliffe summoned his comrades, and Wiltshire recognised in the sportsman young ———, one of Lee's soldiers, who had been wounded at Gettysburg, and had the night before entertained him at his father's house. He had brought with him food and several bottles of whisky. Thus supplied, life in the woods was pleasant enough—a good breakfast, a glass of inspiring liquor, a war-dance, and then the oyster story. When Lieutenant Bowie returned, he brought with him information that a large garrison had been sent to Annapolis, which rendered the abduction of Governor Bradford impossible.

He determined without delay to make his way back to Virginia. Passing through Beltville, the partisans marched for forty miles in the direction of the Sugar-loaf Mountain, which is near the Potomac, and about opposite to Leesburg. At night they slept in a body of pines, and at eight o'clock in the morning were aroused by the tramp of horses. It was discovered that an armed band of about thirty citizens was approaching the bivouac by the public road, who had been roused to retaliate for an act of aggression which had been committed by the Rangers the day before. A fight with Mosby's men is always in order, so they hastily formed on foot, and charged their assailants with a yell. The citizen soldiers fled with precipitation, in their fright firing their guns and pistols in the air.

Before the fight had begun, the valiant citizens, with the exception of eight or ten who were reserved for the cavalry service, had all dismounted. The consequence was that they ran away, leaving their horses for the guerrillas. Bowie, Vest, and Wiltshire, mounted on abandoned horses, pressed hard in the pursuit, the lieutenant being considerably in advance. As he passed near a thicket, he was mortally wounded by a charge of buckshot. When the men gathered around him, he told them that he must die, and ordered them at once to leave him, but they first moved him to the house of a citizen near by, and left him in the custody of his brother.

The command then devolved on Jack Randolph, who struck for the Sugar-loaf, from whence he proceeded to Virginia.

Thus ended a daring but fruitless expedition, or fruitful only in misfortune, for in the death of Lieutenant Bowie the battalion sustained a heavy loss. If he had defects as a commander, they were such as a soldier knows best how to excuse, and as a gentleman and a soldier, he was a model upon which others might form themselves.

Chapter 40: The Hanging Raid

Upper Fauquier, September 30th, 1864.

Dear Percy,—As soon as Company "F" was organised, three expeditions started from Piedmont; the one to Maryland, an account of which I gave you in my last letter, and two to the Valley, with an account of which I will begin my narrative today.

With eight men. Captain William Chapman crossed the Shenandoah for the purpose of attacking Sheridan's line of communication, extending from Winchester to the Potomac. On the old Winchester and Harper's Ferry Dirt Road he discovered, about ten miles from the former place, an immense supply-train passing, escorted by a heavy guard, which he followed until it reached the Winchester and Martinsburg Turnpike, capturing on the way the commissary of Chapman's brigade and two cavalrymen. He then halted his party, and, it being night, went forward to reconnoitre.

He discovered a house, around which were standing a number of horses, and proposed to the proprietor to allow him to stop for the night, but was told that the house was full. "There is, however, in the stable-yard," said he, "a wagon belonging to the 6th Army Corps. Perhaps you can find quarters' with the driver." Possessed of this information, Captain Chapman returned to his command, and sent Lieutenant Fray, with two men, to search the house before mentioned, while with the rest he went to the stable-yard. There he found a commissary wagon, loaded with hard tack and drawn by six mules, in charge of a sergeant and driver. The mules were quickly bridled and harnessed, and the more so when shooting was threatened as the consequence of hesitation or disobedience on the part of those in charge of them. Lieutenant Fray reported that he had found the house deserted, for the inmates had taken the alarm and fled. Before Chapman could get off with his captures, the sound of approaching hoofs was heard, and soon a voice demanded,

"Who is that?"

Chapman replied that he had in charge a 6th Corps wagon, at the same time advancing with his men.

"But why are you making such a devil of a noise?" again demanded the voice.

With becoming humility, Chapman responded that his wagon had broken down, and then ventured to inquire the names of the strangers. But they treated the question with the contempt so appropriate to official dignity—an ineffectual barrier in war—so this bevy of officers, as it proved to be, were compelled to make an unconditional surrender, all but one, who, in the darkness, made his escape. Major Terry, two captains, a lieutenant, and two privates set off with Chapman for "Mosby's Confederacy."

But the night's adventures were not over, for the party had not proceeded more than a mile before it was halted by a man who stood on the side of the road. Chapman asked if it was a picket-station, but was told that eleven officers, together with a sutler's wagon, had halted there for the night. In a low voice the sentinel was informed that he was a prisoner, and was then ordered to call the officers to him singly. Thus were they all captured, and, with nineteen prisoners and twenty-three horses, Chapman continued his march. The affair was so cleverly managed that, in the darkness, those last captured mistook all who were along for "rebels," while the prisoners first taken believed that their captors had received re-enforcements on the route. All this was done without firing a shot,—a piece of head-work that may well make Glasscock look out for his laurels. So great was the disproportion of blue-coats in the column, that it was near being charged by Mosby's men as it drew near Piedmont.

Lieutenant Turner, as I have mentioned, was sent by Captain Frankland to the valley with six men, and made several captures from a party which he charged from ambush.

Soon after Captain William Chapman returned from the valley, his brother, Captain Sam Chapman, was allowed to take one hundred and twenty men, and attempt the capture of a picket from the 6th New York Cavalry, which he had been informed was stationed in Chester's Gap, one of the breaks in the Blue Ridge, not far from Front Royal. With this intent, he marched his command to a point midway between Front Royal and the mountain pass, where he camped for the night, and was informed that no such picket had been posted at that place, but that a large body of Federal cavalry had the day before marched from Front Royal toward Luray, and furthermore that General Torbert had been repulsed by General Wickham at Milford, a point between Front Royal and Luray.

About daybreak the next morning Chapman called for John Gray, Willie Mosby, and several other Rangers, and rode to Mr. King's, on the Gooney Manor Grade, from which place he could see the Federal camp a mile or two below Milford. In a short time it was reported to him that an ambulance-train, escorted by about one hundred and seventy-five men, had started from the Federal camp, and was moving down the turnpike toward Front Royal. Acting upon this information, Chapman returned in the direction of Front Royal, and, when near it, halted his party midway between the road leading from Chester's Gap and the turnpike leading from Milford. Here he sent for the command to join him. As soon as it arrived, he divided it into two parts; one he put under command of Captain Frankland to make a circuit over Grave-yard Hill, and assail the front of the escort as it was about to enter the village, while with the other moiety he would attack it in rear at the toll-house.

Chapman, whose position placed him nearer the advancing escort, saw them as they turned the angle of the road; but cavalry followed without intermission. One, two, three stands of colours were counted. Turning to Harry Hatcher, in command of Company "A," he ordered him back to the Chester Gap wood without delay, "while I," he said, "will get to Frankland if possible, and call him off before he makes an attack." But, before he could execute this purpose, Frankland had pitched into the front of the escort, driving it back among the ambulances. When Chapman met him, exclaiming, "Call off your men; you are attacking a brigade," he replied, in amazement, "Why, Sam, we have whipped them." The order was repeated, but it was slowly obeyed, for the men had tasted blood.

I must now return to Harry Hatcher, who could not find it in his heart to leave the field while his comrades were fighting, and Fount Beattie and Willie Mosby, who were with him, contributed all in their power to hinder a retrograde movement. When the reverend gentleman discovered this reluctance, in his vexation he exclaimed, "It is all very noble and very pretty, but devilish inconvenient at this time;" and there is a tradition in the command that he even used stronger language. The Yankees, in the mean time, enveloped the devoted band like a cloud. Now the Rangers would charge them in front, now beat them off from the flanks and rear, but still they continued to crowd upon them. In this way Chapman continued the retreat till he reached Criser's house, which stands near Chester's Gap Road, where he discovered a body of Federal cavalry so posted as to cut off retreat in that direction. Things looked blue enough, but the reverend gentleman did not hesitate a moment. His countenance glowed with pleasure as he rallied his men, and by a desperate charge opened again the line of retreat to the Blue Ridge.

A Federal lieutenant, with a small party, had galloped up the Chester Gap Road, that he might intercept some of the fugitives, who, on the side of the mountain, were attempting to make their escape by crossing Hominy Hollow. Finding himself cut off by the interposition of Chapman, he dismounted from his horse, it is supposed, intending to surrender. But he imprudently retained his arms, and was riddled with bullets by the fugitives as they passed him. The fate of this officer was not singular, for it is a fact in the history of this locality that no Yankee has ever visited Hominy Hollow and returned to tell the tale.

In this fight none of Mosby's men were killed, none were wounded, but blood flowed freely enough after the combat was over, for a vindictive and sanguinary spirit prevailed among the Yankees that day. Six prisoners had been captured in the fight; Anderson and Carter from Fauquier, Love from Fredericksburg, Jones from Washington, Overby from Georgia, and Rhodes from Front Royal. Events for many months had been drifting to a catastrophe, and it was now determined to sacrifice these victims to the angry vengeance which prevailed in the Northern army toward Mosby and his men. Anderson, Jones, and Love were marched to the rear of the town and shot, while Overby and Carter were marched off in the direction of Guard Hill, and hung to the branches of a walnut-tree in sight of the village, with this placard fastened on their backs,

Such is the fate of all of Mosby's men.

All of them met their fate with singular firmness, but Overby, who was a famous soldier, hurled defiance at his executioners, and said,

My last moments are sweetened by the reflection that for every man you murder this day Mosby will take a tenfold vengeance.

Rhodes had fled up Happy Creek when he was captured. As he was marched through Front Royal to the place of execution, he passed the residence of his mother, whose only stay he was. With a gush of maternal grief and fondness, she rushed out into the street and caught him in her arms; but her arms were unclasped, and she was rudely driven off by the men who had him in charge. He was then taken beyond the village and put to death.

The citizens of Front Royal had witnessed all the terrors of legitimate warfare, and had learned to regard them with composure; but the execution of these enlisted soldiers produced a deep gloom that was visible on every countenance. Had a new chapter in the horrors of war been opened?

Chapter 41: Ogg's (the Scout) Adventure and Escape

Upper Fauquier, October 30th, 1864.

Dear Percy,—On the 29th of September Colonel Mosby returned to Fauquier, and resumed the command of the Partisan Battalion. He was still on crutches, and unable to ride without being lifted into the saddle. As soon as his convalescence began, his restless spirit induced him to visit Richmond on official business. But when he reached Gordonsville, with the purpose of returning to his father's house, he met three of his captains and many of the men—a circumstance which convinced him that his command imperatively demanded his attention. He at once ordered the officers and men to duty, and to one of the men who asked for a furlough, he replied,

"No, sir; it is more disgraceful for a soldier to go home at this time than to go to the penitentiary."

When Mosby arrived Captain William Chapman was in the Valley, and he immediately sent Captain Sam Chapman, with Company "E," to strike Sheridan's communications near Middletown, from which expedition he returned bringing with him thirteen prisoners.

The battalion was ordered to assemble at Piedmont on the 2nd of October, with the intention of striking Sheridan a heavy blow. But when the day arrived, information was brought to Colonel Mosby that a considerable force of the enemy was advancing up the Orange and Alexandria Railroad. Instead of marching to the Valley, he, with two hundred and fifty men and two howitzers, advanced toward the railroad, for he suspected that the enemy harboured the design of establishing for Sheridan a base east of the Blue Ridge. The most valuable service which Mosby could render in this conjuncture was, he thought, to retard, and, if possible, to defeat this enterprise. The undertaking was great, and his means small; yet, by activity, and courage, and skill, he hoped to accomplish that result.

Before he reached Thoroughfare Gap he dispatched Ogg, a good scout and guide, to Bristoe Station in search of information, with orders to report to him that night at Gainesville. As is his custom, he was marching several miles in advance of the battalion, when he learned at the Gap that the enemy were encamped at Gainesville. Thereupon he sent an order to Mountjoy, who was in command of the battalion, to pass through the Gap, and camp at a designated farmhouse, where he knew forage could be obtained. Mosby then proceeded to Gainesville, feeling very uneasy about Ogg and his party, and, after reconnoitring the Federal camp, sought shelter from the rain in a neighbouring farmhouse. Just as Tommy Love was spreading their blankets on the floor, a volley of musketry was heard in the direction of the Federal camp. Mosby knew what it meant, but could not help laughing as he exclaimed, "Tom, that's Ogg." And, sure enough, it was. Ogg had executed his mission, and had come to report, according to orders, at Gainesville; had seen the camp-fires, and, supposing them to be Mosby's, had rode up to the picket, who inquired, "Who are you?"

"Ogg," was the reply. "Don't you know Ogg?"

Never having heard of that individual, the picket required him to dismount and advance.

"What company do you belong to?" inquired Ogg, never suspecting them to "be Yankees.

"Company 'E,'" was the reply.

"Oh yes," said he, "I thought you belonged to that d—d green company." And then insisted on being carried at once to "the colonel," which was agreed to. But when he advanced, greatly to his surprise, he found himself in the midst of blue-coats and bayonets. But Ogg's presence of mind did not in the least forsake him. He remained master of the situation, and the Yankees had not discovered who he was. In a peremptory manner, the Ranger again demanded to be taken to the colonel, for he had, he said, important information for him, but added that he could not walk, as he was extremely lame. As soon as he was again on horseback, he shouted to his comrades, "Break, boys!" and left the Yankees with the rapidity and brilliancy of a streak of lightning. A volley of musketry followed which did Ogg no harm, nor the Yankees any good.

Early the next morning, Mosby, proceeding on a reconnaissance, discovered that about four hundred cavalry had been sent up the railroad, whereupon he dispatched a courier to Mountjoy, with orders to meet him at Bristoe Station, his plan being to intercept and destroy them on their return. But before the courier arrived a heavy force had been interposed between Mountjoy and Bristoe Station, which induced that officer, instead of going thither, to march toward Markham, first passing through one of the gaps of the Bull Run Mountain. On the night of October 3rd a force of about eighteen hundred infantry camped at Salem, and, from their preparations, it was evident they had

Escape of Ogg from the Yankee camp

come to rebuild and reoccupy the road, for they brought with them trains loaded with construction material.

As he passed the Plains on his way to Salem, Mosby stopped and conferred with his trusty and intelligent friend, James William Foster, and on parting from him said, "Listen for me tomorrow." By three o'clock p.m., on the 4th, he had collected his men, and placed his howitzers in position on Stevenson's Hill, a little to the south of Salem, and about half a mile from the Federal camp. The Yankees, not expecting to be attacked, as soon as the guns opened on them fled toward Rectortown, where the rest of the command had gone that morning. First our sharp-shooters rushed into the deserted camp, soon followed by the mounted men. Mosby told them to help themselves to the plunder before them—tents, rubber-cloths, blankets, and well-filled knapsacks, all new—for I need not remind you that, according to his theory, plunder is the cohesive force in the Ranger service.

He followed the retreating enemy, leaving Chapman, with his squadron and the artillery, to hold the railroad and tear up the track. They were overtaken near Rectortown, and charged impetuously by Mountjoy. The Federal loss was fifty prisoners, including three officers, and several killed and wounded. Mosby's loss was two mortally wounded.

I will conclude the narrative of this fight with an anecdote, which strikingly illustrates the courageous spirit which animates the maidens of "Mosby's Confederacy." While the fight was progressing, Miss Anna Morgan, of Clover Hill, was standing in front of her father's residence, watching the smoke as it rose from the guns on Stevenson's Hill. While thus absorbed, three Confederate soldiers approached, coming from the direction of Salem. As they drew up their horses and saluted the lady, she said,

"You are going in the wrong direction, gentlemen." And, pointing to the scene of combat, added, "Every Southern soldier ought to be there."

If the Federals had heard this, they would say more than ever that the Southern women are the fiends that drive the men into battle.

While the fight was in progress at Salem, a force of twelve hundred Yankees, employed in rebuilding the railroad bridge over Goose Creek, near Piedmont, abandoned their work, and hastily fell back to Rectortown. They were soon joined by their discomfited brethren from Salem, and the night was spent in throwing up earthworks for their protection. In the afternoon of the following day Mosby again opened upon General Augur's force with his howitzers, driving them from their fortifications, and compelling them to take refuge in a deep gorge, through which the railroad at Rectortown passes. He continued the shelling until dark, and renewed it the next day, but without being able to dislodge them, for his guns could not be brought to bear upon either trains or men thus protected.

But the shelling had not been unproductive of results, for the Federal commander the ensuing day sent off a train of cars crowded with infantry toward Salem, which had been again occupied by a large force from Alexandria. It moved slowly, preceded by infantry skirmishers, who carefully removed all obstructions from the track, and protected by flankers, thrown out for the distance of two hundred yards on each side of the railroad, while, the howitzers in vain played on it. Each moment we expected to see the engine thrown from the track, but the cars rolled on slowly and surely until they arrived at the new Federal camp.

It will be remembered that Chapman, with his squadron re-enforced by the artillery, had been left at Salem at the close of the first day's fight. The ensuing morning a force marched up from the Plains to relay the railroad track and open communications with the force which had been cut off at Rectortown. But he opened upon them with his guns, and drove them back to their camps. The enemy, however, determined to strip the border of cavalry, in order to prevent

Mosby from interrupting their working parties, and on the 9th of October their entire force commenced moving up the railroad.

By this time Mosby had received from General Lee a reply to a dispatch announcing the occupation of the road by the enemy, his success at Salem, and his purpose to prevent, if possible, the reconstruction of the railroad. General Lee said, "Your success at Salem gives great satisfaction. Do all in your power to prevent the reconstruction of the road."

The intention of General Augur being now developed, which was not only to establish a base for Sheridan higher up in the Valley, but also to compel Mosby to retire to the district south of the road, which could not support him, and ultimately to drive him from the country, Mosby determined to adopt a counteracting policy. He first sent Captain William Chapman, with three companies (for the artillery had been sent to the mountain for safety), to operate for a few days south of the railroad, for the double purpose of deceiving Augur as to his whereabouts and purposes, and also to deter soldiers from straggling over the country, and then dispatched Richards with a squadron to pay his respects to General Sheridan, while he, with Mountjoy's company, remained to operate on the north of the railroad. Knowing that the only way to prevent the progress of the work on the road was to keep the force stirred up behind, on the night of the 9th of October he sent a detachment, under a lieutenant, to throw off the track a train of cars as it passed between Salem and the Plains. This duty was successfully performed, and many on board were killed and many severely wounded.

In retaliation, the Yankees resorted to the inhuman expedient of arresting prominent citizens of the Southern type residing in Fauquier and Alexandria, and making them ride on every train which ran on the Manassas Gap Railroad. In addition, some of the captured Rangers were sent along. But, with the spirit of an old Roman, Mosby declared, "If my wife and children were on board, I would still throw off the cars." This mode of attack worked like a charm. Most of the cavalry and infantry were taken from rebuilding, and employed in guarding the road, and in constructing blockhouses to enable them to do it the more effectually. As an additional protection, the enemy employed large parties of workmen to clear the margins of the road of wood, so as to afford the Partisans no shelter. But Mosby had now gained his object in putting this new force on the defensive, and he turned again to his warfare on Sheridan's communications. But, before this could be done, several events occurred which I will now relate. The same night that the cars were thrown from the track, Mosby, with about forty of his command, slept on the slope of a mountain near Glen Welby, about two miles from Salem, the beautiful residence of Major Richard H. Carter, now serving with General Lee's army.

After the Federals had fallen back to Rectortown, and the pursuing party had been drawn off, Mosby, with several of the men, proceeded to Glen Welby, where he passed the night. He dispatched Charley Grogan, however, to Rectortown, to ascertain, if possible, definite information of the position of the enemy, with orders to, proceed on foot. The soldier started, and when near the village he descried several objects on the brow of a hill which at first he took to be men, but a reconnaissance informed him of his mistake. The scout again began to advance with cautious step, when, to his surprise, a sentinel suddenly stepped from behind a tree, exclaiming,

"Is that you, captain?"

"Yes," promptly responded Grogan; "and why," he sternly added, "are you not walking your beat?". The soldier made no reply to this rebuke, but stepped off and began to pace his beat. Very soon the scout had drawn and cocked his pistol, and proceeded rapidly to the sentinel's side. He placed the pistol to his temple, and, in a whispered voice, told him that he was a prisoner, and if he raised the least alarm he would meet with instant death. The man appeared to be paralyzed with fear, and neither moved nor spoke, but without resistance accompanied his captor, who took him by the arm and led him down the hill. The picket to which the sentinel belonged was nearby, as was disclosed by their fire and the sound of their voices. Arrived at the base of the hill, Grogan turned to his prisoner and said,

"I am Mosby, and you will do well not to give me any trouble."

The man bowed his head in token of submission, and was conducted to the stable-loft at Glen Welby, where Mosby was passing the night, who quickly extracted from him the desired information. Hurrah for Charley Grogan!

Since General Augur had taken up a position at Rectortown, his cavalry had foraged almost exclusively on the adjoining country. Every corn-house and cornfield in a large area were visited almost daily, and it was only by secreting small quantities of grain in different places that families were enabled to preserve food for themselves and the little stock they had been able to retain. Among the farms most frequently visited by these foragers was Glen Welby, particularly obnoxious because of the entertainment which Mosby's men was known ever to receive beneath its hospitable roof.

Early the next morning, the watchful eye of Colonel Mosby discovered a column of one hundred and fifty of the enemy's cavalry approaching from the direction of Rectortown, the residence of Major Carter. It soon appeared that they were in search of hay, which they tied up in large bundles and placed across their horses. He had caught the Yankees *flagrante delicto,* and he meant to make them pay for it. As the column passed out of the Glen Welby farm through a narrow lane formed by high stone fences, Lieutenant Grogan, with twenty men, charged and was soon in the midst of the surprised and dismayed foragers, pouring into them a destructive fire from their revolvers. At this time Mosby struck the column at another point, and made the route complete. The flight was continued some distance before the Federals recovered from their dismay. Then they rallied, but not until Grogan had drawn off his party in safety. But this farce threatened to end in a tragedy, for soon Colonel Gallop, at the head of his regiment, made his appearance on the scene.

Finding one of his men killed, and a good many lying wounded on the road and in the adjoining field, while others were coming in who had fled to the wood, and learning that it had been all produced by a, mere squad of Mosby's men, he was greatly enraged, and determined that some one should suffer. And whom do you suppose were selected as the victims to be immolated by the wrathful officer? Mosby's men? No. Men capable of bearing arms against them? No. But a houseful of helpless women and a large family of children. Upon them he determined to take vengeance for this ordinary and lawful belligerent act. In accordance with this purpose, Colonel Gallop, with his command, hastened to Glen Welby, in full view of which the fight, if such it can be called, had taken place. Very soon the house was surrounded, sentinels thrown out on every side, while a portion of the regiment dismounted, and, with their commander, entered the house. They were met at the door by Mrs. Carter and her daughter, Mrs. Scott, whose husband, Major R. Taylor Scott, was likewise on duty with Lee's army. The officer's salutation was,

"We have come for the purpose of burning this house, and every building attached to the ground."

Mrs. Carter inquired the cause. Colonel Gallop replied,

"We have just been attacked by a party of Mosby's cut-throats on this place, and I have no doubt you had them concealed somewhere near by, and gave them information."

The ladies assured him that they knew nothing of Colonel Mosby's movements, and that the first knowledge they had had of the presence of his men was the firing of which he complained.

But Colonel Gallop refused to credit a word they uttered, and said,

"I know, madam, you are in the habit of harbouring those miserable cut-throats, and you shall suffer for it."

He immediately ordered a detail to be made to execute his threat to fire the buildings. This was a most trying moment. Mrs. Carter had been recently extremely ill, and was scarcely convalescent. Surrounded by her daughters, a niece, one son—a mere boy, and a tender nursling—she saw the incendiaries about to apply the torch to her home, which was a large and beautiful building, comfortably and tastefully furnished, and had been to herself and family for many years the abode of comfort and happiness. In a few moments she was to witness its total destruction, and herself and family were to be turned out without a shelter. Yet even in this helpless and forlorn situation her fortitude did not desert her. She bore herself with such dignity, resignation, and firmness, that even the rude natures around her were softened by compassion. The simple request was made that time should be allowed to remove some clothing. Colonel Gallop replied, "You may have five minutes!"

A small quantity of clothing was accordingly brought out into the yard, but was seized and carried off by the soldiers in the presence of the officers, under the pretext of searching for something contra-

MRS SCOTT AND HER BOY SAVING THE HOUSE FROM THE FLAMES

band. Soon the family, Mrs. Scott and her little son excepted, left the house condemned to the flames, the children, in extreme terror, hiding themselves in the fields and orchard, while Mrs. Carter started in search of her infant, who, then sick and but imperfectly clothed, was exposed to the raw autumnal air. At this time occurred a scene of the most tragic interest, which would defy the pen even of *Walter* Scott, fully to depict—Mrs. Scott, as heroic as she is gentle and beautiful, taking her little boy by the hand, seated herself in one of the parlours, saying,

"Well, my son, if they will burn this dear old home, we will perish in the flames."

This spectacle was too much even for the flinty hearts of the soldiers. Soon one of them, supposed to be a corporal, was seen to approach his commander, and apparently to expostulate with him. Just then Colonel Gallop inquired for Mrs. Carter, who was summoned from the field, and, in company with her daughter Sophie, known as "The Lily" among the Rangers, approached the officer, who, in a very rough and unfeeling manner, began to address her; but Miss Sophie immediately interposed, saying,

"If I had known you had called for my mother to insult her, she should not have been sent for."

The colonel, thus rebuked, concluded by saying,

"I have determined, madam, to spare your house this time; but if I ever catch or hear of one of these cutthroats being here again, nothing shall save the house or any building on the place."

To this Miss Sophie replied,

"We can not make any promise of the kind; and if we did, it would be impossible for us to keep it, for, when soldiers come, we can not, if we would, order them away."

The next day, with Mountjoy's company, Colonel Mosby was stationed in the woods between Salem and the Plains. With thirteen men, he rode within sight of the latter place, where there was a camp of Yankees. About forty or fifty cavalry came in pursuit of him. They did not venture to come to close quarters, but dismounted, and used their carbines from behind a stone fence. Willie Mosby was sent for Mountjoy, while the colonel, in order to draw the enemy farther out, fell slowly back and disappeared in a wood. The stratagem succeeded, and the Federal charged, supposing he had fled. But suddenly he burst upon them. Of all things, a Yankee fears an ambuscade the most, and accordingly they wheeled and rapidly retreated, followed by Mosby and his party. In the pursuit he passed two of the Federal troopers, one of whom shot his horse in the hip, causing it to fall upon him. Thus prostrate, he was surrounded by the enemy. His men, perceiving that they had lost their leader, returned and extricated him from the wounded animal. The Yankees in the mean time had received reenforcements, but were charged and dispersed by Mountjoy, leaving six of their number killed and wounded. In consequence of this fall Mosby is quite lame, and is still unable to wear a boot.

Chapter 42: "The Greenback Raid"

Clover Hill, November 4th, 1864.

Dear Percy,—We will now accompany Mosby to the Valley on what is known in the command as the "Greenback Raid," undertaken in pursuance of the policy which I indicated in my last letter, With eighty-four men Mosby started on the 13th of October from Hooper's Shop, and soon met Henry Heaton, who had been sent on a scout to the Valley, to get information about the Baltimore and Ohio Railroad. The command under Mountjoy was sent to Snickersville, while Mosby went to Upperville to hear the result of Richards's trip to Newtown, and to issue farther orders. He was informed that Richards had attacked an ambulance with an escort of thirty men, and had killed and wounded twelve, captured an equal number, and had brought off twenty-eight horses. Among the articles captured in the ambulance were many important official papers and two fine maps, one of the country along the Orange and Alexandria Railroad as far as the Rappahannock River, and one of the Manassas Gap Railroad as far as Strasburg. These had been destined for General Sheridan, and threw additional light on the use which the federal government proposed to make of one or both of these roads.

From Upperville Mosby went to join the command at Snickersville, and that night crossed the Shenandoah. The next day, from a position on the Valley Turnpike, he captured fifteen men and horses, and then determined to intercept a train of cars on the Baltimore and Ohio Railroad. The point selected to make this attempt was a deep cut a little west of Brown's Crossing, and about a quarter of a mile from Duffield Depot, so that the passengers might sustain no injury from the sudden stoppage of the cars—a precaution which a cruel nature would not have taken.

Harry Hatcher, with a detail of fifteen men, was then ordered to tear up the rails, and was very particular to destroy both tracks, for he was not unmindful of the mortifying experience of Captain Dolly, or "Southdown," as the men called him after that exploit. As soon as the work was done, Mosby, leaving a small guard with the horses, marched the command to the railroad, and, wrapping his blanket around him, laid his head in the lap of one of the men, and slept soundly, for he was much exhausted, having been almost constantly in the saddle since his return to his command.

Oh, sleep! it is a gentle thing
Beloved from pole to pole;
To Mary, Queen, the praise be given,
She sent the gentle sleep from heaven,
That slid into his soul.

At two o'clock p.m. he was roused by the whistle, followed by the explosion of the boiler. The men were astounded. But, knowing that a prompt attack was the way to prevent resistance, Mosby pushed the men down the embankment as rapidly as possible. Roused from their bewilderment, they sprang into the cars, where a wild scene of confusion was presented. The ladies, of whom there were a good number, screamed with terror, while the male passengers were initiated in the operation of being "gone through."

As soon as the cars were boarded, Jim Wiltshire, who is the luckiest dog on earth with the ladies, had a romantic adventure, which may, some of these days, lead to serious consequences. A young lady, of remarkable beauty, and dressed in mourning, with a very agitated manner called to him,

"Oh, captain, protect me, for I am a Mason's daughter!"

The Ranger, not exactly comprehending the purport of her language, gallantly replied, "And I, miss, am a Mason's son. Be not alarmed."

Thus assured, she approached and laid her hand upon his arm, still violently agitated.

At this moment several of her fellow-passengers gathered around her. As they did so she fainted, and would have fallen but for the supporting arm of her new acquaintance, who laid the maiden's inanimate form softly upon one of the seats, and then quietly withdrew.

As soon as the passengers had gathered on the railroad bank, and the ladies were assured of their personal safety, their spirits revived, and they appeared to enjoy the adventure. It was, indeed, a romantic situation, to be stopped amid those wild scenes by starlight, by the band of the guerrilla chief, Jack Mosby.

When the cars came to be burned, there was one found to be freighted with German emigrants, who, not understanding a word of English, made no motion to leave their seats when ordered to do so.

"They don't understand English," said Puryear; "perhaps they understand fire," and with these words he threw a parcel of lighted *New York Heralds* into the car. Out the Dutch tumbled—men, women, and children—amid a chorus of outlandish curses.

During this scene of agitation and confusion, Mosby sat on his horse, conversing freely with the passengers. He remarked to one of them,

"General Stevenson will not guard the railroad, and I am determined to make him perform his duty." Of a Dutch lieutenant, who had just been commissioned, and was on his way to his regiment, he inquired,

"Why did you come to fight us?"

"Only to learn your tactics," he replied.

A little while after, the lieutenant came to Mosby with the complaint that someone had taken his boots from him.

"Oh," said he, laughing, "that is only an elementary lesson in our tactics."

A lady, hysterical with fright, threw her arms about Munro Heiskell's neck, and begged him to inform Colonel Mosby that her husband was a Mason. When the momentous fact was communicated, the partisan chief quietly replied, "Well, tell her I can't help it."

Billings Steele approached one of the passengers for the purpose of "going through him."

"Why, Billings "said he, "I am your brother; besides, they have robbed me twice already."

"The Greenback Raid"

The passengers were standing on the bank, with the light of the burning cars thrown over them, when one of the guerrillas rode along, holding up a handsome carpet sack, and calling for the owner. After a slight pause, an old gentleman bustled out of the crowd and claimed the property, handing up the key to substantiate his title. The Ranger very quietly put the key in his pocket and rode off. As he did so, some one in the crowd, with a gay laugh, exclaimed, "Sold again!" and right cheap did the old gentleman look.

In the midst of the conflagration, Charlie Dear and West Aldridge approached Colonel Mosby with the information that they had taken from the two paymasters a tin box and a satchel filled with greenbacks. This was a splendid prize, and it was immediately sent off in charge of a party under command of Lieutenant Grogan.

The only casualty was the death of a Federal officer, who, as he attempted to escape from the cars, was killed by John Hearn. The prisoners captured were Major Moore and Major Ruggles, the paymasters before mentioned, a Prussian officer in Federal uniform, two lieutenants, and six privates.

On the return march Mosby was informed by a soldier whom he met that Captain Blazer was encamped near Cabletown. He turned his course in that direction, and at sunrise charged into the camp, but Blazer had left just two hours before, and his fires were still burning brightly.

The next day, at a sequestered spot near Bloomfield, the greenbacks were counted and divided by Beattie, Hall, Grogan, and Briscoe, who had been appointed by Mosby to perform that duty. The amount captured being $168,000 dollars, each man received something over two thousand. When the names of the parties entitled to the prize-money were read out, Colonel Mosby came forward and ordered his name to be struck from the list. Against this act of self-denial the men loudly protested, but to no purpose, for he is inexorable in his determination not to partake of the rich spoil which is daily captured by his command.

This is a great sum to be expended among the citizens of "Mosby's Confederacy," for into their hands it will all ultimately pass, and is one of the advantages conferred upon them by having in their midst the Partisan Battalion.

I will now close my account of the Greenback Raid with a copy of General Lee's dispatch to the Secretary of War in relation to it:

Headquarters, October 17th, 1864.
Hon. Secretary of War: "On the 14th Colonel Mosby struck the Baltimore and Ohio Railroad at Duffield Station, and destroyed a United States mail train, consisting of a locomotive and ten cars, securing twenty prisoners, and fifteen horses. Among the prisoners were two Yankee paymasters, with one hundred and sixty-eight thousand dollars in government bonds.

(Signed),   R. E. Lee, General.

As Mosby was returning from the Greenback Raid, Colonel Gansevoort, of the Federal Army, proceeded to Emory's, on the Cobbler Mountain, under the guidance of a deserter from the battalion, as is believed, and captured the four pieces of artillery which had been deposited there for safety. At the same time Sergeant Babcock, who was in charge of the pieces, and several others, were made prisoners.

The day before Mosby started on the Greenback Raid, he ordered Phil and Fred Smith to dart across the railroad, and carry instructions to Captain Chapman to transfer his command to the north side of the railroad, for the purpose of striking the Baltimore and Ohio Railroad at some point in Maryland. But Phil Smith found it to be too heavily guarded to make darting across an easy matter, and therefore had recourse to stratagem to effect his purpose. Taking off his coat, his checked shirt and blue pantaloons had a Yankee-like appearance. He then cautiously approached the road, but, to his surprise, struck it just where two sentinels were seated around their low watch-fire. He addressed them politely, and was allowed to pass, until, getting out of the range of their guns, he set spurs to his horse, and proceeded to deliver the colonel's order.

During the execution of the order Chapman discovered a strong guard on the road, whom he charged, wounding several of them, and capturing quite a number. He then marched up the railroad, picking up the sentries which were strung along it, until he was interrupted by the arrival of a car-load of soldiers, and compelled to move off. The next morning about dawn he started from his camp in Loudoun, and marched by private roads to White's Ford of the Potomac, where an abundance of game was found. Canal-boats were passing one after another in quick succession, freighted, many of them, with supplies for Sheridan's army. Very soon eight or ten of these boats were in a blaze, and the horses by which they were drawn were sent back to Bloomfield. Chapman's objective point being Adamstown, he could not tarry long on the canal, for a party of Keys's race-riders had seen him cross the river, and had posted off to spread the alarm among the hostile camps within reach. There was an encampment of Delaware troops within a distance of seven miles. There were the troops at Point of Rocks, Berlin, and Harper's Ferry, to say nothing of Keys's myrmidons, one hundred and forty of whom were camped right at Adamstown.

When the squadron reached its objective point, Chapman was disappointed to hear that, on account of the capture of the cars by Mosby, no train would come from Harper's Ferry that day, and the men, to soothe their disappointment, were allowed to plunder two store houses. Meanwhile Captain Keys drew up the Loudoun Rangers in battle array within half a mile of the scene, and awaited the moral effect of his presence on the rebels. The squadron set out to return to Virginia, followed by Captain Keys at the respectful distance of five hundred yards, who occasionally fired a shot to let the Rangers know that he was in pursuit. The Reverend Sam Chapman, who brought up the rear, proposed a fight; but his brother said, "Sam, I haven't time to stop and go off on a fox-hunt after Keys." But instead, he determined to set a trap for the fox. So off the squadron started at a rapid rate, as if anxious to effect its escape.

The Loudoun Rangers were delighted at this evidence of demoralisation, and their military ardour rose to a high pitch. They had been many years in the service, and had never seen any body run from them before. As Chapman entered a lane, down they came, riding and yelling upon him, when, by a sudden counter-march, he turned fiercely upon his pursuers. The Virginia Yankees now found they had made a terrible mistake, and began to scatter like a flock of wild turkeys, scrambling over fences and running like mad to the woods. They were so well mounted, however, that only some four or five were killed, and twelve or fifteen taken prisoners. But Chapman quickly called off his dogs of war, for the prisoners informed him that Keys had been sent to delay his march by skirmishes until the fords of the river could be occupied and the canal bridges destroyed—information which proved to be correct, for when he reached a bridge below the Point of Rocks he found a detachment of infantry employed in tearing it up and throwing the timber into the canal; but a volley from the partisans dispersed this party. The bridge was relaid, and the squadron, with its gallant commander, was soon safe again in Old Virginia. *Fortune always favours the brave,* for the Yankees had put in ambush two hundred infantry at the ford next above the one where the crossing was effected. About nightfall the command passed through Leesburg, and were received with demonstrations of welcome. Hurrah for William Chapman!

CHAPTER 43: JOHN ORRICK'S ADVENTURES

Upper Fauquier, November 7th, 1864.

Dear Percy,—Today I will introduce to you John Orrick, a volunteer from Alabama, who, after being captured by the Federals on the retreat from Gettysburg, effected his escape and made his way to Mosby. He is a good soldier, is cool and brave, and, being well acquainted in Maryland, is often employed by his commander to gain information from that side of the Potomac. His adventurous expeditions, some of which I am about to relate, will remind you of Wat Bowie, and will serve to expose to your view still farther this aspect of Partisan life. Soon after he joined the command, with four comrades he crossed the Potomac below Leesburg, and proceeded through the country to a wood near Middlebrook,, where the party passed the night.

The next morning Orrick stationed himself on the road side to look out for Yankees. He had not been long in that position before a traveller in citizens' clothes, but riding an army saddle and wearing large brass spurs, passed. The man was halted and ordered to surrender, which he did promptly. He was very much frightened, and pleaded to be released because he was a Democrat. But Orrick told him that he did not see much difference between a War Democrat and a Republican, and took from him a good horse and a fine pair of pistols, though it turned out that there was no harm in the man, for he was only a sutler's clerk bound for Frederick City.

That night the Rangers took from the poor clerk a blue jacket which he carried with him, and turned him loose, assured that the Federal Army would gain but little strength from War Democrats of that pattern.

The next day the party took up a position in the vicinity of Darnestown, where they captured three soldiers, and that night proceeded toward Rockville, near which place they concealed themselves in a body of pines.

The succeeding morning Orrick and Riley, dressed in blue jackets, started for the house of old man Spates to get something to eat. As they passed through a meadow they encountered a party of negroes at work. The scouts stopped and inquired of them if they had seen any Rebs about. One of the negroes promptly replied, "Oh yes, massa, we just saw four of dem down in de pines." Orrick replied, "We have just caught six," and then added, "If you see any more of them, come to camp, for we have plenty of coffee and sugar."

The two cavaliers then rode to the house, where they found three gentlemen, one of whom was a minister. At their request a snack was set before them, and soon the disguised Confederates fell into conversation with their entertainers, to whom they represented themselves as soldiers from Chicago. At length one of the company mentioned the name of Orrick, saying that at that time he was scouting in the neighbourhood, and inquired if they had fallen in with him. Orrick then called for a description of himself, which was very correctly given, and added that it would be a good thing for the Reb not to fall in with his party, though it would be a good thing for the camp at Seneca if he were caught. Having finished their meal, the two strangers arose, and Orrick in a very polite manner introduced himself to the company. Their astonishment, of course, was very great, and the only compensation which the scouts demanded for the information which had been volunteered about their presence in the country was a plenty of provisions for their friends in the woods.

As they walked out on the porch, they beheld at the distance of half a mile a cloud of dust, and, bidding their entertainers goodbye, put spurs to their horses and were soon out of sight on their way to rejoin their companions. After some farther adventures, which resulted in the capture of several prisoners, the Rangers started for Howard County, from which place Orrick concluded to make a trip to Baltimore City, which was distant from the point at which they had stopped about eighteen miles.

So, the following morning, dressed in a suit of citizens' clothes which he had borrowed, he started for the city, which he reached without adventure, and where he remained a day and night. While there he gathered much useful information, and purchased gray cloth for a uniform and other articles useful to the Ranger service.

When he was about five miles from Baltimore, on his return, he was stopped by six soldiers, who, after many questions, which he answered to their satisfaction, allowed him to drive on.

That night the Rangers started for Montgomery County by a pale moonlight. As they were riding through a field they passed the frame of a house filled with hay, around which were a number of horses engaged in eating. Orrick was in front, and rode up to them under the belief that they were colts, but soon discovered about twenty of the blue-coats asleep on the ground. He wheeled his horse, but in so doing rode over a plank, the sound of which aroused the sleeping soldiers, who at once sprang to their feet and began a pursuit. But the fugitives found no difficulty in eluding their pursuers, and, after a rapid ride of five miles, allowed their horses to relapse into a slow pace. Soon, however, the sound of hoofs from be. hind was heard, and knowing from what cause it proceeded, they turned into a wood until the Yankees had charged by, and then determined, as they were travelling in the same direction, to act as rear-guard to their pursuers.

They had not proceeded far before they came upon a Yank engaged in adjusting the girths to his saddle. They captured the soldier, who proved to be a good-humoured fellow, for, as he rode off with his captors, he said,

"Well, boys, you are a rare set of fellows. Is your colonel along? for of all men I desire most to see him."

The Rangers answered his question, and, in return, were informed that his party had been sent to watch the house of a citizen who was suspected of being a Southern sympathizer.

The scouts then proceeded to a wood near Darnestown, and the next morning Orrick, leaving his co-mates, went to the house of a citizen in search of information. While engaged in conversation with the young ladies of the family, a knock was heard at the door. The soldier ran into an adjoining room, and mounted the staircase with which it communicated, followed by one of the young ladies. There was an old-fashioned chest in one of the rooms, in which he was hastily concealed, and a large box then placed on the lid. After Orrick had laid there for half an hour, and had become much cramped in his close quarters, he determined rather to risk the chance of capture than to continue in so uncomfortable a position. With a spring he burst open with a loud noise the lid of the chest, and, drawing his revolver, advanced to the head of the stairs, determined there to await his fate, fully assured that in that position he would be a match for several assailants. But instead of the Yankees there approached a lady, who informed him that all danger was past, for that the Federal soldiers, from whom the knock at the door had proceeded, had left the house without being aware of his presence. By an early hour the next day the Rangers had recrossed the Potomac with the information which they had been sent to obtain.

Soon after the Greenback Raid, Mosby directed Orrick to go to Frederick City, and ascertain the force of the enemy at that point, and the situation of their camps. Accompanied by Robinson, of Maryland, he crossed the Potomac at White's Ford, and having procured a suit of citizen's clothes, together with a buggy and horse, from a friend, he started for the camp. As he passed through the little town of Urbana he encountered two Federal soldiers, who allowed him to proceed unmolested; but he had not gone more than a mile when one of them, having had his suspicions aroused, no doubt, overtook him, and demanded of Orrick his place of residence.

"Rocksville," promptly responded the scout, and, in his turn, inquired the news of the day.

The soldier replied, "Sheridan is giving Early h—ll."

Orrick said, "That's right; I wish he would kill them all."

In this way the soldiers chatted until they reached the Monocacy Junction, a point three miles distant from Frederick City, and where there was quite a camp of soldiers. Orrick desired to ascertain the strength of this, but was at a loss to know how to accomplish this object. He drew up his horse, therefore, near the picket, who approached him and demanded what he wanted. The scout replied that he was waiting for the cars to pass, as his horse was wild, and then occupied himself with counting the tents, which he found to be twenty-six in number. Allowing six men to a tent, the inference was drawn that a force of one hundred and fifty-six Yankees was stationed at this point. Possessed of this information, he drove to Frederick City, and stopped at the City Hotel, where he registered himself as William Jones, Montgomery County, Maryland.

He had scarcely taken his seat in the public room before a stranger, who looked, Orrick thought, very much like a detective, walked up to the register, and, after reading the list of fresh arrivals, inquired of the clerk if William Jones was in. Orrick thought certainly that his time had come, and that the Yankees would give him a hempen collar. He determined, however, to put on a bold face; so he walked to the desk, and informed the stranger that he was William Jones, who inquired if he had brought his "hounds" with him, Orrick replied, "You have mistaken your man,"

The stranger, having explained to him that he was expecting his hounds to be sent to him by a gentleman of that name, bowed and retired. That evening the Ranger visited several of his lady friends who resided in the town, and agreed to drive with one of them the next day on the roads on which the troops were encamped. By this drive he possessed himself of the information he was sent to acquire. The day following Orrick attended a large M'Clellan mass meeting, and, in the garb of a citizen, passed in the crowd for a first-rate Democrat. His mission being accomplished, he proceeded to rejoin Robinson, and, resuming his own clothes, the two soldiers started for the river, which they did not reach, however, without several farther adventures with the Yankees, such as were ever recurring with Mosby's men on the other side of the river.

Chapter 44: Capture of General Duffie and Other Exploits.

Upper Fauquier, November 10th, 1864.

Dear Percy,—-In obedience to his policy of extending to the people in whose midst he was waging war all the protection in his power, as far as it was compatible with the higher policy of co-operating with the main armies, Mosby ordered Captain William Chapman, with his squadron, to proceed to Piedmont, to check the ravages of the enemy in that vicinity. The Yankees had a habit of chasing scouts who ventured too near their camp, and accordingly Captain Chapman dispatched Shacklett and an Irishman down Crooked Run to draw them out. The stratagem succeeded. Two squadrons came out from camp. Shacklett escaped, but Pat, who was poorly mounted, was gobbled up. The Yankees then devoted their energies to plundering. Mrs. Fletcher's house was convenient, and they helped themselves liberally to hay first, and then to calves, pigs, sheep, chickens, turkeys, geese, apples, and what not.

The sun had just set when they turned their horses' heads toward camp, as jolly as may be. But, alas for human happiness! a lion had stolen out and concealed himself in their path. Captain William Chapman, from a height, had watched them as they passed, and, while they were busy at Mrs. Fletcher's, had, with his squadron, descended a ravine to an advantageous position on the road between them and their camp. It was nearly dark when they came up. They were charged home with a yell. Sam Chapman, with his company, galloped along their flanks, pistoling them with impunity, while Captain William Chapman crowded their front, now turned to rear, more quickly than it could have possibly been done by any other process. Thus jammed up, seven of the Yankees were killed at that place, and twelve wounded. At length they broke through all obstacles, the Rangers pressing and shooting them at every jump. Night alone prevented the capture or destruction of the whole party. As it was, not less than forty were killed and wounded, and twenty-nine taken prisoners.

The slaughter was so great that a complaint was lodged with the colonel of the regiment that prisoners had been shot after surrender, whereupon he addressed a communication to Mosby, inquiring into it, but was assured there was no truth in the story.

One of Chapman's men, Joe Kennally, from the valley, had, without assistance, taken two prisoners, and, amid the darkness, was conducting them to his command. Seizing a moment when his attention was relaxed, they attacked him, and it was only by the exertion of great courage and strength that he saved his own life and killed both of his assailants.

With Companies "A," "B," and "D," Mosby marched to Fairfax, with the purpose of attacking a large wagon-train near Fairfax Station, but failed to do it, the enemy having been notified of his approach. He then made a demonstration on a fort near Anandale, capturing some pickets, and sent Mountjoy to make a strike near Falls Church, with orders afterward to join him in Loudoun, whither he proceeded. Mountjoy created a great commotion at Falls Church, and returned bringing with him twelve prisoners and horses. Meanwhile Mosby's presence in Fairfax had been telegraphed to General Augur, and he sent his cavalry in pursuit of him, but, as the Yankees marched down to Fairfax, Mosby marched up to Loudoun. Without delay he dispatched Richards, with a squadron, to operate near Winchester, while he, with Mountjoy's company, marched toward Bunker Hill, with the intention of attacking a wagon-train, but found it too heavily guarded. Mosby then returned to Fauquier, and collected the battalion for the purpose of striking a heavy blow at Sheridan's communications.

Camping on the Valley Turnpike, within a few of Bunker Hill, he and Captain Chapman went out to reconnoitre the road, and soon beheld an ambulance coming down, with an escort of twenty cavalry. Chapman was sent, with twelve men, to charge the escort in the rear, while Grogan, with another detachment, was directed to charge in front. About that time a large wagon-train made its appearance, coming from the direction of Martinsburg, which the ambulance and. escort made a strenuous exertion to reach. But Chapman was too quick for them, and overtook the ambulance within two hundred yards of the train. As the train hove in sight, Mosby advanced his command of three hundred and seventy-five men, and, as he galloped toward the turnpike, met Boyd Smith and John Dixon escorting their captives to the rear.

"Colonel, here's your general," said Boyd Smith.

"Who are you?" said Mosby, addressing the captive.

"General Duffie," replied the stranger.

"Take him to the rear," said Mosby, and passed on to attack the train. Not having discovered the overwhelming force which guarded it, he sent Chapman and Mountjoy, with their squadrons, to attack it in front, while he, with Richards's squadron, would attack it in rear. The two officers easily drove the three hundred Federal cavalry in advance back upon the infantry, who, in their turn, drove back the Rangers. Mosby, seeing his men retreating in confusion, rode rapidly up to rally and reform them, but, as he did so, discovered, in addition to the enemy's cavalry and infantry, two pieces of artillery. The guns opened upon him, and he at once drew off, hoping to be followed by the Federal cavalry, which had again advanced. But this hope was disappointed, for the train had in charge a great sum of money, and Colonel Currie, in command of the escort, had been ordered not to make any attacks.

General Duffie occupied a very unpleasant position. When at the head of his brigade in the streets of Paris, he had ordered his men to shoot all prisoners taken from Mosby's command. Sergeant Magner, of Company "D," had fallen into his hands, and was on the point of being executed, in obedience to these bloody instructions, when a citizen testified that he belonged to the 6th Virginia Cavalry— an assertion which carried with it the stronger probability, as he had once belonged to that regiment, and still had about him papers which showed his connection with it. By this device Magner was saved, and was sent as a prisoner of war to Harper's Ferry, from which place he managed to make his escape. Such was General Duffie's antecedents when he found himself in the hands of Mosby. The hanging at Front Royal was fresh in the memory, and the Rangers clamoured for his blood, for the manes of Anderson and Overby had never been avenged. The Southern newspapers also had violently urged retaliation upon ruthless officers whenever they might be captured. But Mosby had resolved to pursue another course, and General Duffie was spared, for what cared he for the declamations of newspaper editors or the angry counsels of his own soldiers?

Richards was dispatched with his squadron to intercept a scouting-party of about one hundred Yankees, who had been in the habit of coming out from the Plains toward Middleburg. He watched for them all day on one road, but, failing to post a vedette on a parallel road, let the opportunity slip of catching them. "Southdown" again!

Chapman, with his squadron, was sent to look after foraging parties which Sheridan was in the habit of sending out in the neighbourhood of White Post and Front Royal, while Mosby, with Companies "D" and "F," proceeded to the vicinity of Sheridan's army, which was then lying between Newtown and Winchester. But his presence was discovered, and he was compelled to withdraw. He then determined in person to look after the foragers, and soon saw a train of wagons, escorted by cavalry and infantry, coming down the road. Mosby halted his command, and went forward to reconnoitre, and fell in with Chapman, who was likewise hovering about the wagons, ready to pounce upon them. Chapman was sent behind the wagons to ascertain the strength of the guard, and soon reported that, if Mosby would agree, he could capture the entire party. Consent was given; and Chapman, deploying his men so as to exaggerate his force, accomplished his purpose without firing a shot.

Meanwhile Lieutenant Frank Turner, with Company "F," had been over about Newtown, and had captured a good many prisoners. Mosby then returned to Fauquier, and after a few days went back to the valley on a trip to Martinsburg, which failed of results on account of being misled by the guide. Captain Chapman also made several raids to Warren County with his usual success, while Richards and Frank Turner, with small detachments, operated frequently on the Valley Turnpike near Newtown. On one of these occasions Richards assumed the character of a provost-guard. All small parties were required to exhibit their passes, none of which would satisfy the scruples of that military constable. He met a small band of horsemen as a command of infantry was in the act of passing. He held them in conversation till the infantry were out of sight, and then, in a tone of authority, demanded their passes. The spokesman of the party produced one signed by Sheridan himself, but was told that it was not sufficient. "The d—l!" replied the Yankee. "Things have come to a high pass when a man can't travel this road on General Sheridan's authority."

"And yet," said Richards, "that is the exact condition of things. You will have to go with me." This was a pretty game for a small party to play at, but hazardous in the midst of a Yankee camp.

About the last of October, when General Augur was preparing to abandon the Manassas Gap Railroad, a detachment of the 8th Illinois Cavalry was sent from Rectortown in the direction of Hatcher's Mill, which, you will remember, is on the Little River Turnpike, between Middleburg and Upperville. With one hundred and seven men, Captain Frankland followed their trail for a short distance, and then, with one man, pursued rapidly, leaving Lieutenant Wren with the column to move on at a slower pace. Upon reaching Hatcher's Mill, the Yankees marched in the direction of Upperville, followed by Frankland, till he fell in with Mosby and Hatcher. He was at once ordered to return to the command, and throw himself between the Yankees and their camp, Mosby adding, "I want you to make it a second Dranesville. I will do the scouting, and keep you informed of the enemy's movements."

From Upperville, the detachment from the 8th Illinois headed toward Rectortown, and marched across the stretch of level pasture-land in which the house of Mr. Henry Dulaney is situated, which enabled Frankland, without difficulty, to occupy a position in their front. But, instead of falling back and forming an ambuscade, as had been done at the second Dranesville, Captain Frankland deliberated whether he should not make the attack in open field, for the Yankees had now reached the Dulaney house. At this conjuncture, Captain Wright James and Lieutenant Hatcher came from Mosby with a repetition of his order. But, having taken counsel with Grogan and Wren, who are always ready for a fight, as to the probability of a victorious result, Captain Frankland assumed the responsibility of engaging the enemy in the open field. Hatcher, offended with this determination, said he would have nothing to do with the affair, and returned to Mosby; but Captain James, who is a fighting quartermaster, embraced the opportunity of uniting in the charge.

The following dispositions for the fight were made. Grogan, with thirty men, was sent around on the right to make a flank attack, while Frankland, with Wren's portion of the command, charged in front. But the combination failed. The two parties struck alternately, and were alternately driven off.

The Federal loss was slight, but that of the battalion was severe— four prisoners and seven wounded, of whom four died—Carrington, Davis, Gulick, and Atkins.

Atkins had but recently come from Ireland, and, in consequence, had been with us but a short time, yet long enough to have earned, with all who knew him, the reputation of a gentleman and a brave soldier.

During the occupation of the Manassas Gap Railroad by Federal troops, the Blue Ridge alone separated them from the army in the Valley, and communication between their respective commanders was maintained by means of small detachments of cavalry. But the result was uncertain, and the means hazardous. On one occasion a party of twenty Yankees going toward the valley were captured in Ashby's Gap by eight of Mosby's men, and a dispatch in cipher for General Sheridan taken from them. This closes the operations during the month of October.

Chapter 45: Retaliation

Gordonsdale, near the Plains, November 25th, 1864.

Dear Percy,—I write this letter from the residence of Dr. Robert E. Peyton, who but recently has been relieved from the painful duress to which he and certain other prominent gentlemen in this neighbourhood have been subjected by the enemy, in consequence of Mosby's attack on the trains which they attempted to run on the Manassas Gap Railroad, and to which I have alluded in a previous letter. Gordonsdale is one of the most beautiful residences I have seen in Fauquier, both on account of the romantic scenery by which it is surrounded, and the taste displayed in its adornment, for it has been in possession of the doctor's family since the first settlement of the country.

After the occupation of the Manassas Gap Railroad for one month. General Augur withdrew his forces, convinced, as it would appear, that, as long as the "Guerrilla Mosby" remained in the country, he could not, by means of it, establish a base for General Sheridan in the Upper Valley.

During this period in which Mosby was enveloped in the enemies' lines, he killed and captured six hundred of their number, with a loss to himself of only thirty men, one of the most brilliant results to be found in the domain of military history when the disproportion of forces is taken into consideration, and the fact that an important combination of the enemy was defeated by it.

Before the road was abandoned, the rails were torn up and sent to Harper's Ferry, Mosby Harassing the baffled and retreating foe at every point until the work of destruction had progressed as far as Manassas.

Early in November, Captain A. E. Richards, with ten men, was sent to the rear of Sheridan's army, then lying between Middletown and Strasburg. From a position near the turnpike, in the course of the day he captured fifteen prisoners, among whom were Captain Brewster, of Custer's staff, and his brother, a lawyer, bound on a canvassing expedition to the army in the interest of General M'Clellan. There were also among the prisoners a newsboy and a drummer-boy. The newsboy had often before been captured by Richards, but had always been released, and on this occasion received the same clemency. The drummer-boy claimed his liberty likewise, and pleaded hard for it; but Richards said, "No, the drum excites men to battle, but the newspaper is often the source of demoralization and defeat." As the prisoners, in charge of Dr. Sowers, were passing through Ashby's Gap, they were met by Mosby, who, when informed that they belonged to General Custer's division, determined to retaliate upon them for the death of the Rangers who had been executed at Front Royal. He therefore ordered them to be kept under close guard until his return to Fauquier.

In a few days Mosby left Mountjoy with twenty-three men in the valley, and proceeded to Rectortown to execute his purpose. Meanwhile another party of Custer's men had been captured by Mountjoy, and left in charge of Jimmy Chilton at the residence of a citizen on the Blue Ridge. These prisoners were confined in a schoolhouse, and appeared to be comfortable and cheerful, expressing their surprise at receiving such kind treatment at the hands of Mosby's men. One of them especially was inclined to talk. He was young, handsome, intelligent, and gentlemanly in appearance. The conversation was so pleasant and friendly that Jimmy quite forgot the belligerent relation in which they stood to each other. But soon the tranquillity of the scene was rudely and painfully disturbed by the entrance of two Rangers, who, without preliminary, demanded of the prisoners to whose command they belonged. Several promptly responded,

"We belong to Custer's division."

"Then," said the men, "you are to be hung. Come along."

The announcement produced a terrible shock; and the prisoner to whom reference has been made rose up, and with great calmness said,

"I understand the reason of this. It is in retaliation for the hanging at Front Royal, and I do not condemn you for it. But I desire to make this statement: though I now belong to General Custer's command, yet I did not belong to it when that deed was perpetrated. I do not think, in justice, that I ought to be punished for the action of that officer before I had any connection with him." The case was a hard one, but he was, nevertheless, marched off with his comrades.

On the day appointed for the execution, the battalion assembled at Rectortown. About 11 o'clock a.m. Mosby arrived, prepared to enter upon his painful task. There were twenty-seven men left after Brewster, the lawyer, was excluded from the lottery, and on the list were the names of two officers—Captain Brewster and a lieutenant of artillery. An officer was detailed to superintend the sad affair, and Mosby withdrew from the painful scene, saying, "This duty must be performed for the protection of my men from the ruthless Custer and Powell." The prisoners were drawn up in single rank, and for each a bit of paper was prepared, but seven only of them were numbered. They were then all put into a hat, and each prisoner was required to draw forth one of them.

Those who drew blanks were to be sent to Richmond as prisoners of war, but those who drew numbers were to be hung. Various were the emotions depicted on the countenance as each man put his hand in the hat. Firmness, with his closed lips and unquailing eye; stolid Indifference; and Fear, with his ashen cheek and trembling hand, were all there. Brewster, the lawyer, was there too, and with agonized looks was watching the fate of his brother, while tears coursed down his cheeks. As each hand was taken from the hat, an expression of joy and relief would brighten the countenance, or a groan of anguish or a cry of despair would burst from the lips.

The condemned men were at once set apart and closely guarded. The two officers had drawn blanks, but not so the drummer-boy. His appeals to Captain Richards were now louder and more eloquent than ever, who, touched with compassion, interceded with Mosby for his release. The application was granted, for the boy, in truth, ought never to have been subjected to the lottery. But another had to be substituted in his place, for Mosby remembered the blackened corpses of Overby and Carter as they hung in the parching wind.

The captives drawing lots

The prisoners, in cruel suspense, again stood in line, but now only one death-warrant was in the hat. Captain Brewster again escaped, but the artillery officer was not so fortunate.

A detail was made to execute the sentence of retaliation, for the condemned soldiers were to be carried to the Valley, and were to be executed in the neighbourhood of Winchester. As the party was passing through Ashby's Gap they were met by Captain Mountjoy, who was returning from the Valley with an additional supply of prisoners taken from General Custer's command. Among the men condemned to death he recognised the artillery officer and one of his companions to be Freemasons, and on his own responsibility substituted in their places two of his own prisoners. The melancholy procession again set forward. Owing to the darkness, the road was lost, and at daylight S——, who was in command of the party, found himself at Rosemont, on the edge of Berryville, and he there determined to execute the sentence, for one prisoner had already escaped, and had not been missed until then.

The man who was first called up begged for delay, and said he was not ready to die. His request was granted, and he was postponed till the last. Three were hung and the others shot. But the last prisoner, when his turn came, was not then prepared to die, and, striking the guard who held him by the collar a blow which felled him to the ground, rushed past him, and, screened by the misty dawn, was soon lost to view.

When the substitution made by Captain Mountjoy was reported to Mosby he was much offended, and with severity told him he must remember in future that his command was not a Masonic lodge.

A few days after this execution Colonel Mosby transmitted to General Sheridan the following communication:

November 11th, 1864:.

Maj. Gen. P. H. Sheridan,
Commanding U. S. Forces in the valley:
General,—Some time in the month of September, during my absence from my command,, six of my men, who had been captured by your forces, were hung and shot in the streets of Front Royal, by the order and in the immediate presence of Brig. Gen. Custer. Since then, another (captured by a Colonel Powell, on a plundering expedition into Rappahannock) shared a similar fate. A label affixed to the coat of one of the

murdered men declared 'that this would be the fate of Mosby and all his men.'

Since the murder of my men, not less than seven hundred prisoners, including many officers of high rank, captured from your army by this command, have been forwarded to Richmond; but the execution of my purpose of retaliation was deferred, in order, as far as possible, to confine its operation to the men of Custer and Powell. Accordingly, on the 6th inst., seven of your men were, by my order, executed on the Valley Turnpike, your highway of travel. Hereafter, any prisoners falling into my hands will be treated with the kindness due to their condition, unless some new act of barbarity shall compel me reluctantly to adopt a line of policy repugnant to humanity.

Very respectfully, your obedient servant,

John S. Mosby, Lieutenant Colonel.

About this time Glasscock made a successful raid about Charlestown, capturing a number of horses, wagons, and prisoners.

A few days later, Lieutenant Frank Turner made a successful strike on the Shenandoah, known in the command as the "Hat Raid," the circumstances of which I will briefly relate. With twenty-five men he had been to Summit Point, in the valley, and had captured, with its guard, a four-mule wagon, loaded with a stove, carpeting, and other articles taken from a neighbouring church. Sending his captures to the trap, he proceeded to a point on the river near the Shanandale Springs for the purpose of capturing a picket stationed there, but, on account of the darkness, abandoned the enterprise, and determined to lie in wait for the relief as it approached the next morning.

At the expected hour. Captain Gary, of Company "I," 12th Pennsylvania Cavalry, drew near, with fifty eight men. Turner charged them. Company "P' broke and scattered, hotly pursued by the Rangers. The result of the fight, if such it might be called, was, six of the Federals killed and wounded, and twenty-seven men and horses captured. The flight was so precipitate that not less than forty hats were dropped by the gallant cavaliers. It was an amusing sight to see Mosby's men marching home, each surmounted with a high-crowned United States regulation hat, with the regimental letters and cross sabres. Turner's loss = 0. Hurrah for Company "I!"

Lieutenant Glasscock was sent about this time to the Valley Turnpike, across which he spread his net, and soon took prisoners four couriers and eight soldiers from Sheridan's army. In the afternoon he was informed that two wagons, escorted by twenty cavalry, had passed up the Front Royal Turnpike on a foraging expedition. He followed them to a field, in which he discovered about fifty Federal soldiers scattered, shucking corn.

About half of the Rangers were clad in overcoats which they had taken from the prisoners, and these Glasscock ordered to the front before the column entered the field. The Yankees were all captured save one, at whom a single shot was fired. But this shot excited the attention of a battalion of United States cavalry which was gathering corn in an adjoining field, but had been concealed from view by a thick growth of sassafras bushes. As soon as he was apprised of the presence of this force, Glasscock, determined to put a bold face on the matter, rode into the field, and was hailed by the major commanding with the inquiry, "Who are you?" In the most natural way he replied, "Captain Blazer;" but of him, it appeared, the major had never heard. During the colloquy which ensued, the prisoner who had escaped galloped up and shouted, "They are Rebels, and I have just escaped from their hands." Deception being no longer possible even for the wily Glasscock, he hauled down the United States colours, and galloped over the hill amid a shower of bullets.

On the retreat, the prisoners, many of whom had been allowed to retain their arms, resisted the guard. A fight ensued, which resulted in the escape of all but eleven, with whom and their horses Lieutenant Glasscock recrossed the Shenandoah.

A few days later John Russell struck a successful blow near Winchester, capturing a considerable number of prisoners and horses; and about the same time, Captain Mountjoy, on the same theatre of action, attacked a body of cavalry, and killed and captured about twenty of them. But on his return he fell in with Captain Blazer, who recaptured the horses and liberated the prisoners. I will recount the circumstances of this reverse, for Blazer has been the most formidable Federal officer with whom we have had to cope in the Valley.

When Mountjoy reached Berryville on the homeward route, he allowed those of his command who boarded in Loudoun to cross the river at Castleman's Ferry, while with about thirty men he marched up its bank, with the intention of crossing at Berry's Ferry.

When he reached the residence of Mr. Frank Whiting, two miles from that crossing, he was attacked by Blazer. The partisans broke and fled toward the river, notwithstanding the strenuous exertions of

Mountjoy and Grogan to rally them.

With a party of his men Captain Mountjoy reached the Vineyard, the residence of Captain Esten Cooke, of Stuart's staff, but more widely known as an accomplished author. There he again attempted to rally his men, but again without success. On the retreat from Whiting's house William Armstead Braxton, of King William County, Va., a gallant soldier who had recently joined the battalion, received a mortal wound, but was able to reach the vineyard, where he was tenderly nursed till he died. As he lay wounded on a sofa, Lieutenant Cole, of Blazer's command, entered the house, and, approaching the dying soldier, expressed commiseration for his condition, and offered such religious consolation as he could command. But his stay was short, for he said Mosby's men would soon return for their dead and wounded.

Nottingham, from Maryland, received also a severe injury, and with difficulty escaped into the large forest which covers the space between the Vineyard and the Shenandoah.

Lieutenant Edward Bredell, from St. Louis, Mo., was killed at Whiting's house. He was a private in the battalion, and derived his title from a staff position which he had filled in the regular service. He was a brave soldier, and his loss is much regretted in the command. Bredell had a midnight funeral on the island, a sand deposit in the Shenandoah, but his remains have since been removed to Cool Spring Church, near Piedmont.

Chapter 46: Defeat and Capture of Captain Blazer

Upper Fauquier, December 1st, 1864.

Dear Percy,—On the day after Mountjoy's reverse, Chapman, with his squadron, crossed into the valley at Ashby's Gap, and Captain Richards, with his squadron, at Snicker's Gap. It was Colonel Mosby's intention to have accompanied Chapman, but he was too much indisposed, on account of a severe cold and excessive exertion. I will now relate with some particularity Captain Richards's expedition, as it resulted in a collision with Captain Blazer.

Captain Blazer is a native of West Virginia, and the opening of the war found him in charge of a boat on the Ohio River. Embracing without hesitation the cause of the Union, he entered the ranks of an Ohio infantry regiment, in which he soon became captain. While this regiment was serving with General Crook in West Virginia, that officer created an irregular command, composed of picked men, to collect intelligence and suppress bushwhackers, which should be responsible to himself alone. It was composed of one hundred men, and Captain Blazer was selected to command the Legion of Honour. In this new field he soon distinguished himself by intelligence, activity, and courage, and along with General Crook was transferred to the Valley of Virginia— a new and more conspicuous theatre of action. Here he was brought into collision with Mosby, and proved himself at one time, it was thought, a foeman worthy of his steel.

His movements were rapid and generally successful. His expeditions lasted about three days, during which time he rarely went into camp until late at night, and always moved before daybreak. He appeared to be ever in the saddle, and was constantly turning up where he was least expected and least desired. Such was his activity that scouts and furloughed soldiers never felt safe within the enemy's lines, or in that broad neutral border which separates the hostile forces.

But these were not the only men who had reason to respect the valour of Captain Blazer. He often assailed the outposts of the Confederate Army, and not infrequently participated in larger combats. Already he had surprised and routed the 1st squadron of the Partisan Battalion, and, to say the least, had won the respect, if he had not excited the apprehension of the rest of it. Scouts who had been sent to the valley would, when they returned, often entertain their comrades with accounts of their escape from Blazer. His kindness to citizens was proverbial, and every where within the range of his activities the citizens were ready to bear honourable testimony to his character. His kindness sprang from the heart, but it might well have been the dictate of a refined policy, for it engendered for him a sympathy among the people which opened to him many a channel of information. Mosby and Blazer could not long inhabit opposite sides of the Blue Ridge Mountain, and Mosby was resolved to bring the rivalry to a speedy and decisive issue.

When the partisan chief parted from Richards, he bade his lieutenant to hunt Blazer up, and take men enough to whip him. Without delay, Bob Walker and Dr. Sowers were sent to the valley to get information as to Blazer's whereabouts, and at the same time Richards ordered the squadron to meet him at Bloomfield the next day. Early in the morning the scouts reported that Blazer had been ordered to Hampshire County, and had not returned. Not satisfied with the correctness of this information, Richards, with John Chew, Charley M'Donough, Puryear, Welt Hatcher, and Henry Heaton, proceeded to the valley, leaving the command to follow, in charge of Lieutenant

Harry Hatcher.

When he reached Snickersville he was told that, so far from being in Hampshire County, Blazer had camped within half a mile of the house in which Walker and Sowers had slept, and before daylight had crossed the mountain at Snicker's Gap, and, descending into Eastern Virginia, had marched in the direction of Hillsboro.

Henry Heaton, with one man, was ordered to follow his trail, and report to Richards at certain points on the west side of the river, who, with the remainder of his party, crossed over to Cabletown, a place to which Blazer had been much attracted by the political sympathies of the inhabitants. Lieutenant Hatcher had been ordered to bring the command to a wood near Castleman's house, which is situated two or three miles south of Cabletown. Learning at this place that Blazer had not yet made his appearance, Richards directed Puryear and M'Donough to proceed toward Charlestown, and ascertain whether his adversary had not crossed at some lower ford of the Shenandoah, while he, with John Chew, went to join Hatcher.

Hearing nothing of Blazer, the scouts returned about daylight to Cabletown, where they tarried until Puryear was surprised and captured by a party of Blazer's men dressed in gray. M'Donough escaped, and by a circuitous route joined his commander, and reported to him the fact of Blazer's presence at Cabletown. The squadron was at once moved from Castleman's Wood to a point near the house of Albert Davis, and concealed under a cliff of the river. While it was in this position, Captain Blazer, whose command had been put in camp at Cabletown, came to Davis's house and discovered its presence. He immediately returned to bring up his command, in order to attack Richards's squadron, while his adversary had gone by another route to charge into his camp. Thus were the two commanders, in search of each other, marching on opposite sections of a circle.

Richards, who was the first to discover this fact, determined to profit by his knowledge, and select a position from which he could charge the enemy's flank. With this object, he formed his men in a depression in a small field about half a mile from Myerstown, and about two hundred yards south of the Myerstown and river road, from which it was concealed by a skirt of wood. But as Richards was about to profit by this stratagem, and burst upon Blazer as he travelled the circle, one of his men, who was intoxicated, dashed suddenly forward, and discharged a pistol at the Federal column. Thus apprised of the presence of his enemy, Blazer at once passed through the wood, and halted to have a fence opened which alone separated his command from the squadron, then distant about seventy-five yards.

This movement was mistaken by Richards for an intention on the part of Blazer to dismount his command, and fight him with rifles from the woodland. Under this impression, he rode to the position of Company "A," and ordered Hatcher to send a party to open a fence on the hill immediately in rear of the squadron, it being Richards's purpose to fall back over this hill, and compel the enemy to fight him in open ground. Blazer, mistaking this movement for a flight or a retreat, hastily moved through the fence into the open field. At that moment Tom Richards, in temporary command of Company "B," assumed the responsibility of ordering a charge up the sloping plane which separated him from Blazer. Harry Hatcher, who witnessed this movement, dashed forward with Company "A," and struck the enemy's right a little after his left had been thrown into confusion by Company "B." A hand-to-hand combat ensued, in which the superiority of the revolving pistol to the rifle was soon demonstrated.

Many of Blazer's men were killed and wounded in the first shock, and the rest of his command soon gave way, flying toward Summit Point through Myerstown and Rippon. At Myerstown Blazer endeavoured, under the shelter of the houses, to rally his men, but the fugitives continued their tumultuous retreat, leaving their dead and wounded strewn along the road.

But it is time to return to Puryear. Being one of Mosby's men, he was roughly treated by his captors, having been stripped of his hat, his overcoat, and other articles of clothing, and in addition, it is said, had been threatened by Lieutenant Cole with hanging. To these indignities the Ranger submitted at least with patience, for he was confident that ere long he would regain his liberty, and be enabled to retaliate, in perhaps another fashion, the injuries which he had received. Under some pretence the prisoner had possessed himself of a stick, with which, as soon as the fight began, he stunned his guard. In the next moment Johnny Foster furnished him with a pistol, in return for a service which Puryear had once rendered him in a fight, and he started in pursuit of Lieutenant Cole.

As that officer approached Myerstown, followed by two of his men, Puryear overtook him, and, after killing one of his attendants, inflicted with a pistol-shot a serious wound upon the lieutenant, which caused him to swerve from the Rippon road and flank around a blacksmith's shop, with the intention, it is supposed, of making his way toward

Cabletown. But his pursuer, inflamed with vengeance, followed close upon him, and, as he saw the pistol levelled again at him, he exclaimed,

"Oh, save me!"

"Yes, I will save you," answered the fierce and implacable Puryear, and, receiving a death-shot, Lieutenant Cole dropped from his saddle.

Blazer's men, after they passed Myerstown, began to use their pistols, and the pursuit from that point became rather a running fight, Richards having seven men wounded beyond that place.

But how fared it with Captain Blazer? Even after the fruitless effort at Myerstown he had attempted to restore the fight, but his efforts served only to delay his own retreat, and render useless the fleetness of his horse. He was singled out by four men, justly ranked among the best soldiers in Mosby's command—Sam Alexander, Syd Ferguson, Cab Maddux, and the terrible Powell. Now do thy speediest, Captain Blazer, for those are upon thy track who smite and spare not! The fight is lost, and all that the bravest can do now is to save himself for another trial of the chances of war.

Indeed, after the pursuit had approached near Rippon, several shots from his pursuers admonished him of this fact, and he bent all of his roused energies toward making his escape. But the superiority of Fer-

CAPTAIN RICHARDS

guson's mare. Fashion, one of the fleetest and hardiest animals in the battalion, enabled her rider to pass in succession all his competitors in that headlong pursuit, and place himself by the side of Blazer, who had thrown himself forward to escape the shots aimed at him from behind. Ferguson, though one of Mosby's "spurless roosters," as the parson calls the juniors, is yet a very powerful man, and, rising in his stirrups, he struck Captain Blazer a blow with his pistol which brought him to the ground. There was one man who proposed to finish the work which Ferguson had begun, but, with the chivalry of a true warrior, he stood up in defence of his captive.

Richards lost, besides his wounded, Hudgins, who was killed. Blazer's loss was twenty-four men killed, twelve wounded, and sixty-two prisoners and horses. When the result was reported to him, Mosby was at the house of Mrs. Waters, near Middleburg. He was overjoyed at the intelligence, and, springing from the sofa on which he was lying, gave a hearty cheer for Dolly Richards.

A little later, Mosby, with a portion of Mountjoy's company, got among the Yankees building winter quarters near Perkins's Mill, on the Front Royal and Winchester grade, and captured about thirty men and horses.

With the 2nd squadron Mosby crossed the Shenandoah at Berry's Ferry for the purpose of extending some protection to the citizens of Warren and Clarke against the foragers from Sheridan's army, and camped for the night in the neighbourhood of White Post. The next morning Captain William Chapman, with a scouting-party, captured four or five prisoners, whom he immediately dispatched to Fauquier in charge of Frank Angelo. He also discovered a train of ten wagons, guarded by thirty-five infantry and fifteen cavalry, which had been foraging in the neighbourhood, returning to the brigade camp near Perkins's Mill.

Chapman returned to the Partisan camp, and Mosby started in pursuit, and overtook the train near a strong outpost, and just as it met another train coming out from the camp heavily guarded. He was not apprised of this casual junction when he ordered the charge, yet such was its impetuosity that it scattered the Federals, and drove them into the brigade not far distant. Both trains were captured—men, horses, wagons—and the Rangers rushed into the camp. It was about 4 o'clock in the afternoon of a Yankee Thanksgiving Day, and the soldiers were having a fine time seated around their camp-fires, and did not at once discover what had burst upon them. Their consternation saved us, and the men had time to rob them of their greenbacks before they rallied. But it was soon time for us to travel. The whole camp turned out to pursue. In the retreat, the coolness and bravery of Captain Chapman saved Mosby, and afforded time for the flying Rangers to make their escape.

Mosby was riding a young, wild horse. The animal became unmanageable, the bridle-bit was broken, and the Yankees were charging and yelling close upon him. In this extremity Chapman rallied a few men, charged the pursuers, and for a time held them in check. Two of the men meanwhile, seeing Mosby's peril, placed themselves one on each side the frantic animal, and, seizing the bridle, held him by the nose-strap, and in this way were enabled to moderate and direct his speed. In the charge Chapman's horse was killed, but John Kernie, of Company "C," sprang from his saddle, and, offering his horse to Chapman, said, "Take him, captain; you are of more service to the cause than I."

When the fugitives had reached a point near the Winchester and Millwood Turnpike, Major Otis, of the 21st New York, who gallantly led the pursuit, accompanied by one hundred men, struck across the angle formed by the two roads, and succeeded in dividing the Rangers. It was a perilous condition for those thus suddenly cut off, but Lieutenant Beattie was equal to the emergency. He gathered about him his men, and, by a charge worthy of Mosby himself, opened the line of retreat. By the time Major Otis reached Berry's Ferry, Lieutenant Russell, with five men, was the only force in front of him, for the rest of the force had scattered, and taken refuge in the woods.

Mosby was stripped of most of his captures, and, in addition, lost three men.

Angelo had loitered on the way, and, in consequence, had not reached Millwood until after Major Otis had passed in pursuit of Russell. As he was proceeding through the street, he perceived a party of Federal cavalry in his front. His men hastily abandoned the prisoners and scattered, but Angelo determined to try the fortunes of war. He dashed forward, shooting right and left, and, being well mounted, succeeded in passing through the party referred to, and was moving in a lively gallop toward Berry's Ferry, when he fell in with Major Otis and was captured. He was carried before General Sheridan, and by him was closely catechised. His life, however, was safe, for the enemy had been taught that it was no light thing to condemn to death prisoners captured from Mosby's command. So Angelo, along with other prisoners, was confined at Martinsburg;

but, by the exercise of ingenuity and boldness, he made his escape, and in a short time rejoined the battalion.

I have omitted to mention that on the 15th of this month, by order of the War Department, the battalion was inspected by Lieutenant Meade, who reported it to be in fine condition, the best mounted and equipped in the service.

Chapter 47: General Merritt Devastating the Valley

Upper Fauquier, December 10th, 1864.

Dear Percy,— About the 25th of November Mosby sent Captain Mountjoy, with thirty-eight men, to the neighbourhood of Berryville, from which place the next day he recrossed the mountain to Snickersville, where he was informed that Keys's men were again across the Potomac, and were committing depredations on the farmers and housekeepers of Loudoun. He marched directly to Waterford, a favourite haunt, as I have before told you, for those warriors; but they were not there, and Mountjoy crossed the hills to a point on the Leesburg and Point of Rocks Road, and from thence proceeded toward Goresville, which lay farther on the road in the direction of Leesburg. As Vendeventer and another Ranger, who were in front, drew near this place, they reported the presence of a party of cavalry, which proved to be the Loudoun Rangers, under the command of Lieutenant Grahame, who had been on a raid to Leesburg, where he had captured Fred Smith and Cleveland Coleman, two of Mosby's men, and was then on his way to the north side of the Potomac.

Mountjoy at once closed up his men, moved rapidly toward Goresville, and, as soon as he came within a short, distance of the Loudoun Rangers, charged them. The Yankees mistook the approaching column for friends, and good-humouredly getting out their liquor-flasks, prepared for a general treat. Their consternation may well be conceived when a furious yell burst upon their ears. The prisoners, it is needless to say, were abandoned, and joined in pursuit of their late captors. But the road was narrow, and could not pass all the fugitives, who broke into two parties, one turning to the right in a road which led to their native hills, the other pressing madly in the direction of the river.

As Captain Mountjoy, mounted on a fleet bay horse, and accompanied by Grogan and Munroe Heiskell, was leading the pursuit near the "Burnt Chimney," one of the fugitives killed him with a pistol shot.

'Tis unnatural,
Even like the deed that's done.

A falcon, towering in her pride of place,
Was by a mousing owl hawked at and killed.

The Loudoun Rangers lost in this fight twenty-five horses and thirteen prisoners, among whom was Lieutenant Grahame.

Captain Mountjoy was buried in the cemetery at Warrenton, and his best epitaph is the following order, issued by Mosby, than whom none knew him better.

General Orders, No. ——.
Headquarters 43rd P. R. B., December 3rd, 1864.

The lieutenant colonel commanding announces to the battalion, with emotions of deep sorrow, the death of Captain R. P. Mountjoy, who fell in action near Leesburg on the 27th *ultimo*, a costly sacrifice to victory. He died too early for liberty and his country's cause, but not too early for his own fame. To his comrades in arms he has bequeathed an immortal example of daring and valour, and to his country a name that will brighten the page of her history.

In obedience to orders issued by the military authorities, all the granaries, stack-yards, stables, and mills in the Valley of Virginia had been burned by General Sheridan's army, and General Merritt, toward the latter part of November, crossed the Blue Ridge at Ashby's and Snicker's Gaps, to carry the work of destruction into Loudoun and Upper Fauquier. This total departure from the usages of modern warfare, to be paralleled only by the example of a Tilly or a Genseric, originated in the conviction that, in addition to European mercenaries and insurrectionary negroes, the alliance of Famine, too, was necessary to subdue the stubborn spirit of resistance which animated the Southern people.

The policy of devastation as a material agent is one of vast power, but its efficacy in restoring affection for the government that invokes it may well be doubted. But this is a question for politicians to ponder. It is mine to give an account, however imperfect, of this act of incendiarism in the most fruitful part of Mosby's Confederacy. From Paris and Snickersville, as central points, strong detachments were sent through the devoted region upon their destructive mission. In this way, Merritt's army of five thousand men was expanded like a fan from the Blue Ridge to the Bull Run Mountain, and each soldier being armed with a torch, that terrible implement of war, this beautiful and productive region was soon reduced to a waste. In order more

Fire and sword in Mosby's Confederacy

certainly to enlist the starving *cohorts* of hunger on the side of the Constitution and the laws, all farm-cattle, including milch-cows with their "white abundance," were carried off and collected in one vast drove at Snickersville.

As soon as night invested the scene, blazing fires were visible in all directions, lighting up with their lucid glare the whole of the vast circumference, while columns of dense black smoke mounted up from the burning piles as though the demons of conflagration, rejoicing in the mischief they had wrought, had assumed those terrible forms in which to manifest themselves. Various were the emotions displayed by the agents of destruction as they would approach a smiling homestead. The most, animated by the spirit which dictated the inhuman orders, would laugh at the despair and wretchedness of the forlorn family; while others, with whom no political object could justify crime, invoked divine vengeance on the men who thus deliberately prepared for the helpless and innocent members of society—the old men, the women, the children, and the young maidens of this once happy land, death in its most revolting, lingering, and painful forms.

As I gazed horror-struck upon the awful spectacle, I was carried back to the dark and savage period when Attila, with his fierce barbarians, burst over the Alps and ravaged the plains of Italy, adorned with vineyards and villas, and cities which in magnificence and population were hardly secondary to Rome herself. When I remembered the ties of consanguinity which united the hostile peoples, the startling theory of my friend the Philosopher forced itself into my mind:

> That republican institutions are imbued with an uncontrollable tendency to barbarize and degrade the human character, and that, instead of mounting higher in the ascending circles of civilization, society, from the relaxation of the imposed and wholesome discipline of well-ordered states, sinks lower and lower in the moral scale, till Anarchy, with its devouring jaws, engulfs all things, returning man, the pride of the creation, for a season at least, to his savage state.
>
> Under its malign influence, the nicer shades of personal honour first disappear; then follows morality, the substance of all things; and, finally, the spirit of humanity flies from the accursed land."

As the different corps of incendiaries proceeded through the country, Mosby's men, with orders to take no prisoners, hounded their tracks, watching for opportunities to attack them, as smaller bodies, inflamed by a spirit of rapine, would detach themselves.

After the work of desolation had been accomplished, General Merritt's army was camped at Snickersville. The residence of Dr. Lacy stood on the outer edge of the encampment. A small party of Yankees had approached it with an insolent demand for food. In order to rid himself of their insults and importunities, he advised them to return to their camps, saying Mosby's men might at any moment dart upon them and bear them off to the woods. The soldiers, deeming themselves safe, laughed at this cautionary advice, yet, as if a little persuaded by it, they moved to go away, when John Orrick, accompanied by H——— dashed up, and, as an eagle would bear away a kid to his cliff, hurried them off to a neighbouring forest.

The day before the expedition recrossed the Blue Ridge many prisoners were brought before Captain Barnes, the provost-marshal, at Snickersville. With one exception, they all denied having any connection with Mosby. This man was Newton Jackson. As he was carried before the seat of military justice, it was whispered among the prisoners that he was one of Mosby's men. But Mr. Burwell, of Clarke County, replied,

"No, he is too badly dressed, and is too much of a rough, to belong to the Partisan Battalion."

When Jackson was questioned on that point, he boldly acknowledged that he belonged to Mosby; but when charged with having on previous occasions traded to Alexandria under Federal passports, he roughly denied it. He was threatened with hanging, but in a spirit of haughty defiance the prisoner told Captain Barnes that he dared not execute his threat, for Mosby was provided with the means of retaliation. As Jackson passed out under guard to be confined with the other captives, Mr. Burwell remarked,

"I was mistaken. That is one of Mosby's men."

Among the immense congregation of four-footed animals at Snickersville was a noted thoroughbred bull, which had belonged to Captain Robert Carter, of Number Six. It was in the nature of a compensation to the inhabitants of that vicinity for their many calamities that the Yankees carried off that animal, for he had for many years been a notorious trespasser on every cornfield and garden within reach. As the drove would pass a cottage-door, an old woman would put her head out of the window and exclaim, "Thank God, the Yankees have got Carter's bull." In truth, so confirmed a nuisance had he become, that the people had determined to take the thing in hand, and make Mr. Bull a candidate for the Legislature; for the people of Upper Fauquier have a merry custom, I hear, of sending a man to the Legislature as soon as he becomes a little seedy and an unprofitable member of society. As the animal was driven past Mr. Burwell, he remarked to Captain Carter that it was a pity that so valuable a bull should be lost to the neighbourhood.

"Never fear," replied Carter; "that bull will go home tonight, and carry with him all the cattle from that part of the country."

And so it happened. About two o'clock in the morning the camp was alarmed by the cry of "Mosby." An astounding uproar followed, producing a general stampede in the herd. The next morning Captain Barnes instituted an inquiry for that "impudent guerrilla," Jackson. When Burwell was called upon, he testified that when he saw Jackson last he was mounted on Carter's white bull making his way to Number Six.

CHAPTER 48: MOSBY AGAIN WOUNDED.

Upper Fauquier, December 27th, 1864.

Dear Percy,—About the 1st of December Colonel Mosby left us to visit Richmond, to propose a reorganisation of his battalion. Soon after his departure, Captain Wm. Chapman determined to attack a scouting-party of the enemy, about one hundred in number, who, from their camp at Winchester, daily visited Berry's Ferry. Sometimes the scout would approach the ferry from the direction of White Post, and, marching down the riverbank, would return to Winchester through Millwood, but at other times would approach through Millwood and return by White Post. Chapman's plan was to strike the party front and rear, and, in order to be prepared for their approach from either direction, posted Captain Richards, with half the command, at the base of a wooded bluff on the road side between Berry's Ferry and Millwood, while with the other half he concealed himself on the road which leads from White Post to the ferry. Each party then put out vedettes to report the route taken by the enemy. The two portions of the command were thus held like hounds straining in the leash until the quarry should come within striking distance.

About eleven o'clock Robert Walker, who had been posted near Millwood, announced the approach of the Federals, who proved to be a detachment of the 14th Pennsylvania, commanded by Captain Myers. He had been informed on the way that Mosby's men were lying in wait for him, but had discredited the information till it was repeated by one of Burwell's negroes at a point not far above Richards's ambuscade. By way of precaution, he then sent forward, or rather accompanied, an advance-guard of twenty men, with flankers thrown out. In this order the march proceeded down the turnpike until the advance-guard and flankers had passed the ambuscade. Mistaking them for the main column, Richards burst upon them. But he soon discovered his mistake, and turned his men toward the main body of the enemy. But it had already been fiercely attacked by Russell, Taliafero, Walker, and several others. Before the vigour of Richards's onset the Yankees soon began to give way, and fled toward Millwood, leaving their killed and wounded strewn along the road.

About six of the Rangers had pursued the enemy a mile beyond Millwood. As they returned, fatigued and encumbered with prisoners and horses, they were suddenly met by twenty Yankees, who had been passed by in the pursuit, but had not been disarmed. These men, with arms in their hands, felt little inclined to submit without another struggle to the weary fate of captives. So they rallied, formed their ranks, and, sword in hand, broke through all obstacles to their retreat.

Captain Myers, as I have told you, had accompanied his advance-guard, and, when Richards cut them off, endeavoured to regain his column by making a circuit through the pasture-land that borders the south side of the turnpike. He was followed by Puryear and Jim Wiltshire, who were attracted by his fine charger and officer's uniform, and, after a gallant defence, was killed.

During the pursuit. Bob Walker had a hand-to-hand fight with a Federal soldier, the latter using his sabre, the other clubbing his carbine. Both combatants were severely bruised and cut, but Walker, who is very strong and active, as well as very brave, succeeded in disarming and capturing his opponent.

Richards sustained no loss in this fight, but the loss of the enemy was considerable—twenty-six killed and wounded, fifty-four taken prisoners, and eighty horses.

About this time Sergeant Charley Hall, from Fredericksburg, performed an exploit which I record as illustrative of the adventurous spirit which prevails in our battalion. A cavalry force was encamped within three hundred yards of a picket of three men. One of them was absent, plundering a neighbouring garden, when Hall surprised his two comrades and bore them off, together with the horses and equipments belonging to the three. This is only one of Hall's many daring exploits.

During the month of November, while the battalion was operating in the valley, Colonel Mosby sent Bush Underwood, with a few men, on detached service to Fairfax. He was so successful during this period that he was allowed, during Mosby's absence in Richmond, to remain on the same field of activity. I will give you a brief sketch of Underwood, as he is ranked among the heroes of the battalion. He is now about twenty years of age, and was born in Maryland, but, since early childhood, has resided in Fairfax County. In the beginning of the war he entered the service in an artillery company which went from Loudoun, and participated in the two battles at Manassas, the Seven Days' Fight around Richmond, and other engagements of less magnitude. But the artillery service did not suit Underwood's enterprising temper, and, without the ceremony of a transfer, he betook himself to White's battalion of cavalry, which he in turn left to join Mosby, as early as April, 1863.

At last in a congenial element, he soon drew upon him the attention of all by a display of some of the best qualities of a soldier. Quiet and unobtrusive in deportment, he was ever prompt and faithful in the discharge of duty. In action he is cool, resolute, and always among the foremost to strike the enemy. He has a latent energy and fire in his nature which qualify him, almost beyond any other man, for the wild career he has chosen. As soon as Underwood had displayed these high qualities, a regular transfer was procured for him to the partisan command, for Bush was then too much of a free trapper for Mosby's taste.

One of his first adventures on detached service occurred while General Meade was marching through Loudoun. With two men—his brother, Sam Underwood, and Dave Hixson—he proceeded to Benton's Ford, on Goose Creek, where he saw three horsemen enter the water from the opposite bank. They proved to be a lieutenant colonel and a major, attended by an orderly, who had come to ascertain whether that was an eligible point at which Goose Creek could be crossed. Mistaking the Rangers for citizens, they advanced without hesitation or suspicion. Followed by his comrades, Bush pushed forward to meet the officers, and within ten steps of them levelled his pistol and ordered a surrender. The surprise was complete, the emergency pressing, and the surrender prompt.

Bush took charge of the major, whom, from the splendour of his uniform, he supposed to be certainly a general, the lieutenant colonel fell to Sam's lot, and Dave Hixson had to put up with the orderly. When his arms were demanded, the lieutenant colonel was disposed to stand upon a point of etiquette. He said it was unbecoming in an officer to surrender to a private; but Bush relieved his scruples by informing him that in his command all were officers. He next, evidently to produce delay, objected to giving up his sword, which he said was as much a badge of his rank as his shoulder-straps; but Bush knew little of military etiquette, so he cocked his revolver, and threatened, if he hesitated for another moment, to shoot him through the head. The prisoners were then conducted to a neighbouring wood, where the rest of Underwood's command had been left, and the horses and equipments were sold to the highest bidder.

On another occasion, while he was operating with a command of twenty men, a vedette reported the approach of an ambulance and two wagons, with an escort of twenty-five cavalry. Underwood directed Newcombe to take a portion of the command and strike the rear of the escort, while he, with the rest of it, would charge in front; but by some mistake, all but two of the men went off with Newcombe. With these two, nothing daunted, Bush Underwood made the attack, and, contrary to every reasonable expectation, drove the escort before him.

During the fight. Colonel Switzer, with a captain, escaped from the ambulance into the pines, but left behind for a ransom trunks, which contained a considerable sum of money, and, what a soldier would be least likely to leave, the colonel's sabre. It was, however, time for the officers to leave, for Bush is a rude soldier, and not a respecter of persons.

With three hundred cavalry the Federals pursued Underwood to Mount Zion Church, but to no purpose, for the guerrillas were "*over the hills and far away*," as Charles Augustus would say. This is only one of the many attacks which Underwood has made on the Federals in Fairfax. He has become so obnoxious to them that they devised the following expedient for his destruction. A blockade runner had agreed to deliver to Underwood, at a house near the Potomac, a parcel of merchandise. In company with Trammell, he went to the rendezvous. Soon after their arrival, a lady reported that a party of mounted soldiers were rapidly approaching the house, and before the two Rangers could mount their horses, the Yankees, for such they proved to be, had entered the yard, and with their revolvers had begun the assault. , There was a body of wood, cut off from the yard by a fence, for which the Rangers made, closely pursued.

But Underwood and Trammell were bold riders, and, setting spurs to their horses, cleared the obstacle at a flying leap. "They didn't catch us that time" said Underwood, as they drew up their horses. But a quick succession of shots informed them that the race was not yet over, nor the goal of safety won. Still they were hotly pursued, and headed off on every side until they were driven to Broad Run, at a point where the bank was abrupt, and more than ten feet from the water's surface. It was a hazardous leap, but Underwood and Trammell did not hesitate. When their pursuers reached the stream they durst not follow, but contented themselves with firing a volley at the Rangers as they disappeared from sight.

It is my painful duty to record a third wounding of our chieftain, and to relate the circumstances which attended it.

Colonel Gamble, of the 8th Illinois, commanded a brigade of cavalry, with his headquarters at Fairfax Courthouse. On the 17th of December he sent a raiding-party, comprising detachments of the 13th and 16th New York and 8th Illinois Cavalry, under command of Lieutenant Colonel Clendennin, in search of Mosby. On arriving at Aldie the command separated, and, pursuing different routes, united at Salem. One of these parties visited Kinloch, the residence of Mr. Edward Turner, where they found Lieutenant Grogan and another member of the battalion. Although the house was surrounded, yet, with that deliberate valour which ever characterizes him, Grogan determined to fight his way to his horse, which was tied not far off, preferring to take the chances of death rather than the certainty of confinement in the dreary prison at Johnson's Island, from which, under circumstances of so much hazard, he had once effected his escape. But his fortune was not equal to his valour. He was so severely wounded in the leg that the Federal surgeon pronounced him disabled from farther military service, and he was, in consequence, left with his kind friends at Kinloch.

The Federals then marched to Salem, from which they drove a few of Mosby's men, and then, filing to the right, moved toward Rectortown. When within a mile of this town the flankers encountered two horsemen, who seemed intent on observing closely the moving column. One of them was conspicuous from the scarlet lining of his overcoat, as well as for the reckless exposure of his person. This man was identified as Mosby, and, as he dashed rapidly along the flank toward the front of the column, he was pursued by a private of the 16th New York, noted for his unusual courage. As the two passed through

Rectortown, "Scarlet Cloak," as he was called by the Yankees, turned in his saddle, and by a shot from his revolver killed his pursuer's horse. At Rectortown the Federals halted, built fires, and the men prepared their suppers as if to camp for the night.

Mosby, in the meantime, accompanied by Tommy Love, one of his most favoured and devoted followers, after reconnoitring the camp, proceeded to the house of Ludwell Lake, who lives within a mile of Rector's Cross-roads.

Instead of remaining in camp for the night, the raiders were soon in the saddle again, with the purpose of proceeding to Upperville; but, from the ignorance of the guide, took the road leading to Rector's Cross-roads. As they passed the house of Mr. Lake they discovered two horses, with cavalry equipments, fastened to his gate. Captain Taylor's company of the 13th New York surrounded the house, and through one of the windows Corporal Kane discharged his carbine at a man within. This was Mosby. The ball struck him in the abdomen, but fortunately, without penetrating, ranged around and came out just above and back of the hip. The lights were extinguished as the enemy rushed into the house; but, with a self-possession which never deserts him, Mosby determined to affect the dying man, and by that stratagem to baffle his enemies. Throwing his coat which denoted his rank under the bed, his first act in this tragic performance was to besmear his lips with blood from his wound, to give the appearance of internal haemorrhage, and then to stretch himself on a couch as if exhausted.

One of the men proposed to finish the rebel; but the Federal officers gathered around him, and Captain Taylor and Major Frazer, after examining the wound, pronounced it to be mortal. They then inquired his name, his rank, his regiment. The wounded man, gasping, replied, Lieutenant Johnson, of the 6th Virginia Cavalry. A negro belonging to Mr. Lake was then introduced, and, failing to recognise Mosby, pronounced him to be a stranger in the neighbourhood. This testimony removed all doubt, and the column proceeded in their search for the "guerrilla chief" As soon as Mosby discovered from the conversation of the family assembled in an adjoining room that the Federals had taken their departure, he arose and appeared among them, creating almost as much astonishment as if they had seen one risen from the dead. He immediately ordered preparations to be made for his removal to the house of Mr. Aquila Glasscock, not far off; for he surmised that the enemy, detecting in some way the imposition which had been practiced upon them, would send back a detachment for his recapture.

Nor was this precaution ill-timed, for, upon leaving, the raiders had divested the wounded man of his boots, and carried with them his cloak. These they examined upon the march, and finding the cloak, which was of rich gray cloth trimmed with English scarlet and gold clasps, to correspond with the one which they had often heard described by the citizens of the valley as worn by Mosby, and the boots to agree exactly in make and maker's name with a pair taken from his headquarters when burned last summer, they concluded that they had let the object of their search slip through their fingers, and at once dispatched a squadron to repair the error.

Mosby in the meantime had been conveyed away by the only means of transportation at hand—a cart drawn by two half-broken oxen, and driven by a negro, who, although he faithfully performed this duty, a few days later deserted to the enemy. From Glasscock's a courier was sent to the residence of a citizen near Piedmont, where Jake Lavender, of the command, was that night to be married, and where a large number of the men were likely to be assembled. As soon as the tidings were received the marriage was postponed, the party broken up, and the Rangers hastened to the couch of their wounded chief.

Without delay, Captain Richards dispatched runners to collect a force which might prove sufficient to protect Mosby from a pursuing enemy, and the next day Captain William Chapman appeared and took command. His first act was to send Tom Richards with a party to ascertain the whereabouts of the raiders, who soon reported that they had passed through Aldie on their homeward march. Mosby remained at Glasscock's for several days, suffering great pain, and attended by Doctors Dunn and Eliason, both of the command, during which time his men from every direction thronged in to see him. Among them was West Aldridge, who reported that with two comrades, Roger and Bobby Chew, he had fallen in with a party of the Loudoun Rangers near Waterford, and had killed one and captured three of them. Chew had been wounded, which Mosby the more regretted as he is one of the most daring soldiers in the battalion.

A division of Federal cavalry, commanded by General Torbert, had made an attempt to capture Gordonsville, but Had been driven off by General Lomax's command. At Warrenton they divided and went back to the valley, through different crossings of the Blue Ridge. One of these fractions on their homeward route camped within a mile or two of Glen Welby, whither Mosby had been removed. As soon as the presence of the Federals in the neighbourhood was ascertained, he was conveyed by a circuitous route to Culpepper Court-house, and from thence to Amherst County. About the time of his removal from Glen Welby, the Federals had been told that he was at Salem, and started in pursuit of him. At one time the Rangers who had him in charge were so hard pressed by the enemy that Mosby told them they would be compelled to scatter. They inquired, "What shall we do with you?" He answered, "Bury me."

CHAPTER 49: MOSBY'S MODE OF WARFARE

January 10th, 1865.

Dear Percy,—As early as the middle of October, Colonel Mosby determined to winter a portion of the battalion in the Northern Neck of Virginia, not being able to keep the command together in its usual field of operations on account of the destruction which had been wrought by the incendiaries of General Merritt. Accordingly, about the 1st of January, Lieutenant Colonel Chapman departed for that district of country, taking with him Companies "C, E, F, and G," the latter of which was organised at Salem preliminary to his departure. For this new company the following officers had been indicated by Mosby: T. W. T. Richards, Captain; John Murphy, First Lieutenant; Garland Smith, Second Lieutenant; and William Puryear, Junior Second Lieutenant.

At the time of secession, Captain Richards was a student at Columbia College, in Washington City; he promptly returned to Virginia, and enlisted in the Eighth Virginia Infantry, commanded by Colonel, now General Eppa Hunton. After twelve months' service with this regiment, during which he participated in all the battles in which it was engaged, he left the infantry service and attached himself conditionally to the Seventh Virginia Cavalry, with which he remained till Colonel Jones was promoted to the command of a brigade. Richards was then authorized by him to recruit a company to operate within the enemy's lines, and with this view returned to Loudoun County, where he was attracted to Mosby, of whom he had heard Colonel Jones speak in very high terms. Not being bound by any military engagement to the regular service, he seized this opportunity to enter partisan life, and joined Mosby with twelve recruits.

He served with the command till the fight at Warrenton Junction, where, in an attempt to create a diversion among the enemy, he was severely wounded three times, and did not regain his liberty until after an imprisonment of twelve months. This accounts for his having been so lately made an officer in the battalion; for, as showing the estimation in which he is held by his commander, I will mention that when General Lee requested a suitable officer to be recommended to organise a command to protect the citizens in the Northern Neck, and the counties south of the Rappahannock, from the incursions of raiding parties of the enemy, Mosby nominated Richards. He went on the mission, but soon returned, and reported that it was impracticable.

Murphy entered the service in the Ninth Virginia Cavalry, in which he was subsequently promoted to a captaincy. He had recently joined the command, and was nominated to the lieutenancy by Mosby at the solicitations of Major and Captain Richards.

Garland Smith had been with the battalion for a considerable period, and had proved himself a brave and energetic soldier. Previous to his connection with the command he had been a lieutenant of infantry, and had been honourably discharged in consequence of a painful wound.

Puryear had also served in the regular army before his connection with Mosby, and had earned his promotion by the display of unquestionable gallantry on all occasions.

This interval of comparative repose I am spending at my abode on the Blue Ridge Mountain, enjoying the society of congenial friends, and, in compliance with a promise, will give you an interior view of our organisation, and also an account of Mosby's military policy and civil administration.

As early as September, 1863, Mosby concluded a report to General Stuart by reminding him that "the military value of the species of warfare I am waging is not to be measured by the number of prisoners and material of war captured from the enemy, but by the heavy details it compels him to make in order to guard his communications, and to that extent diminish his aggressive strength." The system which he has devised for carrying into execution the policy which he has thus concisely stated involves the consideration and explanation of the manner in which his command is organised, or, in other words, the principle of the Partisan Ranger law, and his mode of quartering, and subsisting, and disciplining his troops, and also his mode of conducting hostilities.

The principle which distinguishes the Partisan Ranger service is the distribution among the officers and men of the spoil captured from the enemy, and, though Mosby refuses to avail himself of it for his own enrichment, he yet values it as a powerful magnet to attract and bind adventurous spirits to his standard. The dreaming statesman may indulge the reverie that in republics the patriotic principle is sufficient to impel men to the discharge of military duty, but the practical and clear-sighted genius of Mosby knows that mankind are governed by the grosser motive of immediate self-interest, and, impressed with this belief, he made the strenuous efforts of which I have told you to construct his command on this basis.

As an advantageous theatre of operations, he selected Upper Fauquier and Loudoun, a district of great agricultural fertility and salubrity of climate, having pasturelands which, during nine months of the year, resemble in verdancy an oasis, while they are peopled by an offshoot of the Saxon stem—a brave, generous, hospitable people, and devoted to the cause of Southern independence. From this as a central point he has struck the enemy in Fairfax, on the line of the Potomac, in the Valley, and on the Orange and Alexandria Railroad. With the efficiency of his mode of warfare, as original as daring in its plan of execution, you have already been made acquainted, as well as with the vigorous and sometimes sanguinary and despotic means to which Federal commanders have resorted in order to counteract and suppress it.

This system of warfare, defensive in its object, yet aggressive in its principle, has baffled all these attempts, because, as soon as the blow is inflicted, the assailants are at once scattered, before time is afforded to strike them in return. The angry cloud gathers, the thunders roll through the sky, the fatal flash is emitted, and the discharged vapours disperse into thin air. Mosby was followed by Wyndham, by Stahl, and by many others, eager to inflict vengeance upon their tormenting adversary, but the band had been broken, and the men composing the command were dispersed over the large area they inhabited, to be collected, perhaps on the morrow, again to strike Achilles in the heel.

The citizens sometimes murmur, that Mosby, who is ever in an aggressive attitude, so seldom fights the enemy at home; but they do not consider that by doing so he would abandon the object which brought him among them and insure his own destruction, for nothing would gratify the Federal generals more than for him to fight pitched battles with their overwhelming odds.

Robin Hood concealed his men in the solitudes of Sherwood Forest; Marion took refuge in the inaccessible swamps of Carolina, which on every river and lagoon offered an asylum; but Mosby, in an open country, finds security in dispersion among a friendly and chivalrous people. With them the members of the battalion live as boarders and friends, the farmers for a moderate compensation, and sometimes without compensation at all, providing food and shelter for the soldier and his horse. But in some instances, in order to insure greater security, the men have built themselves huts in the mountains. This familiar association between the soldiers and the citizens has developed a very peculiar and romantic state of society, and its elevating effects upon the former are very marked. It has imparted to their deportment and appearance refinement and dignity, with a tincture of knightly courtesy, and, as in a former age, woman again awards the prize to valour. Thus woman, the spectator and sometimes the actor in the fierce drama, is a golden thread woven into the battalion for beauty and ornament, but yielding it strength also.

Distributed through the community, the men select their own boarding-houses, restricted only to certain limits, which contain now an area of twenty miles square. Instead of the discipline of the camp, they are restrained by the discipline of society; but if that prove too feeble a means of government, a military authority is near at hand, prompt to interpose and swift to strike. The officers of the battalion are likewise scattered, in proper proportions, among the men, and are required to keep a strict supervision over them. The rule of discipline is comprehensive and concise: the men must promptly attend the rendezvous, and conduct themselves as soldiers on duty and as gentlemen off duty.

Violations of this rule are at once reported to Mosby, who is ever ready to hear complaints, sometimes by officers, sometimes by soldiers, sometimes by citizens, and, as supreme arbiter, are dealt with by him. If an officer or man is found by this despotic tribunal to be deficient in courage or obedience, or not to be an orderly member of this military community, one of two punishments is inflicted; he is reprimanded for the first offense, or he is pronounced unfit for partisan life and sent to the regular army—regarded, as I have told you before, in the light of a Botany Bay. One of the bravest men in Company "B" was recently sent off for breaking into a Quaker's milk-house, notwithstanding the earnest intercession of his captain.

It must sometimes happen that, even with the strictest vigilance, unworthy men will insinuate themselves into the battalion, but, as soon as discovered, the diseased limb is amputated. To aid in this work, company inspections have been instituted, and on one occasion an inspection of the battalion was made, at which more than fifty names were struck from the rolls.

From their boarding-houses the men collect at various places of rendezvous, which are always selected with reference to the vicinity of a blacksmith's shop. From these points issue daily detachments, varying in strength, commanded generally by officers, but sometimes by privates who enjoy the confidence of their commander. Thus, in one day, we find portions of Mosby's command operating at Accotink, in the valley, on the Baltimore and Ohio Railroad, at Poolesville, and several other points, or scouting in Baltimore, Washington, and in the camps of the enemy. Sometimes a few of his followers are shot or captured, but for every one lost to him the enemy's loss is tenfold. Brave, but never rash, ever vigilant, but never incautious, Mosby soon signalised himself as a leader, but it was not until he obtained a large and stable command, and was able to avail himself of the agency of subordinates, that his unrivalled genius for Partisan warfare shone forth. If his command had been proportioned to the emergency, and to his capacity to employ it, I have thought that when Meade marched through Loudoun and Fauquier with vulnerable rear and flanks, with Lee in his front, the march of his army might have been stayed, or even thrown back beyond the Potomac; and it is past a doubt that, had such a command as I speak of been under Mosby's control, General Sheridan's long line of communications in the valley might have been broken up.

Mosby knows every man in the battalion, his appearance, his name, his general character, where he boards, and to what company he belongs. It is an object with him to gain this information, for by it he has been enabled to surround himself with efficient officers, and select leaders for the small bands which he casts like a quiver of arrows among the enemy. It is this faculty of discernment which has given him the hundred arms of Briareus. He has another quality which comes in aid of this—his inaccessibility to flattery, and consequent exemption from its blinding and disturbing effects. He has, of course, his friendships and personal partialities, but it is astonishing to see how destitute they are of all influence over his public conduct. These favourites eat with him, scout with him, sleep with him, and follow him in the headlong charge. But there is not an instance in which one of them has been promoted to command.

His promotions are always from another class. If a man is honourable, brave, and capable, he looks no farther, for he regards power simply as a trust, and would as soon convert to his own use the public money as the public patronage. You ask if it is by love that he controls his men? No; he is not weak enough to be cheated by that fallacy. Love, he knows, is an inconstant charmer, whose power, from the nature of things, can not be made to pervade and control large masses of men. Fear and Confidence are the *genii* he invokes, and, united to a conviction of his incorruptible integrity, they have enabled him to enchain followers to his standard.

As the battalion grew in strength, and his sphere of action was extended, the difficulty of disciplining and controlling it increased, and Mosby proposed, in consequence, to divide it into two battalions, each to be commanded by a major, while he retained the rank of lieutenant colonel, who should be responsible for the discipline and efficiency of his corps, while the emulation which would necessarily spring up between the two divisions of the command—the officers being of equal rank—would not be without its advantage to the public service. In order to obtain the sanction of law for this plan of reorganisation, early in December, 1864, he visited Richmond. But upon developing his scheme to General Lee, he found him opposed to it, and to favour instead the regimental organisation.

Besides, the Secretary of War was of opinion that no authority for such a division of the command was given by any existing law, and that a special act of Congress would have to be obtained. He therefore suggested as a substitute, which was accepted by Mosby, to give him a lieutenant colonel and a major, between whom the command could practically be divided, although the divisions could not be recognised by the department. After an absence of ten days, Mosby returned to Fauquier with authority to increase his battalion to a regiment, and bringing with him a colonel's commission for himself, a lieutenant colonel's for Chapman, and a major's commission for Richards.

But it is now time to speak of his civil administration. The civil structure in the district over which his power extends had been totally subverted, and there was no law to maintain the recognised rights of property, or to protect the weak from the aggressions of the strong. Finding himself in the possession of power, he regards it as a trust to be exercised for the benefit of those over whom his military jurisdiction extends. To him, as the recognised depository of authority, all men repair, preferring complaints, representations, and applications. The ordinary place for the transaction of such business is at a rendezvous for the command, while the men are assembling. But this is not always the case, for he often gives audiences and makes decisions at other places and at other times. Thus Mosby has reigned in the Upper Piedmont for nearly two years undisputed dictator; and the evidence of Mr. Edward Marshall, of Markham, one of the most prominent and respectable citizens of Fauquier, is but a merited testimonial to the enlightened use which he makes of his great authority.

Says Mr. Marshall:

Mosby has for nearly two years been king of Fauquier, and I have never known the county so well governed.

His education and experience as a lawyer come greatly to his aid in fulfilling these civil duties. The following incident will illustrate, I think, the vigour of his administration. Horse-stealing and cattle-lifting had become a prevalent nuisance in Fauquier and Loudoun and, unless restrained, would, beyond doubt, have been followed by other and more violent forms of lawlessness. But Mosby is just the man to deal with a distemper like that. He published an order authorizing and commanding horse-thieves and cattle-lifters to be shot wherever caught. It was not long before the rude administrators of this military code were called upon to act, and the only investigation that ensued was as to the guilt of the man who had been killed.

Lying outside of the army lines, it is only natural that this district of country should be infested by deserters, blockade-runners, and other disreputable characters, as well as by horse-thieves and cattle-lifters. To meet this evil, he has authorized the arrest of all soldiers not having regular leaves of absence, and awards their horses as prizes to their captors, while strangers are required to exhibit evidence of the lawfulness of their business. It is by the employment of vigorous and enlightened measures such as these, as well as by the brilliancy and success of his military exploits, that Mosby has won, and will ever maintain, a deep hold on the confidence and affection of the people of Northern Virginia.

Chapter 50: "Gog in the Land of Magog"

My dear Percy,—I have another exploit of our friend the chaplain's to relate to you today, and, if I am not mistaken, it will excite in your breast feelings of compassion for the holy man. That you may have no fear of exaggeration in any of its circumstances, I will tell you beforehand that I have gotten all the facts from that oracle of truth, Mr. Blackwell Magog!

The chaplain was on a visit to "Heartland," the classic abode of his relative, Mr. Blackwell Magog. The weather was cold, for it was the inhospitable month of January, the season when Boreas delights to bluster over this northern temperate zone.

Present, besides the host and his family, and a bevy of fair damsels, Dr. Gog, Jake Lavender, Johnny Edmunds, Johnny Munson, George Edmonds, Wyndham Lucas. The day before the one on which occurred the notable events about to be related was devoted to canonical games of cards. The result between the reverend man and his especial antagonist,. Munson, had been the loss by the latter of a large bottle of blockade whisky, which had been promptly paid up, according to the rule which the parson invariably observed with those young guerrillas.

He was opposed, he said, to debt, and would not, in consequence, trust one of them for a shilling. But his success had brought with it but little happiness, for he had to be as much on his guard as if he had been in a camp of gipsies. The young scamps, instigated and encouraged by the master of the house and Jake, who ought to have known better, had concocted many a plot to obtain possession of the vessel which contained the liquor, but, as the sequel will show, unhappily in vain.

In some way, it was never certainly known how, though the chaplain always accused Sam Thomas, the reverend man had contracted that one of the eruptive diseases known to science as *scabies*, but in the vernacular as itch. Every one who is acquainted with this tormenting companion, and the mode in which it ought to be treated, knows that for its cure the application of unguents to the surface of the body is highly recommended. This is one of the particulars of the healing art in which science condescends to agree with unlettered practice—one in which the learned disciples of Æsculapius concur with those kind, excellent physicians, the old women.

But, in order to apply this highly popular remedy, it was necessary for the doctor to disrobe his person, or, as Hamlet, the Dane, would express it, "Unmask his beauty to the moon." By this process our churchman had been reduced to what a philosopher might call a state of nature. While he was in this Adamic condition, as unadorned in truth as our grandparents before the Fall, Munson and Johnny Edmunds rushed wildly into the apartment, which was situated on the second floor, crying out, "The Yankees are coming, and are flanking round the house." Out again they went, with terror in every line of their faces, and the great anointed beheld them through the window, scampering toward Goose Creek, which flows at the base of the eminence on which the house stands. A moment after the voice of his kinsman was heard below urging an immediate retreat; and soon, as if in confirmation of his advice, he himself was seen, with Jake and the others, to hurry off in the same direction. The doctor's clothes had, by his own direction, been removed, to be subjected to a process of fumigation, nor had others been substituted.

Here was a terrible dilemma. It would never do to be captured by the Yankees if the thing could be avoided, for they had sworn to hang the fat priest for plundering their supply-trains if ever they laid their hands on him—yes, to hang him with a grape-vine. After these threats had been communicated to him, and Munson had even seen them in a General Order issued from Winchester, as he had stated that morning at breakfast, Doctor Gog had often thought of hanging with a grape-vine, and the more he. thought of it the less he liked it. He was very indignant, and so expressed himself. It would, he said, be a clear violation of the usages of civilized warfare, and ought not to be tolerated by the nations of Christendom; it was, moreover, the death of a dog, and carried with it disgrace as well as punishment. But what was all this to the parson if the Vandals executed their threat? He would be dead, and nothing could compensate him for that calamity. After much reflection, he had come to the conclusion not to fall into their hands; indeed, this resolution might be said to have become with him a fixed principle of action.

But what was to be done? He had no time for councils of war. The case was one which demanded immediate action. What was to be done? Great God! what was to be done? Even now it might be too late. "Run, Doctor Gog, run!" some good angel whispered; "run! for a human life hangs on thy heels—run, run, run!" How could he resist these moving appeals? for already he felt the felon vine tightening around his throat. Off he started, grasping at a blue counterpane as he passed by the bed. But it was an ample coverlet, and had been closely tucked. It would have taken him five minutes to get that blue counterpane off the bed. Five minutes! he hadn't as many seconds to lose. Out of the room he bolted; down the stairs he leaped, or rather tumbled, and rushed through the porch into the enclosed area which surrounds the house. How cold the air was! but it served only to brace Doctor Gog for more strenuous exertions.

Through the yard he sped like an apparition. The children screamed, the dogs barked, the geese uttered their dissonant cries, and rose up, expanding their great wings, as the doctor flew by them; one, a gander, and the patriarch of the poultry-yard, showed fight, and ran hissing

THE CHAPLAIN'S HASTY RETREAT

after the fugitive. The maid-servants hid their faces and turned away, they were so shocked at the unhandsome spectacle so suddenly presented to their eyes. But what cared the doctor for a country wench, or a score of them for that matter, when the Yankees were flanking round the house?

Children, dogs, maid-servants, ganders, all stand aside for the chaplain of Mosby's Battalion as he bounds toward the garden. Behold him now, through intemperate haste, involved in a labyrinth of raspberry-bushes, with their long, prickly arms reaching out on every side; how they lacerate his soft, greasy skin! But a raspberry-bush, what is it to a grape-vine, if those terrible Yankees have hold of it? He does not stop to disengage their clasping arms, but rudely breaks away. His sides bleed like a spurred courser; but better that than worse, thought the parson, as he continued his retreat, or rather flight. But whether a retreat or flight, what matters it? For the parson, never over-scrupulous, has no time now to higgle over words. All he asks is a clear track.

He has scrambled over the garden fence, and down the hill he goes, encountering in his passage the running briers which, during the war, have spread over the land. How they tear his feet and ankles, and the flints how they cut his flesh! No matter, no matter; what are a few scratches when a man's life is at stake! When he reached the bottom of the hill he came upon the rest of the fugitives, all dressed in their nice warm clothes and long cavalry boots, while he was as naked as a cherub! The Lord, how cold it was! and nobody would lend him a thread—a thing not reasonably to be expected by a man afflicted with *scabies*. The others hid among water-sedges and alder-bushes, which grew on the hither side of the stream; but the parson, with that spectre grapevine about his neck, determined to effect a crossing of Goose Creek at all hazards. Nor did he wait for the arrival of his pontoon-train, but at once plunged in the stream, about waist deep, and, having gained its opposite bank, was soon lost in the undergrowth which offered its friendly shelter.

The doctor was vividly impressed with the imminent perils from which he had just escaped, for had he not distinctly heard the tramp of horses, mingled with the confused sound of human voices? So he laid down very close to a large log, or trunk of what had once been a stately tree, but which now lay prostrate among the weeds and grass like a fallen monarch, abandoned by those who, in the days of his prosperity, had gathered about him, and found shelter in its lordly boughs. But the poor fugitive was not too proud to ask protection from the oak in the days of its adversity; so he crept close to its side, and laid him down at full length, shivering with cold. His teeth chattered, and that was the only noise he made, and that he could not help, poor man! It was so cold that January day! Soon a voice was wafted to his ear, which he thought syllabled his name, and the denuded churchman crouched closer than ever to the frozen earth and the rough bark of the tree, Between the ague of fear and the ague of cold he suffered pangs almost as keen as death.

There is an end, however, of human endurance, and the parson made up his mind to surrender. The Yankees might not, if he spoke them fair, be so hard on him, after all. It would be better, at all events, he reasoned, to take that chance, small as it might be, than to perish with cold. Under this impulse, he had risen to his hands and knees, when, for the first time, his eyes fell upon a wild grape, that sent forth in many a grateful fold its long, tough vines. Down he fell, for it looked like a fatality. The victim and the altar, by a mysterious Providence, had been brought together, and the priest to offer him up was alone wanting, and he, alas! was not far off. "Oh!" groaned Dr. Grog, and he buried his face in his hands ancl tried to pray.

The work of repentance, though long delayed, is swift when it begins. Misdeed after misdeed rose up before the defaulting chaplain like banditti springing out from every brake. Each day produced its band of accusing memories—his broken vows, his profanity, his revels, his gaming, all, all stood before him with menacing brow—a dark array, that confronted the chaplain of Mosby's Battalion, standing on the verge of eternity, a boundless sea shrouded with impenetrable cloud. Plundered quartermasters and violated sutler-wagons were there, to haunt him with their confiscated stores. How horrible thus, "unhouseled and unanneleaed," to be hurried out of life—life, which is so sweet to the voluptuary!

He heard again his own name pronounced, and this time with a distinctness that left no room for doubt, no hope, for the Yankees were as familiar with his name as his own guerrillas.

But, Yankee or no Yankee, grape-vine or no grape-vine, he could stand the cold no longer, for the state of quiescence in which he had lain had generated a numbness which might be the precursor of that drowsiness which precedes death from freezing. As soon as this horrible thought occurred to him he sprang to his feet, but still cautiously went forth to reconnoitre, for the parson had at least this quality of a good soldier, great caution in the presence of the enemy. Unspeakable was his relief when he discovered that the voice proceeded from his own friends, who were calling him to join them, which with painful steps he proceeded to do. By this time the wind had risen, stirred by some demon, or had been released from its barred prison for some uncharitable end. The forlorn divine suffered horribly on his exposed flanks, as the cutting blast with icy breath came whistling from the snow-clad Blue Ridge.

Friends are the kind ministers of Fortune, and those of Dr. Gog, the most welcome of their class, now summoned him to surmount the cross-flowing stream and rejoin them. But, benumbed with cold, how could he accomplish the task? It was a serious question that winter's day which was presented for solution to a church dignitary divested of raiment. Had he been bred in the wilderness, and been a great *sachem* of an Indian tribe, he could have done it, and not have thought of it a moment after. But the chaplain was not a North American savage, but was a child of civilization, and had been nurtured in luxury.

There was no pass way—not even the slender footing of a rail thrown across some narrow belt of the creek. No, there was no help for it; so he plunged in the waters, over which a film of ice had formed. Though an excellent divine, and instructed in all the lore of the Church, Dr. Gog was not an accomplished engineer, for he selected for the crossing of the stream a place where the waters were both broad and deep. A concealed snag caught his foot when he was about midway, and souse he went under. Having expelled the water from his ears and nose, he heard a loud laugh. He gnashed his teeth with rage, for Munson, he knew, with a hundred glosses and exaggerations, would tell the thing over the whole country.

It was, then, in no amiable mood that the chaplain emerged from Goose Creek, sinking knee-deep as he approached the oozy bank. The moisture which had begun to freeze in his drowned locks rattled at every turn of his head. A mariner cast away on the inhospitable coast of Spitzbergen could not be more an object of compassion than was Dr. Gog, as with dripping sides he emerged from the water. His nose and lips were drawn and blue, and with shaking limbs he approached his companions with the salutation,

"Well, boys, I suppose the d—d Yankees are gone?"

Replied Johnny Munson, in a very impertinent manner, "Why, doctor, the affair turned out to be a false alarm; there were no Yankees at all." And they all looked at Dr. Gog and laughed, he standing there forlorn, and covered with goose-bumps.

A new light then broke on his mind—not the cheerful ray shining on a benighted land, but a sulphurous and infernal light, which makes Knowledge, an angel of consolation on earth, one of the furies to torment man in hell. The wrath of the invincible Greek was an amiable feeling compared with the mood which spread like an angry cloud over the parson. His brow darkened, his eyes emitted a strange fire. Without uttering a word, he stooped and grasped one of the smooth enamelled stones which the torrent had piled in that place. Missile after missile hurled he at his tormentors, who instantly decamped—Jake, with his long legs, leading the way. One of the projectiles was better aimed, or was launched with a more auspicious fortune, for the churchman had the inexpressible satisfaction of seeing Mr. Blackwell Magog knocked off the fence which lay across his line of retreat. But he was soon on his feet again, though it gave the parson no little satisfaction to behold the treacherous scoundrel, as he climbed the hill, rub his bushy head, as hard and shaggy as the frontlet of a bison.

It is a consolation to reflect that in the most calamitous situations there is always some circumstance to alleviate our misery— one drop of the sweet in every cup of the bitter. Remember this, children of Adam! and oh, Philosophy! in their weary pilgrimage, teach them to find the single drop of honey, or rather thou divine Chemistry!

An impartial observer could not deny that the parson had achieved a complete victory. The field of battle was abandoned to him, and at his leisure he could proceed to erect his trophy, that undeniable evidence of success. But, after all, was it a success? Could it with any propriety be placed in the catalogue of martial triumphs, thought the chaplain, as he was seated on a decayed stump, with his back turned on the breath of winter, as it came from those blue hills, so beautiful and cold in their wavy outline? Was it not rather a defeat, for had he not driven from him those who alone could serve him?

Children of men, why will ye so torment one another? Is it not better to bring relief than to inflict misery? Inquire of the angels of mercy, those brightest of created beings! Would it not have been far better to have given the parson, benumbed with cold, a glass of Cogniac, or one of his own favourite Downing?

Downing resides near Linden Station, on the Manassas Gap Railway, at the western extremity of Poverty Hollow, pleasantly so called, because it is one of the very richest indentations of the eastern slope of the Blue Ridge. There, in Poverty Hollow, the maidens are, or used to be, the fairest—there the flowers blow the sweetest, and the rivulets, as they dance their wayward round, murmur of a gentle love, and chant their wild minstrelsy to the stars. But the best and brightest is gone—the gentle, the blue-eyed Lucy. She sleeps now under the stars, near the country church where she worshiped God, and has left behind only this memory.

Write for the "Grog" brand; it is the purest and sweetest distillation. It is true, ill-natured persons say the devil taught Downing to make this Grog liquor, and that, on his part, Downing entered into certain covenants to be complied with beyond the grave. But I believe not the story. It is the invention of malice and jealousy, for Downing is a first-rate fellow, and is the last man in Fauquier to deal in the black art.

But, bless me! where is Doctor Gog during this unexpected, but, I trust, not uninteresting episode? Where is the doctor? amiable friend, while thou wert in the airy regions of speculation, or, fancy bound, wert in Poverty Hollow, or the Happy Valley, or Dreamland, as the Hollow used in the olden time to be called— that is, twenty years ago— by the joyous young people who laughed life away and loved under the blue sky, ah! too well—while thou wert thus beguiling the time. Doctor Gog, obedient to the law of self-preservation, was limping, foot-sore, to the barn of Mr. Blackwell Magog. What a contrast to his headlong descent!

Arrived at the barn—let us call it instead a temple of Ceres, as being the heaped altar at which that goddess loves best to be worshiped— the denuded parson could neither see nor hear of living wight. The presence of ladies prevented a nearer approach to the house. A negro wench or two, when the Yankees were flanking round the house,

Adolphus Adam Gog could encounter; but a house full of ladies of good English blood, filtered through several generations of Virginian ancestors, was a different thing. There is always some one act which a man will not do, and to enter the presence of ladies thus divested of raiment was with the parson that one act. He would visit the palace of the winter god, and beard that hoary monarch, throned amid arctic snows, before he would paint the cheek of modesty with a blush.

So, instead of approaching the dwelling, he sought the sunny side of the barn, there to wait until his clothes could be brought him. As the sun bathed the parson's form in his bright beams, sending the freezing blood through each artery and throbbing vein, how delicious were the sensations they produced. How like a god he looked, throned in the heavens, ever in his zenith, reigning amid burning constellations and dazzling splendours, and sending throughout creation those resplendent rays—the ministers of his grace and mercy. From the bottom of his heart he thanked the kind Father who kindled those soft, eternal fires in which all living things might rejoice—yes, all—the worm and the soaring eagle; the beggar upon whom fortune never smiled, and the prince upon whom she never frowned.

But it was not long ere the doctor heard the sound of approaching footsteps. It was Munson. Overjoyed he ran toward the young guerrilla, but undue haste scared him away, or, as the doctor phrased it, "knocked the fat in the fire."

"Johnny, dear Johnny," said the divine, who determined to try the effect of soft words. Reassured, Munson ventured nearer, and, seating himself on a fragment of a plough, the following colloquy ensued:

Doctor Gog. "Johnny, my boy, of this be sure, you need never be afraid of me. You are my favourite in the whole battalion, and for my right arm I wouldn't hurt a hair of your head. But, sweet youth, bring my clothes, or I'll catch my death, and then, you know, the command would break up."

Munson. "Catch your death, parson! I never saw you in a finer glow. But I have always heard mountain breezes recommended for health. Catch your death! I understand you well enough; you want to catch me, and then you'd mash every bone in my body. When you want to fool a man with such chaff as you carry in your wallet, I advise you not to begin with one of Mosby's men."

Doctor Gog. "No, no, dear boy, I swear by the honour of a Christian minister, and that is an oath of credit, I will not hurt a hair of your head."

Munson. "What made you, then, throw those stones at me in the meadow? Don't you suppose you hurt a hair of Mr. Blackwell Magog's head when you knocked him off the fence? If that's what you mean by your fair promises, I think I had better look after my own safety. No, sir, I didn't take your clothes from you, and I'll have nothing to do with the affair; for once in my life I'll attend to my own business." And, so saying, the young man rose to depart.

Doctor Gog. "Johnny Munson, for God's sake don't leave me. I swear by the crucifix that I will not hurt you, and that oath would bind the devil himself."

Munson then resumed his seat and said,

"But, sir, you are not a Catholic, and that makes you so very convenient on the subject of oaths; but I have no sort of confidence in these Universalist preachers. It is the next thing to having no religion at all."

Doctor Gog. "I convenient on the subject of oaths! Why, that's an aspersion on the whole command. What would the world say of the morality of the men if you tell them their chaplain has a seared conscience? But, Johnny, you are wrong in the fact; I have a touch of the Catholic too."

Munson. "Yes, no doubt, just as you are a Baptist or a Presbyterian, or a Methodist, or a Swedenborgian, or what not. No, sir, your religious principles afford no sort of security."

Doctor Gog. "Ungrateful guerrilla! Out of the whole command you have ever been my favourite. Yes, I have taken twice the pains with your religious education that I have with that of any other man in the battalion. But, my boy, won't you bring me my clothes?"

Munson. "No doubt you love me devotedly, since you can scarce refrain from knocking me down in company. If what you say be true, why didn't you let me have some of the liquor today?"

Doctor Gog. "Why, my boy, I was keeping it for a hobnob between us tonight.' Do you suppose I would let that long legged guerrilla, Jake, and that pudding-faced fellow, Mr. Blackwell Magog, and the young thieves around them, have any of it? No, Blockade should be kept for gentlemen. Apple-jack and new dip are good enough for them. D—n it, Johnny, have you lost your penetration?"

Munson. "Not as much, perhaps, as you think."

Doctor Gog. "Oh, Johnny, have you too grown suspicious? I have always loved and admired you for the unaffected simplicity of your nature. Of all the charms of youth, ingenuousness is most endearing to me."

Munson. "Parson, it's no use to talk to me in that way. We had as well get to business at once. I know not how it is with you, basking there in the sun, but it's devilish cold out here. You remember the gray horse you cheated me out of at 'Seven up' last Sunday two weeks? Well, I must have him back, and the calico horse too, that we got in the Fairfax raid."

Doctor Gog. "Why, Johnny, both the horses were fairly won, and surely you would not unravel such old transactions? But, as I always like to have a man satisfied—"

Munson. "Particularly a great favourite."

Doctor Gog, "I am willing to play for the stakes again."

Munson. "That you may have, I suppose, the pleasure of again cheating me. No, I must have both horses back, and no conditions. And then there's the bottle of liquor. I must have that back."

Doctor Gog. "You shall have them all, dear boy, and may they do you more good than they've done me, particularly the liquor. Now, lad, for the clothes!"

'*Munson,* "Not yet. I must have the roll of cloth you got from the sutler in the valley, as well as the lot of smoking tobacco that you brought from Richmond, or hang me if I bring you the clothes."

Doctor Gog. "Johnny, you shall have them all—the horses, the cloth, the liquor, the tobacco. Anything more?"

Munson. "Yes. I never saw you so accommodating before. The pleasant morning and your summer apparel have produced a fine effect upon you. I must have the watch and chain, and the greenbacks too, which you took from the Yankee parson."

Doctor Gog, "John Munson, how thou liest! I have no recollection of such a transaction, but have always heard that '*hawks winna pike out hawks' eyes,*' as the Scotch proverb hath it."

Munson, "No lie about it. It was just as I say. I witnessed the affair, and never laughed more in my life. The Yankee was of the Beecher school, and did the preaching of a Massachusetts regiment. You went through him like a dose of salts. As he couldn't answer certain Scripture questions which you propounded, you pronounced him an impostor, and confiscated his watch and chain. His pocket-book you had taken on general principles. I must have the watch and chain, at least, for that's the best way, I find, to settle the differences of the Church. I will have to play Judge Monkey, and adjudicate between you."

Doctor Gog, "Johnny Munson, you take advantage of my misfortunes! But take the trinkets; you know they were always yours for the asking."

These concessions appeared to satisfy the Ranger, for he moved off in the direction of the house, but soon returned and reopened negotiations.

Doctor Gog, "Why, what the h—ll do you want now?"

Munson. "I must have a pair of cavalry boots, for mine (stretching out his legs) are almost gone. You know, as the government money is worth nothing, we are compelled up here to adopt Bonaparte's maxim, and make '*war support war.*' I must have the boots, and good ones too."

Doctor Gog (aside). "The unconscionable rogue! He would rob me of the last shilling, and leave me to make a livelihood by preaching the Gospel to a gang of thieves. That fellow was born for a money-lender. However, I must speak him fair, though I never mean to be bound by one of the extorted promises. (To Munson.) Certainly, Johnny; how could I refuse you anything? Yes, you shall have a nice, new pair of cavalry boots. But I must have my clothes first."

This time Munson started off as if in earnest, and soon disappeared. He staid, the parson thought, unreasonably long, and when he reappeared it was without the clothes. It was with difficulty that the doctor could suppress his rage as he saw the young man deliberately resume his former seat.

Doctor Gog, "In the name of ten thousand furies, what will you have next? I shall die of cold behind this d—d old barn, and that would make a pretty paragraph in the newspapers!"

Munson, "Be not disturbed on that score, parson, for I engage to write your obituary. Let me see how it will run: 'Departed this life, on the — day of ——, the Rev. Doctor Adolphus Adam Gog, CM. B., at Heartland. He died of a violent attack of—modesty.' Ha, ha, ha! No, doctor, I am not satisfied. I must have security that you will perform your engagements."

In the most provoking manner, Munson began to whistle a popular love-song.

Doctor Gog, "John Munson, what security can I give in this situation? Are you going to be another Shylock, and demand your pound of flesh?"

"Yes," responded Munson, coolly, "several of them, for I must have Mr. Blackwell Magog and Jake for the bail."

"Jake, I suppose, for the leg-bail," said the parson, smiling.

Munson, "Ha, ha, ha! Excellent. Yes, Jake for the leg-bail. I am glad to find that your wit, at least, is not congealed. There is nothing, I see, like a change of climate for the wit."

This point settled, Munson started off once more, and soon returned, bringing a bundle, and followed by Mr. Blackwell Magog and Jake, who found seats near Munson's former place of negotiation; but the securities manifested much reluctance to becoming bound for the chaplain, Jake objecting that he had a way of slipping out of his engagements, like an eel through a fisherman's hand. The complications of the Congress of Vienna were not so difficult to arrange, and the treaty was about being broken off, when, Munson relaxing his attention for a moment, the parson sprang forward, and, knocking his two securities to the ground, possessed himself of the bundle, and then retreated to his former position, fetching, as he did so, an ineffectual blow at Munson. The proposed securities arose from the ground, and in a very ill humour walked away, leaving Munson again alone with the chaplain.

When Dr. Gog examined the bundle he found it contained only his boots and waistcoat, with which he was not much more presentable than before.

"Knocked the fat in the fire again," quoth the doctor, in a sorrowful voice, and, seating himself on a projecting log in the floor of the building, buried his face in his hands as one bereft of hope.

From sheer compassion at his sad plight Munson then brought the rest of the clothes, but their owner would take no notice of him. Fearing lest he had carried the joke too far, the young man approached the parson and shook him roughly by the shoulder. In a moment he found himself in a Herculean grasp, and felt keenly the blows of a hickory withe that had lain near.

"So you want the calico horse, do you?" shouted the parson, "and the cloth, and the tobacco?"

The blows fell heavy and fast, and Munson began to think it was not such a good joke after all.

"The watch, and the chain too," exclaimed the doctor, pausing to recover his breath. "You say you must have them, for it's the best way to settle the disputes of the Church. So you mean to play Judge Monkey, do you, between two quarrelling cats? But your honour will find that one, at least, of the parties litigant has claws."

As he uttered these words the parson paused in the castigation, still holding his tormentor by the collar.

"How do you like this security?" growled he, shaking Munson with his left hand by the collar. "It suits me very well."

Again the thrashing began, and the action might have lasted till the ammunition was exhausted, for the parson had entered on a regular campaign, but for Munson's presence of mind. He kicked the bundle of clothes as if to send it under the barn, which induced Dr. Gog to relax his hold, thus enabling the Ranger to make his escape.

When the injured chaplain returned to the apartment from which he had made so sudden an exit to solace himself with a glass of Blockade, not a drop could he find. In his absence the liquor had been confiscated, and its lawful owner announced his intention of retiring in disgust from the world.

CHAPTER 51: PRISON EXPERIENCES OF MOSBY'S MEN.

Upper Fauquier, February 15th, 1865.

Dear Percy,— Feeling that my chronicle will be incomplete without some account of prison life as experienced by Mosby's men, I have procured from Tom Richards an account of his long captivity, some particulars of which I will introduce in this letter, and also several escapes from prison effected by members of the battalion under circumstances of great peril.

Richards, along with fourteen wounded comrades, was captured in the fight at Warrenton Junction and carried to Alexandria, where they were placed in a hospital with Federal soldiers, and were allowed to receive kind attentions from the ladies of that town, many of whom sympathized warmly with the Southern cause. Of their noble and untiring efforts in behalf of the prisoners Richards speaks in the most admiring and grateful terms. From the hospital he was removed to the Old Capitol Prison, from which place, at the close of two uneventful months, he was sent to Point Lookout, where he tasted all the horrors of prison life north of the Potomac for the space of seven months.

When he reached Point Lookout the number of prisoners was small. They were encamped on Chesapeake Bay, and a line of sentries was stationed around the camp except on the bay side. But, in consequence of the escape of several prisoners— among others, Tom Lake and his party—the additional precaution was taken of inclosing the prison with a fence sixteen feet high, made of plank set on end. About three feet from the top of this enclosure was a platform on which a line of sentries walked their beat. On the bay side were two gates, which were left open during the day, but at night were strongly barred and guarded. As the prospects of a cartel of exchange became more gloomy, some of the captives, from that strong desire of freedom planted in every breast, began to contrive plans of escape.

Among these I will mention the case of five prisoners who were bound to each other by ties of friendship. One of them, in behalf of the party, approached during the day the sentinel on duty at one of the gates which I have referred to, and, after some preliminary conversation, proposed to him, in consideration of a large reward, to allow himself and four others to escape through the gate during the next night. The guard was not averse to the proposition, yet doubted its feasibility, and urged the fatal result to himself in case of detection, but promised to give a definite answer when on duty later in the day. In the afternoon, as soon as the sentinel was seen pacing his customary round, the prisoner, with anxious heart, inquired his determination. He replied that he would open the prison gate, but that he must be well paid for it. The price finally agreed upon was one gold watch, two silver watches, and forty dollars in greenbacks, which was the sum of the valuables which the party could muster. At the hour agreed upon the price was paid, the gate was opened, and the prisoners walked forth. To return to their homes? No! The sentinel had played them false.

As soon as he had been relieved from duty in the forenoon, he had hurried to the provost-marshal. Captain Patterson, of the 14th New Hampshire Infantry, and had communicated to him the overture he had just received. Captain Patterson instructed him to accept the bribe, and to allow the men at the appointed hour to pass to the outside of the prison. About half an hour in advance of the hour agreed upon, the provost-marshal concealed twelve cavalrymen, armed with carbines and pistols, under the bank of the bay, at a distance of twelve feet from the gate at which the Confederates were to make their exit. As soon as the prisoners had passed through the portal, the gate was closed and barred behind them, and Captain Patterson and his twelve men rose from ambush and fired upon the defenceless men.

"For a moment," says Richards, "the firing was rapid; but above the sound of fire-arms and the shout of the blood-thirsty wretches I could distinctly hear one of the Confederates exclaim, 'For God's sake, don't kill me! I give up.' In a moment more the firing ceased, and all was again still, save the cries and groans of the wounded men. Stretchers were now brought on which to transport them to the prison. Cary, of Martinsburg, Virginia, was desperately wounded, two others less severely, while the rest of the party escaped the same fate by falling prostrate on the ground, as if dead. These facts can be vouched for by almost any number of witnesses."

In the month of November four hundred officers were brought to Point Lookout, and shortly afterward two regiments of negroes were put to guard the prisoners. They treated them with great insolence and brutality, and in this they were encouraged by the prison authorities. Here is an example. About eleven o'clock at night one of these negro sentinels who was pacing his beat fired his musket into the encampment. The ball passed through the head of a prisoner who was asleep in his tent, causing immediate death, and also inflicted a mortal wound on a companion lying at his side. As soon as the circumstances of this case were known, the indignation of the prisoners was so great that the officer of the guard, under pretence of sending the negro to the guard-house for punishment, hurried him off. But the next day he was seen again on duty with corporal's stripes on his arm, for he had been promoted for this outrage upon humanity. When asked by the officer upon his arrival why he fired, he replied, "I hearn a noise over dar."

Many other cases occurred quite as shocking, which can be authenticated by thousands of witnesses. For several weeks, at one period, this wanton shooting continued, averaging a death of at least one prisoner a day. To so great an extent was it carried that the tyrants in command at Point Lookout, fearing lest rumours of their connivance at these atrocious deeds might reach the ears of the higher authorities, issued an order prohibiting the shooting of prisoners, except when they attempted to make their escape.

The mechanical ingenuity exhibited by the captives was manifested in various ways, not only for the purpose of whiling away the tedious hours, but in order to obtain funds with which to purchase some of the necessaries of life. Trinkets of almost every description, finger-rings, breast-pins, ear-drops, watch-chains, and miniature books were carved in the most beautiful style. One of the prisoners made with his penknife, in half of a canteen, a clock, which kept good time; while another, with a small coffee-pot for a boiler, made a steam-engine, and had it running on a short track for the amusement of his companions. The Yankees would buy these trinkets, and send them as curiosities to their friends, or to be sold on a speculation. About the fourth month of Richards's captivity he was sent from the prison-camp to the Hammond General Hospital, and there he remained till he was exchanged.

Tom Lake, one of Mosby's men, to whose escape from the prison at Point Lookout I have already alluded, effected it in company with three companions, in the following manner. With their boots under their arms and their money in the crowns of their hats, they managed to elude the sentry, who was pacing his beat. Arrived on the beach, their difficulties were just begun, for they had to go out some distance into the bay in order to pass around the guard posted on the narrow peninsula which separates the waters of the bay from the waters of the Potomac River. They attempted first to wade, the tallest in front, all linked together by clasped hands. In this way they proceeded through the sparkling water until it so far increased in depth as to oblige them to swim. But they fortunately soon reached a sand-bar which ran parallel to the shore, and were again enabled to wade.

They followed the sand-bar through the dark rolling waters, not knowing at what moment they might be engulfed; but after a slow and toilsome march of two miles, which carried them past the sentinels, they struck for; the beach. The moon then rose, like a mountain of fire, from amid the waters, and enabled them with safety to reach the shore. At midnight they landed, having been five hours in the water, and hastened forward through swamps and woodland. Taking the precaution only to travel by night until they got out of the enemy's lines, by the aid of friendly citizens they were helped along their journey, and reached in safety their friends on the Virginia shore.

I will now relate the circumstances of Charley Grogan's escape from the prison on Johnson's Island, which was appropriated to officers, of whom there were about two thousand in confinement there at the time about which I am writing.

Grogan was captured at Gettysburg, along with General Trimble, on whose staff he was then serving, and after a short imprisonment in Fort M'Henry was removed to Johnson's Island. This island, about three hundred acres in extent, is for the most part covered with wood, and is situated in Lake Erie, about three miles from Sandusky, and one mile from the nearest point on the Ohio shore. The prison, as at Point Lookout, is surrounded by a plank enclosure, on the top of which sentinels were mounted, with orders to shoot anyone who approached within twenty feet of the wall. There was but one gateway to this enclosure, which was never used but to admit prisoners and rations. The garrison was quartered outside of the prison walls. The rations furnished the prisoners were insufficient, but those who had money were allowed to make purchases from sutlers.

In consequence of a conspiracy which was formed among the officers confined on this island to overpower the garrison, and, seizing the transportation at the wharf, to escape to Canada, which was revealed to the authorities by a prison spy, a gun-boat was stationed so as to bear on the prison, and prevent the execution of any such design. At the expiration of four weeks' confinement, Grogan, whose thoughts were still bent on regaining his liberty, discovered a collection of prisoners at the outer gate, and, upon inquiring the cause, was informed that they were going under guard to a building on the wharf for the purpose of refilling their beds with straw. He saw in this an opportunity at least for getting beyond the prison walls, and slipping on a citizen's coat, so as to be ready to take advantage of anything that might occur, he joined the party.

Arrived at the building, which was of rough plank, and near the water's edge, he was the last to enter, for he was busy in observing the island. When he went in, unobserved by the sentinel, but aided by his friends, who soon discovered his purpose, he hid himself in the straw, and when the order to return to the prison was given he was not missed by the guard, who quietly locked the door upon him. Grogan remained perfectly quiet, and occupied himself with cutting his bed-tick into strips for future use, until he found that all was still for the night on the island. He then carefully examined the door, and climbed to the roof of the building in which he was confined, but could discover no means of escape from either. He then saw an opening in the side of the house which had been a window, but then had planks nailed over it. To this he directed all his energy, and, with a pocket-knife, succeeded in making an opening large enough for him to creep through. The moon was shining brightly, and there was a sentinel pacing his beat at a short distance in front of the building from which the captive had escaped.

Waiting until the sentinel's back was turned, he managed to pass him without discovery, and reached the shore, where he crept along, hid by the bushes, until he passed around the building and was sheltered by it. He then rose to his feet, but on reaching the rear of the building came in sight of the garrison sentinels, and was again forced to get on his hands and knees, and crawl to a piece of wood. From this he emerged into an open field, and passed rapidly on, his object being to gain the nearest point on the island to the Ohio shore. He then went to work to construct a raft by the aid of the strips of bed-tick, but before it was completed day dawned, and, fearing detection, he pushed off. But the raft soon began to go to pieces, and, in the effort to regain the island, Grogan was let into the water and obliged to wade to the shore. Thoroughly wet and greatly discouraged, he determined to build a better raft the next night, but first pulled the one he had made to pieces to avoid its being noticed. Proceeding along the shore, he made the circuit of the island, but soon discovered that he was followed by a Yankee, who was evidently suspicious of him.

Boldness alone could then save him, and, assuming an air of indifference, he approached the man, whose suspicions he disarmed by his coolness, and walked toward the prison. There he encountered two men at work on the roof of a garrison building, from whom he inquired when the passenger-boat would leave for Sandusky, for he had by this time concluded to try that chance of escape. Passing the quarters of the garrison he came upon the lawn, where an artillery company was drilling, and paused to observe them. He then moved on, and in his way encountered a sutler with whom he had often traded, and also met face to face Major Schovell, the commanding officer, to whom he bowed respectfully. To his great relief, the sentinel on duty at the boat did not demand passes from the passengers going from the island to Sandusky, and Grogan quietly went on board, entered into pleasant conversation with the captain, and then took his seat at the stove. At eight o'clock, to his infinite relief, the boat pushed off, and in less than an hour he was landed at Sandusky. From thence he proceeded by railway to Baltimore, where he lay concealed during the day in the house of a friend, but at night went forth for exercise and pleasure. In a few days he started for Dixie, and, crossing the Potomac near Leesburg, in a short time joined Mosby's command.

I will let John Munson tell his own story:

✶✶✶✶✶✶

I was captured in the fight at the Dulaney House, with eight others of our command, on the 29th of October, 1864, and was confined in the Old Capitol Prison, in Washington. If prison life went harder with any one class of prisoners than another, it was with the 'guerrillas,' for they were being deprived of so much pleasure and 'plunder.' At all events, it was hard to me, and I watched every opportunity of putting an end to my sufferings. I saw one thing, that to escape I would be compelled to deceive some of the sentinels, and that jumping, running, and the like expedients were out of the question. The Yankees had made preparations for all suck attempts.

After a confinement in prison of nearly two months, I thought I had at last found a means of escape. A wagon came into the yard every other night, and along with it were generally three negroes. On one of these occasions, while the sentinel had his back turned to me, I approached the driver, and proposed to him that the next time he came he should leave in the prison-yard one of his attendants, and let me pass out in his place. For the promise of a handsome reward the man consented.

So the night agreed upon I burned a piece of cork, and picked the roughest looking overcoat in the prison, and the shabbiest hat, leaving a new one in its place, and, thus provided, sallied forth to where the wagon was already in waiting. I then blacked up, walked boldly to the wagon, which was standing near a gas-lamp by one of the sentinel's beats, and mounted on the seat. Very soon two negroes came and took their places beside me, and, with a smack of the whip, we started to leave the Old Capitol. We had to pass several sentry-posts; one, two, three were all right, but when we came to number four the soldier on duty stopped us, saying, 'Only two men came in with this wagon; one of you get down.' We all tried persuasion, and this failing, I dismounted, and offered to pay him a large reward if he would let me pass. But no, he wouldn't budge, and I was compelled to go to the hydrant, wash the nigger off, and return to my quarters, in my own estimation worth about five cents.

It was fortunate for me that I had happened to encounter a kind-hearted fellow, for he let the affair drop, and I heard no more of it, while he could either have fired on me, or have reported me to the prison authorities, by whom I would have been put in irons and confined to one of the cells. Though foiled in this attempt, yet I consoled myself with the thought that it might have been worse, and maybe I would have better luck another time. Christmas came; no escape yet. In order to keep our spirits up, and to celebrate the great festival of the Christian world, a few of us made a bucketful of hot whisky punch, and issued invitations to the occupants of several of the rooms to join in our festivity. So we killed Christmas night very dead, and I retired, with the assistance of several of the fellows, not caring whether I ever got out of prison or not.

But with the New Year revived the old longing for liberty, and my powers of invention were employed in devising a plan for escape. I observed that the hospital steward—a Yankee, of course—was allowed to pass in and out without the countersign, the sentinels recognising him by his uniform, which was the ordinary army pants and blouse, having on the sleeves, as a badge or insignia of rank, a strip of green flannel bordered with yellow, and in the centre something like an anchor and coil. This is my man, I thought; I must be hospital steward. But how to get the uniform was a question which I could not, for my life, answer. However, the plan looked well, and kept me in splendid spirits. Two weeks passed, and no uniform. At the end of that time there was an arrival in prison of a party of Yankee bounty-jumpers, one of whom wore a blouse. That is my blouse, I thought, and sure enough it was. This was the way I got it:

I had formed the acquaintance of a Yankee prisoner—a Scotchman, who had promised me to do any thing in his power for me. I went to Sawney, and told him to buy the Yankee bounty-jumper's blouse for me. Giving me a sly wink and a nod, he told me to come down into the yard in an hour, and he would have the fellow out to see me. I went, and found my two Yankees waiting for me, and was not long in striking a bargain. I gave two dollars and a half for the garment, stowed it away under my jacket, carried it to my room, and hid it under my bunk, to await future consideration. The pantaloons didn't give me much trouble, for I traded my gray ones with one of our boys for a dark pair, which answered my purpose very well. Now for the strip of green flannel. I believe I looked all over the Old Capitol Prison for a piece of green flannel, but without success.

I knew what every man's coat was lined with, and some thick coats I had ripped open, while the owners, were asleep, to see if there was any green flannel inside. I would then go to work to sew them up again. Another week was spent in this vain search, when, as I happened to be in the sutler's shop one morning, I noticed a green pasteboard box, just the colour I wanted. I asked him to give it to me to keep roasted coffee in. He emptied the box and handed it to me. I almost flew up stairs, cut it up into two slips, the size of those worn by the steward, and trimmed the edge of the green paper off, which left the yellow paper showing underneath. I next tried my powers as an engraver on the anchor and coil with perfect success; and lastly, when I bent the pasteboard around the sleeves and pinned it on my coat, it was the steward's out and out.

Of the thirty-seven men in our room, I only told one of them of my plan, and he admired it. It was Dennis Darden, who consented to go down with me into the yard and bring back the overcoat, which I would be compelled to wear in order to pass the sentinels in the house. After dressing myself as hospital steward, I substituted my new light hat for Tom Love's old black one, and started. I had chosen night as the time to make the experiment, having discovered that the steward got his meals outside, and I determined to pass for him going to his supper.

But there was one great objection to the whole plan. I was no more like the hospital steward than a monkey was like a man. He was low and fleshy, had black eyes and hair, and, worse than all, had a moustache and a goatee; while I had been starved till I was about the size of a pipe-stem, stood nearly six feet, had a fair complexion, and had not even a sprig of hair growing on my face. In other words, the hospital steward was a tolerably good-looking *man*, and I was a hard-looking boy. Yet my confidant assured me that all that was necessary would be to keep a stiff upper lip, and, if I was stopped, to put a bold face on the matter, and, pushing my arms out at the guard, bid him look at that badge. The old folks had always told me that Friday was an unlucky day to begin an enterprise, but, being one of Mosby's men, I determined to treat the idea as a prejudice, and to make my grand effort on Friday, for on that day I would have been in ward and keep just three months.

In the yard I took leave of Dennis, and told him to hasten to the upstairs window, and he would soon see me walk across the street as free as if I were in Fauquier. I felt just then a very disagreeable weakness about my knees, but one or two drinks from the sutler's "chain lightning" steadied them. From the direction of the hospital I advanced boldly up to the door of the prison, which opened on the passage leading to the street, with my hands in my pockets, and my elbows stuck out so that the badges could be plainly seep. Here I encountered the first sentinel, who looked hard at me, but I kept my arms full in view and walked briskly on, passing the second and third without looking at them. When I approached the fourth, he stepped toward me, but it was only to open the door, that the hospital steward might pass out.

I then heard the door of the Old Capitol Prison close on me, I hoped forever. But there was one more sentinel, whose beat was on the pavement in front of the house. I passed him, and was once more a free Ranger. I soon tore the badges from my sleeves, threw them into the Capitol grounds, and walked down Pennsylvania Avenue with a light and joyous heart. Having been furnished by Dennis with all necessary directions before I left him, in an hour I was transformed into a fashionable cit from Baltimore. I remained in Washington four days with the Southern men, who wished me to stay longer, but the

Potomac was then frozen over, and that was my opportunity to cross. I walked thirty-five miles through Maryland, and the third day after I left the city arrived at Leesburg.

In half an hour after I left the prison my absence was discovered, and the authorities commenced a search. They found out the Yankee who had sold me the blouse, put him in irons, and sent him to Fort Delaware, but I don't think they ever knew how I had managed to get off.

✶✶✶✶✶✶

Chapter 52: Mosby's Early Life and Character

Upper Fauquier, January 27th, 1865.

Dear Percy,—I will devote this letter to a narration of the facts which I have been at pains to collect, to enable me to gratify the very natural desire you have expressed to know something of Mosby's origin and training, as well as of his military life previous to his entering the partisan service.

John Singleton Mosby is the son of Alfred D. Mosby, of Amherst County, and was born on the 6th of December, 1833, at Edgemont, in Powhatan County, the residence of his maternal grandfather, the Rev. Mr. M'Laurin, of the Episcopal Church. At the immature age of sixteen he entered the University of Virginia, where he displayed great aptitude in several branches of learning, particularly in the study of the Greek language, in which he graduated at an early period of his course. But his college life was suddenly and rudely interrupted by a personal difficulty, in which self preservation compelled him to shoot his assailant, inflicting upon him a painful but not dangerous wound. For this act he was tried by the Criminal Court of Albemarle County, and adjudged to suffer six months' imprisonment, and pay a fine of one thousand dollars.

This harsh sentence was referable to the uncommon ability with which he was prosecuted by William J. Robertson, then Commonwealth's Attorney, now the ornament of the Court of Appeals of Virginia, in connection with a strong feeling of prejudice entertained by the citizens of Albemarle against the students of the university—a feeling which always springs up where a community, peculiar in its characteristics and pursuits, resides in the bosom of another community. As an evidence of the injustice of the verdict of the jury, the Legislature of Virginia, before whom all the facts of the case were laid, annulled it, at the recommendation of the governor, in so far as it had not been executed at the time of their assembly. When the offender was called up to receive the judgment of the court, some of the over-righteous of the community were much scandalized when the stripling stood up, in the midst of frowning brows, with no sign of penitence, and looked upon his judges with eyes as bold and bright as ever. It is but justice to the distinguished prosecutor to add, that when he took his seat, he remarked that he had never performed so disagreeable a duty, and had he been in Mosby's place he was quite sure he would have acted as Mosby had done.

This was the beginning of an acquaintance between the two, for Judge Robertson often visited the prisoner during his confinement, and furnished him with books with which to begin the study of law. As soon as his legal studies were completed he settled in Bristol, a small town intersected by the boundary-line of Virginia and Tennessee. Here he soon achieved success in his profession, and married Miss Pauline Clarke, a lady distinguished for her personal attractions, and the daughter of the Honourable Beverley J. Clarke, of Kentucky, late United States Minister to Central America, for many years a member of the United States Congress, and a criminal lawyer of great distinction.

Toward the close of the session of the Virginia Convention of 1861, Mr. Beverley Johnston, brother of the illustrious General Joseph E. Johnston, and a distinguished lawyer of the Southwest, read aloud in Abingdon, Virginia, to an excited crowd, a telegraphic dispatch announcing the secession of the state. He then inquired if they ratified the act. With one voice they said, "We do ratify it." Mosby was in this crowd. Without delay he joined a volunteer company of cavalry, the Washington Mounted Rifles, commanded by Captain William E. Jones, of the old army, and was granted a furlough to return home to settle up his unfinished business, and bid farewell to his wife and children. As soon as he had enrolled his name he visited the Honourable John B. Floyd, who had been but recently Secretary of War of the United States, to hear his views about the condition of the country. Amid the general excitement, that able statesman wore a grave and ominous brow. He said:

> The leaders of this movement in the South know not whither they are going. Some of them talk of a short war; some of them talk of no war; while other visionaries admit the possibility of war, yet say the battles of the South will be fought by the fleets

of England and the bayonets of France. There are no reveries and conjectures that are too wild and improbable for the dreamers at Montgomery to indulge in.

Instead, of there being no war or a short war, or a war which will be fought for us by foreign powers, it will prove to be one of the longest and most sanguinary conflicts between the North and South that ever desolated the earth. The men who prevented the secession of Virginia three months ago, and those at Montgomery who have fooled away the season of preparation, will be responsible for the tears of every widow and orphan.

About the middle of June Captain Jones's company reported to Governor Letcher at Richmond. During the march Mosby formed an acquaintance with Fountain Beattie which proved to be fruitful of results to both the young soldiers. While the company was camped near Richmond, he met on the street Honourable Tim Rives, the great Douglas orator in Virginia, with whom he had been brought into association by a similarity of political opinion. Mr. Rives proposed to the young soldier to apply for a commission in some of the cavalry regiments then being formed, but, with a modesty and disinterestedness quite uncommon in republican states, Mosby declined, saying that he was without any knowledge of military affairs, and preferred serving as private under an able commander like Captain Jones. Another incident occurred about this time which strikingly illustrates his independent spirit.

An ugly, ill-cut uniform, of a dingy, drab-coloured cloth, which had been manufactured in the looms of the State Prison, was distributed among the men. It had well-nigh produced a mutiny, and the clothes, amid murmurs and complaints, were deposited in a pile near the captain's tent by all to whom they had been issued save Mosby and Beattie. They laughed at the anger of their comrades, and dressed in the "penitentiary cloth," as it was called in derision, rode into Richmond to the store-House of Mr. George S. Palmer, where they found one of the company officers engaged in purchasing a handsome "but less durable uniform. But, after the battle of Manassas, the whole company were glad enough to obtain the discarded clothes.

From Richmond Captain Jones marched to Bunker Hill, where his company was incorporated in the 1st Regiment of Virginia Cavalry, commanded by Colonel J. E. B. Stuart. This regiment, after serving in the Valley, accompanied General Johnston to the battlefield of Manassas.

Before it left the valley a lot of cavalry pistols was distributed among the several companies. Six of them fell to Captain Jones, who selected six men to whom the arms were to be given, but he said, by way of qualification when they were delivered, "I shall always put these men in front. I shall always place them in the post of greatest danger." While the regiment was stationed on Bull Run, Captain Jones had occasion to send a scout across the stream into McDowell's lines. He called for the men who had the six pistols. Mosby was the first who obeyed the summons. *This was his first scout.*

During the long period of inactivity which followed the battle of Manassas he performed outpost service with his regiment, and was distinguished in the company for the punctuality and cheerfulness with which he discharged his duty. Entertaining a high opinion of Captain Jones's military capacity, he used to spend many evenings in that officer's tent, conversing about military affairs and discussing with him military problems. The result of this intercourse was, that Mosby was appointed adjutant of the regiment as soon as Jones was promoted to the command of it. He also spent much of his time in the perusal of Noland's work on the *Employment of Cavalry*, Mahan on *Outpost Duty*, Marmont's *Institutes*, and Napoleon's *Maxims*, besides several works on partisan warfare. This ushered him into a new world of ideas, for till then he had been conversant only with the affairs of peace.

On the 8th of March the regiment broke up its encampment, and, prepared, along with the rest of the Confederate army, to abandon to the enemy the Piedmont region, richly stored with agricultural produce, and fall back to the defence of the capital— the remarkable result of one of the most decisive victories in modern warfare.

While the brigade was lying at Warrenton Junction, General Stuart, through Lieutenant Mosby, ordered Colonel Jones to take the First and Second Regiments, and cross Cedar Run, and proceed as far as Bristoe Station, on a reconnaissance. On account of the swollen condition of that stream. Colonel Jones replied, through the same channel, that it would consume an entire day to swim the horses of two regiments across it. When Mosby delivered this response, he proposed to Stuart to send him, with a party of eight men, to effect the object in view, which was to ascertain the position of M'Clellan's advance. His proposition was agreed to, and the next day he reported to Stuart the desired information.

Pleased with the manner in which this duty had been performed. General Stuart, a few days later, sent Lieutenant Mosby, with a small party, to ascertain the position of the enemy as far back as Bull Pun. On this expedition. Ayer, of Cherry Pectoral celebrity, and a bridge contractor, were captured—the first of the many thousand prisoners captured by Mosby. From these prisoners Stuart learned that M'Clellan had collected at Alexandria a great fleet of transports, and that the bulk of his army had fallen back to that point.

Mosby was again dispatched to the picket-line on Cedar Run, and while at the bridge over this stream a boy from the Federal army approached, as if by mistake, and very glibly informed him that there was a large Federal force over the hill. But the artifice was detected, and the boy sent to Stuart, accompanied by a dispatch from Mosby, giving the opinion that the force on Cedar Run was a demonstration to cover some other movement, thus confirming the statement which had been made by Ayer. After some farther observations, which tended to strengthen his impression, he, in person, reported to Stuart that the division of Federal troops on Cedar Run was commanded by General Blenker, who soon after occupied Warrenton Junction, Stuart in the mean time having fallen back to the west bank of the Rappahannock River, To remove all doubt from Stuart's mind as to the correctness of his information, Mosby went on a scout to Blenker's rear, and ascertained with certainty the isolated condition of his division. Possessed of information which he deemed so important, he swam alone the Rappahannock River, to reach without delay Stuart's headquarters, while he sent the party under his command to cross at a ford higher up.

Together with the information he reported, he expressed the opinion that no operation was more feasible than for General Ewell, with his command of eight thousand infantry and Stuart's cavalry, by a rapid and secret march, to pass, under cover of a wooded country, to Blenker's rear, and capture or destroy his entire division. In this opinion Stuart, ever full of enterprise, entirely concurred; and why the effort was not made is one of the mysteries of this war. Having proved the intelligence, activity, and courage of Lieutenant Mosby, Stuart desired to employ him again as a scout, but Colonel Jones objected, and his adjutant was retained to make out monthly returns, a duty fit only for a clerk.

A little after this. Colonel Jones, although one of the most accomplished officers in the cavalry service, was dismissed from his command in virtue of one of those military elections ordained by the Confederate Government, and returned to private life. Proud and reserved by nature, and educated in the ideas of West Point, Jones was the last man to struggle with success in a military election, for:

> He would not flatter Neptune for his trident,
> Nor or Jove for his power to thunder.

With him was discharged Mosby, as far as any military engagement was concerned, but he accepted an invitation from Stuart to remain at his headquarters in the capacity of a scout.

The Battle of Seven Pines has been fought, M'Clellan is in front of Richmond, General Lee is on the Chickahominy, and Stuart's headquarters are on the Charles City Road, near Richmond, when Mosby is invited by the latter to take breakfast with him. Stuart then informed him that he wished him to go to the Totapotamie Creek, and discover whether M'Clellan was fortifying. With four companions, the scout started; but, meeting a flag of truce, he made a detour toward Hanover Courthouse. A vague idea had been floating through his mind that an enterprise such as Stuart soon after undertook might be accomplished, and, before setting out, Mosby remarked to one of the staff officers that, before his return, he expected to visit M'Clellan's headquarters. At the end of three days he returned, having gone from Hanover Court-house down the Pamunkey to Old Church, and having discovered that M'Clellan's communications with the White House were guarded by a small cavalry force, and that those communications were but an extension of his right flank.

He reported to General Stuart; and as they sat on the grass together, he gave a detailed account of his adventures, and the reasons in favour of the opinion that a successful raid could be made on M'Clellan's communications. The general requested the scout to reduce his report to writing. As soon as it was done, Stuart carried it in a sweeping gallop to General Lee, to whom he unfolded the enterprise in all its parts; and the next day, with two thousand cavalry and four pieces of artillery, set forth, with Mosby for a guide, to test the correctness of his opinion. With the brilliant success which crowned this expedition you are doubtless acquainted, but I shall pass over its attendant circumstances, as they belong rather to Stuart's than Mosby's history. In his letter of congratulation to Stuart, General Lee makes complimentary mention of the gallantry displayed on the expedition by two privates, John S. Mosby and Theophilus P. Clapp.

In his first interview with Stuart after the return of the expedition, he was greeted by him with warmth, and assured that there would be no difficulty in getting him promotion on account of the extraordinary service he had rendered. But nothing came of it, and Mosby retained his position as scout.

With the two armies jammed up against each other in so small a compass, the field of enterprise was necessarily circumscribed, and Mosby determined, about the time of the Battle of Port Republic, to go to Jackson, for he thought he recognised in him one who would appreciate the value of the idea he wished to develop. This plan was, however, defeated by the transfer of Jackson's army from the valley to Richmond, and he again returned to Stuart, and was again employed in the old way. His first scout was with a party of three or four men to M'Clellan's rear, from which he brought back information which enabled Stuart to attack and drive away with his artillery the transports which were at Harrison's Landing, and had opened communications with the Federal Army.

Soon after, Stuart's cavalry was moved to Atlee's Station, on the Central Railroad, for the purpose of reorganisation. From that camp Mosby was sent in the direction of Fredericksburg, to acquire for General Lee information about the distribution of Pope's army, which he reported to be as follows: He had troops at Fredericksburg, troops at Manassas, Warrenton, Luray, Winchester, and Front Royal, and between these several points communications had to be maintained. With the eye of a soldier, Mosby beheld a splendid field of operations thus opened, and besought Stuart to furnish him with a detail of fifteen men, with whom to proceed to Fauquier, and enter upon a partisan career, for he argued that with such a nucleus he could soon recruit a large command; for there had been then no conscription in the region to which he proposed to go, and it was well supplied with subsistence. This request was peremptorily refused, but instead he was furnished with a complimentary letter to General Jackson, who was then near Gordonsville. With this letter in his pocket he set forth, but was taken prisoner near Beaver Dam by a raiding-party commanded by Colonel Davies, and carried to Fredericksburg.

Conscious that he would soon be exchanged, the prisoner was on the alert to obtain information that would prove serviceable to the Confederate generals. He was carried to Washington, where he was confined about ten days, and then sent to Hampton Roads to be exchanged, according to the cartel which had just been arranged between General Dix and General D. H. Hill.

But, during his imprisonment at Washington, he had been summoned to his presence by General Pope, and interrogated in relation to the Confederate army. When he was introduced to General Smith, of Pope's staff, many courtesies were' shown him, and among them an offer was made to lend him money. This he promptly declined. Then followed direct questions. But Mosby plainly told him that he should communicate nothing that could be of any service to General Pope. The Federal officer took the refusal in very good part, and appeared to appreciate the honourable motives of his captive, whom he remanded to prison, there to resume the study of Napoleon's *Maxims*, a copy of which he had brought with him.

While he lay in the prison transport in Hampton Roads, Mosby was still on the scout. He did not fail to ingratiate himself with the captain and mate of the vessel, and on their return on one occasion from Fortress Monroe, gained from them knowledge of a fact which he deemed of great importance, for Burnside had arrived from the South, and his transports were then at anchor in the Roads. But to what point was Burnside bound? Would he re-enforce M'Clellan, or would he proceed up the Rappahannock, and, disembarking at Fredericksburg, unite with Pope, then on the Rapidan, in his march on Richmond? This was the problem which that inquisitive mind was engaged in solving, as he lay sweltering in the prison-ship *Georgia*. He boldly inquired of the captain of his ship for what point Burnside was destined. He replied, "Fredericksburg," and soon after Mosby saw the fleet weigh anchor and enter the waters of Chesapeake Bay. With impatience he counted the lazy hours till he leaped ashore at Verina, where the exchange of prisoners was effected.

As soon as he informed Commissioner Ould that he had important information for General Lee, he was allowed to proceed at once on his way. Weary and footsore, he had dropped by the road side not far from Richmond, when a private from Hampton's legion, detailed as courier, rode past. Mosby hailed the soldier, who, as soon as he informed him that he had important information to communicate, allowed him to ride his horse to army headquarters, where he was received by General Lee with a kindness of manner which is ever characteristic of that great man. He reported to the general the information he had acquired, and was both surprised and confused when asked from what direction he thought the next advance would be made. He replied,

"Pope will coalesce with Burnside at Fredericksburg, and from that point advance upon Richmond."

A courier was at once ordered to be in attendance, and a dispatch was soon sent to Jackson, for Lee had taken notes of the communication he had received. As Mosby rose to depart, he said to the general,

"You will know better what weight to attach to my information when I tell you that I am one of the men mentioned in your general order made in connection with Stuart's raid around M'Clellan."

"Oh yes," replied the general, "I remember you well."

Very soon Jackson crossed the Rapidan, and engaged Pope at Cedar Mountain. Mosby had gone to the First Virginia Cavalry, then on duty at Mount Carmel Church, in Caroline County. As he stood on an outpost with Beattie, he heard Jackson's guns. "I brought on that battle, at least," said the scout.

As soon as Jackson recrossed the Rapidan Mosby again set out to join him, but was met by Stuart, and went with him to a mountain on the Orange side of the river, which was used as an observatory by the Southern army. From that high point they saw the Federals falling back toward Culpepper Court-house, and very soon Stuart crossed the Rapidan and pressed on to the Rappahannock. From that time until Stuart's raid on Catlett's Station Mosby served with his cavalry, for he did not apply, as he had intended, for service with Jackson.

In Jackson's flank movement to Pope's rear Mosby participated, and from Manassas Junction was sent by Stuart in the direction of Alexandria to ascertain whether re-enforcements were coming to Pope. With Jasper Jones and two others he crossed Bull Run, and proceeded in the direction of Fairfax Court-house. From thence he returned alone to the army, for his companions had been sent back in charge of captures he had made on the route.

At the second battle of Manassas he was still with Stuart's cavalry, doing duty in the ranks of his old regiment.

At the Battle of Sharpsburg, which occurred next in order, he was on the staff of Stuart, who on that occasion was in command of the artillery which was massed on Jackson's left.

Mosby's horse having been disabled at the battle of Sharpsburg, he was compelled to return to his father's home to procure another, and rejoined Stuart at Barbee's Cross roads, in Fauquier County, where he was skirmishing with M'Clellan's advance, Lee being then in the act of falling back from the camp at Bunker Hill to the line of the Rappahannock.

M'Clellan crossed the Rappahannock, and Lee took up his position on the Hazel River, which thus became the dividing line for the hostile armies. Here M'Clellan stopped, and his adversary did not know but that, under cover of that front, he might be sending troops to the Peninsula. In this condition of affairs, Mosby proposed to Stuart to let him have a command strong enough to raid on M'Clellan's rear, but he was refused. A scout was then proposed by him in search of information, and this being agreed to, he took with him Beattie and another, and crossed the Rappahannock. He reported, on his return to General Lee, that no troops had been sent to the Peninsula, and that the Northern army was still distributed around Warrenton. In addition, he had learned that M'Clellan had been superseded by Burnside.

A few days later, with one companion, he again crossed into Fauquier, and made the additional discovery that Burnside's army was moving toward Fredericksburg, but this fact had been communicated to General Stuart before Mosby's return.[1] From the cavalry headquarters at Warrenton he was sent with nine men to ascertain the position of Siegel's corps. By a skilful disposition of his men, he deceived the large picket at Groveton into the belief that Stuart's cavalry were advancing, in consequence of which the regiment to which it belonged fell back toward Centreville.

During the progress of the battle at Fredericksburg, Mosby, with six men, was ordered to scout, on the Little River Turnpike. At Mat Lee's he encountered a party of Federals about equal in number to his own, and killed the sergeant in command and one private, and put the others to flight. From the camp at Fredericksburg he accompanied Stuart on an unsuccessful raid on Dumfries, and soon afterward on an expedition to Fairfax Station. When the corps reached Middleburg Mosby was left on detached duty, and entered upon the adventurous career of a Partisan Ranger.

But my sketch would be incomplete without some account of my hero's personal characteristics.

He is scarcely of medium height, and his frame is slight, indicating activity, but not strength. He weighs about one hundred and twenty-

---

1. The author was at that time in command of the picket line on the Upper Hazel. With a party he had crossed the river on a reconnaissance, and discovered that the enemy had fallen back to Amissville. He was informed by Mr. M——tt, an intelligent citizen, who had just returned from Warrenton, that Burnside was in command of the Federal army, and was moving toward Fredericksburg. The information was at once sent to General Rosser, and through him reached army headquarters. The guide was a Baptist preacher.

five pounds, and is capable of undergoing great fatigue. His complexion is fair, and his features delicate, which contribute to the extreme youthfulness of his appearance, for the cares of his eventful career have left no trace on his countenance. His most remarkable feature is a brilliant gray eye, which indicates great intelligence and quick penetration.

His deportment is quiet and unobtrusive, and he is rather a thinker than a talker. Yet are his powers of pleasing unusual, and his conversation is racy, witty, and entertaining. He relates an anecdote with great zest, and his smile is almost irresistible. His manners are not demonstrative, yet he is warm and tenacious in his attachments, and generous to a fault. Such is Mosby in private; his public character you must gather from his career.

Chapter 53: The Mount Carmel Fight

Upper Fauquier, February 27th, 1865.

Dear Percy,—When Major Richards was left in command in "Mosby's Confederacy," he turned his attention to the lower valley, and, with sixty men, crossed the Shenandoah at Myers's Ford. Here he met Lieutenant Baylor, with Company "B" of the Twelfth Virginia Cavalry, accompanied by Colonel Preston Chew, commanding the Horse Artillery of the Army of Northern Virginia, who agreed to join the Rangers in the expedition.

Colonel Chew is one of the most distinguished artillery officers in the Confederate service, and is a graduate of the Virginia Military Institute. At the beginning of the war he commanded the artillery attached to Ashby's Cavalry, and displayed both skill and courage in Ashby's numberless encounters with the invaders along the Valley Turnpike. The horse artillery has been distributed in winter quarters at various points in the interior, and Chew has obtained permission to spend the interval with Mosby's Rangers.

Once foiled in an attempt to capture a train of cars on the Baltimore and Ohio Railroad, Major Richards determined in the winter solstice to try his fortune again, and approached that great highway of travel and transportation at a point two miles below Duffield Depot. The tracks were torn up, pickets were posted, and the command lay down to sleep, but was soon aroused by the approach of cars from the direction of Harper's Ferry. The engine was thrown down an embankment, leaving on the track a train of fifteen cars, laden, some of them, with sugar, ale, and immense quantities of coffee, not to speak of canned oysters, raisins, wines, and other articles of like kind, which had been intended for an entertainment to be given in Martinsburg. While the train was being plundered, Richards observed a light approaching from the direction of Duffield, which, proved to be borne by the regular night patrol, who, without resistance, were captured.

At the expiration of an hour the train was fired, and the command returned to Fauquier, each man carrying before him one or more sacks of coffee, and such other articles as inclination or convenience induced him to store away. The weather was intensely cold, and the Shenandoah was swollen and was covered with fragments of ice, and many a frostbitten Ranger has good reason to remember the January night when he made the Coffee Raid.

Soon after the Coffee Raid our enterprising major started with forty men from Bloomfield, to make a third attempt to capture the express train on the Baltimore and Ohio Railroad, and halted his command, about ten o'clock at night, near the crossing of the Winchester and Potomac Railroad known as Flowing Springs. With John Chew and another, he proceeded to ascertain an eligible point at which the railroad could be crossed, and, before his return to the command, captured two stragglers from the Twelfth Pennsylvania Cavalry, which, under the command of Colonel Reno, was camped in the neighbourhood. From the prisoners the information was obtained that the Winchester and Potomac Railroad was so strongly patrolled that it would be almost impossible for Richards to cross it, and proceed to the Baltimore and Ohio Railroad, six miles distant, and capture a train of cars, without being intercepted on his return by superior numbers. Abandoning, for this reason, the object which had brought him across the mountain, he resolved upon the more daring enterprise of visiting Colonel Reno in his camp.

One of the prisoners consented to act as guide, and from him the countersign for the night was obtained, and other useful information. Retaining fifteen men, Richards sent the rest of the command home, when, following the "North Star," as the men denominated the guide, the Rangers started on the expedition. It was a still and cloudless night as they rode in among the sleeping soldiers. Wiltshire and Sheppard without difficulty captured the sentinel, whose post they passed, as they were mistaken for the returning patrol.

There were about forty horses fastened around the guard-tent, which belonged to the men who had been detailed for patrol duty that night. These were at once seized, and might without difficulty have been carried off, but the partisans were not satisfied with this, exploit. They determined to give the Yankees a parting shot—16 leave their cards for Colonel Reno, they said. So they rode among the tents, firing at everything that appeared. But this amusement could not last long, and Richards was compelled to retreat amid a shower of bullets. The firing, though it hurt no one, yet occasioned the loss of all the booty save six horses.

The next morning Colonel Reno, it is said, addressed a speech to his men, whom he censured in severe terms for allowing such a nocturnal visit to be paid his camp with impunity, and in the course of it said, "With such men as Mosby's I could go any where." This was no idle boast, for Colonel Reno enjoys in the army the reputation of a gallant officer, and by strict discipline and justice has won the good opinion of the citizens of Jefferson County.

After his visit to Colonel Reno, Major Richards, with ten men, attempted the exploit of making a visit to Alexandria, but, as he approached the town, was diverted from his purpose by a fall of snow, which would have enabled the enemy to track him. As he returned, he attacked a train of carts proceeding toward the town, under the escort of negroes, commanded by a white officer. A fight ensued, the result of which was the dispersion of the negroes, after three of them had been wounded and eight taken prisoners.

I will now give you an account of the Mount Carmel fight, which occurred about the middle of February.

Spotts, a deserter from the Eleventh Virginia Cavalry, had been instrumental in the capture, at their homes, of about thirty officers and men belonging to the brigade of which he had been a member. Emboldened by success, the deserter had crossed the mountain into Fauquier, to collect information which would lead to farther captures. At Simpers's Mill, which is situated in a gorge of the Blue Ridge, on the mountain-track which leads from Paris to Markham, the spy stopped to have his horse shod, and learned from several of his old acquaintances, who had not yet heard of his desertion, the presence in the neighbourhood of Colonel White and also of several members of the Partisan Battalion. From Simpers's Mill Spotts, habited like a Confederate soldier, proceeded to the neighbourhood of Upperville, where he was informed that Major Richards was at home.

From this place he recrossed the mountain, and reported his discoveries at the headquarters of Tibberts's cavalry brigade. In consequence, with Spotts for a guide, a raiding-party of one hundred and twenty-five men from the 1st New York Cavalry and an equal number from the 14th Pennsylvania was dispatched to Fauquier, under command of Major Gibson, of the latter regiment, who was accompanied by several of General Merritt's staff officers. Major Gibson forded the Shenandoah at Sheppard's Mill and proceeded to Paris, where he arrived at midnight. Here he divided his command; the New Yorkers he sent to Upperville, with orders there to remain until he joined them, while with the Pennsylvanians he went toward Markham by the road which passes Simpers's Mill.

As soon as the detachment arrived at Upperville, a party was dispatched to capture Major Richards, at the residence of his father, and Captain Robert Walker, who was understood to be with him. The house was surrounded and closely searched, but the two officers, together with John Hipkins, had been successfully concealed, by means of a trapdoor, which had been constructed in view of such an emergency. Satisfied that Richards and his comrade had received notification of their approach, the nocturnal visitors returned to their command, which, during their absence, had been likewise active in searching for soldiers. They had captured several, but, what was of far more importance, had discovered several barrels of apple brandy, on which almost the entire command had gotten drunk. For this reason, instead of waiting for Major Gibson, the detachment was marched across the Shenandoah and back to their camp, followed by Major Richards, with a small party, as far as the river.

We will now follow Major Gibson, who, before his return to the river, fell in with something much less agreeable than a barrel of apple brandy. Arrived at Simpers's Mill, he was disappointed in not finding Colonel White, as the deserter had reported, but succeeded in capturing his adjutant and Jerry Wilson, of Mosby's Battalion. The raiding-party, after visiting Markham, marched to Upperville, as had been agreed upon, and on the route made prisoner Mosby's fighting quartermaster.

Jerry Wilson was in the depths of despair, for his marriage was to have been consummated the next day, until he cast up his eyes and beheld Slice Barbour's Jim Banks horse, which, like Jerry, had been picked up on the march. Hope at once revived in the breast of the despondent bridegroom; for, said he, "if I can only induce this rascal of a guard to let me mount Slice Barbour's horse, my escape, as we cross the mountain, is almost certain." So Jerry put on his blandest smile, and obtained from his guard permission to exchange the cob he was riding for the celebrated steed of his friend and neighbour.

On the return march, when the Federal column reached Paris, Major Gibson was besieged by the tears and entreaties of the mountain beauty to whom Jerry Wilson was betrothed. But he turned a deaf ear to them, and Jerry, mounted on the Jim Banks horse, with a cocked pistol at his ear, accompanied the Federal column, reflecting on the vicissitudes to which true love is ever exposed.

Lieutenant Wren, who has a touch of the bloodhound about him, with a small party, had followed Major Gibson on his circuitous route, harassing his march at every step, and by the time he returned to Paris had collected as many as thirty men. At this place he was joined by Major Richards, who was welcomed with huzzas by the men. They demanded to be led without delay against the enemy's rear-guard, which was about equal in number to themselves. But Richards, rising in his saddle, proudly told them that he meant to attack the column. Leaving a man in Paris to send to the front the Rangers as fast as they arrived at that place, he formed his command into column and swiftly followed the track of the enemy, who could yet be seen slowly proceeding up the mountain toward Ashby's Gap. When he reached the tollgate the rear-guard was visible at the next bend of the road, about one hundred yards in advance, but the main body was concealed from view.

On either side of the turnpike at this point the Blue Ridge lifts its towering heights, and, together with the serpentine course of the road, prevented the enemy from discovering the strength of their pursuers, and at the same time prevented them from making use of their own superiority in numbers. Here Richards resolved to make the fight, and gave the order to charge. The enemy's rear-guard faced about, fired an ineffectual volley from their carbines, and then turned to retreat. The Confederates, however, continued the charge until the rear-guard was driven into the column, which had just begun to form in an open space in front of Mount Carmel Church, which stands at the junction of the turnpike with the road leading to Sheppard's Mill.

They fiercely assaulted the Federals with revolvers at close range, who replied with the carbines. But the superiority of the revolver, as in the case with Captain Blazer, was soon evident. As the partisans mingled with the enemy, the latter began to retire toward Sheppard's Mill, at first slowly, then more rapidly—a walk, a trot, a gallop, and then a headlong flight. The road appears to have been dug out of the mountain, is narrow, rough, and hilly, and is crossed at short intervals by streams of water that gush from the mountain side. Not more than two men could ride abreast—a fact which greatly protected the retreat of the enemy.

While the pursuit was in progress, Major Richards observed a Federal soldier endeavouring to protect his comrades by firing back on the pursuers. He turned to Jack Robinson, of the 6th Virginia, and inquired if he could not shoot that man. Syd Ferguson, who was immediately behind Robinson, gave Fashion the spur, and at one bound placed himself next to the enemy.

"Which one did you say, major?"

"The man on the dun horse," Richards replied.

Ferguson at once dashed forward, but succeeded only in capturing Lieutenant Baker, of General Merritt's staff, for the man on the dun horse, who was Spotts, hearing himself singled out, soon made off, and was lost among the fugitives.

The Rangers had been compelled from time to time to stop in order to prevent their prisoners from escaping to the mountain. In consequence, Major Richards, after the chase had continued for four miles, found himself entirely alone. He had captured a sergeant and a private, whom he left under a promise to remain where they were until his return. But, as he rode off, he perceived that they had broken their compact, for, again mounted, they were preparing to strike into the woods. Richards returned, and would have killed them for their breach of faith but for the appearance of Jim Wiltshire and a comrade. The prisoners were turned over to the custody of the latter, and Richards and Wiltshire continued the pursuit. Wiltshire stipulated that he should have the next chance, and was soon gratified. Approaching the river, they came again in sight of the enemy. The Ranger singled out his man, and, starting his horse at full speed, shot him dead at the distance of a few paces, for Wiltshire always prefers short range.

I will in this connection describe with particularity the process of "going through" a Yankee.

Several prisoners were captured on the river bank, and several, in the act of crossing, were ordered by Wiltshire to return, which they did without hesitation. His first act was to demand their greenbacks, his second to demand their pistols.

"How much money have you?" said he to one of the captives.

"Twenty-five dollars," responded the Yankee, in dolorous tones.

"Good," said Jim; "my friend, it is the very sum I stand in need of," and the Ranger smiled complacently at his prisoner, for this is one of the amenities of war which Wiltshire always practices when he gets hold of a fat Yankee.

During this dialogue and transfer of property, the enemy from the opposite bank kept up a brisk fire at the Ranger, but he was so deeply engaged in counting his money that he did not so much as raise his eyes as the balls whistled about him. The prisoners were turned over to a member of the command who had just come up, and Richards and Wiltshire, again hunting in couples, crossed the river, and captured a number of horses that had been abandoned by their riders. With this booty they returned to Mount Carmel Church.

The results of the fight were thirteen of the enemy killed, and about an equal number wounded, sixty-four taken prisoners, and ninety horses captured. Among the prisoners was a wounded captain, who had commanded the Federal rear-guard. He was a parson by trade, and his arm had been shattered. Richards released him from captivity that he might return to his friends, but he did not get farther than Berry's Ferry, where he died. The only loss which Major Richards sustained was Iden, of Lee's army, who was accidentally shot, and Dr. Sowers, who was wounded in the beginning of the fight. This gallant fight was complimented by General Lee in a dispatch to the Department.

Major Gibson had gathered on his raid about fifteen prisoners and twenty horses, which, having been recovered, ought to be credited to Major Richards.

But you will be curious to know how it fared with Jerry Wilson and the Jim Banks horse amid the hurly-burly. As soon as the fight at Mount Carmel began, Jerry at once looked out for a chance to make a break, but the Yankee who had him in charge cocked his pistol, and compelled the captive reluctantly to move forward in the direction of Sheppard's Mill, determined, let the fight go as it might, to carry him off. Presently the rout began, and off Jerry and his Yankee started. At first Jerry thought to outrun him on the Jim Banks horse, but the Yankee rather had the foot of him. Jerry then determined again to have recourse to stratagem; so, when the guard was looking another way, he broke off to the right hand in the mountain, but closely followed by his inevitable Yankee.

The fugitive soon found his course up the mountain side barred by a frowning ledge of rocks, which he could not flank, and with a sad heart abandoned his horse and continued his flight on foot, and without looking behind him, expecting every moment to be shot through the head by his villainous guard. He scrambled up the ledge, and was about to conceal himself under one of its projecting eaves, when he heard the sound of the pursuer on his tracks. Off he again started, and continued his flight until he reached a clearing on the top of the mountain, where, exhausted, the luckless bridegroom sank upon the ground, unable to proceed farther. But great was Jerry's astonishment and delight when, instead of the horrid Yankee with a cocked pistol in his hand, he saw his faithful companion, the Jim Banks horse, gallop up. In another moment he mounted on his steed, and was making his way with the unerring sagacity of a lover along the mountain to Simpers's Mill, near which dwelt his dark-eyed beauty.

Chapter 54: The Ganttt House and Harmony Fights.

Upper Fauquier, March 25th, 1865.

Dear Percy,—Early in March Major Richards directed Jim Wiltshire to take fourteen men and proceed to the Baltimore and Ohio Railroad, and ascertain whether re-enforcements were coming from the West to General Grant. After crossing the river, Wiltshire sent three men on a scout to Charlestown, with orders to report the condition of affairs at that place to him at a designated house. Gallagher and Anderson obtained permission to stop by the wayside to get supper, and as they approached the rendezvous, Anderson, who was riding alone, was met by two men of the Twelfth Pennsylvania, whom he mistook for friends. But he was soon undeceived, for the Federals, with presented pistols, demanded his surrender.

In the surrender Anderson reserved one of his pistols, by the aid of which he subsequently made his escape. As he dashed off from his captors, the shots which they fired at him brought Wiltshire and his party to the spot. One of the Yankees got off, but the other was repeatedly shot and killed, while attempting to climb over a garden fence. The dead body was then thrown across a horse and conveyed to the main road, for it would have compromised the safety of the citizen had the corpse been discovered in his garden the next morning.

Arrived at the Baltimore and Ohio Railroad, Wiltshire's first act was to throw off a train of cars, and then to obtain from a citizen the military information of which he was in search. On his return, he reported to his commanding officer that sixteen thousand of Thomas's army had moved eastward to join Grant. It was well for the Valley Scout, as Wiltshire is sometimes called, that he did not cross at Keys's Ford, which was directly in his route, but instead went higher up, for two companies of the Twelfth Pennsylvania had been sent out to waylay him at the river. One was placed in ambuscade at Keys's Ford, while the other was directed to strike the river at a point higher up, and charge any troops it might encounter. This last order produced a collision between the two companies, in which one man was killed. The unfortunate Twelfth!

Soon after this Colonel Mosby returned to his command, having entirely recovered from his wound. One of his first acts was to fill the vacancy caused in Company C by the promotion of Captain William H. Chapman to the rank of lieutenant colonel. For this post he designed Lieutenant George Baylor, of the Sixth Virginia Cavalry, and, to facilitate his transfer, furnished him with a letter of recommendation to the Secretary of War. But the secretary thought that the appointment would be illegal, and Baylor returned to report the failure of his application to Mosby, who, determined not to be foiled, told that gallant young officer that he should be captain of Company H, soon to be organised.

Lieutenant Frank Carter, with Bush Underwood for a guide, and twenty-two men, was sent to Fairfax in search of Yankees. He took up a position on the road leading from the court-house to Vienna, about one mile from the former place, and about an equal distance from a blockhouse in the direction of Vienna, which was garrisoned by several companies of infantry. About midday the patrol approached from the block-house, and was charged by Carter's men in silence. The Yankees halted, gazed at the advancing cavalry for a minute, and then broke and fled with precipitation, pursued by the Rangers.

CAPTAIN GLASSCOCK.

Bush Underwood was mounted on the best horse in the command, and well did he use his advantage, for before the fugitives could reach the shelter of the blockhouse he had killed three and wounded two of them. In addition, the Federals lost three prisoners and six horses.

I will now pass to the fight at Gantt's house, or a piece of Captain Glasscock's handiwork.

With thirty-six men he took up a concealed position near the Vienna and Luenville road, not far from the point where it crosses the Alexandria and Leesburg Turnpike. At the point of junction of the two roads was a blockhouse garrisoned by infantry, a string of blockhouses being a precaution to which Mosby has compelled the Federals to resort, in addition to employing other defences. After a while a patrol of twenty-two men, commanded by a lieutenant, and accompanied by a lieutenant colonel and a surgeon, passed Glasscock's position, going toward Vienna. Bush Underwood, with fourteen men, had been stationed under cover of a hill to attack them in rear, while Glasscock, with the rest of the command, would charge them in front, and, the road being enclosed on either side by a high fence, by this disposition the patrol would be placed in considerable danger.

As soon as Underwood heard the signal shots he dashed forward, and met the Federals, who had been surprised and driven back by Glasscock. The pursuit was pressed with vigour until the entire party was killed or captured, with the exception of two officers, one the lieutenant colonel, whose fine Irish hunter overleaped the fences and bore off his rider in safety. Glasscock's loss was Yates, of Rappahannock, shot in the melee by one of his comrades, and O'Brien, of Fairfax, wounded in the leg. The man who shot O'Brien was killed by Moss, and it is worthy of mention that the soldier who wounded Mosby at Centreville was killed in this fight. John Hipkins, better known as "Glorious John," distinguished himself on this occasion.

Next in order comes the Harmony fight, so called from Harmony Church, near which it took place.

Mosby had ordered a detail of men to be sent to Loudoun for the purpose of collecting corn for distribution among the command, who, during this service, were quartered among the Quakers. They were ordered to assemble every day at Hamilton, and were immediately disbanded by Captain Glasscock if no business demanded attention.

On the 20th of March, John Chew, with three men, was directed to proceed to Hillsboro and collect information, and after the usual number of chicken-fights and dogfights, at which Bob Ridley presided as ring-master, the men were dismissed to their respective boarding-houses.

As Chew entered Hillsboro he was notified by a lady that a Federal command was in the other end of the town, which turned out to be Byrd's regiment of infantry and the 12th Pennsylvania Cavalry, re-enforced by the Loudoun Rangers, all under command of Colonel Rives. After being fired upon the scouts retreated, but, re-enforced by fourteen of their comrades, and ignorant of the strength of the Federals, returned and skirmished with their advance-guard almost to Purcellville.

In the meantime, Captain Glasscock, having collected a command of one hundred and twenty men, was ordered by Mosby to take a position a mile beyond Hamilton, through which, the Federals would pass going toward Leesburg. A picket which had been thrown out retreated before Colonel Reno's cavalry past Glasscock's position, who had been ordered by Mosby to fall back deeper in the woods, that he might not be discovered, and thus would be able to attack the Federals in rear. This order was being executed when the enemy came in sight, and the rear of Glasscock's column, not understanding the movement, was thrown into disorder. Fearing the effect upon his men of appearing to retreat in the face of the enemy, Glasscock determined to counter-march, and charge back on the Federal cavalry. This was done in the most gallant style, and the Yankees, thrown into confusion by the unexpected onset, retreated toward their infantry, still at Hamilton. When the Rangers had gone several hundred yards in pursuit, they were stopped by Mosby, who had discovered the overwhelming odds in reserve—all but twenty-five, who followed the cavalry close to their infantry supports.

John Chew, with reckless gallantry, pressed on toward the village, and received a disabling shot, whether from friend or foe is not known.

Glasscock's. loss in this engagement was Keith and Binford killed, Chew disabled, and Griffin slightly wounded. The enemy's loss was ten prisoners, and, according to the report of citizens, fifteen or twenty killed, and as many wounded.

For this fight Colonel Reno was made a brigadier general. From Hamilton the Yankees marched toward Upperville, one of Mosby's depots for grain, but they were pressed so closely that they did not succeed in getting any of it. On this skirmishing march Johnny Foster received a severe wound in the knee, but was brought off the field by Hefflebower, who mounted him on his own horse.

Chapter 55: Gallant Action of a Yankee Lieutenant

Upper Fauquier, April 18th, 1865.

Dear Percy,—Richmond has fallen, the cause is lost, and Mosby, in the hour of victory, is negotiating for the disbandment of the Partisan Battalion. The sun which rose in such brightness, rode in such splendour through the sky, is, in the inscrutable providence of God, destined, like the transient meteor, to be extinguished forever.

> Those golden palaces, those golden halls
> With furniture superfluously fair;
> Those stately courts, those high encountering walls,
> Evanish all like vapours in the air.

In the midst of my preparations for departure, and with a sorrowful heart, I will complete my account of the military operations of the command with which I have been connected, some of which occurred after the evacuation of Richmond, but before that event was known in the Upper Piedmont. The people of other portions of the Southern Confederacy may have been prepared for the catastrophe by the gradual stages of decline which they witnessed, but here, amid a continual round of successes, they saw the Confederated banner waving triumphantly. Hope was in every eye, confidence was on every lip, and when the catastrophe was announced it came with the suddenness and violence of an earthquake. Now all is doubt and dismay. Every countenance reflects the calamity which has befallen the country.

As Charles B. Wiltshire about the first of April was returning from Leesburg, he was met by Colonel Mosby, who apprised him of his intention of making him a lieutenant in Company "H," and at the same time ordered him to take a party and make a scout to Stevenson's Depot, on the Winchester and Potomac Railroad. With a few men, Wiltshire was approaching through a lane which leads from Berryville, the residence of Colonel Daniel Bonham, as a Federal officer, who proved to be Lieutenant Eugene Ferris, of the 30th Massachusetts Infantry, was seen to pass rapidly from the house to the stable, which was situated in a corner of the yard. Wiltshire and Gill, who were riding fifty paces in advance of their comrades, passing through the gate which admitted them to the yard, dashed up to the stable-door in which Ferris was standing. Without drawing his pistol from the holster, Wiltshire demanded a surrender.

"Never with life," replied Ferris; and, as his adversary was attempting to disengage his pistol, he inflicted on him a mortal wound in the neck. A little after. Gill, who was somewhat to Wiltshire's left, fired, but Ferris, being protected by the door-post, was not struck, and at once fired on Gill, and inflicted upon him a disabling wound. By this time the rest of the party had arrived on the scene of combat, and opened a rapid fire on the Federal officer, who, disdaining to "fight from a cover, stepped into the open space in front of the stable, and engaged in what appeared to be a hopeless contest. But it was hopeless only in appearance, for, begirt with pistols, he was a skilful shot, and had the additional advantage of being on foot, so that almost all his balls took effect. Soon the gallant officer was master of the field. It was death to stand before that unerring pistol. Orrick and Bartlett Bolling had both been wounded, and Orrick, in addition, had been thrown from his horse.

Seizing Wiltshire's horse, which he found at the gate, Ferris directed his orderly, who, crouched in the stable, had taken no part in the conflict, to mount and follow him, but, before taking his departure, he advanced some paces toward his adversaries, who had retreated back to the lane, and fired at them two parting shots. He then sprang into his saddle, and turned his face toward his camp. Two of the Rangers, one wounded, who were waiting until he mounted his horse, started in pursuit. A running fight was kept up until Lieutenant Ferris (for his orderly was captured in the pursuit) passed the Federal picket-post, but not until he had received a slight wound. When the facts of this encounter were related to Grogan, he remarked that the lieutenant ought to be invited to join the battalion. When they were related to Mosby, he said, "Why, he is as brave as Grogan."[1]

After the encounter was over. Gill attempted, notwithstanding his wound, to return to his friends at Middleburg, but was compelled to stop at the house of a citizen in the Blue Ridge, where in a few days he died. He received the announcement of his approaching end with calmness, and said,

"I die at least in a good cause."

George Murray Gill was from Baltimore, and son of the distinguished gentleman of that name, and at the time of his death had just entered his twenty-fourth year. He was graduated at Princeton College, where he exhibited unusual talent for public speaking, a fine omen of success in the profession of law, to which he had devoted his talents and energy. Moved by the spirit of chivalry which animated so many of the young gentlemen of Maryland, he crossed the Potomac, and at an early period of the war enlisted in the Southern army, and served first in the infantry, then in the cavalry arm of the service. He participated in many of the great battles, and was every where conspicuous for the highest qualities of a soldier.

The day after the second battle of Manassas, he received in a skirmish on the Little River Turnpike a severe wound, which compelled him to absent himself from the army until the middle of November. From that time till after the disaster at Gettysburg he was constantly with Stuart's cavalry, but was taken prisoner at Hagerstown on the retreat of Lee's army. He spent five dreary months in prison, first at Fort Delaware, then at Point Lookout. At the end of this time he was sent to Richmond, and soon after rejoined his regiment, from which he was transferred to the Partisan Battalion. The elements in him were finely blended, for manly courage was united to intelligence, a high morality, and great gentleness of disposition.

On the 5th of April, Company "H" was organised at North Fork Church, in Loudoun County. At the last of Mosby's elections, George Baylor was made Captain; Edward Thompson, First Lieutenant; James Wiltshire, Second Lieutenant; and Franklin Carter, Junior Second Lieutenant.

---

1. There are many different accounts of this fight, and I have taken great pains to ascertain the truth. Colonel Bonham is a witness of unimpeachable veracity, besides being a gentleman of decided Southern principles. He witnessed the whole affair, and his account I have adopted.

George Baylor is a native of Jefferson County, Virginia, and served the first year of the war in the ranks of the Stonewall Brigade, from which he was transferred to the 12th Virginia Cavalry, a component of Ashby's brigade, and was soon made lieutenant. While on detached service he captured a company of cavalry, and performed other exploits, which induced Mosby to tender him the captaincy of this new company.

Lieutenant Thompson was born in Fairfax County, and had recommended himself to promotion by valuable service in the battalion.

Lieutenant Wiltshire is from Jefferson, and has long ago introduced himself to your acquaintance.

Lieutenant Carter is from Loudoun, and, though only nineteen years of age, is a veteran in the battalion. His promotion by Mosby is a sufficient testimony to his merit.

As soon as the company was organised, Captain Baylor started with fifty men to the valley. When he arrived at Charlestown, he was informed that the enemy's cavalry had gone up the valley, with the exception of the Loudoun Rangers, who were camped near Halltown. "Now for the Loudoun Rangers," said Baylor, as at the head of his command he galloped off in the direction of their camp, which was situated on the southern slope of a hill. He took the precaution to pass in between Halltown (where there was a brigade of infantry) and the camp. When within fifty yards of the Loudoun Rangers the order to charge was given. Two of them were killed, four wounded, sixty-five

CAPTAIN BAYLOR

taken prisoners, together with eighty-one horses, with their equipments. The rest of the command sought refuge in the bushes. The only loss which Baylor sustained was Frank Helm, of Warrenton, wounded as he charged among the foremost into the camp.

When Major General Hancock, so distinguished in the Federal army, heard of Baylor's exploit, he laughed heartily, and exclaimed,

"Well, that is the last of the Loudoun Rangers."

The expedition from the Northern Neck has recently returned, and I will give you the facts which I have obtained with reference to its sojourn in that district.

The Northern Neck constituted a part of the crown grant to Lord Fairfax, which still forms the basis of all the land-titles in that part of the state. As defined in this Fairfax Charter, it embraced the great breadth of land between the Potomac and the Rappahannock Rivers, from their head springs to their outlets. But now the name is used in a more restricted sense, and is applied to a narrow strip of land extending for seventy-five miles between those rivers below tide-water.

Colonel Chapman quartered his men among the citizens of Westmoreland, Lancaster, and Richmond Counties, by whom they were received with hospitality, and the Partisans led a pleasant and easy life until about the first of March.

About this time a force under Colonel Sumner was dispatched from Grant's army to capture seventy-five thousand boxes of tobacco which the Confederate government had deposited at Fredericksburg to be exchanged with the Yankees for bacon. After this service was performed, and the tobacco carried off or destroyed, the expedition sailed for Fortress Monroe, from whence, with ten days' rations, it proceeded up the Potomac, and landed at Kinsale, in Westmoreland County, a force of infantry and two hundred and fifty cavalry. It is stated that the object of the expeditionary force was to ravage the Northern Neck, and compel Mosby's men to find refuge elsewhere.

The morning after they landed the Federal cavalry advanced toward the Hague, a few miles distant, but were met on the march by so determined a resistance from small parties of Rangers that they deemed it prudent to return to their infantry supports. In the retreat, Captain Sam Chapman, with a party, assaulted their rear, and received a painful wound in the side, which was the only injury sustained by the Partisans.

Wat Bowie, of Westmoreland, was among the first to resist the invaders, for soon after the Federal cavalry began their march from Kinsale he collected a band of four or five men, and drove the advance-guard back on the column, killing and wounding several of their number. Such is the spirit which Mosby has infused into his men, and so obedient are they to his standing order, "Fight the Yankees wherever you meet them."

In retaliation for this act a wicked deed was perpetrated. The cottage of a helpless widow and an only daughter, which stood near the road, was burned to the ground. It was a pitiable spectacle to behold these houseless women, utterly forlorn, sitting by the blackened ruins of what had been their humble dwelling. This act of vengeance was without any show of justification or excuse, for the women were too poor to give aid and comfort to a soldier, and had been much frightened by the attack which Bowie had made upon the Federal column.

But for the fact that his men were scattered over a large area, Colonel Chapman was confident that the Federal cavalry would not have returned to their camp except as fugitives. He believed and hoped that the experiment would be repeated the next day, by which time his command could be assembled. But he was disappointed, for the invading force embarked on their transports and crossed to Point Lookout.

The resistance which this force met with from Colonel Chapman saved the Northern Neck. As soon as this cloud of war had passed away, the Partisans again bestowed their whole thoughts on the social scenes by which they were surrounded.

About ten days after the events which have been just detailed,

LIEUTENANT COLONEL CHAPMAN

Captain Tom Richards, with seven men, paid a nocturnal visit to Williamsburg, the seat of government during the colonial existence of Virginia, and the residence of all her royal governors. In order to reach the town, he was compelled to travel one hundred and twenty-five miles, and ferry three rivers, one of which was three miles in width. From a scout whom he met in the vicinity of Williamsburg he learned that there was in and about the town a force of three hundred men, and that the approach to it was guarded by a chain of picket-posts.

Lieutenant Puryear and Charlie Vest were sent a hundred yards in advance, with orders to capture the picket, if possible, without firing a shot. It was the hour of midnight, and not a cloud obscured the face of the heavens. The moon rode in her zenith, and bathed the landscape in floods of tender light. There was nothing to interrupt the quietude of the scene save the cautious movement of the Rangers. Presently the challenge of the sentinel rang out clear and sharp,

"Halt!"

"All right," replied Puryear, moving on.

"Halt!" repeated the sentinel, in a sterner voice.

"We are all right," said Puryear.

"Halt, or I'll shoot," shouted the man.

"Don't shoot. I tell you we are all right."

At this stage of the dialogue Puryear and Vest closed upon the soldier, who attempted to escape, but was shot dead. The order to charge was given, and right gallantly did the partisans dash in among the startled garrison, who began to retreat through the town toward the fort not far distant. A Federal officer rushed into the street and attempted

CAPTAIN RICHARDS

to rally his men, but in vain. The conflict with the rear of the retreating enemy was brief, but sharp. In a short time almost all the horses of Richards's command were wounded, while five Federal soldiers lay dead in the streets, and from six to ten wounded. Soon not a moving Yankee was to be seen in Williamsburg. They had all retreated to the fort or within the walls of the burned college. The partisans soon collected all the horses within reach, and, giving three cheers for the garrison of Williamsburg, left the scene of their bold exploit.

The next day a party of the enemy pursued them up the New Kent Road, but it would have taken a wild duck or a kingfisher to have caught Tom Richards.

On the 29th of March, John W. M'Cue, with five other Rangers, was sent across the Potomac to ascertain the force of the enemy at Leonardstown. After performing that duty, M'Cue and two of his comrades made an effort to get possession of the post-office at a place called Croom, which was defended by four government detectives and the postmaster, all armed. His comrades, when fired upon, fled, leaving M'Cue to fight the battle alone. In the rencounter which ensued, Coffun, the postmaster, was struck in the shoulder, and Ryon, one of the detectives, was mortally wounded in a hand-to-hand fight in the dark The other detectives rushed upon and overpowered M'Cue. His hands were at once tied behind him, and he was put for the night under guard in the room with the men he had wounded.

Lying upon his pallet, he saw on the mantlepiece a small seven-shooter, which suggested to him the idea of escape. He attempted to slip his hands from the rope, but found it was too tightly drawn. Then, by a powerful effort, he attempted to burst it, but in vain, and the guard, detecting his object, threw him back on the pallet, and drew the ropes more tightly than before. About four o'clock in the morning, Ryon, in the prospect of death, and in the presence of his wife and others, requested to have M'Cue brought to his bedside, when he addressed the prisoner with these words:

"Sir, you have but done your duty. I don't blame you. You were in Confederate uniform, and fought me bravely and well. I hope you will be treated as a prisoner of war."

The next morning M'Cue's captors, or rather those into whose hands he had been delivered, sent for a rope, and threatened with it to hang the Ranger unless he told the names of his confederates, for they suspected that citizens of Maryland were implicated in the act. But the young soldier stood firm. He said that his attack on the post-office was a legitimate act of war, and that, if they took his life, Mosby, who was across the river, would hang several Union soldiers or citizens in retaliation. This brought the Federals to the conclusion that it would be expedient to deal with the prisoner in another mode, and from Croom he was sent to Annapolis.[2]

Chapter 56: The Last Review

Upper Fauquier, April 22nd, 1865.

Dear Percy,—The deed is accomplished. I give you today the last act in this eventful history.

The Wednesday after the surrender of General Lee, Major General Hancock, whose headquarters were at Winchester, sent Major Moon, of General Torbert's staff, to communicate under a flag of truce with Colonel Mosby. The official papers were deposited by the intermediary in the hands of Mr. J. H. Clarke, at Millwood, by whom they were forwarded to Colonel Mosby. These papers contained a proposition for the surrender of the Partisan Battalion on the terms which had been accepted by General Lee, and were accompanied by an address from General Hancock to the citizens residing in the vicinity of his lines. The circular contained, among other particulars, an offer of the parole to all stragglers and detachments from the Army of Northern Virginia, but excluded from that benefit the "guerrilla chief Mosby," as our commander was denominated. It will doubtless strike you, as an Englishman, with surprise that Major General Hancock should have been directed by the authorities at Washington to conclude a military negotiation with an officer whom they refused to acknowledge as a lawful warrior. But it affords additional evidence of the resentful feelings which they cherish toward Mosby.

On the receipt of these papers. Colonel Mosby dispatched Lieutenant Colonel Chapman with a letter addressed to Major General Hancock, of which this is a copy:

April 15th, 1865.

Major General W. S. Hancock, Commanding, etc.:

General,—I am in receipt of a letter from your Chief of Staff, Brigadier General Morgan, inclosing copies of correspondence between Generals Grant and Lee, and informing me that you would appoint an officer of equal rank with myself to arrange details for the surrender of the forces under my command. As

---

2. See Appendix.

yet I have no notice through any other source of the facts concerning the surrender of the Army of Northern Virginia; nor, in my opinion, has the emergency yet arisen which would justify the surrender of my command. With no disposition, however, to cause the useless effusion of blood, or to inflict on a war-worn population any unnecessary distress, I am ready to agree to a suspension of hostilities for a short time, in order to enable me to communicate with my own authorities, or until I can obtain sufficient intelligence to determine my future action. Should you accede to this proposition, I am ready to meet any person you may designate to arrange the terms of an armistice.

I am, very respectfully, your obedient servant,

John S. Mosby, Colonel C. S. A.

In reply to this letter, Colonel Chapman brought back the following communication from Major General Hancock:

Headquarters Middle Military Division,
Winchester, Va., April 16th, 1865.

To Colonel John S. Mosby, C. S. A.:

Colonel,—Major General Hancock directs me to acknowledge the receipt of your communication, by the hand of Lieutenant Colonel Chapman, of the 15th instant, in reply to mine of the 11th.

The general does not think it is necessary to designate an officer to meet you to arrange an armistice, as you suggest.

Understanding, however, your motives in hesitating to surrender your command without definite intelligence from your former superiors, the general is very willing to allow a reasonable time for you to acquire the information you desire. It is not practicable for you to communicate with General Lee, as he is no longer in authority. Lieutenant Colonel Chapman, the bearer of your communication, has been furnished with such evidence as will undoubtedly satisfy you that farther resistance on the part of your command can result in no good to the cause in which you have been engaged.

In view of these facts, the general will not operate against your command until Tuesday next, at 12 m., provided there are no hostilities from your command.

This agreement to he understood to include the Department of Washington and the Potomac River line. It is possible some difficulty may arise from the operation of guerrilla parties not of your command, but the general hopes you can control the whole matter.

On Tuesday, at noon, the general will send an officer of equal rank with yourself to Millwood, to meet you and ascertain your determination, and, if you conclude to surrender your command, to arrange the details. Lieutenant Colonel Chapman will be able to give all the information you desire as to the probable terms.

If you consent to the above arrangements, please notify Brigadier General Chapman, at Berryville, as soon as practicable.

Very respectfully, your obedient servant,

C. H. Morgan,
Brevet Brig. Gen. and Chief of Staff.

Mosby at once communicated with General Chapman, whose headquarters were at Berryville, and on the 18th of April, at 11 a.m., a conference was agreed to be held at Millwood. Not being able, on account of unforeseen causes, to reach Millwood at the appointed hour. Colonel Mosby sent Captain Tom Richards and Captain Robert Walker in advance to acquaint the Federal officers delegated to meet him with the reasons for his detention. Walker and Richards, in accordance with this order, crossed the Shenandoah, and, with a handkerchief unfurled for a flag, galloped rapidly toward Millwood. The Federals were on the ground, and the two harbingers were conducted at Mr. Clarke's house to the presence of General Chapman and other Federal officers. Soon Mosby arrived with an escort of fifteen men, and all eyes were riveted on him.[1]

The result of the conference was a stipulation that there should be a cessation of hostilities for two days, ending at noon on the 20th of April. The agreement concluded with this covenant:

> Colonel Mosby to use his influence and authority in the mean time to prevent any acts of hostility by bands or organisations of Confederate soldiers operating from Loudoun or Fauquier counties.
>
> (Signed), George H. Chapman, Brig. General U. S. Vols.
> John S. Mosby, Colonel C. S. A.
> Millwood, April 18th, 1865.

---

1. The author, at the request of Colonel Mosby, was present on this occasion, as it had been already arranged that he should write this history.

At the same time the following compact was signed by the two officers, subject to Major General Hancock's approval, which was withheld, as will be seen from his letter, as given below.

A cessation of hostilities is hereby agreed upon between the forces of the United States commanded by General Hancock, and the forces of the Confederate States commanded by Colonel John S. Mosby.

This cessation to be subject to the approval of General Hancock; if approved, to be in force for ten (10) days, commencing on the 20th of April at 12 m., and ending on the 30th at 12 m.

Colonel Mosby to be notified at Millwood of the approval or disapproval of this agreement by 12 noon of April 20th.

Colonel Mosby to use his authority and influence to prevent any acts of hostility being perpetrated or attempted by any bands or organisations of Confederate soldiers operating, from Loudoun or Fauquier counties.

This agreement is made with the understanding that, in case during this interval the army opposed to the army of General Sherman shall capitulate or be dispersed. Colonel Mosby will disband his organisation (the 43rd Virginia Battalion).

      Geo. H. Chapman, Brig. General U. S. Vols.
      John S. Mosby, Colonel C. S. A.
Millwood, April 18, 1865.

      Headquarters Middle Military Division,
        19th April, 1865.

Colonel,—Major General Hancock, commanding Middle Military Division, directs me to say that he has confirmed the extension of the cessation of hostilities until noon of the 20th, arranged at Millwood on the 18th between Brigadier General Chapman, U. S. Volunteers, and yourself; but General Hancock can see no sufficient reasons why the cessation of hostilities should be continued. The truce will therefore cease at noon on the 20th between the forces commanded by Major General Hancock and your troops, unless you should decide to surrender at or before that time on the conditions previously offered and explained by Lieutenant General Grant, which are enclosed.

The officer bearing the flag will wait at Millwood until 12 m. to hear your decision. Unless you then announce your immediate surrender, he will return. In case of your surrender, the arrangements will be immediately perfected at Millwood. Truce of hostilities in such case will only refer to that point, and be of such duration as only to allow time to prepare and sign the paroles and receive the public property. After the expiration of this truce, General Hancock is commanded not to offer you or your men terms again. I am, sir, very respectfully, your obedient servant,

W. G. Mitchell, Brevet Colonel and A. D. C.

To Colonel John S. Mosby, C. S. A.,
Commanding, etc., Millwood, Va.

On the 20th of April, when Colonel Mosby returned to Millwood, the following letter from General Hancock was placed in his hands, which you will perceive extends to him the same terms offered to other Confederate officers:

Headquarters Cavalry. Middle Military Division,
April 19th, 1865.

Colonel,—Major General Hancock directs me to say to you that the following instructions have been telegraphed to him in reference to Confederate officers or soldiers who surrender:

Washington, D. C, April 19th, 1865.

To Major General Hancock:

You may receive all rebel officers or soldiers who surrender to you on exactly the same terms that were given to General Lee, except have it distinctly understood that all who claim homes in states that never passed Ordinances of Secession have forfeited them, and can only return on compliance with the amnesty proclamation. Maryland, Kentucky, Delaware, and Missouri are such states. They may return to West Virginia on their parole.

(Signed), U. S. Grant, Lieutenant General.

I am, colonel, very respectfully,

C. McK. Groser, A. A. A. G.

Colonel J. S. Mosby, C. S. A.

At Salem, the 21st of April, 1865, Mosby assembled the Partisan Battalion for the last time. It contained at this date on its muster-rolls the names of seven hundred men, of whom one hundred were in prison. The rest were present for duty, dressed in Confederate gray, with drab hats and nodding black plumes, and mounted on the best horses, and supplied with the best arms and equipments which the Northern cavalry could furnish. As for the last time Mosby glanced his experienced eye along their serried ranks, drawn up in the level field to the south of the town, they presented an appearance of which any commander might justly be proud, for in point of style, arms, equipment, and efficiency, the Partisan Battalion was, without doubt, the foremost body of cavalry in either army; and when contrasted with the handful of borrowed men with whom their leader began his glorious career, his extraordinary talents, exercised under adverse influences, for organisation, preservation, and command stood confessed. Indeed, he had plunged the infant Mars in a bath of fire and blood, and the child had come forth a renowned warrior, invigorated for the contest and adorned with glory, though seamed with many a scar.

A copy of the following address was then given to the commanding officers of the squadrons, and by them read to their men:

Fauquier County, April 21st, 1865.

Soldiers,—I have summoned you together for the last time. The vision we cherished of a free and independent country has vanished, and that country is now the spoil of a conqueror. I disband your organisation in preference to surrendering to our enemies. I am no longer your commander. After an association of more than two eventful years, I part from you with a just pride in the fame of your achievements, and grateful recollections of your generous kindness to myself And now, at this moment of bidding you a final *adieu*, accept the assurance of my unchanging confidence and regard. Farewell!

John S. Mosby, Colonel.

As soon as the military bond was severed, there followed a scene which beggars description. The sternest natures dissolved in tears, for the men then discovered how strong were the personal sympathies which bound them to each other and to the chieftain of whom they were so proud. In broken ranks they crowded around him, and, amid tears and protestations of confidence and fidelity, assured him that at the first bugle-note they would rally again to his standard.

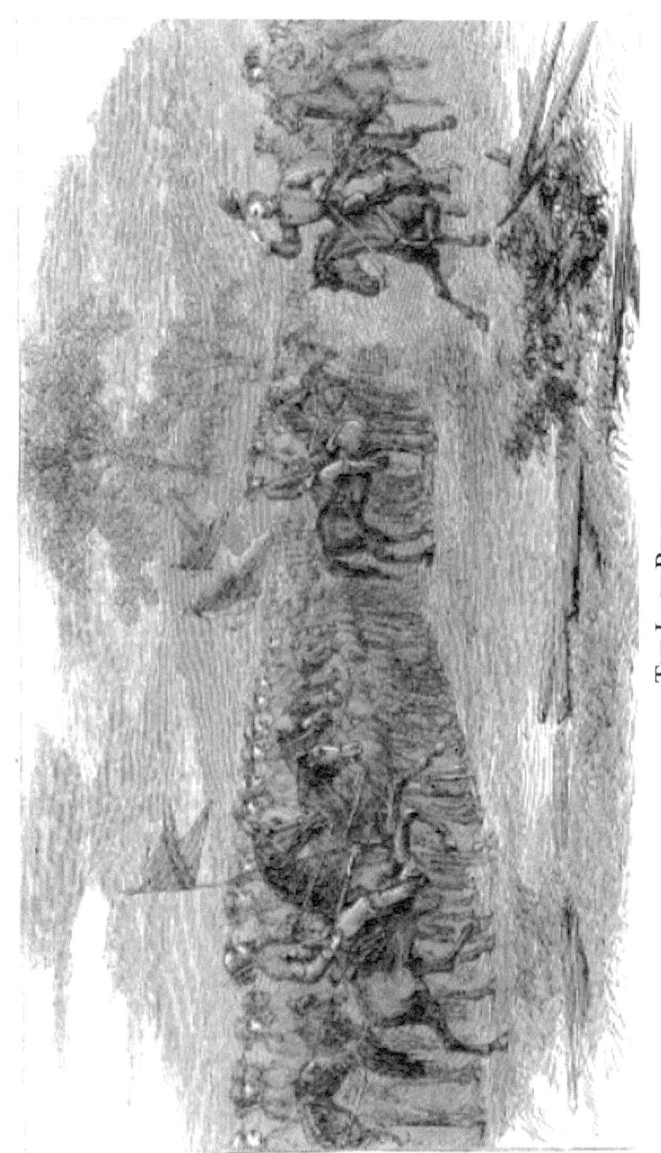

The Last Review

Appendix

Account of Private M'Cue's Imprisonment

(The following facts in regard to the treatment of M'Cue have, at my request, been furnished me by a gentleman well acquainted with them. They present a picture of despotism and cruelty rarely witnessed in a Christian country, but they bear, at the same time, honourable testimony to the fidelity with which General Grant adhered to the engagements which he contracted at Appomattox Court-house.—Original Editor.)

From Annapolis he was removed to Baltimore and cast into a negro jail, where his treatment was that of a convict. He was heavily ironed, and confined in a dark, cold cell, and when a fellow-prisoner, through the iron-bars of his dungeon, gave him a blanket, the order was given to the prison-guard to take it away. Very soon a man dressed in Confederate uniform was put in the cell with M'Cue, and left to spend the night with him. The stranger made advances toward an acquaintance, asked his fellow-prisoner his name, to what command he belonged, and the charges preferred against him, and at the same time told him that he himself was under charges as a Confederate, and was to be tried by a military commission.

He doubted not, he added, that both of them would be sentenced to the gallows. "I have a proposition to make to you, for there is but one way in which we can save our lives—to rush upon the guard, seize their arms, and murder them. In the confusion thus created, an opportunity may occur for our escape." The proposition was so wild and impossible of execution that M'Cue at once saw in it a snare prepared for his destruction. So he very quietly said to his companion, "You may attempt to murder the guard and make your escape, but I will have nothing to do with it." He knew he was a detective.

This conspiracy having failed, he was then carried before the provost-marshal, who told him that the only chance for life afforded was to confess his guilt and throw himself upon the mercy of the court. To this he replied, "I am a Confederate soldier, engaged in legitimate warfare. I belong to Mosby's Partisan Battalion, which is not a guerrilla band. I believe there is a predetermined purpose to take my life, and I will not appear before my Maker with a false plea stamped upon my conscience. I am a lawful soldier, and have no excuse, apology, or confession to make."

The provost-marshal left him, saying that he was the most hardened villain he had ever come in contact with, and that death by the gallows inevitably awaited him.

At the end of four days the Partisan Ranger was removed to .the city jail of Baltimore, where he received from the keeper humane treatment. An order for a military commission to assemble at Baltimore was soon issued for the trial of such offenders as might be brought before it. The charges on which M'Cue was arraigned were as follows:

> 1st. The murder of Richard N.. Ryon, a detective officer in the service of the United States.
>
> 2nd. Assault with intent to kill and murder one Jeremiah Coffron, by discharging at the head of said Coffron a loaded pistol, thereby inflicting a serious and dangerous wound.
>
> 3rd. Violation of the laws of war as laid down in general orders, etc.

The plea of the prisoner was, of course, "Not guilty."

The finding in reference to the first charge—murder—is so singular and unprecedented in criminal jurisprudence, that I can not forbear giving it *verbatim*: "Guilty, except with malice aforethought."

The court acquitted the prisoner of malice aforethought, and to acquit him of the malice is to acquit him of the crime, for malice every tyro in law knows is the essential element of murder.

After this finding the record goes on to say,

> And the commission do *therefore* sentence him, the said John W. M'Cue, to be imprisoned at *hard labour* for and during the period of his *natural life*, in such penitentiary or place of confinement as the commanding general may designate.

At a subsequent date the following order was published, to wit:

Headquarters, Middle Department, 8th Army Corps,
Baltimore, May 18th, 1865.

"The proceedings, finding, and sentence in the foregoing case of John W. M'Cue are approved and confirmed, and the sentence will be carried into execution. The commanding general designates Clinton Prison, New York, as the place of confinement of the prisoner.

(Signed), Lew. Wallace,
Major General Commanding.

The trial was suspended a few days, that the father of the prisoner and Captain Halsey, then confined as prisoners of war at Fort Delaware, might be summoned to testify in behalf of the defence.

The prisoner was brought into court heavily ironed, and the examination of the witnesses was begun. The point on which the examination chiefly turned was as to the status of Mosby's command in the Confederate Government. Their evidence was clear and decided: that Mosby was a commissioned officer, his command organised by virtue of an act of Congress, and that it was part and parcel of the Army of Northern Virginia, under the supreme control of General Lee, which negatived the idea that the Partisan Battalion was a band of lawless *banditti*. But it all went for naught with the military commission, and they sentenced this brave soldier of General Lee to spend the remainder of his life in expiating among felons an offense which he had not committed.

On the 17th of July, 1865, he was removed in chains to Clinton Prison, New York, near Lake Champlain, where he was shaved, washed, hair cut, and coarse prison clothes put upon him; was first put to striking in the blacksmith's shop, and then put to cutting nails by machinery. Each day he was required to work eleven hours. One hour was allowed for meals; and the prisoner was forbidden, under a heavy penalty, to speak to any one except to his keeper, and then only on business. This was the routine for the day, and the night was no relief to the day, for he was locked up alone in a cell ten feet by four. The only relaxation of this severity was that he was allowed on Sunday to attend religious exercises in the chapel. The Reverend Mr. Canfield was chaplain of the prison, who extended to the prisoner, in his deep affliction, kindness and sympathy. He was a Christian gentleman, which embraces every virtue.

With a negro convict M'Cue worked side by side, and was required to walk to and from the mess-hall with him. Together they daily took their meals. His name was Joseph Oliver, the best friend and more of a gentleman than any man the prisoner met with, except the chaplain and the foreman, Mr. Gay.

During this period of suffering the unfortunate young man received from his parents and friends in Virginia letters assuring him that every effort was being made to procure his pardon. His father was released from the military prison about the 1st of July, and went vigorously to work in his son's behalf, and did not relax his efforts until his liberation was accomplished. The means with which he worked were petitions signed by many thousand citizens of Virginia, including some of the best names in the state, addressed to the President, to which were added the weight of letters and personal appeals. Among these letters was one which deserves your especial attention, an extract from which I give. It is from Colonel S. M. Bowman, president of the commission that tried him, dated New York, October 6th, 1865, and is addressed to the President of the United States. Here is the extract:

> He had a trial before a court composed chiefly of young officers, not one of whom (except myself) had ever read a law-book, and knew but little about any system of jurisprudence—had never sat on a jury, and probably never witnessed a trial of a case in court. *The time of the trial was just after the assassination of President Lincoln, when the temper of the country was averse to anything like leniency.*

But these efforts in the cause of justice and humanity appear to have been fruitless, until the case was brought to the attention of General Grant, to whom, and to Captain James M'Guire, of Washington City—a big-hearted and big-brained Irishman— the great secular head of the Catholic Church in and about Washington, the prisoner was indebted for the consummation of his pardon. On the 8th of November, 1865, they appeared together before the President, and did not leave him till the object was accomplished. General Grant took the bold position that there had been suffering enough occasioned by this war, and the time had come for the prison-doors to be thrown open and the captives set free. The eloquent and energetic appeal was not unavailing, for before they left him the President had granted the pardon for which they petitioned. It is but just to the claims of nature to add that it was maternal solicitude and love which procured this powerful intercession, and revealed to General Grant this act of despotism and cruelty which had been practiced under the colour of military law.

Description of the Shenandoah Valley.

(By the express permission of Lieutenant General Early, I introduce here the comprehensive and lucid description of the Valley of the Shenandoah given by that distinguished officer in his able and interesting *Memoir of the Last Year of the War for Independence.*—Original Editor.)

The Valley of Virginia, in its largest sense, embraces all that country lying between the Blue Ridge and Alleghany Mountains, which unite at its southwestern end.

The Shenandoah Valley, which is a part of the Valley of Virginia, embraces the counties of Augusta, Rockingham, Shenandoah, Page, Warren, Clarke, Frederick, Jefferson, and Berkeley. This valley is bounded on the north by the Potomac, on the south by the county of Rockbridge, on the east by the Blue Ridge, and on the west by the Great North Mountain and its ranges.

The Shenandoah River is composed of two branches, called, respectively, the 'North Fork' and the 'South Fork,' which unite near Front Royal, in Warren County. The North Fork rises in the Great North Mountain, and runs eastwardly to within a short distance of New Market, in Shenandoah County, and thence northeast by Mount Jackson to Strasburg, where it turns east to Front Royal. The South Fork is formed by the union of North River, Middle River, and South River. North River and Middle River, running from the west, unite near Port Republic, in Rockingham County. South River rises in the southeastern part of Augusta, and runs by Waynesboro, along the western base of the Blue Ridge, to Port Republic, where it unites with the stream formed by the junction of the North and Middle Rivers. From Port Republic the South Fork of the Shenandoah runs northeast, through the eastern border of Rockingham and the county of Page, to Front Royal, in Warren County.'

The North Fork and South Fork are separated by the Massanutten Mountain, which is connected with no other mountain, but terminates abruptly at both ends. Its northern end is washed at its base, just below Strasburg, by the North Fork. Its southern end terminates near the road between Harrisonburg and Conrad's Store on the South Fork, at which latter place the road through Swift Run Gap, in the Blue Ridge, crosses that stream. Two valleys are thus formed, the one on the North Fork being called 'The Main Valley,' and the other on the South Fork, and embracing the county of Page and part of the county of Warren, being usually known by the name of 'The Luray Valley.' The Luray Valley unites with the main valley at both ends of the mountain. There is a good road across Massanutten Mountain from one valley to the other, through a gap near New Market.

South of this gap there is no road across the mountain, and north of it the roads are very rugged, and not practicable for the march of a large army with its trains. At the northern or lower end of Massanutten Mountain, and between two branches of it, is a valley called 'Powell's Fort Valley,' or more commonly 'The Fort.' This valley is accessible only by the very rugged roads over the mountain which have been mentioned, and through a ravine at its lower end. From its isolated position, it was not the theatre of military operations of any consequence, but merely furnished a refuge for deserters, stragglers, and fugitives from the battlefields.

From Front Royal the Shenandoah River runs along the western base of the Blue Ridge to Harper's Ferry, where it unites with the Potomac, which here bursts through the mountains. The mountain in extension of the range of the Blue Ridge from this point through Maryland and Pennsylvania is called 'South Mountain.'

Strictly speaking, the county of Berkeley and the greater part of Frederick are not in the valley of the Shenandoah. The Opequon, rising southwest of Winchester, and crossing the Valley Pike four or five miles south of that place, turns to the north and empties into the Potomac some distance above its junction with the Shenandoah; the greater part of Frederick and nearly the whole of Berkeley being on the western side of the Opequon.

Little North Mountain, called in the lower valley 'North Mountain,' runs northeast through the western portions of Shenandoah, Frederick, and Berkeley counties to the Potomac. At its northern end, where it is called North Mountain, it separates the waters of the Opequon from those of Back Creek.

Cedar Creek rises in Shenandoah County, west of Little North Mountain, and, running northeast along its western base, passes through that mountain four or five miles from Strasburg, and, then making a circuit, empties into the North Fork of the Shenandoah about two miles below Strasburg.

The Baltimore and Ohio Railroad crosses the Potomac at Harper's Ferry, and, passing through Martinsburg, in Berkeley County, crosses

Back Creek near its mouth, runs up the Potomac, crossing the south branch of that river near its mouth, and then the North Branch to Cumberland, in Maryland. From this place it runs into Virginia again, and, passing through North western Virginia, strikes the Ohio River by two stems terminating at Wheeling and Parkersburg respectively.

There is a railroad from Harper's Ferry to Winchester, called 'The Winchester and Potomac Railroad,' and also one from Manassas Junction, on the Orange and Alexandria Railroad, through Manassas Gap in the Blue Ridge, by Front Royal and Strasburg, to Mount Jackson, called 'The Manassas Gap Railroad;' but both of these roads were torn up and rendered unserviceable in the year 1862, under the orders of General Jackson.

From Staunton, in Augusta County, there is a fine macadamized road called 'The Valley Pike,' running through Mount Sydney, Mount Crawford, Harrisonburg, New Market, Mount Jackson, Edinburg, Woodstock, Strasburg, Middletown, Newtown, Bartonsville, and Kearnstown to Winchester, in Frederick County, and crossing Middle River seven miles from Staunton, North River at Mount Crawford, eighteen miles from Staunton, the North Fork of the Shenandoah at Mount Jackson, Cedar Creek, between Strasburg and Middletown, and the Opequon at Bartonsville, four or five miles from Winchester. There is also another road west of the Valley Pike, connecting these several villages, called the 'Back Road,' and, in some places, another road between the Valley Pike and the Back Road, which is called the 'Middle Road.'

From Winchester there is a macadamized road, *via* Martinsburg, to Williamsport, on the Potomac, in Maryland, and another *via* Berryville, in Clarke County, and Charlestown, in Jefferson County, to Harper's Ferry. There is also a good pike from Winchester to Front Royal, which crosses both forks of the Shenandoah just above their junction; and from Front Royal there are good roads up the Luray Valley, and by the way of Conrad's Store and Port Republic, to Harrisonburg and Staunton.

From Staunton south there are good roads passing through Lexington in Rockbridge County, and Buchanan in Botetourt County, to several points on the Virginia and Tennessee Railroad, and others direct from Staunton and Lexington to Lynchburg.

The Central Railroad, from Richmond, passes through the Blue Ridge, with a tunnel at Rock-fish Gap, and runs through Waynesboro and Staunton westwardly to Jackson's River, which is one of the head streams of James River.

This description of the country is given in order to render the following narrative intelligible without too much repetition.

In the spring of 1864, before the opening of the campaign, the lower Shenandoah Valley was held by the Federal troops under Major General Sigel, with his headquarters at Winchester, while the upper valley was held by Brigadier General Imboden, of the Confederate Army, with one brigade of cavalry or mounted infantry, and a battery of artillery. When the campaign opened Sigel moved up the Valley, and Major General Breckinridge moved from Southwestern Virginia, with two brigades of infantry and a battalion of artillery, to meet him. Breckinridge, having united his forces with Imboden's, met and defeated Sigel at New Market on the 15th day of May, driving him back toward Winchester. Breckinridge then crossed the Blue Ridge, and joined General Lee at Hanover Junction with his two brigades of infantry and the battalion of artillery.

Subsequently the Federal General Hunter organised another and larger force than Sigel's, and moved up the valley, and on the 6th day of June defeated Brigadier General William E. Jones at Piedmont, between Port Republic and Staunton, Jones's force being composed of a very small body of infantry, and a cavalry force which had been brought from Southwestern Virginia after Breckinridge's departure from the valley. Jones was killed, and the remnant of his force, under Brigadier General Vaughan, fell back to Waynesboro. Hunter's force then united with another column which had moved from Lewisburg, in Western Virginia, under the Federal General Crook. As soon as information was received of Jones's defeat and death, Breckinridge was sent back to the valley with the force he had brought with him."

    THE CONQUERED BANNER.
        By Father Ryan.

Furl that banner, for 'tis weary;
Round its staff 'tis drooping dreary;
Furl it—fold it—it is best,
For there's not a man to wave it,
And there's not a sword to save it.
And there's not one left to lave it
In the blood which heroes gave it.
And its foes now scorn and brave it—
Furl it—hide it—let it rest.

Furl that banner, for 'tis tattered;
Broken is its staff, and shattered,
And the valiant hosts lie scattered
O'er whom it floated high.
Oh, 'tis hard for us to fold it.
Hard that there is none to hold it,
Hard that those who once unrolled it
Now must furl it with a sigh.

Furl that banner, furl it sadly;
Once ten thousands hailed it gladly.
And ten thousands wildly, madly
Swore it should forever wave.
Swore that foemen's swords should never
Hearts entwined like theirs dissever
Till that flag should float forever
O'er their freedom or their graves.

Furl it, for the hands that grasped it,
And the hearts that fondly clasped it.
Cold and dead are lying low;
And that banner it is trailing,
While around it sounds the wailing
Of its people in their woe;
For, though conquered, they adore it;
Love the cold, dead hands that bore it;
Weep for those who fell before it;
Pardon those who trailed and tore it;
For oh, wildly we deplore it,
Now to furl and fold it so.

Furl that banner, for 'tis gory,
Yet 'tis wreathed around with glory,
And 'twill live in song and story
Though its folds are in the dust;
For its fame on brightest pages.
Penned by poets and by sages.
Shall go sounding down the ages.
Furl its folds though now we must.

Furl that banner, furl it slowly;
Treat it gently—for 'tis holy,
For it droops above our dead;

Touch it not—unfurl it never—
Let it droop thus furled forever.
For its people's hopes are fled.

Reply To "The Conquered Banner."
By Sir H. Houghton, Bart., England.

Gallant nation, foiled by numbers,
Say not that your hopes are fled
Keep that glorious flag that slumbers
One day to avenge your dead.
Keep it widowed, sonless mothers,
Keep it sisters, mourning brothers
Furl it with an iron will;
Furl it now, but—keep it still.
Think not that its work is done.
Keep it till your children take it
Once again to hail and make it
All their sires have bled and fought for,
All their noble hearts have sought for,
Bled and fought for all alone.
All alone! ay, shame the story—
Millions here deplore the stain—
Shame, alas! for England's glory—
Freedom called, and called in vain.
Furl that banner sadly, slowly,
Treat it gently, for 'tis holy,
Till that day—yes, furl it sadly.
Then once more unfurl it gladly—
Conquered banner, keep it still

Gettysburg.
By Edward Warren, M.D., late Surgeon General, N. C.

From the hills of the West to the shores of the sea,
From the yellow Roanoke to the distant Pedee,
A wild wail of sorrow ascendeth on high
For the heroes who bleed, and the martyrs who die.

The hearts of our fathers are breaking with pain,
And the tears of our mothers descending like rain,
For the loved and the lost who homeward no more
Return from the field so red with their gore.

That banner of bars, which so proudly hath flown
Where the demon of carnage claimed all as his own,
Now droops in its gloom, while the cypress is seen
Entwined with the laurels on its glittering sheen.

The foemen exult as they bury the slain
Who fell in the charge on that terrible plain;
For Carolina's brave sons—the pride of the South—
Lie covered with glory at the dread cannon's mouth.

Ah! well may they gloat o'er the work they have done,
And boast of the field they so dearly have won,
When the hearts of such heroes forever are still
As fought at Manassas, and Malvern's proud hill;

And at Bethel and Sharpsburg, all reckless of death,
Came down on the foe like the hurricane's breath,
And scattered his legions o'er mountain and lea,
As the leaves, of the forest or foam of the sea.

But hark! as we mourn for the "good and the true"—
For Marshall, Burgwin, and the brave Pettigrew,
Through forest and city, o'er river and plain,
A wild cry for vengeance re-echoes again.

For the noble old state—thank God for the sight!—
Is burning and arming once more for the fight;
And, dashing the tear from her sorrowing eye,
By Jehovah she swears to conquer or die.

Proud men of the North, from the rebels ye spurn,
A lesson of blood you will speedily learn;
And though jubilant now, beware! oh, beware!
For your boastings shall turn to wails of despair.

Somebody's Darling.
By a Young Lady of Savannah.

Into a ward of whitewashed walls,
Where the dead and the dying lay,
Wounded by bayonets, shells, and balls,
Somebody's darling was borne one day.
Somebody's darling, so young and so brave,
Wearing yet on his pale, sweet face.
Soon to be hid by the dust of the grave,
The lingering light of his boyhood's grace.

*Matted and damp are the curls of gold
Kissing the snow of that fair young brow;
Pale are the lips of delicate mould—
Somebody's darling is dying now.
Back from his beautiful blue-veined brow
Brush all the wandering waves of gold.
Cross his hands on his bosom now—
Somebody's darling is still and cold.*

ALSO FROM LEONAUR
AVAILABLE IN SOFTCOVER OR HARDCOVER WITH DUST JACKET

LIFE IN THE ARMY OF NORTHERN VIRGINIA by *Carlton McCarthy*—The Observations of a Confederate Artilleryman of Cutshaw's Battalion During the American Civil War 1861-1865.

HISTORY OF THE CAVALRY OF THE ARMY OF THE POTOMAC by *Charles D. Rhodes*—Including Pope's Army of Virginia and the Cavalry Operations in West Virginia During the American Civil War.

CAMP-FIRE AND COTTON-FIELD by *Thomas W. Knox*—A New York Herald Correspondent's View of the American Civil War.

SERGEANT STILLWELL by *Leander Stillwell*—The Experiences of a Union Army Soldier of the 61st Illinois Infantry During the American Civil War.

STONEWALL'S CANNONEER by *Edward A. Moore*—Experiences with the Rockbridge Artillery, Confederate Army of Northern Virginia, During the American Civil War.

THE SIXTH CORPS by *George Stevens*—The Army of the Potomac, Union Army, During the American Civil War.

THE RAILROAD RAIDERS by *William Pittenger*—An Ohio Volunteers Recollections of the Andrews Raid to Disrupt the Confederate Railroad in Georgia During the American Civil War.

CITIZEN SOLDIER by *John Beatty*—An Account of the American Civil War by a Union Infantry Officer of Ohio Volunteers Who Became a Brigadier General.

COX: PERSONAL RECOLLECTIONS OF THE CIVIL WAR--VOLUME 1 by *Jacob Dolson Cox*—West Virginia, Kanawha Valley, Gauley Bridge, Cotton Mountain, South Mountain, Antietam, the Morgan Raid & the East Tennessee Campaign.

COX: PERSONAL RECOLLECTIONS OF THE CIVIL WAR--VOLUME 2 by *Jacob Dolson Cox*—Siege of Knoxville, East Tennessee, Atlanta Campaign, the Nashville Campaign & the North Carolina Campaign.

KERSHAW'S BRIGADE VOLUME 1 by *D. Augustus Dickert*—Manassas, Seven Pines, Sharpsburg (Antietam), Fredricksburg, Chancellorsville, Gettysburg, Chickamauga, Chattanooga, Fort Sanders & Bean Station.

KERSHAW'S BRIGADE VOLUME 2 by *D. Augustus Dickert*—At the wilderness, Cold Harbour, Petersburg, The Shenandoah Valley and Cedar Creek..

AVAILABLE ONLINE AT **www.leonaur.com**
AND FROM ALL GOOD BOOK STORES

www.ingramcontent.com/pod-product-compliance
Lightning Source LLC
Chambersburg PA
CBHW020938230426
43666CB00005B/73